Communications
in Computer and Information Science   1936

Rationale

The CCIS series is devoted to the publication of proceedings of computer science conferences. Its aim is to efficiently disseminate original research results in informatics in printed and electronic form. While the focus is on publication of peer-reviewed full papers presenting mature work, inclusion of reviewed short papers reporting on work in progress is welcome, too. Besides globally relevant meetings with internationally representative program committees guaranteeing a strict peer-reviewing and paper selection process, conferences run by societies or of high regional or national relevance are also considered for publication.

Topics

The topical scope of CCIS spans the entire spectrum of informatics ranging from foundational topics in the theory of computing to information and communications science and technology and a broad variety of interdisciplinary application fields.

Information for Volume Editors and Authors

Publication in CCIS is free of charge. No royalties are paid, however, we offer registered conference participants temporary free access to the online version of the conference proceedings on SpringerLink (http://link.springer.com) by means of an http referrer from the conference website and/or a number of complimentary printed copies, as specified in the official acceptance email of the event.

CCIS proceedings can be published in time for distribution at conferences or as post-proceedings, and delivered in the form of printed books and/or electronically as USBs and/or e-content licenses for accessing proceedings at SpringerLink. Furthermore, CCIS proceedings are included in the CCIS electronic book series hosted in the SpringerLink digital library at http://link.springer.com/bookseries/7899. Conferences publishing in CCIS are allowed to use Online Conference Service (OCS) for managing the whole proceedings lifecycle (from submission and reviewing to preparing for publication) free of charge.

Publication process

The language of publication is exclusively English. Authors publishing in CCIS have to sign the Springer CCIS copyright transfer form, however, they are free to use their material published in CCIS for substantially changed, more elaborate subsequent publications elsewhere. For the preparation of the camera-ready papers/files, authors have to strictly adhere to the Springer CCIS Authors' Instructions and are strongly encouraged to use the CCIS LaTeX style files or templates.

Abstracting/Indexing

CCIS is abstracted/indexed in DBLP, Google Scholar, EI-Compendex, Mathematical Reviews, SCImago, Scopus. CCIS volumes are also submitted for the inclusion in ISI Proceedings.

How to start

To start the evaluation of your proposal for inclusion in the CCIS series, please send an e-mail to ccis@springer.com.

Teresa Guarda · Filipe Portela ·
Jose Maria Diaz-Nafria
Editors

Advanced Research in Technologies, Information, Innovation and Sustainability

Third International Conference, ARTIIS 2023
Madrid, Spain, October 18–20, 2023
Proceedings, Part II

 Springer

Editors
Teresa Guarda [iD]
Universidad Estatal Peninsula de Santa Elena
Campus Matriz
La Libertad, Ecuador

Filipe Portela [iD]
Algoritmi Research Centre
University of Minho
Guimarães, Portugal

Jose Maria Diaz-Nafria [iD]
Universidad a Distancia de Madrid
Madrid, Spain

ISSN 1865-0929   ISSN 1865-0937 (electronic)
Communications in Computer and Information Science
ISBN 978-3-031-48854-2   ISBN 978-3-031-48855-9 (eBook)
https://doi.org/10.1007/978-3-031-48855-9

Preface

The need for a greener and more digital world leads academia, governments, industry and citizens to look for emerging, sustainable, intelligent solutions and trends.

These new solutions and ideas must promote communication and ubiquitous computing between society agents, i.e., citizens, industry, organizations, net-worked machines and physical objects, and provide a promising vision of the future integrating the real world of knowledge agents and things with the virtual world of information. The emerging approaches in study or development can address several dimensions with a technological focus like Information, Innovation and Sustainability and topics: Computing Solutions, Data Intelligence, Ethics, Security, Privacy and Sustainability.

These topics are closely related to the field of Information Systems (IS) because all of them involve the use and management of technology and data to achieve specific purposes or goals. Computing Solutions are a crucial aspect of information systems as they provide the technical infrastructure and tools for organizations to manage and process data. Data Intelligence is also a key area of information systems as it involves the collection, analysis and interpretation of data to support decision-making and problem-solving. Sustainability is becoming an increasingly important aspect of information systems as organizations are recognizing the impact of technology on the environment and are looking for ways to reduce their carbon footprint. Ethics, Security and Privacy are also essential aspects of information systems as they involve the responsible and secure use of technology and data to protect individuals and organizations from potential harm.

The change observed in society modifies the landscape of human activity, particularly regarding knowledge acquisition and production, offering new possibilities and challenges that need to be explored, assessed and disseminated.

To expose and disseminate this, ARTIIS arose in 2021. ARTIIS is an international forum for researchers and practitioners to present and discuss the most recent innovations, trends, results, experiences and concerns from several perspectives of Technologies, Information, Innovation and Sustainability. This book is split into three volumes and contains a selection of 113 papers accepted for presentation and discussion at the International Conference on Advanced Research in Technologies, Information, Innovation and Sustainability (ARTIIS 2023) and its workshops. The third edition of ARTIIS, realized in 2023, received 297 contributions from 44 countries worldwide. The acceptance rate was 38.04%, 98 regular papers and 15 short papers.

The papers accepted to ARTIIS 2023 are published in the Communications in Computer and Information Science series (Springer CCIS). It is indexed in DBLP, Google Scholar, EI-Compendex, SCImago and Scopus. CCIS volumes are also submitted for inclusion in ISI Proceedings.

The conference proceedings are published in 3 CCIS volumes. The first 2 volumes (CCIS volumes 1935, 1936) consist of the peer-reviewed papers from the main conference track. In addition, 1 volume (CCIS 1937) contains the peer-reviewed papers of the 10 Special Sessions.

The first volume of the book contains all the papers on two topics: Computing Solutions and Data Intelligence:

- Computing Solutions addresses the development of applications and platforms involving computing and concerning some area of knowledge or society. It includes topics like Networks, Pervasive Computing, Gamification and Software Engineering.
- Data Intelligence focuses on data (e.g., text, images) acquisition and processing using smart techniques or tools. It includes topics like Computing Intelligence, Artificial Intelligence, Data Science and Computer Vision.

The second volume contains all the papers about Sustainability, and Ethics, Security and Privacy:

- Ethics, Security and Privacy shows a more strict and secure area of Information Systems where the end-user is the main concern. Vulnerabilities, Data Privacy and Cybersecurity are the main subjects of this topic.
- Sustainability explores a new type of computing: more green, connected, efficient and sustainable. Topics like Immersive Tech, Smart Cities and Sustainable Infrastructures are part of this topic.

The third volume contains the papers from the ten Special Sessions:

- Applications of Computational Mathematics to Simulation and Data Analysis (ACMaSDA 2023)
- Challenges and the Impact of Communication and Information Technologies on Education (CICITE 2023)
- Workshop on Gamification Application and Technologies (GAT 2023)
- Bridging Knowledge in a Fragmented World (glossaLAB 2023)
- Intelligent Systems for Health and Medical Care (ISHMC 2023)
- Intelligent Systems in Forensic Engineering (ISIFE 2023)
- International Symposium on Technological Innovations for Industry and Society (ISTIIS 2023)
- International Workshop on Electronic and Telecommunications (IWET 2023)
- Innovation in Educational Technology (JIUTE 2023)
- Smart Tourism and Information Systems (SMARTTIS 2023)

ARTIIS 2023 had the support of Universidad a Distancia de Madrid, Madrid, Spain; Universidad Estatal Península de Santa Elena, Ecuador; and the Algoritmi Research Center of Minho University, Portugal. It was realized in a hybrid format: face-to-face and virtual at Universidad a Distancia de Madrid – UDIMA, P.º del Gral. Martínez Campos, 5, 28010 Madrid, Spain – between the 18th and 20th of October 2023. Besides the main conference, ARTIIS 2023 also hosted ten special sessions.

The Program Committee was composed of a multidisciplinary group of more than 457 experts from 60 countries, with the responsibility for evaluating, in a double-blind review process, the submissions received for each of the main themes proposed for the conference and special sessions.

We acknowledge those who contributed to this book: authors, organizing chairs, steering committee, program committee, special sessions chairs, and editors. We sincerely appreciate their involvement and support, which were crucial for the success of the International Conference on Advanced Research in Technologies, Information, Innovation and Sustainability (ARTIIS 2023). We also wish to thank our publisher, Springer, for agreeing to publish the proceedings.

The success of this third edition gives us a lot of confidence to continue the work. So, we hope to see you in the fourth edition in 2024, which will be in Chile.

We cordially invite you to visit the ARTIIS website https://artiis.org.

September 2023

Teresa Guarda
Filipe Portela
Jose Maria Diaz-Nafria

Organization

General Chairs

Teresa Guarda   Universidad Estatal Península de Santa Elena, Ecuador/Universidad a Distancia de Madrid, Spain

Filipe Portela   Algoritmi Research Centre, UM, Portugal/Minho University, Portugal

Program Committee Chairs

Teresa Guarda   Universidad Estatal Península de Santa Elena, Ecuador

Filipe Portela   Minho University, Portugal

José María Díaz-Nafría   Universidad a Distancia de Madrid, Spain

Organizing Chairs

Isaac Seoane Pujol   Universidad a Distancia de Madrid, Spain

Jorge Morato Lara   Universidad Carlos III de Madrid, Spain

José María Díaz-Nafría   Universidad a Distancia de Madrid, Spain

Maria Fernanda Augusto   BITrum Research Group, Spain

Silvia Prieto Preboste   Universidad a Distancia de Madrid, Spain

Steering Committee

Andrei Tchernykh   CICESE Research Center, Mexico

Beatriz De La Iglesia   University of East Anglia, UK

Bruno Sousa   University of Coimbra, Portugal

Enrique Carrera   Universidad de las Fuerzas Armadas ESPE, Ecuador

Modestos Stavrakis   University of the Aegean, Greece

Ricardo Vardasca   ISLA Santarem, Portugal

Wolfgang Hofkirchner   Technische Universität Wien, Austria

Special Sessions Chairs

Abrar Ullah	Heriot-Watt University, Dubai
Teresa Guarda	Universidad Estatal Península de Santa Elena, Ecuador

ARTIIS Program Committee

A. Manuela Gonçalves	University of Minho, Portugal
Abbas Aljuboori	Al Zahra College for Women, Oman
Alberto Simões	Instituto Politécnico do Cávado e do Ave, Portugal
Alejandro Rodriguez	Universidad Politécnica de Madrid, Spain
Aleksandra Djordjevic	University of Belgrade, Serbia
Alfredo Cuzzocrea	University of Calabria, Italy
Alfredo Milani	University of Perugia, Italy
Ana Azevedo	Polytechnic Institute of Porto, Portugal
Ana Cláudia Campos	University of Algarve, Portugal
Ana Paula Teixeira	Universidade de Trás-os-Montes e Alto Douro, Portugal
Ana Pereira	Polytechnic Institute of Bragança, Portugal
Ana Ramires	Universidade Europeia, Portugal
Anacleto Correia	CINAV/Escola Naval, Portugal
Andreas Fricke	University of Potsdam, Germany
Andrei Tchernykh	CICESE Research Center, Mexico
Angel Dacal-Nieto	CTAG Centro Tecnológico de Automoción de Galicia, Spain
Anisha Kumari	National Institute of Technology Rourkela, India
Antonio Dourado	University of Coimbra, Portugal
António Fernandes	Instituto Politécnico de Bragança, Portugal
Antonio Jesús Muñoz-Montoro	Universidad de Málaga, Spain
Antonio Silva Sprock	Universidad Central de Venezuela, Venezuela
António Trigo	Instituto Politécnico de Coimbra, ISCAC, Portugal
Arnulfo Alanis Garza	Instituto Tecnológico de Tijuana, Mexico
Asma Patel	Staffordshire University, UK
Attila Körei	University of Miskolc, Hungary
Babar Shah	Zayed University, United Arab Emirates
Barna Iantovics	University of Medicine, Pharmacy, Science, and Technology of Târgu Mureş, Romania
Beatriz De La Iglesia	University of East Anglia, UK
Benedetto Barabino	Università degli Studi di Brescia, Italy

Bertil P. Marques	Instituto Superior de Engenharia do Porto, Portugal
Biswajeeban Mishra	University of Szeged, Hungary
Bruno Sousa	University of Coimbra, Portugal
Camille Salinesi	Université de Paris1 Panthéon-Sorbonne, France
Carina Pimentel	University of Aveiro, Portugal
Carina Silva	Escola Superior de Tecnologia da Saúde de Lisboa, Portugal
Carla Cavallo	University of Naples Federico II, Italy
Carlos Balsa	Instituto Politécnico de Bragança, Portugal
Carlos Costa	Universidade de Lisboa, Portugal
Carlos Fajardo	Fundación Universitaria Konrad Lorenz, Colombia
Carlos H. F. Alves	Federal Center of Technological Education, Brazil
Carlos Lopezosa	Universitat Pompeu Fabra Barcelona, Spain
Carlos R. Cunha	Instituto Politécnico de Bragança, Portugal
Carmen Guida	Università degli Studi di Napoli Federico II, Italy
Cecilia Avila	Fundación Universitaria Konrad Lorenz, Colombia
Cecilia Castro	Universidade do Minho, Portugal
Celia Ramos	University of the Algarve, Portugal
Chien-Sing Lee	Sunway University, Malaysia
Christian Grévisse	University of Luxembourg, Luxembourg
Christoph Schütz	Johannes Kepler University Linz, Austria
Christos Anagnostopoulos	University of Glasgow, UK
Clara Bento Vaz	Instituto Politécnico de Bragança, Portugal
Clarice Maraschin	Universidade Federal do Rio Grande do Sul, Brazil
Claudia Seabra	University of Coimbra, Portugal
Corrado Rindone	Università degli studi Mediterranea di Reggio Calabria, Italy
Daniele Granata	Università della Campania "Luigi Vanvitelli", Italy
Dasa Munkova	Constantine the Philosopher University in Nitra, Slovakia
Dimos Pantazis	Technological Education Institution of Athens, Greece
Elena Cantatore	Politecnico di Bari, Italy
Elena Cocuzza	University of Catania, Italy
Elisabetta Ronchieri	INFN CNAF, Italy
Elisete Mourão	Universidade de Trás-os-Montes e Alto Douro, Portugal
Emmanuel Okewu	University of Lagos, Nigeria

Enrique Carrera	Universidad de las Fuerzas Armadas, Ecuador
Erica Isa Mosca	Politecnico di Milano, Italy
Ester Scotto di Perta	University of Naples Federico II, Italy
Estrella Diaz	Castilla-La Mancha University, Spain
Eugen Rusu	Dunarea de Jos University of Galati, Romania
Fabio Alberto Schreiber	Politecnico di Milano, Italy
Fabio Rocha	Universidade Tiradentes, Brazil
Fabio Silveira	Federal University of São Paulo, Brazil
Fakhri Alam Khan	King Fahd University of Petroleum & Minerals, Saudi Arabia
Federica Gaglione	Università degli Studi del Sannio, Italy
Felipe S. Semaan	Fluminense Federal University, Brazil
Felix Härer	University of Fribourg, Switzerland
Fernanda A. Ferreira	Polytechnic Institute of Porto, Portugal
Fezile Ozdamli	Near East University, Turkey
Filipe Mota Pinto	Polytechnic Institute of Leiria, Portugal
Filipe Portela	University of Minho, Portugal
Flavia Marzano	Link Campus University, Italy
Flora Ferreira	University of Minho, Portugal
Florin Pop	University Politehnica of Bucharest, Romania
Francesco Mercaldo	University of Sannio, Italy
Francesco Palmieri	University of Salerno, Italy
Francesco Santini	Università di Perugia, Italy
Francisco Alvarez	Universidad Autónoma de Aguascalientes, Mexico
Frederico Branco	Universidade de Trás-os-Montes e Alto Douro, Portugal
Frederico Lopes	Universidade Federal do Rio Grande do Norte, Brazil
Gabriel Hornink	Federal University of Alfenas, Brazil
Geert Poels	Ghent University, Belgium
George Stalidis	Alexander Technological Educational Institute of Thessaloniki, Greece
Georgios Georgiadis	Aristotle University of Thessaloniki, Greece
Gerardo Carpentieri	University of Naples Federico II, Italy
Gianni D'Angelo	University of Salerno, Italy
Giovanni Paragliola	ICAR-CNR, Italy
Guillermo Rodriguez	ISISTAN-UNICEN, Argentina
Gustavo Gatica	Universidad Andrés Bello, Chile
Héctor Bedón	Universidad a Distancia de Madrid, Spain
Helia Guerra	University of Azores, Portugal
Henrique Vicente	Universidade de Évora, Portugal

Hugo Peixoto	University of Minho, Portugal
Humberto Rocha	Universidade de Coimbra, Portugal
Ilaria Matteucci	IIT-CNR, Italy
Inna Skarga-Bandurova	Oxford Brookes University, UK
Ioan Ciumasu	Université de Versailles Saint-Quentin, France
Ioannis Politis	Aristotle University of Thessaloniki, Greece
Ioannis Vrellis	University of Ioannina, Greece
Iqbal H. Sarker	Edith Cowan University, Australia
Isabel Lopes	Instituto Politécnico de Bragança, Portugal
J. Luis Luviano-Ortiz	University of Guanajuato, Mexico
Jakub Swacha	University of Szczecin, Poland
Joanna Kolodziej	NASK Warsaw and Cracow University of Technology, Poland
Jordi Vallverdú	Universitat Autònoma de Barcelona, Spain
Jorge Buele	Universidad Tecnológica Indoamerica, Ecuador
Jorge Herrera-Tapia	Universidad Laica Eloy Alfaro de Manabí, Ecuador
Jorge Luis Bacca Acosta	University of Girona, Spain
Jorge Oliveira e Sá	University of Minho, Portugal
José Carlos Paiva	University of Porto, Portugal
Jose Guillermo Guarnizo Marin	Santo Tomás University, Colombia
José Machado	University of Minho, Portugal
José María Díaz-Nafría	Madrid Open University, Spain
José Méndez Reboredo	University of Vigo, Spain
José Rufino	Polytechnic Institute of Bragança, Portugal
Juan-Ignacio Latorre-Biel	Public University of Navarre, Spain
Kalinka Kaloyanova	University of Sofia, Bulgaria
Kanchana Rajaram	SSN College of Engineering, India
Karine Ferreira	Instituto Nacional de Pesquisas Espaciais, Brazil
Kazuaki Tanaka	Kyushu Institute of Technology, Japan
Laura Verde	Università della Campania Luigi Vanvitelli, Italy
Lelio Campanile	Università degli Studi della Campania Luigi Vanvitelli, Italy
Leonardo Soto-Sumuano	Universidad de Guadalajara, Mexico
Leticia Vaca-Cardenas	Universidad Técnica de Manabí, Ecuador
L'ubomír Benko	Constantine the Philosopher University in Nitra, Slovakia
Luigi Piero Di Bonito	University of Campania Luigi Vanvitelli, Italy
Luis Gomes	Universidade dos Açores, Portugal
Luís Matos	Universidade do Minho, Portugal
Luiza de Macedo Mourelle	State University of Rio de Janeiro, Brazil
M. Filomena Teodoro	Portuguese Naval Academy, Portugal

Manuela Cañizares Espada	Universidad a Distancia de Madrid, Spain
Manuele Kirsch-Pinheiro	Université Paris 1 Panthéon-Sorbonne, France
Marcelo Fajardo-Pruna	Escuela Superior Politécnica del Litoral, Ecuador
Marcelo Leon	Universidad Tecnológica Empresarial de Guayaquil, Ecuador
Marcin Woźniak	Silesian University of Technology, Poland
Marco Gribaudo	Politecnico di Milano, Italy
Marco Zucca	University of Cagliari, Italy
Marco Cabezas González	Universidad de Salamanca, Spain
Margherita Lasorella	Polytechnic University of Bari, Italy
Maria Isabel Ribeiro	Instituto Politécnico Bragança, Portugal
Maria João Fernandes Polidoro	Politécnico do Porto, Portugal
Maria João Rodrigues	Universidade do Porto, Portugal
Maria José Abreu	Universidade do Minho, Portugal
Maria Macchiaroli	University of Salerno, Italy
Maria Sousa	CIEO Centre for Spatial and Organizational Dynamics, Portugal
Maria Stella de Biase	Università degli Studi della Campania Luigi Vanvitelli, Italy
Mariapia Raimondo	Università degli Studi della Campania Luigi Vanvitelli, Italy
Marílio Cardoso	Instituto Superior de Engenharia do Porto, Portugal
Marilisa Botte	University of Naples Federico II, Italy
Marina Alexandra Andrade	ISCTE Instituto Universitário de Lisboa, Portugal
Mario Pérez-Montoro	University of Barcelona, Spain
Mario Pinto	Politécnico do Porto, Portugal
Maritza Placencia	Universidad Nacional Mayor de San Marco, Peru
Martinha Piteira	Instituto Politécnico de Setúbal, Portugal
Mauro Iacono	Università degli Studi della Campania Luigi Vanvitelli, Italy
Michal Baczynski	University of Silesia in Katowice, Poland
Michal Munk	Constantine the Philosopher University in Nitra, Slovakia
Michel Soares	Universidade Federal de Sergipe, Brazil
Michele Mastroianni	University of Salerno, Italy
Milliam Maxime	Zekeng Ndadji University of Dschang, Cameroon
Mirka Mobilia	University of Salerno, Italy
Modestos Stavrakis	University of the Aegean, Greece
Mohamad Molaei Qelichi	University of Tehran, Iran
Mohammadsadegh Mohagheghi	Vali-e-Asr University of Rafsanjan, Iran
Mónica Pinto	Universidad de Málaga, Spain
Muhammad Younas	Oxford Brookes University, UK

Naveed Abbas	Islamia College, Peshawar, Malaysia
Naveenbalaji Gowthaman	University of KwaZulu-Natal, South Africa
Neelam Gohar	Shaheed Benazir Bhutto Women University, Pakistan
Nguyen D. Thanh	Banking University of Ho Chi Minh City, Vietnam
Nikolaos Matsatsinis	Technical University of Crete, Greece
Nishu Gupta	Norwegian University of Science and Technology in Gjøvik, Norway
Nuno C. Marques	Universidade Nova de Lisboa, Portugal
Nuno Pombo	University of Beira Interior, Portugal
Olivier Parisot	Luxembourg Institute of Science and Technology, Luxembourg
Omar Castellanos	Universidad Estatal Península de Santa Elena, Ecuador
Omid Fatahi Valilai	Constructor University, Germany
Oscar Dias	University of Minho, Portugal
Pankaj Mishra	G. B. Pant University of Agriculture and Technology, India
Paola Britos	Universidad Nacional de Río Negro - Sede Andina/Atlántica, Argentina
Paolino Di Felice	University of L'Aquila, Italy
Patricia Cano-Olivos	Universidad Popular Autónoma del Estado de Puebla, Mexico
Paula Amaral	Universidade Nova de Lisboa, Portugal
Paula Odete Fernandes	Instituto Politécnico de Bragança, Portugal
Paulo Piloto	Polytechnic Institute of Bragança, Portugal
Paulo Vasconcelos	University of Porto, Portugal
Pedro Gago	Polytechnic Institute of Leiria, Portugal
Piedade Carvalho	Instituto Superior de Engenharia do Porto, Portugal
Rafal Scherer	Częstochowa University of Technology, Poland
Raphael Gomes	Instituto Federal de Goiás, Brazil
Ricardo Cajo	Escuela Superior Politécnica del Litoral, Ecuador
Ricardo Correia	Instituto Politécnico de Bragança, Portugal
Ricardo Queirós	Politécnico do Porto, Portugal
Ricardo Vardasca	ISLA Santarem, Portugal
Robertas Damasevicius	Silesian University of Technology, Poland
Roberto Andrade	Escuela Politécnica Nacional, Ecuador
Roberto Nardone	University of Naples "Parthenope", Italy
Roman Chertovskih	University of Porto, Portugal
Ronan Guivarch	Université de Toulouse, France
Rosa Reis	Instituto Superior de Engenharia do Porto, Portugal

Rytis Maskeliunas, Kaunas	University of Technology, Lithuania
S. B. Kulkarni	SDMCET, India
Said Broumi	Hassan II University Mohammedia-Casablanca, Morocco
Samson Oruma	Østfold University College, Norway
Sanjay Misra	Østfold University, Norway
Sanket Mishra	BITS Pilani Hyderabad Campus, India
Sara Paiva	Instituto Politécnico de Viana do Castelo, Portugal
Sergio Cappucci	ENEA, Italy
Sergio Ilarri	University of Zaragoza, Spain
Shelly Sachdeva	National Institute of Technology Delhi, India
Sherali Zeadally	University of Kentucky, USA
Shuhei Kimura	Tottori University, Japan
Silvia Araújo	University of Minho, Portugal
Silvia Rossetti	Università degli Studi di Parma, Italy
Simone Belli	Universidad Complutense de Madrid, Spain
Simone Corrado	Università degli Studi della Basilicata, Italy
Smriti Agrawal	Chaitanya Bharathi Institute of Technology, India
Socrates Basbas	Aristotle University of Thessaloniki, Greece
Sofia Almeida	Universidade Europeia, Portugal
Sonia Casillas Martín	Universidad de Salamanca, Spain
Spyros Panagiotakis	Hellenic Mediterranean University, Greece
Stefania Regalbuto	Ca' Foscari University of Venice, Italy
Stefano Falcinelli	University of Perugia, Italy
Stephan Scheele	Fraunhofer IIS, Germany
Sumit Babu	Harcourt Butler Technical University, India
Syeda Sumbul Hossain	Daffodil International University, Bangladesh
Sylwia Krzysztofik	Lodz University of Technology, Poland
Tapiwa Gundu	Sol Plaatje University, South Africa
Telmo Pinto	University of Minho, Portugal
Tengku Adil Tengku Izhar	Universiti Teknologi MARA, Malaysia
Teresa Guarda	Universidad Estatal Península de Santa Elena, Ecuador
Tetiana Biloborodova	Volodymyr Dahl East Ukraine National University, Ukraine
Tiziana Campisi	Kore University of Enna, Italy
Ugo Fiore	Federico II University, Italy
Ulises Ruiz	Instituto Nacional de Astrofisica Óptica y Electrónica, Mexico
Vanda Lourenco	NOVA University of Lisbon, Portugal
Vasileios Gkioulos	Norwegian University of Science and Technology, Norway

Vicente Ferreira De Lucena Jr.	Federal University of Amazonas, Brazil
Victor Alves	University of Minho, Portugal
Victor Darriba	Universidade de Vigo, Spain
Virginie Felizardo	Universidade da Beira Interior, Portugal
Vitor Monteiro	University of Minho, Portugal
Vladimir Tcheverda	Institute of Petroleum Geology and Geophysics, Russia

Special Session Organizers

Applications of Computational Mathematics to Simulation and Data Analysis (ACMaSDA 2023)

Carlos Balsa	CEDRI-IPB, Portugal
Victoria Espinar	CITMaga - USC, Spain
Ronan Guivarch	IRIT-UFTMiP, France
Sílvio Gama	Universidade do Porto, Portugal

Challenges and the Impact of Communication and Information Technologies on Education (CICITE 2023)

| Teresa Guarda | Universidad Estatal Península de Santa Elena, Ecuador |
| Maria Fernanda Augusto | BITrum Research Group, Spain |

3rd Workshop on Gamification Application and Technologies (GAT 2023)

Ricardo Queirós	ESMAD, Portugal
Mário Pinto	ESMAD, Portugal
Filipe Portela	University of Minho, Portugal

Bridging Knowledge in a Fragmented World (glossaLAB 2023)

José María Díaz-Nafría	Universidad a Distancia de Madrid, Spain
Jorge Morato Lara	Universidad a Distancia de Madrid, Spain
Sonia Sánchez-Cuadrado	Universidad a Distancia de Madrid, Spain
Manuela Cañizares	Universidad a Distancia de Madrid, Spain
Héctor Bedón	Universidad a Distancia de Madrid, Spain
Isaac Seoane-Pujol	Universidad a Distancia de Madrid, Spain

Intelligent Systems for Health and Medical Care (ISHMC 2023)

Arnulfo Alanis   National Technological Institute of Mexico,
                                  Mexico
Bogart Yail Marquez   National Technological Institute of Mexico,
                                  Mexico
Rosario Baltazar   National Technological Institute of Mexico,
                                  Mexico

Intelligent Systems in Forensic Engineering (ISIFE 2023)

Alessia Amelio   University "G. d'Annunzio" Chieti-Pescara, Italy
Samuele Biondi   University "G. d'Annunzio" Chieti-Pescara, Italy
Regina Finocchiaro   University "G. d'Annunzio" Chieti-Pescara, Italy
Luciano Caroprese   University "G. d'Annunzio" Chieti-Pescara, Italy
Samantha Di Loreto   University "G. d'Annunzio" Chieti-Pescara, Italy
Sergio Montelpare   University "G. d'Annunzio" Chieti-Pescara, Italy

International Symposium on Technological Innovations for Industry and Society (ISTIIS 2023)

Filipe Portela   University of Minho, Portugal and IOTECH,
                                  Portugal
Rita Miranda   IOTECH, Portugal

International Workshop on Electronic and Telecommunications (IWET 2023)

Luis Chuquimarca   Universidad Estatal Península de Santa Elena,
                                  Ecuador
Carlos Peñafiel   Universidad Nacional del Chimborazo, Ecuador
Leticia Vaca   Universidad Técnica Manabí, Ecuador
Ricardo Cajo   Escuela Superior Politécnica del Litoral, Ecuador

Innovation in Educational Technology (JIUTE 2023)

Alba García Barrera   Universidad a Distancia de Madrid, Spain
Francisco David de la Peña   Universidad a Distancia de Madrid, Spain
  Esteban
Lucas Castro Martínez   Universidad a Distancia de Madrid, Spain
Verónica Nistal Anta   Universidad a Distancia de Madrid, Spain

Smart Tourism and Information Systems (SMARTTIS 2023)

Isabel Lopes	Instituto Politécnico de Bragança, Portugal
Isabel Ribeiro	Instituto Politécnico de Bragança, Portugal
Carlos Rompante Cunha	Instituto Politécnico de Bragança, Portugal

Special Sessions Program Committee

Adriano Mancini	Universitá Politecnica delle Marche, Italy
Ahmad Ali	Shenzhen University, China
Alba Garcia Barrera	Universidad a Distancia de Madrid, Spain
Ana Azevedo	CEOS.PP, ISCAP, Polytechnic of Porto, Portugal
Ana Dopico	Universidade de Vigo, Spain
Andres Muñoz	Universidad de Cádiz, Spain
Angel Recalde	Escuela Superior Politécnica del Litoral, Ecuador
Angel Torres Toukoumidis	Universidad Politécnica Salesiana, Ecuador
António Fernandes	Instituto Politécnico de Bragança, Portugal
Antonio Jesús Muñoz-Montoro	Universidad de Málaga, Spain
Antonio Mauricio Silva Sprock	Universidad Central de Venezuela, Venezuela
Antonio Moreira	Polytechnic Institute of Cávado and Ave, Portugal
Asma Patel	Aston University, UK
Barna Iantovics	UMFST, Romania
Benito Mendoza Trujillo	Universidada Nacional de Chimborazo, Ecuador
Bertil P. Marques	Polytechnic Institute of Porto, Portugal
Bogart Yail Marquez	Instituto Tecnológico Tijauna, Mexico
Bráulio Alturas	Instituto Universitário de Lisboa, Portugal
Carlos Balsa	Instituto Politécnico de Bragança, Portugal
Carlos Gordon	Universidad Técnica de Ambato, Ecuador
Carlos H. F. Alves	Federal Center of Technological Education, Brazil
Carlos Peñafiel	Universidad Nacional del Chimborazo, Ecuador
Carlos R. Cunha	Instituto Politécnico de Bragança, Portugal
Celia Ramos	University of the Algarve, Portugal
Chiara Braghin	Università degli Studi di Milano, Italy
Cristian Javier Rocha Jácome	Universidad de Sevilla, Spain
Daniel Santillán	UNACH, Ecuador
Datzania Villao	Universidad Estatal Península de Santa Elena, Ecuador
David Lizcano Casas	Madrid Open University, Spain
David Moreno	ESPOCH, Ecuador
Diego Paredes	UTN, Ecuador
Douglas Plaza	ESPOL, Ecuador

Eleni Christopoulou	Ionian University, Greece
Enrique-Javier Díez-Gutiérrez	Universidad de León, Spain
Estevan Gomez	Universidad de las Fuerzas Armadas, Ecuador
Fabrizio Messina	University of Catania, Italy
Fausto Calderón Pineda	Universidad Estatal Península de Santa Elena, Ecuador
Fernando Rodríguez Varela	Universidad Rey Juan Carlos, Spain
Filipe Pinto	Polytechnic Institute of Leiria, Portugal
Filipe Portela	University of Minho, Portugal
Francesco Cauteruccio	Polytechnic University of Marche, Italy
Franklin Eduardo Samaniego Riera	Universidad Nacional de Chimborazo, Ecuador
Frederico Branco	Universidade de Trás-Os-Montes e Alto Douro, Portugal
Frederico Lopes	UFRN, Brazil
Gerhard Chroust	Johannes Kepler University Linz, Austria
Giada Gasparini	University of Bologna, Italy
Giuseppe Festa	University of Salerno, Italy
Gunta Grinberga-Zalite	University of Life Sciences and Technologies, Latvia
Hector Bedon	Universidad a Distancia de Madrid, Spain
Hugo Moreno Aviles	Escuela Superior Politécnica de Chimborazo, Ecuador
Hugo Peixoto	University of Minho, Portugal
Ijaz Ahmad	Università Telematica "Leonardo Da Vinci", Italy
Ingars Eriņš	Riga Technical University, Latvia
Inna Skarga-Bandurova	Oxford Brookes University, UK
Ioan Ciumasu	UVSQ, France
Ioannis Vrellis	University of Ioannina, Greece
Isaac Seoane Pujol	Madrid Open University, Spain
Isabel Lopes	Instituto Politécnico de Bragança, Portugal
Isabel Pedrosa	Instituto Politécnico de Coimbra, Portugal
Jaciel Gustavo Kunz	FURG, Brazil
Jeniffer García Mendoza	Grupo Ananke, Ecuador
Jessica S. Ortiz	Universidad de las Fuerzas Armada, Ecuador
Jezreel Mejía Miranda	CIMAT, Mexico
Jhonattan Javier Barriga Andrade	IT Systems Security, Ecuador
João Cordeiro	University of Beira Interior, Portugal
Jorge Bernardino	Polytechnic Institute of Coimbra, Portugal
Jorge L. Hernandez-Ambato	Escuela Superior Politécnica de Chimborazo, Ecuador
Jorge Morato	Universidad Carlos III, Spain

Jorge Oliveira e Sá	University of Minho, Portugal
Jorge Oliveira	NOVA School of Science and Technology, Portugal
José Israel Hernández Vázquez	Instituto Tecnológico de León, Mexico
José María Díaz-Nafría	Madrid Open University, Spain
José Matos	University of Porto, Portugal
José Omar Hernández Vázquez	Instituto Tecnológico de León, Mexico
José Rufino	Polytechnic Institute of Bragança, Portugal
Jose Xavier Tomalá	Universidad Estatal Península de Santa Elena, Ecuador
Juan Pablo Ciafardini	UNLP, Argentina
Juan Rodriguez-Fernandez	Universidad de León, Spain
Juan V. Capella	Universitat Politècnica de València, Spain
Karolina Baras	University of Madeira, Portugal
Lasma Licite-Kurbe	Latvia University of Life Sciences and Technologies, Latvia
Leonardo Chancay-García	Universidad Técnica de Manabí, Ecuador
Leonardo Renteria	UNACH, Ecuador
Leticia Vaca-Cardenas	Universidad Técnica de Manabí, Ecuador
Lidice Haz	Universidad Estatal Península de Santa Elena, Ecuador
Linda Groma	Latvia University of Life Sciences and Technologies, Latvia
Lorena Molina Valdiviezo	Universidad Nacional de Chimborazo, Ecuador
Luis Alfonso Gaxiola	Universidad Autónoma de Baja California, Mexico
Luis Amaya	Universidad Estatal Península de Santa Elena, Ecuador
Luis Enrique Chuquimarca Jimenez	Universidad Estatal Península de Santa Elena, Ecuador
Luís Matos	Universidade do Minho, Portugal
Luis Mazon	BITrum Research Group, Ecuador
Manuel Montaño	Universidad Estatal Península de Santa Elena, Ecuador
Manuela Cañizares Espada	UDIMA, Spain
Manuele Kirsch Pinheiro	Paris 1 Panthéon-Sorbonne University, France
Marcela Palacios	Instituto Tecnológico Superior de Purísima del Rincón, Mexico
Marcelo Zambrano	Universidad Técnica del Norte, Ecuador
Marcia Marisol Bayas Sampedro	Universidad Estatal Península de Santa Elena, Ecuador
Marcos Cevallos	UCAB, Ecuador
Maria Covelo	UA, Portugal

María del Carmen Messina Scolaro — Universidad de la República, Uruguay

Maria Isabel Ribeiro — Instituto Politécnico Bragança, Portugal

Maria João Rodrigues — Universidade do Porto, Portugal

María Verdeja Muñiz — Universidad de Oviedo, Spain

Mario Pérez-Montoro — Universitat de Barcelona, Spain

Mario Pinto — ESMAD.IPP, Portugal

Mehran Pourvahab — University of Beira Interior, Portugal

Miguel Efraín Sangurima Pacheco — Universidad Nacional de Chimborazo, Ecuador

Mirna Muñoz Mata — Centro de Investigación en Matemáticas - Unidad Zacatecas, Mexico

Modestos Stavrakis — University of the Aegean, Greece

Nelia Gonzalez — Universidad Espíritu Santo, Ecuador

Nuno Pombo — University of Beira Interior, Portugal

Omar Castellanos — Universidad Estatal Península de Santa Elena, Ecuador

Panos Fitsilis — University of Thessaly, Greece

Paul Diaz — Universidad de las Fuerzas Armadas, Ecuador

Paula Odete Fernandes — Instituto Politécnico de Bragança, Portugal

Paulo Vasconcelos — University of Porto, Portugal

Pedro Aguado — Universidad de León, Spain

Pedro Gago — Polytechnic Institute of Leiria, Portugal

Pedro Oliveira — Instituto Politécnico de Bragança, Portugal

Piedade Carvalho — Instituto Superior de Engenharia do Porto, Portugal

Radmila Jankovic — Mathematical Institute of Serbian Academy of Sciences and Arts, Serbia

Rafael Angarita — Isep, Inria, France

Rainer E. Zimmermann — UAS for Technology and Economics Berlin (HTW), Germany

Regina Finocchiaro — "Gabriele d'Annunzio" Università di Chieti-Pescara, Italy

René Faruk Garzozi-Pincay — Universidad Estatal Península de Santa Elena, Ecuador

Ricardo Cajo — Escuela Superior Politécnica del Litoral, Ecuador

Ricardo Correia — Instituto Politécnico de Bragança, Portugal

Ricardo Godinho Bilro — ISCTE-Instituto Universitário de Lisboa, Portugal

Ricardo Queirós — Polytechnic Institute of Porto & CRACS - INESC TEC, Portugal

Roberth Abel Alcivar Cevallos — Universidad Técnica de Manabí, Ecuador

Roger Idrovo — Universidad de Navarra, Spain

Roman Chertovskih — University of Porto, Portugal

Ronan Guivarch — IRIT - Université de Toulouse, France

Rosa María Martínez	University of Almería, Spain
Rosa Reis	ISEP, Portugal
Rosario Baltazar Flores	Instituto Tecnológico de León, Mexico
Sang Guun Yoo	Escuela Politécnica Nacional, Ecuador
Sebastião Pais	University of Beira Interior, Portugal
Senka Borovac Zekan	University of Split, Croatia
Sergio Magdaleno	Instituto Tecnológico de Tijuana, Mexico
Silvia Prieto Preboste	Universidad a Distancia de Madrid, Spain
Sílvio Gama	Universidade do Porto, Portugal
Simone Belli	Universidad Complutense de Madrid, Spain
Siu Ming Yiu	University of Hong Kong, China
Surendrabikram Thapa	Virginia Tech, USA
Susana Burnes R.	Universidad Autónoma de Zacatecas, Mexico
Teresa Guarda	Universidad Estatal Península de Santa Elena, Ecuador
Tiago C. Pereira	University of Minho, Portugal
Ulises Ruiz	INAOE, Mexico
Verónica Crespo	Universidade da Coruña, Spain
Victor Huilcapi	Universidad Politécnica Salesiana, Ecuador
Victoria Otero-Espinar	University of Santiago de Compostela, Spain
Virginie Felizardo	Universidade da Beira Interior, Portugal
Wendoly Julieta Guadalupe Romero Rodriguez	Instituto Tecnológico Superior de Guanajuato, Mexico
Wolfgang Hofkirchner	Institute for a Global Sustainable Information Society, Austria

Sponsors

Universidad Estatal Península de Santa Elena, Ecuador
Universidade do Minho, Portugal
Universidad a Distancia de Madrid, Spain
Algoritmi Research Centre, Portugal
BITrum Research Group, Spain
The Institute for a Global Sustainable Information Society GSIS, Austria

Contents – Part II

Ethics, Security, and Privacy

Sustainability

Exploring the Relationship Between Innovation, Entry Modes and Destination Countries

Mónica Azevedo[1,2] , Carla Azevedo Lobo[1,2(✉)] , Carla Santos Pereira[1,2] , and Natércia Durão[1,2]

[1] Universidade Portucalense, Porto, Portugal
cadsa@upt.pt

[2] REMIT- Research on Economics, Management and Information Technologies, Porto, Portugal

Abstract. In a world characterized by globalization, where the internationalization of businesses is pivotal for their prosperity, innovation is emerging as a pivotal strategic choice influencing their growth and competitive edge. Despite the broad consensus on the growing importance of internationalization and innovation, some questions arise about the relationship of innovation with entry modes with less commitment to the market and with destination markets with less risks. In order to determine whether there is a pattern of relationship between internationalization modes, destination markets, and innovation for Portuguese firms, the objective is to study this possibility. To achieve this goal, we carried out an online questionnaire survey to collect data. The questionnaire was carefully designed based on a literature review and included various variables related to the internationalization of firms. It was sent to all 8183 firms listed in the AICEP database of Portuguese internationalized firms through Google Forms tool. The data was collected over an 8-month period, starting in May 2019. To analyze the data, we used IBM SPSS Statistics 27.0 software, applying a quantitative approach. We employed Quantitative Analysis Methodologies: Univariate and Multivariate Exploratory Factorial Analysis (EFA), Correlation analysis and the nonparametric tests Chi-square and Mann-Whitney. Based on the findings, the empirical evidence clearly demonstrates that firms employing internationalization modes demanding higher commitment, along with those targeting geographically and psychologically distant markets, place significantly greater emphasis on innovation as a pivotal factor driving their international expansion.

Keywords: Innovation · Internationalization · Internationalization Modes

1 Introduction

Researchers generally agree that internationalization is crucial to a firm's survival and expansion. Likewise, innovation is acknowledged as a critical factor driving a firm's progress and competitive edge. In light of the aforementioned, the literature has begun to pay more attention to the connection between innovation and internationalization. This link can be examined from two distinct perspectives: innovation as a cause of or a result of a firm's international expansion [1–7]. Additionally, a sizable body of literature

T. Guarda et al. (Eds.): ARTIIS 2023, CCIS 1936, pp. 3–16, 2024.
https://doi.org/10.1007/978-3-031-48855-9_1

has given this group of businesses extra attention due to the significant contribution that small and medium-sized enterprises (SMEs) make to economic growth. In a global market context, the significance of innovation becomes even more pronounced. The basic relevance of the innovation process is emphasized by Sapienza, Autio, George, and Zahra [8], who stress that businesses must constantly adapt to the dynamic changes in their environment. They place a special emphasis on product innovation. Innovative resources and competencies are essential for a firm's growth, according to Zucchella and Siano [1], both in domestic and international markets. Researchers like Genc, Dayan and Genc [2] and Saridakis, Idris, Hansen and Dana [4], when discussing the product life cycle, underscore the necessity for firms to constantly explore new products (or services) to offer, given that these cycles are getting shorter. Moreover, there is a widespread agreement among researchers that internationalization and innovation (often referred to as Research and Development (R&D) [1, 9–11]) are two pivotal strategic decisions for business success [3, 9]. Furthermore, the synergistic effect of internationalization and innovation is considered crucial for the success and endurance of firms in global markets [12]. The relationship between internationalization and innovation is frequently described as a dynamic virtuous circle, whereby they mutually reinforce one another and produce even more advantages [13]. However, despite the general agreement that internationalization and innovation are becoming increasingly important to firms, and the existence of a link between the two, certain questions arise:

Q1: Does the relationship between internationalization and innovation differ according to entry modes?
Q2: Are the most innovative firms those that opt for internationalization modes with greater commitment?
Q3: Are the firms that opt for internationalization modes with greater commitment, those that reveal a greater willingness to take risks?
Q4: Are the firms that opt for internationalization modalities with greater commitment, the ones that internationalize to more distant countries geographically and psychologically?

Taking into account a sample of Portuguese firms, from different sectors of activity (three predominant sectors - 83% of the firms) and of different sizes, this study seeks to address all these inquiries. Therefore, the objective of this paper is to determine whether there is a clear relationship between internationalization strategies and innovation among Portuguese firms. The remainder of this paper is structured as follows. After these introductory remarks, next section presents a literature review. Section 3 is devoted to methodology and results. Finally, Sect. 4 summarizes the main findings of the study and its limitations. It also outlines suggestions for further research in this area.

2   Literature Review

2.1   Internationalization

Internationalization is becoming increasingly important for firms in the modern global economy. With the development of technology and globalization, firms must be able to operate in different markets and cultures. Internationalization opens up new opportunities for firms to expand their customer base, increase revenue, and become more competitive. It also helps to develop new markets, discover new sources of raw materials, and create new partnerships. By building relationships with diverse stakeholders, firms can better understand customer needs and develop strategies to meet them. Internationalization also helps firms to gain access to new talent, capital, and technology. Additionally, it allows firms to diversify their portfolio and reduce risk. By taking advantage of internationalization, firms can remain competitive and achieve sustainable success [14].

2.2 Innovation and Internationalization

So, knowing that firms compete in a complex and uncertain environment with growing global competition, innovation has assumed an increasingly important role in corporate strategy. This fact has been addressed by several authors who, theoretically and/or empirically, underline that innovation is fundamental for the growth of firms, and even for their survival [1, 2, 10, 11]. In addition to studies addressing the effects of internationalization and innovation separately, there are some that focus on internationalization-innovation relationship. Among the latter, it is possible to find those that study the impact of innovation on internationalization, those concerned with the reverse causal relationship and others which consider innovation and internationalization as complementary strategies [1–3, 5–7, 15].

Access to New Technologies or Resources as a Tool of Innovation. Mathews [16] presents various reasons why firms may choose to internationalize. These motives can be categorized as relational, resource-based, or government-incentive-driven. Responding to competition, following customers' internationalization processes, or replicating foreign firms' techniques are examples of relational motives. Resource-based motivations, on the other hand, include pursuing reduced manufacturing costs abroad and gaining access to technological expertise through overseas branches. Additionally, government incentives provided by either the home country or host country can also influence internationalization decisions. Furthermore, Gjergji et al. [3] underscore the paramount importance of resources obtained and cultivated throughout the internationalization journey, with a particular focus on gaining access to novel technological expertise and knowledge through forging alliances with foreign partners. According to these scholars, the resources and skills obtained and/or developed by exporting firms play a critical role in supporting organizational innovation. This perspective finds support from other researchers who assert that small and medium-sized enterprises (SMEs) often lack the necessary resources and capabilities [2, 17] making it challenging for them to invest in research departments [18]. In such a context, engaging in innovation activities through collaborative partnerships established in international markets becomes essential for SMEs. The questionnaire survey used in this study asked entrepreneurs to assess the importance they attach to various factors when deciding to internationalize their firms. These factors were classified into two categories: those related to the Internal Market (such as the need to discover new markets/customers, take advantage of internal resources, reduce/diversify risks, and gain from economies of scale) and those related to the External Market (such as low competition in the target market, favorable growth prospects in a new market, access to new technologies or resources, tracking customers, following partners, and keeping track of competitors). For the purpose of this study, the concept of innovation was operationalized through the variable "Allow access to new technologies or resources," (from now on designated as "ANTR") which is considered to be associated with entrepreneurs' propensity to innovate. Moreover, Klass and Wood [19, pp. 3] offer a comprehensive definition of "propensity to innovate" as the readiness to explore, embrace, and incorporate external ideas, taking calculated risks without trepidation, even in domains beyond the organization's immediate scope. This outlook involves valuing the capacity to think divergently and exhibiting a willingness to endorse and invest in occasionally revolutionary concepts. In turn, Wan, Ong and Lee [20] find that organizational innovation is positively correlated with autonomous structure, organizational resources, conviction in the value of innovation, risk-taking propensity, and openness to sharing ideas. Thus, we consider that it would also be interesting to analyze whether the entrepreneurs who most value internationalization as access to new technologies and resources are those who attach the greatest importance to the propensity to take risks.

Innovation and Internationalization Entry Modes. The readiness to assume risks may also be reflected in the internationalization strategy chosen by entrepreneurs, with exporting being the one that implies a lower commitment by the firm and, consequently, involves less risk. In most of the empirical works that study internationalization, and in particular in those addressing the relationship between internationalization and innovation, exports are considered as 'measure' of internationalization. This can be stated, for example, by analyzing the summary of main articles on the innovation-internationalization relationship presented by Gjergji et al. [3], who even recognize that "export activity" is the most commonly used measure of the degree of the internationalization; they also stress that the degree of internationalization is a complex measure since it depends on several factors and, in their own study, on the grounds of the limited nature of the data, they focus only on export intensity. Furthermore, Zucchella and Siano [1] emphasize that exporting is the typical way of entering foreign markets. Some authors put forward as a possible explanation for this: exporting is still often the initial phase of the internationalization process of SMEs [4, 13, 21]. Notwithstanding, some works have addressed other internationalization modes. Using data from 220 Italian SMEs, Majocchi and Zucchella [22] find that firms' performance owes more to their capability to reach specific markets (such as North America) than to the export intensity and number of international agreements. The results also show that firms' performance tends to be negatively affected when SMEs internationalize through non-export entry modes (namely Foreign Direct Investment (FDI)) - called the 'liability of foreignness' effect, which occurs at an early stage of international expansion. Nevertheless, according to the authors, this negative effect can be outweighed by the international skills that SMEs develop through intensive export activity, that is, when FDI is associated with high levels of export intensity. Moreover, the authors consider that the latter result is in line with the hypothesis that the "knowledge gap" is the biggest obstacle to the international expansion of SMEs. In fact, they explain that by exporting intensively in distant markets (both from a physical and psychological point of view) a value creation process is generated. This process results not only from the contribution of the profitability of the export activity, but also from the positive effects of the accumulated knowledge about other modes of internationalization. Therefore, in order to shed light on this issue, we wanted to analyze whether there is a relationship between innovation, internationalization and the different internationalization strategies. Consequently, we proposed this first hypothesis.

H1: The relationship between internationalization and innovation differ according to entry modes.

Innovation and Commitments Levels of Internationalization. According to Vila and Kuster [23], a firm's internationalization process can progress to the point where it employs more complex and riskier entrance techniques. Furthermore, the authors suggest that a firm achieves its highest innovation potential when it engages in creating new products, implementing new strategies, adopting new processes, and entering new markets. However, they also point out that while many firms may be either international or innovative, only a select few achieve a high level of both internationalization and superior innovations. These exceptional firms are characterized by their willingness to invest abroad and allocate substantial resources to innovate across all four dimensions: products, strategies, processes, and markets. Analyzing a sample of 154 Spanish firms in the textile sector, the authors grouped firms according to their level of internationalization from zero to four, where higher levels of internationalization imply greater risk, control and commitment: firm does not go abroad; firm adopts indirect export; firm uses the direct export formula; firm has export agreements; and firm directly manufactures in the overseas market. Among the conclusions reached by them is the fact that "the internationalization strategy of the firm affects innovation and depends on its international commitment" [23, pp. 32]. Firms that take more risks in entering foreign markets need to continually seek new strategies and processes to gain a better understanding of their new countries. Consequently, it can be said that firms at a higher stage of internationalization tend to have a higher propensity to innovate. Nonetheless, the authors emphasize that firms with higher levels of internationalization are not necessarily the most "product" and "market" innovative businesses, as well as for the specific characteristics of the sector under consideration. The authors also conclude that both internationalization and innovation should be presented in incremental terms because when a firm chooses to venture abroad or innovate, its commitment can be gradually enhanced as more and more resources are allocated to its purpose - this is related to the presence of different levels of internationalization and dimensions of innovation. Stoian, Rialp and Dimitratos [14] consider that different modes of market entry can lead to different network strategies, having a different impact on innovative behavior and foreign market knowledge. Furthermore, in their study analyzing a sample of internationalized British SMEs, they find that there is a positive and significant relationship between international performance and the adoption of innovative behavior. They claim that this is possible because understanding how innovation in foreign markets is related to both exporting and more intensive foreign market servicing will enable SMEs to select the best internationalization strategy, ultimately resulting in improved international performance. Additionally, the authors draw the conclusion that understanding international markets has a favorable and significant impact on innovative behavior. They note in particular that improved understanding of the global business environment, efficient distribution methods, and foreign marketing strategies enable innovation. Abubakar, Hand, Smallbone and Saridakis [24] use a sample of 1058 manufacturing SMEs from least developed Sub-Saharan countries (LDCs) in order to understand what specific modes of internationalization influence SMEs innovation. Building on the work of Zahra, Ireland, and Hitt [25], Kafouros, Buckley, Sharp, and Wang [26], as well as Rada and Božić [27], the study examines three key international entry modes that can impact firm innovation: foreign technology licensing, imports of intermediate production inputs, and exporting. The investigation further distinguishes between process and product innovation. Regarding foreign technology licensing, the results reveal a positive and statistically significant correlation with both product and process innovation. In the case of imports, the authors identify a significant influence on product innovation in certain scenarios, while finding no significant impact of imports of intermediate goods on SME process innovation. Finally, regarding exports, evidence shows that exports do not seem to significantly influence manufacturing SMEs' process and product innovation. Using information gathered from 384 US-based SMEs, Zahra, Ucbasaran, and Newey [28] investigate how SMEs' strategic decisions regarding the extent of their international activities and routes of entrance influence future product innovation for exporting and international expansion. To accomplish that, they deal with two critical aspects of SMEs' internationalization: the international market's expansion (as measured by the number of foreign countries entered) and the mode of entry into the foreign market (licensing, exporting, alliances, acquisitions, and Greenfield investments). The authors especially mention how the techniques SMEs use to reach overseas markets might influence their potential to introduce new items that are suitable to worldwide expansion and export. The analysis leads them to the conclusion that a broader international business environment is more likely to produce effective product innovation in the future, particularly when SMEs have the essential social understanding about their targeted foreign markets. Furthermore, these authors discover a link between higher control and deeper involvement modes of foreign market entry and SMEs' social knowledge that will boost future innovations. Using data from multinational enterprises (MNEs) from developed and developing countries, Álvarez and Marín [29] examine the relationship between national systems of innovation (of host countries) and the diverse ways that firms have to internationalize. Exports, Greenfield FDI and cross-border Mergers and Acquisition are the entry mode considered. These authors even note that the mode of entry can affect the extent of knowledge transfer. Golovko and Valentini [13] investigate the potential complementarity between innovation and export for SMEs' growth. By analyzing a sample of Spanish manufacturing firms, they confirm the existence of a virtuous cycle between the two strategies. Specifically, they find that the positive impact of innovation activity on the growth rate of firms tends to be higher for firms that also export, and vice versa. The findings further point out that, ceteris paribus, the adoption by firms of one growth strategy (such as entry into export markets) have positively affect the adoption of another (such as innovation). In Li's [30] literature review is stressed that internationalization influences innovation through imports, FDI and technology trade: while, by intensifying competition, imports, FDI and technology transfer act as an incentive for innovation, exports provide firms with learning opportunities and incentives to innovate, i.e., provide decision-makers with valuable information to help new firms acquire competitive advantage abroad. Therefore, the literature suggests that there is a relationship between innovation and internationalization modes with greater commitment. So, we proposed the following hypothesis.

H2: The most innovative firms are those that opt for internationalization modes with greater commitment.

Innovation and the Risks of Internationalization. As previously said, firms that take greater risks in entering overseas markets must constantly seek new strategies and processes in order to obtain a deeper grasp of the new country. Therefore, firms at a higher stage of internationalization tend to have a higher propensity to innovate [23]. This risk can be addressed by the distance to the destination country. This distance may be geographic or even psychologic. Thus, in the internationalization process, the choice of destination countries may also be related to the willingness to take risks, being that more than physical distance, psychological distance is associated with greater risk. In this regard, Sass [31] refer that foreign locations are chosen primarily based on the attractiveness of their markets, with firms usually going in stages from countries with less psychic distance to those that are further away. According to Azar and Drogendijk [32] research, cultural distance is a significant cause of uncertainty for firms during the internationalization process. Therefore, knowing which are the main destination countries in the internationalization process could be an interesting clue about the risk readiness and the innovative profile of the entrepreneur. These authors emphasize the work developed by Alvarez and Robertson [33] where they divide export destinations into developing and developed markets and argue that export destination impacts firms' innovation activity. Azar and Drogendijk [32] develop a framework where it is suggested that psychic distance and innovation are directed related, and the latter is directly related to firm performance. Furthermore, they believe that innovation mediates the association between psychic distance and firm performance. In fact, Sass [31] also points out that selling to neighboring countries with low psychic distance usually does not involve specific efforts such as language knowledge, marketing and advertisement. They conclude that firms who export to developing nations are more likely to have R&D units and make investments in product design. On the other hand, firms that export to developed countries are more likely to invest in new products and production processes. Therefore, we wanted to ensure that firms at a higher stage of internationalization tend to have a higher propensity to innovate and that this risk can be addressed by the distance to the destination country, according to the following hypotheses.

H3: The firms that opt for internationalization modes with greater commitment, are those that reveal a greater readiness to take risks.
H4: The firms that opt for internationalization modalities with greater commitment, are the ones that internationalize to more distant countries geographically and psychologically.

3 Methodology

For this research a questionnaire was carried out to collect the data. The questionnaire was carefully designed based on a literature review and included various variables related to the internationalization of firms. It was distributed to all 8183 firms listed in the AICEP database of Portuguese internationalized firms through Google Forms tool. The data was collected over an 8-month period, starting in May 2019. To analyze the data, we employed IBM SPSS Statistics 27.0 software, applying a quantitative approach. We employed Quantitative Analysis Methodologies: Univariate and Multivariate Exploratory Factorial Analysis (EFA), Correlation analysis and the nonparametric tests Chi-square and Mann-Whitney. The study focused on the following variables:

– Internationalization drivers: "ANTR" and "Strong Entrepreneurial and risk-taking propensity" (from now on designated as "SERTP"). These variables were rated by respondents using a 5-point Likert scale from "1-not important" to "5-extremely important"."
– Internationalization modes that indicate the strategies the firm has chosen to internationalize: "One-off export", "Medium-long term exports", "Export through agents", "Technology or brand licensing", "Franchising", "Joint-venture", "Subsidiary", "Project", "Foreign Direct Investment (FDI)" and "other". These variables were chosen accordingly with the literature review [14, 25, 29].

4 Results

In an attempt to answer our Research Questions, we tested the data gathered on the questionnaire. The following table (Table 1) presents, for each of the internationalization modes, the most appropriate statistic measures to assess the importance of the factor "ANTR", that we use to operationalize the innovation of Portuguese firms.

Table 1. Median and mode for "*ANTR*" by internationalization mode.

	One-off export	Medium-long term exports	Export through agents or dealers	Technology or brand licensing	Franchising	Joint-venture	Subsidiary	Project	Foreign Direct Investment (FDI)	Other
Median	3	3	3	4	4	2.5	2.5	3	3	3
Mode	3	3	3	4	4	2 or 3	2	2	1 or 3	4
n	88	126	153	12	5	6	24	47	16	33

According to the collected data, and to address our Hypothesis 1, we can highlight the Export Modalities as those most used by the respondent firms. We can also emphasize the value 4 (very important) for the Median and Mode associated to "Licensing of technology or brand" and "Franchising". However, given the small sample size in these two modalities we cannot draw conclusions with statistical significance.

For this reason and in order to assess whether the modalities with the highest commitment attach a different degree of importance to "ANTR", and thereby test our hypothesis

2, we decided to group the 10 modalities into two groups: group 1- exports group (which includes the first three modalities) and group 2- others (consisting of the remaining 7 modalities). Table 2 presents the achieved results.

Table 2. Median and mode for "*ANTR*" by groups.

	Group 1	Group 2
Median	3	3
Mode	3	2

Table 3. Contingency table and Chi-square test for "*ANTR*" vs groups.

			ANTR					Total
			Not important	Not very important	Important	Very important	Extremely important	
Groups	1	Count	34	43	66	34	11	188
		% within Groups	18,1%	22,9%	35,1%	18,1%	5,9%	100,0%
		% within *Allow access to new technologies or resources*	64,2%	56,6%	73,3%	54,8%	39,3%	60,8%
	2	Count	19	33	24	28	17	121
		% within Groups	15,7%	27,3%	19,8%	23,1%	14,0%	100,0%
		% within *Allow access to new technologies or resources*	35,8%	43,4%	26,7%	45,2%	60,7%	39,2%
Total		Count	53	76	90	62	28	309
		% within Groups	17,2%	24,6%	29,1%	20,1%	9,1%	100,0%
		% within *Allow access to new technologies or resources*	100,0%	100,0%	100,0%	100,0%	100,0%	100,0%

Chi-Square Tests

	Value	df	Asymptotic Significance (2-sided)
Pearson Chi-Square	13,117[a]	4	,011
Likelihood Ratio	13,239	4	,010
Linear-by-Linear Association	2,405	1	,121
N of Valid Cases	309		

a. 0 cells (0,0%) have expected count less than 5. The minimum expected count is 10,96.

The results indicate that there are almost no differences between the 2 groups. The same fact can be observed in Table 3, which crosses the two variables. On one hand, the percentage of firms that consider "ANTR" at least important is 59.1% in group 1 and 56.9% in group 2. On the other hand, we also observe that, amongst the firms that consider "access to new technologies or resources" not at all or not very important, the highest percentages are concentrated on the firms in group 1. Among the firms that consider that factor as extremely important, 60.7% belong to group 2. Moreover, the result of the Chi-square test (p-value = 0.011 < 0.05) allows us to conclude that there are significant differences in the degree of importance granted to "ANTR" according to the groups. Briefly, the firms in group 2 are those that attach more importance the innovation factor.

To test our hypothesis 3, we then decided to carry out statistical analyses that would allow us to assess a possible correlation between the two factors: "SERTP" and "ANTR".

Table 4 shows that, at a significance level of 1%, there is a positive correlation between the two variables (rs = 0.471), in other words, the respondents who most value one variable are those who most value the other.

Table 4. Spearman's correlations between "*SERTP*" and "*ANTR*".

Correlations			Strong entrepreneurial and risk-taking propensity	Allow access to new technologies or resources
Spearman's rho	Strong entrepreneurial and risk-taking propensity	Correlation Coefficient	1,000	,471[**]
		Sig. (2-tailed)		,000
		N	62	62
	Allow access to new technologies or resources	Correlation Coefficient	,471[**]	1,000
		Sig. (2-tailed)	,000	
		N	62	62

[**]. Correlation is significant at the 0.01 level (2-tailed).

Given these results we believe it would be important to know which internationalization destinations have greater relevance regarding these internationalization factors (SERTP and ANTR), and thus test our hypothesis 4. For the Multivariate Exploratory Factorial Analysis – EFA we used the principal components method, followed by a Varimax rotation for extraction, as it produced a more interpretable solution. This analysis generated scores that condensed the information into a smaller set of factors. Table 5 presents the factorial weights of each indicator in the two retained factors (KMO = 0.7). Factorial weights with an absolute value greater than 0.4 are highlighted in bold (Table 5).

Factor 1 (Component 1) is clearly defined by destinations that assign greater relevance to innovation and entrepreneurship factors for internationalization and more

Table 5. Factorial weights of each variable in the 2 retained factors, after EFA.

Rotated Component Matrix[a]

	Component	
	1	2
Spain	,073	,544
Euro zone excluding Spain	,369	**,744**
Europe excluding euro zone	**,590**	,361
Africa	,181	**-,707**
America	**,681**	,029
Asia	**,694**	-,042
Oceania	**,721**	-,127
Allow access to new technologies or resources	**,461**	,287
Strong entrepreneurial and risk-taking propensity	**,439**	,171

Extraction Method: Principal Component Analysis.
Rotation Method: Varimax with Kaiser Normalization.
a. Rotation converged in 3 iterations.

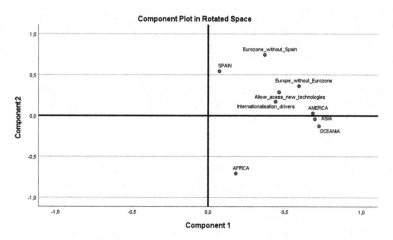

Fig. 1. Component plot in the rotated space.

distant countries. While factor 2 (Component 2) is clearly defined by Africa and Euro Zone destinations excluding Spain.

Thus, the first factor presents higher factor weights in the internationalization destinations Europe excluding euro zone, America, Asia and Oceania and in the variables associated with innovation "ANTR" and "SERTP". These are the destinations with greater geographical and psychological distance, i.e. those requiring less risk aversion.

The second factor have high factor weight, but of opposite direction, in the Eurozone excluding Spain and Africa, and essentially summarizes the inverse position of the firms when the choice of destinations refers to these 2 continents.

5 Discussion

The aim of this study was to investigate the relevance of different modalities associated with exporting for internationalized firms. Additionally, the study explored the importance that firms attach to innovation and access to new technologies or resources when choosing their internationalization mode. The analysis of the statistical results is presented in this discussion.

The data analysis revealed that for the internationalized firms in the sample, the modalities associated with exporting were particularly relevant, supporting Hypothesis 1 - The relationship between internationalization and innovation differ according to entry modes. This finding is consistent with previous literature that highlights the importance of exporting in international business [1, 24].

Regarding Hypothesis 2 - The most innovative firms are those that opt for internationalization modes with greater commitment, the results indicated that both the firms that chose export modes and those that chose internationalization modes with greater commitment placed some importance on "ANTR". However, the firms in group 2 placed greater importance on the innovation factor. These findings supported Hypothesis 2, suggesting that firms that prioritize innovation are more likely to choose more committed internationalization modes [14, 23].

The analysis also supported Hypothesis 3 - The firms that opt for internationalization modes with greater commitment, are those that reveal a greater readiness to take risks. The data showed a positive correlation between entrepreneurial propensity and innovation, indicating that those managers who had a greater readiness for risk-taking were more likely to value innovation.

Finally, Hypothesis 4 - The firms that opt for internationalization modalities with greater commitment, are the ones that internationalize to more distant countries geographically and psychologically suggested that firms that choose to internationalize in countries with more economic and technological potential are those firms for which innovation factors are more significant. The results showed that firms tended to choose Europe excluding euro zone, America, Asia, and Oceania, which are technologically more developed and have more economic potential. In contrast, firms that internationalized their operations to the Eurozone excluding Spain, chose countries with high economic and technological potential as opposed to the African continent which predominantly comprised of countries with low economic and technological power.

6 Conclusion

In summary, the results of this study provide valuable insights into the decision-making processes of internationalized firms. The findings support the literature on the importance of exporting in international business and the significance of innovation and access to new technologies or resources when choosing internationalization modes [1, 3, 16]. The study also highlights the importance of entrepreneurial and risk-taking propensity in determining a firm's approach to innovation. It is important for managers to recognize the value of innovation in international business and be willing to take risks in order to achieve it.The results of the study also suggest that firms choose to internationalize in countries with greater economic and technological potential, especially when they opt for internationalization modalities with greater commitment. In such cases they tend to establish their businesses in these locations. This is consistent with the notion that firms seek out locations that offer potential for growth and development.

Notwithstanding the results presented, some limitations can be recognized to this study, although many of them constitute suggestive avenues for future work. For example, in this paper firms are not distinguished according to their size. A possible improvement of this work, could be to conduct the study by classifying the firms into SMEs and large firms, to understand how the results differ according to the size of the firms. More detailed information on these differences could be useful for the formulation of government policies towards internationalization as a way to stimulate economic development in Portugal, as well as for all managers and CEOs interested in developing their firms.

Acknowledgments. This work was supported by the FCT Fundação para a Ciência e a Tecnologia, I.P. [Project UIDB/05105/2020].

References

1. Zucchella, A., Siano, A.: Internationalization and innovation as resources for SME growth in foreign markets: a focus on textile and clothing firms in the Campania Region. Int. Stud. Manag. Organ. **44**(1), 21–41 (2014)
2. Genc, E., Dayan, M., Genc, O.F.: The impact of SME internationalization on innovation: the mediating role of market and entrepreneurial orientation. Ind. Mark. Manage. **82**, 253–264 (2019)
3. Gjergji, R., Lazzarotti, V., Visconti, F., Saha, P.: Internationalization and innovation performance: the role of family management. Economia Aziendale Online- **10**(2), 321–343 (2019)
4. Saridakis, G., Idris, B., Hansen, J.M., Dana, L.P.: SMEs' internationalisation: when does innovation matter? J. Bus. Res. **96**, 250–263 (2019)
5. Alayo, M., Iturralde, T., Maseda, A.: Innovation and internationalization in family SMEs: analyzing the role of family involvement. Eur. J. Innov. Manag. **25**(2), 454–478 (2022)
6. Do, H., Nguyen, B., Shipton, H.: Innovation and internationalization in an emerging market context: moderating effects of interpersonal and organizational social networks. J. Int. Manag. **29**(2), 101014 (2023)
7. Lee, Y., Hemmert, M.: Performance implications of combining innovation and internationalization for Korean small-and medium-sized manufacturing firms: an exploration–exploitation perspective. Asian Bus. Manag. **22**(1), 1–25 (2023)
8. Sapienza, H.J., Autio, E., George, G., Zahra, S.A.: A capabilities perspective on the effects of early internationalization on firm survival and growth. Acad. Manag. Rev. **31**, 914–933 (2006)
9. Chang, C.H., Chang, C.H., Hsu, P.K., Yang, S.Y.: The catalytic effect of internationalization on innovation. Eur. Financ. Manag. **25**(4), 942–977 (2019)
10. Heunks, F.J.: Innovation, creativity and success. Small Bus. Econ. **10**, 263–272 (1998)

11. Audretsch, D.B., Coad, A., Segarra, A.: Firm growth and innovation. Small Bus. Econ. **43**, 743–749 (2014)
12. Onetti, A., Zucchella, A., Jones, M.V., McDougall-Covin, P.P.: Guest editor's introduction to the special issue: entrepreneurship and strategic management in new technology based companies. J. Manage. Governance **16**(3), 333–336 (2012)
13. Golovko, E., Valentini, G.: Exploring the complementarity between innovation and export for SMEs' growth. J. Int. Bus. Stud. **42**(3), 362–380 (2011)
14. Stoian, M.C., Rialp, J., Dimitratos, P.: SME networks and international performance: unveiling the significance of foreign market entry mode. J. Small Bus. Manage. **55**(1), 128–148 (2017)
15. Du, J., Zhu, S., Li, W.H.: Innovation through internationalization: a systematic review and research agenda. Asia Pac. J. Manage. 1–35 (2022)
16. Mathews, J.: Dragon multinationals: new players in 21st century globalization. Asia Pac. J. Manage. **23**(1), 5–27 (2006)
17. Bagheri, M., Mitchelmore, S., Bamiatzi, V., Nikolopoulos, K.: Internationalization orientation in SMEs: the mediating role of technological innovation. J. Int. Manag. **25**(1), 121–139 (2019)
18. Sarkar, S.: Empreendedorismo e Inovação. Third Edition. Escolar Editora (2014)
19. Klass, D., Wood, M.: Propensity to innovate: driving innovation in a professional services firm. In: 23rd ANZAM Conference 2009: Sustainable Management and Marketing (2009)
20. Wan, D., Ong, C.H., Lee, F.: Determinants of firm innovation in Singapore. Technovation **25**(3), 261–268 (2005)
21. Jones, M.V.: First steps in internationalisation: concepts and evidence from a sample of small high-technology firms. J. Int. Manag. **7**(3), 191–210 (2001)
22. Majocchi, A., Zucchella, A.: Internationalization and performance: findings from a set of Italian SMEs. Int. Small Bus. J. **21**(3), 249–268 (2003)
23. Vila, N., Kuster, I.: The importance of innovation in international textile firms. Eur. J. Mark. **41**(1/2), 17–36 (2007)
24. Abubakar, Y.A., Hand, C., Smallbone, D., Saridakis, G.: What specific modes of internationalization influence SME innovation in sub-saharan least developed countries (LDCs)? Technovation **79**, 56–70 (2019)
25. Zahra, S.A., Ireland, R.D., Hitt, M.A.: International expansion by new venture firms: international diversity, mode of market entry, technological learning, and performance. Acad. Manag. J. **43**(5), 925–950 (2000)
26. Kafouros, M.I., Buckley, P.J., Sharp, J.A., Wang, C.: The role of internationalization in explaining innovation performance. Technovation **28**(1–2), 63–74 (2008)
27. Radas, S., Božić, L.: The antecedents of SME innovativeness in an emerging transition economy. Technovation **29**(6–7), 438–450 (2009)
28. Zahra, S.A., Ucbasaran, D., Newey, L.R.: Social knowledge and SMEs' innovative gains from internationalization. Eur. Manag. Rev. **6**(2), 81–93 (2009)
29. Álvarez, I., Marín, R.: Entry modes and national systems of innovation. J. Int. Manag. **16**(4), 340–353 (2010)
30. Li, G.: A review of the literature of the relationship between innovation and internationalization of SMEs and future prospects. Am. J. Ind. Bus. Manag. **10**(03), 619 (2020)
31. Sass, M.: Internationalisation of innovative SMEs in the Hungarian medical precision instruments industry. Post-Communist Econ. **24**(3), 365–382 (2012)
32. Azar, G., Drogendijk, R.: Psychic distance, innovation, and firm performance. Manag. Int. Rev.. Int. Rev. **54**, 581–613 (2014)
33. Alvarez, R., Robertson, R.: Exposure to foreign markets and plant-level innovation: evidence from Chile and Mexico. J. Int. Trade Econ. Dev. **13**(1), 57–87 (2004)

Flexibility and Productivity in IoT Programming: A Case Study with Mruby

Kazuaki Tanaka[1]([⊠])(iD), Sota Ogura[1], R. Krishnamoorthy[2](iD),
Ko-ichiro Sugiyama[3], and Miyu Kawahara[3,4]

[1] Kyushu Institute of Technology, Kitakyushu, Japan
`kazuaki@ics.kyutech.ac.jp`
[2] Chennai Institute of Technology, Chennai, India
[3] National Institute of Technology, Matsue College, Matsue, Japan
[4] Okayama University, Okayama, Japan

Abstract. This paper explores the use of data flow-based design in IoT application development and its integration with the Node-RED programming tool. Node-RED provides a visual interface for creating programs based on the flow of data between nodes. However, Node-RED is not suitable for resource-constrained devices like micro-controllers. To address this, we propose a method of generating mruby code from Node-RED's data flow programs. The generated mruby code can be compiled into device-independent byte-code and executed on the mruby VM. To facilitate the implementation, we introduce the RBoard, a prototyping micro-controller board equipped with the mruby VM firmware. This approach combines the intuitive data flow design of Node-RED with the power of mruby for embedded systems. Through this integration, developers can rapidly prototype IoT applications and leverage the flexibility of scripting languages. Our findings demonstrate the feasibility and benefits of using data flow-based design and mruby code generation in IoT application development. This research contributes to the advancement of efficient and scalable IoT programming methodologies and enables the creation of innovative IoT solutions on micro-controller platforms.

Keywords: Embedded software development · Data flow programming · IoT · mruby

1 Introduction

In IoT programming, a combination of knowledge about embedded systems and the integration of software and hardware components is essential to realize a functioning system. On the other hand, IoT applications are naturally designed by considering the flow of data, rather than designing each individual process separately. This includes data acquisition from sensors, data processing, communication for data transmission, and data analysis.

Designing IoT applications based on data flow provides an intuitive approach that aligns with the natural progression of data within the system. Instead of

T. Guarda et al. (Eds.): ARTIIS 2023, CCIS 1936, pp. 17–27, 2024.
https://doi.org/10.1007/978-3-031-48855-9_2

treating each process as isolated entities, a data flow design allows for a holistic view of how data moves and undergoes transformations throughout the application.

In a data flow design, the emphasis is on understanding the path that data takes from its source (e.g., sensors) to its destination (e.g., data processing modules, communication channels, analytics). This design approach enables developers to visualize the interconnections of various components and the flow of information between them.

By considering data flow as a central aspect of IoT application development, developers can better organize the design and implementation of different processes. It facilitates the identification of data dependencies, enables efficient routing and processing of information, and enhances the overall system's scalability and flexibility.

Overall, designing IoT applications based on data flow provides a natural and intuitive approach to development. It allows for a more widely understanding of how data moves and is processed through the system, promoting efficient and effective implementation of IoT applications.

This paper introduces a methodology to convert asynchronous data flow programming into procedural languages, specifically adopting mruby in our research, for execution on micro-controllers. The implementation of the approach shown in this paper is released as open-source software. The research is expected to contribute to the advancement of IoT programming by bridging the gap between asynchronous data flow design and procedural execution, thereby enhancing the capabilities of micro-controllers in IoT applications.

2   IoT Programming Environment

In traditional embedded software development, C/C++ has been widely used. However, there is a growing trend of incorporating scripting languages such as micro-Python, mruby, and Lua as alternatives to C/C++.

In our research and development efforts, we have been focusing on applying the object-oriented programming language Ruby to embedded software development through the use of mruby.

Mruby is a lightweight implementation of the Ruby programming language that is specifically designed for embedded systems. It provides a smaller memory footprint and faster execution compared to the full Ruby implementation, making it well-suited for resource-constrained environments [1,2].

By utilizing mruby, we aim to bring the benefits of Ruby's expressive and flexible syntax, as well as its object-oriented programming paradigm, to the field of embedded software development. This allows developers to leverage the productivity and readability advantages offered by Ruby while developing software for embedded systems.

Our research and development activities focus to the capabilities of mruby, optimizing its performance for embedded applications, and providing tooling and libraries to support its integration into embedded systems. Through these efforts, we strive to enable developers to use the power and versatility of Ruby in the development of embedded software, expanding the range of options available for creating efficient and feature-rich embedded applications.

2.1 Mruby

Mruby is an embedded implementation of the Ruby programming language, and is released as open-source software, which is available under the MIT and BSD License [4,5].

It is designed to be lightweight and efficient, making it suitable for resource-constrained environments like IoT devices. The operation mechanism of mruby involves the following key aspects:

Memory Efficiency Mruby uses a smaller memory footprint compared to the full Ruby implementation. It achieves this by excluding some features and optimizing the run-time environment for embedded systems.

Garbage Collection Mruby incorporates garbage collection to automatically manage memory allocation and release. This helps simplify memory management tasks for developers, reducing the risk of memory leaks and enhancing overall system stability.

Flexibility and Productivity Ruby is known for its expressive and flexible syntax, which can significantly enhance development productivity. By using mruby in IoT applications, developers can leverage the familiar and powerful Ruby programming language to create applications quickly and efficiently.

Rapid Prototyping Lightweight concept of mruby, and ease of use make it suitable for rapid prototyping in IoT development. Developers can rapidly iterate and test their ideas using the dynamic and interactive nature of Ruby, accelerating the development cycle.

Enhanced Readability Ruby's clean and readable syntax can improve the maintainability and understandable of IoT application code. This is especially beneficial when working on complex IoT projects that involve multiple modules and interactions.

In summary, applying mruby in IoT applications, we get benefits such as rapid prototyping, and enhanced readability, and reduced resource consumption. These advantages make mruby a valuable tool for developing efficient and feature-rich IoT applications.

Listing 1.1 shows an example of mruby program. When this program is executed on micro-controller board, the LED connected to pin 1, which works as GPIO, blinks in one second cycle.

Listing 1.1. mruby sample

```
1 led = GPIO.new(1)
2 while true do
3   led.write GPIO::HIGH
4   sleep 0.5
5   led.write GPIO::LOW
6   sleep 0.5
7 end
```

2.2   Node-RED

In IoT application development, designing based on data-flow is intuitive and effective. One programming tool that utilizes data flow is Node-RED [7].

Node-RED is a visual programming tool that allows developers to create applications by defining the flow of data between nodes. Nodes represent various functionalities and operations, such as data input, processing, and output. Developers can use a web browser to access the Node-RED interface and design the application by connecting these nodes together to define the desired data flow(Fig. 1).

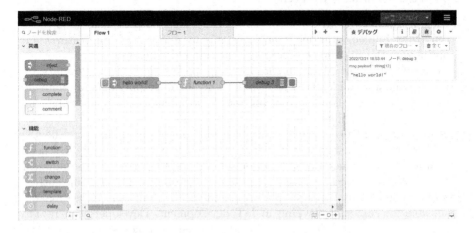

Fig. 1. Node-RED development environment

However, Node-RED operates within a web browser environment and is not compatible with micro-controllers or devices with limited resources typically found in IoT devices.

Once the data flow design is created, the information about the nodes and their connections can be obtained in the form of a JSON file. This JSON file serves as a configuration file that captures the entire structure and properties of the nodes and their relationships.

With the data flow representation stored in the JSON file, we propose the generation of procedural code. The code generator will parse the JSON file and generate code in a procedural programming language, such as scripting language. This generated code represents the translation of the data flow design into a procedural program.

By utilizing Node-RED, developers can intuitively design IoT applications based on data flow. The resulting data flow design can be saved as a JSON file, which can then be used to generate procedural code for execution. This approach simplifies the development process and provides a visual and intuitive way to create IoT applications with efficient data flow management.

2.3   RBoard

From a data flow program created in Node-RED, mruby code can be generated (Node-RED to mruby code generator). The generated mruby program is compiled into device-independent byte-code. This byte-code is designed to be executed on the mruby VM (mruby Virtual Machine).

A prototyping micro-controller board called RBoard is equipped with the mruby VM as part of its firmware, enabling the execution of the generated byte-code.

The RBoard is a micro-controller board designed and developed by the authors with the primary objective of executing mruby programs. Its specifications is commonly found in micro-controllers intended for embedded systems, and its design aligns with the standards of micro-controllers within embedded systems (Table 1). The RBoard schematics are available under Creative Commons(CC-BY-NC-SA 3.0) [6].

Table 1. RBoard Specifications

Micro-controller chip	PIC32MX170F256B (Microchip Technology)
SRAM	64KB
Flash	256KB
I/Os	Digital, PWM, ADC, I2C, UART
Firmware	mruby/c VM 3.0.1

The RBoard microcontroller board is equipped with various interfaces to control sensors and actuators, including GPIO and I2C (Fig. 2).

The GPIO(General Purpose Input/Output) interface allows the RBoard to communicate with and control external devices, such as sensors, through digital input and output signals. It provides a versatile way to interface with a wide range of components and peripherals.

Additionally, the RBoard features an I2C (Inter-Integrated Circuit) interface, which is a serial communication protocol commonly used for connecting sensors, actuators, and other devices. The I2C interface enables the RBoard to interact with I2C-compatible devices, allowing for efficient data exchange and control.

By incorporating these interfaces into the RBoard, developers can easily connect and control various sensors and actuators in their IoT applications. This versatility and compatibility enhance the board's capabilities and enable seamless integration with a wide range of devices and peripherals.

Fig. 2. RBoard, mruby ready micro-controller board

3   Integrating Data-Flow Design and Mruby

A NodeRED-to-mruby code generator enables the generation of corresponding mruby code from the JSON file obtained through the design process in Node-RED [3]. This JSON file encompasses the necessary descriptions for accessing the RBoard's interfaces, allowing for seamless integration of RBoard's functionalities into the Node-RED environment.

3.1   NodeRED-to-mruby Code Generator

The code generator takes the JSON file as input and processes the information to produce mruby code that can be executed on the RBoard micro-controller board. This generated code incorporates the requisite instructions for interfacing with the RBoard's interfaces and effectively controlling connected sensors and actuators.

By adopting this approach, developers can design their IoT applications within the Node-RED platform, incorporating the functionalities provided by the RBoard micro-controller board. The resulting design can be saved as a JSON file, serving as input to the code generator. The generated mruby code facilitates the optimal utilization of the RBoard's interface capabilities and seamless interaction with connected devices.

The integration of Node-RED design with the RBoard, along with the development of the NodeRED-to-mruby code generator, offers a comprehensive solution for the design and deployment of IoT applications. This solution leverages the intuitive data flow design of Node-RED, the interface capabilities of the RBoard, and the execution environment of mruby. It empowers developers to create sophisticated IoT applications with enhanced control and efficiency, bridging the gap between visual programming and embedded systems.

3.2   Asynchronous Execution on Mruby

While Node-RED is not a procedural programming language, mruby is a procedural language. One key distinction between the two executions is handling asynchronous execution or not.

In Node-RED, each node operates asynchronously, meaning that the execution order of nodes is non-deterministic. This allows for concurrent processing and event-driven execution, enabling the flexible and dynamic nature of data flow programming.

On the other hand, mruby is a procedural language and typically follows a sequential execution model. It is designed to handle synchronous operations by default. To achieve asynchronous processing and handle the non-deterministic nature of Node-RED's data flow execution, special considerations need to be made within NodeRED-to-mruby code generation.

By incorporating the necessary constructs for asynchronous processing in mruby, developers can effectively development within the data flow paradigm of Node-RED while executing in the procedural capabilities of mruby. This enables the seamless integration of both paradigms and facilitates the development of robust and responsive IoT applications within the Node-RED environment.

3.3   Implementation of NodeRED-to-mruby

The generation of mruby code is based on the information of nodes and their connections, known as wires, within the data flow design.

Since nodes in the data flow are executed asynchronously, the order in which data flows through the wires is non-deterministic. To handle the asynchronous nature of data flow execution and generate mruby code accordingly, each node is implemented as a function, and the wires are implemented using First-In-First-Out (FIFO) data structures.

Using one global FIFO (named pipe), the functions of each node are invoked in any order. The execution order of nodes is not predetermined. The function of each node retrieves data (i.e., the data flowing through the wires) from the global FIFO and performs the operations specific to the node.

If there is output that needs to be propagated, it is then en-queue the output into the FIFO. This process is repeated, allowing for the pseudo-asynchronous execution of data flow processing.

The figure shown in Fig. 3 represents the design of a data flow and the architectural diagram of the program generated using NodeRED-to-mruby.

The NodeRED-to-mruby code generator takes this JSON representation as input and processes it to generate the actual mruby code. This generated code encompasses the necessary functions, data structures, and logic to implement the desired data flow behavior as defined in the design. The combination of the data flow design, NodeRED-to-mruby conversion, and the resulting program architecture depicted in Fig. 3 shows the result of translating a high-level design into a procedural mruby program.

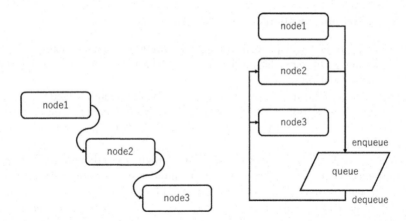

Fig. 3. Node and wire in data flow design(left), its implementation diagram using queue (right)

Within the context of asynchronous execution, an exception to the non-deterministic nature of data flow is the "inject" node, which generates triggers at regular time intervals.

The inject node serves as a mechanism to introduce time-based control into the data flow design. Unlike other nodes that rely on the flow of data for execution, the inject node operates on a predetermined schedule or timing. By configuring the inject node, developers can specify the time interval between triggers, allowing for the periodic initiation of data flow execution. This ensures that certain actions or processes occur at regular intervals, regardless of the non-deterministic execution order of other nodes.

In applications where there is a need to periodically retrieve sensor values at fixed time intervals, the inject node becomes essential. The inject node plays a crucial role in time-sensitive applications, allowing for the precise timing of data acquisition and ensuring the availability of sensor readings at fixed intervals.

The following shows the pseudo-code of the function dispatch in executing data-flow nodes.

Listing 1.2. Dispatching nodes

```
1 global_queue @$\gets$@ []
2
3 Procedure inject_node_process
4   Foreach inject_node @$\in$@ inject_nodes Do
5     data @$\gets$@ @{\it Call}@ inject_node
6     global_queue.enqueue(data)
7   End
8 End
9
10 Do forever
11   @{\it Call}@ inject_node_process
12   data @$\gets$@ global_queue.dequeue
13   Case data.node_name Of
```

```
14      inject: @{\it Call}@ inject(data)
15      node1: @{\it Call}@ node1(data)
16      ...
17   End
18 End
```

By this approach, the generated mruby code can simulate the asynchronous execution of the data flow design.

4   Implementation Results and Evaluation

We conducted validation of the NodeRED-to-mruby generator by generating a mruby program from a data flow design for sensing using a temperature sensor.

The data flow design consists of several nodes, including an inject node, a sensor node, a Ruby function node, a branching node, and GPIO output nodes (Fig. 4).

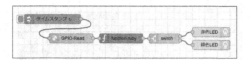

Fig. 4. RBoard, mruby ready micro-controller board

inject node The inject node generates a trigger signal every second, serving as the source of the data flow.

sensor node The sensor node utilizes the ADC interface to acquire the voltage value from the temperature sensor.

ruby function node The Ruby function node is responsible for converting the voltage value to Celsius temperature. The content of the Ruby function node is directly outputted as a mruby function (Fig. 5).

branch node The branching node performs conditional branching based on the temperature value, determining which of the two GPIO nodes to execute subsequently.

GPIO node The GPIO node outputs signal to specified I/O pin.

Through this design, the data flow is established, starting from the inject node, acquiring temperature values through the sensor node, applying temperature conversion using the Ruby function node, and performing conditional branching using the branching node. The GPIO output nodes enable control of external devices based on the branching result.

The NodeRED-to-mruby generator processes the data flow design and generates a mruby program that incorporates the necessary functions and logic to implement the desired behavior. This validation confirms the successful generation of the mruby program based on the given data flow design for temperature sensing (Fig. 6).

Fig. 5. Ruby function node, contains ruby code for converting from voltage to temperature

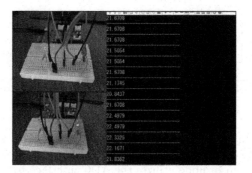

Fig. 6. Execution result on RBoard

5 Conclusion

In this research, we focused on the validation of the NodeRED-to-mruby generator by creating an mruby program from a data flow design centered around temperature sensing using a temperature sensor.

By developing and validating the NodeRED-to-mruby generator, we demonstrated its ability to transform the data flow design into an mruby program. This research focuses to the potential of data flow design such as a visual programming tool Node-RED for IoT application development, with the added advantage of generating code for mruby-enabled micro-controller boards like RBoard.

A public course aimed at high school students was organized utilizing the RBoard. This initiative provided an opportunity for programming novices to engage in sensor-based programming. The course enabled even those new to programming to experience the world of sensors. Describing data flows proved particularly effective for comprehending the combination of sensors and actuators, as commonly encountered in IoT programming. Spanning the past two years, this public course has reached over 150 students. By using the RBoard and emphasizing data flow programming, the course empowered high school attendees with practical skills and insights into IoT field, fostering a deeper understanding of sensor and actuator combinations.

The findings presented here contribute to the field of IoT programming, showcasing the effectiveness of data flow-based designs and the seamless integration of Node-RED and mruby in the development process. This work opens up new possibilities for efficient and intuitive programming in the realm of IoT applications, combining the benefits of visual programming with the power of embedded systems.

The work products of this research are available as open-source software [8].

References

1. Tanaka, K., Higashi, H.: mruby - rapid IoT software development. In: Computational Science and Its Applications - ICCSA 2017. Lecture Notes in Computer Science, vol. 10404. Springer, Cham. (2017) https://doi.org/10.1007/978-3-319-62392-4_53+
2. Tanaka, K., Tsujino, C., Maeda, H.: IoT software by dataflow programming in Mruby programming environment. In: Computational Science and Its Applications - ICCSA 2020. Lecture Notes in Computer Science, vol. 12252. Springer, Cham. (2020) https://doi.org/10.1007/978-3-030-58811-3_15+
3. Sugiyama, K.-i., et al.: Development of a visual programming tool called SmrAI for function testing to mitigate the shortage of programming personnel in the manufacturing, Computer Software, vol. 39, no. 4 (2022). Released on J-STAGE December 25, 2022 (in Japanese). https://doi.org/10.11309/jssst.39.4_61+
4. mruby: https://github.com/mruby/mruby+
5. mruby/c: https://github.com/mrubyc/mrubyc+
6. RBoard schematic: https://oshwlab.com/YoshihiroOgura/rboard+
7. Node-RED: https://nodered.org/+
8. mruby/c ide: https://github.com/mruby-lab/mrubyc-ide+

Agile Model for the Gradual and Short-Term Deployment of an Enterprise Architecture in the Financial Sector

Kevin Avalos-Varillas(✉) ⬡, Rafael Rivas-Carillo⬡, and Daniel Burga-Durango⬡

Universidad Peruana de Ciencias Aplicadas, Lima, Peru
{U201514123,U201614625}@upc.edu.pe, daniel.burga@upc.pe

Abstract. New technologies are being decisive in opening up the financial services market, historically stagnant, to new providers, which has generated a new competitive environment that is booming. Companies must adopt new organizational forms, optimize resources, establish policies, and best practices with clients, so organizations respond to these challenges through the practice of Enterprise Architecture. This methodology allows us to align processes, data, applications, and technological infrastructure with the strategic objectives of the organization. Despite the growing impact, ignorance means that only a small number of companies obtain a digital transformation. For this reason, it seeks to develop an agile model for a gradual deployment and in a short term in an effective manner, which is fully accessible to entities within the financial sector. The objectives include analyzing the current situation of the financial sector, designing the model for the enterprise architecture, validating the proposed agile model and developing a continuity plan for the investigation. A model based on the agile SAFe methodology and the TOGAF business architecture framework will be developed, whose objective is to provide agile results without sacrificing good management and control. In addition, it also seeks to provide an easily adaptable guide so that companies interested in the field can begin to undertake the use of agile methodologies.

Keywords: enterprise architecture · agile model · SAFe · TOGAF

1 Introduction

According to BBVA Research, recent technological advances are being decisive in the way that the financial services market generates new providers, which has generated a new competitive environment that is booming [1]. Companies have begun to adopt new organizational forms, optimize their resources, establish policies and best practices with clients, so organizations can respond to these challenges through the practice of Enterprise Architecture.

Enterprise Architecture is a discipline that seeks to comprehensively design and plan the processes, systems, technologies and human resources of an organization, to align them with its business strategy and achieve its objectives. However, implementing an enterprise architecture in the financial industry can present unique challenges, such as the

T. Guarda et al. (Eds.): ARTIIS 2023, CCIS 1936, pp. 28–44, 2024.
https://doi.org/10.1007/978-3-031-48855-9_3

need to adapt to an ever-changing and highly regulated environment. To address these challenges, an agile model has been proposed that allows the gradual and short-term deployment of an enterprise architecture in the financial sector. The main objective of this is to create an easily adaptable model that can be implemented by companies interested in the financial sector. According to a recent study [2], adopting an agile approach to enterprise architecture implementation in financial firms can improve the organization's ability to quickly adapt to market and regulatory changes, as well as take advantage of emerging opportunities. Another study suggests that [3], the use of agile methodologies in the implementation of enterprise architecture in the financial sector can improve the efficiency and effectiveness of business processes, as well as improve the organization's ability to respond quickly to changes in the business environment. Taking an agile approach to deploying an enterprise architecture in the financial industry can provide a number of benefits. According to a study carried out by [4], this approach also helps financial companies to meet changing market requirements and improve collaboration between work teams.

In the financial industry, where innovation and speed are critical, implementing an agile enterprise architecture can help companies stay competitive in a dynamic and complex marketplace. According to a study conducted by [5], the agile approach is an effective way to manage complexity and uncertainty in the financial sector and can help companies quickly adapt to changes in the business environment. According to [6], adopting an agile approach to implementing EA can help organizations adapt quickly to market changes and customer needs, and can improve organizational efficiency and effectiveness. Furthermore [7], they highlight that adopting an agile approach to the implementation of an EA in the Financial Sector can enhance the organization's ability to innovate and improve the customer experience. On the other hand [8], emphasize that the use of an agile model in EA can improve the organization's ability to adapt to market changes and customer needs, while allowing greater alignment of information technology systems with business objectives. Likewise [9], they highlight that the use of an agile model for the implementation of an EA in the Financial Sector can enable organizations to make more informed decisions, increase transparency and improve collaboration between the different departments of the organization. Finally, according to [10], the use of an agile model for the implementation of an EA can enable organizations in the Financial Sector to achieve greater speed, flexibility, and adaptability, which is essential to compete in today's changing business environment.

2 Related Work

It has been possible to identify different investigations and successful case studies, which directly support the research topic. In [11], the use of agile methods in IT projects in the German banking sector is examined, including which tools are used and what expectations are associated with the use of agile methods in terms of cost savings, quality improvement, acceleration of project delivery or improvement of innovation performance. In addition, barriers to the adoption of agile practices are investigated and the differences between established banks and young fintech companies are compared. In [12] an approach for generating test cases for business services based on enterprise architecture design is proposed. The approach is based on the identification of business services and their dependencies through the business architecture, which allows for more efficient and effective test case generation. In [13, 14] a systematic review of the literature on agile enterprise architecture is presented, with the aim of identifying the main approaches, practices and tools used in the implementation of agile enterprise architecture. This provides an overview of the approaches and practices used in implementing agile enterprise architecture and can be helpful in understanding how to implement agile enterprise architecture in the financial industry. In [15] a case study of a financial services company that implemented an agile approach to enterprise architecture is presented. It describes how the company used an iterative and incremental approach to develop its enterprise architecture, and how agile principles were applied. to improve collaboration between IT and business teams.

3   Method

This section will analyze possible agile methodologies, enterprise architecture frameworks, and scalable frameworks that can be applied for the short-term and gradual deployment of an enterprise architecture within the financial sector, using the benchmarking technique. These points were chosen for comparison due to the reasons that's provide different characteristics in terms of focus, benefits, productivity, and functionality. The Likert scale was chosen as a measurement method to express neutrality when making comparisons between two or more things. First, the methodologies and frameworks will be identified; second, selection criteria will be defined; and finally, each will be chosen based on benchmarking results.

3.1   Benchmarking Agile Methodologies

For this comparison, there are four continuous improvement and project management methodologies: Lean, Scrum, Kanban and Six Sigma. Lean focuses on maximizing benefits through five basic concepts. Scrum is used to solve complex problems and requires a Scrum Master to ensure the achievement of objectives. Kanban is a visual tool for project and task management, with the aim of improving efficiency and reducing waiting time. Finally, Six Sigma focuses on improving quality and reducing variability through the identification and elimination of defects (Table 1).

In the benchmarking, four criteria with different attributes were used: Use, Agility capacity, Applicability and Processes and products. After the evaluation, Scrum was the methodology selected as the winner due to its high level of end-user satisfaction, increased productivity, ability to adapt to changes, people-centeredness, and responsiveness. Furthermore, Scrum proved to be applicable to projects of different sizes and complexities, with seamless interaction between team members, the customer, and end users. Its ability for project management and quality control, and its emphasis on testing and continuous integration, were also highlighted.

Table 1. Comparative Benchmarking of Agile Methodologies.

Lacovelli Point of View	LEAN	SCRUM	Kanban	XP
Use (5)	2	4	2	2
Agility Ability (12)	11	9	10	10
Applicability (9)	4	6	4	7
Processes and Products (12)	7	8	5	7
Total (38)	24	27	21	26

3.2 Benchmarking of Scalable Frameworks

For this comparison, LeSS, Nexus and SAFe are scalable frameworks. Nexus extends Scrum to unify multiple teams into a larger, more consistent unit. SAFe is a framework based on systems thinking, agility and lean thinking. It consists of three levels: Portfolio, Large Solution and Essential. SAFe's principles include economic vision, systems thinking and decentralization of decision-making (Table 2).

Table 2. Comparative Benchmarking of Scalable Frameworks

Criteria	LeSS	Nexus	SAFe
Feasibility	3	2	4
Applicability	3	2	4
Reliability	4	3	3
Adaptability	2	2	4
Total	12	9	15

Based on the criteria of feasibility, applicability factor, reliability and adaptability, the SAFe framework is positioned as the winner in the benchmarking carried out. This framework is viable to carry out the objectives of the project, it has applicability in real projects, its information is reliable and accurate, and it has the ability to adapt to different solutions, models, methodologies, and sectors.

3.3 Benchmarking of Enterprise Architecture Frameworks

For this comparison, the four Enterprise Architecture Frameworks, Zachman, TOGAF, FEAF and Gartner, are frameworks used to develop, design, implement and manage enterprise architectures. Zachman is based on an ontological framework that provides a comprehensive description of an enterprise information infrastructure from six different perspectives, while TOGAF focuses on four interrelated areas that fully describe what enterprise architectures should contain. FEAF is a framework designed by the United States government to improve the efficiency and effectiveness of its business systems. GEAF, for its part, is an architectural framework created by Gartner that helps organizations align their enterprise architecture with their strategic objectives (Table 3).

Table 3. Comparative Benchmarking of Enterprise Architecture Frameworks.

Criteria	Zachman	TOGAF	FEAF	Gartner
Taxonomic Integrity	4	2	2	1
Process Integrity	1	4	2	3
Reference Models	1	3	4	1
Orientation To Practice	1	2	2	4
Maturity Models	1	1	3	2
Focus On The Government	1	2	1	4
Government Guidance	1	2	3	3
Orientation To Partitions	1	2	4	3
Prescriptive Catalog	1	2	4	2
Supplier Neutrality	1	4	3	1
Information Availability	2	4	2	1
Valuation Time	2	3	1	4
Prestige	2	4	2	3
Total	19	35	33	32

According to the evaluation carried out by TOGAF, the Enterprise Architecture Framework stands out in the benchmarking for its high taxonomic and process integrity, useful reference models, practical and governance orientation, and focus on the business and the effective partitioning of the company. It also offers a prescriptive catalog and is vendor neutral. The free information and its prestige in the market make it a valuable choice, with a reasonable time to value before generating high-value business solutions.

3.4   The SAFe Implementation Roadmap

After extensive research on agile methodologies, the SAFe framework was selected for the gradual and short-term deployment of an agile enterprise architecture. To achieve business agility, you must adopt lean-agile standards and requirements and establish mechanisms for continuous value delivery. You will focus on moves critical to SAFe adoption, using a standard pattern and implementation path to achieve organizational change. The SAFe (Scaled Agile Framework) Implementation Roadmap follows a structured and goal-oriented path, consisting of ten steps. This detailed process helps companies implement SAFe effectively and achieve desired outcomes.

Reaching the Tipping Point:
In this step, organizations aim to build awareness and create a sense of urgency for change. Key activities include executive sponsorship, identifying Agile change agents, and conducting initial Agile training.

Train Lean-Agile Change Agents:
Organizations train a group of change agents who will lead the SAFe implementation. These individuals will become the coaches, mentors, and trainers for Agile teams and leaders throughout the organization.

Train Executives, Managers, and Leaders:
This step focuses on providing training to executives, managers, and leaders to help them understand their roles and responsibilities within the SAFe implementation. They learn how to support Agile teams, foster an Agile culture, and drive the necessary changes.

Create the Implementation Plan:
A comprehensive implementation plan is created, taking into account the organization's specific needs and context. This plan includes the identification of Agile Release Trains (ARTs), establishing the Agile program management office, and defining the necessary milestones and timelines.

Prepare for ART Launch:
This step involves preparing the identified ARTs for launch. Activities include selecting and preparing the Agile teams, defining the Agile program management processes, establishing the necessary infrastructure, and aligning with the enterprise strategy.

Train Teams and Launch ARTs:
Agile teams receive training on SAFe principles, practices, and processes. Once adequately prepared, the ARTs are launched, and the teams begin their first Program Increment (PI) to deliver value and align with the program objectives.

Coach ART Execution:
Agile coaches work closely with the ARTs, providing guidance and support to ensure successful execution. They help teams apply SAFe practices, resolve impediments, and continuously improve their performance.

Launch More ARTs and Value Streams:
Organizations expand the implementation by launching additional ARTs and establishing more value streams. This step involves repeating the previous steps for each new ART and ensuring alignment across ARTs and value streams.

Extend to the Portfolio:
The SAFe implementation extends to the portfolio level, aligning strategic initiatives, defining value streams, and implementing Lean portfolio management practices. This step ensures the organization's ability to prioritize, fund, and track the delivery of value across the portfolio.

Sustain and Improve:
The final step focuses on continuously improving the SAFe implementation and ensuring its long-term sustainability. Organizations establish Communities of Practice, conduct periodic assessments, and adapt their practices based on feedback and lessons learned.

3.5   Design of the Agile Model

In order to design an agile Model for a gradual and short-term use of a business architecture framework for entities in the financial sector, a series of requirements will be defined based on the line of business, considering as fundamental sources: the agile principles of business architecture and the destination line. These will be tailored alongside the TOGAF-based AE framework targets and the SAFe scalable framework. Figure 1 shows all the stages of the design of the agile model for the implementation of the EA framework for the financial sector.

For the Input, the destination line for financial entities is defined according to the investigation carried out in detail in the previous chapters. Then, the agility principles based on the SAFe framework and its implementation phases are described and finally, it analyzes the general concepts of a TOGAF Business Architecture, where it will take the structure of the phases, its objectives and which are the appropriate deliverables for the processes of a financial institution.

Destination Line
It is defined based on research carried out on financial entities. This structure is as follows:

- Manage the credit information system of the financial institution.
- Strengthen the quality of service provided to build a competitive advantage.
- Strengthen sustainability through risk and operations management.
- Improve, optimize, and modernize customer-oriented processes.

Agile Approach
The main requirement is to define the agility principles proposed by the SAFE framework to adapt the agile model to the AE framework. For the design, it consists of 5 stages to create the agile framework:

Stage 1: An analysis of each of the objectives of the TOGAF framework stages is carried out. Cross tables are used, where the objectives will be related to the requirements belonging to the target line and the agility approach.

Stage 2: From stage 1, the main objectives that are necessary for the design of the framework of the agility model are acquired.

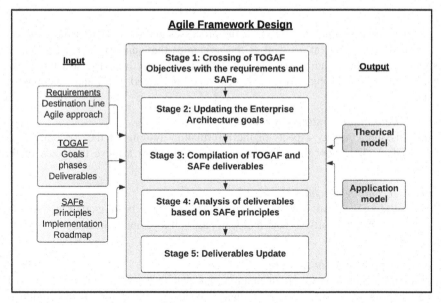

Fig. 1. Integration Strategy

Stage 3: An analysis of all the deliverables proposed by TOGAF for the new model is prepared.

Stage 4: According to the criteria of the SAFe agile principles and target line, the list of deliverables will be simplified.

Stage 5: The TOGAF deliverables are modified, acquiring the detailed final list for the agile model of the EA framework.

For the output, the agile model will be divided into 2 model stages:

Theoretical model: Contains the principles, scope, preliminary studies, scope, etc.

Application model: Contains solutions, governance, migration, etc.

3.6 Base Framework

The TOGAF framework will be used as the basis for the design of the business architecture model. The TOGAF framework is divided into the following phases.

Preliminary Phase
In this phase, the governance structure is established, and it is agreed to implement the method and framework of reference, where the corporation is formed so that the business architecture plan achieves success, in addition, the business environment is understood and the scope is agreed upon, confirming the principles of EA.

Phase A: Architectural Vision
Within this initial phase of the architecture, the constraints, expectations, and scope are defined to generate the vision of the architecture confirming the business environment and producing a governance document that shows what the enterprise architecture will be.

Phase B: Business Architecture
It examines the personnel, the business, the processes and their relationships between them and the environment, as well as the principles that support their development, design and how the organization achieves its business objectives. The structure of the organization, business objectives, processes, services offered, roles and functions are defined.

Phase C: Information Systems Architecture
Within this step, the key aspects of the information systems of the corporation are established to show how the information systems help to achieve the goals of the corporation.

Phase D: Technology Architecture
Within this step, we detail how the information system will be supported by the component based on both software and hardware, as well as communication and business relationships.

Phase E: Opportunities and Solutions
We draw up a preliminary implementation plan, where we define the project implementation priority, as well as their mutual dependence. To decide to buy, build or recycle.

Phase F: Migration Planning
We prepare an implementation plan, and a detailed transition plan is produced where a profitability analysis and a risk analysis are carried out.

Phase G: Governance of Implementation
Within this phase, the verification of the architectural implementation is carried out, in addition we define the limits of the implementation projects and monitor their implementation.

Phase H: Architecture Change Management
Changes within the architecture, people, and potential changes are managed in this phase. It is continuously monitored to ensure that architectural changes are used in an intelligent and integrated way. Providing support to business architecture and thus be flexible to technological or commercial changes.

Requirements Management
Within the TOGAF project, each of its phases is based on business requirements, including their validation. Claims are logged, identified, and managed as they enter and exit the appropriate stages of the ADM, which are eliminated, processed, and prioritized.

3.7 Agile Modeling Design

A set of enterprise architecture deliverables is presented using the TOGAF methodology and SAFe implementation principles for each of the phases. The next thing will be to analyze all the deliverables to be able to summarize and shorten them, in order to have greater simplicity and agility for the progress of the ADM of the architecture, based on the principles of the SAFe approach (Table 4).

Table 4. TOGAF - SAFe Framework Schema

Agile EA framework in the financial sector	
Preliminary Phase	Deliverable originated in the phase
	Preliminary framework
	Architectural Work Request
A	Architectural Work Statement
	Communications Plan
	Capacity Assessment
	Value stream management and ART implementation
	Risk Management
B C D	Architecture Definition Document
E	Architecture Roadmap
	Gap Analysis
	Architectural Views and Viewpoints
	Building Blocks of Architecture
	Solution Building Blocks
F	Capacity-based planning
	Implementation and Migration Plan
G	Implementation Governance Model
	Architectural Contracts and Agreements
H	Change Requests
	Conformity Assessment
Requirements Management	Requirements Impact Assessment

3.8   Agile Model for Enterprise Architecture

Now, we will begin to detail the proposed agile Model divided into a Theoretical Model and an Application Model that are composed of each its objectives, phases and deliverables according to what is described and copied in the research.

THEORETICAL MODEL
PRELIMINARY PHASE
   Objectives
   Establish the Architectural Capabilities required by the company.
   Analyze the organizational environment used to develop the Enterprise Architecture
   Recognize and establish the elements of the organization that are affected by the capabilities of the architecture.
   Recognize the proposed frameworks, processes and methods that are crossed with the capacity of the architecture.

Define architecture capabilities.
Establish and develop the organizational model used in enterprise architecture.
Specify and detail the processes and resources used in architecture governance.
Choose which tools to develop that support the capabilities of the architecture.
PHASE A: VISION OF ARCHITECTURE.

Objectives

Establish a higher-level view of the capabilities and value of the business in order to be delivered as a consequence of the company's proposed architecture.

Acquire the acceptance of a Declaration of Work of Architecture which defines a project of works to promote and develop the architecture indicated within the Vision of Architecture.

PHASE B: BUSINESS ARCHITECTURE

Objectives

Implement the target Business Architecture by describing how the company operates to achieve its business objectives in such a way that it can respond to the strategic objectives defined within the Architecture Vision, as well as respond to Architecture Work requests and stakeholder requirements.

PHASE C: INFORMATION SYSTEMS ARCHITECTURE

Objectives

Implement the functional objective information systems architecture by describing how it will enable Enterprise Architecture and architecture vision by answering the Architecture Work Request and stakeholder concerns.

Recognize from the Roadmap Architecture its candidate components based on the differences between the architecture of objective information systems and the baseline. (Applications and data)

PHASE D: TECHNOLOGY ARCHITECTURE

Objectives

Implement the functional target technology architecture by describing how it will enable the Enterprise Architecture and architecture vision by answering the Architecture Work Request and stakeholder concerns.

Recognize from the Architecture Roadmap its candidate components based on the differences between the target information systems architecture and the baseline.

APPLICATION MODEL

PHASE E: OPPORTUNITIES AND SOLUTIONS

Objectives

Design the initial version of the complete architecture roadmap based on gap analysis and candidate components of the Phase B, C and D Architecture roadmap.

Validate that the phased approach is necessary, to recognize transition architectures that can provide ongoing business value.

PHASE F: MIGRATION PLANNING

Objectives

Finalize the Architecture work plan together with the Migration and Implementation Support Plan

Validate that the Migration and Implementation Plan is coordinated with the system for the application and management of changes of the company.

Ensure that the virtue of the business as well as the price of the work packages and that the transition architectures are understandable by the important stakeholders.

PHASE G: GOVERNANCE OF IMPLEMENTATION

Objectives

Consolidate compliance through deployment projects with the target architecture.

Develop appropriate architecture governance functions for the solution and applications driven by architecture change requests.

PHASE H: ARCHITECTURE CHANGE MANAGEMENT

Objectives

Consolidate that the architecture lifecycle can be maintained.

Ensure that the Architecture Governance Framework can be executed.

Ensure that enterprise architecture capability can meet current requirements.

REQUIREMENTS MANAGEMENT

Objectives

Consolidate that the Requirements Management process sustains and operates all crucial phases of ADM.

Manage that configuration requirements detected throughout all elaborations of the cycle or phase of an ADM.

Consolidate that the crucial requirements for its use are available when each stage is executed.

4 Case Study

The implementation of an agile model based on the SAFe Roadmap for enterprise architectures in the financial sector can have a significant impact on process efficiency and flexibility in the development of products and services in a financial savings and credit cooperative. For this, an analysis of the processes, risks and problems of a savings and credit cooperative was carried out. Then the implementation was carried out following all the phases and deliverables of the proposed model, and in order to validate this hypothesis, a survey was carried out among the employees of a financial savings and credit cooperative.

4.1 Scenario 1

The Financial Savings and Credit Cooperative currently employs a traditional enterprise architecture model for the implementation of new processes and services. This model has encountered limitations in terms of its ability to adapt to rapid and efficient changes, resulting in delays in the implementation of new solutions and, consequently, missed business opportunities. The objective of the research is to measure process improvement through the implementation of the agile model.

Six questions directly related to the operational dimensions of the credit and collection processes of the cooperative were designed. The questions were asked logically and evaluated according to the guidelines for the validity of an instrument.

Once the survey was validated, a sample of ten workers from the Savings and Credit Financial Cooperative was selected to participate in the survey. Workers from different areas and hierarchical levels were included to obtain a more complete view of the employees' perception of the implementation of the agile model. The reliability of the survey will be verified with the crombach alpha formula. Where the reliability coefficient oscillates between 0 and 1. The magnitude of the reliability coefficient of an instrument is interpreted from null with ranges from 0.01 to 0.52, to valid with ranges from 0.72 to 1.00. When calculating the reliability of the instrument, an internal correlation of 0.79 (α) is shown. This demonstrates the representativeness and coherence of each of the questions.

$$\alpha = \frac{K}{K-1}\left[1 - \frac{\sum S_i^2}{S_T^2}\right]$$

4.2 Scenario 2

The Financial Savings and Credit Cooperative offers savings and credit services to its clients. With the implementation of the agile model, the aim is to achieve greater adaptability to changes and improved efficiency in the implementation of new processes and services.

The business process with the agile model begins with the identification of improvement opportunities by the company's staff. Once the need is identified, a rapid assessment is conducted to determine if a short-term solution is possible. The Jira Atlassian tool will be used to manage the user implementation process and, to a lesser extent, improve communication with the credit processes and partner collection process. For this purpose, the trial version of the platform was utilized so that those responsible for the credit and collection area could use it for a few weeks.

The results of the AS-IS survey carried out on the savings and credit cooperative gave unfavorable but expected results, due to the current situation of the company. A series of 6 questions were asked that are related to a series of criteria about the capacity of the business architecture of the credit and collection process of the cooperative. This survey was carried out on 10 cooperative workers who are directly related to these processes (Table 5).

Table 5. As-Is Survey Result

	Criteria	1	2	3	4	5	Total (50)	Percentage (100%)
AS-IS	Efficiency of current processes	3	3	4	0	0	21	42%
	Flexibility and adaptability to changes	0	4	3	3	0	29	58%
	Communication and collaboration between the different areas	1	4	4	1	0	25	50%
	Customer satisfaction level	0	5	4	1	0	26	52%
	Fulfillment of established deadlines	2	3	5	0	0	23	46%
	Workflow efficiency	0	4	5	1	0	27	54%
							25.17	**50%**

The results of the To-Be survey reveal a remarkable improvement compared to the results of the As-Is survey. This survey was applied after presenting a detailed implementation plan of the agile enterprise architecture model along with its deliverables, strategies, and in-depth risk analysis. A joint test of the Jira Atlassian process management tool was also carried out to improve communication and collaboration between credit processes. This increasing the level of satisfaction among respondents (Table 6).

Table 6. To-Be Survey Result

	Criteria	1	2	3	4	5	Total (50)	Percentage (100%)
TO-BE	Efficiency of current processes	0	0	2	4	4	42	84%
	Flexibility and adaptability to changes	0	0	2	5	3	41	82%
	Communication and collaboration between the different areas	0	0	1	6	3	42	84%
	Customer satisfaction level	0	0	2	4	4	42	84%
	Fulfillment of established deadlines	0	0	2	3	5	43	86%
	Workflow efficiency	0	0	2	4	4	42	84%
							42	**84%**

The results of the comparison of the as-is surveys against the to-be survey carried out present interesting results. The indicators show a significant increase of 34% in the level of agreement and efficiency in all evaluated areas. This suggests that the implementation of the agile model for the gradual and short-term deployment of an enterprise architecture in the financial sector can lead to increased efficiency and satisfaction in the processes of the financial cooperative (Table 7).

Table 7. As-Is Survey Vs To-Be Survey Result

	Criteria	Percentage (AS-IS)	Percentage (TO-BE)	Increase
AS-IS VS TO-BE	Efficiency of current processes	42%	84%	42%
	Flexibility and adaptability to changes	58%	82%	24%
	Communication and collaboration between the different areas	50%	84%	34%
	Customer satisfaction level	52%	84%	32%
	Fulfillment of established deadlines	46%	86%	40%
	Workflow efficiency	54%	84%	30%
		50%	**84%**	**34%**

5   Conclusion

Through the case study of the savings and credit cooperative in the financial sector, it is evident that the implementation of an agile model of Business Architecture based on the SAFe methodology can result in significant benefits for organizations in the financial sector.

First, the main objective of the implementation of the SAFe methodology and the Enterprise Architecture was to align the different processes, systems and people in the organization to improve the efficiency and effectiveness of operations. In addition to the improvement in efficiency, the implementation of the agile Enterprise Architecture model also led to an improvement in the quality of the products and services offered by the credit union. The SAFe methodology allowed a more effective integration of team members and a focus on the continuous delivery of value to clients through the different workflows. As a result, there was an increase in customer satisfaction and greater loyalty to the cooperative.

In terms of values, the implementation of an agile Enterprise Architecture model and the SAFe methodology also brought clear benefits by increasing customer satisfaction and providing faster and more predictable delivery of value, while improving the organization's capacity for innovation. By focusing on agile principles and team collaboration, the credit union was able to increase its productivity, also improved the ability to make informed and strategic decisions, while maintaining transparency throughout the organization's operations.

We can conclude that the implementation of an agile Enterprise Architecture model based on the SAFe methodology is an excellent option for organizations seeking to improve quality, productivity, speed in value delivery and commitment to the team. It is also recommended to carry out similar case studies in different industries and business settings to assess the applicability of the model in different contexts and further improve its implementation in future projects.

References

1. Urbiola, P., Fernandez, S.: Transformación digital y competencia en el sector financiero. BBVA Research (2018). https://www.bbvaresearch.com/wp-content/uploads/2019/01/Transf ormacion-digital-y-competencia-en-el-sector-financiero-vf3_edi.pdf
2. Ghaffari, A., Ahmadi, P., Ebrahimi, A., Zarei, B.: An agile approach to enterprise architecture implementation in financial institutions. J. Enterp. Archit. **17**(1), 19–32 (2021). https://essay. utwente.nl/68228/1/Hensema_MA_EEMCS.pdf
3. Miah, S.J., Gammack, J., McGrath, K.: Agile enterprise architecture: a review of the literature and roadmap for future research. J. Enterp. Archit. **16**(3), 35–42 (2020). https://pdfs.semant icscholar.org/e6a3/d161b0120f692f457d4d4e352161490085be.pdf
4. Chen, Y., Liu, H., Liu, Y., Yang, Y.: Agile enterprise architecture development for collaborative innovation. J. Syst. Softw. **137**, 520–530 (2018). https://doi.org/10.1016/j.jss.2017.12.020
5. Bera, P., Ravanan, R.: Agile enterprise architecture for financial institutions: an exploratory study. J. Enterp. Archit. **16**(3), 36–43 (2020). https://www.jofea.org/wp-content/uploads/ 2020/09/JEA_Volume16_Issue3.pdf#page=36
6. Sohrabi, S., Asghari, S., Alizadeh, M.: The impact of agile approach on enterprise architecture implementation. Procedia Computer Science **143**, 170–175 (2018)
7. Al Shaikhli, A.A., Kautz, K., Schneider, A.W.: Agile enterprise architecture: an exploratory study. J. Syst. Softw. **150**, 11–34 (2019)
8. Abid, F., Iqbal, S., Saeed, S., Nazir, S.: Agile enterprise architecture: a systematic review. IEEE Access **8**, 22988–23005 (2020)
9. Vojta, M., Basl, J., Halaška, P.: Agile enterprise architecture in the financial industry: challenges and benefits. J. Univ. Comput. Sci. **27**(5), 425–446 (2021)
10. Habbal, M.A., Rahim, A.R.A., Ali, M.A.M.: An agile enterprise architecture approach for digital transformation: a case study of a financial institution. J. Enterp. Inf. Manag. **34**(1), 1–23 (2021)
11. Brühl, V.: Agile methods in the German banking sector: some evidence on expectations, experiences and success factors. J. Bus. Econ. **92**(8), 1337–1372 (2022). https://doi.org/10. 1007/s11573-022-01102-y
12. Rahmanian, M., Nassiri, R., Mohsenzadeh, M., Ravanmehr, R.: Test case generation for enterprise business services based on enterprise architecture design. J. Supercomput. **79**, 1877–1907 (2022). https://doi.org/10.1007/s11227-022-04742-7

13. Kassa, E.A., Mentz, J.C.: Towards a human capabilities conscious enterprise architecture. Information **12**(8), 327 (2021). https://doi.org/10.3390/info12080327
14. Tamm, T., Seddon, P.B., Shanks, G.: How enterprise architecture leads to organisational benefits. Int. J. Inf. Manage. **67**, 102554 (2022). https://doi.org/10.1016/j.ijinfomgt.2022.102554
15. Beese, J., Haki, K., Schilling, R., Kraus, M., Aier, S., Winter, R.: Strategic alignment of enterprise architecture management – how portfolios of control mechanisms track a decade of enterprise transformation at Commerzbank. Eur. J. Inf. Syst. **32**, 92–105 (2022). https://doi.org/10.1080/0960085X.2022.2085200

Digital Master Plan as a Tool for Generating Territory Development Requirements

Tatiana Churiakova$^{(\boxtimes)}$, Vasilii Starikov, Vladislava Sudakova,
Aleksandr Morozov , and Sergey Mityagin

ITMO University, 197101 Saint Petersburg, Russia
tanufry@gmail.com

Abstract. The article considers the approach to creating such a tool as a Digital Master Plan and using it to generate the requirements for the development of territories automatically. The specificity of the Digital Master Plan is that it takes into account the context of the city, or, more precisely, the conditions of placement of the territory to be developed in the context of the entire city. Digital Master Plan provides a multifaceted evaluation of the outcome of suggested or already implemented urban changes. The tool was applied on the territory of Metallostroy settlement of Saint Petersburg (Russia) to calculate school provision. Based on the results of the experiment, a territory change option was proposed.

Keywords: Network modeling · City model · Master Plan · Urban development · Digitalization

1 Introduction

Spontaneous urban development has become an obstacle to the implementation of the "classic" urban policy of the twentieth century, where the future of the territory was determined by the strict framework of General Plans, which ignored the speed of urbanization, progress, as well as the values and needs of people [1]. The "conservative" General Plans have been replaced by strategic spatial planning, which develops an interdisciplinary approach to the design of territories. Its main task is to create a program of territorial development, which allows to manage urban development in the rapidly changing conditions of the contemporary world. The primary tool of strategic planning in territorial development has become a Master Plan of the territory, a document of spatial territorial development. However, the development of draft Master Plans for a particular area is a time-consuming and long-term process, limited by the capabilities of the project team. At the same time, the result runs the risk of being subjective due to the human factor or irrelevant in the context of rapidly changing urban factors. In this case, adapting to future territorial changes will be most effective if digital tools are used to support decision-making [2–4]. At the stage of digitalization,

T. Guarda et al. (Eds.): ARTIIS 2023, CCIS 1936, pp. 45–57, 2024.
https://doi.org/10.1007/978-3-031-48855-9_4

we can use a tool that has already proven itself as an effective tool for assessing potential changes. The proposed vision of the Digital Master Plan allows us to automate the selection of technical and economic parameters and simulate several scenarios of development of the territory, taking into account the objective functions, reflecting the concept of the socio-economic strategy of the region.

In the second chapter, we review the existing methods of generating requirements for the development of territories, known methods of automatization. The third chapter describes the concept of the Digital Master Plan as a management tool, how it differs from the traditional Master Plan of the territory, and how it affects decision-making. Further, the proposed method of generating requirements for the development of territories in the context of the creation of the Digital Master Plan tool is described. An experiment describing the work of the method on the example of the territory in the city of Saint Petersburg (Russia) is conducted. In conclusion, a discussion on the availability of necessary data is offered and a conclusion on the viability of the Digital Master Plan tool in the management of urban development is made.

2   Literature Review

In the context of modern urbanism, a Master Plan is a spatial development strategy containing an urban planning component, designed by the public authorities with the participation of representatives of various interest groups [5]. It covers the economic, social and spatial aspects of urban development, including the necessary management mechanisms for implementing the goals and objectives [6]. A Master Plan is a flexible long-term planning document that provides a conceptual framework for the future growth and development of an area [7]. It conceptualizes space and determines the vector of the city's future development, setting the basis for the development of more detailed solutions, documents, and projects. Urban management is a process of finding a compromise between government, business, and residents [8].

Urban regions around the world are turning to scenario-based modeling to understand and cope with uncertain land use changes and future land use needs [4]. While scenarios take into account various drivers to simulate land change, spatial planning has received limited attention. The paper [9] considers spatial planning in scenarios through strategic development planning intentions expressed in various spatial plans. The four simulated scenarios take into account possible trends in future needs expressed in areas for residential, built-up, green space, and agricultural land (using population data and making predictions based on it), and the strategic planning intentions that are characterized by spatial development documents. Scenarios take into account increases and decreases in future needs, including or excluding spatial planning intentions.

Depending on the purpose of the Master Plan, it can consist of different sections and be developed in different ways. However, there are two fundamentally important stages in the creation of a Master Plan - a feasibility study and a strategic framework (Fig. 1) [7]. The feasibility study includes an objective review of the available options for the development of the city, presented on the basis of the analysis of the existing situation and indicators. The strategic framework is a framing for the concept to be developed.

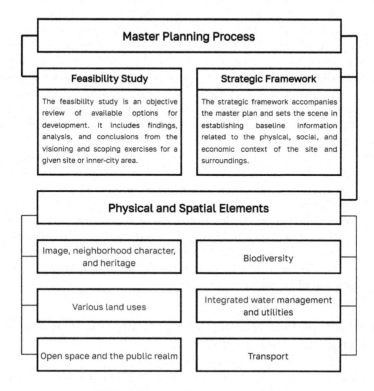

Fig. 1. Master Planning process [7]

In connection with the continuing growth of urbanization, the most relevant is the scenario of urban adaptation to the increase in density and compactness of buildings [10]. The integrated vision of Master Plans used in the digital space also opens up opportunities to help plan for sustainable adaptation to climate change and the environment. For example, in [11], urban water demand is projected to optimize resource management. Findings show the potential of digitalization to support more effective early warning and emergency response systems, improve food and water security, increase the productivity of energy infrastructure, ensure citizen participation and adaptation measures, and minimize the impact of climate risks [11]. There are also assessments of territories, which are also built on data and can give estimates for many cities at once, such as The Urban Environment Quality Index [12]. But what are the assessments aimed at, the Index shows the current state of the urban environment, if we look at other assessments, we will find little information about the provision of the population. Sociological surveys are used to determine the level of satisfaction of the population, but it is an even more time-consuming process, difficult to process and quite subjective.

In the process of creating a Master Plan, urban analytics technologies can be used. Typically, such analytics involves the creation of a digital model of the city or a digital twin. Despite the fact that often between these concepts is put an equal sign, it is important to understand the differences between them: "a digital twin without a physical twin is a model" [13]. Key aspects of the digital twin is an accurate model of the data of real objects (in this case, the objects of the urban system), as well as the means of updating this model. The use of a digital twin is appropriate if such data change over time in a way that makes it irrelevant to use the model of objects. Since the city is a huge complex system, the main difficulty in creating a digital twin of the city is the collection and processing of a huge array of urban data [14]. An alternative, accordingly, is to use an urban model that uses data close to real, but not necessarily up-to-date.

The creation of a digital model opens up the possibilities of basic urban analytics: construction of isochrons of urban accessibility, service coverage zones. On this basis, more complex methods of analysis are created: calculation of the provision of urban services, determination of the morphotype of the urban environment, etc. In general, the approach based on AI and data analysis can offer a fast, efficient and data-driven method for determining development needs to improve urban areas, which facilitates the prioritization of investments and efficient allocation of resources.

3   Methods of Generating and Setting the Requirements of a Digital Master Plan

A Digital Master Plan is a scenario in a digital city model for spatial analysis of the urban environment's current quality and assessment of potential changes' impact to support decision-making on urban development management.

Unlike the traditional Master Plan, the Digital Master Plan automates the initial data collection processes and generates requirements based on specified coefficients or context conditions, which speeds up the process and avoids human error in the calculation of indicators. An up-to-date city database is used for data analysis, where the method of handling the missing data is used to distribute the number of residents by house [15]. Service capacity values are used to estimate the provision of services to the population. Scenarios of changes in the area allow assessing the effects of changes not only in the context of the projected area, but also how the changes will affect the entire city.

The management of spatial development of urban areas includes both the development of vacant space and the development of existing built-up areas under constraints. Figure 2 shows the stages of using the Digital Master Plan in the spatial planning decision-making process.

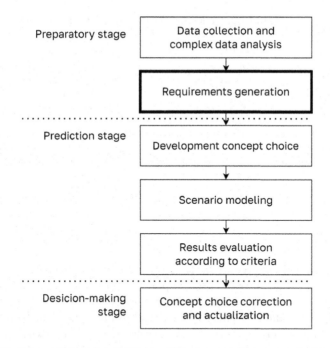

Fig. 2. The place of the Digital Master Plan in spatial planning decision-making

3.1 Data Collection and Comprehensive Analysis

Information about the urban context is collected from various sources with characteristic features (Table 1). For example, the existing objects of cultural heritage on the territory imply a ban on their demolition. Information on area constraints is also collected from several sources (Table 2) to obtain a range of values as part of the requirements generation.

Table 1. Territory data collection

Source	Relevance	Cost	Examples	Automation
Open Data	Inaccurate	Free	OSM; local, regional and state statistical agencies	Overpassturbo, geocoding (provided the data are digitized)
Map service	Updated	Paid	Google Maps, Yandex Maps, 2GIS	Parsing (Legitimacy Issue)
Government	Updated	Free on request	Topography, engineering networks, cadastre	Depends on the source (digitized or not)
Sociology	Updated	Free	Interview, observation	Geographic information systems of public participation

Table 2. Collecting data on restrictions

Source	Feature	Where to get
Regulatory documents	Obligatory	Available upon request or online
Methodological recommendations	Aimed at creating a comfortable urban environment	May be developed with the participation of the authorities by research institutes or other organizations
The demands of the citizens of the local community	May not be expressed clearly	Sociological research (surveys, social network analysis, etc.)
Environmental parameters	Can be partially covered by regulatory documents	The result of the environmental analysis is either provided by the authorities
Territory context requirements	Shaping the face of the city and the urban environment	The data are provided by the authorities or are the result of the work of a specialist from the

The dominant design paradigm today is to create artificial intelligence technologies that can scale and promote component reuse. This thinking is outdated. Today, it is possible to create technologies that work under certain conditions (scenarios) in a flexible and cost-effective way. Process automation includes automating the collection of current metrics and the selection of techno-economic metrics.

Basic documents of city regulation, in its essence, stated in the legislation, are designed to provide complexity, the basis of which are calculated areas of acceptable ratios between (a) maximum volumes of construction and (b) minimum volumes-capabilities of various types of infrastructure to serve the maximum volumes of the planned construction, including in the local areas, including the areas of complex development. The complexity of the development occurs only on the basis of the calculated modeling of balances between the volumes of construction and the volumes-capabilities of its service infrastructure of various kinds.

An approach to the automatic formation of requirements for the development of urban areas can be based on the use of artificial intelligence and data analysis methods. This approach involves the collection and analysis of data on various aspects of urban development, including demographics, infrastructure, transportation and the environment, to identify areas for improvement.

Researchers from Georgia Institute of Technology, Emory University and the University of California, Irvine, in collaboration with the Atlanta Fire and Rescue Department (AFRD), developed an algorithm that can predict fire risk in buildings. Using data from 2010-2014, the algorithm incorporated more than 50 variables including property location, building size, structure, age and fire history to predict fire risk [16]. Researchers at Carnegie Mellon University collaborated with the City of Pittsburgh to develop the Scalable Urban Traffic Control system (SURTRAC), which could simultaneously monitor and control traffic flows [17].

The proposed tool - a Digital Master Plan allows to automate the selection of technical and economic parameters of the territory and simulates several scenarios of territory development, taking into account the objective functions, reflecting the concept of the socio-economic strategy of the region.

3.2 Requirements Generation

1. Preparation of initial data. At this stage, an information model of the city is formed on the basis of a graph. The vertices of the graph are the city blocks, and the edges are the paths by public transport, private transport and on foot. In this case, for simplicity, it is assumed that the residents of the block are accessible to all services in this block.
2. Determination of environmental requirements. This step comes down to the calculation of the "Value Standard" environmental indicators [18]. In this case, it is also necessary to consider the support of these values in other areas of the city in the zone of ecological and anthropological impact from the area.
3. Determination of normative requirements. At this stage, we calculate the indicators of normative provision of residents of the territory of transformation and the city as a whole. The result of calculating the indicators of security is the requirements for the composition and capacity of urban services for each quarter of the selected area.
4. Determination of contextual constraints. This stage involves the use of methodological recommendations in the context of the morphotype of the territory. The result at this stage is a list of limitations of the key parameters of the recommendations.
5. Determination of behavioral requirements of the population. This stage involves assessing the support for the life of citizens in the context of the model of life situations [19]. The result at this stage is the additional requirements for the composition and capacity of urban services, which may not be fixed in regulation.

Thus, the result of the method is a spatial layer with the neighborhoods included in the development area.

3.3 Prediction Stage - Selection of the Concept

Strategic urban planning must take into account the interests of all stakeholders. Balancing the interests and desires of society, business and government is still a major problem and challenge in regional and urban planning [8]. Different stakeholders such as residents, businesses, government agencies, environmental organizations, and other stakeholders have different needs and expectations for the use of the urban area. Balancing their interests allows you to consider a wide range of factors and create a Master Plan that meets multiple needs [20,21]. For example, planning must pay attention to the preservation of natural resources, the improvement of the quality of life of residents and the promotion of economic development [21]. Traditionally, sustainable development encompasses three areas: economic, social and environmental. In the context of the city, economic sustainability can be expressed in the efficient and responsible use of resources for long-term benefits [22]. Social sustainability, in turn, means actively maintaining the ability of present and future generations to create healthy and prosperous communities by promoting equity, diversity and other

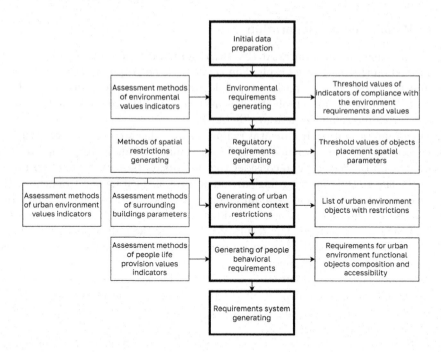

Fig. 3. Method of generating requirements for the development of territories

aspects [22]. Environmental sustainability is about making decisions to preserve the environment [22]. It should be noted that there is a growing need to consider the "institutional" dimension of sustainability - the governance structures and regulations that play an important role in sustainable urban development and planning [22, 23].

In this paper, we use a scenario where we maximize social, economic and environmental effects. The directions of development are:

- Healthy City. This scenario takes into account indicators such as the provision and accessibility of hospitals, clinics, recreational areas (parks, sports grounds) and pharmacies.
- Comfortable city/yard. This scenario takes into account the provision of food stores and basic social infrastructure of residential areas (playgrounds, sports fields, etc.).
- The Sustainable city scenario involves assessing the provision of green areas, taking into account the area of green areas and the percentage of residents living within walking distance of the public transport network. Diversity of services in a residential area and the provision of social infrastructure facilities are also important indicators.
- Social equality involves assessing the diversity of services in the residential area, public and business areas, the provision of social infrastructure facilities and accessibility of social infrastructure facilities.

– Business City. This scenario focuses on the percentage of developed land classified as industrial and mixed-use, accessibility to places/areas of employment, diversity of services in public and business areas, and the percentage of residents living within walking distance of the public transport network.

The main advantages of the Digital Master Plan include automation, saving time, the ability to use different options for the development of the area, a built-in function to find the best solution, as well as the ability to assess the impact of changes on the entire city.

3.4 Scenario-Modeling and Results Evaluation According to Criteria

Optimization of the spatial structure of land use with a focus on sustainable development involves identifying the most efficient and sustainable use of land resources. This approach is aimed at minimizing the negative impact of land use on the environment while meeting the needs of society and the economy. Methods of optimization, which are aimed at achieving several goals in land use [10]:

– Multi-objective genetic algorithm (MOGA): This method involves using genetic algorithms to optimize multiple targets.
– Multi-objective Particle Swarm Optimization (MOPSO): This method involves using particle swarm optimization to optimize multiple targets.
– Non-dominant Sorting Genetic Algorithm-II (NSGA-II): This method involves the use of genetic algorithms to identify non-dominant solutions in multi-objective optimization.
– Strength Pareto Evolutionary Algorithm (SPEA2): This method involves the use of evolutionary algorithms to determine Pareto-optimal solutions in multi-objective optimization.

These methods assist in making decisions for efficient and sustainable land use that can simultaneously meet various social, economic, and environmental objectives.

3.5 Decision-Making Stage

The requirements selected according to the chosen scenario represent the optimal solution within the framework of the task. At the next stage, they are submitted to the urban planners for verification. If there are no comments from them, the resulting requirements become the basis for the development of specific project proposals.

4 Experiment

The experiment is being carried out on a local territory of Metallostroy settlement of Saint Petersburg (Russia). The local territory consists of 9 urban blocks shown in Fig. 4.

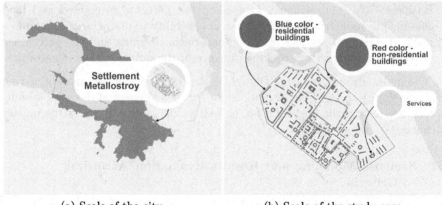

(a) Scale of the city   (b) Scale of the study area

Fig. 4. The initial local territory of Metallostroy settlement

The first step of the method includes environmental values support assessment. It is necessary to build an Environmental and Anthropological Impact zone (EAI zone). The EAI zone represents an isochrone of 30 min of travel time from any point within the territory. The second step represents the generating of regulatory requirements for the territory (Table 3). According to the methodological recommendation, the following territory consists of two morphotypes: mid-rise model and low-rise model. City services provision assessment was carried out for schools.

Table 3. Generating of regulatory requirements for the territory

Requirements	Value
Number of landfills in EAI zone	3
Specially protected natural territories area in EAI zone	0
Number of natural heritage objects in EAI zone	0
Additional capacity needed for schools	609
Pedestrian accessibility (meters)	500
Territory morphotype	Mid-rise model, low-rise model

As a result of the collected requirements, the area requires the construction of a school within an accessibility radius for at least 609 students (Fig. 5a).

4.1 Scenario for the Addition of a New School

Consider an area change scenario in which a 600-seat school was built to meet the needs of the residents. Figure 5 shows the distribution of school load between the residential buildings before and after the change.

As can be seen in Fig. 5a, there is a shortage of schools in the northeast of the area in the accessibility zone, so in the provision of schools it is necessary to build a school in a vacant location so that it crosses the accessibility zones of the homes as much as possible. In Fig. 5b it can be seen how the provision of schools for residential buildings in the area has changed. It is clear that the provision situation has changed for the better, but this transformation is the result of working with the requirements of the local area.

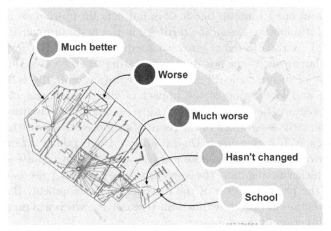

(a) School provision in the study area before the addition of a new school

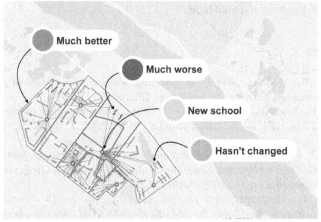

(b) School provision in the study area after the addition of a new school

Fig. 5. School provision in the study area

5   Discussion

The proposed method of requirements generation for the Master Plan, first of all, solves the problem of structuring heterogeneous requirements for the development of the territory. One of the advantages of the method is the possibility to automate the collection of requirements at all levels by creating an information model of the city, as well as taking into account the impact of possible development scenarios on other areas. The issue of initial data collection remains open, as the gathering of information for the territory and the city itself can be automated from open sources, but it does not contain up-to-date information. Nevertheless, it allows to assess the territory in the first approximation.

Automation of the process of generating requirements for the development of the Master Plan opens up the possibility of creating a new tool - a Digital Master Plan. The use of such a tool will allow the integration of digital technologies in the planning and forecasting of the impact of the development of territories, taking into account the requirements of all stakeholders. In addition, this tool will allow a versatile assessment of the result of proposed or already implemented urban changes. When creating a Digital Master Plan, taking into account the requirements of various parties becomes possible through the use of objective functions, which can regulate the spectrum of all existing needs of the city, highlighting the priority vector of the direction of development. However, it is necessary to define the objective functions themselves, which will properly reflect the desired direction of development.

Acknowledgments. This research is financially supported by the Russian Science Foundation, Agreement 17-71-30029 (https://rscf.ru/en/project/17-71-30029/), with co-financing of Bank Saint-Petersburg.

References

1. Pelorosso, R.: Modeling and urban planning: a systematic review of performance-based approaches. Sustain. Urban Areas **52**, 101867 (2020)
2. Nummi, P., Staffans, A., Helenius, O.: Digitalizing planning culture: A change towards information model-based planning in Finland. J. Urban Manage. **12**, 44–56 (2023)
3. Fertner, C., et al.: Emerging digital plan data - new research perspectives on planning practice and evaluation. Geografisk Tidsskrift-Danish J. Geography **119**, 6–16 (2018). https://doi.org/10.1080/00167223.2018.1528555
4. Bullivant, L.: Masterplanning futures, 1st edn., pp. 1–313. Routledge (2012). www.taylorfrancis.com/books/mono/10.4324/9780203720684/masterplanning-futures-lucy-bullivant
5. Strategic Master Plan: A Tool for Managing the Future. Strelka Press (in Russian), Moscow (2014)
6. Tuzovsky, V.S.: Formation of the concept ≪master plan≫ in national urban planning theory and practice (in Russian). Nohma (Architecture. Urbanism. Art.) (**S3**(3)), 29–43 (2019)

7. Master Planning — Urban Regeneration. https://urban-regeneration.worldbank. org/node/51

8. Ma, S., Wen, Z.: Optimization of land use structure to balance economic benefits and ecosystem services under uncertainties: a case study in Wuhan, China. J. Cleaner Product. **311**, 127537 (2021)

9. Bacău, S., Domingo, D., Palka, G., Pellissier, L., Kienast, F.: Integrating strategic planning intentions into land-change simulations: designing and assessing scenarios for Bucharest. Sustain. Urban Areas **76**, 103446 (2022)

10. Rahman, M.M., SzabÓ, G.: Multi-objective urban land use optimization using spatial data: a systematic review. Sustain. Urban Areas **74**, 103214 (2021)

11. Zubaidi, S.L., et al.: Urban water demand prediction for a city that suffers from climate change and population growth: Gauteng province case study. Water **12**(7), 1885 (2020)

12. Urban Environment Quality Index. https://cities-index.ru/#/

13. Wright, L., Davidson, S.: How to tell the difference between a model and a digital twin. Adv. Model. Simul. Eng. Sci. **7**(1), 1–13 (2020)

14. Shahat, E., Hyun, C.T., Yeom, C.: City digital twin potentials: a review and research agenda. Sustainability **13**(6), 3386 (2021)

15. Khrulkov, A.A., Mishina, M.E., Mityagin, S.A.: Approach to imputation multi-variate missing data of urban buildings by chained equations based on geospatial information. In: Groen, D., de Mulatier, C., Paszynski, M., Krzhizhanovskaya, V.V., Dongarra, J.J., Sloot, P.M.A. (eds.) Computational Science – ICCS 2022. ICCS 2022. LNCS, vol. 13352. Springer, Cham (2022). https://doi.org/10.1007/978-3-031-08757-8_21

16. Madaio, M., et al.: Identifying and prioritizing fire inspections: a case study of predicting fire risk in Atlanta. Bloomberg Data for Good Exchange, New York, NY, USA (2015)

17. Smith, S., Barlow, G., Xie, X.F., Rubinstein, Z.: Smart urban signal Networks: initial application of the Surtrac adaptive traffic signal control system, vol. 23, pp. 434–442 (2013)

18. Mityagin, S.A., Gornova, G., Drozhzhin, A., Sokol, A.: Value-based in a smart city (in Russian). Int. J. Open Inf. Technol. **9**(12), 104–110 (2021)

19. Tikhonova, O., Yakimuk, I., Mityagin, S.A.: Detection the relevance of urban functions for value-based smart city management. In: Alexandrov, D.A., et al. (eds.) DTGS 2021. CCIS, vol. 1503, pp. 193–206. Springer, Cham (2022). https://doi. org/10.1007/978-3-030-93715-7_14

20. Metternicht, G.: Land use planning. Global Land Outlook (Working Paper) (2017)

21. Riddell, R.: Sustainable urban planning: tipping the balance. Wiley (2008)

22. Komeily, A., Srinivasan, R.S.: A need for balanced approach to neighborhood sustainability assessments: a critical review and analysis. Sustain. Urban Areas **18**, 32–43 (2015)

23. Spangenberg, J.H., Pfahl, S., Deller, K.: Towards indicators for institutional sustainability: lessons from an analysis of agenda 21. Ecol. Ind. **2**(1–2), 61–77 (2002)

Cooperation and Technological Capacity Development Among Companies: Evidence from Ecuador

Gustavo Hermosa-Vega[1]([⊠]) [iD], Astrid Aguilar-Vega[2] [iD], Marianela Reina-Cherrez[2] [iD], and Myriam Moreno-Achig[2] [iD]

[1] Instituto Superior Tecnológico San Antonio, Quito, Ecuador
ghermosa@itsa.edu.ec
[2] Universidad Central del Ecuador UCE, Quito, Ecuador

Abstract. This study aims to understand the relationship between cooperation and the development of technological capacities among companies, considering the way innovation is introduced, the type of innovation activity, as well as the regional location. The data source for this study is the National Innovation Survey (ENAI) 2012–2014, which provides a sample of 2,544 innovative companies, meaning those that introduced a new or improved product, service, or process. This research utilizes a multivariate probit estimation method, which allows for analyzing the effect of cooperation on the way companies introduce innovation through four dependent variables. The results show that companies should not be considered at the same level of innovation since the effects vary depending on the degree of technological capacity. Innovation research in developing countries is scarce, the contribution of this investigation is to empirically contribute by applying this study to the case of Ecuadorian companies, within the context of emerging innovation systems.

Keywords: Innovation · Multivariate-Probit · Cooperation

1 Introduction

The ability of companies to identify solutions in an uncertain, dynamic, and global environment requires an improvement in their innovative capacity (Rubio & Abril 2023) related to the performance of the economy to which they belong (Freeman & Soete 1997; Verspagen 2004). This ability, known as "technological capacity," generates innovation based on science and technology (Parrilla, Balayac & Radicic 2020) and is defined as the ability to develop and introduce new products, services, and processes in the market through the application of scientific and technical knowledge (Pavitt, 2004). Promoting technological capacities does not depend solely on the companies themselves; they arise through the interaction that companies have with various types of agents involved in the innovation process (suppliers, customers, competitors, scientific institutions, etc.) (Lundvall 2010). Technological capabilities are influenced by the specific characteristics of companies, the characteristics of their sector and the characteristics of the environment

T. Guarda et al. (Eds.): ARTIIS 2023, CCIS 1936, pp. 58–71, 2024.
https://doi.org/10.1007/978-3-031-48855-9_5

in which they operate (Arnold and Thuriaux 1997; Malerba 2004; Lundvall 2010). And they become vital for their permanence in the market (Liu 2020).

Research examining the factors that influence the technological capacities of companies in developing countries is limited. This leaves room for development in the literature since their innovation processes differ from those of companies in developed countries (Padilla et al. 2009; Makkonen 2015). The present study aims to examine how cooperative relationships, based on the type of innovation activity, condition the development of technological capacities in companies according to their modes of innovation within a developing country context.

The way innovations are developed within companies varies according to the technological capacities they have acquired and accumulated (Divella 2016). Technological capacities are a set of skills that allow for the assimilation, use, adaptation, and modification of existing technologies through knowledge development (Dutrénit 2004). The absorption and application of knowledge in companies enable them to develop and accumulate technological capacities to carry out innovation activities. Various empirical research studies interested in assessing these capacities in companies use outcome variables such as the introduction of new products and/or processes (Iammarino et al. 2012). However, Divella (2016) argues that this indicator can be misleading as it fails to differentiate between different levels of technological capacities and incorrectly assumes that all companies develop their innovation activities in the same way, thereby losing information regarding how innovations are generated within the company.

The development of technological capabilities in companies is directly related to their learning and absorption capacity, determined by their ability to generate and assimilate knowledge both internally and through cooperation with other companies (Ortega 2005) and rapid technological change has transformed the way companies innovate, demonstrating the need for cooperation between companies in knowledge markets (Senguta & Sena 2020). The learning process leads to the "accumulation" of technological capacities necessary for the development of innovation activities (Albu 1997). When companies manage to develop these capacities, they have the necessary resources for the generation of new or improved products, services, and processes, resulting from the adaptive and innovative capacity they have developed (Fernández and Vaca 2017). However, this process of acquiring technological capacities is not linear; it is a complex process as intermediate states and "embryonic" technological capacities emerge (Dutrénit 2004). When companies are in a phase of minimum technological capacities, their competition is based on their production capabilities. On the other hand, companies that have developed strategic technological capacities compete based on their innovative skills using new and diverse knowledge and the combination of that knowledge (Segarra 2006).

In developing countries, companies often lack sufficient technological capacities (Garcia, Pineda & Andrade 2015), which means their cooperative relationships are not focused on generating R&D activities but rather on obtaining information as a requirement to initiate the process of accumulating technological capacities (Zhou and Wu, 2010). According to Fernández and Vaca (2017), cooperative agreements established for the development of these types of activities lead companies to create basic capacities that would enable them to implement innovations in the future. Non-R&D-related

cooperative agreements have a dual connotation. On one hand, they can incentivize companies to increase investment in innovation activities not directly related to research and development itself. On the other hand, they can lead to increased investment in R&D activities aimed at building R&D capacities. If companies invest and establish cooperative relationships in activities not directly related to R&D, their type of innovation is adaptive, involving the assimilation and modification of existing technology. Conversely, if companies cooperate in R&D activities, they develop higher technological capacities that allow them to generate innovations on their own.

Companies whose cooperative relationships are not focused on R&D activities should be distinguished between those whose cooperative relationships are oriented towards the development of basic activities for innovation, such as information, technical assistance, and training, with a low level of technological capacities. Their interest lies in investing in and cooperating in these types of activities to absorb knowledge. On the other hand, there are companies whose cooperative relationships are oriented towards the development of activities related to engineering and design, as well as product testing. These companies have an intermediate level of technological capacities, but it is not decisive in determining the mode of technological innovation development.

This research revolves around two hypotheses: Hypothesis 1 states that the greater the complexity of innovative activities in which companies cooperate, such as R&D, the higher the probability that technological development will occur through internal processes of the companies or through "cooperative generation". In cases of cooperation involving moderately complex innovative activities such as engineering and design, and product testing, the lower the level of complexity of the innovative activities of the companies cooperating in areas such as training, technical assistance, and information, the more likely the companies are to develop innovations through "adaptation" and "adoption" of technologies. Therefore, they have a lower probability of developing innovations internally.

Hypothesis 2 states that companies located in more advanced regions of a country positively influence the development of technological capacities through cooperation. This is because advanced economies have a more developed regional innovation system, with more institutions, more companies, more economic activity, and more networks, facilitating the strengthening of technological capacities in companies.

2 Data and Variables

2.1 Data

This study uses data from the National Innovation Survey 2012–2014 of Ecuador (ENAI), which collects information at the firm level regarding the characteristics, inputs, and outcomes of the innovation process. Additionally, the survey provides information on the types of innovative activities in which companies cooperated with external partners. It also provides information on the importance of internal and external sources of information for the development of innovation activities in companies. Lastly, in order to analyze the regional factors that influence the technological capacities of companies, information from the two main provinces of Ecuador, Guayaquil and Quito, is used to construct the regional-level variable.

2.2 Variables

Given that the objective is to analyze the factors that influence the construction of technological capacities, the dependent variable will be a binary variable reflecting the technological capacities of the companies based on the way they carry out innovation activities and the type of innovations they introduce in the market. Following Divella (2016), this variable of technological capacities can be constructed through four binary variables that take values of 0 or 1. The definition of each of these variables is described in Table 1.

Table 1. Variable List

Variable Values	Description	% companies
Internal Generation **"Internal_Generation" = 1"**	The company has successfully introduced a new or improved product, service, or process developed internally by the company	66,5%
Generation in cooperation *"generation_coop = 1"*	The company has successfully introduced a new or improved product, service, or process developed in collaboration with other companies or institutions	20,3%
Innovation adoption *"adaptation = 1"*	The company has successfully introduced a new or improved product, service, or process primarily developed by the company, adapting, or modifying goods or services originally developed by another company or institution	6,8%
External Generation *"adoption = 1"*	The company has successfully introduced a new or improved product, service, or process primarily developed by another company or institution	6,4%

Companies that have internally generated innovations or innovations through cooperation are considered to have higher technological capacities compared to those that mainly rely on technological adaptation or adoption developed by another company or institution (Barreto & Pettit 2017). The independent variables include individual, sectoral, and regional factors. According to the literature, the individual characteristics that influence technological capacities are described in the following table:

The technological capabilities of companies are also influenced by the sector in which they operate. Therefore, a set of sectoral binary variables is included based on a classification system that reflects technological intensity. This classification system considers the different technological opportunities available to companies within each industrial sector. The following table displays the types of activities that constitute each of the sectoral categories based on a CIIU classification.

The environment in which companies operate influences their technological capabilities, therefore, a regional control variable is included. For this purpose, a binary variable called "advanced region" is defined. It takes a value of 1 if the company operates in either of the two most advanced provinces in Ecuador, which are Pichincha and Guayaquil. It takes a value of 0 if the company is in the rest of the country. The analysis focuses

Table 2. Individual characteristics of companies

Name	Description
size	Natural logarithm of the number of employees of the company in the year 2012
start_up	Binary variable that takes a value of 1 if the company was created during the period from 2012 to 2014, and 0 otherwise
khum	Total number of employees with a tertiary-level degree or higher divided by the total number of employees in the year 2014
cluster	Binary variable that takes a value of 1 if the company is part of a business group whose parent company is located outside of Ecuador, and 0 otherwise
export	Binary variable that takes a value of 1 if the company exported in at least one of the three years during the period 2012–2014, and 0 otherwise
ln_intensity_intra	Natural logarithm of the research and development (R&D) expenditure conducted within the company divided by the total number of employees, for the year 2012
ln_intensity_extra	Natural logarithm of the research and development (R&D) expenditure conducted outside the company or with external personnel divided by the total number of employees, for the year 2012
ln_intensity_spent	Natural logarithm of the overall expenditure on other innovation activities excluding R&D divided by the total number of employees, for the year 2012
Int_sources	Ordinal categorical variable that takes values from 1 to 7, indicating the intensity of the indirect effects of knowledge input from internal areas of the companies
Ext_sources	Ordinal categorical variable that takes values from 1 to 13, indicating the intensity of the indirect effects of knowledge input from external sources of the companies, such as suppliers, competitors, research institutions, trade fairs, internet, among others
s_coop_high	Binary variable that takes the value 1 if the company collaborated in R&D activities with any external partner or organization during the period from 2012 to 2014, and 0 otherwise
s_coop_half	Binary variable that takes the value 1 if the company collaborated in "Engineering and Design" or "Product Testing" activities with any external partner or organization during the period from 2012 to 2014, and 0 otherwise
s_coop_basic	Binary variable that takes the value 1 if the company collaborated in "Training," "Technical Assistance," or "Information" activities with any external partner or organization during the period from 2012 to 2014, and 0 otherwise

(*continued*)

Table 2. (*continued*)

Name	Description
multi_activ	Ordinal categorical variable that takes values between 1 and 6, indicating the total number of innovation activities that the company has undertaken during the period from 2012 to 2014

Table 3. Sectoral Variables

Name	Sectoral Category	Economic activities that make up
low_manuf_intensity	Manufactures of low technological intensity	C10, C11, C12, C13, C14, C15, C16, C17, C18, C31 y C32
half_low_manuf_intensity	Manufactures of medium-low technological intensity	C19, C23, C24, C13, C25, C33 y S95
half_high_manuf_intensity	Medium-high technological intensity manufacturing	C20, C22, C27, C28, C29, C30
high_manuf_intensity	High technological intensity manufacturing	C21, C26
servic_no_inten_con oc	Non-knowledge intensive services	B09, G45, G46, G47, H49, H50, H51, H52, H53, I55; I56, L68, M73, N77, N78, N79, N81, N82, O84, S94, S96, T97, T98, U99
servic_inten_knowledge	Knowledge-intensive services	J58, J59, J60, J61, J62, J63, K64, K65, K66, M69, M70, M71, M72, M74, M75, N80, P85, Q86, Q87, Q88, R90, R91, R92, R93
services_provider	Service providers	D35, E35, E36, E37, E38, E39
extractive_sectors	Extractive sectors	B05, B06, B07, B08
construction	Construction	F41, F42, F43

on companies capable of introducing or improving at least one new product, service, or process during the period of 2012–2014. Specifically, 2,544 companies are considered as "innovators" for the scope of this study.

2.3 Estimation Strategy

For the estimation, a multivariate probit model is used because it allows predicting multiple correlated binary outcomes jointly and controlling for potential correlation of error terms (Green 2012). It is considered that the four variables are highly correlated and that the effects of unobserved characteristics, included in the error terms, are also correlated. Methodologically, prior to estimating the model, tests were conducted to discard multicollinearity, and controls were applied to avoid heteroscedasticity. The model is presented below:

$$if_i = \alpha + \beta_E X_i + \beta_S S_i + \beta_R R_i + \varepsilon$$

where if_i represents the way in which companies develop innovations, X represents the firm-level characteristics described in Table 2, S represents the sectoral binary variables described in Table 3, R represents the regional control, and ε represents the error term.

3   Results

After creating the dependent and independent variables, and after estimating the proposed econometric model, the following results are obtained, with an effective sample of 2,536 companies.

Table 4. Results of Multivariate Probit Model. Degree of Cooperation by Type of Innovative Activity of Ecuadorian Companies, 2012–2014.

Independent Variables	Dependent variables			
	Internal Generation	generation_coop	adaptation	adoption
size	−0.0022793	0.0486972*	0.0460149	0.0370913
	(0.0234141)	(0.0230697)	(0.0281043)	(0.0295943)
start_up	0.2685112	0.02659	0.0568225	−0.1296517
	(0.1482025)	(0.1464902)	(0.1903961)	(0.1894277)
khum	−0.2497345*	−0.0070969	−0.0665313	0.2271238
	(0.124661)	(0.1274419)	(0.1673927)	(0.1680316)
cluster	−0.2200677**	0.1036431	0.2605**	0.1068525
	(0.0755255)	(0.0762554)	(0.0911965)	(0.1063711)
export	0.0823698	−0.2456401**	0.0506577	−0.1098156
	(0.0894621)	(0.0862487)	(0.1069269)	(0.112028)
ln_intra_intensity	0.0523099***	0.0072013	−0.0172486	−0.0617237**
	(0.0149694)	(0.0135393)	(0.0169511)	(0.02273)
ln_extra_intensity	−0.0756054***	0.0423594*	0.0306934	0.0754932**
	(0.017953)	(0.0185776)	(0.0224192)	(0.0241846)
ln_spent_intensity	0.0158011	0.0151039	0.0117575	−0.0087824
	(0.0087419)	(0.0089244)	(0.0116678)	(0.0118861)

(continued)

Table 4. (*continued*)

Independent Variables	Dependent variables			
	Internal Generation	generation_coop	adaptation	adoption
int_sources	0.0132603	0.0633438**	−0.0117963	−0.0939065**
	(0.0211285)	(0.0211636)	(0.0279128)	(0.029771)
ext_sources	0.0247169*	−0.0127976	0.0310121	−0.0044765
	(0.0123323)	(0.0119843)	(0.0158922)	(0.0165772)
s_high_coop	−0.1015587	0.2537713	0.1904745	−0.0288248
	(0.1297969)	(0.1307568)	(0.1579851)	(0.1916688)
s_half_coop	−0.1578759	0.1370553	0.1216769	−0.6870329*
	(0.1606015)	(0.1670431)	(0.2044783)	(0.3005245)
S_basic__coop	−0.1631281*	0.139733	0.1953635*	−0.1436359
	(0.0761478)	(0.0791977)	(0.095438)	(0.1045883)
multi_activ	−0.1563471***	0.185748***	0.126167***	0.128806***
	(0.0195669)	(0.0193321)	(0.0247266)	(0.0268711)
Low_intensity_manuf	0.4369916***	−0.2939614***	−0.0713725	−0.3807846***
	(0.0836623)	(0.085359)	(0.112531)	(0.1111587)
Half_low_intensity_manuf	0.4328099**	−0.2264413	0.0462832	−0.8923149***
	(0.1365046)	(0.1336449)	(0.164376)	(0.2654988)
Half_high_intensity_	0.3504889**	−0.0560424	−0.2880095	−0.1664409
	(0.1227183)	(0.1184029)	(0.1785373)	(0.1638376)
manuf_alta_intensid	0.3619638	−0.2902015	0.1726564	0.0627587
	(0.2785365)	(0.2623173)	(0.2781021)	(0.3147012)
servic_inten_conocim	0.1112489	0.1834892*	0.1102233	−0.2467998*
	(0.082319)	(0.0818507)	(0.10814)	(0.1140148)
Service_provider	0.0123714	−0.2506121	0.1115731	−0.027969
	(0.1887959)	(0.2239089)	(0.3077544)	(0.2621167)
Extractive_sectors	0.0160004	0.288981	−0.0424754	−3617925***
	(0.2391678)	(0.2502884)	(0.3481231)	(0.2183952)
construction	0.0850113	−0.1878219	0.2345307	−0.2441178
	(0.1149836)	(0.1290278)	(0.145829)	(0.1572358)
Advanced_regional	−0.0490841	−0.1679427**	0.1837813*	0.235315**
	(0.0631442)	(0.0633197)	(0.0837186)	(0.0844324)

(*continued*)

Table 4. (*continued*)

Independent Variables	Dependent variables			
	Internal Generation	generation_coop	adaptation	adoption
_cons	0.9537381***	−1465958***	−2329795***	−1573658***
	(0.1080004)	(0.1082697)	(0.1438553)	(0.143628)
	rho1	rho2	rho3	rho4
rho1	1			
rho2	−0.6704917***	1		
rho3	−0.4377388***	0.0130958	1	
rho4	−0.4690721***	0.0207054	0.0895994*	1

Likelihood ratio test of rho21 = rho31 = rho41 = rho32 = rho42 = rho43 = 0; chi2(6) = 857.939 Prob > chi2 = 0.0000; Number of obs = 2536; Wald chi2(92) = 1247.66 Log pseudolikelihood = -3366.6125; Prob > chi2 = 0.0000 Note: Standard errors are shown in parentheses. *$p <$ 0.10;**$p < 0.05$; ***$p < 0.001$; t-test dos colas. The grouping criteria for the sectorial variables follow the classification based on the technological intensity of industries, based on a 2-digit CIIU classification, with the following typology: 1 Low technological intensity manufacturing, 2 Medium-low technological intensity manufacturing, 3Medium-high technological intensity manufacturing, 4 High technological intensity manufacturing, 5 Non-knowledge-intensive services, 6 Knowledge-intensive services, 7 Service providers, 8 Extractive sectors, 9 Construction.

One notable result is the covariance matrix at the end of Table 4, which shows a high and significant correlation among the standard errors of the four dependent binary variables, confirming the relevance of applying a multivariate probit model. This indicates that the decisions or ways of developing innovations in products, services, or processes are interdependent. As mentioned in Hypothesis 1, when the level of complexity of the innovative activities that companies cooperate in, such as training, technical assistance, and information, is lower, it is less likely that they will develop innovations internally. This result is evident in the Ecuadorian case with the negative and significant coefficient of "internal generation." It may be due to the fact that companies are in a phase of building technological capabilities to be able to innovate in the future. They are currently gathering information about technologies, undergoing training, and often require technical assistance, indicating that they are not yet capable of internal innovation. Ecuadorian companies engage in less formal innovation activities by adapting or modifying existing technologies, which is reflected in the significant and positive coefficient of technological adaptation.

The firms that cooperate in medium innovation activities, including engineering and design, and product testing, are companies that have moderate technological capabilities to develop their product and process innovations internally. Therefore, a positive and significant effect would be expected in their strategies to generate technological capabilities through cooperation. However, the results show a positive but not significant effect. On the other hand, the results indicate a significant negative effect of innovation through technology adoption, meaning that companies that cooperate in these types of innovative activities are less likely to adopt technology. Overall, the results reflect that companies are not developing product and process technologies when engaging in intermediate innovation activities, which is characteristic of emerging innovation systems.

For high cooperation, which includes more formal innovation activities such as R&D, all four modes of technological capability are not significant. This indicates that companies that cooperate in R&D have a lower likelihood of generating product and/or process innovations internally. Regarding the variable that captures the multiple activities in which companies cooperate to carry out their innovations, it shows that a higher number of cooperation activities leads to a lower probability that innovations are the result of internal generation. Additionally, it is observed that engaging in multiple cooperative activities increases the likelihood that company innovations are achieved through cooperation.

Regarding the influence of firm-specific characteristics, the results show that not all factors are determinants in defining the type of innovation that companies develop. Contrary to Schumpeter's view that it is large companies that independently develop innovations due to their technological capabilities and greater resources for R&D activities, the results indicate that firm size positively influences the generation of cooperative innovations and is negatively associated with internal generation. This could be explained when considering the results in the context of an emerging innovation system, where the reasons guiding these large companies to innovate through cooperation are linked to reducing and sharing the costs they would incur in the development of innovation activities that inherently carry a higher level of risk (Navarro 2002). On the other hand, the significant positive coefficient of cooperative generation confirms the hypothesis that large companies are prone to innovate through cooperation due to their greater technological capabilities.

Regarding the age of the firms, the non-significant results indicate that in Ecuador, new companies do not have a different mode of technological capability compared to "older" companies. Startups are less likely to adopt technology, and the non-significant positive relationship between being a new company and the probability of generating innovation through cooperation suggests that new companies have not yet built sufficient technological capabilities and are more inclined to seek other sources of knowledge (Sorensen & Stuart 2000). While it is relevant for new companies to generate innovation through cooperation, it is not statistically significant in the Ecuadorian context, reflecting the characteristics of an emerging innovation system with weak technological linkages.

Regarding human capital, measured in terms of the logarithm of the number of employees with higher education available in the companies, one would expect a positive relationship with internal generation, as the development of new innovations requires highly qualified personnel. Similarly, for generation through cooperation and adaptation, a higher level of qualification is needed to better absorb the knowledge generated through cooperative relationships. Lastly, adapting to new technologies requires a certain level of employee qualification to successfully implement changes in products and processes. However, the obtained results differ from each other. There is a significant negative relationship with internal generation and a non-significant negative relationship with generation through cooperation and adaptation. This suggests that the level of qualification is not directly related to the mode of technological development. In the context of developing countries with emerging innovation systems, these results indicate that the organizational routines of companies in these countries are not effectively leveraging the technological capabilities and competencies of their employees, and the human capital available is not being fully integrated into the innovation processes.

Membership in a business group (external partners) increases opportunities to develop technological capabilities, as companies can more easily benefit from indirect knowledge effects within the group (Filatotchev, Piga, & Dyomina 2003). Therefore, belonging to a group should be more closely related to the mode of technological development through adaptation or modification. The significant and positive result of this relationship confirms the positive influence of the parent company, which develops the technology, while the subsidiary companies adapt or modify it, increasing the probability of improving their technological capabilities.

In the case of internal generation, there should not be a positive relationship, and the results of the model support this. Regarding the propensity of companies to export, the significant negative association with generation through cooperation indicates that Ecuadorian companies do not possess sufficient capabilities to benefit from external knowledge through "learning by exporting." Consequently, their export activities do not allow them to increase their technological capabilities in a way that enables them to develop innovations through cooperation.

Regarding the intensity of internal R&D expenditure in logarithmic terms ("ln_intensidad_intra"), the significant coefficients are quite logical. The intensity of internal R&D expenditure is strongly positively related to internal innovation development and negatively related to technology adoption. However, it is important to mention that one would expect the generation of innovations through cooperation to also have a positive and significant effect, as companies absorb knowledge from their partners. Nevertheless, the insignificance of the coefficient indicates weak cooperation relationships or a lack of cooperation networks in developing countries.

The intensity of expenditure on research and development (R&D) in external activities is negatively and significantly associated with internal generation of innovations. This means that if companies are allocating resources to enhance research outside their departments, there is a lower probability of generating innovations within the company. On the other hand, there is a significant positive effect on adoption and generation through cooperation, which is consistent with the idea that investing externally leads to innovation development through collaboration with external partners.

In relation to the intensity of expenditure on innovation, specifically investments in activities other than R&D (ln_intensidad_gasto), the results are not significant. This indicates weaknesses in the organizational routines of companies in developing countries. Companies that give importance to internal sources are more likely to develop innovations through cooperation. The adoption of technologies, on the other hand, is not related to the importance given to internal sources and, in fact, is negatively significant. This suggests that companies emphasizing internal sources are less likely to adopt technologies developed by others.

External sources of information are expected to be related to the mode of innovation through adaptation. However, a significant positive relationship was found with internal generation, indicating that companies are not solely relying on external information but also using it to generate innovations internally.

The inclusion of sectoral variables in the model allows for controlling for fixed effects. The results indicate that companies in manufacturing sectors with medium-high, medium-low, and low technological intensity are more likely to develop innovations through internal generation compared to the services sector, where innovations tend to be primarily adopted, especially in non-knowledge-intensive services. The result obtained for the high-tech manufacturing sector is noteworthy, as it suggests that companies in this sector are not more inclined to generate innovations on their own. This reflects the characteristics of emerging innovation systems that pose challenges for technological development in these sectors.

On the other hand, it is not surprising that sectors related to services do not show a significant coefficient for internal generation. This is expected because the services sector primarily focuses on technology adaptation.

Regarding generation through cooperation, manufacturing sectors with low technological intensity show a significant negative coefficient, indicating a lower propensity to generate innovations through cooperation compared to the services sector. No sectoral differences are found in terms of innovation generation through adaptation. In the case of adoption, companies within the sectors related to low and medium-low technological intensity manufacturing have a lower probability of innovating through adoption.

Regarding the advanced regional variable (Pichincha and Guayaquil), it would be expected to have a positive influence on the mode of innovation generation through cooperation, as these regions have more institutions, companies, economic activities, and networks. However, the results indicate that the companies that rely more on cooperation to innovate are not located in the more advanced regions; instead, they are found in the less advanced regions. These companies face greater difficulty in developing innovations internally and require more cooperation. On the other hand, the more advanced regions of Ecuador have a significant and positive effect on technology modification and adoption. This is because these regions have more technological information, technology availability, and institutions that facilitate technology transfer, thereby increasing the likelihood of improving their technological capabilities through product modification or adoption.

4 Conclusions

The way innovations develop in companies differs according to the technological capabilities they have acquired and accumulated. The type of activity in which companies cooperate conditions the development of their technological capabilities. If companies are cooperating to obtain information, training, and technical assistance, they are in a phase of building technological capabilities in order to innovate in the future, meaning they have a low technological level. On the other hand, if the activities in which they are cooperating are related to product testing or engineering and design, it is said that the companies have acquired an intermediate level of technological capabilities. Finally, if the cooperative relationships are aimed at carrying out R&D activities, then the companies have reached a higher level in the development of their technological capabilities.

The analysis conducted for the Ecuadorian case contributes to determining whether the type of activity in which companies cooperate with other agents effectively conditions the development of their technological capabilities and whether being located within an advanced geographical area positively influences the development of such capabilities. The results obtained confirm that the differences between companies regarding the degree of developed technological capacity and the type of activity for which they establish cooperative relationships cannot be fully appreciated if all innovative companies are considered equal. The greater technological capabilities of companies would derive from their ability to generate innovations internally and/or in cooperation, which is directly associated with cooperation in the development of R&D activities. An intermediate degree of cooperation is associated with companies' ability to adapt products or processes, for which it is necessary to enhance activities related to product testing and engineering and design of new products and/or processes.

Lastly, companies that establish cooperative relationships for information search, training, and technical assistance have limited technological capabilities, and their innovations are linked to technology adoption. In an emerging innovation system, particularly in the case of Ecuador, there is a higher probability that innovations are generated in cooperation with different partners of the company. This is because companies take advantage of these partnerships to build their technological capabilities. In the case of companies located in less advanced regions of Ecuador, they are more likely to develop innovations through cooperation.

It is important to consider that this study is conducted for a developing economy and provides a guide for potential interventions by public and private policies to promote the development of innovative activities based on cooperation between companies. Future research should delve deeper into the study, considering the pandemic that led to a change in the business innovation landscape across various sectors. The limitations of this study are related to the database used (ACTI), which was last applied in 2014, and the lack of updated data to further enhance the research.

References

Albu, M.: Technological learning and innovation clusters in the south.: In: Electronic Working Papers. Science policy Research Unit, vol. 7, pp. 1–54. Brighton (1997)

Arnold, E., Thuriaux, B.: Developing firms technological capabilities. In: Researchgate, Informe de la OCDE, vol. 25, pp. 1–43. Technopolis (2016)

Barreto, J., Petit, T.: Modelos explicativos del proceso de innovación tecnológica en las organizaciones (2017)

Divella, M.: Cooperation linkages and technological capabilities development across firms. In: Regional Studies, vol. 51, pp. 1494–1506 (2017)

Dutrénit, G.: Building technological capabilities in latecomer firms. In: Science, Technology and Society, vol. 9, pp. 209–241 (2004)

Fernandez, S., Vaca, C.: Cooperation for innovation in developing countries and its effects: evidence from Ecuador. J. Technol. Manag. Innov. **12**(3), 1–10 (2017)

Filatotchev, I., Piga, C., Dyomina, N.: Network positioning and R&D activity: a study of Italian groups. R&D Manage. **33**(1), 37–48 (2003)

Freeman, C., Soete, L.: The economics of industrial innovation, 3rd edn. Routledge (1997)

Green, W.: Econometric analysis, 7th edn. New York (2012)

Iammarino, S., Piva, M., Vivarelli, M., Tunzelmann, N.: Technological capabilities and patterns of innovative cooperation of firm in the UK regions. In: Regional Studies, Discussion Paper (2009), vol. 46, pp. 1283–1301. Germany (2012)

INEC: Encuesta Nacional de Actividades de Innovación. In: ENAI, Ecuador (2014)

Liu, Y.: Contextualizing risk and building resilience: returnees versus local entrepreneurs in China. Appl. Psychol. **69**(2), 415–443 (2020)

Lundvall, B.: National systems of innovation. toward a theory of innovation and interactive learning, 1st edn. Anthem Press, New York (2010)

Makonen, T.: National innovation system capabilities among leader and follower countries: widening gaps or global convergence. In: Tandfonline, Innovation and Development, vol. 5, pp. 113–129 (2015)

Malerba, F.: How and why innovation differs across sectors. In: Fagerberg, J., Mowery, D., Nelson, R. (eds.) The Oxford handbook of innovation, vol. 1, pp. 380–406 (2009)

Navarro, M.: La Cooperación para la Innovación en la Empresa Española. Desde una perspectiva internacional comparada. In: Dialnet. Economía Industrial, vol. 346, pp. 47–66 (2002)

Padilla, R., Vang, J.: Regional innovation systems in developing countries: integrating micro and meso level capabilities. In: Lundvall, B.-A., Joseph, K., Chaminade, C., Vang, J. (eds.), Handbook of Innovation Systems and Developing, vol. 1, pp. 217–290. UK (2009)

Parrilli, M., Balavac, M., Radicic.: Business innovation modes and their impact on innovation outputs: regional variations and the nature of innovation across EU regions. Res. Policy **49**(8), 104047 (2020)

Ortega, R.: Aprendizaje y acumulación de capacidades tecnológicas en un grupo del sector siderúrgico. Innovar **15**(25), 90–102 (2005)

Pavitt, K.: Innovation processes. In: Fagerberg, J., Mowery, D., Nelson, R. (eds.) The Oxford handbook of innovation, vol. 1, pp. 86–114. Oslo (2004)

Rubio, M., Abril, C.: Sustainability oriented innovation and organizational values: a cluster analysis. J. Technol. Transfer (2023). https://doi.org/10.1007/s10961-022-09979-1

Segarra, M.: Estudio De La Naturaleza Estratégica Del Conocimiento Y Las Capacidades De Gestión Del Conocimiento: Aplicación A Empresas Innovadoras De Base Tecnológica. In: Tesis Doctoral. Jaume, España (2006)

Senguta, A, Sena, V.: Impact of open innovation on industries and firms - a dynamic complex systems view. Technol. Forecast. Soc. Change **159** (1), 120199 (2020)

Sorensen, J., Stuart, T.: Aging, obsolescence, and organizational innovation. In: Sage Publications. Administrative Science Quarterly, vol. 45, pp. 81–112. Chicago (2000)

Verspagen, B.: Innovation and Economic Growth. In:University Press. The Oxford handbook of innovation, vol. 1, pp. 487–513 (2004)

Zhou, K., Wu, F.: Technological capability, strategic flexibility, and product innovation. Strateg. Manag. J. **31**(5), 547–561 (2016)

Technological Solution in Real Time Based on IoT Devices to Optimize Soccer Team Training

Hiro Macuri, Rodrigo Castro, and Juan-Pablo Mansilla$^{(\boxtimes)}$

Universidad Peruana de Ciencias Aplicadas, Lima, Peru, USA
{u201618149,u201715323,juan.mansilla}@upc.edu.pe

Abstract. Currently, the soccer players of the youth clubs of the university community are engaged in constant physical training to improve their skills before an official match, requiring technological tools to man- age the physical preparation of each soccer player. For this reason, in this scientific article a technological solution will be proposed to optimize the training of soccer teams using IoT devices in real time. Its design based on technological architectures will be explained to detail the flow of the system and the components to be used to carry out the development and programming of the solution. Therefore, the functionality of the system will be validated based on 2 types of indicators based on the use of the solution in reality. The test indicators establish both the percentage of improvement in the level of physical performance of the amateur player for each weekly training session, as well as the weekly comparison of high performance levels of the amateur with a recognized and referential elite soccer player; all this to verify if the amateur is already physically pre- pared to play a championship. On the other hand, a series of questions were asked about the viability of the solution to interview selected users and experts, whose answers were finally mostly satisfactory.

Keywords: IoT · Football · Monitoring · Training · Portable Devices

1 Introduction

Today it is known that soccer is the king of sports globally, and in Peru thou- sands of people play it practicing it as a habit in their daily life or professionally as a representative of a national team [1]. In the latter case, it is essential that the footballer is in the best possible physical and mental condition in order to obtain great results for his team. Likewise, for soccer clubs, it is essential that the training sessions of their professional teams are optimized in order to be properly prepared for an official match. For example, the case of Fútbol Club Barcelona (FCB) is presented, which proposed a methodology called optimizer training (OE) whose purpose is to seek the development and stimulation of the abilities of the human being athlete through practice, according to its physical-cognitive level characteristics [2]. For this reason, there are certain sports institutions that decide to acquire technological devices to use and/or implement them during the training phase. The HUMANOX company developed the famous HUOX 50 smart shin guards

T. Guarda et al. (Eds.): ARTIIS 2023, CCIS 1936, pp. 72–86, 2024.
https://doi.org/10.1007/978-3-031-48855-9_6

that report the corresponding input data of the professional soccer player such as speed, distance covered, heart rate, temperature and GPS, which contribute to the athlete's activity history, as well as the injury prevention [3]. For this reason, it is essential to optimize the level of physical performance in soccer team training through technological methods so that clubs in the university youth category can better manage the control and monitoring of the case. Likewise, after reviewing various scientific articles, it has been taken into account that there is no proposal that optimizes soccer team training through IoT devices in real time. In the following lines, the scientific articles cited in the related documents section (Sect. 2) will be explained in detail, then the technological solution to be proposed (Sect. 3) and its development process (Sect. 4), its process validation (Sect. 5) and conclusions (Sect. 6).

2   Related Documents

In this section, an analysis has been developed through various approaches aligned to the object of study and contributed by various authors in their respective scientific articles, which in turn will strengthen the development of this project in an organized and efficient manner, saving time, cost and effort.

In [4] it is proposed to build a new physical education platform using 5G- based IoT technologies for universities and colleges.

In [5], the authors propose to monitor sports activity by big data visualization method (SAM-BDV) in sports athletic fitness tracking systems using IoT.

In [6], the combination of short-term memory (LSTM) and genetic algorithm (GA) concepts based on deep learning and IoT smart wearable devices was proposed to improve the efficiency of college football training.

In [7], the author's goal was to propose a sensor with a corresponding algorithm that allows receivers to automatically detect whether they caught or dropped a pass during football practice.

In [8], the authors' goal is to develop smart shin guards based on machine learning and microelectromechanical systems (MEMS) accelerometers for the analysis of the performance of a soccer team positioned through Global Navigation Satellite Systems.

In [9], a motion tracking system based on AI, IoT, and MEMS sensing technologies is proposed for the next generation of foot-powered sports talent training and selection.

In [10], the authors propose an efficient framework based on deep learning in IoT-enabled fintech environments for the recognition of prominent multi-person football events.

In [11], the main objective is to build a movement prediction model of aerobics athletes based on the Wearable Inertial Sensor of the Internet of Things and Bidirectional Long-Term Memory (BiLSTM) network.

In [12], a multi-criteria decision-making model based on a three-layer virtual IoT algorithm is proposed to automatically track and evaluate the performance of professional soccer players over the Internet.

In [13], the author proposes a new deep learning method to monitor the health of soccer players using real-time wearable sensors and recurrent neural networks.

In [14], a sensor fusion technique based on wearable technologies is proposed to measure and provide high-quality analysis data of athletic performance of soccer players.

In [15], a prediction model based on portable GPS sensors is proposed to collect data on injuries of a soccer player produced during training.

3   Proposal for a Technological Solution in Real Time Using IoT Devices

The contribution of this study is a technological solution that allows optimizing soccer team training. The aim is to improve the level of physical performance of all the amateur soccer players that make up a team once the planned exercises have been carried out, using GPS vests as an IOT device that will provide high sports performance data for each player and then synchronize them to the system. Likewise, a comparative analysis is carried out between the amateur player analyzed and the ideal level taking an elite (professional) player as a reference, to provide coaches and/or physical trainers with the aspect in which the amateur player needs to improve to prioritize their physical performance through continuous improvement monitoring.

4   Development

The technological solution proposal will include the design of technological architecture models, mockups and a database diagram for its development.

In the first place, the business architecture divided into 4 layers that will explain the flow of the technological solution associated with the business and application processes was designed. The first layer is the motivation layer, as shown in Fig. 1, centrally oriented to the general objective of this project. The second layer, the business layer in Fig. 2, focuses on the 4 macro-processes of the web application flow. The application layer (the third), as illustrated in Fig. 3, details the required business functions and data object in each application process handled by the corresponding interface modules. The fourth and last layer, the technology layer as shown in Fig. 4, focuses on components such as the web server (user interface), application server (collects the information from the web server and is subsequently processed through business logic) and database server (for the backend of the web application), all of them interconnected in a LAN with internet access.

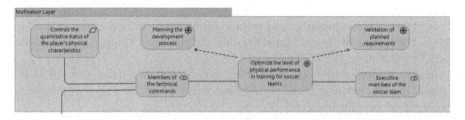

Fig. 1. Motivation Layer of Enterprise Architecture

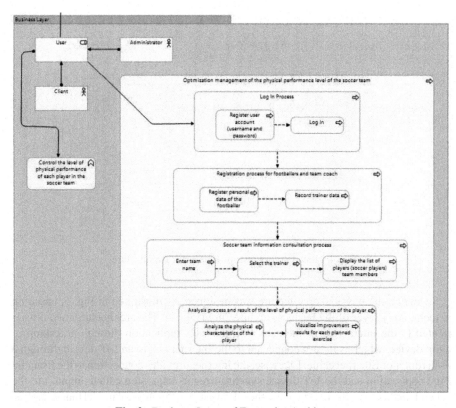

Fig. 2. Business Layer of Enterprise Architecture

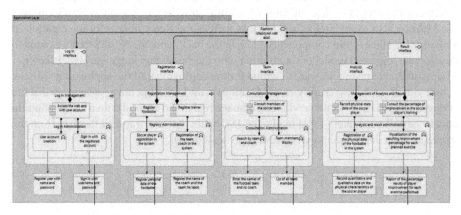

Fig. 3. Application Layer of Enterprise Architecture

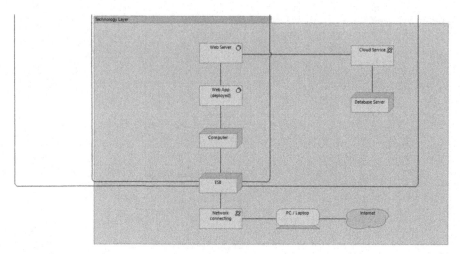

Fig. 4. Technology Layer of Enterprise Architecture

Secondly, the physical architecture was designed, as illustrated in Fig. 5, based on the technology layer of the business architecture (Fig. 4). The architecture modeling is oriented to the interaction of the user with the web application through a desktop or laptop device, which is in turn connected to the Internet and to an IoT device through a Wi-Fi router or Ethernet cable; Likewise, the internet provides connection to the frontend of the application and the IoT device synchronizes its data (step called "input") to the backend. In this case, the IoT device is the GPS vest, a technological model that is applied during the soccer player's training to monitor the response of his body while he is doing his exercises or some sporting activity [16]. In the frontend, for the development of the interfaces, the programming language of the Bootstrap library known as JavaScript was used (this is also usable in the backend), as well as the React library for the creation of web user interfaces from components. [17]. In the back- end, the NestJS tool was used to develop the logic and model of the solution with the JavaScript language [18]. Likewise, Microsoft Azure resources were essential for the deployment of the application with the Azure virtual machine (Azure Virtual Machine) in the Linux operating system, so that the Azure Cosmos DB database service can manage registered users and their corresponding data to be collected later [19]. Finally, the JSON file that will transmit the data from the frontend to the backend and vice versa is presented [20].

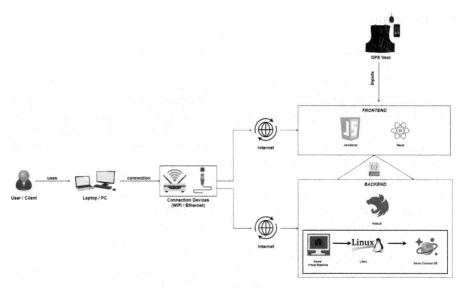

Fig. 5. Physical Architecture

Subsequently, we proceeded to design the prototypes (mockups) of the so- lution (Figs. 6 and 7), according to the 4 architecture models, detailing the respective functionalities of each part of the system flow.

Fig. 6. Web App Artifact Registration Interface

5   Validation

During the soccer team training sessions at the Proamateur Soccer Institute, GPS vests (wearables) were placed on the 11 amateur players so that they could carry out the planned exercises while the corresponding physical performance level measurements were carried out. Likewise, all the resulting measurements obtained from the wearables were synchronized to the web application system to finally corroborate the improvement percentages of each physical performance data of each player. Said percentages are calculated based on a comparative analysis between the real high-performance data of the amateur player and that of the elite (professional) player, whose data of the latter is registered by de- fault in the system database as a reference. After having used the application, the coaches, physical trainers, the owner and the administrative coordinators of Proamateur and other sports institutions gave us their respective points of view on the functionality of the system through survey forms that were sent to them via email. For all of the above, two types of indicators have been defined to carry out this validation process: test indicators and survey indicators.

Fig. 7. Player physical performance level results

5.1   Definition of Test Indicators

The following indicators have been defined for this testing phase in Table 1:

Table 1. Table of Test Indicators.

Test Indicators	
1	Percentage improvement in the level of physical performance of the analyzed amateur Player
2	Weekly comparison of values of the physical performance levels of amateur and elite Players

Additionally, in Table 2 the high performance data of each amateur player obtained from the GPS vest are defined:

On the other hand, for the analysis result of the level of performance of the amateur player, expressed as a percentage, it will be calculated using the logic of the rule of three (illustrated in Fig. 8) comparing each data of the amateur with that of the elite player (the which will be taken as reference) respectively. The logic is based on the position of the player on the field (forward, midfielder, goalkeeper or defender). It is important to specify that it is only possible to compare the 2 types of players as long as both assume the same position.

Table 2. GPS Vest Sports High Performance Data.

GPS Vest Sports High Performance Data	
Average speed	It is the average speed of the soccer player during training Its range varies between 5 to 20 km/h
Maximum speed	It is the greatest possible speed of the footballer It is usually twice the average speed or greater than the average speed by a difference of 5 km/h
Distance traveled	Space covered by the soccer player during training Its range varies between 2 to 7 km
Sprint	It is the short maximum speed race of the footballer Its range varies between 2 to 6 sprints
Heart rate	Number of times of the footballer's heartbeat per minute Its range varies between 50 to 200 bpm (beats per minute)
Time played	Duration of the footballer's training Its range varies between 30 to 100 min

Rule of Three Logic				
Analytical procedure to obtain the percentage improvement of the level of physical performance of the amateur player in the system.	**Rule of Three Formula**	*Let "a" be the value of high performance of the amateur and "b" that of the elite*	$a \rightarrow 100\%$ $b \rightarrow x\%$	$x = \dfrac{b}{a}(100)$
	Formulas for the Improvement Percentage (depends on the result of the Rule of Three)	*For average speed, maximum speed and sprints*	Para a > b	$y = -100 + x$
			Para a < b	
			Para a = b	$y = +100 - x$
		For distance covered, average heart rate and time played	Para a > b	
			Para a < b	$y = +100 - x$
			Para a = b	

Fig. 8. Rule of Three Logic Table

Likewise, it is necessary to mention the high performance data of 4 recognized elite Champions League players, with their respective positions illustrated in Fig. 9, which are registered by default in the system database.

	Erling Haaland (Forward)		Luka Modric (Midfielder)	
Renowned professional (elite) players of the Champions League registered by default in the system	Average speed	15 km/h	Average speed	15 km/h
	Maximum speed	35 km/h	Maximum speed	35 km/h
	Distance traveled	6 km	Distance traveled	5.97 km
	Sprint	7	Sprint	4
	Heart rate	200 lpm	Heart rate	180 lpm
	Time played	60 minutes	Time played	60 minutes
	Thibaut Courtois (Goalkeeper)		Virgil Van Dijk (Defense)	
	Average speed	12 km/h	Average speed	15 km/h
	Maximum speed	24 km/h	Maximum speed	31 km/h
	Distance traveled	3.1 km	Distance traveled	6.22 km
	Sprint	2	Sprint	3
	Heart rate	130 lpm	Heart rate	150 lpm
	Time played	60 minutes	Time played	60 minutes

Fig. 9. 4 Recognized Footballers of the Champions League

Case Study. We present the case of an amateur player named George Frazer, with goalkeeper position, who performed his exercises during 3 weekly training sessions, whose high performance data (average speed, maximum speed, distance covered, sprint, heart rate and time played) were synchronized from the GPS vest to the system.

George Frazer (Goalkeeper)	Week 1	Average Speed	8,33%
		Maximum speed	8,33%
		Distance Traveled	-76,77%
		Sprint	150,00%
		Average Heart Rate	-7,69%
		Time Played	8,33%
	Week 2	Average Speed	-8,33%
		Maximum speed	-8,33%
		Distance Traveled	-70,65%
		Sprint	-50,00%
		Average Heart Rate	0,00%
		Time Played	13,33%
	Week 3	Average Speed	-16,67%
		Maximum speed	-12,50%
		Distance Traveled	-67,10%
		Sprint	100,00%
		Average Heart Rate	-30,77%
		Time Played	6,67%

Fig. 10. Percentages of improvement of the amateur goalkeeper player in weeks 1, 2 and 3.

For the first test indicator (percentage improvement in the level of physical performance of the amateur player) and taking the elite soccer player Thibaut Courtois as a reference, with the same goalkeeper position, the following percentage improvement results were obtained in the web application of each data on high sports performance of the amateur player in weeks 1, 2 and 3 (Fig. 10), derived from the comparative analysis of the amateur data with those of Courtois according to the logic of the rule of three.

For the second test indicator (weekly comparison of values of the physical performance levels of the amateur and elite players), the comparisons of the high sports performance data of both the amateur and the elite player per week were statistically obtained. For the case study, the web application shows in a bar graph the comparisons of the average speed values (the example is the same with any other high performance sports value) of George Frazer (amateur) and Thibaut Courtois (elite). For each weekly session, both with the same goalkeeper position (Fig. 11). It should be noted that Courtois's average speed value remains constant for every week, as shown in the following graphs, because the high performance values of Courtois and the other elite footballers, in addition to the fact that they are registered by defect in the system database, they are referential to compare them weekly with Frazer's level of physical performance and know how physically prepared he is to be able to play an official soccer match in the best possible way.

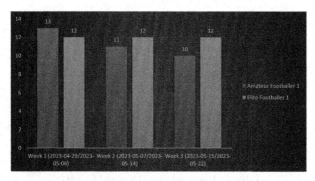

Fig. 11. Comparison of mean speed values between soccer players George Frazer (am- ateur) and Thibaut Courtois (elite) in weeks 1, 2 and 3.

5.2   Definition of Indicators for Surveys

The following indicators have been defined for the survey, as illustrated in Table 3.

Table 3. Table of Indicators for Surveys

Indicators for Surveys	
1	Response time
2	Reliability
3	Security
4	Usability
5	Functionality
6	General satisfaction of the experience

Likewise, the people interviewed are classified as follows (Fig. 12):

3 Users	3 Experts
1 Physical Trainer of Proamateur Futbol	1 Owner of Proamateur Futbol
2 Soccer Coaches from the UPC	2 Administrative Coordinators of Club Sportivo Huracán

Fig. 12. Conformation of Users and Experts for the Interview

5.3 Questions Format for Interviews

A series of questions were formulated for each indicator for the interviews.

Likewise, for the score the Likert scale of 5 variables was used, which is illustrated in Table 4:

Table 4. Likert Scale of 5 Variables

1	Strongly disagree
2	In disagreement
3	Neither agree nor disagree
4	Agree
5	Totally agree

The question posed in the "Response time" indicator, for users and experts, is shown in Table 5:

Table 5. Response time (User and Expert)

Response time (User and Expert)	
1	The web app shows the analysis of the player by his position in real time

The questions posed in the "Reliability" indicator, for users and experts, are shown in Table 6:

Table 6. Reliability (User and Expert)

Reliability (User and Expert)	
1	Feel the web app allows you to optimize workouts and reduce injuries
2	The web app allows you to perform a better analysis of the players in training
3	The web app allows you to improve the relationship you have with soccer players

The questions posed in the "Security" indicator, for users and experts, are shown in Table 7:

The questions posed in the "Usability" indicator, for users and experts, are shown in Table 8:

Table 8. Usability (User and Expert)

Usability (User and Expert)	
1	It was easy for me to register the IoT device. (User)
2	It was easy for me to register the data of the player, team and coach. (User)
3	It was easy for me to interact with the web app throughout the IoT registration process. (Expert)
4	I would recommend to my friends or specialized soccer academies that use IoT devices such as a GPS vest in their training to use the web application to have better control and analysis of the player. (Expert)

The questions posed in the "Functionality" indicator, for users and experts, are shown in Table 9:

Table 9. Functionality (User and Expert)

Functionality (User and Expert)	
1	Options within the web app were available throughout the test. (User)
2	The options within the web app in the registration of the IoT device were in accordance with the GPS vest. (Expert)

The questions posed in the "General satisfaction of the experience" indicator, for users and experts, are shown in Table 10:

Table 10. General satisfaction of the experience (User and Expert)

General satisfaction of the experience (User and Expert)	
1	You are satisfied with the ease of use of the web app
2	You are satisfied with the efficiency of the solution
3	I would like to continue interacting with the web app to control and monitor my players

All the questions formulated above focused on the viability of the web app within the training session on the soccer field.

Table 7. Security (User and Expert)

Security (User and Expert)	
1	Perceives that the personal data of the players are protected
2	Perceives that the information provided is confidential between the player and the Physical Trainer/Coach

Both users and experts agree on 3 indicators: the sampling of the player's analysis according to position (response time), the functionalities of the training optimization system and analysis of the level of physical performance of each amateur soccer player (reliability), and the availability of IoT options during testing (functionality). The result of all the aforementioned is displayed in Fig. 13.

Fig. 13. Percentage of users and experts who are satisfied with the response time, reliability and functionality of the web app.

However, it was possible to corroborate that both the user and the expert do not agree or disagree with the security because the confidentiality of the information registered in the system was not considered. The result is displayed in Fig. 14.

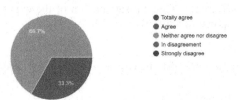

Fig. 14. Percentage of users and experts who neither agree nor disagree with the security of the web app.

Regarding usability, user and expert fully agree with the recording of all equipment and IoT artifact data. Likewise, they are totally satisfied with the qualities of the application in terms of ease of use, the efficiency of the solution and the interaction of the clients with the system for the control and monitoring of the high performance of amateur players. The result of all the aforementioned is displayed in Fig. 15.

Fig. 15. Percentage of users and experts who fully agree with the indicators of usability and general satisfaction of the web app experience.

6   Conclusion

In conclusion, the main objective of this work is to propose a technological solution to optimize the training of the soccer team. Its development is based on the design of two types of architecture: business, to detail the flow of the system; and physical, to diagram the software part of the solution indicating the required components to be used for its subsequent deployment. In the validation phase, two types of indicators were defined based on the proposal: test and survey. With the first, an analysis was carried out in the system to obtain results of the percentage improvement in the performance of an amateur player and comparative values of high performance between the amateur and an elite footballer in the Champions League, to find out if the first has the physical preparation necessary to play a soccer match. With the second, users and experts were consulted on the feasibility of the solution and were satisfied with the ease of use, efficiency and customer interaction with monitoring the high performance of amateur players.

Financing Universidad Peruana de Ciencias Aplicadas / UPC-EXPOST-2023-2.

Acknowledgements. The authors thank the evaluators for their important suggestions that have allowed a significant improvement of the present work. Likewise, to the Research Directorate of the Universidad Peruana de Ciencias Aplicadas for the support provided to carry out this research work through the UPC- EXPOST-2023-2 incentive.

References

1. Muñoz Blázquez, P: El derecho del fútbol ante los clubes Estado: el caso Mbappé. Final Degree Project presented at the Universidad Pontificia Comillas to obtain the title of Lawyer, specializing in Law. Universidad Pontificia Comillas (2022)
2. Pons, E., et al.: Training in Team Sports: Optimising Training at FCB. Apunts. Educación Física y Deportes **142**, 55–66 (2020). https://doi.org/10.5672/apunts.2014-0983.es.(2020/4).142.07
3. Humanox Soccer: HUOX 50 las primeras espinilleras inteligentes, https://humanox.com/esp inilleras-inteligentes-hx50/. Accessed 15 Jun 2023
4. Wang, J.: Application of 5G Internet of Things Technology in the Design of Physical Education Platform. Computational Intelligence and Neuroscience, **2022** (2022). https://doi.org/10.1155/2022/9382048
5. Li, W., Karthik, C., Rajalakshmi, M.: Big data visualization for in-situ data exploration for sportsperson. Computers and Electrical Engineering, **99** (2022). https://doi.org/10.1016/j.com peleceng.2022.107829

6. Guan, Y., Qiu, Y., Tian, C.: Trajectory planning in college football training using deep learning and the internet of things. J. Supercomput. (2022)https://doi.org/10.1007/s11227-022-046 19-9

7. Hollaus, B., Stabinger, S., Mehrle, A., Raschner, C.: Using wearable sensors and a convolutional neural network for catch detection in American football. Sensors (Switzerland) 20(23), 1–16 (2020). https://doi.org/10.3390/s20236722

8. Mascher, K., Laller, S., Wieser, M.: Development of smart shin guards for soccer performance analysis based on mems accelerometers, machine learning, and GNSs. In: CEUR Workshop Proceedings, vol. 2880 (2020). http://ceur-ws.org/Vol-2880/paper5.pdf

9. Lu, S., Zhang, X., Wang, J., Wang, Y., Fan, M., Zhou, Y.: An IoT-based motion tracking system for next-generation foot-related sports training and talent selection. J. Healthcare Eng. 2021 (2021). https://doi.org/10.1155/2021/9958256

10. Muhammad, K. et al.: AI-driven salient soccer events recognition framework for next generation IoT-enabled environments. IEEE Internet Things J. (2021). https://doi.org/10.1109/JIOT.2021.3110341

11. Ye, J., Wang, H., Li, M., Wang, N.: IoT-based wearable sensors and bidi rectional LSTM network for action recognition of aerobics athletes. J. Healthcare Eng. 2021 (2021). https://doi.org/10.1155/2021/9601420

12. Chang, C.-W.: Developing a multicriteria decision-making model based on a three-layer virtual Internet of Things Algorithm Model to Rank Players' Value. Mathematics 10(14) (2002). https://doi.org/10.3390/math10142369

13. Alghamdi, W. Y.: A novel deep learning method for predicting athletes' health using wearable sensors and recurrent neural networks. Decis. Anal. J. 7 (2023). https://doi.org/10.1016/j.dajour.2023.100213

14. Kim, M., Park, C., Yoon, J.: The design of GNSS/IMU loosely-coupled integration filter for wearable EPTS of football players. Sensors 23(4) (2023). https://doi.org/10.3390/s23041749

15. Piłka, T., Grzelak, B., Sadurska, A., Górecki, T., Dyczkowski, K.: Predicting injuries in football based on data collected from GPS-based wearable sensors. Sensors 23(3) (2023). https://doi.org/10.3390/s23031227

16. Betancourt Vásquez, V.A., Hernández Villarreal, M.J., Dávila Matute, M.F.: Medición de los parámetros de rendimiento físico en tiempo real a través de un chaleco de neopreno equipado con rastreador GPS PLAYR para monitorizar las cargas de trabajo y forma física de los jugadores de la Sub 13 del club de futbol templo FC. Final Degree Project presented at the Unidades Tecnológicas de Santander to obtain the title of Sports Technologist, specializing in Natural Sciences and Engineering. Unidades Tecnológicas de Santander (2020)

17. Meta Open Source: React, https://es.react.dev/. Accessed 16 Jun 2023

18. Mysliwiec, K.: Documentation|NestJS-A node.js framework built on top of TypeScript. Official NestJS Consulting. https://docs.nestjs.com/. Accessed 16 Jun 2023

19. Ruiz Caldas, A.J.: Migración de servidores a la nube de Microsoft Azure para mejorar la continuidad de los servicios TI, de la fiduciaria en el año 2018. Thesis presented at the Universidad San Ignacio de Loyola to obtain the title of Business and Systems Engineer, specializing in Engineering. Universidad San Ignacio de Loyola (2019)

20. IBM Corporation: Formato JSON (JavaScript Object Notation). https://www.ibm.com/docs/es/baw/20.x?topic=formats-javascript-object-notation-json-format. Accessed 17 Jun 2023

Methods of Allocation of Urban Centers

Aleksandr Katynsus$^{(\boxtimes)}$ (iD), Ekaterina Shapovalenko (iD), Anna Pavlova (iD),
Inna Arseneva (iD), and Sergey Mityagin (iD)

ITMO University, Birzhevaya Line 14, Saint-Petersburg, Russia
267882@niuitmo.ru

Abstract. The paper considers a set of methods that solve the problem of identifying central places in the current urban environment. The problems of research are caused by the need to consider the proximity and location of the actual central places of cities and settlements in almost all processes of planning development and transformation of the environment. Errors in determining the location of the territory to be transformed in the system of central places of the city lead to significant financial and temporary losses. However, there are currently no common approaches to defining central locations. The paper presents the result of research on the systematization of methods based on information about the distribution system in the city, the placement of city services, as well as information about the actual activities of citizens based on spontaneous data. The developed methods are summarized in a general application scenario and experimentally demonstrated on the data of the city of Miass.

Keywords: Network modeling · Information modeling · Graph algorithms · Urban quarter modeling · Urban environment modeling · Centrality of urban quarters · Urban quarter profiling · NLP · Open data

1 Introduction

The paper focuses on identifying central locations in modern cities, a crucial concept in urban planning. These locations arise from natural resource variations, spatial clustering, urban service collocation, competition, and citizens' activities [1]. The absence of central places leads to a blurred urban environment, reduced quality, limited leisure access, and spontaneous migration [2]. Identifying central locations is crucial during preliminary urban studies. Neglecting transformable territory can lead to financial losses and functional difficulties [2]. However, due to the concept's ambiguity, there is a lack of established methodological approaches.

The paper examines the central places of a city based on various characteristics. Thus, central residential areas with a high concentration of population and urban centers of daily activities and places for recreation are defined. There are also quasi-central locations [3] like transport hubs or monofunctional areas, and potential central locations indicated by accessibility and connectivity, requiring methods for determining agglomeration boundaries. Therefore, identifying central locations in the urban environment is a complex task. Use of a systematic approach will prevent loss of accuracy in the analysis and ensure effective urban planning for sustainable development.

The article consists of the following sections: review of the, relevant literature review, methodology for determining central locations, experimental studies of the methods, and finally a discussion of the considered methods and conclusions.

2   City Central Places Allocation Problems Background

The issue of identifying central locations in the urban environment is well known in the scientific literature, as it is one of the key tasks of information and analytical support for the process of planning the development of modern cities. Based on the studies carried out in the following sections, it can be stated that the previously created methods do not simultaneously take into account a lot of data, and also do not fully use new technologies that appear in the modern world.

2.1   Definition of the Urban Central Place

The problem lies in the fact that in the planning of urban areas, central places are not defined properly. Historically, this concept came from the theory of central places by Christaller-Lösch [4], which states that a central place is a designation of a city center for other settlements that provides them with goods and services. Although the Christaller-Lösch theory was developed for the supra-urban level, the concept of a central place proved to be useful for analyzing intra-urban processes.

At the intra-urban level, the concept of a central place is closely related to the concepts of attraction points or points of interest (POI) [5]. Considering the possible types of activity, different criteria for the centrality of such points can be identified. The concept of a point of interest gives a social meaning to the concept of a central place from the perspective of urban science and links it to the concept of "third places" [6] a place that can unite, create an atmosphere of interaction, communication, and creativity.

Thus, the identifying and planning central places includes the following parts:

- Identification of already established central places with social activity.
- Determination of places that are central from the perspective of urban planning without social activity.
- Identification of places with high centrality potential.
- Planning the creation of new central places and public.

2.2   Spatial Division of Territory for Centrality Assessment

From an urban planning perspective, central places are primarily areas with defined boundaries. Each central place has a certain service radius, which is determined by the degree of centrality according to Christaller [7] or the catchment area [6]. These characteristics give a rise to different approaches to spatially delineate central places and determine their boundaries. The most typical approaches are described in Table 1.

In spatial planning tasks, the approach based on the assessment of territorial planning units has demonstrated the greatest potential.

Table 1. Approaches to geographical delineation of central places.

Description	Illustrations

Native delineation of central place boundaries using clustering and grouping of phenomena on a map. In this case, the boundaries themselves are not explicitly delineated, and the results require additional processing for use in spatial planning.

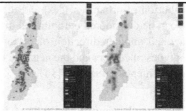

Fig. 1. - Approach 1

Territory decomposition based on a grid of regular geometric shapes with the assignment of centrality scores for each shape [8]. This approach contradicts the established urban planning as it goes against the existing urban layout.

Fig. 2. - Approach 2

Ranking of linear objects [9]

Fig. 3. - Approach 3

Ranking of territorial planning units [10]

Fig. 4. - Approach 4

2.3   Criteria for Assessing Centrality of Places

There are various approaches to assessing the degree of centrality of territorial units. The first approach is based on definition of coverage area formed by the composition and strength of services located in the respective territory [11]. This method is applied to both individual planning units and linear objects. Another approach involves assessing the density of the resident population [12]. These methods aim to identify the structure of the settlement system and serve to align demand and supply in the territory.

Analyzing the correspondence between the first type of central places (based on the distribution of urban services) and the second type of places (based on residential centers) can be considered a traditional urban planning task [13]. Solving this problem has generated another direction of research aimed at identifying disparities between different types of centers and the negative effects they generate. One of the most notable effects is counter-urbanization [14].

2.4 Literature Review of Methods of Allocation of Central Places

The task of determining central places is closely related to the task of determining the actual boundaries of the territory. There are two principal approaches for determining the boundaries of methods for highlighting central places:

- Methods based on clustering spatial units with high centrality indices [15].
- Methods based on network models that reproduce the spatial dynamics of citizens between central places of different types, such as residential and service centers [16].

The application of these methods is associated with the use of modern information technologies and the search for the most appropriate data and information resources.

Moreover, there is a wide range of analytical methods to measure spatial distribution of urban centers: use of local knowledge to identify city centers, examinations of the spatial distribution with identifying local peaks as possible sub-centers, use of a regression model based on density and distance, space syntax [9].

All these methods have very significant drawbacks: due to their age, they do not take into account all the data generated by city actors. Therefore, scientists decided to develop new methods based on data and information technology.

The first method "Identification of the changing spatial structure of cities by patterns of human activity" [17] based on various data on human activity was proposed by students of the Massachusetts Institute of Technology. In the article, the researchers presented a new centrality index applied to large-scale data for city analysis. The index combined the number of people attracted to a place and the range of their activities, and the smoothed density function helped to detect spatial clusters of locations. The identified clusters can be understood as functional centers that create a complete picture of the spatial structure of the city.

The second method is defined in the study "Measure of centrality for city networks based on the concept of eigenvector centrality" [18]. The article discusses a method for localizing key areas of activity in urban areas of various shapes and sizes, and also proposes a new algorithm for measuring centrality for certain types of extended urban networks based on the eigenvector centrality index.

All other methods can be defined as methods within some software packages and programming tools, since all fields of science have become very dependent on modern technologies. Only in Python there are at least 3 libraries with which you can measure the centrality of urban areas. The first is OSMnx [19], which has algorithms for measuring the shortest path between network nodes and finding centers by connectivity based on graph theory. The NetworkX library [19] is designed for deep learning calculations.

Another software is Cityseer-api [20], which is used for network-based city analysis at the pedestrian scale. A very important feature here is that the computation of network centrality uses either the shortest or simplest path heuristics in the primary or dual network, including special methods such as harmonic proximity centrality.

3   Methodology of Identifying Central Locations

After the analysis of the existing methods there were defined new ones based on modern approaches, practices, and technologies. In this paper we propose to use 4 new methods in one complex algorithm to reveal urban centers. The scheme of the process can be seen in Fig. 5.

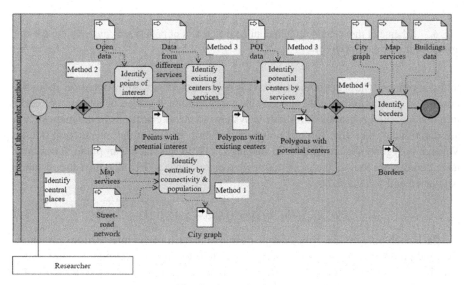

Fig. 5. General scheme

3.1   Method for Determining the Centers of Population Congestion in the City and Assessing their Connectivity. Method 1

This method represents the city model as a complex network consisting of planar graphs – nodes and undirected edges. The point is to use the graph to determine the central places of settlement in the city not only based on topological data, but also on population data. This method uses open spatial attributive data on population and street and road networks. The data sources are the population census data (in Russia, this is the reform of housing and communal services and Rosstat), the OpenStreetMap database. In general, the method is presented in the flowchart on Fig. 6.

The input for this part is topographic data which is used to build the network: the street and road network of the city, it is a layer of lines with the type of street embedded

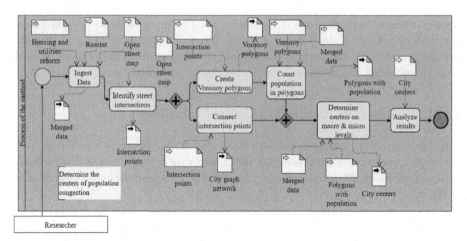

Fig. 6. - Scheme of the method for determining the centers of population congestion in the city and assessing their connectivity.

in the attributes. The second input dataset is population data with information about the number of people living in the area under consideration. Further, these data is loaded into one file into geographic information system, so the intersections of the main streets are determined, then the Voronoi polygons are built based on the intersection points. Voronoi polygons use the Euclidean distance [21]. In the Euclidean plane, let point a have coordinates (a1, a2) and let point b have coordinates (b1, b2), then the distance between a and b is given by:

$$l = d[(a_1, a_2), (b_1, b_2)] = \sqrt{(a_1 - a_2)^2 + (b_1 - b_2)^2} \tag{1}$$

Each such polygon describes the nearest area at each of the intersections, in which the total population in each polygon is calculated, forming one common point. After that, links are built from each point to each other in a straight line within a radius of a comfortable walking distance, which is taken as 1 km.

The output of this method is a map with the connected nodes and located centers. It can be used to assess how dense the connections between the nodes are, compare this with data on the population, as well as building characteristics. To analyze a graph network, the criterion of centrality by degree can be used, the closer it is to 1.0, the more central the place of settlement.

3.2 Method of Defining Centers of Urban Spaces Based on Extraction of Points of Interest. Method 2

The next method is based on the open data from social networks and cartographical services which is analyzed for extracting points of interest in a city. It is proposed to measure the centrality of urban spaces based on the number of points, their attractiveness and quality.

There are at least two types of input data used in the algorithm: data from social networks and data from maps. Map data is represented by reviews of the point in the city. With the help of official API, the method receives all the reviews from places. Every row in the table where this data is stored is represented by the name of the place, review, and address to geocode it. Inappropriate content is filtered and cut from the dataset.

Data ingested from social networks is the most complicated because of the manner of writing and unofficial way of sharing the information with users. It can contain spam and advertisements. To filter the data, it is very important to use NLP (Natural Language Processing) models for classification of spam, advertisement and unwanted content to prevent false results after the execution of the algorithm. The scheme of the method can be seen in Fig. 7.

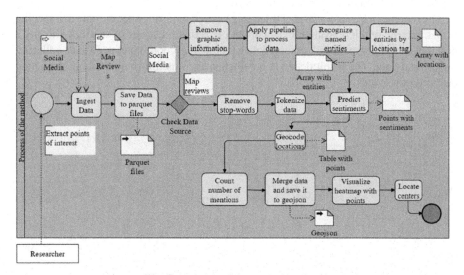

Fig. 7. Schema of the second method

The first step in this new method is data ingestion. All the data is stored in the parquet files. This format has been chosen due to the possibility of compressing the data. To start the algorithm, users need to choose a city, and define time periods to get the data. Then comes data processing. As it is text data, we need to use methods of text processing like tokenization to split sentences by tokens, lemmatization to find words' original forms. One of the most important tasks here is to remove all the stop words.

The most interesting step in this method is recognizing named entities (NER) from the social networks' posts. There are some Python packages with pre-trained models that can do this task: DaData, Pullenti, Abbyy, In-foextractor, Dictum, and Stanza. In this method the main model is Stanza with its' pipelines, where it is possible to define all the processes the data should go through. All the extracted entities are filtered by locations and organizations.

Data coming from maps has no need in NER. The only process here is sentiment analysis to define the attractiveness of the point. The number of reviews and the sentiment of each review are combined in one metric.

The last step of the method is to geocode all extracted points and put them on the map. Geocoding is made with the help of GeoPy library and ArcGis geo-coder, what takes text address and converts it to coordinates. The output here is a map with points split by colors: positive - green, neutral - gray, and negative - red.

3.3 Method of Automatic Identification of Central Locations in a City. Method 3

The next method is used for displaying existing service centers and identifying potential service locations based on a set of accompanying characteristics.

The main task that needs to be solved is the automatic identification of central places in the city. The output should be a map with polygons whose sizes correspond to the degree of saturation of each place with services.

The scheme in Fig. 8 consists of three stages, each requiring specific data in a specific format. Firstly, publicly available data about the actual locations of services, the city's master plan, the city map, and reviews with geographical coordinates need to be collected as the input data. The result depends on whether there is information about the actual locations of services.

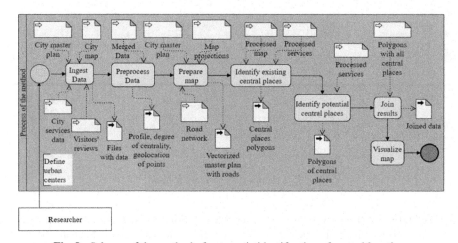

Fig. 8. Schema of the method of automatic identification of central locations

If there is no information, then potential central places can be identified based on the combined characteristics of existing central places. If there is information about the actual locations of services, it needs to be processed to obtain the coordinates of the service, its profile, and the degree of centrality using the K-means method. In the third stage, the map needs to be prepared using the QGIS open-source geographic information system. The output is a map with polygons displaying existing or potential central places. This method is a universal tool for design organizations, private entrepreneurs, and active citizens.

3.4 Method for Delimiting Agglomeration Boundaries: Leveraging Open Data and Identifying Urban Centers. Method 4

This study employs a method focused on delineating the boundaries of urban agglomerations using an unevenly zoned model. The developed method relies on two crucial parameters: patterns of development and the stability of transport connectivity.

The analysis of the agglomeration's planning structure is based on the principle of the unevenly zoned Vysokovsky model. This model serves as the foundation for understanding the distribution and organization of different zones within the agglomeration. By examining the patterns of development and the connectivity of transportation networks, the methodology aims to provide insights into the spatial dynamics and functional characteristics of urban agglomerations.

To facilitate this analysis, a classifier of building morphotypes was specifically developed for this study. This classifier aids in categorizing the different types of buildings found within the study area, providing valuable insights into the built environment and its relationship with urban centers.

To gather the necessary data for the analysis, open data sources such as the housing and communal services reform, OpenStreetMap, and urban planning documents will be utilized as the input data. These data sources provide comprehensive information on the built environment, infrastructure, and urban development plans, enabling a detailed examination of the study area. The scheme of the method is in Fig. 9.

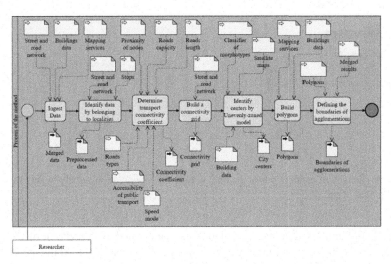

Fig. 9. Method for Delimiting Agglomeration Boundaries

By combining information on building morphotypes and transport connectivity, this methodology offers a comprehensive understanding of the characteristics and spatial organization of urban centers. The integration of open data sources ensures a robust and transparent analysis process, facilitating accurate assessments and informed decision-making in urban planning. The output of this step is the spatial distribution of urban centers and the delineation of agglomeration boundaries.

4 Experimental Studies of Methods

All 4 methods were tested on the city in Chelyabinsk region - Miass. This is a small city with the population of approximately 150000 people. It is the best choice due to the volume of data generated in the city.

4.1 Validation of Method for Determining the Centers of Population Congestion in the City and Assessing their Connectivity

In Fig. 10 you can see where the links between the nodes are most densely located – there is a good connection between population clusters. Most of the population is in medium and high-rise residential buildings, but this does not mean the centrality of the place. Areas with denser mid-rise development take center stage as they tend to have a more connected pedestrian network, distances and spaces that are commensurate and comfortable for people. The private residential sector is rarely the center since there is a very low density of both population and buildings.

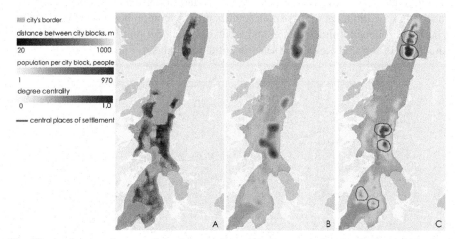

Fig. 10. A - density of connections of the road network, B - population density by city blocks, C - central places of the city

Residential areas with a large population can be defined as POI (Point of Interest). Due to the low density, they can only form centers at the micro level. At the macro level of the city, densely built-up quarters will still be considered centers of attraction.

4.2 Validation of the Method Based on Points of Interest

All the data was ingested on a local machine, saved in parquet format, and then analyzed. There were 998 groups about Miass city in VK (Russian online social media network) what were scrapped for the data. Moreover, all posts what contain the name of the city in Russian were also added to the dataset. After the data ingestion, all the texts were tokenized and converted to numbers to extract named entities. The only entity needed was location; hence, there was a filter to save only locations in the final dataset. At the same time, all the texts have been processed semantically to define the attractiveness of the point.

Final maps with the extracted points of interest can be seen in Fig. 11.

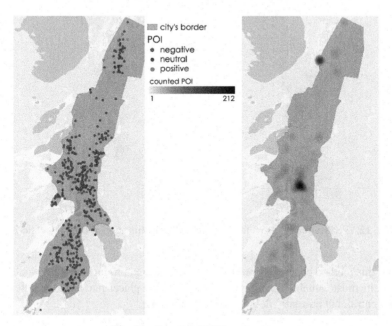

Fig. 11. Results of POI's extraction

The first map shows the distribution of points of all kinds. The second one is a heat map drawn by the number of mentions of every point. It shows the most popular points in the city, what are the centers of urban spaces. There are at least two main and some minor centers in the city.

4.3 Validation of the Method of Automatic Identification of Central Locations in a City

Based on the location of all services of the profile of interest on the map, a heat map is created showing where the concentration of services is highest, as shown in Fig. 8.

Subsequently, the K-means method is applied to cluster the existing services, using its coordinates. After identifying the clusters, the degree of popularity of the central places is determined according to the heat map. On the final visualization, the central places are represented in different colors according to their popularity.

To identify potential central places, it is necessary to collect reviews mentioning specific points on the map and geocode them. Then, they are also displayed as a heat map, clustered, and added to the final map. As shown in Fig. 12 right., potential central places have lower popularity. This may be due to the absence of services on their territory that attract a large people flow.

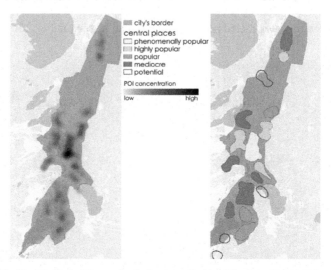

Fig. 12. Verification of the method of automatic identification of central locations

Thus, this method can be utilized for various tasks and produces different outcomes. However, its most valuable function is to identify those places that have the potential to become central, but currently do not have some service.

4.4 Validation of the Method for Delimiting Agglomeration Boundaries: Leveraging Open Data and Identifying Urban Centers

The method for determining agglomeration boundaries and identifying urban centers using transport infrastructure analysis revealed highly connected areas that could be potential urban centers in the city. These areas displayed a concentration of road networks and transportation routes, emphasizing their importance for the overall transport links in the city.

By employing a classifier, the processed data successfully categorized urban centers based on population density, commercial activity, and access to public facilities. These identified urban centers matched the characteristics of developed and densely populated areas, highlighting their significance in the city's spatial structure.

The correlation analysis between the obtained results and the boundaries defined in the master plan for Miass's development by 2030 demonstrated a strong agreement. The agglomeration boundaries identified based on transport infrastructure connectivity aligned with the long-term vision outlined in the master plan. This correlation confirmed the accuracy and reliability of the proposed method in defining agglomeration boundaries that align with the city's strategic objectives. Refer to Fig. 13 for the results and workflow.

The results offer valuable insights into urban center distribution and agglomeration boundaries in Miass. They inform urban planning, resource allocation, and decision-making for sustainable development and efficient urban resource utilization.

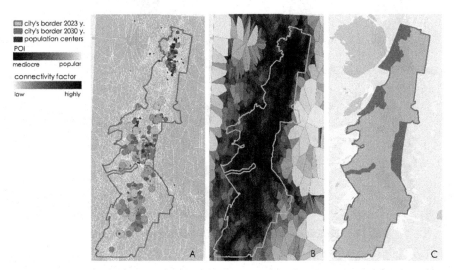

Fig. 13. Verification of the method for Delimiting Agglomeration Boundaries: Leveraging Open Data and Identifying Urban Centers

5   Discussion

This article presents four new urban center allocation methods that collectively form a powerful tool for comprehensive city analysis, overcoming previous limitations in existing research. These methods enable a holistic understanding of urban centers, significantly enhancing geo-analysis and urban center definition and extraction (Fig. 14e).

Comparing the individual methods with existing literature, Fig. 14a efficiently identifies central settlement places based on connectivity and population density, while Fig. 14b introduces innovative attraction point clustering to enhance precision. Figure 14c provides a nuanced understanding of POI dynamics, and Fig. 14d visualizes city development directions. In conclusion, these four methods offer a comprehensive urban analysis toolset, providing valuable insights for city planning and development. Their integration bridges research gaps and opens avenues for further exploration in this field.

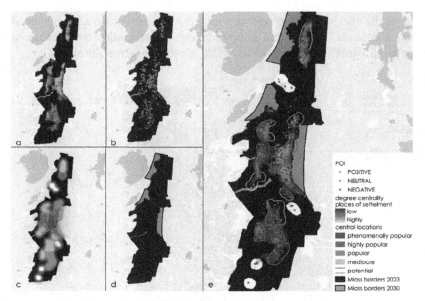

Fig. 14. Verification of the methods of allocation of urban centers

6   Conclusion

This article proposed a new approach of identifying existing urban centers and subcenters based on open data. This methodology can be used to gain a deeper understanding of urban dynamics and pave the way for more informed decision-making in urban development and management. The proposed method is very flexible due to the use of open data and NLP models, so in the future it can be easily upgraded and applied in different areas. The only limitation is that it uses open data, and it means that not all groups of people are represented by this data. It will be a good advantage to find a way of ingesting relevant data from all citizens.

Acknowledgements. This research is financially supported by The Russian Science Foundation, Agreement №17–71-30029 (https://rscf.ru/en/project/17-71-30029/), with co-financing of Bank Saint-Petersburg.

References

1. Wong, Z., Li, R., Zhang, Y., Kong, Q., Cai, M.: Financial services, spatial agglomeration, and the quality of urban economic growth–based on an empirical analysis of 268 cities in China. Financ. Res. Lett. **43**, 101993 (2021). https://doi.org/10.1016/j.frl.2021.101993
2. Mohammad Firoz, K., Subia, A., Bapon, B.: Quality of Urban Environment: A Critical Review of Approaches and Methodologies. Current Urban Studies. 3. (2015)
3. Dickinson, J.: Quasi-public place-governance: an exploration of shopping centres. Bus. Law Rev. **40**(Issue 4), 161–169 (2019). https://doi.org/10.54648/BULA2019021

4. Dmitriev, R.V.: Theory of central places: abstract constructions and/or applied developments. In: Conference "Theoretical and Applied Problems of Geographic Science: Demographic, Social, Legal, Economic, and Ecological Aspects", pp. 62–66 (2019)
5. Katynsus, A.V.: Study of methods for identifying points of public interest based on open data. In: Conference "12th Congress of Young Scientists". - St. Petersburg (2023)
6. Oldenburg, R.: The Great Good Place: Cafes, Coffee Shops, Bookstores, Bars, Hair Salons and Other, 3rd edn. Marlowe & Company, US (1989)
7. Berliant, M.: Central place theory. In: Durlauf, S.N., Blume, L.E. (eds.) The New Palgrave: Dictionary of Economics, pp. 734–736. Palgrave Macmillan UK, London (2008). https://doi.org/10.1007/978-1-349-58802-2_211
8. Ghadiri, M., Rassafi, A.A., Mirbaha, B.: The effects of traffic zoning with regular geometric shapes on the precision of trip production models. J. Transp. Geogr. **78**, 150–159 (2019). https://doi.org/10.1016/j.jtrangeo.2019.05.018
9. Yamu, H.C.: Space syntax: a method to measure urban space related to social, economic and cognitive factors. In: The Virtual And The Real in Planning and Urban Design: Perspectives, Practices and Applications, Routledge, Oxon, UK/New York, USA, pp. 136–150 (2018)
10. Hudec, M., Vujosevic, M.: Integration of a fuzzy system and an information system for the territorial units ranking, pp. 374–377 (2007)
11. Gehl, J.: Cities for People. Island Press (2010)
12. Pereira, R., Nadalin, V., Monasterio, L., Albuquerque, P.: Urban centrality: a simple index. Geogr. Anal. **45**, 77–89 (2013)
13. Em, P.P.: A big city as an independent central place system, a case study of Moscow. Reg. Res. Russ. **8**(2), 151–157 (2018). https://doi.org/10.1134/S2079970518020041
14. Šimon, M.: Counterurbanization: condemned to be a chaotic conception? Geografie. **116**(3), 231–255 (2011)
15. Jain, A.K., Murty, M.N., Flynn, P.J.: Data clustering: a review. ACM Comput. Surv. **31**(3), 264–323 (1999)
16. Newman, M.E.J.: Mathematics of networks. In: Durlauf, S.N., Blume, L.E. (eds.) The New Palgrave: Dictionary of Economics, pp. 4059–4064. Palgrave Macmillan, London (2008). https://doi.org/10.1007/978-1-349-58802-2_1061
17. Zhong, C., Schläpfer, M., Arisona, S.A., Batty, M., Ratti, C., Schmitt, G.: Revealing the changing spatial structure of cities from human activity patterns. Urban Stud. **54**(2), 437–455 (2016)
18. Agryzkov, T., Tortosa, L., Vicent, J.F., Wilson, R.: A centrality measure for urban networks based on the eigenvector centrality concept. Urban Stud. **46**(4), 668–689 (2017)
19. Geoff Boeing, Urban Street Network Centrality. https://geoffboeing.com/2018/01/urban-street-network-centrality/. Accessed 15 May 2023
20. Simons, G.: The Cityseer Python package for pedestrian-scale network-based urban analysis. Environ. Plann. B: Urban Anal. City Sci. **50**(5), 1328–1344 (2022). https://doi.org/10.1177/23998083221133827
21. Deza, M.M., Deza, E.: Encyclopedia of Distances. Springer Berlin Heidelberg, Berlin, Heidelberg (2016). https://doi.org/10.1007/978-3-662-52844-0

Characterization and Comparison of Maximum Isometric Strength and Vertical Jump Among Novice Runners, Long Distance Runners, and Ultramarathoners

Mailyn Calderón Díaz[1,2,3]([✉]), Ricardo Ulloa-Jiménez[4,5], Nicole Castro Laroze[6], Juan Pablo Vásconez[1], Jairo R. Coronado-Hernández[7], Mónica Acuña Rodríguez[7], and Samir F. Umaña Ibáñez[7]

[1] Faculty of Engineering, Universidad Andres Bello, Santiago, Chile
{mailyn.calderon,juan.vasconez}@unab.cl
[2] PhD in Health Sciences and Engineering, Universidad de Valparaíso, Valparaíso, Chile
[3] Millennium Institute for Intelligent Healthcare Engineering (iHealth), Valparaíso, Chile
[4] Academia Biomecánica Deportiva, Santiago, Chile
[5] Physical Therapy and Training Center Forza, Santiago, Chile
[6] Escuela de Kinesiología, Facultad de Salud, Universidad Santo Tomás, Santiago, Chile
[7] Universidad de la Costa CUC, Barranquilla, Colombia

Abstract. The main objective of this paper is to explore and compare the characteristics of the maximum isometric force (FIM) of the hip and knee musculature in runners with different years and volume of training, as well as the manifestation of the stretch-shortening cycle (CEA) through the evaluation of the vertical jump. The participants of this study are 10 novice runners (N), 8 long distance (LD) and 6 mountain ultramarathoners (U), belonging to Team Mora, from Santiago, Chile. The main measures for this study are: Dominant (D) and non-dominant (ND) hip extensors and abductors FIM; FIM of knee extensors and flexors D and ND were measured using a load cell. The squat jump (SJ), as well as the bipodal and unipodal D and ND countermovement jump (CMJ) were measured with a force platform, as a measure of explosive (FE) and elastic explosive (FEE) strength.as results, the main significant differences are given in the hip extensor muscles D (N < LD, LD < U, U > N); in the hip extensor muscles ND (LD < U and U > N); in the hip abductor muscles D and ND (N < LD and U > N) and in the knee extensor muscles D (U > N). The U have less ability to jump than LD and N. it can be concluded that runners with higher training volume have higher levels of FIM and lower levels of FEE than those with lower volume. The N runners are characterized by having a lower FIM than the LD runners.

Keywords: Vertical Jump · maximum isometric strength · hip and knee musculature

T. Guarda et al. (Eds.): ARTIIS 2023, CCIS 1936, pp. 102–112, 2024.
https://doi.org/10.1007/978-3-031-48855-9_8

1 Introduction

Running in recent years has become a booming sport in much of the world, generating a social and fitness phenomenon around it [1]. It is a discipline that can be done over different distances, with the marathon (42 km) and the ultramarathon (usually 50–150 km) being popular races that have increased tremendously in the last two decades [2].

Given this increase, many attempts have been made to describe the factors that determine or influence running success, from the novice to the elite runner [3–5]. Variables such as maximum oxygen consumption (VO2max), lactate threshold, as well as running economy are factors that are correlated with running performance [6, 7]. From a mechanical and energetic perspective, running economy is influenced by physiological factors [7, 8], biomechanical efficiency [4, 9, 10], neuromuscular [4, 5, 11, 12] and training [7, 13, 14].

Both the physiological and biomechanical determining factors in running have been widely studied, both by categories of runners, as well as at different levels of training [15], however, the neuromuscular characteristics of the sport discipline have been less explored, partly ignoring the behavior of these variables in relation to the type of runner and the characteristics of the training. The interaction between the neural and muscular systems (neuromuscular system) is essential in movement, being effective in translating cardio-respiratory capacities into mechanical efficiency and sports performance [7, 12, 16].

Another neuromuscular factor described as a determinant in running is the stretch-shortening cycle (CEA) [4], which is manifested in the elastic explosive force (FEE) usually studied through jump tests such as the Countermovement jump (CMJ) [17]. During CEA, energy storage occurs through elastic tendon elongation and subsequent release of part of the stored energy to reduce the energy cost of locomotion and running [18]. As with muscular strength parameters, there is little evidence to indicate what the explosive force generation (EF) and FEE characteristics are in different types of runners.

The purpose of this investigation was to explore and compare the characteristics of maximal isometric strength of the hip and knee muscles in runners who differ in years of training and weekly training volume, such as novice, long-distance, and ultramarathon runners. as well as the manifestation of the CEA through the evaluation of the vertical jump.

2 Materials and Methods

2.1 Participants

The study followed a cross-sectional design. The sample consisted of 24 runners belonging to the "Team Mora" running club from the city of Santiago, Chile. These were divided into 3 groups according to the definition described by Kluitenberg et al.: Novices (N) (n = 10); Long Distance (LD) (n = 8) and Mountain Ultramarathoners (U) (n = 6). Prior to their participation, the subjects read and signed an informed consent. All the research was carried out following the principles established in the Declaration of Helsinki. The descriptive statistics of the sample are presented in Table 1.

Table 1. Mean values and standard deviation of the characteristics of the participants.

Category	Age	Size (m)	Weight(kg)	Training Time (years)	Training Volume (km*week^{-1})	Competition Distance (km)
Novice	30,83 ± 10,23	1,73 + 0,12	76,5 + 13,23	0,246 ± 0,168	20,83 ± 8,01	-
Long Distance	32 ± 6,36	1,705 ± 0,02	68 + 6,63	4,2 ± 2,77	51,2 ± 27,698	10 – < 42
ultramarathoners	39,67 ± 7,64	1,58 + 0,04	55,67 + 6,66	13,33 ± 8,32	106,667 ± 23,094	> 50

2.2 Instruments

For the measurement of maximum isometric force (FIM), a 1000 N type S load cell and an FMON-1 model force monitor (artOficio limitada, Santiago, Chile) were used. The jumpability evaluation was carried out through a force platform, model PF 4000/50 (artOficio limitada, Santiago, Chile) with a sampling frequency of 200 Hz. The acquisition and processing of the kinetic data was carried out in the Igor software. Pro 6.1 (Wavemetrics Inc. Portland, OR, USA).

2.3 Procedures

Prior to the measurements in this study, all the runners performed a standard warm-up that consisted of 8 min of continuous running on a treadmill (LifeFitness T3, USA) at 8 km*h-1, general mobility and muscle activation exercises.

The FIM was evaluated bilaterally in the hip extensor and abductor groups, as well as in the knee flexors and extensors. To record the strength of each runner, 3 maximal isometric contractions held for 3 s were performed for each muscle group, with a 1-min pause between each repetition. Before evaluating the next muscle group, a 2-min pause was made. Each attempt was recorded in Newton's and normalized to the subject's body weight (BW) (percentage of BW).

For the evaluation of the hip extensor musculature, the subjects were positioned on a clinical table in the prone position with the distal third of the thigh outside the table, with a knee flexion of 90° in the extremity to be evaluated, with both arms free outside of the table. The stretcher. In order to stabilize the pelvis and limit its movements during the evaluation, a support strap was placed at the lumbo-pelvic level, which is fixed in the lower area of the stretcher. The load cell was placed vertically, with one end anchored to the ground and the other fixed to a leg strap using anti-deforming steel cables. The hip angle during the FIM test was 0° in tension (Fig. 1a).

For the evaluation of the hip abductor musculature, the subjects were positioned on a clinical table in lateral decubitus with the extremity to be evaluated supralaterally, with the distal third of the extremity outside it. The lower limb (LI) not evaluated was positioned infralateral, with the hip and knee flexed at 45° and 90° respectively. To protect the area between the femoral condyles and neutrally position the hip in the frontal plane, a cushion was placed between both lower limbs. In order to stabilize the pelvis and limit its movements during the evaluation, a support strap was placed at the level of the iliac crest, which is fixed in the lower area of the stretcher. The load cell was placed vertically, with one end anchored to the ground and the other is fixed through anti-deforming steel cables to an ankle brace in the intermalleolar line. The hip angle in the frontal plane during the FIM test was 0° in tension (Fig. 1b).

The evaluation of the knee flexor musculature was carried out with the subjects on a clinical table in the prone position, with the knees on the lower edge of the table, with both arms free outside of it. The untested MI is extended with support, while the tested MI is positioned in 60° of flexion at the time of performing the FIM. In order to stabilize the pelvis and limit its movements during the evaluation, a support strap was placed at the lumbo-pelvic level, which is fixed in the lower area of the stretcher. The load cell was placed vertically, with one end anchored to the ground and the other fixed to an ankle brace through anti-deforming steel cables (Fig. 1c).

To assess the knee extensor musculature, the subjects were seated on a clinical table, with the popliteal angle at the edge of the table. The arms were crossed at chest level with both hands on the contralateral shoulder. The evaluated MI was positioned in 90° hip and knee flexion. An ankle brace connected to the load cell was placed in the intermalleolar line by means of anti-deforming steel cables in an anteroposterior direction, being anchored to a metal structure on the wall. The knee angle was 70° in tension during the FIM (Fig. 1d).

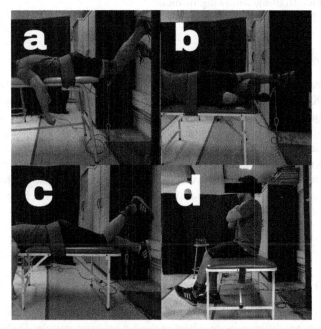

Fig. 1. Maximal Isometric Strength (FIM) Assessment. A) FIM of hip extensors. B) FIM of hip abductors. C) FIM of knee flexors. D) FIM of knee extensors.

2.4 Vertical Jump

Each subject underwent an evaluation of: a) explosive strength (FE), through the Squat Jump (SJ), which starts with the hands on the waist and flexion of 90° of the knees, after 3 s jumps the as high as possible keeping the lower limbs extended during the entire flight phase; b) elastic explosive force (FEE), through the countermovement jump (CMJ), which is executed with the hands on the waist, performing a countermovement until a knee flexion of 90°, jumping as high as possible and keeping the limbs lower legs extended throughout the flight phase; c) FEE of the dominant limb (D) and non-dominant (ND), this jump is performed in the same way as the CMJ, but unilaterally. In each of the conditions, 2 jumps were recorded, with a 1-min pause between each repetition.

The data obtained for each jump on the force platform were: a) output force (Fs), which represents the maximum value of force before the flight phase, measured in newtons, being normalized with the body weight of the subjects (% of body weight; b) flight time (Tv), expressed in seconds; c) Maximum height (Hmax), which represents the highest point reached during the flight phase, measured in meters; d) output velocity (Vs), expressed in m*sec-1, which represents the velocity before the flight phase coinciding with the moment of the output force and, e) Output power (Ps), expressed in watts*kg-1, which is obtained from the following formula:

Ps: output force (in newtons) * output velocity (m* sec-1)/body weight (kg).

2.5 Statistical Analysis

To check the assumptions of normality and the equality of the variances in the described variables, the Kolmogorov-Smirnov tests and the Levene test were used, respectively. To compare the means based on the type of runner and dominance in the FIM, CMJ D and CMJ ND tests, a two-factor analysis of variance (univariate ANOVA) was performed. To compare the means according to the type of runner in the SJ and CMJ tests, a one-factor analysis of variance (unifactorial ANOVA) was performed. Tukey's post hoc test was used to observe differences between the groups of runners. The confidence level established was 95% ($p < 0.05$). The results were estimated with the help of the IBM SPSS Statistics 20 software (IBM Corporation, USA).

3   Results

3.1   Maximal Isometric Strength

The results of the univariate ANOVA test for these evaluations are observed in Table 2. The main significant differences are given in the hip extensor muscles D (N < LD, LD < U, U > N); in the hip extensor muscles ND (LD < U and U > N); in the hip abductor muscles D and ND (N < LD and U > N) and in the knee extensor muscles D (U > N).

Table 2. Two-way ANOVA results for the FIM test. F represents the Fisher-Snedecor F-statistic; p represents the significance value ($< .05$) for the total anova and Tukey's post hoc in limb D and ND.

Muscle group	ANOVA			N vs LD		LD vs U		U vs N
	F	**p total**	**p D**	**p ND**	**p D**	**p ND**	**p D**	**p ND**
Hip extensors	1,729	0,138	0,034*	0,556	0,006*	< 0,001*	< 0,001*	< 0,001*
Hip abductors	0,819	0,540	0,004*	0,008*	0,756	0,356	0,005*	0,001*
Knee flexors	1,071	0,383	0,935	0,757	0,105	0,327	0,108	0,203
Knee extensors	1,535	0,189	0,296	0,678	0,149	0,235	0,019*	0,383

N: novice; LD: long distance; U: ultramarathoners; D: dominant; ND: non-dominant
*significant differences

3.2 Vertical Jump

Table 3 presents the results of the complete evaluation of jumpability (mean and standard deviation), organized by category of runners and jump executed. Table 4 shows the statistical results of the one-factor anova test for the SJ and CMJ jumps. In these, it is observed that, surprisingly, there were only statistically significant differences in the Fs of the CMJ jump (total p and LD vs U).

Table 3. Mean values and standard deviation of the jumpability results

Jump	Variables	Catergory of Runners		
		Novice	Long distance	Ultramarathoners
Squat Jump	Fs (% PC)	217,86 + 43,89	218,89 + 13,21	210,95 + 15,06
	Tv (s)	0,432 + 0,034	0,423 + 0,042	0,418 + 0,037
	Hmax (m)	0,23 + 0,036	0,219 + 0,044	0,215 + 0,036
	Vs ($m*s^{-1}$)	2,119 + 0,167	2,072 + 0,209	2,049 + 0,184
	Ps ($w*kg^{-1}$)	45,813 + 12,44	44,103 + 5,465	41,889 + 4,342
Counter Movement Jump	Fs (% PC)	208,82 + 26,71	206,05 + 10,65	187,45 + 12,17
	Tv (s)	0,446 + 0,043	0,442 + 0,046	0,431 + 0,036

(continued)

Table 3. (*continued*)

Jump	Variables	Catergory of Runners		
		Novice	Long distance	Ultramarathoners
	Hmax (m)	0,246 + 0,046	0,241 + 0,050	0,229 + 0,038
	Vs (m*s^{-1})	2,188 + 0,213	2,165 + 0,226	2,115 + 0,179
	Ps (w*kg^{-1})	45,222 + 9,907	43,895 + 6,328	38,998 + 5,538
Counter Movement Jump Dominante	Fs (% PC)	177,37 + 22,74	177,30 + 10,39	158,95 + 3,47
	Tv (s)	0,312 + 0,035	0,3 + 0,027	0,27 + 0,030
	Hmax (m)	0,121 + 0,028	0,111 + 0,020	0,090 + 0,019
	Vs (m*s^{-1})	1,531 + 0,173	1,425 + 0,155	1,323 + 0,148
	Ps (w*kg^{-1})	26,931 + 6,568	25,597 + 3,318	20,622 + 2,509
Counter Movement Jump No Dominante	Fs (% PC)	176,06 + 17,54	180,70 + 17,31	161,37 + 10,43
	Tv (s)	0,305 + 0,032	0,29 + 0,022	0,28 + 0,022
	Hmax (m)	0,115 + 0,024	0,103 + 0,015	0,096 + 0,014
	Vs (m*s^{-1})	1,498 + 0,161	1,421 + 0,108	1,372 + 0,102
	Ps (w*kg^{-1})	26,047 + 5,095	25,139 + 2,728	21,753 + 2,761

Fs: output force; BP: body weight; Tv: flight time; Hmax: maximum height; Vs: output speed; PS: output power

Table 4. One-way ANOVA results for SJ and CMJ jumps. F represents the Fisher-Snedecor F-statistic; p represents the significance value ($< .05$) for the total anova and tukey's post hoc.

Jump	Variables	ANOVA		NvsLD	LDvsU	UvsN
		F	p total	p	p	p
Squat Jump	Fs(%PC)	0,169	0,846	0,937	0,836	0,952
	Tv (s)	0,327	0,724	0,831	0,970	0,740
	Hmax (m)	0,359	0,702	0,782	0,986	0,743
	Vs (m*s^{-1})	0,327	0,724	0,831	0,970	0,740
	Ps (w*kg^{-1})	0,379	0,688	0,900	0,885	0,668
Counter Movement Jump	Fs (% PC)	3,794	0,036*	0,725	0,031*	0,103
	Tv (s)	0,241	0,788	0,966	0,889	0,769
	Hmax (m)	0,269	0,766	0,973	0,861	0,748
	Vs (m*s^{-1})	0,258	0,774	0,959	0,887	0,755

(*continued*)

Table 4. (*continued*)

Jump	Variables	ANOVA		NvsLD	LDvsU	UvsN
		F	p total	p	p	p
	Ps (w*kg^{-1})	1,244	0,305	0,920	0,471	0,281

N: novices; LD: long distance; U: ultramarathon runners; Fs: output force; BP: body weight; Tv: flight time; Hmax: maximum height; Vs: output velocity; PS: output power. *significant differences.

Table 5 shows the results of the univariate anova test for the CMJ D and ND jumps. There are no significant differences in any variable when comparing the unipodal jumps between N vs LD. When contrasting the results of the LD vs U groups, significant differences were found in the Fs D and ND, as well as in the Ps D. Finally, significant differences were found in all the variables of the CMJ D jump between U vs N, as well as in the Ps of the jump CMJ ND of these categories of runners.

Table 5. Two-way ANOVA results for the single leg jump test. F represents the Fisher-Snedecor F-statistic; p represents the significance value (< .05) for the total anova and Tukey's post hoc in limb D and ND.

Jump	Variables	ANOVA		N vs LD		LD vs U		U vs N	
		F	p total	p D	p ND	p D	p ND	p D	p ND
CMJ	Fs (% PC)	2,193	0,070	0,991	0,510	0,034*	0,026*	0,029*	0,078
	Tv (s)	0,708	0,620	0,329	0,218	0,056	0,516	0,006*	0,087
	Hmax (m)	1,118	0,363	0,296	0,213	0,072	0,516	0,007*	0,085
	Vs (m*s^{-1})	0,691	0,633	0,101	0,228	0,190	0,526	0,007*	0,095
	Ps (w*kg^{-1})	1,743	0,142	0,636	0,740	0,016*	0,096	0,004*	0,047*

CMJ: Countermovement Jump; N: novices; LD: long distance; U: ultramarathon runners; D: dominant; ND: non-dominant; Fs: output force; BP: body weight; Tv: flight time; Hmax: maximum height; Vs: output velocity; PS: output power. *Significant differences

4 Discussion

The purpose of this study was to characterize and compare running-determining neuromuscular factors such as FIM, FE, and FEE in N, LD, and U runners, who differ in years and weekly training volume. Although it has been established that neuromuscular characteristics such as muscle strength and power, as well as the stretch-shortening cycle (SSC) of the lower body musculature would play a fundamental role in the efficiency of energy absorption and generation during running, there is no characterization of the behavior of these factors in relation to the type of runner and the volume of training, so the behavior of these variables in different running disciplines is unknown.

4.1 The U Generated Higher Levels of FIM Than Runners N and LD

The results of the FIM tests of this study indicate that the U generated higher levels of force than N and LD runners, mainly in the hip extensor and abductor musculature. Various authors have described the importance of the gluteal musculature in running, as well as its relationship with injuries, fulfilling a stabilizing role during the support phase of the race [19–21]. Neuromuscular factors such as hip abductor weakness have primarily been proposed to increase the risk of lower extremity injuries such as patellofemoral pain and IT band syndrome [21, 22]. [23] found that recreational runners had FIM values of hip abductors and extensors of 35% and 28% PC respectively. The results obtained in our study indicate that the N runners in all conditions presented lower FIM than the LD and U runners, both in hip extensors and hip abductors (see Fig. 2). On the other hand, when contrasting the results of LD versus U, the latter present higher levels of FIM in the hip extensors (close to 30% of the FIM normalized to body weight with a difference of $p < 0.05$), without finding differences in hip abductors. One of the most important findings is found in the FIM levels of hip extensors in the U group, which reach records greater than 50% of the PC, which doubles the results of the N and LD. A possible explanation for this could be given by the characteristics of the volume (> 100 km*wk-1) and training surfaces of the U, which involve mountains with positive and negative slopes. On positive slopes (uphill running) the muscles of the lower leg perform more mechanical work than on flat surfaces or negative slopes (downhill), this implies a greater requirement of activity and muscular power, particularly around the hip [6, 16]. Therefore, it can be assumed that the FIM levels of U-shaped hip extensors are the result of training volume under highly demanding environmental conditions.

The results for the knee flexor and extensor muscles surprisingly did not present significant differences, with the exception of the dominant extensor FIM between U and N (76.39% PC vs. 59.38% PC). [24] suggested that functional hamstring: quadriceps ratio and not muscle strength per se in these groups would be associated with metabolic cost during running. Our results suggest that the hip musculature is influenced to a greater extent by the volume and training surface in runners than the knee musculature.

4.2 The U Presented Lower FEE Capacity Than the N and LD Corridors

The results of the jump tests indicate that the three study groups do not present differences in the different variables quantified in the SJ jumps. This confirms that EF would be more related to speed races than resistance [17]. When contrasting the results of the bipodal CMJ jump, these indicate that the U have less generation of Fs than the LD. However, the most striking results are found in the D and ND unipodal CMJ jump, in which the U have lower values of Fs and Ps than the N and LD runners, as well as a worse performance in the variables Tv, Hmax and Vs. When compared with the N in the D extremity. As in the FIM results, these could be associated with the training characteristics of the U, those who present a greater weekly volume, in variable altitude conditions, lower speeds than others types of runners and longer duration times in the support phase [6]. Running is basically a series of horizontal jumps that requires strong and efficient extensor muscles [24]. During the race and as in the jump, CEA occurs repetitively, which generates an increase in muscle mechanical efficiency as a result of the accumulation of elastic potential energy in muscles and tendons, events that have been related to economy of the race [4]. Our results indicate that the U have a lower capacity for FEE production with the correct use of CEA, possibly influenced by the described characteristics of their training.

Some limitations of this research are the following: first, our study sample is small, which makes it difficult to extrapolate our results to a larger population, so even the behavior of these neuromuscular parameters in different types of runners cannot be generalized. Second, our FIM measurement was limited to the maximum value obtained by each subject, which we consider an incomplete measure for the study of force production. Future studies should focus on studying the rate of strength development in these types of runners to gain a better understanding of neuromuscular adaptations to training, as well as the correlation between training characteristics and performance of these variables.

5 Conclusions

The results of this research show that the runners with the highest training volume, the U have a greater capacity to produce FIM in the hip extensor and abductor musculature, but less capacity to generate FEE than LD and N runners. Along with this, we found that LD runners produce greater FIM of the hip musculature than N runners, without presenting differences in the characteristics of the vertical jump. These results suggest that the FIM is positively influenced by the high volume of training, as well as by the uphill type training characteristic of the U. Along with this, there would be associated with these characteristics, a negative influence on the use of CEA and FEE generation.

Acknowledgments. ANID funded this work – Millennium Science Initiative Program CN2021_004 and ANID - Subdirección de Capital Humano 21221478.

References

1. Burfoot, A.: The history of the marathon: 1976-Present. Sport. Med. **37**(4–5), 284–287 (2007)
2. Cejka, N., Rüst, C.A., Lepers, R., Onywera, V., Rosemann, T., Knechtle, B.: Participation and performance trends in 100-km ultra-marathons worldwide. J. Sports Sci. **32**(4), 354–366 (2014)
3. Tawa, N., Louw, Q.: Biomechanical factors associated with running economy and performance of elite Kenyan distance runners: a systematic review. J. Bodyw. Mov. Ther. **22**(1), 1–10 (2018)
4. Barnes, K.R., Kilding, A.E.: Strategies to improve running economy. Sport. Med. **45**(1), 37–56 (2015)
5. Brandon, L.J.: Physiological factors associated with middle distance running performance. Sport. Med. **19**(4), 268–277 (1995)

6. Vernillo, G., et al.: Effects of ultratrail running on skeletal-muscle oxygenation dynamics. Int. J. Sports Physiol. Perform. **12**(4), 496–504 (2017)

7. Barnes, K.R., McGuigan, M.R., Kilding, A.E.: Lower-body determinants of running economy in male and female distance runners. J. Strength Cond. Res. **28**(5), 1289–1297 (2014)

8. Damasceno, M.V., et al.: Effects of resistance training on neuromuscular characteristics and pacing during 10-km running time trial. Eur. J. Appl. Physiol. **115**(7), 1513–1522 (2015)

9. Stöggl, T., Wunsch, T.: Biomechanics of marathon running. In: Zinner, C., Sperlich, B. (eds.) Marathon Running: Physiology, Psychology, Nutrition and Training Aspects, pp. 13–45. Springer International Publishing, Cham (2016). https://doi.org/10.1007/978-3-319-297 28-6_2

10. Hamill, J., Palmer, C., Van Emmerik, R.E.A.: Coordinative variability and overuse injury. Sport. Med. Arthrosc. Rehabil. Ther. Technol., **4**(1) (2012)

11. Anderson, T.: Biomechanics and running economy. Sport. Med. **22**(2), 76–89 (1996)

12. Paavolainen, L., Nummela, A., Rusko, H., Häkkinen, K.: Neuromuscular characteristics and fatigue during 10 km running. Int. J. Sports Med. **20**(8), 516–521 (1999)

13. Knechtle, B., Tanda, G.: Effects of training and anthropometric factors on marathon and 100 km ultramarathon race performance. Open Access J. Sport. Med., 129 (2015)

14. McLaren, S.J., Macpherson, T.W., Coutts, A.J., Hurst, C., Spears, I.R., Weston, M.: The relationships between internal and external measures of training load and intensity in team sports: a meta-analysis. Sport. Med. **48**(3), 641–658 (2018)

15. De Aguiar, R.A., Lisbôa, F.D., Turnes, T., De Oliveira Cruz, R.S., Caputo, F.: The effects of different training backgrounds on VO2 responses to all-out and supramaximal constant-velocity running bouts. PLoS One **10**(8) (2015)

16. Giandolini, M., et al.: Effect of the fatigue induced by a 110-km ultramarathon on tibial impact acceleration and lower leg kinematics. PLoS One **11**(3) (2016)

17. Hudgins, B., Scharfenberg, J., Triplett, N.T., McBride, J.M.: Relationship between jumping ability and running performance in events of varying distance. J. Strength Cond. Res. **27**(3), 563–567 (2013)

18. Ache-Dias, J., Dal Pupo, J., Dellagrana, R.A., Teixeira, A.S., Mochizuki, L., Moro, A.R.P.: Effect of jump interval training on kinematics of the lower limbs and running economy. J. Strength Cond. Res. **32**(2), 416–422 (2018)

19. Lenhart, R., Thelen, D., Heiderscheit, B.: Hip muscle loads during running at various step rates. J. Orthop. Sports Phys. Ther. **44**(10), 766–774 (2014)

20. Vannatta, C.N., Kernozek, T.W., Gheidi, N.: Changes in gluteal muscle forces with alteration of footstrike pattern during running. Gait Posture **58**, 240–245 (2017)

21. Mucha, M.D., Caldwell, W., Schlueter, E.L., Walters, C., Hassen, A.: Hip abductor strength and lower extremity running related injury in distance runners: a systematic review. J. Sci. Med. Sport **20**(4), 349–355 (2017)

22. Barton, C.J., Lack, S., Malliaras, P., Morrissey, D.: Gluteal muscle activity and patellofemoral pain syndrome: a systematic review. Br. J. Sports Med. **47**(4), 207–214 (2013)

23. Brund, R.B.K., Rasmussen, S., Nielsen, R.O., Kersting, U.G., Laessoe, U., Voigt, M.: The association between eccentric hip abduction strength and hip and knee angular movements in recreational male runners: An explorative study. Scand. J. Med. Sci. Sport. **28**(2), 473–478 (2018)

24. Sundby, O.H., Gorelick, M.L.S.: Relationship between functional hamstring: quadriceps ratios and running economy in highly trained and recreational female runners. J. Strength Cond. Res. **28**(8), 2214–2227 (2014)

Energy Efficient Fill-Level Monitoring for Recycling Glass Containers

Nikola Marković[1](✉)[iD], Ali Raza[2], Thomas Wolf[2], Pascal Romahn[2], Arndt-Hendrik Zinn[2], and Dorothea Kolossa[1][iD]

[1] Institute of Energy and Automation Technology, Tu Berlin 10587, Berlin, Germany
{nikola.markovic,dorothea.kolossa}@tu-berlin.de
[2] Zolitron - Internet of Things Company GmbH, Bochum, Germany
{araza,twol}@zolitron.com

Abstract. Monitoring the fill levels of glass containers is important for smart cities, to simultaneously save energy and traffic by preventing unneeded pick-up routes, and to support the circular economy by ensuring that containers are always available for new recycling glass. Here, we present a novel and highly energy-efficient method for reliable monitoring of glass container fill levels. This was achieved by framing the problem as a classification problem of the container fill state, and by using a dataset consisting of over 100,000 accelerometer recordings from 106 different containers for training hybrid models that combine the best aspects of deep learning and probabilistic inference. We propose the use of hybrid models, via optimal sequential decision making based on a probabilistic output of the deep neural network. With this approach, the overall accuracy increases by more than 10% while preventing sudden changes in state prediction. Finally, we have optimized the network efficiency. For this purpose, we investigated four techniques of explainable artificial intelligence methods for time series to investigate which feature are important for classification. The final results show that this allows for training a classification model of roughly comparable performance by using only 5% of the input features, which leads to an additional improvement of 97 % in terms of energy consumption of the smart sensor.

Keywords: Condition monitoring · Smart city · Neural-probabilistic learning · Explainable AI · Energy-efficient sensing

1 Introduction

The global city population has doubled in the last seventy years and currently makes up almost half of the entire world's inhabitants. Although the growth rate has declined, it is estimated that the number of people in cities will continue to rise in the next fifty years, reaching almost 60% of the world population in the year 2070 [28]. One of the biggest challenges that come with such changes is solid waste management (SWM). It is estimated, that global waste generation

T. Guarda et al. (Eds.): ARTIIS 2023, CCIS 1936, pp. 113–127, 2024.
https://doi.org/10.1007/978-3-031-48855-9_9

has increased by 70% in the last ten years, the majority of which was generated by high and upper-middle income societies [16]. SWM includes four main components: sorting and collection, recycling, transportation, treatment and disposal [21]. Among these, transportation represent 50% − 70% of the operational costs [2], which makes optimization of this SWM component desirable. Additionally, waste collection optimization reduces the greenhouse gas emissions incurred during waste collection [21]. A prerequisite for collection optimization is reliable information about the current fill level of containers. This problem is not easy to solve; only a few methods for glass containers have been proposed, and fewer yet are field-tested.

1.1   Waste Fill Level Detection Methods

A commonly applied approach for fill level monitoring is an ultrasonic sensor attached to the top of a waste bin and a load sensor at the bottom of the bin [9, 20, 22]. Even though ultrasonic sensors are used in the field, they have some drawbacks as they need to be installed inside the container, which is hard to do and can damage the container's roof. Furthermore, they do not perform well in a closed environment. In [7], the waste fill level is monitored by employing two infrared (IR) sensors, one in the middle and one at the top of the container, and a load sensor for measuring the weight of the waste. In our experience, IR sensors have a problem of the laser being reflected because of glass causing unreliable readings. Recently, data-based approaches have also emerged. In [4], the authors used images of the waste bins to train a classifier to recognize if the bins are empty, partially full, or full. A support vector machine (SVM) model was trained and tested on 200 images, achieving very high accuracy. The authors in [24] have analyzed the use of an accelerometer for the application of measuring a fill level of the container via vibration produced usage of the container. In a range of fill levels from 0 to 15%, they have shown that the peak frequencies computed through the Fast Fourier Transform (FFT) of the recorded vibrations are a good indicator of the fill level change, but a scalable algorithm that can be used in a production environment could not be realized. Recordings from an accelerometer were also employed in [30]. In this approach, the authors extract features using available recordings and a physical model of vibrations. Then, fill levels are clustered into three classes. However, this approach requires a vibration model, which is specific to the container and would require additional experiments for its derivation.

The task discussed in this paper can also be regarded as one of time-series classification. In recent years, there has been increased research interest in this topic, as it has many practical applications. The following subsection provides an overview of state-of-the-art methods in this field.

1.2   Deep Learning Methods for Time-Series Classification

Most recent methods are based on deep neural network (DNN) architectures, inspired by computer vision or natural language processing applications. For example, in [29], a fully convolutional network (FCN) is proposed, which extracts features using three convolutional layers, each followed by a batch normalization layer. Then, a global average pooling layer and a softmax output layer are applied for classification. Parallel use of the long-short-term memory cell [13] and an FCN model for feature extraction, proposed in [15], has shown an improvement in results for both univariate and multivariate time series. In [12], the authors present an ensemble of five DNN models, where the final prediction is then computed as an average of the five model outputs, which decreases uncertainty. However, as with previously described deep learning (DL) models, the number of parameters is quite high and significant computing power is needed to train the model. A computationally less costly approach called $ROCKET$ was proposed in [10]. Features extracted via a large number of convolutional kernels are not learned but are randomly initialized. Then, logistic or ridge regression is trained for classification. Nonetheless, as each kernel produces features, using a large number of kernels, which is often needed, can still make the number of trainable parameters of the classifier large. The evaluation of various techniques for time series classification on univariate and multivariate time series datasets [11], has shown that, given sufficient training data, the DL methods have superior performance in comparison to more classical machine learning techniques that require heavy data prepossessing and feature engineering [23]. Besides that, as shown in this paper, convolutional neural networks (CNN) in particular, can learn features during optimization with, for modern standards, a small number of parameters.

1.3 Explainable Artificial Intelligence Methods

In addition to designing novel systems for vibration-based fill level analysis in an IoT context, our second contribution is analyzing the effectiveness of *explainable artificial intelligence* (XAI) methods within such systems. Concretely, we evaluate the performance of these methods in finding the most important parts of input features. In this way, we can apply XAI methods for dimension reduction with the goal of designing an energy-efficient solution, through minimizing the size of the network and the number of computations.

The main focus of XAI methods is interpreting the inference of an AI model and computing *attribution maps*, which highlight the parts of input that are most important for the model's decision. For classification tasks, an attribution map can be computed with respect to each classification output. It highlights those features that contribute to selecting a particular class, represented by that output. Most XAI methods were originally developed for computer vision tasks, but have been employed in other areas, including time-series classification [1,26]. For our analysis, we have applied and compared several known methods, representing different approaches in XAI, as further described in Sect. 5.

In this paper, a hybrid neural/probabilistic method for classifying the fill level of a glass container is proposed. Using vibration signals recorded by an accelerometer as the input, a two-stage classification procedure is implemented. In the first stage, a neural network, i.e. a CNN, is applied as a density estimator for the current fill level. The second stage uses dynamic programming for integrating the past outputs of the network, to make the final decision. Although trained on an imbalanced and imperfectly labeled dataset and having less than 5000 parameters, the classification model can perform accurate and reliable monitoring of the container fill level in this manner. Subsequently, we consider different XAI methods for finding the most informative parts of the input. We find that by applying the DeepLift method, only 5% percent of the original features can be used for training a classification model, with a small performance drop but a major impact on energy efficiency when implemented in an edge device.

The remainder of the paper is organized as follows: Sect. 2 describes the methodology for data collection as well as the structure of the resulting dataset. The considered feature types and the proposed classification method are introduced in Sect. 3, while implementation details and results are given in Sect. 4. Application and comparison of different XAI methods are described in Sect. 5, before providing conclusions and an outlook on future work in Sect. 6.

2   Dataset Description

The vibration data was captured using the Z-Node sensor developed by the company Zolitron[1]. The sensor is a solar-powered Narrow-Band-Internet-of-Things (NB-IoT) device with multiple types of sensors onboard, including a 3-axis accelerometer.

Table 1. Dataset distribution

Fill level	Training Data		Test Data	
0–9%	19,523	17.0%	1,302	14.4%
10–19%	16,052	14.0%	890	9.9%
20–29%	15,318	13.3%	1,072	11.9%
30–39%	13,143	11.4%	772	8.6%
40–49%	12,715	11.1%	839	9.3%
50–59%	11,090	9.7%	807	8.9%
60–69%	9,895	8.6%	789	8.8%
70–79%	7,407	6.4%	1,024	11.3%
80–89%	5,894	5.1%	706	7.8%
90–99%	3,877	3.4%	819	9.1%
Total	114,914		9,020	

The containers used in the study were manufactured by Rhland[2], and the sensor was glued to the top of each container. When the vibration magnitude

---

[1] www.zolitron.com.

[2] www.ruehland.com.

exceeds 0.2 g, the sensor wakes up from a deep sleep, and a measurement is triggered. The accelerometer recorded a 640 ms long trace in X, Y, and Z axis, which made 1,920 samples in each recording.

The reference fill levels were collected by regularly sending an employee to visually inspect and note the current fullness of each container. An additional inspection was also conducted to estimate the uncertainty of human assessment. Multiple annotators were asked to estimate the fill level of 24 different containers. An analysis of their labels shows that the average inter-annotator-difference was around 10%. This shows that the collected labels are not highly precise.

The dataset comprises the vibration data recorded from 106 glass containers. The training data includes recordings from 93 containers, while the data from the remaining 13 containers are included in the test set. In total, there are 114,914 traces in the training set and 9,020 traces in the test set. Although this is a relatively large dataset, it is also imbalanced, as shown in Table 1. This data imbalance is specifically problematic for this task, as the reliable recognition of high fill levels is of great practical importance. However, as described in Sect. 4.1, we have successfully addressed this data scarcity issue in our optimization approach.

3 Proposed Method

The primary goal of the proposed method is to monitor the fill level of the glass container and reliably recognize two or three different levels of fullness. There are three main classification steps: feature extraction, probabilistic classification, and integration of the classifier output via dynamic programming. This approach is adapted from our previous work on condition-monitoring for power converters, see [19] for details.

3.1 Features

Two different feature types were used. The first, *time-based-features*, are formed by first reshaping the recorded traces into a matrix where each row corresponds to one vibration axis. Then, eight consecutive traces are averaged, finally forming a two-dimensional vector with dimensions 3×640, where the three represents the three axes and the 640 is the number of samples per trace. The second feature type is *frequency-based-features*. These are formed by applying an FFT to the X, Y, and Z axis of each trace, separately. Then, traces are arranged into a matrix, with each row corresponding to the absolute value of the FFT of one axis. As with time-based features, eight consecutive FFTs of traces are averaged. Finally, this yields a two-dimensional matrix of shape 3×320. The averaging of the traces is motivated by reducing the computational effort, as our experience has shown that it does not affect the classifier performance.

3.2   Probabilistic Classifier

A CNN-based classifier with a VGG architecture [27] was applied to obtain density estimates for the discrete fill level. The fundamental block of this architecture consists of two or three convolutional layers, followed by a max-pooling layer. Each convolutional layer consists of kernels with dimension 3×3 and uses the ReLU activation function. After applying several such blocks, the output is flattened and passed first to a dense layer and finally to the output softmax layer for density estimation. The advantage of stacking convolutional layers is the increase of the effective receptive field while applying nonlinear rectification, which makes the decision function more discriminating. In this work, the applied architecture contained four blocks with two convolutional layers followed by a max pooling layer, with a pooling size of 1×4. Each convolutional layer had eight kernels. Additionally, in order to decrease the number of parameters, there is no dense layer between the flattening and the *softmax* output layer, as this has been shown not to improve the classification.

3.3   Finding the Best Fill Level via Dynamic Programming

Classifying the current fill level based only on the recently available measurement is not sufficiently reliable, as there can be different external disturbances that affect the quality of the recording. For example, recording of the vibration might be affected by rain or nearby traffic. We, therefore, propose to improve the decision-making process by integrating consecutive outputs of the classifier via search through a lattice of possible container fill state sequences. We can make this search computationally highly efficient via dynamic programming, specifically choosing the Viterbi algorithm as our approach to search.

Principal Idea. In order to frame the search problem in a way that is amenable to dynamic programming, we need to make some statistical independence assumptions. This can be easily achieved by describing the evolution of the container fill state (which is not directly observable in practice) in the form of the Hidden Markov Model (HMM). This statistical model was designed to deal specifically with cases like this, where an unobservable state needs to be estimated *across time*. It makes two simplifying assumptions regarding the sequential data that it describes:

- At each time-point, the observation is only dependent on the current model state, but not on any previous states or observations.
- Model states evolve from time step to time step, according to a transition matrix γ. The model state at time $t + 1$ thus only depends on the model state at time t, but not on any longer context, nor on observations.

Both model assumptions taken together, the first-order Markov model allows for the application of simple dynamic programming algorithms in searching for an optimal state sequence.

Characteristics of HMMs. Having selected the HMM as our model, we then need to learn the characteristics of our sequential data, which boils down to estimating the parameters of an HMM. An HMM with N states is described by three parameters: 1) *prior probability* - P_0, of each state at the first time step, 2) *transition matrix* - γ, describing the probability of transition between states, with $\gamma_{i,j}$ denoting probability of transitioning from state i to state j, and 3) *emission distributions* - $p(o_t|s_n)$, describing how an observation o_t is generated in state s_n.

Application to Fill State Classification. Our classification task, container fill state classification across time, can be solved through inference in a hidden Markov model by considering recorded vibration data as observations and different fill-level classes as the states of the HMM.

Parameters P_0 and γ are learned during optimization, as described in the following section. The emission distributions are computed using Bayes' Theorem: $p(o_t|s_t = j) = \frac{p(s_t=i|o_t)p(o_t)}{p(s_t=j)} \approx \frac{p(s_t=i|o_t)}{p(s_t=j)}$, where the last approximation is used since the term $p(o_t)$ is independent of the state. During test time, the posterior distribution over the states—$p(s_t = i|o_t)$—is obtained as the output of the trained DNN, while the state probability $p(s_t = j)$ is estimated based on the frequency of that state in the training set.

After defining an HMM and estimating its parameters P_0 and γ, given a vector of T observations $\mathbf{O_T} = \{ o_1, o_2, ..., o_T \}$, we are interested in finding that sequence of hidden states $\mathbf{S_T} = \{ s_1, s_2, ..., s_T \}$, which is most likely to have generated this observation sequence. This problem is efficiently solved using dynamic programming, in its specific instantiation of the *Viterbi algorithm* [8]. In the first step, the log-probabilities $\omega_{t,j}$ of each of the N states are computed for at every timesteps $t = 1 ... T$. The obtained $T \times N$ matrix is then used to find the most probable path of states by applying the *back-tracking* procedure. The detailed sequence of computations is given in Algorithm 1.

Algorithm 1. Viterbi algorithm

$T \leftarrow$ number of observations
$N \leftarrow$ number of states
for $t = 1..T$ **do**
    for $j = 1..N$ **do**
        $\omega_{t,j} \leftarrow \log p(o_t|s_t = j) + \max_{i=1..N} (w_{t-1,i} + \log \gamma_{i,j})$
    end for
end for
$s_T \leftarrow \arg \max_{i=1..N}(\omega_{T,i})$
for $t = T - 1..1$ **do**
    $s_t \leftarrow \arg \max_{i=1..N}(\omega_{t,i} + \log \gamma_{i,s_{t+1}})$
end for

---

4   Evaluation and Results

Two classification tasks were considered. The first task was a two-state classification where the first state included traces with fill level labels below 80%, with the second state included traces corresponding to the remaining levels equal or above 80%. The second task was a three-state classification, where the first state was composed of traces corresponding to fill levels below 30%, the second state included traces with labels between 30% and 70%, and the third state contained traces labeled with fill levels above 70%.

4.1   Classifier Optimization and Implementation Details

The performance on both tasks was compared in cases with time and frequency-based features. In all of test cases, the same classifier structure given in Subsect. 3.2, was applied. For the two-state classification task, this yielded 4314 parameters in the case of time-based features and 4218 parameters in the case of frequency-based features. For the three-state classification, there were 4387 network parameters when time-based features were used and 4243 parameters for frequency-based features. As described in Subsect. 3.3, the *Viterbi algorithm* was used to integrate the outputs of the classifier for obtaining the final container state classification. The learnable parameters of the HMM are the initial distribution of states P_0 and the state transition matrix γ.

The training procedure consists of two parts. First, the neural network was trained on the entire training dataset for four epochs, using a batch size of 64. Secondly, the parameters of the network were jointly optimized with the parameters of the HMM, using backpropagation through the Viterbi algorithm, for 10 more epochs. During the second part of the optimization, the network input was fed by traces from each container separately in chronological order. Alternatively, the parameters of the HMM could have been learned using the Baum-Welch algorithm [6]. But as inference is efficiently implemented in the form of the Viterbi algorithm, we decided instead to backpropagate through the algorithm that is ultimately employed in our classification as well. The entire training and test of the proposed method were implemented in the PyTorch framework. The cross-entropy loss function was applied, where the imbalance of the training set was addressed by weighting the loss depending on the classifier decisions. If the classification is correct the weight is equal to one, but for different misclassifications the loss is weighted according to a pre-defined weight matrix W, with element $W_{i,j}$ denoting the weight of misclassifying state i as state j. The weights corresponding to misclassifying each class are considered to be the same. In terms of the weight matrix this means that all of the off-diagonal elements in each row are equal. The values of $W_{i,j}$ were determined through a grid-search of values ranging from 1 to 10, with step equal to 1. To learn the parameters, we employed an Adam optimizer with a learning rate of $5 \cdot 10^{-3}$ during the first phase, and 10^{-3} during the second phase of optimization.

Table 2. Confusion matrices of instant and Viterbi classification, for the two-state classification task. s_1 denotes fill levels below 80% with s_2 covering the remaining fill levels above 80%. Predicted states are denoted as $\hat{s}_1$ and $\hat{s}_2$

		Time features		FFT features	
		s_1	s_2	s_1	s_2
Instant classification	$\hat{s}_1$	**82.2**	17.8	**87.2**	12.7
	$\hat{s}_2$	18.8	**81.2**	12.0	**88.0**
Viterbi classification	$\hat{s}_1$	**88.0**	12.0	**93.6**	6.4
	$\hat{s}_2$	12.9	**87.1**	5.8	**94.2**

4.2   HMM Parameter Optimization

The parameters of the HMM were optimized, starting from different initial points. For both classification tasks, the self-transition probabilities for each state s_i denoted as - $\gamma_{i,i}$, were varied from 0.1 to 0.9, with a step size of 0.1. The transition probabilities between different classes were set to $(1 - \gamma_{i,i})$ for two-state classification and $(1 - \gamma_{i,i})/2$, in the case of three-state classification. Despite using a wide range of initial values, the HMM parameters always converged to very similar final values.

Concretely, for the first classification task, the initial probabilities and transition matrix converged to:

$$P_0 = [0.99, 0.01], \gamma = \begin{bmatrix} 0.96 & 0.04 \\ 0.02 & 0.98 \end{bmatrix}.$$

For the three-state classification, the estimated HMM parameters were:

$$P_0 = [0.99, 0.01, 0.0], \gamma = \begin{bmatrix} 0.97 & 0.02 & 0.01 \\ 0.0 & 0.99 & 0.01 \\ 0.01 & 0.0 & 0.99 \end{bmatrix}.$$

4.3   Results

In the following, we present and analyze the classification results of our suggested approach, and compare it to the instant-classification baseline.

Two-State Classification. The results for the two-state classification are shown in Table 2. The instant classification results show that both feature types allow for classification accuracies above 80% for both classes. The frequency-based features achieve better results, with an accuracy that is around 5% higher than for the time-based features. From cross-temporal integration via the Viterbi algorithm, the overall results improve significantly. The effect is similar in both cases, so the frequency-based features still perform better, achieving an accuracy above 90% for both classes.

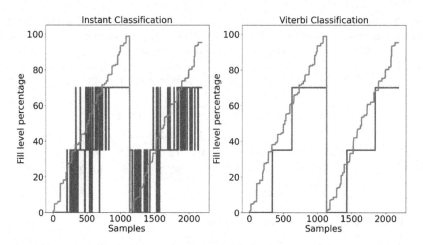

Fig. 1. True fill level (orange) and classification output (blue). Classification without (left) and with (right) applying cross-temporal integration via the Viterbi algorithm on the CNN outputs (Color figure online)

Three-Class Classification. Table 3 shows the results of the three-state classification. The frequency-based features again show better performance in comparison to the time-based features, although the difference is smaller than in the case of the two-state classification. Application of the Viterbi algorithm for this task again brings a notable improvement. For both feature types, the accuracy increased by 10%, achieving a state recognition rate of over 80%. As can also be seen, the overall accuracy decreases by around 9% in comparison to the two-state classification. This comes as a consequence of having one more state and of the fact that the classes are not well separated. Additionally, the sequential decision-making of the Viterbi algorithm causes a slight decision latency, which also affects accuracy, as illustrated in Fig. 1. However, this figure also reveals information that is not obvious from the confusion matrix. The Viterbi algorithm makes the classification much more reliable and allows clear recognition of different states.

5   Application of XAI Methods

As mentioned above, a number of XAI methods have been applied for dimension reduction. The first of these, *Grad-CAM*, falls into the class of backpropagation-based XAI [25]. In this approach, the attribution map of a CNN layer is computed as the weighted sum of all kernel activations in that layer. Each kernel activation is given a weight proportional to the average gradient of kernel activations with respect to the desired output. Most commonly as well as in this paper, the attribution map is computed only for the last convolutional layer and then upsampled to the size of the input.

Table 3. Confusion matrices of instant and Viterbi classification for the three-class classification task. s_1, s_2 and s_3 denote the fill levels below 30%, between 30% and 70%, and above 70%, respectively. Predicted states are denoted as $\hat{s}_1$, $\hat{s}_2$ and $\hat{s}_3$

		Time features			FFT features		
		s_1	s_2	s_3	s_1	s_2	s_3
Instant classification	$\hat{s}_1$	**73.2**	23.5	2.3	**75.8**	22.9	1.2
	$\hat{s}_2$	14.9	**70.3**	13.8	13.6	**73.1**	13.3
	$\hat{s}_3$	2.3	24.8	**72.9**	1.9	22.2	**75.9**
Viterbi classification	$\hat{s}_1$	**83.4**	16.4	0.2	**85.6**	14.4	0.0
	$\hat{s}_2$	13.4	**80.0**	6.6	8.3	**83.7**	8.0
	$\hat{s}_3$	1.0	15.3	**83.7**	0.9	14.1	**85.0**

As a second XAI method, we consider *Layer-wise relevance propagation* (LRP) [5]. After propagating the input through the entire forward path of the network, LRP computes a relevance score of each neuron. The relevance of the neurons in the last layer is set to their output value. Then, a backward pass is performed and the relevance of each neuron is redistributed to the neurons in the previous layer, according to the strength of their connection. The final attribution map is then equal to the relevance of the input layer. A similar approach, *DeepLift*, was proposed in [3]. Here, the attribution of each neuron is equal to the difference between the unit activation when the current and the reference input are propagated. Depending on the application, a reference input denotes a neutral, non-informative input. Finally, the *gradient SHAP* (GSHAP) [18] technique is used. Firstly, a modified input is created by adding noise to the given network input. Then the applied input is randomly selected from a linear path between a reference value and the changed input. This is repeated for multiple samples. The attribution of a feature is then approximated by multiplying the expected size of the gradient with respect to that feature and the difference between the current and reference input. Additionally, a *Random* strategy is used as a simple and uninformed baseline, which randomly selects features as important. An implementation of all these XAI methods is available in the PyTorch-compatible *Captum* library [17], which is employed in all XAI experiments described below.

5.1 Feature Selection

XAI methods are mostly developed for image analysis, where attribution maps help discover pixel areas that are important for classification. Since the structure of the considered data is different, the procedure for selecting the most important features was modified. Firstly, attribution maps were computed for the entire training dataset. Then, the relevance score of features is summed column-wise, and a pre-determined percentage of the most important points are selected. In the time domain, this corresponded to selecting the most important time points, while in the frequency domain, it corresponds to selecting the most important

Table 4. Comparison of performance for models trained on 5% of the most important features, selected with various XAI methods. The results are shown as accuracy (in %) of instant classification for the three-class classification task

	Original	GradCAM	LRP	DeepLIFT	GSHAP	Random
Time features	72.1	48.4	50.3	49.9	**51.5**	42.6
FFT features	74.9	40.6	67.5	**71.1**	68.2	38.6

frequencies. For computing reference input, it was found, that the best choice for a non-informative value of a feature was zero, for both types of features.

5.2   Training Classifiers After Feature Selection

To compare the efficacy of the considered XAI methods, the classification model is retrained using only the most important features (selected according to all above attribution approaches). We keep the top 5% percent of both feature types for three-state classification task and analyze the resulting performance. The classification results are shown in Table 4. In the case of time-based features, the application of XAI methods yielded similar results. In the case of all four methods, the accuracy is around 50%, which still proved better than randomly choosing which features to keep. The selected frequency-based features showed a much better performance, except in the case of GradCAM. Training on features chosen by DeepLift showed the best performance, as the accuracy drop is only 3%, without 95% of the original features. The performance of using LRP and GSHAP is on a similar level, retaining a relatively small accuracy drop.

Table 5. Comparison of different models performance on the Z-Node sensor, for the three-class classification task. Classification results are shown as accuracy (in %)

	Full model	Full quant.	XAI model	XAI quant.
Energy cons. (mJ)	57.4	6.6	3.3	1.5
Inference time (s)	3.5	0.4	0.2	0.1
Instant classification	74.9	74.8	71.2	71.0
Viterbi classification	85.8	85.5	81.6	81.2

5.3   Energy Efficiency Improvements

The effect of input dimension reduction on the energy efficacy was tested on the Z-Node sensor. The performance of the full model, which uses all of the extracted FFT features as inputs was compared with the one of the model using only 5% of the most important features, selected via the DeepLift method. Before implementation on the sensor, trained models were transformed into the appropriate format. The first step in this process is to convert models from the PyTorch to the TensorFlow (TF) format using the ONNX library [14] for Python. Then, the model is converted to TensorFlow Lite (TFLite) format to be ready for deployment on the sensor. Two different versions of each model were implemented and tested on the sensor. The first version is produced as a plain conversion to TFLite. In the second version, quantization of the network parameters was additionally applied during the model conversion. This means that instead of storing network parameters as 32-bit float values, activations of the network were quantized to 16-bit integer values while weights were quantized to 8-bit integer values. To evaluate the four models, the test data was processed and classified for the three-class classification task. Since the data processing is the same for all models, the energy consumption was compared only for the inference part. Table 5 shows the overall results, including energy consumption per inference, average inference time per input, and classification accuracy for the tested models. For the case of the full model, the quantization preservers model performance, while allowing for almost 90% of decrease in energy consumption and inference time. Using the XAI model decreases energy consumption and inference time by 50% in comparison to the quantized full model, with a performance drop of around 4%. Finally, the quantized XAI model keeps the performance of the non-quantized XAI model with further computing resource optimization. In comparison with the full model, the quantized XAI model achieves a 4% lower classification accuracy but allows a drastic, 97% decrease in energy consumption and inference time.

6   Conclusion

We have presented a novel method for determining the fill level of recycling glass containers. Recordings from an accelerometer were used to optimize the parameters of a CNN-based instantaneous classifier. To integrate information across time in a statistically sound and learnable manner, the filling process of the container was modeled as an HMM, which allowed the application of the Viterbi algorithm to improve the decision-making process. Training and testing were conducted on real-world data collected from 106 glass containers. The results show that a model with less than 5000 parameters, using FFT-based features, can achieve over 90% accuracy for two-state classification and 85% accuracy for three-state classification.

For optimization of energy consumption, we also compared XAI methods in their capability of identifying the most informative features. A new model was trained using only 5% of the original features selected by the DeepLift method, at an accuracy that is only 4% lower than that of the original model. On our IoT hardware, the Z-Node sensor, combining XAI methods with parameter quantization resulted in a reduced model with comparable classification performance using just 3% of computational resources of the full model.

References

1. Abdelsalam, I.A., Mohamed, G., Corrada, B.H., Soheil, F.: Benchmarking deep learning interpretability in time series predictions. In: Proceedings of the 34th International Conference on Neural Information Processing Systems. NIPS'20 (2020)
2. Aremu, A.: In-town tour optimization of conventional mode for municipalsolid waste collection. Niger. J. Technol. **32**(3), 443–449 (2013)
3. Avanti, S., Peyton, G., Anshul, K.: Learning important features through propagating activation differences. In: Proceedings of the 34th International Conference on Machine Learning (2017)
4. Aziz, F., et al.: Waste level detection and HMM based collection scheduling of multiple bins. PLoS ONE **13**(8), e0202092 (2018). https://doi.org/10.1371/journal.pone.0202092
5. Bach, S., Binder, A., Montavon, G., Klauschen, F., Müller, K.R., Samek, W.: On pixel-wise explanations for non-linear classifier decisions by layer-wise relevance propagation. PLOS ONE **10**(7), e0130140 (2015). https://doi.org/10.1371/journal.pone.0130140
6. Baum, L., Eagon, J.: An inequality with applications to statistical estimation for probabilistic functions of Markov processes and to a model for ecology. Bull. Am. Math. Soc. **73**(3), 360–363 (1972). https://doi.org/10.1090/s0002-9904-1967-11751-8
7. Bharadwaj, A., Rego, R., Chowdhury, A.: IoT based solid waste management system: a conceptual approach with an architectural solution as a smart city application. In: 2016 IEEE Annual India Conference (INDICON). IEEE (2016). https://doi.org/10.1109/indicon.2016.7839147
8. Bishop, C.M.: Pattern Recognition and Machine Learning. Springer Science + Business Media (2006)
9. Chaudhari, M., Patil, B., Raut, V.: IoT based waste collection management system for smart cities: An overview. In: 2019 3rd International Conference on Computing Methodologies and Communication (ICCMC). IEEE (2019). https://doi.org/10.1109/iccmc.2019.8819776
10. Dempster, A., Petitjean, F., Webb, G.: ROCKET: exceptionally fast and accurate time series classification using random convolutional kernels. Data Min. Knowl. Disc. **34**(5), 1454–1495 (2020). https://doi.org/10.1007/s10618-020-00701-z
11. Fawaz, H., Forestier, G., Weber, J., Idoumghar, L., Muller, P.: Deep learning for time series classification: a review. Data Min. Knowl. Disc. **33**(4), 917–963 (2019). https://doi.org/10.1007/s10618-019-00619-1
12. Fawaz, H., et al.: InceptionTime: finding AlexNet for time series classification. Data Min. Knowl. Disc. **34**(6), 1936–1962 (2020). https://doi.org/10.1007/s10618-020-00710-y
13. Hochreiter, S., Schmidhuber, J.: Long short-term memory. Neural Comput. **9**(8), 1735–1780 (1997). https://doi.org/10.1162/neco.1997.9.8.1735
14. Junjie, B., et al.: Onnx: Open neural network exchange. www.github.com/onnx/onnx (2019)
15. Karim, F., Majumdar, S., Darabi, H., Harford, S.: Multivariate LSTM-FCNs for time series classification. Neural Netw. **116**, 237–245 (2019). https://doi.org/10.1016/j.neunet.2019.04.014
16. Kaza, S., Yao, L., Bhada-Tata, P., Woerden, F.: What a Waste 2.0: A Global Snapshot of Solid Waste Management to 2050. Washington, DC: World Bank (2018). https://doi.org/10.1596/978-1-4648-1329-0

17. Kokhlikyan, N., et al.: Captum: a unified and generic model interpretability library for pytorch (2020)
18. Lundberg, S., Su-In, L.: A unified approach to interpreting model predictions. In: Proceedings of the 31st International Conference on Neural Information Processing Systems. NIPS'17 (2017)
19. Markovic, N., Stoetzel, T., Staudt, V., Kolossa, D.: Hybrid condition monitoring for power converters: learning-based methods with statistical guarantees. IEEE Access **11**, 31855–31865 (2023). https://doi.org/10.1109/access.2023.3262986
20. Misra, D., Das, G., Chakrabortty, T., Das, D.: An IoT-based waste management system monitored by cloud. J. Mater. Cycles Waste Manage. **20**(3), 1574–1582 (2018). https://doi.org/10.1007/s10163-018-0720-y
21. Oteng-Ababio, M., Annepu, R., Bourtsalas, T., Intharathirat, R., Charoenkit, S.: Climate Change and Cities: Second Assessment Report of the Urban Climate Change Research Network, chap. 15, pp. 553–582. Cambridge University Press (2018)
22. Pardini, K., Rodrigues, J., Diallo, O., Das, A.K., Albuquerque, V., Kozlov, S.: A smart waste management solution geared towards citizens. Sensors **20**(8), 2380 (2020). https://doi.org/10.3390/s20082380
23. Ruiz, A., Flynn, M., Large, J., Middlehurst, M., Bagnall, A.: The great multivariate time series classification bake off: a review and experimental evaluation of recent algorithmic advances. Data Min. Knowl. Disc. **35**(2), 401–449 (2020). https://doi.org/10.1007/s10618-020-00727-3
24. Schmelter, S., Fuhner, C., Rohrig, C.: Container filling level estimation using vibration resonance behavior. In: 2020 IEEE 5th International Symposium on Smart and Wireless Systems within the Conferences on Intelligent Data Acquisition and Advanced Computing Systems (IDAACS-SWS). IEEE (2020). https://doi.org/10.1109/idaacs-sws50031.2020.9297051
25. Selvaraju, R.R., Cogswell, M., Das, A., Vedantam, R., Parikh, D., Batra, D.: Grad-CAM: Visual explanations from deep networks via gradient-based localization. In: 2017 IEEE International Conference on Computer Vision (ICCV). IEEE (2017). https://doi.org/10.1109/iccv.2017.74
26. Siddiqui, S., Mercier, D., Munir, M., Dengel, A., Ahmed, S.: TSViz: demystification of deep learning models for time-series analysis. IEEE Access **7**, 67027–67040 (2019). https://doi.org/10.1109/access.2019.2912823
27. Simonyan, K., Zisserman, A.: Very deep convolutional networks for large-scale image recognition. In: ICLR (2015)
28. UN-Habitat: World Cities Report 2022: Envisaging the Future of Cities. United Nations Human Settlements Programme (2022)
29. Wang, Z., Yan, W., Oates, T.: Time series classification from scratch with deep neural networks: a strong baseline. In: 2017 International Joint Conference on Neural Networks (IJCNN). IEEE (2017). https://doi.org/10.1109/ijcnn.2017.7966039
30. Zhao, Y., Yao, S., Li, S., Hu, S., Shao, H., Abdelzaher, T.: Vibebin: a vibration-basedwaste bin level detection system. Proceedings of the ACM on Interactive, Mobile, Wearable and Ubiquitous Technologies **1**(3), 1–22 (2017). https://doi.org/10.1145/3132027

Impact of Biometric Sensors on Physical Activity

Teresa Guarda[1,2,3,4(✉)] ⓘ, Datzania Villao[1] ⓘ, and Maria Fernanda Augusto[4] ⓘ

[1] Universidad Estatal Península de Santa Elena, La Libertad, Ecuador
tguarda@gmail.com
[2] Universidad a Distancia de Madrid, Madrid, Spain
[3] Algoritmi Centre, Minho University, Guimarães, Portugal
[4] BiTrum Research Group, Leon, Spain

Abstract. Currently, the use of biometric sensors in physical activity has received considerable interest from academics and industry. Biometric sensors such as heart rate monitors, accelerometers and GPS trackers will provide immediate data on physiological responses, movement patterns and performance metrics. This paper intends to examine the impact of biometric sensors concerning physical training and analyze its use, benefits, and challenges. In addition, the paper discusses the potential of biometric sensors to optimize training methods, improve performance, prevent injuries, and personalize training programs, addressing challenges of data interpretation, privacy concerns, and barriers a it deals with redemption. By analyzing previous research and case studies, this paper provides valuable insights into the use of biometric sensors in physical training and highlights future directions for research and development.

Keywords: Biometric sensors · Physical training · Performance optimization · Injury prevention · Personalization

1 Introduction

Biometric sensors incorporated into physical training in recent years have helped athletes, fitness enthusiasts and coaches monitor and optimize their performance [1]. Biometric sensors encompassing heart rate monitors, accelerometers, GPS trackers, and motion sensors serve to furnish instantaneous data on different physiological and biomechanical parameters in the course of exercising and engaging in physical activity. [2, 3]. This paper intends to examine the impact of biometric sensors concerning physical training and analyze its use, benefits, and challenges.

Biometric sensors have emerged as valuable tools in the fitness industry, providing detailed physiological responses to exercise and movement [1, 4]. These sensors enable the measurement and analysis of biometric data points, such as heart rate, oxygen consumption, number of steps, speed, distance, muscle activity [4]. By capturing these data points, biometric sensors will provide a more complete understanding of an individual's physiological and biomechanical states during training [5].

Biometric sensors have the ability to provide objective information in real-time, allowing athletes, trainers and coaches, to make the most appropriate decisions regarding

T. Guarda et al. (Eds.): ARTIIS 2023, CCIS 1936, pp. 128–139, 2024.
https://doi.org/10.1007/978-3-031-48855-9_10

training intensity, techniques and strategies. Biometric sensors possess the ability to optimize training strategies, enhance athletic performance, mitigate the risk of injuries, and personalize training programs to individual needs. The usage of biometric sensors in revolutionizing bodily activity has sparked interest among various stakeholders, inclusive of researchers, specialists, and engineers [6].

The primary goal of this paper is to furnish a complete assessment of the effect on exerted through biometric sensors on physical training. This work attempts to investigate the application of biometric sensors in physical training by conducting an analysis of literature, and research findings. Specifically, the aim is to explore the advantages and benefits, and challenges of integrating biometric sensors into physical training.

In addition, this paper will discuss data interpretation, privacy concerns and adoption barriers arising from biometric sensor integration.

2 Biometric Sensors

Biometric sensors have received huge prominence in the realm of physical training, revolutionizing the manner athletes, fitness enthusiasts, and trainers monitor and analyze numerous physiological and biomechanical parameters during exercise and physical [7]. This section offers an assessment of the common biometric sensors utilized in physical training, the sorts of statistics they acquire, and the advantages they provide.

There are various types of biometric sensors utilized in physical education that capture special components of physiological and biomechanical statistics. Figure 1 and Table 1 provide an overview of commonly used biometric sensors in physical training [8, 9, 10, 11].

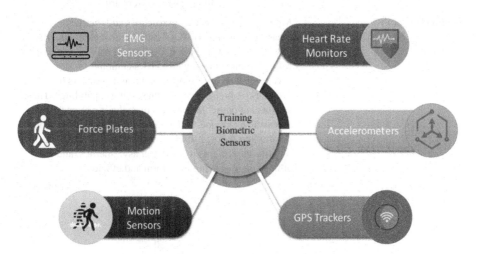

Fig. 1. Physical training biometric sensors.

Table 1. Physical training biometric sensors.

Sensor	Description
Heart Rate Monitors	Heart rate monitors measure the electrical signals produced by the heart. They can be worn as chest straps or wristbands and utilize either contact-based electrodes or optical sensors to measure heart rate. Heart rate monitors provide real-time feedback on heart rate and heart rate variability, which can help monitor exercise intensity, track cardiovascular fitness, and assess recovery
Accelerometers	Accelerometers are motion sensors that measure acceleration and movement in multiple directions. They are often found in wearable devices like fitness trackers and smart watches. Accelerometers track changes in velocity, direction, and amplitude of movement, providing data on steps taken, distance traveled, and even estimating calorie expenditure. These sensors are useful for monitoring activity levels and analyzing overall movement patterns
GPS Trackers	GPS (Global Positioning System) trackers utilize satellite signals to determine geographical location and movement speed. They are commonly used in outdoor activities and sports to track routes, analyze pace, and measure distances covered. GPS trackers provide accurate data on speed, elevation, and geographic coordinates, enabling athletes to monitor their performance in real-time and analyze their training sessions afterward
Motion Sensors	Motion sensors, such as gyroscopes and inertial measurement units (IMUs), capture movement patterns, orientation, and changes in position. Gyroscopes measure rotational movement, while IMUs combine accelerometers, gyroscopes, and magnetometers to provide comprehensive motion sensing capabilities. These sensors are particularly useful in analyzing biomechanics, assessing technique, and monitoring joint angles and body positioning during exercises. Motion sensors can help identify movement errors, detect asymmetries, and guide athletes in improving their form and efficiency

(*continued*)

Table 1. (*continued*)

Sensor	Description
Force Plates	Force plates are specialized sensors embedded in the ground or platforms that measure ground reaction forces during movements like jumping, landing, and running. They can quantify variables such as ground contact time, vertical force, and weight distribution. Force plates provide valuable insights into biomechanical parameters, such as power output, balance, and symmetry, allowing trainers and coaches to assess movement quality, identify potential injury risks, and optimize performance
EMG (Electromyography) Sensors	EMG sensors measure electrical activity in muscles. They detect and record the electrical signals generated by muscle contractions during exercise. EMG sensors help assess muscle activation patterns, muscle imbalances, and muscular fatigue. By monitoring muscle activity, trainers can optimize training techniques, improve muscle recruitment, and prevent overuse injuries

3 Applications of Biometric Sensors

Biometric sensors have observed numerous applications in physical training, providing precious insights into a character's physiological responses, movement patterns, and performance metrics. By utilizing the data collected from biometric sensors, athletes, trainers, and coaches can optimize training methodologies, enhance performance, prevent injuries, and personalize training programs [5, 12, 13] (see Fig. 2).

The applications of biometric sensors in physical training are tremendous and proceed to extend as technology advances. By leveraging the data given by these sensors, athletes and trainers can optimize their training strategies, upgrade execution, enhance performance, reduce the risk of injuries, and personalize preparing programs to meet personal needs. The integration of biometric sensors in physical training has revolutionized the way athletes plan, prepare, and perform, driving progressed results and a more productive and compelling training process.

Biometric sensors play a critical function in optimizing training methods by way of providing real-time feedback and goal measurements. For example, heart rate monitors allow athletes to monitor their heart rate zones, assisting to manipulate their heart rate during training. Accelerometers and GPS trackers allow athletes to track their velocity, distance, and pace, permitting them to adjust training volume and intensity based totally on specific performance goals. With the use of those sensors running trainers and coaches can layout and modify training programs to gain the desired consequences results.

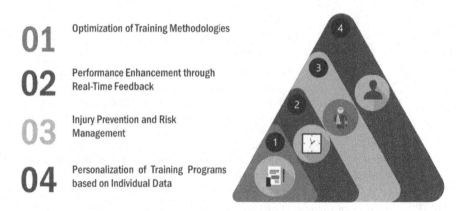

01 Optimization of Training Methodologies

02 Performance Enhancement through Real-Time Feedback

03 Injury Prevention and Risk Management

04 Personalization of Training Programs based on Individual Data

Fig. 2. Biometric applications insights.

Biometric sensors provide real-time feedback on performance metrics, allowing athletes to make instant adjustments during training [3]. For example, motion sensors provide real-time information about movement and joint angles, helping athletes optimize their technique and movements. Heart rate monitors allow athletes to measure their effort, ensuring that they are training in their target areas for maximum performance. With instant feedback from biometric sensors, athletes can make timely adjustments to their physiology, movement and overall performance to improve results [5, 13].

Biometric sensors help in injury prevention and risk management by providing insights into movement quality, imbalances, and excessive strains on the body. For example, motion sensors can detect abnormalities in the movement patterns or joints angles, and identify areas of potential injury risk [5]. Force plates provide valuable information about the forces acting on the ground, helping to identify imbalances and abnormal mechanical movements that can lead to overuse injuries. Analyzing data collected from biometric sensors, trainers and coaches can implement corrective exercises, adjust training loads, and modify strategies to reduce injury risk [13, 14].

Biometric sensors permit the personalization of training programs with the aid of capturing individual data and adapting training plans as needed. By analyzing an individual's physiological and biomechanical responses, trainers can identify strengths, weaknesses, and regions for improvement. Heart rate monitors, accelerometers, and movement sensors provide precious statistics that may be used to increase customized training programs that deal with an individual's abilities, allowing effective progress and better results.

Specific biometric sensors may be used individually or combined, congregating comprehensive data on an athlete's physiological and biomechanical responses. The integration of more than one sensor affords a greater holistic understanding of individual performance, allowing better decision-making and personalized training program.

Biometric sensors gather a huge range of data associated with an individual physiological response, biomechanics, and environmental elements. Figure 3 and Table 2 highlight some types of data collected [15, 16, 17].

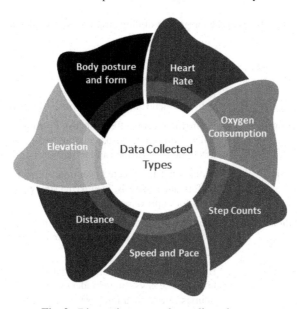

Fig. 3. Biometric sensors data collected types.

Table 2. Biometric sensors data collected types.

Type	Description
Heart rate	Provides insights into cardiovascular intensity, recovery, and overall fitness levels
Oxygen consumption	Reflects the body's energy expenditure and aerobic capacity during exercise
Step counts	Tracks the number of steps taken, which is used to estimate distance traveled and overall activity levels
Speed and pace	Measures the rate at which an individual is moving, aiding in performance analysis and goal setting
Distance	Calculates the total distance covered during an activity or training session
Elevation	Determines changes in altitude, which is crucial for activities like hiking, trail running, or cycling
Body posture and form	Assesses movement patterns, body alignment, and technique during exercises and sports-specific movements

The integration of biometric sensors in physical training offers several advantages: real-time feedback; objective monitoring; performance analysis; training optimization; injury prevention; and personalized training programs [16, 18] (Table 3).

Table 3. Advantages of the integration of biometric sensors in physical training.

Advantage	Description
Real-time feedback	Biometric sensors provide immediate feedback on key parameters, allowing individuals to make adjustments and optimize their training in real-time
Objective monitoring	Biometric sensors offer objective measurements, reducing reliance on subjective perceptions and enhancing accuracy in assessing performance and progress
Performance analysis	Biometric data collected over time allows for in-depth performance analysis, identifying strengths, weaknesses, and areas for improvement
Training optimization	Biometric sensors help optimize training methodologies by providing insights into training intensity, recovery, and adaptation
Injury prevention	By monitoring biomechanics and detecting unusual patterns, biometric sensors can help identify and prevent potential injuries caused by improper form or excessive strain
Personalized training programs	Biometric data facilitates the development of personalized training programs tailored to individual needs, goals, and capabilities

The integration of biometric sensors in physical training empowers individuals to monitor, analyze, and optimize their performance, enabling more effective and personalized training experiences.

4   Benefits of Biometric Sensor Integration

The integration of biometric sensors in physical training brings about numerous benefits for athletes, trainers, and coaches. By leveraging the data collected from these sensors, individuals can gain valuable insights into their physiological responses, movement patterns, and performance metrics.

This section outlines the key benefits of integrating biometric sensors in physical training highlighting: real-time monitoring and feedback; objective measurements and data-driven decisions; enhanced training efficiency and optimization; personalized training programs; injury prevention and risk management; and motivation and accountability.

The real-time monitoring and feedback provided by biometric sensors, enable athletes to make immediate adjustments during training sessions [3, 19]. For example, heart rate monitors allow athletes to monitor their heart rate zones, ensuring they are training at the desired intensity levels for optimal performance. Accelerometers and motion sensors provide instant feedback on movement patterns and technique, helping athlete's correct form and improve efficiency. Real-time monitoring and feedback enhance performance by enabling athletes to maintain appropriate intensity, optimize technique, and make necessary adjustments on the spot.

Biometric sensors offer objective measurements of physiological and biomechanical parameters, eliminating subjective interpretations. This objective data allows for more accurate assessments of progress, performance, and training effectiveness. Athletes, trainers, and coaches can rely on the quantifiable data from biometric sensors to set goals, track improvements, and make data-driven decisions [3]. Objective measurements provide a solid foundation for evaluating performance, optimizing training protocols, and identifying areas for improvement [20].

The integration of biometric sensors allows for enhanced training efficiency and optimization. By monitoring biometric data, trainers can identify patterns, trends, and performance indicators to tailor training programs more effectively. Heart rate monitors, accelerometers, and GPS trackers help optimize training volume, intensity, and recovery periods based on individual responses and goals. This leads to improved training efficiency, better adaptation, and enhanced overall performance outcomes [21, 22].

Biometric sensors enable the development of personalized training programs based on individual data. Trainers and coaches, based on the results of the athletes' physiological and biomechanical data, can adjust individual training programs appropriate to the needs, strengths and weaknesses of the athletes.. Personalization enhances training effectiveness, reduces the risk of overtraining or undertraining, and maximizes performance gains [3].

The role of biometric sensors are crucial in injury prevention and risk management. By monitoring movement patterns, joint angles, and ground reaction forces, trainers can identify potential imbalances, faulty mechanics, or excessive stress that may lead to injuries. With this information, appropriate interventions can be implemented, such as corrective exercises, technique modifications, and targeted strength and conditioning programs. Biometric sensors facilitate proactive injury prevention strategies, allowing athletes to train safely and minimize the risk of sports-related injuries [23].

Biometric sensors can enhance motivation and accountability by providing tangible data on progress and performance. Athletes can track their improvements over time, set goals, and celebrate milestones based on objective measurements. The availability of real-time data and feedback keeps athletes engaged and motivated, driving them to achieve their full potential. Additionally, the use of biometric sensors promotes accountability as athletes can objectively assess their efforts, adherence to training plans, and the impact of lifestyle factors on their performance [24].

The integration of biometric sensors in physical training offers numerous benefits that optimize performance, enhance training efficiency, and reduce the risk of injuries. Real-time monitoring, objective measurements, personalized training programs, and motivation-driven feedback empower athletes and trainers to make informed decisions, maximize their training outcomes, and achieve peak performance levels [21, 22, 24].

5 Challenges and Limitations

While the integration of biometric sensors in physical training brings numerous benefits, there are also several challenges and limitations that need to be considered.

Factors such as sensor calibration, sensor placement, signal interference, and variations in individual physiology can affect data accuracy. It is crucial to validate the accuracy and reliability of biometric sensors to ensure that the data collected is consistent and can be relied upon for making informed decisions [25].

Another challenge is the compatibility and integration of different biometric sensors and their associated technologies. Integrating multiple sensors into a cohesive system may require complex data synchronization and interoperability between different sensor devices and software platforms. Standardization of data formats and protocols is necessary to facilitate seamless integration and data exchange across different sensor technologies [26].

Biometric sensors capture sensitive personal data, including physiological and biomechanical information. This raises concerns regarding privacy and data security. Adequate measures must be applied to protect the privacy and confidentiality of individual biometric data. Encryption, secure data storage, and data protection regulations are essential to maintain the privacy and safety of the collected data These advancements are poised to augment the precision, efficacy, and influence of biometric sensors toward enhancing athletic performance, optimizing training methodologies, and promoting holistic health and well-being [27].

Cost and accessibility can be limiting factors when considering the adoption of biometric sensors. Some high-end biometric sensor technologies can be expensive, making them inaccessible for certain individuals or organizations with limited resources. Cost-effective solutions and advancements in technology are needed to ensure broader accessibility and affordability of biometric sensors in physical training settings.

Ethical considerations related to data usage, consent, and the potential for misuse of biometric information must be addressed [28]. Clear guidelines and ethical frameworks should be established to ensure responsible and ethical use of biometric sensor data. Athletes' informed consent should be obtained, and data usage should be transparently communicated to maintain trust and uphold ethical standards.

It is important to acknowledge and address these challenges and limitations to fully harness the potential of biometric sensors in physical training.

6 Conclusions

The adoption of biometric sensors in the realm of physical training has brought about a transformation in the methodology employed by athletes and their trainers to oversee, assess, and enhance performance. The current study delves into the influence of implementing biometric sensors in physical exercise by analyzing their various applications, advantages, obstacles, and prospects for future research.

The implementation of biometric sensors provides a noteworthy understanding of the physiological reactions, movement sequences, and performance measures of athletes, effectively supporting trainers in their capacity to utilize data-centric strategies and construct customized training regimens. The application of biometric sensors has exhibited remarkable benefits, such as improved management of training load, optimization of techniques, prevention of injuries, and enhancement of performance.

Notwithstanding, a multitude of obstacles and restrictions necessitate resolution in order to optimally employ biometric sensors to their fullest capacity. The successful implementation of data-driven technologies necessitates the meticulous consideration and scrutiny of various factors, such as data accuracy and reliability, sensor compatibility and integration, data management and interpretation, privacy and data security, user acceptance and comfort, cost and accessibility, and ethical considerations.

Anticipating the future, the potential of sensor technology, amalgamation with artificial intelligence and machine learning algorithms, virtual and augmented reality, longitudinal tracking, and merger with wearable technology and smart devices presents a highly advantageous prospect for the area of physical training. These advances will make it possible to increase the accuracy and effectiveness of biometric sensors, enabling the optimization of training methodologies and the consequent improvement in the performance of athletes, and the promotion of health and well-being.

The use of biometric sensors in training has revolutionized and continues to revolutionize the way athletes commit to training, through the assessment of their progress and consequent improvement in their performance.

The data collected from the biometric sensors are fundamental for the adequate decision making, which is base for the adaptation of the training protocols aligned with the individual needs of athletes, and consequent improvement in performance.

Through ongoing research, technological innovations, and scrupulous ethical considerations, the incorporation of biometric sensors is poised to play an increasingly influential role in the landscape of physical training, enabling athletes to scale previously unattainable heights of achievement and attain their optimal capacity.

References

1. Alghamdi, W.Y.: A novel deep learning method for predicting athletes' health using wearable sensors and recurrent neural networks. Decis. Anal. J. **7**, 1–13 (2023). https://doi.org/10.1016/j.dajour.2023.100213
2. Ancillao, A., Tedesco, S., Barton, J., O'Flynn, B.: Indirect measurement of ground reaction forces and moments by means of wearable inertial sensors: a systematic review. Sensors **18**(8), 2564 (2018). https://doi.org/10.3390/s18082564
3. Aroganam, G., Manivannan, N., Harrison, D.: Review on wearable technology sensors used in consumer sport applications. Sensors **19**(9), 1–26 (2019). https://doi.org/10.3390/s19091983
4. Bates, M.: The rise of biometrics in sports. IEEE Pulse **11**(3), 25–28 (2020). https://doi.org/10.1109/MPULS.2020.2993708
5. Blasco, J., Chen, T.M., Tapiador, J., Peris-Lopez, P.: A survey of wearable biometric recognition systems. ACM Comput. Surv. (CSUR) **49**(3), 1–35 (2016). https://doi.org/10.1145/2968215
6. Browne, J.D., et al.: Lifestyle modification using a wearable biometric ring and guided feedback improve sleep and exercise behaviors: a 12-Month randomized, placebo-controlled study. Front. Physiol. **2**, 1–16 (2021). https://doi.org/10.3389/fphys.2021.777874
7. Buller, M.J., Delves, S.K., Fogarty, A.L., Veenstra, B.J.: On the real-time prevention and monitoring of exertional heat illness in military personnel. J. Sci. Med. Sport **24**(10), 975–981 (2021). https://doi.org/10.1016/j.jsams.2021.04.008
8. Cilliers, L.: Wearable devices in healthcare: privacy and information security issues. Health Inf. Manage. J. **49**(2–3), 150–156 (2020). https://doi.org/10.1177/1833358319851684
9. Foster, C., Rodriguez-Marroyo, J.A., De Koning, J.J.: Monitoring training loads: the past, the present, and the future. Int. J. Sports Physiol. Perform. **12**, 1–7 (2017). https://doi.org/10.1123/IJSPP.2016-0388

10. Gravina, R., Fortino, G.: Wearable body sensor networks: state-of-the-art and research directions. IEEE Sens. J. **21**(11), 12511–12522 (2020). https://doi.org/10.1109/JSEN.2020.304 4447

11. Gupta, S., Kacimi, M., Crispo, B.: Step & turn—a novel bimodal behavioral biometric-based user verification scheme for physical access control. Comput. Secur. **118**, 1–14 (2022). https://doi.org/10.1016/j.cose.2022.102722

12. Hill, C.: Wearables–the future of biometric technology? Biometric Technol. Today **2015**(8), 5–9 (2015). https://doi.org/10.1016/S0969-4765(15)30138-7

13. Jeon, H., Lee, C.: Internet of Things Technology: Balancing privacy concerns with convenience. Telematics Inform. **70**, 1–12 (2022). https://doi.org/10.1016/j.tele.2022.101816

14. Khan, S., Parkinson, S., Grant, L., Liu, N., Mcguire, S.: Biometric systems utilising health data from wearable devices: applications and future challenges in computer security. ACM Comput. Surv. (CSUR) **53**(4), 1–29 (2020). https://doi.org/10.1145/3400030

15. Kristoffersson, A., Lindén, M.: A systematic review of wearable sensors for monitoring physical activity. Sensors **22**(2), 573 (2022). https://doi.org/10.3390/s22020573

16. Li, R.T., Kling, S.R., Salata, M.J., Cupp, S.A., Sheehan, J., Voos, J.E.: Wearable performance devices in sports medicine. Sports Health **8**(1), 74–78 (2016). https://doi.org/10.1177/194173 8115616917

17. Liu, J., Huang, G., Hyyppä, J., Li, J., Gong, X., Jiang, X.: A survey on location and motion tracking technologies, methodologies and applications in precision sports. Expert Syst. Appl. **229**, 1–19 (2023). https://doi.org/10.1016/j.eswa.2023.120492

18. Mekruksavanich, S., Jitpattanakul, A.: Biometric user identification based on human activity recognition using wearable sensors: an experiment using deep learning models. Electronics **10**(3)(308), 1–21 (2021). https://doi.org/10.3390/electronics10030308

19. Nithya, N., Nallavan, G.: Role of wearables in sports based on activity recognition and biometric parameters: a survey. En IEEE (Ed.), In: 2021 International Conference on Artificial Intelligence and Smart Systems (ICAIS) (pp. 1700–1705). IEEE, (págs. 1700–1705) (2021). Obtenido de https://ieeexplore.ieee.org/stamp/stamp.jsp?tp=&arnumber=9395761

20. Ometov, A., Shubina, V., Klus, L.S., Saafi, S., Pascacio, P., Lohan, E.S.: A survey on wearable technology: History, state-of-the-art and current challenges. Comput. Netw. **193**, 108074 (2021). https://doi.org/10.1016/j.comnet.2021.108074

21. Patel, V., Chesmore, A., Legner, C.M., Pandey, S.: Trends in workplace wearable technologies and connected-worker solutions for next-generation occupational safety, health, and productivity. Adv. Intell. Syst. **4**(1), 1–20 (2022). https://doi.org/10.1002/aisy.202100099

22. Rana, M., Mittal, V.: Wearable sensors for real-time kinematics analysis in sports: a review. IEEE Sens. J. **21**(2), 1187–1207 (2020). https://doi.org/10.1109/JSEN.2020.3019016

23. Sazonov, E.: Wearable sensors: fundamentals, implementation and applications. Academic Press (2020)

24. Siekańska, M., Bondar, R.Z., di Fronso, S., Blecharz, J., Bertollo, M.: Integrating technology in psychological skills training for performance optimization in elite athletes: A systematic review. Psychol. Sport Exerc. **57**, 1–24 (2021). https://doi.org/10.1016/j.psychsport.2021. 102008

25. Su, X., Tong, H., Ji, P.: Activity recognition with smartphone sensors. Tsinghua Sci. Technol. **19**(3), 235–249 (2014). Obtenido de https://ieeexplore.ieee.org/stamp/stamp.jsp?arnumber=6838194

26. Tan, T., et al.: A scoping review of portable sensing for out-of-lab anterior cruciate ligament injury prevention and rehabilitation. npj Digital Med. **6**(1)(46), 1–13 (2023). https://doi.org/10.1038/s41746-023-00782-2

27. Vijayan, V., Connolly, J.P., Kelvey, N., Gardiner, P.: Review of wearable devices and data collection considerations for connected health. Sensors **21**(16), 5589 (2021)
28. Zadeh, A., Taylor, D., Bertsos, M., Tillman, T., Nosoudi, N., Bruce, S.: Predicting sports injuries with wearable technology and data analysis. Inf. Syst. Front. **23**, 1023–1037 (2021). https://doi.org/10.1007/s10796-020-10018-3

A Domain Specific Language Proposal for Internet of Things Oriented to Smart Agro

Alexander Guerrero[1], Daniel Samaniego[1], Darwin Alulema[1][(⊠)] [ID],
Mayerly Saenz[2] [ID], and Verónica Alulema[1]

[1] Universidad de Las Fuerzas Armadas-ESPE, Sangolquí, Ecuador
doalulema@espe.edu.ec
[2] Universidad Politécnica Salesiana, Quito, Ecuador

Abstract. Currently, the convergence of hardware and software is aimed at future smart cities through the use of the Internet of Things, which will need to bring together various technologies, and where television has great potential to remotely control domestic objects and indicate detailed information about them. This technological development in all productive sectors, especially agriculture, can be taken to a higher level through the automation of processes, by generating detailed information in real time for decision making. This work proposes an automatic mechanism for the development of applications focused on the Smart Agro domain through the use of a metamodel, graphical DSL and source code generation. For the verification of the operation, a system test scenario has been implemented based on the monitoring of a home orchard.

Keywords: – Web of Things · Domain Specific Leanguage · Metamodel · Smart Agro · Digital Terrestrial Television

1 Introduction

The technological transition resulting from the advent of Industry 4 uses technologies such as WoT to achieve the integration of information obtained from sensors and actuators that are integrated in very diverse fields such as transportation, industry, education, agriculture, among others (Efeagro, 2020). In this context, MDE (Model Driven Engineering) can be useful to achieve convergence between heterogeneous technologies. The Smart Agro concept proposes the use of low-cost power consumption devices and the use of the Web of things for the standardization of services so that the system is compatible with other projects.

The following work proposes the design of a graphical DSL for which we propose: a metamodel that complies with the abstract syntax according to the interactivity characteristics of DTT (Carvalho, 2007) together with WoT, a graphical editor consisting of a canvas and tool palette, finally a model to text transformation engine in order to generate software artifacts for DTT, web services and arduino. In summary, model-driven engineering (MDE) is a useful methodology for the development of IoT applications in smart agro. These mode-los capture the different aspects of the system and allow abstracting

T. Guarda et al. (Eds.): ARTIIS 2023, CCIS 1936, pp. 140–148, 2024.
https://doi.org/10.1007/978-3-031-48855-9_11

its complexity. In the context of smart agro, models can represent IoT devices, sensors, actuators, business rules and other relevant elements.

M2T, on the other hand, is a technique used in DEM to automatically generate code (Ciccozzi, 2017), documentation or other artifacts from the models. In the case of IoT applications in smart agro, M2T can be used to generate the source code that implements the specific functionality of IoT devices and their interaction with backend systems.

This paper presents sections such as the work previously done where a bibliometric analysis is performed in order to obtain current information on the topics related to the project. In the design stage, the general architecture of the project is presented. The implementation stage details the process of creating the graphic editor and code generation based on the design architecture. In the functional tests section, the usability, load and function point tests to which the system was subjected are detailed. Finally, conclusions and future work are presented to present the results of the research.

2   Architecture Design

The DSL consists of a metamodel, a graphical editor and a model-to-text transformation. These are in accordance with the system architecture as follows: For the system called IoTV focused on Smart Agro, the orchestrator has been arranged as the backbone which handles requests and requests from sensors and actuators, which are managed by the controller. It also allows the operation of the web service based on REST services. With this architecture, it opens the way to the inclusion of the Digital Terrestrial Television domain, especially to the creation of remote interactive applications (Fig. 1).

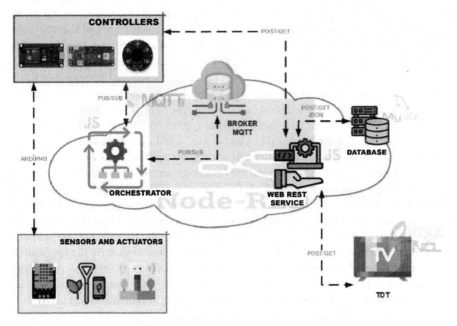

Fig. 1. Proposed system architecture

For the abstraction of the characteristics corresponding to the DTT, the Ginga middleware is considered, with which templates are defined for the user interface. These templates facilitate the design of interactive applications, allowing to establish different multimedia resources and modifying their dimension and position parameters. For the modeling of the API Rest, the host and port are considered, to make HTTP requests from the required resources. In the case of the Database, it allows to file data in separate tables, one for sensors in an incremental way with established measurement parameters for Smart Agro such as: temperature, humidity (environmental), lighting and moisture, which is the soil moisture; and another for actuators, which in this case should consist of tables corresponding to LED, irrigation and fan, which should store their states, being these: ON or OFF, these states are updated and are not stored in an incremental way.

The orchestrator establishes controls the interaction between the DTT and the hardware elements under threshold values defined by the user. The actions that the orchestrator performs are set by the specifier. The hardware must be connected via Wi-Fi to the Internet, must be able to read analog and digital data, and must be low power consumption devices so that they can be powered by a portable power supply.

2.1 Metamodel

For the construction of the metamodel, several modules that describe the parameters of each element are considered in the metamodel (Fig. 2): (a) Controller, is a parent class that has attributes to establish communication to the Internet and the entire system; (b) Sensors, this parent class is composed of a denoted attribute name of EString type to identify the sensors to be used in the systems, in addition three daughter classes have been established depending on the types of sensors compatible with the controllers used in the system. The first daughter class is called dht and corresponds to the digital sensor dht11 which can deliver both the measurement of temperature and humidity, also details an atribute called pin EString type which defines the pin through which it will be connected to the controller. The second daughter class called senanalogic corresponds to the analog type sensors. The third child class called sendigital corresponds to the digital type sensors, it has similar attributes to those of the senanalogic class with the difference that the pin to be used must be of digital type. The parent class Actuators has a child class called actdigital with name attribute type of option typeactuator to identify the actuators (led, fan, irrigation) that can be used within the system. For the REST services the class apirest has been defined with attributes host, port to connect to the web server that contains this service and the parameter textotal to identify the maximum number of crops to interact within the DTT application. The parent class called Tdt in which the name of the device and the programming (video) to be played will be defined by means of the attributes name and program correspondingly. Once the parent class is defined, the subclass called App is defined to establish the background that will host the other elements of the DTT with attributes such as name to identify the application, background to establish an image that will be superimposed on the current programming, the extension of the image must be established (jpg or png), the remaining attributes are to position and delimit the background. Child classes are also obtained that co-

Respond to the different buttons and elements (text, image and video) that can be visualized through their action, an abstract class called Buttons is defined, which contains

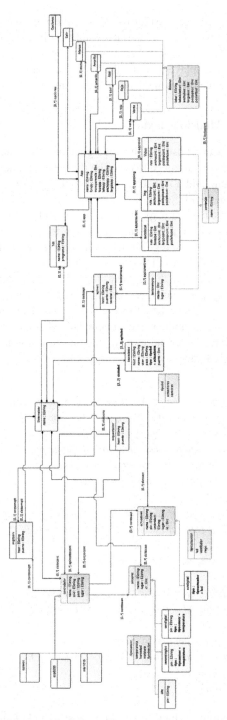

Fig. 2. Metamodel of the architecture of the proposed system

attributes for the configuration of the buttons. Among the main ones are label to define the labels, labelsizebot to define the size of the labels and the remaining parameters determine the position and size. The Img class allows inserting images, the path attribute defines the name of the image to be displayed. While the Video class allows inserting.mp4 format videos only by defining the file name inside the path attribute.

2.2 Transformación Modelo a Texto

The Acceleo tool has been chosen as the code generation engine because it allows to establish a general-purpose language to describe the behavior and functionality of each component of the system, and also because it allows to access the characteristics of the graphical model designed with Sirius.

For the creation of the files corresponding to the controllers, the "for" function allows the creation of the code of the n elements belonging to the controller class while the "if" function allows the code to be generated from the existence of a specific controller (MKR 1010, ESP8266 or OPLA IoT).

In the following lines of code, the variables that will occupy each sensor and actuator directly related to each type of controller are established, by means of the "for" statement the classes defined for sensors or actuators are accessed and according to their type the name corresponding to the attribute name and pin defined as attributes in the metamodel are assigned as a variable. Under the same logic, the subscriptions of these variables to the MQTT server are created.

```
[for (tiposen : senanalogico | cont. conttosen)]
[if (tiposen.tipo.toString() = 'iluminacion')]
int [tiposen.name/];
int const [tiposen.name/]pin=[tiposen.pin/];
[for (tipoact : actdigital | cont.conttoact))
[if (tipoact.tipo.toString() = 'led')]
int [tipoact.name/];
const int [tipoact.name/]pin=[tiposact.pin/];
[for (tipoact : actdigital | cont.conttoact))
[if (tipoact.tipo.toString() = 'led')]
client.subscribe("jardin/[tipoact.name/]");
[/if]
[if (tipoact.tipo.toString() = 'ventilador')]
client.subscribe("jardin/[tipoact.name/]");
[/if]
[if (tipoact.tipo.toString() = 'riego')]
client.subscribe("jardin/[tipoact.name/]");
[/if]
[/for]
```

Defining the above logic, which is based on the sweep of elements and comparison with each type of sensor or actuator, we can see in the following lines of code, the general codes for reading data from the physical quantities and change of state on the actuator pins.

```
[for (tiposen : senanalogico | cont. conttosen)]
[if (tiposen.tipo.toString() = 'humedad')]
//read humidity value
int [tiposen.name/]aux = analogRead([tiposen.name/]pin);
[tiposen.name/]aux1 = [tiposen.name/]aux * ((3.3 / 1023.0) * 100);
client.publish("jardin/[tiposen.name/]", [tiposen.name/]aux1);
[/if]
[/for]
[for (tipoact : actdigital | cont.conttoact)]
[if (tipoact.tipo.toString()='led')]
if(topic=="jardin/[tipoact.name/]"){
    Serial.print("[tipoact.name/]: ");
    if(messageTemp == "true"){
       digitalWrite([tipoact.name/], HIGH);
       Serial.print("On");
    }
    else if(messageTemp == "false"){
       digitalWrite([tipoact.name/], LOW);
       Serial.print("Off");
    }
}
```

For the generation of the database files as shown in the following code lines, the existence of the created element is verified in the graphic editor and the databases are created with the name according to the assigned class (sensors or actuators), each table within the databases will be created with the name of the attribute name of the sensors or actuators and two columns will be defined with initial data 1 (id) and 0 (value of the sensor magnitude or actuator status).

```
[for (auxbd : basedatos | a.sisttobd)]
 [if (auxbd.tipo.toString()='sensores')]
 [file ('basedatos/'.concat('sensores.sql'), false)]
 CREATE TABLE [tiposen.name/]hum` (
    `id` int(11) NOT NULL,
    `dato` float DEFAULT NULL
 ) Engine = InnoDB DEFAULT CHARSET = utf8mb4;
 INSERT INTO `[tiposen.name/]hum` (`id`, `dato`) VALUES (1, 0);
```

After creating the ".ncl" file, it is also necessary to generate the ". Lua" file that will contain the script to perform the remote connection with the web server, for this purpose it is first verified that the remote text element is defined within the DTT app, then the attributes of the APIREST, sensors and actuators classes are used in order to perform GET and POST requests to access and modify the information within the database so that the actuators can operate manually or for the activation of the orchestrator that will allow the system to operate automatically.

3 Proposal Validation

Two types of tests have been proposed: (a) Function point testing and (b) Usability testing. The function points are based on the analysis of the software measurement, they try to determine the functionality that an application or software provides to the final users, the aspects that must be considered to carry out this analysis are the following ones:

- Function Point count planning.
- Collection of current system information.
- Calculation of the adjustment factor and weight factor.
- Performing the counting of transactions and logical files.
- Organization and classification of the components.
- Review of the general characteristics of the system.
- Tabulation and validation of the results.

The procedure to perform these tests begins with the determination of the types of count and functional components, the IFPUG-FPA defines 5 elements: internal logical file, external interface file, external input, external output, and external query, the latter two differ in the output produce aggregate values, while the queries only refer to the content of the files and present them in lists.

Subsequently, a level of complexity is assigned to each component, these levels depend on factors such as repetition of elements, number of files created, number of external outputs, among others. The higher the number of elements, the higher the complexity level should be assigned.

Once the function points have been assigned, the number of unadjusted function points (FPAS) is summed, and the number of unadjusted function points is obtained. Finally, an adjustment factor defined by IFPUG-FPA is applied, obtained from all the components of the system, and represented by a table of parameters, the adjusted function points (FPA) will be:

$$FPA = FPAS * [0.65 + (0.01 * Factor)].$$

To estimate man-hours or man-days from the FPA results, a conversion factor must be applied, which is obtained from historical equipment productivity data for each functionality described in the previous tables.

Usability tests (SUS) are used to evaluate how easy a product is to use for end users, allowing the developer to know the degree of user satisfaction in a specific scenario. The main characteristics of these tests are the following:

- They are based on a short questionnaire that does not require many resources to administer.
- It is a quick method to implement and analyze, just copy, paste, and modify according to the scenario.

- It is a method that requires between 8 to 12 people to perform the analysis.

Once the questionnaire is completed, the evaluation process of the SUS tests consists of the following steps:

- Subtract 1 from the score of each odd question.
- Subtract 5 from the score of each even numbered question.
- Add up the scores obtained.
- Multiply the total by 2.5.

The total SUS test score can be compared to the following metrics:

- Scores above 80.3 corresponds to an "A" grade, which means that people are satisfied with the application and will recommend it to their friends.
- Scores greater than, equal to or less than 68 corresponds to a grade of "C", which means that the application was performed correctly, but could be improved.
- Scores below 51 correspond to a grade of "F", which means that the application should be corrected immediately, and usability should be prioritized.

4 Conclusions

A DSL was developed based on Model Driven Engineering, which consists of a meta-model defined by parent and child classes, the corresponding relationships were used for composition, reference and supertype elements, these relationships describe the convergence between DTT, IOT, Smart Agro and different software tools (API REST, Orchestrator, MQTT, Node-RED), IOT, Smart Agro and different software tools (API REST, Orchestrator, MQTT, Node-RED), in addition, the use of classifiers by numbering was used for the classes that determined execution limits in terms of types of sensors, actuators and databases; The attributes within each class were obtained through a high level of abstraction, analyzing the constitution of each of the hardware and software elements through previous performance tests.

With the use of the Sirius tool in Eclipse it was possible to develop a graphical editor based on the classes and relationships previously defined, from this was created in the first instance the representation by which the editor is attached with the properties arranged in the metamodel, it highlights the importance of the use of containers that allowed the generation of grouped nodes and connectors under common characteristics such as Digital Television, This favored the establishment of the tool palette in an orderly and assimilable way for the user, in this same sense, the Sirius tool provides the ease of use of restrictions with respect to the number of elements, connections, deletion and reconnection actions, always under the logic established by the metamodel.

With the use of the function points it was verified that designing and implementing the system would take approximately 648 h or an equivalent of 4.67 months, due to the number of tools used, while with the use of the DSL it would take approximately 4 h, thus minimizing the effort and time of the developers.

Acknowledgments. This work has been supported by the Universidad de las Fuerzas Armadas ESPE grant 2022-EXT-003 ESPE and by the Universidad Tecnológica Indoamérica through the project "Cyber-Physical Systems for Smart Environments-SCEIN" with funding code INV-0012-031.

References

1. Ciccozzi.: MDE4IoT: Supporting the Internet of Things with Model-Driven Engineering. In: International, S. (ed.) Intelligent Distributed Computing X, Badica, pp. 67–76. Publishing, Cham (2017)
2. Czarnecki, K., Helsen, S.: Classification of Model Transformation Approaches. (2003)
3. Brajesh De. 2017. API Testing Strategy. 153–164. https://doi.org/10.1007/978-1- 4842-1305-6_9
4. de Carvalho, E.R.: The Brazilian digital television system access device architecture. J. Braz. Comput. Soc. 12(4), 95–113 (2007). https://doi.org/10.1590/S0104-65002007000100009
5. EFEAGRO. 2020. "Smart Agro", la tecnología al servicio de la agricultura en América Latina. https://efeagro.com/smart-agro-tecnologia-agricultura/
6. Gonzalez Garcia, C, 2014. Midgar: domain-specific language to generate smart objects for an internet of things platform. In: 2014 Eighth International Conference on Innovative Mobile and Internet Services in Ubiquitous Computing . IEEE. https://doi.org/10.1109/imis.2014.48
7. Jutadhamakorn, P., Pillavas, T., Visoottiviseth, V., Takano, R., Haga, J., Kobayashi, D. A scalable and low-cost MQTT broker clustering system, pp 1–5. https://doi.org/10.1109/INCIT. 2017.8257870 (2017)
8. Lara, J., Guerra, E., Sanchez Cuadrado, J. 2015. Model-driven engineering with domain-specific meta-modelling languages. Softw. Syst. Model. 14, 1 (Feb 2015), 429–459. https:// doi.org/10.1007/s10270-013-0367-z
9. León, J.: Contributions to the design and development process of interactive applications for digital TV based on Ging ga-NCL. Ph. D. Dissertation (2011)
10. Niknejad, N.: Understanding Service-Oriented Architecture (SOA): A systematic literature review and directions for further investigation. Inf. Syst. 91, 101491 (2020). https://doi.org/ 10.1016/j.is.2020.101491
11. OMG. 2001. MDA (Model Driven Architecture). www.omg.org/mda/
12. da Silva, A.R.: Model-driven engineering: a survey supported by the unified conceptual model. Comput. Lang. Syst. Struct. 43(2015), 139–155 (2015). https://doi.org/10.1016/j.cl.2015. 06.001
13. Rodriguez. 1999. Los Puntos de Funcionalidad (Function Points). Universidad de Castilla-La Mancha. (1999), 9 – 34.
14. Alencar, M.S.: Digital Television Systems. Cambridge University Press (2009). https://doi. org/10.1017/CBO9780511609732
15. Soares, L.F.G., Rodrigues, R.F., Moreno, M.F.: Ginga-NCL: the declarative environment of the Brazilian digital TV system. J. Braz. Compu. Soc. 12(4), 37–46 (2007). https://doi.org/ 10.1590/S0104-65002007000100005
16. Daniel, F., Matera, M.: Model-Driven Software Development. In: Mashups. DSA, pp. 71–93. Springer, Heidelberg (2014). https://doi.org/10.1007/978-3-642-55049-2_4
17. Sun, L., Li, Y., Memon, R.A.: An open IoT framework based on microservices architecture. China Commun. 14(2), 154–162 (2017). https://doi.org/10.1109/CC.2017.7868163

Survey Based Analysis on Processed Food and Organic Consumption Pattern in India

Kushi Jain[1], Jose Swaminathan[1]([⊠]) [iD], and Dewar Rico-Bautista[2] [iD]

[1] Vellore Institute of Technology, Vellore, India
jose.s@vit.ac.in
[2] Universidad Francisco de Paula Santander, Ocaña, Colombia
dwricob@ufpso.edu.co

Abstract. When pandemic is making inroads into every nation and India being affected much in the second wave, it is necessary to investigate the factors that would add to the immunity and nutritional value of the human being. Changes in food consumption are characterized by an increased awareness in reducing calories intakes and a change in the food habits towards more meat and dairy products. Work from home has brought awareness among public to improve the immunity and the diets containing more protein is considered as a better option. Sedentary working environment is taking a toll on the normal functioning of a family and a lot of time is spent on the professional work, and an easy option for a nuclear family is to depend more on processed or semi-processed food. However, processed food has its own merits and demerits. In some cases, it cannot replace the nutritional values present in fresh fruits and vegetables. This study aims at finding out the purchase pattern of consumers and analyses the purchase pattern using statistical tools. Study was conducted using survey methods in the southern part of India and it would help the reader to understand the prevailing situation better.

Keywords: Processed Food · Semi-Processed Food · Nutritional Value · Purchase Pattern

1 Introduction

Changes in food consumption are characterized by an increased awareness in reducing calories intakes and a change in the food habits towards more meat and dairy products. Onset of pandemic has brought awareness among public to improve the immunity and the diets containing more protein is considered as a better option. It is noted that the young adults are more towards food richer in saturated fats and cholesterol. Young adults were more inclined to eating less fruits and vegetables as their income is less compared to peers [1]. An individual's decision making, and behavior also plays an important role in food selection and consumption. World Health Organization's (WHO) guideline suggests that eating seasonal fruits, green vegetables, lentils, beans, unprocessed maize, whole grains, millet, oats, brown rice, or roots such as potato, yam, taro or cassava,

T. Guarda et al. (Eds.): ARTIIS 2023, CCIS 1936, pp. 149–158, 2024.
https://doi.org/10.1007/978-3-031-48855-9_12

and meat, fish, eggs, and milk is very important to maintain good immunity during pandemic [2]. However, the consumer preferences and demand driven by changing food environments makes the food industry to produce processed food to cater to the customer needs. In the past two decades there is huge transformation of the food sector, and the growth is driven by changes in food consumption and the entry of women into workforce. Processed food offers an easy solution to the busy lifestyle. Even during pandemic driven lockdowns work from home is driving many customers to opt for processed food which is easily available. Processed food in this study refers to the cooked, semi-cooked, canned, packaged or food with preservatives. Organic food refers to the natural and unaltered food without any added ingredients.

Bigger markets or super and shopping complexes are built in huge areas on a single and multilevel and is near many residential areas within the reach of many consumers. This gives a huge choice of food under a single roof at an affordable price. Some of these markets are open throughout the year and allocates huge budgets for advertising thereby attracting many customers and luring them to buy processed food for easy consumption. This research focuses on the consumption patter of the customers. A questionnaire based study was conducted and the results are presented.

2 Literature Review

A thorough study of literature was conducted to compare the food consumption pattern of various customers; research [3] has pointed out that the living area affects people's food choices and nutrition. This study has presented that promoting health benefits of fruits and vegetables would help the consumers to buy more products that add desirable nutrients to their food intake. This study also analyzed the customers of supermarkets and established the fact that higher consumption of processed food is by these customers, and they consume less quantity of unprocessed foods. Regression model is used in this study. This study also investigated the connection between purchase of processed food and the impact of that on people's body mass index, as well as on other important health indicators such as fasting blood glucose, hyper blood pressure, and the metabolic syndrome data. [4] have studied the purchasing pattern of customers in supermarkets and the connection of the food and child nutrition from urban Kenya. This study presented the results related to the height, age, weight scores based on the data collected. Finding show that the obesity in children is not connected with purchase in supermarkets. Varieties of food and dietary guide provided by the supermarkets have had a positive effect on children nutrition.

From the research paper published [5] based on a study in Indonesia points out that it was found that there was no conclusive evidence of proven significance or direct connection between the purchase in supermarkets and food diversity and diet diversity in the households. Rather, it was found that super market food expenditure may have a significant association with diet quality through indirect linkages. [6] analysed 1800 responses from urban Indonesian consumers and presented the fact that there is no relationship between food expenditure and healthiness of customers food purchase. Regression models were employed in this study. [7] conducted a study in Zambia to find out the influence of modern retailers on consumers' choice of food purchase and pattern of diet. It was found that consumers were positively influenced by the modern retailers and they were moving towards buying more of processed food. Income and social economic factors were also playing a major role in this pattern of purchase. Other major stores and kiosk also played a major role in consumers buying processed food and it clearly depicts the fact that not only modern retailers, but other stores and kiosks were also a part of this pattern of purchasesa.

Based on the study conducted [8] it is found out that more consumption of food and decrease in calories intake has led to increased weight, obesity and other non-communicable sicknesses. Price of the commodities, consumer goods, incentives to promote correct body mass index were a few of the factors taken for analysis in this study. [9] found that special offers, discounts, assured quality, easily available local brands, attractive display of commodities in a super market, friendly behavior of salesmen, good choice for children, ample parking space are considered as vital factors while designing a super market and it is definitely having a huge impact on the Indian customers and is changing their purchase behavior. [10] found that easy access to a well stacked super market or a convenience store was not having a significant impact on the fruits consumption of customers. Similarly proximity of a supermarket was not impacting the purchase of food or consumption pattern. In a study by Popkin [11], it is vividly mentioned that the food value chain is shifting quickly and a few issues are left unattended to that are related to the nutrition of communities and health concerns. Analyzing various studies has not presented a very clear picture on the consumption of processed food or the dietary pattern of the consumers. This study is designed to address this problem with a systematic survey and analysis.

3 Methodology

Increasing consumption of processed and fast food is a challenge to nutrition security. The main issue is to find out how fast-moving life has influenced the dietary pattern. The study is carried out to determine processed and unprocessed food consumption pattern of consumers of various age groups. Main objective is to study the consumption pattern of processed food and unprocessed food of consumers; To evaluate the purchasing frequency of processed and unprocessed food; To study the factors influencing the food consumption patterns of consumers; To study how supermarket shopping affects the diet and nutrition consumption of consumers.

This study has used descriptive research including survey and fact finding by consulting the respondents through questionnaire (close ended questions). This type of research uses questions asked to the respondent to know about their preferences related to the study. This becomes the most important tool for carrying out the research. Surveys conducted give a clear insight into proposed study and are very useful while conducting no experimental studies/design. It is considered as a traditional way of research to present the real facts.

A sample size of 200 respondents was taken in this research and the respondents were from the southern part of India. Through questionnaire; responses were collected. Personal interviews, face to face interaction with consumers, and field works were used to collect the data. After collecting the primary data, published reports related to this study, were considered to collect secondary data. Simple percentage analysis, chi-square analysis, correlation techniques, were the various tools used in this study for analysis and interpretation of results.

4 Analysis and Interpretation

In the responses collected 47% of the respondents were male and 53% female, the responses were of the age group of 25 to 60 years. Among the respondents 61% were married. 55% of the respondents were at least a university degree holder. It shows that many of the respondents were well educated and well-informed group in the society. Income of the respondents varies from 150 to 1000 USD per month. 35% of the respondents have an income less than 150 USD per month.

Employees from private, government, constitute to 60%, self-employed 14% and 11% were students. 9% of the respondents went to the nearby supermarket more than four times a month. 63% of the respondents visited two times per month. It is noticed that 68% of the consumers purchased processed and semi-processed food. Only 21% purchased fresh food. Personal interviews with the consumers revealed the fact that processed foods are time saving (21%), tasty (30%), convenient to use, healthy and nutritional (5%). Only 19% of the consumers pointed out that processed or semi processed food is unhealthy.

It is found that 35% of the respondents consumed processed or semi-processed occasionally and 6% took processed food daily. 59% of the respondents consumed processed food a few times in a month. On the flip side 9% of the consumers bought fresh food daily, 74% purchased fresh food a few times per month. 83% of the respondents accepted the fact that fresh good is tasty and it is easily available in the southern part of India. 17% preferred fresh food, because of the nutritional quality available. 26% of the consumers found that processed food easily available in the supermarkets close to their residence and it drove them to buy processed food. 54% of the consumers were influenced by affordable price and attractive advertisements for processed food. 61% of the consumers came out with a very valid reason that processed food makes cooking much easier and paves way for them to spend more time with the family. 21% have presented that even children could be independent and have food of their choice if processed food is available at home. 27% of the consumers have seen an increase in their expenditure as they are buying processed food.

However, 42% of the consumers were able to balance the budget and keep it same even though they were buying processed food. 52% of the respondents have given up the habit of eating fresh fruits and vegetables, because of the frequent usage of processed or semi-processed food. 33% of the consumers have reduced or eliminated the usage of raw spices in their cooking, because of the easy availability of processed food. Even though usage of processed or semi-processed food has increased 39% of the respondents feel that it is not helping in improving the time with the family. Only 33% of the consumers express those using processed or semi-processed food increases the time they spent with the family. Half of the respondents have declared that their diet plan has changed because of the ready and easy availability of processed food. 55% of the respondents have pointed out that their food consumption pattern itself has significantly changed as processed food is available easily. Food habits are also changing considerably is the take of 68% of respondents.

Using the data collected a chi-square test was conducted to establish the fact that the food consumption pattern changed in both genders due to processed food use.

H 1: There is association between consumption patterns in both the genders due to processed food use. It was noted that Chi-Square statistic, $\chi 2 = 1.021$, df $= 3$ and p > 0.05; Chi-square value is more than the table value. Hence there is no association between food consumption pattern changes in both genders due to processed food use. Hence null hypothesis is accepted, and alternative hypothesis is rejected.

H 2: There is an association between age and other factors (easy availability, price, advertisement) influencing the purchase of processed food products. The minimum expected count is .68. Chi-Square statistic, value $= 11.606$, df $= 12$, and p < 0.05; Chi-square value is less than the table value. There is association between age and factors (easy availability, price, advertisement) influencing the purchase of processed food products. Hence the null hypothesis is rejected, and alternative hypothesis is accepted.

Pearson correlation was used to find out whether any association existed between age, frequency of purchase and unprocessed food.

H 1: There is an association between age and frequency of purchasing and purchase of unprocessed food products.

H 2: There is no association between age and frequency of purchasing and purchase of unprocessed food products. The correlation is found to be 0.11, which means there is a positive relation between age and frequency of purchasing and purchase of unprocessed food products.

H 3: There is an association between gender and frequency of purchasing of unprocessed food products.

H 4: There is no association between gender and frequency of purchasing of unprocessed food products.

Table 1. Gender [*] changes in food consumption pattern Cross Tabulation.

Count

		Changes in food consumption pattern[*]				Total
		More time available for family	Cooking has become easier	Cooking method has changed	Children can also cook for themselves	
Gender	Male	18	38	13	21	90
	Female	19	52	18	21	110
Total		37	90	31	42	200

[*]Chi-Square test, Table 1 below shows the Gender and food consumption pattern changed due to processed food use. H1: There is association between the gender and food consumption pattern changed due to processed food use.

Gender and purchase of unprocessed food has the correlation of −123 which means there is a negative relation between gender and unprocessed food. So, hypothesis H 3 is rejected, and H 4 is accepted. On the flip side gender and purchase of processed food has the correlation of .094 which means there is a positive relation between gender and processed food.

Table 2. Chi square tests with df 3.

Heading level	Value	df	Asymptotic significance (2-sided)
Pearson Chi-Square	1.021[*]	3	.796
Likelihood Ratio	1.020	3	.796
Linear-by-Linear Association	.071	1	.796
N of Valid Cases	200		

[*]0 cells (0.0%) have expected count less than 5. The minimum expected count is 13.95.

Table 3. Age [*] factor influencing the purchase of processed food products Crosstabulation.

Count

		Factor influencing the purchase of processed food products[*]				Total
		Easy availability	Price	Advertisements	Others	
Age	Below 25	19	13	24	12	68
	25–35	19	22	21	8	70
	35–45	9	9	11	9	38
	45–55	4	4	7	5	20
	Above 55	3	0	1	0	4
Total		54	48	64	34	200

The results presented in Table 3 are related to age of the people purchasing processed food.
[*]Chi-Square statistic, $\chi2 = 1.021$, df = 3 and p > 0.05; Chi – square value is more than the table value. There is no association between gender and food consumption pattern changed due to processed food use. Hence null hypothesis is accepted, and alternative hypothesis is rejected. The above given Table 2 indicates the food consumption pattern changed due to processed food use on gender of 200 respondents, 90 respondents are female, and 110 respondents are male. Table 3 below shows the Age and factor influencing the purchase of processed food products. H2: There is an association between age and factor influencing the purchase of processed food products.

Table 4. Chi square tests with df12.

Heading level	Value	df	Asymptotic Significance (2-sided)
Pearson Chi-Square	11.606[*]	12	.048
Likelihood Ratio	12.044	12	.042
Linear-by-Linear Association	.024	1	.078
N of Valid Cases	200		

[*]6 cells (30.0%) have expected count less than 5. The minimum expected count is .68. Chi-Square statistic, value = 11.606, df = 12, and p < 0.05; Chi – square value is less than the Table 4 value. There is association between age and factor influencing the purchase of processed food products. Hence the null hypothesis is rejected, and alternative hypothesis is accepted, see Table 5.
Pearson correlation.
Hypothesis 0 (H0)- Null hypothesis.
Hypothesis 1 (H1)- The is association between age and frequency of purchasing unprocessed food products.
Hypothesis 2 (H2)- The is association between age and frequency of purchasing processed food products.

Table 5. Correlations.

		Age	Frequency of purchasing unprocessed food products	Frequency of purchasing processed food products
Age	Pearson Correlation	1	.011	.004[*]
	Sig. (2-tailed)		.877	.960
	N	200	200	200
Frequency of purchasing unprocessed food products	Pearson Correlation	.011	1	.092
	Sig. (2-tailed)	.877		.195
	N	200	200	200
Frequency of purchasing processed food products	Pearson Correlation	.004	.092	1
	Sig. (2-tailed)	.960	.195	
	N	200	200	200

[*]Hypothesis: H1 is accepted, Age and purchase of processed food has the correlation of 0.004 which means there is a positive relation between age and processed food.
Hypothesis: H2 is accepted, Hypothesis (H3) - The association between gender and frequency of purchasing unprocessed food products.

5 Conclusions

In this study the responses from 200 respondents across age groups and different sections of people based on occupation and income were collected and analyzed scientifically. Age group varies from 25 to 60 years. Respondents below 25 years of age constituted 35% of the respondents and in the 26 to 35 years group we had 35%. Among the respondents 61% were married. 55% of the respondents were at least a university degree holder. All these details play a significant role in food consumption, and it may be noted that education, marital status, and age are also vital factors that influence food consumption. It shows that many of the respondents were well educated and well-informed group in the society. Income of the respondents varies from 150 to 1000 USD per month. It is noticed that 68% of the consumers purchased processed and semi-processed food. It is found that 35% of the respondents consumed processed or semi-processed occasionally and 6% took processed food daily.

The analysis shows an increase in consumption of processed food in the age groups of children and working population irrespective of their gender. This suggests that the dietary pattern has changed due to processed food as cooking methods became easier to cope up with their busy life. Many respondents perceive processed food to be tasty and time saving. Also, it is noted that the different age groups people have their own purchasing frequency. Their choices are mainly guided by taste, convenient to use and the ease of access. Therefore, awareness can be created among consumers to make right choices amidst the taste and convenience.

Disclosures. Author Contributions: All the authors have contributed equally.

Funding: . No funding.

Conflicts of Interest:. The authors declare there is no conflict of interest.

Questionnaire a Study on Processed and Unprocessed Food Consumption Pattern of Customers

(*Processed Food* - Examples: Tinned vegetables "convenience foods" ready to eat meals Instant meals sausage rolls, pies and pasties, Processed meat products, and soft drinks). (*Unprocessed Food* - Examples: Fruits and vegetables, Whole grain, milk, cheese, unsweetened yogurt, eggs, nuts and seeds).

NAME
1. Gender
a) Male b) Female
2. Age
a) Below 25 b) 25–35 c) 35–45 d) 45–55 e) Above55
3. Marital status
a) Married b) Unmarried
4. Qualification
a) SSLC/HSC b) UG c) PG d) Diploma/ITI e) Others
5. Income in INR per month
a) Below 10000 b) 10000–25000 c) 25000–40000 d) Above40000
6. Occupation
a) Private b) Government c) Self-employed d) Students e) Other
7. Number of visit made in a month
a) 1 Time b) 2 Time c) 3 Time d) 4 Time e) More than 4
8. Type of food purchasing from the market
a) Raw food b) Processed food c) Semi processed food d) Others
9. How do you perceive new processed foods?
a) Time saving b) Tasty c) Unhealthy d) Convenient to use e) Healthy and nutritional
10. How often you purchased the processed food products?
a) Daily b) Weekly c) Monthly d) Occasionally
11. How often you purchased unprocessed food?
a) Daily b) Weekly c) Monthly d) Occasionally
12. What is the main reason for consumption of processed food products?
a) Nutritional quality b) Tasty c) Easy available
13. What are the main factors which influence the purchasing of processed food products?
a) Easy availability b) Price c) Advertisements d) Others
14. How has your food consumption pattern changed due to the processed foods use?
a) More time available for family b) Cooking has become easier c) Cooking method has changed d) Children can also cook for themselves
15. How has your food budget changed due to processed food buying?

a) Increased b) Decreased c) Remains the same

16. What all have been replaced in your regular grocery list due to processed foods?

a) Fresh fruits b) Fresh vegetables c) Raw spices d) Other raw food Material

17. How have the social relations changed due to use of processed foods?

a) More time available for family b) Less time available for family c) Dependency on other resources has increased

18. Has your dietary pattern changed due to processed food?

a) Yes b) No

19. Does your food consumption pattern have a link with supermarkets?

a) Yes b) No

20. Do you think that the food habits are changing due to modern retailers?

a) Yes b) No

References

1. Perera, T., Madhujith, T.: The pattern of consumption of fruits and vegetables by undergraduate students: a case study. Trop. Agricult. Res. **23**, 261 (2012)
2. Galeano-Barrera, C.J., Ospina, M.E.A., García, E.M.M., Rico-Bautista, D., Romero-Riaño, E.: Exploring the evolution of the topics and research fields of territorial development from a comprehensive bibliometric analysis. Sustainability **14**, 6515 (2022)
3. Demmler, K.M., Ecker, O., Qaim, M.: Supermarket shopping and nutritional outcomes: a panel data analysis for urban Kenya. World Dev. **102**, 292–303 (2018)
4. Debela, B.L., Demmler, K.M., Klasen, S., Qaim, M.: Supermarket food purchases and child nutrition in Kenya. Glob. Food Sec. **25**, 100341 (2020)
5. Rupa, J.A., Umberger, W.J., Zeng, D.: Does food market modernisation lead to improved dietary diversity and diet quality for urban Vietnamese households? Austral. J. Agricult. Resour. Econ. **63**, 499–520 (2019)
6. Toiba, H., Umberger, W.J., Minot, N.: Diet transition and supermarket shopping behaviour: is there a link? Bull. Indones. Econ. Stud. **51**, 389–403 (2015)
7. Khonje, M.G., Qaim, M.: Modernization of African food retailing and (un)healthy food consumption. Sustainability **11**, 4306 (2019)
8. Schmidhuber, J., Schmidhuber, J.: The growing global obesity problem: some policy options to address it. Electron. J. Agricult. Develop. Econ. **1**, 272–290 (2004)
9. Rishi, B., Singh, H.: Determinants of supermarket shopping behaviour in an emerging market. J. Bus. Retail Manag. Res. **7** (2012)
10. Pearce, J., Hiscock, R., Blakely, T., Witten, K.: The contextual effects of neighbourhood access to supermarkets and convenience stores on individual fruit and vegetable consumption. J. Epidemiol. Commun. Health **62**, 198–201 (2008)
11. Popkin, B.M.: Nutrition, agriculture and the global food system in low and middle income countries. Food Policy **47**, 91–96 (2014)

Technology and the Generation Gap: How E-Expertise Present in Youths Positively Affects Online Purchases

José Magano[1,2] , Manuel Au-Yong-Oliveira[3,4(✉)] ,
and José Pedro Teixeira Fernandes[2,5]

[1] Research Center in Business and Economics (CICEE), Universidade Autónoma de Lisboa,
1150-293 Lisboa, Portugal
jmagano@iscet.pt
[2] Higher Institute of Business and Tourism Sciences (ISCET), 4050-180 Porto, Portugal
jfernandes@iscet.pt
[3] INESC TEC—Institute for Systems and Computer Engineering, Technology and Science,
4200-465 Porto, Portugal
mao@ua.pt
[4] GOVCOPP, Department of Economics, Management, Industrial Engineering and Tourism,
University of Aveiro, 3810-193 Aveiro, Portugal
[5] Portuguese Institute for International Relations, Nova University of Lisbon (IPRI-Nova),
Lisbon, Portugal

Abstract. This cross-sectional study addresses Portuguese online shoppers'
behavior toward Chinese online retailers, assessing the impact of financial, product, and time-convenience risks and demographic traits on their willingness to
buy from those e-stores. The research relies on a survey of 1,432 participants who
have shopped online at least once. Approximately half of the sample already buys
from Chinese websites; age, financial, and time-convenience risks explain 21.5%
of the variance of their purchase intention. On the other hand, participants who
buy on Chinese websites present significantly lower values of all risks and the
intention to buy from Chinese websites, possibly reflecting a satisfactory transaction experience. Furthermore, a generation gap is evident as younger people feel
more confident in dealing intuitively with and solving online issues, giving them
the confidence necessary to purchase online from Chinese e-stores – perhaps geographically and ideologically distant – but brought closer by e-expertise (online
dexterity).

Keywords: Internet Consumer · Online Shopping · Perceived risk · Online
purchasing intention

1 Introduction

A recent survey held in Portugal [1] documents that the Portuguese public opinion is
somehow suspicious and critical of [Superpower] China in several aspects, namely,
Chinese foreign policy, technology infrastructure, and other Chinese investments in the

T. Guarda et al. (Eds.): ARTIIS 2023, CCIS 1936, pp. 159–174, 2024.
https://doi.org/10.1007/978-3-031-48855-9_13

country, and even China's somewhat ambiguous role during the Covid-19 pandemic, leading to a generally negative image. The above may and should be understood as perhaps part of a greater and very significant growth and evolution path followed by the Chinese economy, which has had side-effects in what is a very specific context and in view of other more lagging economies. Situational involvement influences perceived risk and consumers' trust expectation, which predicts the intention to purchase from an e-retailer [2]. We question whether the subsequent distrust may add to consumers' perceived risk of buying from Chinese websites, thus deterring their online purchase intentions. As such, this research addresses Portuguese online shoppers' behavior toward Chinese online stores. Specifically, it intends to assess if financial, product, and time-convenience risks and demographic traits impact Portuguese online consumers' willingness to buy from Chinese e-retailers.

Consumers' perceived risks impact attitudes toward online shopping and purchase behaviors, as published studies on this theme are still scarce and inconclusive [3]. Among the most frequent issues affecting online purchase intentions are financial apprehensions and low understanding or comfort with the technology or Internet resources, such as vendor rating sites [4, 5] or inability to see or touch the product before purchase [6, 7]. In addition, several authors highlight, among others, three types of risks related to the frequency of online searches with the intent to purchase: financial risk, product performance risk [4, 8, 9] and time-convenience-related issues [5, 6, 10]. Those perceived risks in online shopping negatively influence the intention to buy products online [11].

1.1 Financial Risk

Financial risk conveys the fear of monetary loss from online purchasing [12] and the consumers' accounts being hacked by dishonest elements [8]. Perceived financial risk is the most common risk associated with the online shopping experience [4, 12] and may prevent consumers from spending money online, fearing online scams, identity theft, leaking of confidential information, no money-back guarantee, or manipulation of credit card information by sellers [12]. According to Swinyard and Smith [6], shopper's credit card information should be isolated from the online retailer, as online consumers prefer online stores they associate with financial security; providing an independent and certified declaration of safety attached to the website can mitigate security risk and diminish shoppers' fears. The absence of security in an online shopping environment leads to lower trust and deters intentions toward online shopping [13]. Therefore, we hypothesize:

Hypothesis 1: Financial risk will negatively impact online shopping intentions.

1.2 Product Risk

Product risk conveys the risk perceived from product performance, quality, and value [7], arising from the consumer's inability to inspect products when buying online [8, 14]. Furthermore, there is the risk that, despite all the consumer's effort in online search-ing for information about the product, once delivered, the product will not match the consumer's expectations based on what was initially displayed on the website [3, 15]. In addition, consumers may perceive product risk if the product price is higher with limited information displayed on the website [3]. A study by Han and Kim on consumer purchase intentions at a major Chinese online marketplace found that product risk was negatively associated with consumers' trust and purchase intention, regardless of their degree of product involvement [16]. Hence:

Hypothesis 2: Product risk will negatively impact online shopping intentions.

1.3 Time and Convenience Risk

Convenience risk includes issues experienced during online transactions, frequently resulting from the difficulty of browsing or submitting orders, delays in receiving products, or the lack of adequate product cancellation procedures after ordering [4], resulting in the perception of wasted time or effort put into the purchasing process [10]. In addition, consumers can find a vast number of products and services information on a wide variety of websites; searching and locating the correct information about those products and services and even learning how to use specific online stores can be time-consuming. Time risk is also associated with the time and effort needed to return a product that needs repair and replacement [17]. Therefore:

Hypothesis 3: Time and convenience risk will negatively impact online shopping intentions.

1.4 Demographic Factors

According to several authors, consumer gender and age influence the intention to buy online [e.g., 18–20], being that risk attitude is considered a personality's characteristic standing on the continuum from risk aversion to risk-taking. Prior research has revealed gender differences in risk perceptions; women have higher perceived risks in various domains, including financial, suggesting greater risk aversion and may perceive purchasing online as riskier than men [18]. In addition, Rogers [19] documented women found online shopping less convenient than men, looking at online shopping as a weak social activity compared with shopping in traditional stores; also, they did not shop online because they could not find the products that were convenient for them [20, 21]. However, a study by McKay-Nesbit [22] found that men have more online purchase intentions for hedonic products; still, there were no differences concerning utilitarian products, and in specific product categories, women seem more active online purchasers than men, namely, clothing, food, and fashion-oriented brands [12]. Age is another demographic factor that can be seen as a predictor of online shopping behavior, being that older people are less likely to take risks and more likely to avoid uncertainty [21]. On the other hand, young people are active consumers of online products, namely mobile covers, shoes and clothing, gadgets, music, books, and other articles not available in their local market [12]. Furthermore, Bhatnagar and Ghose found that more educated consumers should be aware of financial and security risks and better understand vendors' efforts to protect their privacy [8]. Hence, we hypothesize:

Hypothesis 4: Differences will be found in the willingness to purchase online between men and women.

Hypothesis 5: Age will impact the willingness to purchase online.

Hypothesis 6: The education level will impact the willingness to purchase online.

2 Methods

2.1 Procedures

All the procedures carried out were based on the principles of the Declaration of Helsinki and its later amendments. A survey was prepared based on a questionnaire with items used in published works by Forsythe et al. [4], Lewis [5], Swinyard and Smith [6], and Chen [7]. All items were translated and back translated into Portuguese by bilingual experts, and the questionnaire protocol was established, to which a section with sociodemographic questions was added. The questionnaire was distributed over the Internet, using the Survey Monkey software, following a convenience and snowball-sampling procedure between 18 January and 17 February 2023. The research protocol included informed consent, and confidentiality and anonymity of the data were guaranteed. The inclusion criteria consisted of Portuguese online shoppers aged 18 or over.

2.2 Measures

The research protocol included a sociodemographic questionnaire (whose questions related to gender, age, education, and job status); a questionnaire related to the type of products purchased online (clothing, shoes, electronics and computers, travel, food and beverage, books, music, games, furniture, other); and items to assess the risk of online buying (financial, product, time-convenience purchase risks) and the intention to buy. Five items that assessed financial risk ($\alpha = 0.72$) were based on Forsythe et al. [4] ("can't trust the online company"; "may not get the product"; "may purchase something by accident"; "my personal information may not be kept"; "my credit card number may not be secure") and one item on Lewis [5] ("I do not purchase online if there is no money back guarantee"). Three items that assess product risk ($\alpha = 0.82$) were adapted from Swinyard and Smith [6] ("I might not get what I ordered through online shopping"; "I might receive malfunctioning merchandise"; "It's hard to judge the quality of merchandise on the Internet") and another two items from Chen et al. [7] ("I am worried about the quality of the products sold online"; "I am worried about the true value of the product I bought online is lower than my expectation"). Time convenience risk ($\alpha = 0.56$) was assessed by four items from Swinyard and Smith [6] ("finding the right product online is difficult"; "if I shop online, I cannot wait till the product arrives"; "I feel that it will be difficult settling disputes when I shop online"; "it's hard to cancel orders") and one from Lewis [5] ("I do not purchase online if there is no free return shipment service available"). All 18 items were rated on a 7-point Likert scale, where 1 corresponds to "totally disagree" and 7 to "completely agree", except item 17, which has a reversed quote. A high score suggests a higher perception of risk. Finally, two items created by the authors assessed the intention to buy ($\alpha = 0.60$) ("I will buy from Chinese online stores"; "the COVID-19 pandemic has reduced my intention to purchase from Chinese online stores").

2.3 Data Analysis

Data were analyzed using SPSS Version 28 and AMOS Version 28, and included specific procedures of descriptive statistics (mean, standard deviation, minimum and maximum) to characterize the sample and items and dimensions, and inferential statistics (group comparison tests, chi-squared tests, *t*-tests for independent proportions, used to examine sociodemographic characteristics, products bought online, and scores concerning financial risk, product risk, time convenience risk, and intention to buy constructs). To assess the constructs' reliability, Cronbach's alpha coefficients were determined ($\alpha >$ 0.6) [18]. In addition, multivariate regression models, one without demographic variables as covariates and another with covariates were conducted to assess the association between risks independent variables and the intention to buy dependent variable.

3 Results

3.1 Sample

The sample comprises 1,423 Portuguese participants who, at least once, have already shopped online. This sample was characterized according to sociodemographic characteristics and participants who have already used and who have never used Chinese sites to make their online purchases (Table 1). More than half of the sample already purchased goods or services from Chinese e-stores; this group of participants is composed of 50 percent of men and 50 percent of women, with university attendance or degree, professionally active, and with an average of 37.7 years old. However, proportionally, there are more women not buying on Chinese sites than buying, as well as more inactive than active people (Table 1).

Table 1. Sample - sociodemographic characteristics.

Socio-demographic variables		N (%)	n (%)	n (%)			
		Total	Purchased from Chinese e-stores				
			No	Yes			
Sample		1423 (100.0)	691 (48.6)	732 (51.4)			
					χ^2	p	Φ
Gender	Female	745 (52.4)	379 (54.8)	366 (50.0)	3.349	0.067	0.049
	Male	678 (47.6)	312 (45.2)	366 (50.0)			
Education	Primary	92 (6.5)	44 (6.4)	48 (6.6)	**8.731**	**0.033**	**0.078**
	Secondary	418 (29.4)	194 (28.1)	224 (30.6)			
	University student	320 (22.5)	139 (20.1)	181 (24.7)			
	University graduate	593 (41.7)	314 (45.4)	279 (38.1)			
Job status	Inactive	242 (17.0)	123 (17.8)	119 (16.3)	0.600	0.439	0.021

(continued)

Table 1. (*continued*)

Socio-demographic variables		N (%)	n (%)	n (%)			
		Total	Purchased from Chinese e-stores				
			No	Yes			
Sample		1423 (100.0)	691 (48.6)	732 (51.4)			
					χ^2	p	Φ
	Active	1181 (83.0)	568 (82.2)	613 (83.7)			
					t	p	d
Age	M ± SD; Min-Max	38.98 ± 16.79; 18–85	40.36 ± 16.85; 18–85	37.68 ± 16.64; 18–85	**3.021**	**0.003**	**0.160**

Notes: N = frequencies; % - percentage; χ^2 = Chi-squared test; t = t-test; p = p-value; d = Cohen effect size; Φ = Phi effect size. In **bold**: statistically significant values

3.2 Products Purchased Online

Whether in the total sample or the different groups (those who have already purchased from Chinese e-stores and those who have not), the most purchased product category is clothing, followed at a distance by computers and electronics; the least bought products are music, furniture, games, and travel (Table 2). Most people that purchase in all product categories, except for shoes and books, also buy from Chinese online stores (Table 2).

Men significantly purchase more than women in electronics and computers, music, games, and other product categories; in contrast, women significantly buy more than men in clothing, food and beverage, books, and furniture categories. In addition, in the product categories where most respondents have purchased (clothing, electronics and computers), the percentage of buyers is significantly higher among the more educated respondents (University attendees or graduates); the same happens in the categories where most respondents have not purchased online, that is, travel, food and beverage, books, music, games, furniture, and other products categories. Table 2 also documents that online consumers are significantly younger concerning clothing, shoes, electronics and computers, and games categories.

3.3 Scales and Items

Item 8 ("it's hard to judge the quality of merchandise on the Internet") has the highest mean value, followed by item 16 ("I do not purchase online if there is no money back guarantee"), item 10 ("If I shop online I cannot wait till the product arrives"), and item 11 ("I am worried about the quality of the products sold on line"), while item 3 has the lowest ("May purchase something by accident") (Table 3). Product risk items' scale scores the highest mean, followed by time-convenience risk scale, and financial risk scale. For all scales, Cronbach's alpha coefficient is above 0.60, confirming the reliability of these instruments.

Table 4 documents scales frequencies and comparison between groups. In all groups, the scale product risk presents the highest mean value, and the subscale intention to buy

Table 2. Products purchased online.

Products		Total	Purchased from Chinese e-stores		Gender		Education				Age
			No	Yes	Female	Male	Basic	Secondary	University attendee	University graduate	
		N (%)	N (%)	N (%)	N (%)	N (%)	N (%)	N (%)	N (%)	N (%)	$M \pm SD$
Clothing	No	547 (38.4)	270 (39.1)	277 (36.5)	197 (26.4)	350 (51.1)	47 (51.1)	169 (40.4)	112 (35.0)	219 (36.9)	41.53 ± 17.20
	Yes	876 (61.6)	421 (60.9)	455 (62.2)	548 (73.6)	328 (48.4)	45 (48.9)	249 (59.6)	208 (65.0)	374 (63.1)	37.38 ± 16.34
					$\chi^2(1) = 95.103; p < 0.001; \Phi = -0.259$		$\chi^2(3) = 9.089; p = 0.028; \Phi = 0.080$					$t(1421) = 4.567; p < 0.001; d = 0.249$
Shoes	No	996 (70.0)	477(69.0)	519 (70.9)	506 (67.9)	490 (72.3)	72 (78.3)	289 (69.1)	232 (72.5)	403 (68.0)	39.58 ± 17.16
	Yes	427 (30.0)	214 (31.0)	213 (29.1)	239 (32.1)	188 (27.7)	20 (21.7)	129 (30.9)	88 (27.5)	190 (32.0)	37.58 ± 15.84
											$t(1421) = 2.126; p = 0.034; d = 0.119$
Electronics and computers	No	711 (50.0)	377 (54.6)	334 (45.6)	455 (61.1)	256 (37.8)	53 (57.6)	244 (58.4)	148 (46.3)	266 (44.9)	39.97 ± 17.43
	Yes	712 (50.0)	314 (45.4)	398 (54.4)	290 (38.9)	422 (62.2)	39 (42.4)	174 (41.6)	172 (53.8)	327 (55.1)	37.99 ± 16.08
			$\chi^2(1) = 11.339; p = 0.001; \Phi = 0.089$		$\chi^2(1) = 77.186; p < 0.001; \Phi = 0.233$		$\chi^2(3) = 9.089; p < 0.001; \Phi = 0.124$					$t(1421) = 2.229; p = 0.026; d = 0.118$

(continued)

Table 2. (*continued*)

Products		Total N (%)	Purchased from Chinese e-stores		Gender		Education				Age
			No N (%)	Yes N (%)	Female N (%)	Male N (%)	Basic N (%)	Secondary N (%)	University attendee N (%)	University graduate N (%)	M ± SD
Travel	No	1151 (80.9)	565 (81.8)	586 (80.1)	606 (81.3)	545 (80.4)	80 (87.0)	364 (87.1)	266 (83.1)	441 (74.4)	38.84 ± 17.05
	Yes	272 (19.1)	126 (18.2)	146 (18.2)	139 (18.7)	133 (19.6)	12 (13.0)	54 (12.9)	54 (16.9)	152 (25.6)	39.56 ± 15.67
							$\chi^2(3) = 29.904; p < 0.001; \Phi = 0.145$				
Food and beverage	No	1059 (74.4)	517 (74.8)	542 (74.0)	531 (71.3)	528 (77.9)	72 (78.3)	335 (80.1)	244 (76.3)	408 (68.8)	38.76 ± 16.75
	Yes	364 (25.6)	174 (25.2)	190 (26.0)	214 (28.7)	150 (22.1)	20 (21.7)	83 (19.9)	76 (23.8)	185 (31.2)	39.61 ± 16.92
					$\chi^2(1) = 8.125; p = 0.004; \Phi = -0.076$		$\chi^2(3) = 18.298; p < 0.001; \Phi = 0.113$				
Books	No	934 (65.6)	439 (63.5)	495 (67.6)	469 (63.0)	465 (68.6)	71 (77.2)	338 (80.9)	206 (64.4)	319 (53.8)	38.45 ± 16.98
	Yes	489 (34.4)	252 (36.5)	237 (32.4)	276 (37.0)	213 (31.4)	21 (22.8)	80 (19.1)	114 (35.6)	274 (46.2)	39.98 ± 16.40
					$\chi^2(1) = 4.990; p = 0.025; \Phi = -0.059$		$\chi^2(3) = 85.482; p < 0.001; \Phi = 0.245$				

(continued)

Table 2. (continued)

Products		Total	Purchased from Chinese e-stores		Gender		Education				Age
			No	Yes	Female	Male	Basic	Secondary	University attendee	University graduate	
		N (%)	N (%)	N (%)	N (%)	N (%)	N (%)	N (%)	N (%)	N (%)	M ± SD
Music	No	1306 (91.8)	634 (91.8)	672 (91.8)	695 (93.3)	611 (90.1)	87 (94.6)	396 (94.7)	299 (93.4)	523 (88.2)	38.80 ± 16.87
	Yes	117 (8.2)	57 (8.2)	60 (8.2)	50 (6.7)	67 (9.9)	5 (5.4)	22 (5.3)	21 (6.6)	70 (11.8)	40.93 ± 15.78
					$\chi^2(1) = 4.729; p = 0.030; \Phi = 0.058$		$\chi^2(3) = 17.932; p < 0.001; \Phi = 0.112$				
Games	No	1185 (83.3)	582 (84.2)	603 (82.4)	670 (89.9)	515 (76.0)	84 (91.3)	359 (85.9)	246 (76.9)	496 (83.6)	40.14 ± 16.95
	Yes	238 (16.7)	109 (15.8)	129 (17.6)	75 (10.1)	163 (24.0)	8 (8.7)	59 (14.1)	74 (23.1)	97 (16.4)	33.19 ± 14.69
					$\chi^2(1) = 49.768; p < 0.001; \Phi = 0.187$		$\chi^2(3) = 15.772; p = 0.001; \Phi = 0.105$				$t(1421) = 6.486; p < 0.001; d = 0.419$
Furniture	No	1257 (88.3)	614 (88.9)	643 (87.8)	646 (86.7)	611 (90.1)	83 (90.2)	380 (90.9)	291 (90.9)	503 (84.8)	39.00 ± 16.87
	Yes	166 (11.7)	77 (11.1)	89 (12.2)	99 (13.3)	67 (9.9)	9 (9.8)	38 (9.1)	29 (9.1)	90 (15.2)	38.80 ± 16.27
					$\chi^2(1) = 3.997; p = 0.046; \Phi = -0.053$		$\chi^2(3) = 12.206; p = 0.007; \Phi = 0.093$				

(continued)

Table 2. (*continued*)

Products		Total	Purchased from Chinese e-stores		Gender		Education				Age
			No	Yes	Female	Male	Basic	Secondary	University attendee	University graduate	
		N (%)	N (%)	N (%)	N (%)	N (%)	N (%)	N (%)	N (%)	N (%)	M ± SD
Other products	No	945 (66.4)	474 (68.6)	471 (64.3)	508 (68.2)	437 (64.5)	68 (73.9)	268 (64.1)	229 (71.6)	380 (64.1)	38.45 ± 17.06
	Yes	478 (33.6)	217 (31.4)	261 (35.7)	237 (31.8)	241 (35.5)	24 (26.1)	150 (35.9)	91 (28.4)	213 (35.9)	40.02 ± 16.22
							$\chi^2(3) = 8.559; p = 0.036; \Phi = 0.078$				

Notes: M = mean; SD = standard deviation; N = frequencies; % - percentage; t = t-test; p = p-value; χ^2 = Chi-squared test; d = Cohen effect size; Φ = Phi effect size. In **bold**: statistically significant values

Table 3. Scales and items frequencies.

	M	SD	N %						
			1	2	3	4	5	6	7
Financial risk ($\alpha = 0.72$) ($M = 4.25$; $SD = 1.68$)									
1 Can't trust the online company	3.5	1.5	126	295	273	351	243	87	47
			8.9	20.7	19.2	24.7	17.1	6.1	3.3
2 May not get the product	4.4	1.5	50	162	184	291	366	278	91
			3.5	11.4	12.9	20.4	25.7	19.5	6.4
3 May purchase something by accident	3.2	1.7	236	368	156	343	150	134	35
			16.6	25.9	11.0	24.1	10.5	9.4	2.5
4 My personal information may not be kept	4.7	1.5	45	109	88	328	394	339	119
			3.2	7.7	6.2	23.0	27.7	23.8	8.4
5 My credit card number may not be secure	4.7	1.6	54	124	105	301	363	322	153
			3.8	8.7	7.4	21.2	25.5	22.6	10.8
16 I do not purchase online if there is no money back guarantee	5.1	1.6	32	88	82	315	225	415	265
			2.2	6.2	5.8	22.1	15.8	29.2	18.6
Product risk ($\alpha = 0.82$) ($M = 4.88$; $SD = 1.47$)									
6 I might not get what I ordered through online shopping	4.7	1.6	43	141	116	272	369	344	137
			3.0	9.9	8.2	19.1	25.9	24.2	9.6
7 I might receive malfunctioning merchandise	4.8	1.4	32	104	97	277	413	371	128
			2.2	7.3	6.8	19.5	29.0	26.1	9.0
8 It's hard to judge the quality of merchandise on the Internet	5.4	1.3	16	48	58	205	309	517	269
			1.1	3.4	4.1	14.4	21.7	36.3	18.9
11 I am worried about the quality of the products sold online	5.0	1.5	36	94	92	247	286	447	220
			2.5	6.6	6.5	17.4	20.1	31.4	15.5
14 I am worried about the true value of the product I bought online is lower than my expectation	4.6	1.4	43	158	117	403	221	308	172
			3.0	11.1	8.2	28.3	15.5	21.6	12.1
Time-convenience risk ($\alpha = 0.61$) ($M = 4.49$; $SD = 1.65$)									
9 Finding right product online is difficult	3.8	1.6	44	105	68	284	273	379	269
			3.1	7.4	4.8	20.0	19.2	26.6	18.9

(*continued*)

Table 3. (*continued*)

		M	SD	N %						
				1	2	3	4	5	6	7
10	If I shop online, I cannot wait till the product arrives	5.0	1.6	27	83	84	282	343	404	199
				1.9	5.8	5.9	19.8	24.1	28.4	14.0
12	I feel that it will be difficult settling disputes when I shop online	5.0	1.5	64	192	156	496	223	213	78
				4.5	13.5	11.0	34.9	15.7	15.0	5.5
13	It's hard to cancel orders	4.1	1.5	29	124	113	410	334	309	103
				2.0	8.7	7.9	28.8	23.5	21.7	7.2
15	I do not purchase online if there is no free return shipment service available	4.6	1.6	43	158	117	403	221	308	172
				3.0	11.1	8.2	28.3	15.5	21.6	12.1
Intention to buy ($\alpha = 0.61$) ($M = 4.58$; $SD = 1.74$)										
17	I will buy from Chinese online stores	4.7	1.6	103	76	57	388	258	384	156
				7.2	5.3	4.0	27.3	18.1	27.0	11.0
18	The COVID-19 pandemic has reduced my intention to purchase from Chinese online stores[a]	4.5	1.8	110	132	149	389	116	289	238
				7.7	9.3	10.5	27.3	8.2	20.3	16.7

Notes: [a] Reverse item. M = mean; SD – Standard deviation; N = frequency; % = percentage; 1 - Strongly disagree; 2 - Disagree; 3 - Somewhat disagree; 4 - Neither agree nor disagree; 5 - Somewhat agree; 6 - Agree; 7 - Strongly agree

stands the lowest. Participants who have bought on Chinese websites present significantly lower values in all subscales (financial risk, product risk, time convenience risk, and intention to buy; Table 4). Participants who buy on Portuguese and Chinese websites present lower values than those who do not buy concerning financial risk, time convenience risk, and intention to buy.

3.4 Regressions

A hierarchical multiple regression was carried out to analyze the effects of demographic and risk variables on the intention to buy from Chinese e-stores. Those independent variables were entered in two blocks; as a consequence, two nested models were generated. Model 1 estimated the effect of the demographic variables, being that gender, education level, and job status effects were not statistically significant. Model 2 added risks, being that Product risk was not statistically significant. Thus, in the final full model for the total sample, age, financial risk, and time convenience risk contributed significantly to explaining 21.3% of the intention to buy from Chinese websites (Table 5). The variable with the most weight to explain the variance of the intention to buy was the financial risk.

Table 4. Scales frequencies and comparison between groups.

Scale variables	Total	Purchased from Chinese e-stores		Gender		Education			
		No	Yes	Female	Male	Basic	Secondary	University attendee	University graduate
	M *(SD)*	*M* *(SD)*	*M* *(SD)*	*M* *(SD)*	*M* *(SD)*	*M* *(SD)*	*M* *(SD)*	*M* *(SD)*	*M* *(SD)*
Financial risk	4.25 (1.68)	**4.34 (1.03)**	**4.19 (0.97)**	4.26 (1.02)	4.24 (0.99)	**4.47 (1.00)**	**4.35 (0.97)**	**4.13 (0.94)**	**4.24 (1.05)**
		$t(1420) = 2.824; p = 0.005; d = 0.150$				$F(3) = 4.378; p = 0.004; \eta^2 = 0.009$			
Product risk	4.88 (1.47)	**4.95 (1.10)**	**4.81 (1.10)**	**5.01 (1.09)**	**4.74 (1.10)**	4.85 (1.13)	4.87 (1.10)	4.92 (1.05)	4.87 (1.13)
		$t(1420) = 2.299; p = 0.022; d = 0.122$		$t(1420) = 4.518; p < 0.001; d = 0.240$					
Time-convenience risk	4.49 (1.65)	**4.59 (0.96)**	**4.40 (0.97)**	**4.60 (0.95)**	**4.37 (0.98)**	4.68 (0.95)	4.52 (0.96)	4.48 (0.92)	4.45 (1.00)
		$t(1420) = 3.678; p < 0.001; d = 0.195$		$t(1420) = 4.635; p < 0.001; d = 0.246$					
Intention to buy from Chinese e-stores	4.58 (1.74)	**4.05 (0.96)**	**4.17 (0.88)**	**4.12 (0.95)**	**4.09 (0.90)**	4.20 (1.13)	4.18 (0.97)	4.10 (0.84)	4.05 (0.90)
		$t(1420) = -2.504; p = 0.012; d = -0.133$							

Notes: M = mean; SD – Standard deviation; t = t-test; d = Cohen effect size; F = ANOVA; η^2 = eta squared size; p = p-value. In **bold**: statistically significant values

Table 5. Variables that contribute to intention to buy from Chinese websites (total sample).

	Model 1			Model 2		
	B	*EP B*	β	*B*	*EP B*	β
Age	0.017	0.003	0.192	0.011	0.002	0.121
Financial risk				–0.490	0.042	–0.333
Time-convenience risk				–0.298	0.061	–0.139
R^2 (R^2 Adj.)	0.038 (0.037)			0.215 (0.213)		
F for change in R^2	42.514**			126.681**		

R^2 = R squared; R^2 Adj. = R squared adjusted; B = unstandardized regression coefficients; EP B = unstandardized error of B; β = standardized regression coefficients; $**p < 0.001$.

4 Discussion and Conclusions

The results show that, for the total sample, financial and time-convenience risk significantly predict the intention to buy from Chinese e-stores, thus supporting hypotheses H1 and H3, in line with Arshad et al. [12], Forsythe et al. [4], Javadi et al. [19], Masoud [20], and Swinyard and Smith [6]; as such, the higher the financial and time-convenience risks, the lower inclination people have toward buying from Chinese e-stores. However, though an association exists between product risk and that intention, it is not statistically significant, in contrast with Forsythe et al. [4]; accordingly, H2 could not be confirmed, which also occurred in a study by Javadi et al. [19].

Furthermore, contrary to expectations, neither gender [21–23] nor education level [8] were significant predictors of the intention to buy from Chinese e-stores; thus, hypotheses H4 and H6 were not supported. These results, however, are in line with Hernández et al. [24], who claim that the progress of the online environment has created the "experienced" e-shopper [including of course reactions to fake news and misinformation, present on the Internet, and which may lead to confusion in some quarters and the avoidance of certain e-commerce websites due to the COO or country-of-origin effect – in this case of China], whose behavior is similar, independently of their socioeconomic characteristics; as all respondents had prior experience with buying from e-retailers, to some extent that experience status could explain why gender, among other sociodemographic characteristics, did not predict the intention to buy from online Chinese vendors. Nevertheless, it is interesting to notice significant differences in terms of gender concerning product categories purchased online; men tend to purchase more electronics and computers, music, and games than women (in consonance with their hobbies and leisure activities), whereas women buy more clothing, food and beverage, books, and furniture than men (in consonance with their interests, around social and more homely activities), in line with Chekima et al. [25]. Also, still possibly because of prior experience, participants who have purchased from Chinese websites consistently score lower in financial, product, and time-convenience risks, and higher in the intention to buy from those vendors.

Yet age was found to be a statistically significant predictor of that intention, in line with Stafford et al. [26], confirming hypothesis H5. The findings document differences between those who have bought and have not bought products from Chinese e-stores, in that, on average, those who have to tend to be younger, more educated, and more active. Being younger suggests e-consumers have more time – more time to follow up in case of problems with delivery, for example, *vis-a-vis* older counterparts who (most often with children and other such related responsibilities) do not have this time to spare. Such results are aligned with Swinyard and Smith [6], who concluded in addition to having higher computer skills, spending more time on the Internet, and finding online shopping more accessible and fun, we could expect online consumers to be younger, better educated, and be less fearsome about financial loss associated with online transactions (as they also feel more able to "single-handedly", and independently, solve their online problem(s), which may be too complex and time-consuming to be solved by generations who have not dealt intuitively with the Internet their entire adolescent/adult lives). We would add another possible interpretation, as in contrast with the pessimism and reservations of the older generations regarding the Chinese (because of the Cold War and the ideological confrontation between liberal democracy and communism) [1], Portuguese younger people may tend to have a better perspective toward China, and thus Chinese vendors, as a result of the lack of adverse experiences and prior memories about China.

Purchasing perceived risk is of paramount importance for online transactions. This study intended to provide evidence of how Portuguese online consumers perceived risk influenced their intention to purchase from Chinese websites. As such, it examined three dimensions of perceived risk in buying online from those e-retailers: financial risk, product risk, and time-convenience risk. Two of them, financial and time-convenience risks, impact Portuguese online consumers' buying intention negatively; product risk does not significantly influence that intention. Also, most sample sociodemographic characteristics (gender, job status, and education) do not impact purchasing intention, except for age, as younger consumers perceive less risk and are more inclined to buy from Chinese e-stores. If Chinese e-retailers want to diminish the consumers' perception of risk and increase the likelihood of purchase, they must increase website quality, improve user interface, and better security and privacy perceptions, as this impacts information satisfaction and significantly relates to consumers' purchase behavior [27].

A limitation of this study is that only three risk dimensions were explored. Future research could include other variables, namely delivery, social, performance, psychological and health risks, or trust. Also, our findings only coincide partially with empirical studies carried out in other countries found in the scientific literature, possibly due to cultural differences - an aspect that should be investigated. In future works, the influence of online consumers' experience on the intention to buy from Chinese websites should be further explored, as well as their specific hedonic or utilitarian motives, perceived benefits, and differences in their attitude towards buying from other international e-retailers.

Finally, the increasing number of Chinese tourists in foreign countries is also beneficial as Portugal's younger generations (also avid of travel) meet and mingle with them more and more frequently - in popular foreign, as well as in popular domestic, destinations. Suddenly, China and Chinese citizens are not so far away, and this may also positively influence Chinese e-store purchases and may warrant further research on the topic.

Acknowledgements. This work was financially supported by the Honourable Mention prize for the Social Sciences – University of Aveiro Researcher Awards for 2022, attributed to Manuel Au-Yong-Oliveira, on 1st March 2023.

References

1. Fernandes, J.P.T., Magano, J., Turcsanyi, R.Q., Leite, Â.: Portugal-China relations: a shot in the dark? Eur. Rev. Bus. Econ. **2**, 47–71 (2022)
2. Hong, I.B.: Understanding the consumer's online merchant selection process: the roles of product involvement, perceived risk, and trust expectation. Int. J. Inf. Manag. **35**, 322–336 (2015)
3. Kamalul Ariffin, S., Mohan, T., Goh, Y.-N.: Influence of consumers' perceived risk on consumers' online purchase intention. J. Res. Interact. Mark. **12**, 309–327 (2018)

4. Forsythe, S., Liu, C., Shannon, D., Gardner, L.C.: Development of a scale to measure the perceived benefits and risks of online shopping. J. Interact. Mark. **20**, 55–75 (2006)
5. Lewis, M.: The effect of shipping fees on customer acquisition, customer retention, and purchase quantities. J. Retail. **82**, 13–23 (2006)
6. Swinyard, W.R., Smith, S.M.: Why people (don't) shop online: a lifestyle study of the internet consumer. Psychol. Mark. **20**, 567–597 (2003)
7. Chen, Y., Yan, X., Fan, W.: Examining the effects of decomposed perceived risk on consumer's online shopping behavior: a field study in China. Eng. Econ. **26**, 315–326 (2015)
8. Bhatnagar, A., Ghose, S.: Segmenting consumers based on the benefits and risks of Internet shopping. J. Bus. Res. **57**, 1352–1360 (2004)
9. Wani, S.N., Malik, S.: A comparative study of online shopping behaviour: effects of perceived risks and benefits. Int. J. Market. Bus. Commun. **2** (2013)
10. Mathur, N.: Perceived Risks towards Online Shopping. Int. J. Eng. Develop. Res. **2**, 262 (2015)
11. Almousa, M.: Perceived risk in apparel online shopping: a multi dimensional perspective. Can. Soc. Sci. **7**, 23–31 (2011)
12. Arshad, A., Zafar, M., Fatima, I., Khan, S.K.: The impact of perceived risk on online buying behavior. Int. J. New Technol. Res. **1**, 13–18 (2015)
13. Chetioui, Y., Benlafqih, H., Lebdaoui, H.: How fashion influencers contribute to consumers' purchase intention. J. Fashion Market. Manag. Int. J. **24**(3), 361–380 (2020)
14. Popli, A., Mishra, S.: Factors of perceived risk affecting online purchase decisions of consumers. Pacific Bus. Rev. Int. **8**, 49–58 (2015)
15. Zhang, L., Tan, W., Xu, Y., Tan, G.: Dimensions of perceived risk and their influence on consumers' purchasing behavior in the overall process of B2C. In: Engineering Education and Management: Results of the 2011 International Conference on Engineering Education and Management (ICEEM2011), vol. 1, pp. 1–10. Springer, Guangzhou (2011)
16. Han, M.C., Kim, Y.: Why consumers hesitate to shop online: perceived risk and product involvement on Taobao.com. J. Promot. Manag. **23**, 24–44 (2017)
17. Ko, H., Jung, J., Kim, J., Shim, S.W.: Cross-cultural differences in perceived risk of online shopping. J. Interact. Advert. **4**, 20–29 (2004)
18. DeVellis, R.F.: Scale Development: Theory and Applications. Sage Publications (2016)
19. Javadi, M.H.M., Dolatabadi, H.R., Nourbakhsh, M., Poursaeedi, A., Asadollahi, A.R.: An analysis of factors affecting on online shopping behavior of consumers. Int. J. Market. Stud. **4**, 81 (2012)
20. Masoud, E.Y.: The effect of perceived risk on online shopping in Jordan. Eur. J. Bus. Manag. **5**, 76–87 (2013)
21. Weber, E.U., Blais, A.R., Betz, N.E.: A domain-specific risk-attitude scale: measuring risk perceptions and risk behaviors. J. Behav. Decis. Mak. **15**, 263–290 (2002)
22. Rogers, D., Wong, A., Nelson, J.: Public perceptions of foreign and Chinese real estate investment: intercultural relations in Global Sydney. Aust. Geogr. **48**, 437–455 (2017)
23. Van Slyke, C., Comunale, C.L., Belanger, F.: Gender differences in perceptions of web-based shopping. Commun. ACM **45**, 82–86 (2002)
24. Hernández, B., Jiménez, J., José Martín, M.: Age, gender and income: do they really moderate online shopping behaviour? Online Inf. Rev. **35**, 113–133 (2011)
25. Chekima, B., Wafa, S.A.W.S.K., Igau, O.A., Chekima, S., Sondoh, Jr, S.L.: Examining green consumerism motivational drivers: does premium price and demographics matter to green purchasing? J. Clean. Prod. **112**, 3436–3450 (2016)
26. Stafford, T.F., Turan, A., Raisinghani, M.S.: International and cross-cultural influences on online shopping behavior. J. Glob. Inf. Technol. Manag. **7**, 70–87 (2004)
27. Park, C.H., Kim, Y.G.: Identifying key factors affecting consumer purchase behavior in an online shopping context. Int. J. Retail Distrib. Manag. **31**, 16–29 (2003)

Internet of Things in Business & Management: Current Trends, Opportunities and Future Scope

Swati Sharma$^{(\boxtimes)}$ ⓘ

Jindal Global Business School, O. P. Jindal Global University, Sonipat, India
swati@jgu.edu.in

Abstract. The study explores the theme of Internet of Things in business and management by conducting bibliometric analysis of extant literature on the topic. SPAR-4-SLR protocol methodology of systematic literature review is employed for bibliometric analysis. Year-wise, Author-wise, Citation-wise, Country-wise, Source-wise, Affiliation-wise, Sponsoring institutions-wise and keywords-wise listing are the parameters to identify the trend, opportunities, and future scope of this theme. We use Scopus database to list the extant literature. The study suggests that IoT in business and management is going to be explored in relation to digital transformation, fog computing, soft computing, embedded system, industry 4.0, circular economy, sustainable development, and smart cities and subsequently this wide-spread application of IoT in Business & Management also brings certain challenges like cyber-security, reliability, privacy, and complexity in working. This study provides insights on current trends and the future scope of IoT in business and management which is equally useful for researchers and policy makers.

Keywords: Internet of Things · Literature review · Bibliometric analysis · SPAR-4-SLR · IoT

1 Introduction

The term IoT (Internet of Things) is not new to the Information & technology domain. The need for digitalization of business brings IoT & business operation work closely to each other. However, the use of this term is not universal in all domains as there is no unique definition for IoT that is acceptable by the world community of users. In fact, there are many different groups including academicians, researchers, practitioners, innovators, developers, and corporate people that have defined the term according to its applicability [1]. IoT refers to the networked interconnection of objects of diverse nature, such as electronic devices, sensors, but also physical objects and beings as well as virtual data and environments [2]. The Internet of Things (IoT) is basically like a system for connecting computer devices, mechanical and digital machines, objects, or individuals provided with the unique system (UIDs) and without transfer to transmit data over an ability human-to-human or computer-to-human relation [3]. The functional aspect of IoT

T. Guarda et al. (Eds.): ARTIIS 2023, CCIS 1936, pp. 175–188, 2024.
https://doi.org/10.1007/978-3-031-48855-9_14

is to unite every object of the world under one common infrastructure; in such a manner that humans not only have the ability to control those objects; but to provide regular and timely updates on the current status [4]. As the definitions of IoT may defer in different studies but the basic idea of IoT remains the same, i.e., to ease the work process for different applications and business and management is one such application where IoT is used dominantly. Some of the IoT applications include smart homes, smart cities, smart grids, smart retail, etc. [5]. These applications require blending of business operations and IoT. Hence, the employment of IoT in business and management is inevitable. Such inevitability of integration attracts researchers' attention that results in studies exploring application of IoT in business and management. These studies are also reviewed based on existing literature. Qawy et.al 2015 [6] provide an overview study of the IoT paradigm, its concepts, principles and potential benefits. Their study focuses on the IoT major technologies, emerging protocols, and widespread applications. The application on IoT in different domain like healthcare, energy, agriculture, thermoelectricity, blockchain, healthcare etc. have been also explored by researchers [7–12]. There is plethora of studies based on literature review of IoT in different domains [6, 13–16]. However, none of existing studies review the extant literature on IoT in business and management. Hence, the present study contributes to literature by conducting systematic review with bibliometric analysis of studies on IoT in business and management. The study frame following research objectives:

RO1. To identify the publication trend on IoT in Business & Management.

RO2. To find most influential articles, top contributing source title, top contributing authors, top contributing country, top contributing sponsoring agency and top contributing affiliation on IoT in Business & Management.

RO3. To draw inferences about future scope of IoT in Business & Management by keyword occurrence analysis.

2   Research Methodology

Literature review studies have been conducted for developing conceptual understanding, checking methodological viability, and for providing insights regarding under researched, over researched, and exhaustive researched questions and objective [17, 18]. This present study employs well-known and widely used method of systematic literature review known as Scientific Procedures and Rationales for Systematic Literature Reviews (SPAR-4-SLR) developed by Paul et al., 2021 [19] to examine the extant literature on Internet of Things in Business & Management. As per google scholar database, the systematic literature review method of SPAR-4-SLR has been used in more than 300 studies ranging from different domains like Medicine, Social-science, Engineering, Management to Psychology & Environmental sciences [20–24]. Paul et al. (2021) also suggests looking for four basic characteristics of existing studies on underlying topic before employing the SPAR-4-SLR method of literature review as unlike empirical studies, literature review studies need to have certain base. These four basic criteria are:

- When a substantial body of work in the domain exists (e.g., at least 40 articles for review).
- When no systematic literature review in the domain exists in recent years (e.g., within the last 5 years).
- When no review of the domain exists in high-quality journals
- When existing systematic literature reviews have gaps or short-changes

The underlying topic i.e., Internet of things in business & management fulfill all four criteria as more than 300 articles exist on topic, no systematic literature review is conducted on exact same topic for given time-period in highly reputed source title. Hence, SPAR-4-SLR method for literature review is suitable for fulfilling research objectives of the present study. Furthermore, the SPAR-4-SLR protocol consists of three stages named assembling, arranging, and assessing. Each of these three stages has 2 sub-stages i.e., identification & acquisition under assembling, organization & purification under arranging, and evaluation & reporting under assessing. All these stages are explained as:

2.1 Assembling

The assembling includes the identification and acquisition of literature on the topic. The sub-stage identification specifies domain, research questions and source type whereas sub-stage acquisition specifies search-title, search source, search period, and filters e.g., keyword, subject etc. Three research objectives as describe in introduction section of this study is put under research question head whereas peer-reviewed research articles are source type of current study. Additionally, as the underlying topic of present paper is Internet of Thing in business & management, we put subject filter of "Business & Management" on searched articles. Other specifications of assembling stage are depicted in Fig. 1. Further, Scopus research database is searched with title Internet of Things, Internet of things, IoT, and IoTs. These search titles have generated 3098 articles ranging from 1997 to May 2023. Out of these 3098 articles, we exclude all article which are not from Business & Management domain. This subject filtering left us with 304 articles in hand that are scrutinized in further stages of arranging & assessing.

2.2 Arranging

The second stage of arranging includes organization and purification of articles assembled in stage 1. The first sub-stage of organization of articles includes organizing code and organizing framework. The present study conducts bibliographic analysis of literature; hence, the organizing code includes year, citation, authors, source-titles, country, affiliation, and keywords analysis. As the present study is not analyzing literature as per any framework, this part is not applicable (NA). The second sub-stage of arranging is the purification of literature. We exclude the article which are non-English language i.e., 4 articles and of unrelated focus i.e., 5 articles. Hence, 304 articles of assembling stage, are further curtailed to 295 articles.

2.3 Assessing

Assessing is the final stage of SPR-4-SLR protocol. It has two sub-stages i.e., Evaluation & Reporting. For evaluation, the present study employs bibliometric analysis and find best practices, gaps, and areas for future research on topic. The result of evaluation is presented in form of tables and figure. Figure 1 describes all these six sub-stages in detail.

Fig. 1. SPAR-4-SLR Protocol

3   Analysis and Findings

This section elaborates on the findings of bibliometric analysis and review of 295 articles as per three research objectives as follows:

3.1   RO1. To Quantify the Trends of Publication on IoT in Business & Management

Table 1 and Fig. 2 summarize the trends of publication on IoT in Business & Management. The publication year ranges from 1997–2023 i.e., twenty-seven years. Average publication per year is 10.93 publications. The highest publication is in the year 2020 with 62 publications followed by the year 2022 with 58 publications. Year 2023 has 31 publications till March i.e., 50% of highest publication year. Hence, there is possibility that 2023 years publication will have more publication recording year for IoT in Business & Management. The lowest number of publications i.e., 0 publication is found in the three years 1998, 2000 and 2008.

Table 1. Descriptive Statistics of Article on Internet of things

Mean	10.93	Kurtosis	3.42
Standard Error	3.32	Skewness	2.02
Median	2	Range	62
Mode	1	Minimum	0
Standard Deviation	17.25	Maximum	62
Sample Variance	297.69	Sum	295

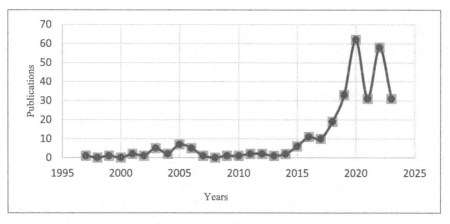

Fig. 2. Publication trends on IoT in Business & Management

3.2 RO2. To Find Most Influential Articles, Top Contributing Source, Top Contributing Authors, Top Contributing Country, Top Contributing Sponsoring Agency and Top Contributing Affiliation on IoT in Business & Management

Most cited articles are the most influential study of the subject area. Out of 295 selected studies, 234 studies are cited. That means 61 studies have 0 citations. Considering the number of citations, Table 2 highlights all publications which have more than 200 citations. Eight such studies have been identified. These eight studies accounted for more than 25% of total publication citation (TPC) i.e., 11,415 for all 295 studies. TC/TPC is ratio of total citation (TC) of single article to total publication citation. TCY is total citation per year. With 839 as TC, Stojkoska et al. 2017 tops the table. Although as per total citation per year, Ben-Daya et al. 2019 study is the most influential article with 188 TCY, followed by Kamble et al. 2020 with 172.50 TCY.

Table 2. Most influential articles on Internet of Things

Author	Title	Year	Source Title	TC	TCY	TC/TPC
Risteska Stojkoska B.L., Trivodaliev K.V	A review of Internet of Things for smart home: Challenges and solutions	2017	Journal of Cleaner Production	839	167.80	7%
Ben-Daya M., Hassini E., Bahroun Z	Internet of things and supply chain management: a literature review	2019	International Journal of Production Research	564	188.00	5%
Atlam H.F., Walters R.J., Wills G.B	Fog computing and the internet of things: A review	2018	Big Data and Cognitive Computing	350	87.50	3%
Kamble S.S., Gunasekaran A., Gawankar S.A	Achieving sustainable performance in a data-driven agriculture supply chain: A review for research and applications	2020	International Journal of Production Economics	345	172.50	3%
Winkelhaus S., Grosse E.H	Logistics 4.0: a systematic review towards a new logistics system	2020	International Journal of Production Research	285	142.50	2%

(continued)

Table 2. (*continued*)

Author	Title	Year	Source Title	TC	TCY	TC/TPC
Feng H., Wang X., Duan Y., Zhang J., Zhang X	Applying blockchain technology to improve agri-food traceability: A review of development methods, benefits and challenges	2020	Journal of Cleaner Production	282	141.00	2%
Yaqoob I., Hashem I.A.T., Gani A., Mokhtar S., Ahmed E., Anuar N.B., Vasilakos A.V	Big data: From beginning to future	2016	International Journal of Information Management	249	41.50	2%
Malhotra A., Melville N.P., Watson R.T	Spurring impactful research on information systems for environmental sustainability	2013	MIS Quarterly: Management Information Systems	202	22.44	2%

Further to finding the most influential articles, the present study also collected data on the title sources which has published minimum five articles on the topic. Such six source titles are identified and listed in Table 3. Internet Of Things Netherlands has published highest TP (Total Publication) i.e., 73 and highest TCP (Total Cited Publication) i.e., 58. However, Journal of Cleaner Production has the highest TC 2323, and International Journal of Production Research has highest TC/TP and TC/TCP i.e., 164.7.

Table 4 present data on top contributing authors and Table 5 present top contributing affiliation on the topic. Authors who have minimum three publications on the topic are listed in Table 4. Seven such authors are identified. Treiblmaier, H. has the highest 6 publication. However, Ben-Daya, M. with 3 TP has highest TC 606 and Gunasekaran, A. with 3 TP has highest TC/TP and TC/TCP 198.33. Interestingly, the highest cited article as per Table 2 is not part of listed author's study of Table 4.

Table 5 lists the affiliation which has minimum 4 studies on IoT in business and management. Such six affiliations are identified. MODUL University Vienna has highest 6 TP. Although Universiti Malaya with 4 TCP has highest TC, highest TC/TP and TC/TCP followed by Friedrich-Alexander-Universität Erlangen-Nürnberg.

Table 6 shows the publication trends country-wise and lists all the countries with more than ten publications. Eleven such countries are identified. United State has highest number of publications i.e., 58 publications followed by India with 45 publications, has

Table 3. Most contributing Source Title on Internet of things

SOURCE TITLE	TP	TCP	TC	TC/TP	TC/TCP	Impact Factor
Internet Of Things Netherlands	73	58	2319	31.77	39.98	8.35
Journal Of Cleaner Production	20	19	2323	116.15	122.26	11.072
Journal Of Management Analytics	8	8	722	90.25	90.25	6.554
International Journal of Production Research	7	7	1152	164.57	164.57	9.018
Strategic Direction	7	3	18	2.57	6	0.14
Big Data And Cognitive Computing	5	4	426	85.2	106.5	3.901

Table 4. Most contributing Authors on Internet of things

AUTHOR NAME	TP	TCP	TC	TC/TP	TC/TCP
Treiblmaier, H	6	5	192	32	38.4
Rejeb, A	5	4	148	29.6	37
Rejeb, K	5	4	148	29.6	37
Atlam, H.F	3	3	424	141.33	141.33
Ben-Daya, M	3	3	606	202	202
Gunasekaran, A	3	3	595	198.33	198.33
Lu, Y	3	3	366	122	122

Table 5. Most contributing Affiliation on Internet of things

AFFILIATION	TP	TCP	TC	TC/TP	TC/TCP
MODUL University Vienna	6	5	192	32	38.4
Friedrich-Alexander-Universität Erlangen-Nürnberg	5	5	210	42	42
Universiti Malaya	5	4	390	78	97.5
CNRS Centre National de la Recherche Scientifique	4	3	20	5	6.67
Universitat Politècnica de València	4	2	13	3.25	6.5
Università degli Studi di Roma Tor Vergata	4	3	123	30.75	41

highest total citation 3443 followed by United Kingdom with 2090 total citation. United Kingdom also has highest TC/TP i.e., 69.67 and TC/TCP ratio i.e., 77.41.

Table 6. Most contributing countries on Internet of things

COUNTRY	TP	TCP	TC	TC/TP	TC/TCP
United States	58	49	3443	59.36	70.27
India	45	40	1370	30.44	34.25
United Kingdom	30	27	2090	69.67	77.41
Canada	19	16	1180	62.11	73.75
China	19	17	1154	60.74	67.88
Australia	18	16	505	28.06	31.56
Italy	17	14	675	39.71	48.21
Malaysia	17	14	601	35.35	42.93
Germany	16	15	769	48.06	51.27
France	12	11	563	46.92	51.18
Brazil	11	9	391	35.55	43.44

Table 7 shows the publications which have been sponsored by some Agency or Institute. It lists all such Agencies which have a minimum of four sponsored publications. Such five agencies are identified. Natural Sciences and Engineering Research Council of Canada has maximum sponsored publication i.e., 7, has highest total citations 880, and highest TC/TP 125.71 and highest TC/TCP 146.67 followed by National Natural Science Foundation of China.

Table 7. Most contributing Agencies on Internet of things

SPONSORING AGENCY	TP	TCP		TC	TC/TP	TC/TCP
Natural Sciences and Engineering Research Council of Canada	7	6	880		125.71	146.67
European Regional Development Fund	5	3	5		1	1.67
Coordenação de Aperfeiçoamento de Pessoal de Nível Superior	4	4	168		42	42
European Commission	4	3	193		48.25	64.33
National Natural Science Foundation of China	4	4	338		84.5	84.5

3.3   RO3. To Draw Inferences About Scope and Opportunities for Studies on Internet of Things in Business & Management

This study investigates the keywords used in literature year-wise and frequency wise to draw inference about current trends and future scope of IoT in business & management. Keywords are analyzed to find under-researched and promising topics, and VOSviewer tool is used for keyword visualization. There are 1673 keywords used in all 295 articles. Table 8 shows frequency of keyword used in articles with number of co-occurrences. As frequency increases, the number of keyword occurrences decreases e.g., 129 keywords appear minimum three times, 84 keywords appear minimum four times and so on.

Table 8. Frequency of Keyword co-occurrences

Frequency	Keyword Co-occurrence	Frequency	Keyword Co-occurrence
1	1674	6	41
2	274	7	34
3	129	8	25
4	84	9	21
5	51	10	18

Table 9 represents the keywords which have appeared minimum 10 times in studied literature and their total strength link. Total strength link represents number of documents which have co-occurrence of two keywords (Guo at. al. 2019). The keyword Internet of things has the highest total link strength i.e., 168 followed by the keyword Industry 4.0.

Figure 3 shows frequency of keywords used in literature in relation to IoT in business & management. For better understanding, the keywords used minimum 5 times are framed in network visualization. The bigger the circle, the higher the frequency of co-occurrence. The line represents link of keyword co-occurrence e.g., how many time keyword Internet of Things and machine learning appear together is represented by the line connecting these two keywords.

As per VOSviewer manual, each link has a strength, represented by a positive numerical value. The higher link value represents the stronger the link. Red represents the keyword Internet of Things i.e., that has total strength link 266 and occurrence 120. Yellow represents keyword Industry 4.0 with total strength link 113 and occurrence 39. Machine learning, cloud computing, block-chain, sustainable development, embedded system, circular economy etc. are the other frequently used keywords.

Figure 4 on overlay visualization of keywords used between 2018–2023 shows how over the years frequency of keywords used have been changed. Keywords like Fog computing, Edge computing, Block-chain, digital transformation, Smart Cities, Embedded system has been frequented in recent years, especially after 2019 whereas Keywords like Internet of Things, Machine Learning, 6g, Circular economy, Industry 4.0 have been used frequently in literature. Based on network and overlay visualization of keyword co-occurrence, i.e., Tables 8–9 & Figs. 3–4, we suggest following topics which are going to be explored substantially by researchers in upcoming studies:

Table 9. Total Link Strength of keywords used minimum 10 times in literature.

Keyword	Occurrence	Total Link Strength
Internet Of Things	122	168
Industry 4.0	40	68
Big Data	25	60
IoT	34	50
Artificial Intelligence	24	48
Block-Chain	21	43
Internet Of Things (IoT)	42	43
Systematic Literature Review	21	43
Cloud Computing	24	40
Machine Learning	23	39
Security	22	38
Sustainable Development	17	33
Data Analysis	12	32
Supply Chain Management	12	24
Sustainability	13	24
Privacy	12	21
Internet	18	15
Literature Review	10	15

- IoT & Industry 4.0
- Role of IoT in sustainable development
- IoT and Fog Computing & Edge Computing
- IoT & Circular Economy
- IoT & Smart cities
- IoT & Digital Transformation (Big data, Blockchain, cloud computing etc.)
- IoT & ethical dilemma (privacy, confidentiality, and security issues)

4 Limitations and Scope of Study

Though present studies reviews 295 articles for presenting a comprehensive view Internet of Things in Business and Management there are few limitations that exists with the study. We search only one research engine for finding literature i.e., Scopus, that may limit the view of the present paper. The keyword used for searching the articles of the topic may also include other non-related keywords as there may be studies on IoT business and management in different domain/industries. These limitations can be overcome by using more keyword and exploring other research databases for finding the articles on the topic. We also strongly suggest doing comprehensive review of all literature with integrated field like social science and Economics to broaden this study horizon.

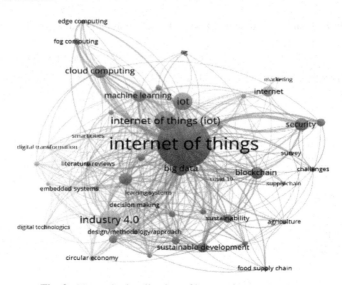

Fig. 3. Network visualization of keyword co-occurrence.

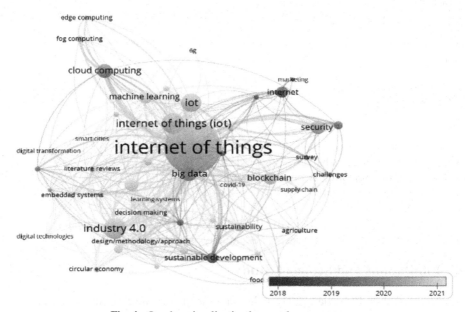

Fig. 4. Overlay visualization keyword co-occurrence.

5   Conclusion

The Internet of Things is now an integral part of the business and management process. Its applicability does not limit itself to traditional stand but expands to inter-related business and management domains like sustainability, socially responsible business, circular economy, industry 4.0 etc. This study presents a comprehensive view on existing literature on IoT in business and management. The bibliographic analysis of literature suggests that IoT is going to be explored in all dimensions of business and management in one way or another. IoT has also been explored in other areas like healthcare, agriculture, defense, energy sector etc. Its widespread application also brings certain challenges like cyber-security, reliability, privacy, and complexity in working [25–27]. Hence, a standardized and efficient regulatory framework needs to be there to ensure smooth integration of IoT in business and management.

References

1. Madakam, S., Ramaswamy, R., Tripathi, S.: Internet of Things (IoT): a literature review. J. Comput. Commun. **3**, 164–173 (2015)
2. Kosmatos, E.A., Tselikas, N.D., Boucouvalas, A.C.: Integrating RFIDs and smart ob-jects into a unified internet of things architecture. Adv. Internet Things Sci. Res. **1**, 5–12 (2011)
3. Laghari, A.A., Wu, K., Laghari, R.A., Ali, M., Khan, A.A.: A Review and State of Art of Internet of Things (IoT). Arch. Comput. Methods Eng. **29**, 1395–1413 (2022). https://doi.org/10.1007/s11831-021-09622-6
4. Khanna, A., Kaur, S.: Internet of Things (IoT), applications and challenges: a comprehensive review. Wirel. Personal Commun. **114**, 1687–1762 (2020). https://doi.org/10.1007/s11277-020-07446-4
5. Sobin, C.C.: A survey on architecture, protocols and challenges in IoT. Wireless Pers. Commun.Commun. **112**(3), 1383–1429 (2020). https://doi.org/10.1007/s11277-020-07108-5
6. Abdul-Qawy, A.S., Pramod, P.J., Magesh, E., Srinivasulu, T.: The internet of things (IoT): an overview. Int. J. Eng. Res. Appl. **5**(12), 71–82 (2015)
7. Gómez-Chabla, R., Real-Avilés, K., Morán, C., Grijalva, P., Recalde, T.: IoT applications in agriculture: a systematic literature review. In: ICT for Agriculture and Environment: Second International Conference, CITAMA 2019, Guayaquil, Ecuador, January 22–25, 2019, Proceedings, pp. 68–76. Springer, Cham (2018)
8. Bedi, G., Venayagamoorthy, G.K., Singh, R., Brooks, R.R., Wang, K.-C.: Review of Internet of Things (IoT) in electric power and energy systems. IEEE Internet Things J. **5**(2), 847–870 (2018)
9. Lee, I.: Internet of Things (IoT) cybersecurity: literature review and IoT cyber risk management. Future Internet **12**, 157 (2020)
10. Azzawi, M.A., Hassan, R., Bakar, K.A.A.: A review on Internet of Things (IoT) in healthcare. Int. J. Appl. Eng. Res. **11**(20), 10216–10221 (2016)
11. Talavera, J.M., et al.: Review of IoT applications in agro-industrial and environmental fields. Comput. Electron. Agric. **142**, 283–297 (2017)
12. Scarpato, N., Pieroni, A.: Luca Di Nunzio, and Francesca Fallucchi. E-health-IoT universe: A review. management **21**(44), 46 (2017)
13. Čolaković, A., Hadžialić, M.: Internet of Things (IoT): a review of enabling technologies, challenges, and open research issues. Comput. Netw.. Netw. **144**, 17–39 (2018)
14. Del Giudice, M.: Discovering the Internet of Things (IoT) within the business process management: a literature review on technological revitalization. Bus. Process. Manag. J. **22**(2), 263–270 (2016)
15. Sadeeq, M.M., Abdulkareem, N.M., Zeebaree, S.R.M., Ahmed, D.M., Sami, A.S., Zebari, R.R.: IoT and Cloud computing issues, challenges and opportunities: a review. Qubahan Acad. J. **1**(2), 1–7 (2021)

16. Rose, K., Eldridge, S., Chapin, L.: The internet of things: an overview. Internet Soc. (ISOC). **15**(80), 1–50 (2015)
17. Hulland, J., Houston, M.: Why systematic review papers and meta-analyses matter: an introduction to the special issue on generalizations in marketing. J. Acad. Mark. Sci. **48**(3), 51–59 (2020)
18. Palmatier, R.W., Houston, M.B., Hulland, J.: Review articles: purpose, process, and structure. J. Acad. Mark. Sci. **46**, 1–5 (2018)
19. Paul, J., Lim, W.M., O'Cass, A., Hao, A.W., Bresciani, S.: Scientific procedures and rationales for systematic literature reviews (SPAR-4-SLR). Int. J. Consum. Stud. **45**(4), O1–O16 (2021)
20. Das, M., Roy, A., Paul, J., Saha, V.: High and low impulsive buying in social commerce: A SPAR-4-SLR and fsQCA approach. IEEE Trans. Eng. Manage., 1 Jun 2022
21. Bhattacharyya, J.: The structure of sustainability marketing research: a bibliometric review and directions for future research. Asia-Pacific J. Bus. Administration. **15**(2), 245–286 (2023)
22. Sreenivasan, A., Suresh, M.: Future of healthcare start-ups in the era of digitalization: Bibliometric analysis. International Journal of Industrial Engineering and Operations Management. **4**(1/2), 1–8 (2022)
23. Lim, W.M., Rasul, T., Kumar, S., Ala, M.: Past, present, and future of customer engagement. J. Bus. Res. 1(140), 439–458 (2022)
24. Tsiotsou, R.H., Koles, B., Paul, J., Loureiro, S.M.: Theory generation from literature reviews: a methodological guidance. Int. J. Consum. Stud. **46**(5), 1505–1516 (2022)
25. Farhan, L., Shukur, S.T., Alissa, A.E., Alrweg, M., Raza, U., Kharel, R.: A survey on the challenges and opportunities of the Internet of Things (IoT). In: 2017 Eleventh International Conference on Sensing Technology (ICST), pp. 1–5. IEEE (2017)
26. Darshan, K.R., Anandakumar, K.R.: A comprehensive review on usage of Internet of Things (IoT) in healthcare system. In: 2015 International Conference on Emerging Research in Electronics, Computer Science and Technology (ICERECT), pp. 132–136. IEEE (2015)
27. Elijah, O., Rahman, T.A., Orikumhi, I., Leow, C.Y., Nour, M.H.D., Hindia.: An overview of Internet of Things (IoT) and data analytics in agriculture: Benefits and challenges. IEEE Internet Things J. **5**, 3758–3773 (2018)

Ethics, Security, and Privacy

Literature Review of SMS Phishing Attacks: Lessons, Addresses, and Future Challenges

Diana Barrera[1] ⓘ, Valery Naranjo[1,3](✉) ⓘ, Walter Fuertes[1] ⓘ,
and Mayra Macas[1,2] ⓘ

[1] Computer Science Department, Universidad de las Fuerzas Armadas ESPE,
Sangolquí, Ecuador
{dfbarrera3,vinaranjo1,wmfuertes}@espe.edu.ec, mayramacas@ieee.org
[2] College of Computer Science and Technology, Zhejiang University, No. 38 Zheda
Road, Hangzhou 310027, China
[3] Research, Development and Innovation, Grupo Radical, Quito, Ecuador

Abstract. Social engineering short message service (SMS) Phishing (smishing) attacks have increased with the rise of smart homes, cities, and devices. Smishing is a form of phishing that involves stealing the victims' private information through the content they send in their SMS, which has become the most widely used function on mobile devices. This paper aims to explore the different solutions implemented to detect and mitigate this type of attack. To that end, we conduct an exhaustive review using the methodological guide of Barbara Kitchenham. The literature search located 40 articles that met the exclusion and inclusion criteria. The results show a variety of implementations of Random Forest, and Deep Learning techniques (in particular, Long-term memory or LSTM). A few researchers solved the smishing problem using Uniform Resource Locator analysis and blacklists. Others used methods such as Bidirectional Encoder Representations from Transformers embedding, Elliptic Curve Digital Signature Algorithm encryption and convolutional neural networks. In addition, we discovered insights, psychological challenges, and future research directions associated with smishing, such as persuasion and urgency, confirmation bias, and unfamiliarity, indicating that solutions for detecting and mitigating smishing attacks must also consider the study of the human mind and its processes.

Keywords: Smishing · SLR · Deep Learning · Attack · Detection · SMS Phishing

1 Introduction

This research comes in response to a critical need in today's digital environment: the growing threat of SMS phishing, commonly known as smishing. Social Engineering is the illegitimate manipulation practice cybercriminals use to obtain

T. Guarda et al. (Eds.): ARTIIS 2023, CCIS 1936, pp. 191–204, 2024.
https://doi.org/10.1007/978-3-031-48855-9_15

confidential information from users or their organizations [1]. One such attack is SMS phishing (smishing), which has been a growing threat to the security of smartphone users over the last decade [3,17]. The term smishing appeared in 2008; it has increased in recent years, not only through text messages but also in messaging applications such as WhatsApp. These scams work by sending messages that manipulate and trick victims into clicking on fraudulent links [4].

To contextualize SMS phishing, COVID-19 increased the use of digital services and online applications for daily activities such as buying, paying, accessing medical services, telework, and online education worldwide. This move to digitization, without knowledge of cybersecurity, has aroused the interest of cybercriminals who intend to commit fraudulent appropriation. For instance, this cybercrime occurred in California in the US, where attackers perpetrated serious cyber-attacks, including a ransomware attack and a smishing attack known as the Cloudflare Case. The Smishing attack involved employees receiving text messages containing a legitimate-looking login page for a newly registered domain. The attacker used four phone numbers associated with T-Mobile-issued SIM cards to send messages to at least 76 employees and their family members [6,7]. Likewise, the employees of a company were the victim of a smishing attack through an SMS on the company phone from a fake messaging service that asked them to download an application to manage delivery. Upon downloading the app, workers found it malicious and sent many SMS, resulting in an unusually high phone bill. [5,10]. According to Proofpoint's 2022 State of the Phish report, 74 % of organizations received smishing attacks in 2021, up 13 percent from 2020 [2].

Faced with this scenario, researchers developed detection tools and models to protect users from these attacks. For example, in the study proposed by [9], a machine learning-based model was developed to classify smishing text messages in Swahili. Likewise, a malicious domain detection method that focuses on the arrival rate of SMS messages with URL links has been proposed, reducing error rates [8]. However, smishing still needs to be solved.

This paper aims to determine the techniques, methods, and algorithms used in Deep Learning to control and mitigate an SMS phishing attack. To accomplish this, we conducted a systematic literature review using the methodological guide of Barbara Kitchenham [27]. We broadly explore SMS phishing by reviewing the literature available. We collect and analyze previous studies addressing different aspects, including the effects on the victims and the techniques used by the attackers. Furthermore, this study recognizes the methods and strategies implemented to mitigate the attack. As a main contribution, we identify the current state of knowledge about SMS phishing, helping to show gaps, challenges, and future research directions. Likewise, these findings can help inform prevention policies by critically evaluating the available scientific evidence.

The remainder of this paper is structured as follows: Sect. 2 describes the theoretical background that supports this investigation. Section 3 explains the research methodology process. Section 4 presents the results obtained. Section 5 discloses the lessons, challenges, and future addresses. Finally, Sect. 6 clarifies the conclusions and future work.

2   Theoretical Background

The origins of neural networks and Deep Learning can be traced back to the early development of artificial neural networks in the late 1950s and 1960s, with the first neural network model, the perceptron, developed in 1958 by Frank Rosenblatt [32]. However, the limitations of this model led to the development of more complex neural network architectures, such as the multilayer perceptron in 1965 [32]. These early neural networks had limited capabilities but laid the foundation for future developments in the field of Deep Learning [35]. The introduction of the backpropagation algorithm in the 1980s was a significant breakthrough in the field of neural networks. This algorithm enables more efficient training of neural networks and supports the development of more deep and more complex neural network architectures [36]. With the advent of such algorithms, neural networks became more capable of performing complex tasks such as image and speech recognition [37]; this ushered in the era of Deep Learning, where multi-layer neural networks were used for complex tasks [39]. Deep Learning techniques continued to advance with the development of convolutional neural networks (CNNs) and recurrent neural networks (RNNs) in the late 1980s [32]. These Deep Learning techniques have been used in various applications, such as natural language processing, computer vision, and speech recognition [40]. The use of neural short-term memory (LSTM) networks has also led to advances in the field of natural language processing [41]. As Deep Learning grows, it has great potential to solve complex problems and revolutionize various industries [42]. In this context, it is crucial to address SMS Phishing attacks and their close relationship with malware. A smishing attack involves the manipulation of users via text messages or messaging applications to induce them to perform harmful actions, such as clicking on malicious links or downloading infected files. These links and files often contain malware, software designed to compromise the security of devices, steal information or cause damage. These attacks can impact the privacy and integrity of users and organizations.

2.1   Deep Learning Algorithms

Deep Learning uses algorithms to analyze data and draw human-like conclusions. It allows machines to manipulate images, text, or audio like humans. It is based on multi-layered neural networks and involves extracting complex information as it goes deeper into the layers. Machines learn to identify features and adapt to changes through iterative learning methods and exposure to large data sets. They can then understand the logic and reach reliable conclusions after repeated exposures [44].

Artificial Neural Networks is a parallel distributed system that attempts to model the brain's connectivity and simple biological processing cells (a.k.a., neurons). The knowledge network of the ANN is determined by the strength of the interconnections, known as the synapses of the neurons in the network. This synapse strength is represented as an accurate number weight connecting the output of one neuron to the input of another neuron [33].

Recurrent Neural Networks can learn features and long-term dependencies from sequential and time-series data. The RNNs have a stack of non-linear units where at least one connection between units forms a directed cycle. A well-trained RNN can model any dynamical system. However, training RNNs is plagued mainly by issues in learning long-term dependencies. More information about RNNs can be found in the survey [34].

Generative Adversarial Networks can learn deep representations without requiring highly annotated training data. This is achieved through a competitive process using backpropagation signals between a pair of networks. GANs can be applied in various areas, such as image synthesis, semantic image editing, style transfer, image super-resolution, and classification. The authors in [38] provide an overview of GANs, using familiar analogies and concepts, and explain different methods for training and building GANs. They also point out future challenges in the theory and application of GANs.

Convolutional Neural Networks it is a Deep Learning model that processes data with a grid structure, such as images. It is designed to automatically and adaptively learn spatial hierarchies of features, from low-level to high-level patterns. The organization of the visual cortex of animals inspires it. CNN mainly comprises three layers: convolution, clustering, and fully connected. The convolution and clustering layers extract features, while the fully connected layers map those extracted features into the final output, such as classification [43]. Figure 1 is a visual abstraction of a CNN that learns from a data set and tries to identify patterns in images to recognize objects, classes, and categories in SMS Phishing attacks.

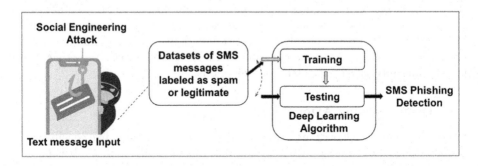

Fig. 1. Visual abstraction of a DL Algorithm that learns an SMS Phishing

2.2   Datasets

Deep Learning (DL) is a powerful tool that can be used to develop application frameworks in the field of SMS phishing. By using artificial systems, such as neural networks, it is possible to simulate the learning processes of the biological brain to identify and mitigate SMS phishing attacks. This approach enables the development of solutions to detect and prevent increasingly frequent SMS phishing attacks in today's digital world. By leveraging DL, organizations can develop more effective mitigation solutions to protect their customers from these attacks. In order to develop mitigation solutions based on DL, it is critical to have proper methodologies in place for the training, validation, and testing of such solutions. Machine learning algorithms are used to train DL models, which require large amounts of data to be effective. This data must be appropriately labeled and preprocessed to ensure accurate results. The models are then validated using cross-validation techniques to stay within the data. Finally, the models are tested using real-world data to evaluate their effectiveness in mitigating SMS phishing attacks.

The results obtained from testing DL-based mitigation solutions have shown promise in identifying and preventing SMS phishing attacks. Fraud analytics, which uses big data analytics techniques to prevent online financial fraud, can be employed to develop practical tests for SMS phishing attacks. Machine learning algorithms can be trained on this data to identify patterns and detect SMS phishing attacks in real time. In addition, machine learning can be used to develop fraud detection models for banking and financial institutions to prevent fraudulent activities. By leveraging DL frameworks and methodologies, organizations can develop practical solutions to combat SMS phishing attacks and protect their customers from financial loss and other security risks. Specifically, data collection can be performed on several items. We include a DL framework for SMS phishing applications and briefly summarize the testbeds that can be used to train, validate and test Deep Learning-based mitigation solutions. Several public datasets contain information about smishing attacks, including malicious messages, attack details, and victim data. These datasets are available for researchers to train and test smishing detection models. Some of the examples of such datasets are as follows:

- UCI Machine Learning Repository. (2012). SMS Spam Collection Dataset. Retrieved from https://www.kaggle.com/datasets/uciml/sms-spam-collection-dataset. The following dataset indicates the collection of text messages categorized as either spam or legitimate.
- Hugging Face Datasets. (2022). sms_spam. Retrieved from https://huggingface.co/datasets/sms_spam. Datasets composed of 5,574 messages in English, real and unencrypted, labeled according to whether they are legitimate (ham) or spam.
- Sid321axn. (2021). Malicious URLs Dataset. Retrieved from https://www.kaggle.com/datasets/sid321axn/malicious-urls-dataset. Data collection of 651,191 URLs, of which 428103 are benign or safe URLs, 96457 are defacement URLs, 94111 are phishing URLs and 32520 are malware URLs.

3   Research Methodology

3.1   Research Questions

To meet our objectives, we have structured this paper into four research queries that seek to address and define our purpose. (i) How is the effectiveness of a socially engineered SMS phishing attack assessed? (ii) What are the techniques employed by researchers to address this problem? (iii) How is the overall impact of phishing attacks assessed? (iv) What are the preventive measures explored to mitigate smishing attacks, and what are the gaps and future lines of research?

3.2   Search the Relevant Documents

We search in the following scientific databases or search engines: IEEExplore, Web of Science, Springer, ACM Digital Library, Elsevier, and Google Scholar.

3.3   Define Search Terms (Search String)

The paper aimed to obtain relevant information from primary sources on methodologies, methods, and techniques for detecting and mitigating SMS phishing attacks. For this purpose, the following search strings were entered into each scientific database, as shown in Table 1.

Table 1. Search Strings in Scientific Databases

Scientific Database	Search String
IEEE Xplore	("Journals & Magazines": Smishing) AND (("Journals & Magazines": Attack) AND ("Journals & Magazines": Detention)), In addition, the year from 2017 to 2023 was filtered using the graphical interface.
Web of Science	TS=Smishing Attack and (TI=system or TI=technology and PY=2017-2023)
SpringerLink	'Smishing Attack Detection AND "Machine Learning" within 2017 - 2023
ACM Digital Library	[All: sms phishing attack detection] AND [All: cnn] AND [All: technology] AND [All: smishing] AND [E-Publication Date: (01/01/2017 TO 04/30/2023)]
Google Scholar	"SMS phishing" or "smishing" + "attacks" + "Machine Learning" or "Deep Learning": > 2017
ScienceDirect	smishing attack AND detection. In addition, the year from 2017 to 2023 was filtered using the graphical interface

3.4   Inclusion and Exclusion Criteria

The analysis period was from 2017 to 2022, as more studies have been conducted due to the increased use of electronic devices during the COVID-19 pandemic. All studies included mathematical calculations and precision measures. In addition, we included only primary English articles obtained from journals and conferences, as they met the search criteria and offered concrete solutions to detect and mitigate smishing attacks.

3.5   Result of Review

Considering that the literature review collects and allows critical analysis of research studies through a systematic process that provides search quality, we ensure the review only in primary works that applied SMS Phishing analysis on the web, ruling out other methods, such as URL analysis, since this was not our object of study. In addition, the review was carried out in scientific databases, eliminating duplicates. Then we checked abstracts and only considered 40 articles that met the inclusion and exclusion criteria (see Fig. 2).

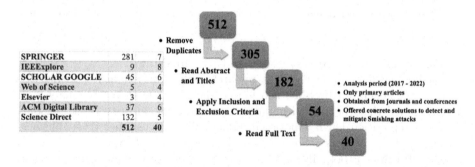

Fig. 2. Number of papers by Scientific Database

4   Evaluation of Results and Discussion

Q1: What is the effectiveness of a phishing attack using messages?

Text message scams are on the rise and are difficult to eradicate because criminals create new forms of deception, exploiting people's psychological vulnerabilities with emotions such as fear, anxiety and excitement [23–25].

Q2: What are the methodologies, methods, and techniques used for smishing detection and mitigation?

Figure 3 illustrates the methods and techniques used in this review. It shows that Machine Learning, the Extra Tree classifier, and Random Forest are the most frequent. In second place are Deep Learning and LSTM Bayes. Eventually, the most minor used are URL and Blacklist. Some researchers solved the smishing problem with URL analysis and blacklisting. A few used methods such as BERT embedding, ECDSA encryption, convolutional neural networks (CNN), multilayer security perception, and TCP-IP traffic analysis.

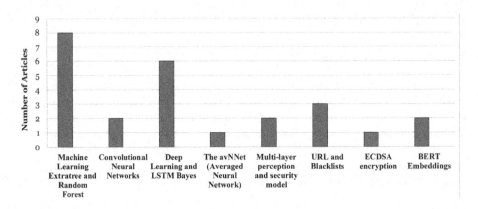

Fig. 3. Methods and techniques used for the detection and mitigation of SMS Phishing

Q3: What is the impact generated by Smishing?

During the development of this research, only some studies described the real impact generated by SMS Phishing attacks. However, in the analysis, it is determined that there is an impact on productivity, identity theft, personal image or reputation harm, emotional damage, loss of customer trust, business income, and loss of money. Some lessons learned are as follows:

Proofpoint.- Proofpoint, a USA security software company that processes more than 80% of North America's mobile messages [28], reported that only 23% of users aged 55+ had been able to define smishing correctly. However, millennials did little better, with only 34% of 23–38-year-olds demonstrating awareness of the term (see Table 2).

Table 2. Percentage of awareness of Smishing [28]

Age	Knowledge
18–22 years	22%
23–38 years	34%
39–54 years	31%
Over 55 years	23%

Wandera.- According to a 2018 report from cloud infrastructure provider Wandera, 17% of its business users encountered phishing links on their mobile devices. Compare this to only 15% of users who received a phishing email and 16% who received phishing links via social media apps [29].

FTC's Fraud Report.- By the Federal Trade Commission (FTC) report [30], many have already received smishing text messages on their phones. This report found that text messages are the most used contact method, with 23% fraud attempts, surpassing all other techniques. Additionally, smishing attacks are costly, with total losses exceeding $130 million in 2021.

Loss of Money.- Victims can be tricked into providing financial information, allowing criminals to make fraudulent transactions with their bank or credit card accounts [18].

Identity Theft.- Smishing obtains personal information to steal identity and open credit accounts, causing financial problems [24].

Reputational Damage.- If personal information is disclosed, such as compromising photographs or text messages, it can harm the victim's reputation [18,31].

Emotional Damage.- Victims of smishing may experience stress and anxiety due to deception and financial loss [25,26].

Q4: What are the prevention measures to mitigate smishing attacks?

As a result of this review, we describe in Table 3 some actions that users and institutions should consider to protect themselves against smishing:

Table 3. Preventive measures to mitigate Smishing

Action	Description
Call the bank or merchant directly	You should call your bank or merchant directly if you are in doubt. Legitimate institutions do not request account updates or login information via text message. In addition, users can verify any urgent notices directly on their online accounts or through an official telephone helpline [45].
Avoid using links or contact information in the message	Avoid using links or contact information in messages that make users feel uncomfortable. Go directly to official contact channels when users can [45].
Verify the phone number	Scammers may use email-to-text services to mask their real phone numbers, evidenced by odd-looking phone numbers such as 4-digit numbers [45].
Use Multi-Factor Authentication (MFA)	MFA or two-factor authentication can protect your account even if your password is exposed. 2FA commonly uses text message verification codes, but stronger variants, like Google Authenticator, are available. Never share your 2FA recovery codes or password with anyone; only use them on official sites [45].
Never provide a password or account recovery code by text message	Passwords and 2FA recovery codes received through text messages can compromise your account if given to the wrong person. It is important to never share this information with anyone and only use it on official sites [45].
Report to the police or the prosecutor's office	All SMS phishing attempts should be reported to the designated authorities; in the case of being a victim of this type of attack, file a complaint with the special cybercrime unit of the police or the prosecutor's office in your country [45].

5   Challenges and Research Directions

SMS phishing presents not only technical challenges but also psychological ones. By understanding these challenges, redirecting, and adopting more careful and aware behavior, individuals can protect themselves against SMS phishing and other online scams. Users should assess the situation and verify the source rather than assume that a text message is legitimate. Therefore, in this review, research is redirected to develop solutions for detecting SMS phishing incorporating algorithms that respond to and consider the user's psychological perception. In other words, researchers must include the scientific study of the human mind and its processes. Furthermore, the developed software should focus on automating how the user processes information based on their perception, acquired knowledge, and how memory, language, attention, and decision-making work. Below are several psychological challenges related to smishing:

Persuasion and Urgency. Phishing messages use persuasion and urgency techniques to get people to make quick, emotional decisions without taking the time to assess the situation or verify the source [46].

Confirmation Bias.- People often have cognitive biases that lead them to seek information confirming their existing beliefs or assumptions, making them more likely to believe phishing messages that appear legitimate or confirm their expectations [47].

Unfamiliarity.- Many people are unfamiliar with online security practices ohr do not fully understand the risks associated with SMS phishing, making tem more vulnerable to online scams [48].

6   Conclusions

This study concludes that SMS Phishing is a growing social engineering attack due to the widespread use of short messages through WhatsApp. A systematic literature analysis was carried out to answer four research questions. The main machine learning techniques used are Random Forest, Deep Learning, and LSTM Bayes, shown to be the most effective ways to mitigate Smishing attacks, according to the analysis of the selected 40 articles. The review also points out that SMS phishing is not only a technical challenge but also a psychological one, as phishing messages use persuasion and urgency techniques to get people to make quick and emotional decisions, taking advantage of confirmation bias and lack of knowledge about online safety practices. Therefore, this research opens new challenges and redirects future research to focus on the scientific study of the human mind and its processes.

We plan to design and implement a CNN-based model to detect and mitigate Smishing attacks for future work. Since smishing attacks are a growing threat that can severely impact individuals and organizations, implementing an accurate and effective detection and mitigation model can help prevent or limit the inflicted damage.

Text classification addresses problems such as predicting sentiments in tweets and reviews, as well as classifying mails as spam. Deep Learning methods are effective in this task and obtain leading results on academic problems. The technique employs a word embedding to represent terms and a Convolutional Neural Network (CNN) to learn to distinguish documents in classification. CNNs are effective in classification, selecting relevant features regardless of their position in the sequence.

The architecture consists of three key elements:

- Word Embedding: distributed representation of terms, similar for words with similar meaning.
- Convolutional Model: Extracts salient features from documents with word embeddings.
- Fully Connected Model: Interprets extracted features to predict results.

Given the growing threat of smishing, an accurate detection and mitigation model can help prevent damage. The methodology developed by Barbara Kitchenham for conducting systematic literature reviews and evidence synthesis offers a structured and organized approach that brings important benefits to research. This methodology ensures thorough identification of relevant evidence, objective assessment of the quality of the studies collected, and effective synthesis of findings. In addition, its scientific basis backed by years of experience in the field guarantees the reliability of the results obtained. The application of this methodology also improves decision making by providing a solid basis for the formulation of evidence-backed conclusions.

References

1. Benavides, E., Fuertes, W., Sanchez, S.: Characterization of phishing attacks and techniques to mitigate them. Attacks: a systematic literature review, June 2020. www.revistas.uteq.edu.ec/index.php/cyt/article/download/357/407
2. Parthy, P.P., Rajendran, G.: Identification and prevention of social engineering attacks on an enterprise. IEEE Xplore, Ocotber 2019. https://doi.org/10.1109/CCST.2019.8888441
3. Macas, M., Wu, C., Fuertes, W.: A survey on deep learning for cybersecurity: Progress, challenges, and opportunities. Comput. Networks (2022). https://doi.org/10.1016/j.comnet.2022.109032
4. Hossain, S.M.M., et al.: Spam filtering of mobile SMS using CNN-LSTM based deep learning model. Springer, March 2022. https://doi.org/10.1007/978-3-030-96305-7_10
5. Eshmawi, A., Nair, S.: The Roving Proxy Framework for SMS Spam and Phishing Detection. IEEE, July 2019. https://doi.org/10.1109/CAIS.2019.8769562
6. Akande, O.N., Akande, H.B., Kayode, A.A., Adeyinka, A.A., Olaiya, F., Oluwadara, G.: Development of a real time smishing detection mobile application using rule based techniques. sciencedirect, February 2023. https://doi.org/10.1016/j.procs.2022.01.012
7. Wahsheh, H.A.M., Al-Zahrani, M.S.: Lightweight cryptographic and artificial intelligence models for anti-smishing. In: Al-Emran, M., Al-Sharafi, M.A., Al-Kabi, M.N., Shaalan, K. (eds.) ICETIS 2021. LNNS, vol. 322, pp. 483–496. Springer, Cham (2022). https://doi.org/10.1007/978-3-030-85990-9_39

8. Saek. R., Kitayama. L., Koga. J., Shimizu. M., Oida. K.: Smishing Strategy Dynamics and Evolving Botnet Activities in Japan, Sept 2022. https://doi.org/10.1109/access.2022.3557572

9. Iddi, M., Jema. N., Kisangiri. M.: Classifying swahili smishing attacks for mobile money users: a machine-learning approach. IEEE, August 2022. https://doi.org/10.1109/access.2022.9849641

10. Oluwatobi, N., Oluwadara, G., Oluwakemi, C., Rasheed, G., Hakeem, B., Abdullateef, B., Anuoluwapo, F.: SMSPROTECT: an automatic smishing detection mobile application. ICT Express (2022). ISSN 2405–9595, https://doi.org/10.1016/j.icte.2022.05.009

11. Sonowal, G., Kuppusamy, K.S.: SmiDCA: an anti-smishing model with machine learning approach. Comput. J. **61**(8), 1143–1157 (2018). https://doi.org/10.1093/comjnl/bxy061

12. Wei, W., Ke, Q., Nowak, J., Korytkowski, M., Scherer, R., Woźniak, M.: Accurate and fast URL phishing detector: a convolutional neural network approach (2020). Computer Networks, 107275. https://doi.org/10.1016/j.comnet.2020.107275

13. Bojjagani, S., Denslin Brabin, D.R., Venkateswara Rao, P.V.: PhishPreventer: a secure authentication protocol for prevention of phishing attacks in mobile environment with formal verification. Procedia Comput. Sci. **171**, 1110–1119 (2020). ISSN 1877–0509. https://doi.org/10.1016/j.procs.2020.04.119

14. Ulfath, R.E., Alqahtani, H., e Iqbal H. Sarker, M.H.: Hybrid CNN-GRU framework with integrated pre-trained language transformer for SMS phishing detection. At the 5th International Conference on Future Networks and Distributed Systems (ICFNDS 2021), pp. 244–251. Association for Computing Machinery, Nueva York, NY, EE.UU. (2022). https://doi.org/10.1145/3508072.3508109

15. Oswald, C., Elza Simon, S., Bhattacharya, A.: SpotSpam: SMS spam detection based on intent analysis using BERT inlays (2022). Web 16, 3, Artículo 14 (agosto de 2022), 27 pages. https://doi.org/10.1145/3538491

16. Li, Y., Xiao, R., Feng, J., Zhao, L.: A semi-supervised learning approach for detection of phishing webpages. Optik **124**(23), 6027–6033 (2013). ISSN 0030–4026, https://doi.org/10.1016/j.ijleo.2013.04.078

17. Mishra, S., Soni, D.: Smishing detector: a security model to detect smishing through SMS content analysis and URL behavior analysis. Future Generation Comput. Syst. **108**, 803–815 (2020). Web. https://doi.org/10.1016/j.future.2020.02.006

18. Soykan, U., Elif, Bagriyanik, M.: The effect of SMiShing attack on security of demand response programs. Energies (Basel) **13**(17), 4542. Web (2020). https://doi.org/10.3390/en13174542

19. Joo, J.W., et al.: S-Detector: an enhanced security model for detecting smishing attack for mobile computing. Telecommun. Syst. **66**(1), 29–38 (2017). Web. https://doi.org/10.1007/s11235-016-0231-6

20. Cyber thefts set off alarm bells in Ecuador, blogsnews, November 2020. www.elcomercio.com/actualidad/seguridad/robos-ciberneticos-alertas-ecuador-denuncias.html

21. Ecuador is among the countries with the most cyber-attacks in Latin America, blogsnews, July 2021. www.elcomercio.com/tendencias/tecnologia/ecuador-ciberataques-america-latina-hacker.html

22. The Internet is the service that has made the most progress in 2020, blogsnews, May 2021. www.elcomercio.com/actualidad/negocios/ecuador-internet-tecnologia-fibra-optica.html

23. Rahman, Md.L., Timko, D., Wali, H., Neupane, A.: Users really do respond to smishing. ACM, April 2023. https://doi.org/10.1145/3577923.3583640

24. Baadel, S., Thabtah, F., Majeed, A.: Avoiding the phishing bait: the need for conventional countermeasures for mobile users. Crowdstrike, January 2019. https://doi.org/10.1109/IEMCON.2018.8615095
25. Caldwell, N.: Smishing: what it is, why it matters, and how to protect yourself, October 2022. www.arcticwolf.com/resources/blog/smishing-what-it-is-how-to-protect-yourself/
26. SMS scam or smishing: what it is, risks, examples and how to avoid it. lisainstitue (2023). www.lisainstitute.com/blogs/blog/smishing-estafa-sms-riesgos-ejemplos#:~:text=El%20enlace%20incluido%20en%20el,del%20usuario%20y%20su%20contrase%C3%B1la
27. Kitchenham, B., Pearl Brereton, O., Budgen, D., Turner, M., Bailey, J., Linkman, S.: Systematic literature reviews in software engineering, a systematic literature review. J. Inf. Softw. Technol., January 2009. https://doi.org/10.1016/j.infsof.2008.09.009
28. Njuguna, D., Kamau, J., Kaburu, D.: Model for mitigating smishing attacks on mobile platforms. IEEE Xplore, February 2022. https://doi.org/10.1109/ICECET52533.2021.9698789
29. Clasen, M., Li, F., Williams, D.: Friend or foe: an investigation into recipient identification of sms-based phishing. In: Furnell, S., Clarke, N. (eds.) HAISA 2021. IAICT, vol. 613, pp. 148–163. Springer, Cham (2021). https://doi.org/10.1007/978-3-030-81111-2_13
30. Ma, K.W.F., McKinnon, T.: COVID-19 and cyber fraud: emerging threats during the pandemic emerald, March 2020. https://doi.org/10.1108/JFC-01-2021-0016
31. Fuertes, W., et al.: Impact of social engineering attacks: a literature review. In: Rocha, Á., Fajardo-Toro, C.H., Rodríguez, J.M.R. (eds) Developments and Advances in Defense and Security. Smart Innovation, Systems and Technologies, vol 255. Springer, Singapore (2022). https://doi.org/10.1007/978-981-16-4884-7_3
32. Rosenblatt, F.: The perceptron: a probabilistic model for information storage and organization in the brain. Psychol. Rev. **65**(6), 386–408 (1958). https://doi.org/10.1037/h0042519
33. Pazikadin, A.R., Rifai, D., Ali, K., Malik, M.Z., Abdalla, A.N., Faraj, M.A.: Solar irradiance measurement instrumentation and power solar generation forecasting based on Artificial Neural Networks (ANN): a review of five years research trend. ScienceDirect, May 2020. https://doi.org/10.1016/j.scitotenv.2020.136848
34. Salehinejad, H., Baarbe, J., Sankar, S., Barfett, J., Colak, E., Valaee, S.: Recent Advances in Recurrent Neural Networks, arxiv, December 2017
35. Nikou, M., Mansourfar, G., Bagherzadeh, J.: Stock price prediction using DEEP learning algorithm and its comparison with machine learning algorithms (2019). https://doi.org/10.1002/isaf.1459
36. Wu, Yc., Feng, Jw.: Development and Application of Artificial Neural Network (2018). https://doi.org/10.1007/s11277-017-5224-x
37. Petridis, S., Li, Z., M, Pantic, End-to-end visual speech recognition with LSTMS. IEEE (2017). doi: https://doi.org/10.1109/ICASSP.2017.7952625
38. Creswell, A., White, T., Dumoulin, V., Arulkumaran, K., Sengupta, B., Bharath, A.A.: Generative adversarial networks: an overview. IEEE, January 2018. https://doi.org/10.1109/MSP.2017.2765202
39. Zenke, F., Ganguli, S., Zenke, F., Ganguli, S.: SuperSpike: supervised learning in multilayer spiking neural networks (2018). https://doi.org/10.1162/neco_a_01086
40. Deng, L., Liu, Y.: Deep learning in natural language processing. Springer (2018). https://doi.org/10.1007/978-981-10-5209-5

41. Yao, L., Guan, Y.: An improved LSTM structure for natural language processing. IEEE (2018). https://doi.org/10.1109/IICSPI.2018.8690387

42. Ahmed, I., Jeon, G., Piccialli, F.: From artificial intelligence to explainable artificial intelligence in industry 4.0: a survey on what, how, and where. IEEE (2022). https://doi.org/10.1109/TII.2022.3146552

43. Yamashita, R., Nishio, M., Do, R.K.G., et al.: Convolutional neural networks: an overview and application in radiology. Springer, June 2018. https://doi.org/10.1007/s13244-018-0639-9

44. Abdel-Jaber, H., Devassy, D., Al Salam, A., Hidaytallah, L., EL-Amir, M.: A Review of Deep Learning Algorithms and Their Applications in Healthcare, MDPI, February 2022. https://doi.org/10.3390/a15020071

45. What is Smishing and How to Defend Against it. www.kaspersky.com/resource-center/threats/what-is-smishing-and-how-to-defend-against-it

46. Stojnic, T., Vatsalan, D., Arachchilage, N.: Phishing email strategies: understanding cybercriminals' strategies of crafting phishing emails (2021). https://doi.org/10.1002/spy2.165

47. Pfleeger, S.L., Caputo, D.D.: Leveraging behavioral science to mitigate cyber security risk (2012). https://doi.org/10.1016/j.cose.2011.12.010

48. Lewis, A.: U.S. international strategy for cybersecurity (2015). www.jstor.org/stable/pdf/resrep37695.pdf

One-Time Passwords: A Literary Review of Different Protocols and Their Applications

Luis E. Almeida[1,2], Brayan A. Fernández[1,2], Daliana Zambrano[1,2], Anthony I. Almachi[1,2], Hilton B. Pillajo[1,2], and Sang Guun Yoo[1,2,3(✉)] ⓘ

[1] Departamento de Informática y Ciencias de la Computación, Escuela Politécnica Nacional, Quito, Ecuador
sang.yoo@epn.edu.ec
[2] Smart Lab, Escuela Politécnica Nacional, Quito, Ecuador
[3] Departamento de Ciencias de la Computación, Universidad de las Fuerzas Armadas ESPE, Sangolquí, Ecuador

Abstract. Currently, user authentication only based on passwords can be inadequate due to different types of vulnerabilities and attacks. To solve this problem, two-factor authentication is commonly used, providing a higher level of security when the user logs into their accounts, and one popular example of two-factor authentication is the combination of password and One-Time Passwords (OTP). Due to the importance and popularity of OTPs, this study analyzed the most widely used OTP protocols and their applications to understand their state of the art. The scientific community can use the analysis carried out in this work to understand why OTP is so popular and to decide on the type of OTP, in case a custom implementation is needed for an authentication system. To achieve this, this work analyzed a large number of previous works methodically through a semi cyclic process based on research action combined with a systematic review process. The most important works were analyzed to identify their specific features and to classify the used technologies. Usage trends in terms of protocols, implementations, algorithms, and OTP generators were also analyzed. In addi-tion, this article has determined a complementary feature guide that must be considered when implementing an OTP authentication system.

Keywords: Authentication process · One-Time Passwords · OTP · OTP protocols · OTP generators · Two-Factor Authentication · 2FA

1 Introduction

Security in different technological areas, such as the Internet of Things [1], networks [2] and software development [3], has given great importance to the authentication process. This process aims to establish trust between users and devices, verifying the identity of users on a platform [4]. Although the use of username and password has been common for authentication [5], the advancement of the Internet has made identity theft a significant security problem [6].

© The Author(s), under exclusive license to Springer Nature Switzerland AG 2024
T. Guarda et al. (Eds.): ARTIIS 2023, CCIS 1936, pp. 205–219, 2024.
https://doi.org/10.1007/978-3-031-48855-9_16

Based on research from the last 30 years, a strong single factor authentication based on passwords has been found to be difficult to implement due to various threats and attacks [7], such as compromised devices with spyware, intercepted communications, brute force attacks, and "Man in the Middle" attacks [8, 9]. As a result, two-factor authentication (2FA) has gained popularity as a more effective security measure [10]. 2FA combines two of the three universal factors: something the user knows, something the user has, and something the user is or does [11]. The key advantage of 2FA is that even if one factor is compromised, the security of the system is maintained [11].

Among the various ways to implement 2FA, the use of One-Time Passwords (OTP) based on software tokens is one of the most popular methods [12, 13]. These programs use OTP algorithms for their implementation and are fundamental to guarantee the security of systems in applications of online banking, electronic commerce, medical care, IoT and other scopes [12, 13]. Lamport [14] proposed the first OTP known as the S/KEY authentication system [15], to authenticate untrusted computers in public use.

Due to the advances in the use of OTP-based systems, this study focuses on analyzing different types of OTP and their algorithms, as well as their respective characteristics, in order to generate a complete document on the state of the art of this technology.

2 Research Methodology

The primary objective of this research is to analyze the current trend regarding OTPs implemented in different solutions. To achieve this, a semi cyclic process based on research action [16] and combined with a systematic review process [17, 18] has been applied. This methodology is the same used in [19]. Each of these phases has specific tasks executed during the research development process (see Fig. 1).

2.1 Planning Phase

This is a preparatory phase prior to starting the research process. The main objective is to reduce the scope and produce accurate searches that are suitable for the present study. To achieve this, the following research questions were proposed: (1) what are the solutions in the current implementations of OTP?, (2) what kinds of algorithms are used in the different implementations of OTP?, and (3) in what areas are OTPs used?

With the defined questions, the following keywords were identified: "One-Time Passwords", "solutions", "implementations", "2FA", "areas". Subsequently, the preliminary search strings were "One-Time Password solutions", and "One-Time Password implementations". These strings resulted in large amounts of documents, and to reduce the number of documents, we used logical connectors to combine the previously mentioned keywords. Additionally, scientific databases were selected to search for articles using the previously defined strings. The selected databases were ACM Digital Library, IEEE Xplore, Springer, and ScienceDirect.

2.2 Perform Review Phase

In this stage of the study, searches were carried out in the digital repositories using specific previously defined strings. Only publications older than 5 years are considered, with some exceptions, as mentioned in the definitions of [18] and [19], because certain algorithms used in the development of solutions based on OTPs were developed in longer than the specified period of time.

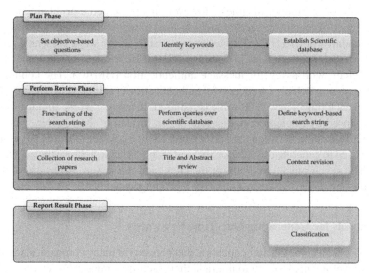

Fig. 1. Detailed research method.

For the collection and management of the articles, the Mendeley tool was used, which allows sharing and managing research papers through labels and filters. In this way, a shared library could be created to facilitate the analysis of the bibliography.

To conclude this stage, an article discard protocol was applied manually. The titles and abstracts of each article are reviewed to identify relevant keywords and details that might answer the research questions posed above. Those documents that did not comply with the terms or did not provide relevant information were discarded.

2.3 Report Result Phase

In the last step of the research methodology, the findings and results were documented and used to build the following sections, which are the central part of this work. Furthermore, new OTP technological solutions and their implementation areas were analyzed and discussed. The results of this phase are shown in the following sections of this document.

3 One-Time Passwords

OWASP Top 10 indicates that an authentication system may be exposed to different types of threats [20]. This situation shows how important is the implementation of 2FA based on OTP. When a system implements only the password-based authentication systems, it can be exposed to different types of attacks. For example, we could mention the attack executed on the PlayStation Network, where a group of attackers gained access to 77 million customer accounts, including credit card information [21].

The study of OTPs began with Lamport [14] in the early 1980s, with a protocol in which both the client and the server agreed to use an algorithm to generate OTPs, which expired once the authentication process was successfully carried out. Lamport's solution used a seed (S) agreed upon by both the client and the server, which passed through a hash function (h) n number of times. However, this presented a problem, since after a certain number of repetitions, hash functions tend to repeat the output values [22].

Subsequently, other OTP solutions emerged, such as the work presented in [23]. In this work, the protocol is based on a counter (C) that increments its value and is applied to a hash chain with a key for message authentication (HMAC). The counter on the server increments each time a successful authentication is achieved, while for the user it increments each time a new OTP value is required. In another work, an improvement of [23] is proposed by implementing the time factor instead of the counter, which avoids the desynchronization between the server's and client's counter [24]. In [24], timestamp marks are used to generate the values to be sent to the server to achieve the authentication process. The synchronization, both for the client and the server, makes use of the Unix time, as it is universally used by Unix type operating systems.

3.1 Protocols for Generating One-Time Passwords

Today, OTPs are a common authentication mechanism for many companies, institutions, and even governments looking to upgrade their security strategy. For example, Google uses the sending of OTP via SMS to authenticate the user after numerous failed login attempts. On the other hand, telecom companies generate a One-Time Password and send it directly to the user's mobile phone as an authentication privilege for using the free internet service in public places such as shopping centers, maritime terminals, or airports, which has a validity of 30 min [25].

OTP algorithms can be classified into two groups, i.e., event based and seed value-based OTPs. Event based OTPs change value whenever an event occurs. The main event-based OTPs are HOTP and TOTP. In the case of HOTP, if the counter value changes by a login attempt event, a new HOTP value is generated. Similar process is done in TOTP, where a new value is generated when the time value changes, invalidating the previous value. On the other hand, seed value-based OTPs are based on a shared seed that is used to generate the OTP value.

3.1.1 HMAC-Based One-Time Password Protocol (HOTP)

HOTP is an event-based OTP algorithm created in 2005 that generates values based on hash message authentication codes (HMAC) [26–28]. For generating HMACs, the Secure Hash Algorithm-2 (SHA-2 or SHA2) is used frequently among the different hash algorithms. However, in 2015, NIST recommended the use of Secure Hash Algorithm-3 (SHA-3 or SHA3) due to known weaknesses that SHA-2 has exhibited over time [27, 28].

HMAC is used to create the HOTP value. The HOTP algorithm works based on an increasing counter value (C) and a static symmetric key (K) known only to the token and validation service [23]. The key (K) must be shared between the client and the server, and the counter (C) must be synchronized between the HOTP generator (client) and the HOTP validator (server) [29][30].

HOTP works with two counters, one on the client side (hardware or software token) and one on the server side. Both counters validate the HOTP value. The server increments its counter after each successful authentication, while the client does so when requesting a new OTP. If the server receives a value that does not match that of the client, the resynchronization protocol is started before another attempt [23], this process can be seen summarized in Fig. 2.

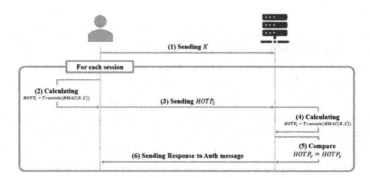

Fig. 2. HOTP algorithm protocol, adapted from [22]

For the user to easily remember the OTP, the most common OTP length is 6 digits, resulting in ten million possible combinations. HOTPs are vulnerable to brute force attacks because their value expires only after successful authentication [23]. In [23], two solutions are proposed to detect and stop brute force attacks on the authentication server: (1) Define a maximum number of possible attempts for HOTP validation and (2) Implement a delay scheme to avoid Multiple parallel divination techniques. For each failed attempt at a login session, the authentication server would wait for: (Number of failed attempts) * (Definite time).

HOTP has no expiration time and can be used for a long period of time, increasing the chances of being attacked. This weakness is solved by the TOTP algorithm, which provides short-lived OTP values to improve security [24].

3.1.2   Time-Based One-Time Password (TOTP)

Time-based One-Time password (TOTP) is an extension of the HOTP algorithm. The main difference is that the HOTP uses a counter (C) while the TOTP uses time (T). The time T can be defined as: TOTP = HOTP(K, T), where T represents the number of time steps between the initial counter time T_0 and the current Unix time (i.e., the number of seconds elapsed since midnight UTC of January 1, 1970) [24]. In general, the time value tends to be the date (YYYY-MM-DD) followed by the time (HH:MM:SS). Both are usually measured in Coordinated Universal Time (UTC) or as well-known as Greenwich Mean Time (GMT) because it can be used depending on the location or the time zone [27, 28].

The HOTP method requires a timer. The validation system receives the TOTP value without knowing the exact OTP generation timestamp, which creates a gap between generation and reception. To address this, an authentication policy is established with an acceptable transmission delay window. A time step of 30 s is recommended as a proper balance between security and usability [24].

TOTP is based on the HOTP algorithm, which is derived from HMAC and uses defined hash functions. That is, part of the security of the TOTP depends on the hash functions used in the HMAC algorithm. Consequently, TOTP implementations choose to use HMAC-SHA-256 or HMAC-SHA-512 instead of the HMAC-SHA-1 functions [24].

3.1.3 Seed Value-Based One-Time Password

In [31], an example of seed-value-based One-Time Password is described. To generate the OTP value, three entities are utilized: user, server, and One-Time Password Generation System (GS). The GS receives data from both the user and the server to generate the OTP. The user provides a number (N) and a secret password phrase (PP), while the server provides a seed (S). The GS uses the user's secret password phrase along with the seed received from the server, applying the secure hash function N times to generate a sequence of OTP values, Eq. 8 describes the formula for generating the OTP.

$$OTP = Hash_{funtion}(PP, S)^N$$

The seed comes from the server in a clear text which is purely alphanumeric of 1 to 16 characters long that must be internally converted to lower case. As with the other OTP algorithms described before, the security of seed value-based OTP also depends on the used hash function.

Another way to use a seed value-based OTP is using pseudorandom numbers. A pseudorandom number generator (PRNG) is commonly used to generate unpredictable OTP values [31]. The pseudo random numbers are values or elements statistically random, derived from a seed [31]. A cryptographically strong pseudorandom number generator is needed by the server to generate the OTP value for each login session [32].

The security of the PRNG depends on the random algorithm used, but also requires a correct implementation, for example, choosing a constant as the seed for the random algorithm, the PRNG could be predictable. For that reason, there are critical randomness rules [3]: (1) do not use a constant or predictable seed to initialize the random function, (2) do not use a static OTP value, and (3) do not generate OTP values according to specific patterns.

In the previous description, we get a wider idea of how OTPs are implemented. Depending on the required complexity and the requirements set by the organization, we can choose one or the other. Nevertheless, we can see that the trend of these protocols is divided into: Time-based OTPs, Hash-chain based OTPs, and Challenge-based Authentication algorithms. Table 1 shows a summary of the type of OTP used in the reviewed articles. The structure of this table is as follows, the first column presents the different types of OTP protocols analyzed in each article, while the second column lists the corresponding articles. In the last row of the table are articles that do not specify the type of OTP protocol used. However, these articles provide valuable information about the operation and applications of OTPs, which allows for a more complete understanding of the topic.

Table 1. OTP Classification.

Type of OTP	References
Time-based OTP	[7] [19] [25] [23] [29] [34] [35] [37] [38] [39] [45] [51] [53]
HMAC based OTP	[7] [12] [14] [19] [25] [23] [33] [40] [10] [41] [42] [43]
Seed value base OTP	[2] [3] [11]
Not specified	[1] [5] [36] [44] [46] [47] [48] [49] [50] [52]

3.1.4 Other OTP Generation Protocols

Although they are not very common, some previous works make use of other types of protocols. The following is a list of some of them:

YSH Protocol: The YSH protocol is an enhancement of the Lamport hash chain protocol for generating One-Time Passwords (OTP). Although it allows the server to be verified, it does not protect against spoofing attacks by not storing certain client parameter values, which compromises authentication. Furthermore, it is vulnerable to "small number attack" [15].

Bicakci Protocol: The protocol is based on asymmetric cryptography to generate and verify OTPs, being an evolution of the HOTP protocol to improve security. However, it has disadvantages such as computational complexity and lack of server authentication, which could allow for phishing attacks [22].

Chefranov's Scheme: The protocol features a complex and secure algorithm with many parameters. However, its high complexity makes it difficult to implement and understand in comparison with previous protocols. Although it is resistant to browsing attacks, it lacks protection against check table modification. Furthermore, the Chefranov scheme allows for server verification, but does not protect against spoofing [22].

3.2 Methods of Receiving One-Time Passwords

The previous works analyzed in this paper shown different ways of sending and receiving the OTPs. In the following, there are the explanation of those methods.

Text Messages: The common method to deliver OTP is via SMS [3]. However, studies such as [31, 33, 34] have shown that SMS is vulnerable to attacks such as SIM card cloning and shoulder surfing. Despite this, companies like Airbnb, Facebook, and Google continue to send OTPs over SMS due to user preference [5]. Alternatives using lightweight cryptography and text steganography have been also proposed [35].

Quick Response Code (QR): According to [36], scanning QR codes is a relevant method to receive OTP which allows saving time by avoiding manual input of characters. Although the average authentication time is 25.8877 s, [37] highlights that QR codes are vulnerable to replacement, modification, and malicious URL attacks.

Piezo-Gyro Channel: A work proposed by [38] presents a unique way to input an OTP using a physical device that automatically sends the OTP to a smartphone through acoustic stimuli on its MEMS gyroscope. The device uses a piezoelectric transducer to induce movements in the internal mass of the gyro sensor, generating artificial angular velocity readings that are translated into the OTP value. This process creates a one-way communication channel between the physical device and the smartphone, allowing authentication without the user having to manually enter the OTP [38].

Proprietary Tokens: Proprietary tokens are small physical devices, such as hardware keys. They do not require passwords but may require a physical or wireless connection to authenticate the user. In addition to cards, there are other tokens such as USB and wireless devices. Cards are more likely to be lost and cloned [39].

Paper: The OTP paper receipt method is a form of authentication that uses a list of printed codes to securely transmit information. It is useful in situations where access to devices is complicated or impossible [10]. For example, Google verification codes work like this. Ten one-time passcodes are generated when 2 Step Verification is enabled on a Google account, and new codes are generated when old ones are used up [41].

Email: Email is a popular way to send OTPs due to its ease of use, speed, and cost effectiveness. According to [25], they propose a virtual OTP keyboard represented as a 4x4 matrix with XY coordinates sent to the user to select on the virtual keyboard. Email based OTPs are secure and allow user identity to be authenticated during login on any Internet enabled device. However, [42] warns that they can be intercepted or compromise the user's account.

3.3 Classification of the Use of One-Time Passwords

One-time password (OTP) passwords are a security tool used to protect information and ensure user authentication in different applications and systems [43]. These passwords are generated randomly and can only be used once, making them an effective security measure against unauthorized access [8]. OTP passwords are commonly used in the access of online bank accounts [44], user authentication in email services [39], and access to private networks and two-factor authentication systems [2, 45]. However, as of the writing of this document, some works were found that utilize OTPs in different ways and in different areas as detailed below.

Use of OTPs in Mobile Applications: Currently, mobile applications have had great success due to their portability and efficiency [5]. One area that has taken advantage of this is online banking, with the implementation of virtual wallets [5]. A study focused on Human-Computer Interaction (HCI) and Computer Supported Cooperative Work (CSCW) of the digital payment apps Paytm and PhonePe was carried out, too [46]; both apps use OTPs to perform the login or user registration process by sending a unique code to the user's registered mobile number [46]. To make a transaction in the Paytm app, a unique QR code must be scanned for each store. However, in several countries, card payments, including those made through digital wallet apps, require a two-factor authentication (2FA) [46]. Both the CVV (the three-digit code on the back of the card) and an OTP delivered to the user via the bank's own app or SMS must be entered [46]. Although methods vary among banks, for the case studied in [46], it indicates that the user has 180 s or less to complete the authentication process.

Use of OTP in Hospitals and Healthcare Centers: In [5], TreC, a platform developed in Northeast Italy to manage personal health records (PHR) is described. In addition to the main web system, TreC offers specific solutions for chronic patients, such as TreC Diario Diabete, which allows recording health data such as blood glucose level and physical activity, and TreC FSE, which allows access to personal health data and medical prescriptions from the phone.

Authentication in TreC is based on a Multi-Factor Authentication (MFA) system that uses One-Time Passwords (OTP). These codes are displayed on the screen of the patient's mobile device and entered into the web system to validate her identity. This OTP authentication approach has also been used in hospital settings, such as emergency care and vehicle services, where tablets enabled with insecure passwords are employed in emergency vehicles to quickly access necessary information.

The use of OTP is essential to protect the patient information payload in the hospital system and prevent cyber attacks that may reveal private information. Many hospital systems are outdated and use outdated operating systems, making them vulnerable to malware attacks. In addition, the lack of personal computers for medical personnel leads to the sharing of potentially infected computers with keyloggers.

The COVID-19 pandemic presented additional challenges as hospitals had to perform tests and deliver results with precision and privacy. It was proposed to use tokens to assign results in electronic government systems, but this could increase costs and exclude people with limited resources or without access to the Internet.

Finally, it is highlighted that people with mental disabilities also use OTP to generate secure access codes to systems, which allows them to authenticate or validate their access through specific applications or devices [48].

Usage of OTP in IoT: In an Internet of Things (IoT) system [49], an approach to improve the security of smart locks using one-time passwords (OTP) is proposed. In this system, when someone rings the doorbell of an apartment equipped with a smart lock, the owner, Bob, receives a notification on his phone. In addition, a camera built into the doorbell takes a photo of the person who has rung the doorbell and sends it to Bob.

To verify the identity of the person, Bob uses the photo to confirm that it is Alice. Instead of sending him the password that he always uses, Bob generates a temporary password (OTP) and sends it to Alice. In this way, Bob keeps the original password for his apartment private, improving the security of the system.

4 Discussion

As shown in Fig. 3, research related to OTPs experienced constant growth from 2017 to 2020, with 2019 and 2020 being the years of greatest research activity. However, starting in 2020, there was a decrease in the number of published works, when we were overcoming the COVID-19 pandemic. It is possible that the priority attention towards projects related to the pandemic has affected the interest in the OTPs. The need for future research is raised to better understand the trend in this area, especially in authentication issues which is of great relevance in computer security.

4.1 One-Time Password Generation Protocol

71% of the relevant research projects focus on the TOTP (Time-Based One-Time Password) protocol for implementation or highlight its use. According to references [32] and [3], TOTP is considered superior to the HOTP protocol in terms of robustness for generating one-time passwords (OTPs). The factors that contribute to this greater robustness are the following:

- OTP Randomness: TOTP uses time as the key to generate cryptographically strong pseudo-random values using HMAC, which results in completely random one-time passwords. This increases the randomness of the one-time passwords generated by TOTP, as mentioned in article [32].
- OTP Expiration: By default, article [38] specifies that after x, a determined time, a new OTP value will be generated (e.g., a recommended time of 30 s). This prevents brute force attacks. However, it is possible that values generated once the time span has expired may still be valid for a short period due to latency and other communication-affecting effects, as mentioned in [3].
- OTP Consumption: Although not a TOTP-specific feature, several systems using two-factor authentication do not limit the number of allowed incorrect OTP entry attempts, as mentioned in article [32]. This can lead to excessive usage of OTPs.

According to Fig. 4 in the research papers, a trend is observed in the OTP generation protocols. The TOTP protocol has the highest percentage of implementations at 71%, followed by HMAC-based One-Time Password (HOTP) at 18%, while value-based OTP implementations are at 11%.

However, there are concerns about the security of one-time password generation due to possible poor implementation practices. For example, the use of basic random number generation functions or predictable initial values could compromise security. An attacker could obtain a bank of values and predict the next value in the sequence if he knows the seed, allowing the entire sequence of values to be generated.

The article [32] mentions that many programming languages have predefined random number generation functions, but these are usually not cryptographically secure. Therefore, it is essential to keep this in mind to ensure the security of one-time password generation.

Figure 5 Shows that the TOTP protocol peaked in publication in 2019, correlating with the data in Fig. 13. However, in 2020, there was a 16% decrease in TOTP-related publications. This could be because some articles mention the use of one-time passwords without making a clean reference to the TOTP protocol.

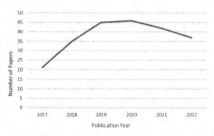

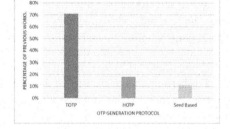

Fig. 3. Trend of number of previous works related to OTP.

Fig. 4. Usage of OTP Protocols.

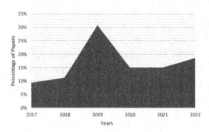

Fig. 5. OTP uses over the years.

5 One-Time Password Selection Strategy

In the context of current research, several features of OTP algorithms have been identified. It is noted that all solutions use hash functions to add an additional layer of security, ensuring that an attacker cannot obtain the original value even if they manage to obtain the resulting hash value.

It is mentioned that HOTP may be vulnerable to brute force attacks once the OTP value is generated and expires on successful validation, potentially allowing an attacker to determine the value if there is no limit on the number of authentication attempts. Failed.

In the case of TOTP, it is mentioned that the vulnerability is reduced thanks to the use of the time value for each OTP value, which disables it after a short period of time and makes a brute force attack almost impossible.

In addition, it is noted that seed-based one-time passwords can be vulnerable to network snooping attacks, where an attacker obtains seed values to generate OTPs and uses them to steal the shared secret or launch attacks.

Despite the aforementioned drawbacks, each OTP generation protocol has ideal scenarios for its implementation. HOTP and seed-based OTP are suitable for systems where the OTP value does not need to be updated quickly and where the level of security is not critical, or where ease of use is a priority. On the other hand, the TOTP is recommended for systems where security is a primary concern, as it limits the time to enter a 6-digit value to just 30 s.

When selecting a one-time password (OTP) it is important to adhere to its ability to meet appropriate security standards [32]. This involves choosing an OTP with a strong cryptographic algorithm and additional security measures. Ease of use and compatibility with existing systems and devices [35] should also be considered, as a difficult-to-use or incompatible OTP can result in low adoption and lower security.

Furthermore, the durability of the OTP value is relevant. An OTP that is resistant to reverse engineering and not easily compromised should be chosen [32], since an OTP that is susceptible to attacks or short-lived might not be suitable for long-term use.

As for the methods of receiving OTP, each has advantages and disadvantages. Paper OTP cards are easy to use and do not require electronic devices or internet connection. However, there is a risk of losing, duplicating, or discarding these cards, which could allow an attacker to authenticate illegitimately.

QR codes are used in messaging applications to authenticate devices when logging in, improving the experience through the use and communication of One-Time Passwords (OTP) without the need to enter codes manually, which increases security. However, some devices without cameras limit accessibility, and security could be compromised if attackers were to steal images with QR codes that contain OTP. Additionally, it is important to consider the cost and availability of OTPs before choosing them, as they may not be feasible for certain organizations. [39].

6 Conclusions

According to the reviewed literature, there are various types of protocols that allow us to make use of OTPs. A clear trend in the use and implementation of the protocols established in different RFCs, such as HOTP, TOTP and Seed value-based OTP was evidenced in the reviewed works.

To achieve a satisfactory authentication process, different OTP protocols can be used. However, the selection and usage conditions of these protocols depend on the advantages and communication frequency between the OTP generator server and the user, as assessed in previous sections.

To effectively implement different types of one-time passwords (OTP), it is important to follow certain recommendations. First, it is essential to ensure that the chosen OTP complies with the appropriate security standards and is compatible with existing systems and devices. It is important to perform compatibility and security tests before implementing the OTP to ensure that it meets the organization's needs.

While the protocols previously discussed the focus on security and increased robustness of different One-Time Password implementations, the user experience of entering the passwords where required is often neglected.

In conclusion, to effectively implement different types of OTPs, it is important to ensure that they comply with appropriate security standards, are compatible with systems and devices, and that there is a balance between the cost and benefit of implementing a two-factor authentication system.

In terms of future work, it is proposed to conduct a study that helps to determine which type of protocol and delivery method the user feels most comfortable with, as well as to implement a solution that makes use of the most widely used protocols.

References

1. Tsai, W.-C., Tsai, T.-H., Wang, T.-J., Chiang, M.-L.: Automatic key update mechanism for lightweight M2M communication and enhancement of iot security: a case study of CoAP using libcoap library. Sensors **22**(1), 340 (2022)
2. Zhou, X., Lu, Y., Wang, Y., Yan, X.: Overview on moving target network defense. In: 2018 IEEE 3rd International Conference on Image, Vision and Computing (ICIVC), pp. 821–827 (2018)
3. Ma, S., et al.: Fine with '1234'? An analysis of SMS one-time password randomness in android apps. In: 2021 IEEE/ACM 43rd International Conference on Software Engineering (ICSE), pp. 1671–1682 (2021)
4. Zhang, J., Tan, X., Wang, X., Yan, A., Qin, Z.: T2FA: transparent two-factor authentication. IEEE Access **6**, 32677–32686 (2018)
5. Sciarretta, G., Carbone, R., Ranise, S., Viganò, L.: Formal analysis of mobile multi-factor authentication with single sign-on login. ACM Trans. Privacy Sec. **23**(3), 1–37 (2020)
6. Ruoti, S., Seamons, K.: End-to-end passwords. In: Proceedings of the 2017 New Security Paradigms Workshop, pp. 107–121 (2017)
7. Wang, D., Li, W., Wang, P.: Measuring two-factor authentication schemes for real-time data access in industrial wireless sensor networks. IEEE Trans. Industr. Inform. **14**(9), 4081–4092 (2018)
8. Aloul, F., Zahidi, S., El-Hajj, W.: Two factor authentication using mobile phones. In: 2009 IEEE/ACS International Conference on Computer Systems and Applications, pp. 641–644 (2009)
9. Shirvanian, M., Agrawal, S.: 2D-2FA: a new dimension in two-factor authentication. In Annual Computer Security Applications Conference, pp. 482–496 (2021)
10. Aravindhan, K.: One-time password: a survey. Inter. J. Emerging Trends Eng. Developm. Issue **3**(1), 3 (2013)
11. Gunson, N., Marshall, D., Morton, H., Jack, M.: User perceptions of security and usability of single-factor and two-factor authentication in automated telephone banking. Comput. Secur. **30**(4), 208–220 (2011)
12. Erdem, E., Sandikkaya, M.T.: OTPaaS—one time password as a service. IEEE Trans. Inf. Forensics Secur. **14**(3), 743–756 (2019)
13. Jin, C., Yang, Z., van Dijk, M., Zhou, J.: Proof of aliveness. In: Proceedings of the 35th Annual Computer Security Applications Conferenc, pp. 1–16 (2019)
14. Lamport, L.: Password authentication with insecure communication. Commun. ACM **24**(11), 770–772 (1981)
15. Leea, W.-B., Chen, T.-H., Sun, W.-R., Ho, K. I.-J.: An S/key-like one-time password authentication scheme using smart cards for smart meter. In: 2014 28th International Conference on Advanced Information Networking and Applications Workshops, pp. 281–286 (2014)
16. Drummond, J.S., Themessl-Huber, M.: The cyclical process of action research. Action Res. **5**(4), 430–448 (2007)
17. Chauhan, S., Agarwal, N., Kar, A.K.: Addressing big data challenges in smart cities: a systematic literature review. Info **18**(4), 73–90 (2016)
18. de Morais, C.M., Sadok, D., Kelner, J.: An IoT sensor and scenario survey for data researchers. J. Brazilian Comput. Soc. **25**(1), 4 (2019)
19. Barriga, J.J., et al.: Smart parking: a literature review from the technological perspective. Appl. Sci. **9**(21), 4569 (2019)
20. The OWASP Foundation, "OWASP Top Ten," OWASP Top Ten, Sep. 30 (2021)
21. Polleit. P., Spreitzenbarth, M.: Defeating the secrets of OTP apps. In: 2018 11th International Conference on IT Security Incident Management & IT Forensics (IMF), pp. 76–88 (2018)

22. Babkin, S., Epishkina, A.: Authentication protocols based on one-time passwords. In: 2019 IEEE Conference of Russian Young Researchers in Electrical and Electronic Engineering (EIConRus), pp. 1794–1798 (2019)

23. M'Raihi, D., Bellare, M., Hoornaert, F., Naccache, D., Ranen, O.: HOTP: an HMAC-Based One-Time Password Algorithm (2005). doi: https://doi.org/10.17487/rfc4226

24. M'Raihi, D., Machani, S., Pei, M., Rydell, J.: TOTP: Time-Based One-Time Password Algorithm (2011). doi: https://doi.org/10.17487/rfc6238

25. Balilo, B.B.B., Gerardo, B.D., Medina, R.P., Byun, Y.: Design of physical authentication based on OTP KeyPad. In: 2017 International Conference on Applied Computer and Communication Technologies (ComCom), pp. 1–5 (2017)

26. Krawczyk, H., Bellare, M., Canetti, R.: HMAC: Keyed-Hashing for Message Authentication (1997). doi: https://doi.org/10.17487/rfc2104

27. Lina, L., Jovana, D., Stefan, A., Trpcheska, M., Vesna, H.D.: A comparative analysis of HOTP and TOTP authentication algorithms. which one to choose?. Inter. Sci. J. Sci. Techn. Union Mech. Eng. "Industry 4.0," **5**(4), 131–136 (2021)

28. Lina, L., Jovana, D., Stefan, A., Trpcheska, H.M., Vesna, D.: comparative analysis of HOTP and TOTP authentication algorithms. which one to choose?. Inter. Sci. J. Sci. Techn. Union Mech. Eng. "Industry 4.0," **5**(4), 131–136 (2021)

29. Haller, N., Metz, C., Nesser, P., Straw, M.: A One-Time Password System (1998). doi: https://doi.org/10.17487/rfc2289

30. Grimes, R.A.: One-Time Password Attacks," in Hacking Multifactor Authentication, pp. 205–226 (2021). doi: https://doi.org/10.1002/9781119672357.ch9

31. Nassar, N., Chen, L.-C.: Seed-based authentication. In: 2015 International Conference on Collaboration Technologies and Systems (CTS), pp. 345–350 (2015)

32. Ma, S., et al.: An empirical study of SMS one-time password authentication in Android apps. In: Proceedings of the 35th Annual Computer Security Applications Conference, pp. 339–354 (2019)

33. Peeters, C., Patton, C., Munyaka, I.N.S., Olszewski, D., Shrimpton, T., Traynor, P.: SMS OTP security (SOS). In: Proceedings of the 2022 ACM on Asia Conference on Computer and Communications Security, pp. 2–16 (2022)

34. Berenjestanaki, Md. H., Conti, M., Gangwal, A.: On the exploitation of online SMS receiving services to forge ID verification. In: Proceedings of the 14th International Conference on Availability, Reliability and Security, pp. 1–5 (2019). doi: https://doi.org/10.1145/3339252. 3339276

35. Sheshasaayee, A., Sumathy, D.: A Framework to Enhance Security for OTP SMS in E-Banking Environment Using Cryptography and Text Steganography, pp. 709–717 (2017). doi: https://doi.org/10.1007/978-981-10-1678-3_68

36. Imanullah, M., Reswan, Y.: Randomized QR-code scanning for a low-cost secured attendance system. Inter. J. Elect. Comput. Eng. (IJECE) **12**(4), 3762 (2022). https://doi.org/10.11591/ijece.v12i4.pp3762-3769

37. Krombholz, K., Frühwirt, P., Kieseberg, P., Kapsalis, I., Huber, M., Weippl, E.: QR Code Security: A Survey of Attacks and Challenges for Usable Security, pp. 79–90 (2014)

38. Oren, Y., Arad, D.: Toward usable and accessible two-factor authentication based on the piezo-gyro channel. IEEE Access **10**, 19551–19557 (2022)

39. Lone, S.A., Mir, A.H.: A novel OTP based tripartite authentication scheme. Inter. J. Perv. Comput. Commun. **18**(4), 437–459 (2022)

40. Fortinet, "FortiToken One-Time Password Token (2022). https://www.fortinet.com/content/dam/fortinet/assets/data-sheets/fortitoken.pdf,

41. Google, "Sign in with backup codes." https://support.google.com/accounts/answer/1187538?hl=en&co=GENIE.Platform%3DAndroid (Accessed 23 Jan 2023)

42. Grimes, R.A.: Types of Authentications. In: Hacking Multifactor Authentication, pp. 59–99. Wiley (2020). doi: https://doi.org/10.1002/9781119672357.ch3

43. Tirfe, D., Anand, V.K.: A Survey on Trends of Two-Factor Authentication, pp. 285–296 (2022). doi: https://doi.org/10.1007/978-981-16-4244-9_23

44. Hassan, M.A., Shukur, Z.: Device identity-based user authentication on electronic payment system for secure E-wallet apps. Electronics (Basel) **11**(1), 4 (2021). https://doi.org/10.3390/electronics11010004

45. Sudar, C., Arjun, S.K., Deepthi, L.R.: Time-based one-time password for Wi-Fi authentication and security. In: 2017 International Conference on Advances in Computing, Communications, and Informatics (ICACCI), pp. 1212–1216 (2017)

46. Kameswaran, V., Hulikal Muralidhar, S.: Cash, digital payments and accessibility. Proc ACM Hum. Comput Interact. 3(CSCW), 1–23 (2019)

47. Singanamalla, S., Potluri, V., Scott, C., Medhi-Thies, I.: PocketATM. In: Proceedings of the Tenth International Conference on Information and Communication Technologies and Development, pp. 1–11 (2019). doi: https://doi.org/10.1145/3287098.3287106

48. Stephens, C.: Why are SMS codes still the global ID solution? Biometric Technology Today **2020**(8), 8 (2020). https://doi.org/10.1016/S0969-4765(20)30110-7

49. Kook, J.: Design and Implementation of a OTP-based IoT Digital Door-lock System and Applications (2019). http://www.irphouse.com

50. Mahboob Alam, T., et al.: OTP-based software-defined cloud architecture for secure dynamic routing. Comput. Mater. Continua **71**(1), 1035–1049 (2022)

51. Luo, J.-N., Wu, C.-M., Yang, M.-H.: A CAN-bus lightweight authentication scheme. Sensors **21**(21), 7069 (2021). https://doi.org/10.3390/s21217069

52. Gawas, M., Patil, H., Govekar, S.S.: An integrative approach for secure data sharing in vehicular edge computing using Blockchain. Peer Peer Netw Appl **14**(5), 2840–2857 (2021). https://doi.org/10.1007/s12083-021-01107-4

53. Cunha, V.A., Corujo, D., Barraca, J.P., Aguiar, R.L.: TOTP Moving Target Defense for sensitive network services. Pervasive Mob. Comput. **74**, 101412 (2021)

Social Engineering Shoulder Surfing Attacks (SSAs): A Literature Review. Lessons, Challenges, and Future Directions

Bryan Zurita[1] , Santiago Bosque[1] , Walter Fuertes[1(✉)] ,
and Mayra Macas[1,2]

[1] Computer Science Department, Universidad de las Fuerzas Armadas ESPE,
Sangolquí, Ecuador
{bazurita2,sdbosque,wmfuertes}@espe.edu.ec, mayramacas@ieee.org
[2] College of Computer Science and Technology, Zhejiang University,
No. 38 Zheda Road, Hangzhou 310027, China

Abstract. Shoulder Surfing Attacks (SSAs) represent a significant threat to user authentication (UA) methods, especially to the process based on the user's knowledge in which the attacker writes down, memorizes, or records the user's credential input. This study aims to offer the scientific community, industry, readers, and users a meta-analysis to understand this problem and develop software solutions for this threat. In this study, we systematically reviewed the literature using the methodological guide of Barbara Kitchenham. The results show that the UA method protected against SSA is based on Physiological Biometrics. Furthermore, this study determined that the primary detection and mitigation tools are the fisheye lens in the front camera for mobile devices, the Vicon system, which captures the position of each person and the orientations of the head and torso concerning the screen that visualizes, using the Kinect 2, computer and laptop cameras to capture images. Likewise, this research evidenced that some works used Deep Learning combined with Face Recognition, relying on the characteristics of electronic devices, such as dimming, device brightness, display of alerts, and activation of the lock screen, among others, to detect and mitigate these attacks. The study also showed some software and hardware artifacts used and studied to solve this problem. Finally, the meta-analysis determined future challenges and research directions for researchers looking for solutions to detect and mitigate SSA attacks.

Keywords: Shoulder surfing · dace recognition · user authentication · Deep Learning · detection · mitigation

1 Introduction

Social engineering is the attack on the weaknesses of the human being, aided by social interaction, to break cyber security, with or without using technological

T. Guarda et al. (Eds.): ARTIIS 2023, CCIS 1936, pp. 220–233, 2024.
https://doi.org/10.1007/978-3-031-48855-9_17

devices [2,32]. This article will focus on Shoulder Surfing Attacks (SSAs). This technique takes advantage of the human essence, attacking the weaknesses of social engineering knowledge and the innocence of the human being.

The attack focuses on subject A, who owns a technological device, being watched or observed without consent by subject B, without the owner user realizing it, to acquire confidential information [27]. SSAs have been increasing since it is notorious how technology has advanced, and human beings have tried to be at the forefront of it. Today, most of the population has a smartphone or a portable device such as a laptop or tablet [18], so the user takes the owner position and needs to protect it through authentication mechanisms.

SSAs have been studied as the most frequent attack model focused on the user [10]. It is visible how subjects outside our environment try to observe our information without our consent. Shoulder surfing attacks occur mainly at work, and university, followed by home and public transport [20]. Faced with this problem, several researchers have created tools to detect and mitigate Shoulder Surfing attacks. For example, in the study proposed by [20], authors developed a tool for smartphones that detect people who are trying to see our information with the help of a lens adapted to a casing that is attached to the cell phone, and It's on the front of it. In the same way, a detection mechanism based on large screens and sensors has been proposed to detect the attacker's presence [6].

This study aims to conduct a systematic literature review using Barbara Kitchenham's [12] methodological guide for studies focused on Shoulder Surfing. We focus on the process that this threat entails to conduct in a traditional and current way, the objectives/benefits to be achieved from the attacker's perspective, and forms of authentication in which there is a greater risk. Likewise, we focus on making known artifacts used to combat this threat, examining parameters, regulations, and rules to consider to develop software focused on this topic. In addition, it is intended to contrast the possible implementation of new technologies, such as Face Recognition, to detect and mitigate this attack. The main contributions of this study are:

- The characterization of shoulder surfing attacks;
- A sustainable approach to be able to solve the challenges that are presented by corrupting facial detection with face impersonation methods (masks, photos, videos);
- The identification of future challenges and research directions to create new tools to solve not only recognition but also impersonation;
- The description of the actual impact caused by these attacks, such as identity theft, financial fraud, extortion, and reputational damage, among others.

The remainder of this article is structured as follows: Sect. 2 presents the theories and work related to this threat. Section 3 describes the research methodological process. Section 4 explains the evaluation of the results, its main findings, the challenges, and directions for future research. Section 5 offers the conclusions and forthcoming work lines.

2   State of the Art

2.1   Shoulder Surfing

Shoulder Surfing at [3,5] is interpreted as an information security threat characterized by an unauthorized observation or spying technique on an authentication method. They intend to steal private information, especially security passwords. Due to the growth of mobile devices, electronic services, web services, monetary movements, studying, working, sending emails, and uploading multimedia content, among other day-to-day activities, users access their bank, student, and work accounts [16,25,26]. They use some form of authentication that falls under this category (e.g., passwords, alphanumeric digit PINs, pattern password lock, image selection, and so on.); this leads to intelligent Shoulder Surfing attackers applying it to extract monetary or even personal benefits from the victim. According to [20], SSAs frequently occur where the victim and attacker have a close relationship. In this way, the possibility of it also happening in the labor and academic field where this closeness exists can be left open. Additionally, this technique has been perfected over the years to the point of moving from the traditional procedure where the attacker stands behind the victim to take notes or memorize their authentication credentials to the use of recording devices [3].

2.2   Authentication

Authentication is the user's action to identify that he is the owner of a device or application and thus be able to protect data and confidential information. Over the years, authentication mechanisms have been created, such as PINs, pattern locks, and passwords [15,20]. The use of these methods has lost its degree of security and confidence. Today there are many mechanisms to counteract this security and break it, for example, guessing attacks that seek the credential by trying common passwords or combinations with public user data. On the other hand, reconstruction attempts focused on attacking the patterns with residues, marks, or traces displayed on the device. Finally, the observation attack, which is our purpose of study, involves attempting to observe the access information when it is being typed without the user noticing [20].

Given these vulnerabilities in common authentication mechanisms, new authentication schemes with biometric features are being sought [7,14]. Thus, for example, fingerprint access is based on scanning the fingerprint of one of the previously registered user's fingers, iris recognition, which involves access through sight. This type of authentication is used in high-security systems since this method is considered one of the most sophisticated and difficult to break. There is also facial recognition, which has become an efficient mechanism and can be applied to all devices that have a front camera with an acceptable resolution. It is a mechanism that detects the user's face and gives them access according to the previous registration of the user's image [30]. This last method has shown great advantages in authentication systems, such as unlocking mobile devices and payments online [31].

2.3   Face Recognition

Facial recognition is a biometric authentication mechanism; that is, it uses the face as a verification tool to gain access [30]. The primary authentication tool is a camera placed on the front of the smartphone or computer, as used by [17,20]. This activity starts the authentication process, captures the image in real time, and processes it. The image projection must be optimal since factors such as light, camera clarity, and the device's position and the user can influence the authentication process to be incorrect [19]. As in any authentication method, some mechanisms try to break it, and facial recognition is no exception. Presentation attacks (PA) are your main enemy, and these are photo impressions, 3D masks, video reproductions, and makeup [31], as well as photo modifications such as moving, joining, and deleting [18] manage to violate the security of the owner user. To mitigate these attacks, researchers and the industry used Convolutional Neural Networks (CNN), which activate the detection of fake faces through PA methods and, in turn, do facial recognition, achieving efficiency and security [29]. However, they are also vulnerable to low pixel attacks [22].

2.4   Deep Learning

According to [23], Deep Learning, as part of machine learning (ML) which in turn corresponds to a subset of Artificial Intelligence (AI), focuses on giving machines the functions that humans perform, such as "learning" and "problem-solving". Deep Learning works with neural networks (NN), where the initial layers learn based on the discrimination of simple features. The acquired insights are then processed by higher layers [23,33]. The inputs go through a process called stochastic gradient descent (SGD). The SGD calculates outputs and errors using a sample to calculate the mean gradient of those examples and adjust the weights accordingly to decrease noise and allow the NN to give consistent responses [13]. Extensive research and experimentation have resulted in new NN architectures. Thus, for example, recurrent neural networks (RNN) are admirable for recovering a stored pattern, and convolutional neural networks (CNN) are characterized by convolutional filters, allowing better data processing in the form of multiple matrices. The CNNs provide an excellent contribution to image processing due to being composed of three 2D matrices that contain the intensities of the pixels in the three channels (RGB) [13], clearing up any doubt about which would be one of the best NNs for apply Face Recognition Technology (FRT) (see Fig. 1).

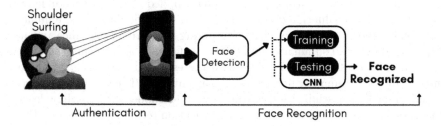

Fig. 1. Compilation of the state of the art

3   Methodological Design

To frame the problem posed in this research and to know in a specific way about shoulder surfing attacks, this systematic literature review addresses the following questions: (i) Determine the techniques, methods, or tools that help mitigate these attacks; (ii) Understand what software artifacts have been developed to combat it; (iii) As to the parameters that must be taken into account to develop software of this type; (iv). Finally, identify the lessons, challenges, and lines of future research to detect and mitigate these types of attacks.

3.1   Search the Relevant Documents

We searched the studies in the following scientific databases: IEEE Explore, ACM Digital Library, ScienceDirect, Springer, and Google Scholar. The study seeks preliminary information on techniques, methods, or algorithms developed to detect and mitigate SSAs during user authentication (UA). Depending on the database, we enter the search strings using boolean operations.

3.2   Inclusion and Exclusion Criteria

We select the primary studies between 2018 to 2023. The main reason for this range was technological advancement in this period due to the notorious development of deep learning, neural networks, and data science. In addition, we decided to include articles from impact journals that met the search criteria. All papers presented accuracy scores using mathematical calculations and contributed significantly to detecting and mitigating shoulder surfing attacks.

3.3   Quality Evaluation of Research

To have a good quality search, we focus on analyzing primary articles within the area of knowledge of Computer Science or related fields. The papers were carefully selected because they contribute to the objective of research on the detection and mitigation of shoulder surfing attacks. We care about the seriousness of the theoretical design, the investigative process, the actions, and methodological decisions in all its stages.

3.4   Result of Review

We ensured a review of primary studies that applied analysis of Shoulder Surfing attacks. The evaluation was carried out in scientific databases, eliminating duplicates. Then we filtered by title, considering its degree of relevance and ambiguity. Itself, we read summaries and full texts. Only 34 articles met the required criteria, of which 29 were published with the established criteria, reflecting an interest by the community in Shoulder Surfing attacks. The remaining five correspond to secondary studies of literature review methodologies, machine learning concepts, and the emergence of user authentication techniques/tools (see Fig. 2).

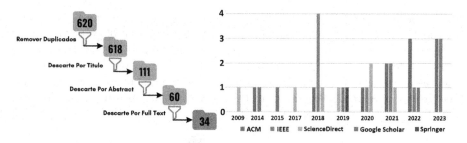

Fig. 2. Primary sources resulted from the search process and the number of articles on scientific databases and their years of publication

4   Evaluation of Results and Discussion

RQ1 *How effective would applying facial recognition be in detecting and mitigating SSAs?*

In [25], the difficulty of the human being to remember good passwords of more than ten characters is evidenced due to the limitations of the human brain in not remembering complex sequences. While in [26], the human being represents the weakest link regarding the choice of good passwords. In general, they are short or significant and easy to memorize, making it easy for them to be easy targets to suffer an attack by SSAs through three types of attack: i) Type I: Naked eyes, ii) Type II: The video captures the entire authentication process once or iii) Type III: The video captures the entire authentication process more than once. In [3], they indicate only two, by visual observation or by recording the password entry process. There are essential factors such as the angle of perception of the attacker [3,26] the object that participates as an observer, be it a person or an electronic device, which allows stealing the credentials of electronic devices. For example, [24] comments on installing spy cameras in ATMs to capture user credentials. However, [4,35] also point out that the PIN form of authentication may be susceptible to observed and recorded SSAs. In short, the first scenario is one of the most used because it is simple compared to the other since it requires more study of the victim, planning, effort, and resources to acquire sufficiently robust devices.

Implementing the FRT in different solutions resulted in great potential in the field of people identification [8]. From the point of view of the first scenario, authors considered the possibility of identifying the possible attacker as shown in Fig. 3. However, what about the second scenario? With the help of CNNs and Deep Learning, the FRT has obtained a compact representation and noise separation in comparing images of faces [21]. The recognition of objects through computerized vision (CV) as an application of Deep Learning allows the recognition of images [23]. When taking them to the digital world, both faces and recording devices are associated with an image, so it is possible to train NN to detect both objects. This can be confirmed in [28], where its authors present a study in which CNNs through CV allow the detection/recognition of generic objects and biometric attributes. All this, plus the different characteristics of personal devices, allow the generation of SSA mitigation processes. For example, the dimming of the device's brightness, the automatic blocking of the device, the display of alerts to the victim to take precautionary measures, and so on.

Fig. 3. Representation SSAs Detection By Face Recognition Technology

RQ2 *What artifacts or tools have been used for detecting and mitigating SSAs?*

Within the process of detecting and mitigating SSAs, there is the software application's logical part. There is the part of the user interface design, the programming code, and the machine learning processing algorithms such as CNN when working with image recognition [29]. As these logical processes are improved, so is the code, as mentioned in [31], whose authors use a central difference convolutional network (CDCN) to extract local texture information and predict the depth of face. Likewise, there is the physical part, which the participant or user uses to enter the data processed in the application. The artifacts capture and send data efficiently so the process continues and culminates with the best results. Several tools are used; for example, in the study [20], a mobile phone case and a personalized model are made for each participant to use their phone, plus is that it includes a fisheye lens on the front camera that expands the camera's field of view from 60 to 90 °C to 180 °C, giving a better view of the attacker. In [6], they focus on high-fidelity movement, which consists of a large screen and a tracking system (Vicon) to identify and capture the position of each person and the orientations of the head and the torso; this defines the exact location regarding the screen. In Fig. 4, it can see that the tools described. Although several mechanisms are expensive, other more accessible and less costly tools have also been added, such as the Kinect 2 [6] or a simple camera, as can be evidenced in face anti-spoofing studies that use the cameras of computers and laptops, to be able to capture images [17,31].

Fig. 4. Large screen with movement system (left); Smartphone with the fisheye lens (right)

RQ3 *What are the authentication methods that protect users against SSAs?*

The study by [30] determined four categories that encompass the authentication methods, which are described below in the Table 1.

Table 1. Classification of Authentication Methods based on the study of [30]

Category	Definition	Authentication forms
Knowledge-based	Requires the user to provide information that only the user should know using his or her memorability	Text-based (e.g., digit PINs and alphanumerical passwords) or Graphic-based (e.g., lock pattern and secret click points on pictures) [20,30]
Based on Physiological Biometrics	Uses unique physical characteristics of the user	Fingerprints, iris patterns, hand geometry, and face contour [30]
Based on Behavioral Biometrics	Analyzes data on how a person interacts with a system or device (behavioral characteristics or habits)	Tapping or swiping on the touch screen, finger movements, walking, and speaking voice patterns (user's daily activities) [30]
Based on Two/multi-factor	Combines two or more authentication metrics to provide more secure authentication	Multiple biometrics, secret knowledge and biometric, pressure and signing speed with graphic-based secret signature shape, etcetera [30]

For [1,30] the knowledge-based authentication category is the most popular, effective, and one of the most used methods throughout history to obtain positive results through SSAs [11,28,30,34]. The first author mentions that several studies show that stealing credential entries through SSAs is possible. The second comments on how memorable passwords are susceptible to SSAs. Specifically, passwords of the image selection type allow the attacker to be easy to remember. The third focuses on increasing the risk to SSAs on mobile devices, considering knowledge-based forms of authentication, here the authors seek to analyze the interaction, the observation angle, the input error, and the observation effort. Finally, the fourth states that some forms of authentication that fall into the knowledge-based category are types of attacks that are easily vulnerable to SSA attacks. Additionally, it was possible to collect information on the effectiveness with which SSAs and other threats are successful. In the Table 2, we present a summary of the effectiveness of the SSAs on the authentication methods to indicate how unprotected users are. We categorized the authentication methods to fit the [30] classification.

Table 2. Effectiveness of Shoulder Surfing in categories based on [11]

Category	Affected By SSA	No Affected By SSA
Knowledge-based	• Dictionary-based method • Leakage-resilient password authentication method • Context-sensitive screen locking application • PIN + touch dynamics • Spinlock • Bimodal PIN + audio based • Drawing a PIN authentication • Graphical authentication password • Powerful sensor + graphics	• IPAS • Graphic-based methods • TMD • Recognition and recall-based method • CCP • Graphical password, VC, PL • CD-GPS scheme
Based on Physiological Biometrics		• LDPC + SHA + IWT • Facial • FIRME • Gait authentication • Hand geometric based biometric system + mobile phone cameras + webcams • SPN + ESPN • NIR light source + charge-coupled device (CCD)+3D vein image • Eyes, nose, mouth, and full face
Based on Behavioral Biometrics	• KDA • GEAT gesture-based authentication • New lightweight, touch dynamics and touch gesture • Signal utilizing weights sensor mounted on the back of the telephone • Touch behavior and miniaturized scale developments of device • Electroencephalography (EEG) + Patterned based authentication scheme • Touch-based authentication systems • Accelerometer-based authentication	• Behavior profiling, keystroke flow, and semantic profiling • Behavioral biometrics + conventional authentication scheme • Keystroke dynamics and accelerator biometric • Swipe gesture • Data acquisition • FAST • Implicit authentication • User touch behavior • Gesture typing behavior • Artificial intelligence, pattern password, touching durations, and biometric traits • CA + IA • Camera-video recording-based attack
Based on Two/multi-factor	• Two-factor face authentication • Pattern • MFA	• Biometric data (inherence factor) + passwords (knowledge factor) • Touch-based biometric authentication • HATS • Graphical authentication, pass code and behavioral biometric • Implicit authentication • Keystroke dynamic authentication • Geographical area + location • NFC and tattoo • Mobsecure

RQ4 *What are the parameters, regulations, and rules for developing software that mitigates SSAs?*

To develop a software tool to combat and mitigate SSAs, we must walk that fine line from being a protector to becoming a victimizer. If the technicians plan to use facial recognition as an essential support, this technology can infringe on the privacy of the attacker, even if it sounds illogical [20]. Automatically taking or capturing photos may be inappropriate, so they only store images locally and do not upload them anytime. It must be considered that some people may accidentally participate in this activity during the testing and production period and can be taken as attackers without being true. That is why users have to abide by the rules and laws of each region. In the case of Ecuador, the organic law on identity management and civil data refers to the fact that the State will guarantee all Ecuadorian and foreign persons, regardless of their immigration status, the right to identity and data protection of information staff. Starting from this premise, it can be defined that the main parameter is the privacy of the human being. Therefore, the attacker can be referenced without exposing his identity. That is, notify the owner user that they want to attack him so that he can take preventive measures, but leave aside the fact of presenting the attacker. Under this precept, the study [9] hypothesizes that intentionally degrading the quality of egocentric photos (i.e., photographs captured from a first-person perspective), such as obfuscating them with a blur filter, can increase the predisposition of people to be captured by portable cameras. In the results, they obtained that it is possible to increase the number of passers-by willing to be captured by 17.5% when a blur filter is applied to these photos.

4.1   Challenges and Future Research Directions

Shoulder Surfing presents some technological, environmental, obtaining and training data, social, security, and privacy policy challenges, especially those that have slowed progress in the development of detection and mitigation of this threat, as detailed in Fig. 5 which outlines in summary the entire process from start to end of what represents the use of FRT for detection and mitigation of SSAs, while Table 3 details the challenges that have been encountered, as well as outlining future directions that can be influenced to eliminate these challenges.

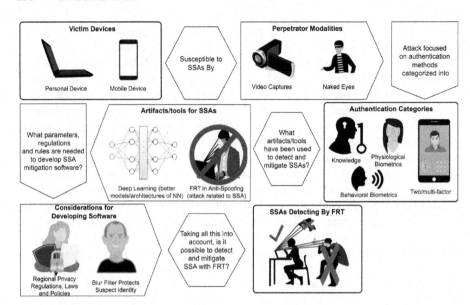

Fig. 5. Illustrative context map of the results of the research questions

Table 3. Challenges and Future Directions

Areas	Challenges	Future Directions
Technologies and Environment	• Influence of other social engineering based attacks [17, 26, 31]	• Two/multi-factor mitigation technologies
	• Ambient lighting conditions [8, 30]	• Infrastructure redesign
	• False positive rates [23]	• Implementation of new technologies, devices and sensors
AI and Data	• Datasets availability (organization employees and repeat offenders)	• Organization partnership and encryption data
	• Age variations [8]	• Improvement and redesign AI models
	• Hide face with face accessories [24]	• Novel AI and Deep Learning algorithms
Society, Security and Privacy Policy	• Social refusal to be video-monitored	• Policy Development
	• FRT is an invasive privacy technology	• Privacy Protection Technologies
	• FRT increases some types of corporate and political risks [21]	• International Policy and Partnership

5   Conclusions and Future Work

This study highlights the ongoing presence of a pervasive threat. Despite the emergence of new forms of technology, the issue remains unresolved. More action is required to bridge the gap between old and new user authentication methods to better protect potential victims and detect potential attackers. Additionally, we must consider the legal framework and its role in regulating data collection. In addition, SW and HW artifacts were found to solve the problem and preserve the main functionality of capturing the user's physical characteristics in an adequate and safe way so that no information is exposed.

In summary, we explore the current studies and seek to promote the development of applications that use current technologies, such as FRT, that help combat this problem. We present a meta-analysis in which challenges and future research directions are found to grant thematic and scientific maturity to this study. Finally, as future work, it is planned to develop an application for a desktop environment with the possibility of scaling to a multiplatform application and being taken to a web or mobile environment, which allows for detecting and mitigating SSAs.

References

1. Ali, M., et al.: A simple and secure reformation-based password scheme. IEEE Access **9**, 11655–11674 (2021)
2. Alizadeh, F., Stevens, G., Jakobi T., Krüger, J.: Catch me if you can: "delaying" as a social engineering technique in the post-attack phase. Proc. ACM Hum. Comput. Interact. **7**(CSCW1), 1–25 (2023)
3. Behera, S.K., Bhoi, S., Dogra, D.P., Roy, P.P.: Robustness analysis of motion sensor guided air authentication system. IEEE Trans. Consum. Electron. **64**(2), 171–179 (2018)
4. Binbeshr, F., Por, L.Y., Mat Kiah, M.L., Zaidan, A.A., Imam, M.: Secure pin-entry method using one-time pin (OTP). IEEE Access **11**, 18121–18133 (2023)
5. Bošnjak, L., Brumen, B.: Shoulder surfing experiments: a systematic literature review. Comput. Secur. **99**, 102023 (2020)
6. Brudy, F., Ledo, D., Greenberg, S., Butz, A.: Is anyone looking? mitigating shoulder surfing on public displays through awareness and protection. In: Proceedings of the International Symposium on Pervasive Displays (PerDis 2014), pp. 1–6. Association for Computing Machinery, New York (2014)
7. Cao, H., Liu, D., Jiang, H., Wang, R., Chen, Z., Xiong, J.: Lipauth: hand-dependent light intensity patterns for resilient user authentication. ACM Trans. Sen. Netw. **19**(3), 1–29 (2023)
8. Cárabe, L., Cermeño, E.: Concealing attacks on face identification algorithms: Stegano-morphing. IEEE Access **9**, 100851–100867 (2021)
9. Dimiccoli, M., Marín, J., Thomaz, E.: Mitigating bystander privacy concerns in egocentric activity recognition with deep learning and intentional image degradation. Proc. ACM Interact. Mob. Wearable Ubiquit. Technol. **1**(4), 1–18 (2018)
10. Harbach, M., Von Zezschwitz, E., Fichtner, A., De Luca, A, Smith, M.: It's a hard lock life: a field study of smartphone (un)locking behavior and risk perception. In: Proceedings of the Tenth USENIX Conference on Usable Privacy and Security (SOUPS 2014), pp. 213–230. USENIX Association, USA (2014)
11. Ibrahim, T.M., et al.: Recent advances in mobile touch screen security authentication methods: a systematic literature review. Comput. Secur. **85**, 1–24 (2019)
12. Kitchenham, B., Pearl Brereton, O., Budgen, D., Turner, M., Bailey, J., Linkman, S.: Systematic literature reviews in software engineering - a systematic literature review. Inf. Softw. Technol. **51**(1), 7–15 (2009). Special Section - Most Cited Articles in 2002 and Regular Research Papers

13. LeCun, Y., Bengio, Y., Hinton, G.: Deep learning. Nature **521**(7553), 436–444 (2015)

14. Liu, S., Shao, W., Li, T., Xu, W., Song, L.: Recent advances in biometrics-based user authentication for wearable devices: a contemporary survey. Digit. Signal Process. **125**, 103120 (2022). Sensing, Signal Processing and Computing for the Era of Wearables

15. Macas, M., Chunming, W., Fuertes, W.: A survey on deep learning for cybersecurity: progress, challenges, and opportunities. Comput. Netw. **212**, 109032 (2022)

16. Otoum, S., Kantarci, B., Mouftah, H.: A comparative study of AI-based intrusion detection techniques in critical infrastructures. ACM Trans. Internet Technol. **21**(4), 1–22 (2021)

17. Qin, L., Peng, F., Long, M., Ramachandra, R., Busch, C.: Vulnerabilities of unattended face verification systems to facial components-based presentation attacks: an empirical study. ACM Trans. Priv. Secur. **25**(1), 1–28 (2021)

18. Ren, R., Niu, S., Ren, H., Zhang, S., Han, T, Tong, X.: Esrnet: efficient search and recognition network for image manipulation detection. ACM Trans. Multim. Comput. Commun. Appl. **18**(4), 1–23 (2022)

19. Samangouei, P., Patel, V.M., Chellappa, R.: Facial attributes for active authentication on mobile devices. Image Vis. Comput. **58**, 181–192 (2017)

20. Schneegass, S., Saad, A., Heger, R., Delgado Rodriguez, S., Poguntke, R., Alt, F.: An investigation of shoulder surfing attacks on touch-based unlock events. Proc. ACM Hum. Comput. Interact. **6**(MHCI), 1–14 (2022)

21. Shao, X.-F., et al.: How does facial recognition as an urban safety technology affect firm performance? the moderating role of the home country's government subsidies. Saf. Sci. **143**, 105434 (2021)

22. Shapira, Y., Avneri, E., Drachsler-Cohen, D.: Deep learning robustness verification for few-pixel attacks. **7**(OOPSLA1), 434–461 (2023)

23. Shinde, P.P., Shah, S.: A review of machine learning and deep learning applications. In: 2018 Fourth International Conference on Computing Communication Control and Automation (ICCUBEA), pp. 1–6 (2018)

24. Sikandar, T., Ghazali, K.H., Rabbi, M.F.: ATM crime detection using image processing integrated video surveillance: a systematic review. Multim. Syst. **25**(3), 229–251 (2019)

25. Sosa Valles, P.A., et al.: My personal images as my graphical password. IEEE Latin Am. Trans. **16**(5), 1516–1523 (2018)

26. Sun, H.-M., Chen, S.-T., Yeh, J.-H., Cheng, C.-Y.: A shoulder surfing resistant graphical authentication system. IEEE Trans. Depend. Secure Comput. **15**(2), 180–193 (2018)

27. Syafitri, W., Shukur, Z., Mokhtar, U.A., Sulaiman, R., Ibrahim, M.A.: Social engineering attacks prevention: a systematic literature review. IEEE Access **10**, 39325–39343 (2022)

28. Toor, A.S., Wechsler, H., Nappi, M., Choo, K.-K.R.: Visual question authentication protocol (VGAP). Comput. Secur. **76**, 285–294 (2018)

29. Tu, X., Ma, Z., Zhao, J., Du, G., Xie, M., Feng, J.: Learning generalizable and identity-discriminative representations for face anti-spoofing. ACM Trans. Intell. Syst. Technol. **11**(5), 1–19 (2020)

30. Wang, C., Wang, Y., Chen, Y., Liu, H., Liu, J.: User authentication on mobile devices: approaches, threats and trends. Comput. Netw. **170**, 107118 (2020)

31. Wang, Z., Xu, Y., Wu, L., Han, H., Ma, Y., Li, Z.: Improving face anti-spoofing via advanced multi-perspective feature learning. ACM Trans. Multim. Comput. Commun. Appl. (2022). Just Accepted

32. Wang, Z., Sun, L., Zhu, H.: Defining social engineering in cybersecurity. IEEE Access **8**, 85094–85115 (2020)
33. Yousefi, N., Alaghband, M., Garibay, I.: A comprehensive survey on machine learning techniques and user authentication approaches for credit card fraud detection (2019)
34. Zhou, L., Wang, K., Lai, J., Zhang, D.: A comparison of a touch-gesture- and a keystroke-based password method: toward shoulder-surfing resistant mobile user authentication. IEEE Trans. Hum. Mach. Syst. **53**(2), 303–314 (2023)
35. Zhou, M.,et al.: Presspin: enabling secure pin authentication on mobile devices via structure-borne sounds. IEEE Trans. Depend. Secure Comput. **20**(2), 1228–1242 (2023)

Adaptive Key Management-Based Privacy Preservation Protocol for Healthcare Data

Pankaj Khatiwada[1] , Nishu Gupta[2]([✉]) , Bian Yang[1] , and Mohammad Derawi[2]

[1] Department of Information Security and Communication Technology,
Norwegian University of Science and Technology (NTNU), Gjøvik, Norway
pankaj.khatiwada@ntnu.no

[2] Department of Electronic Systems, Faculty of IES, Norwegian University of Science and
Technology (NTNU), Gjøvik, Norway
nishu.gupta@ntnu.no

Abstract. With the advent of the concept of smart healthcare emerging out of the Internet of Things applications, the researchers concentrate on proposing a possible solution for exchanging and storing the Patient Health Records (PHR). Current practices over cloud-oriented centralized data centers lead to increased cost of maintenance, need huge storage space, and cause privacy concerns regarding the sharing of information over an exposed network. This urges to model a framework that enables the security as well as real-time sharing of big medical data effectively within a trustless environment. In this context, this article proposes to generate an adaptive patient-centric key management protocol for healthcare monitoring system with the help of blockchain technology. The transmission of PHR from patient to doctor or vice versa is handled through a new key management privacy preservation model. The PHR data is stored in blockchain and is sanitized by the adaptive key agreement protocol with the help of Grey Wolf Optimization (GWO) using a valuable objective model. The restoration process also depends on the adaptive key for retrieving the original information. The proposed protocol is validated by comparing it with the state-of-the-art models with special concentration to the security aspects.

Keywords: Adaptive Key Management · Blockchain Technology · Internet of Things · Privacy Preservation Protocol · Smart healthcare

1 Introduction

The convergence of the communications, information, and the medical industry paves the way for developing precision medicine technologies, which permits personalized healthcare [1]. Specifically, the customized healthcare services are improved with the specialization of personalized medical services since it allows people to have a better and healthier lifestyle [2]. These kind of services are investigated on the basis of user data that is dispersed in a continuous manner, and the prediction and analysis services that are applicable for maintaining the individual behaviour are important [3].

© The Author(s), under exclusive license to Springer Nature Switzerland AG 2024
T. Guarda et al. (Eds.): ARTIIS 2023, CCIS 1936, pp. 234–247, 2024.
https://doi.org/10.1007/978-3-031-48855-9_18

In the present times, several studies on handling as well as investigating the user data effectively are being performed in the medical institutions and university hospitals. Yet, the issues related to the security arise since it is not possible to expose the user data in a public manner [4]. Presently, the blockchain technology is gaining attention towards the banking industry, and several enhancements and studies are in progress continuously in the direction of its commercialization [5]. It can also be subjected to various other industries, in which transactions happen in a frequent manner [6].

Recent advancements in the blockchain technology have led to improved healthcare and critical life-supporting domains in several new ways [7, 8]. It is not possible to falsify this technology by the user. Moreover, effective personalized healthcare services are also permitted in a mobile environment [9]. This technology permits numerous entities of the healthcare ecosystem for sharing data [10]. Integrating healthcare sector with the blockchain offers resilience to various attacks that are linked to "user authentication problem & key management" vulnerabilities like "replay, man-in the- middle, impersonation, password guessing, illegal session key computation, health data disclosure, Denial of Service (DoS), privileged insiders", etc. It also offers better healthcare services in a real time and secured environment. The contributions of the paper are as follows.

- To develop an adaptive patient-centric key management protocol for healthcare monitoring system using blockchain technology.
- To handle the transmission of PHR from patient to doctor or vice versa through the new key management privacy preservation model.
- To store the PHR data in the blockchain and to sanitize it by the adaptive key agreement protocol with the help of Grey Wolf Optimization (GWO) by a valuable objective model.
- To retrieve the original information using the restoration process that is based on the adaptive key and to validate it by comparing it with similar models with respect to computational, restoration, and convergence analysis respectively.

Rest of the article is organized as follows: various related works supporting the blockchain technology for the healthcare sector are discussed in Sect. 2. Section 3 describes the proposed privacy preservation protocol for healthcare sector using optimal key management with blockchain. The optimal key agreement protocol in healthcare sector is explained in Sect. 4. Section 5 returns the results and discussions. Section 6 concludes the paper.

2 Literature Survey

2.1 Related Works

Garg et al. [11] modelled a new blockchain enabled authentication key agreement protocol known as BAKMP-IoMT. The healthcare data can be accessed securely by the legitimate users from the cloud servers. Data is stored in a blockchain that is handled by the cloud servers. It furnishes better functionality as well as security and also requires less computational costs and communication than the remaining schemes. Furthermore, Wang et al. [12] developed a method that ensures the user's trust using Graph Neural Network (GNN) for detecting the malicious nodes. The outcomes reveal that the proposed method is better for smart healthcare systems.

Zhou *et al.* [13] have addressed a method known as Med-PPPHIS that comprises a permission-based as well as permission-less blockchain called Med-DLattice. Medical data is transformed into on-chain tokens, which is an effective and safe channel for establishing the data circulation, while the data privacy is also ensured. A prototype is implemented and a blockchain-oriented closed-loop technique is also introduced for the chronic disease management. It returns high throughput and low latency and proves that the model is applicable for preventing DDoS attacks, Sybil attacks, etc.

Chung and Jung [14] recommend a knowledge-oriented blockchain network. The context information, as well as the log data of the user, is subjected to the blockchain technology. The mechanism enables high security and expandability for securing the mobile environment. It returns 16.5% superior performance in both the reproducibility and accuracy. Gordon and Catalini [15] have facilitated the blockchain technology via five mechanisms such as, "digital access rules, data aggregation, data liquidity, patient identity, and data immutability". The barriers were also found to the incentives, patient engagement, security and privacy.

2.2 Survey

There exists an increasing interest in the healthcare sector because of the latest enhancements in the IoT technologies in view of the 4th industrial revolution. Majority of the services are available for the user's personal health management. Additionally, blockchain technology enables the knowledge base towards establishment of an effective health data management, which is considered as the "next generation information security technology". Table 1 shows the salient features and the challenges associated with traditional blockchain-related healthcare sector methods. BAKMP-IoMT [11] returns minimum communication as well as the communication costs for the key and authentication management phase and also accesses the healthcare data by the legitimate users in a secured format. But various usable models are not found with the identical privacy guarantees. Graph Convolutional Network [12] provides better efficiency, can fulfil the security needs and also constructs a trust model for providing security, and the risks are also minimized. Still, it does not study the privacy issues as well as the effectiveness of the blockchain on the smart health. Med-PPPHIS [13] has the characteristics of high throughput, low latency, tamper-resistance, transaction transparency, and decentralization and can be applied to legal case management, digital archives management, and various particular scenarios. Yet, the keyword query is not supported for the medical data. Knowledge-based blockchain network [14] permits the users to receive the health care services accurately in the mobile platform. But, the big health-data records are not managed with the help of user log data. Institution-driven and patient-driven [15] helps to interact with multiple stakeholders in a secure manner and also facilitates the transaction using immutability, patient identity, liquidity and data availability, data aggregation, and digital access rules management. Still, the clinical transaction volume is not supported by the scaling blockchain. Hence, it is required to propose novel methods for securing the healthcare data by integrating the blockchain technology with the adaptive key management-oriented privacy preservation protocol.

Table 1. Features and Challenges of State-of-the-art Blockchain-Related Healthcare Sector Methods.

Author	Methodology	Features	Challenges
Garg et al. [11]	BAKMP-IoMT	• The healthcare data can be accessed by the legitimate users in a secured format • It returns minimum communication as well as the communication costs for the key and authentication management phase	• It does not find various usable models with the identical privacy guarantees
Wang et al. [12]	Graph Convolutional Network	• A trust model is constructed for providing security and the risks are also minimized • It provides better efficiency and can also fulfil the security needs	• The privacy issues as well as the effectiveness of the blockchain on the smart health are not studied
Zhou et al. [13]	Med-PPPHIS	• It can be applied to legal cases management, digital archives management, and various particular scenarios • It has the characteristics of high throughput, low latency, tamper-resistance, transaction transparency, and decentralization	• It does not support the keyword query for the medical data

(*continued*)

Table 1. (*continued*)

Author	Methodology	Features	Challenges
Chung and Jung [14]	Knowledge-based blockchain network	• It can store a large amount of information in the knowledge base • It permits the users to receive the health care services accurately in the mobile platform	• It does not manage the health big data records with the help of several user log data
Gordon and Catalini [15]	Institution-driven and patient-driven	• The transaction can be facilitated using immutability, patient identity, liquidity and data availability, data aggregation, and digital access rules management • It helps to interact with multiple stakeholders in a secure manner	• It does not support the clinical transaction volume by the scaling blockchain

3 Privacy Preservation Protocol

3.1 Proposed Model

Majority of the healthcare systems depend on the outdated technologies for handling the patient's records in a safe manner. The security-oriented issues existing in the healthcare sector are not lessened. The major challenge prevailing in the Electronic Health Records (EHRs) for the healthcare data mining, medicine investigation, market analysis, patient-centred research, etc. is the data privacy. Providing technological solutions to the preservation of the privacy of patients and maintaining large-scale data seems to be a challenge for the researchers since long. Consequently, the blockchain technology eradicated some of the issues by offering a distributed and protected platform. The traditional EHR management system is limited from trust-less cooperation, delayed communication, and data manipulation in the distribution, storage, and limited data collection. Hence, it is necessary to develop such a mechanism that ensures privacy in healthcare data using blockchain technology. The architecture of the proposed privacy preservation protocol for the healthcare sector is shown in Fig. 1.

The major objective of the proposed protocol is to secure data security in the healthcare sector. The data is stored in blockchain and preserved through proposed key agreement mechanism that ensures the dual security of the health records. This proposed operation is accomplished in two phases, *data hiding* and *data restoration*. Data hiding

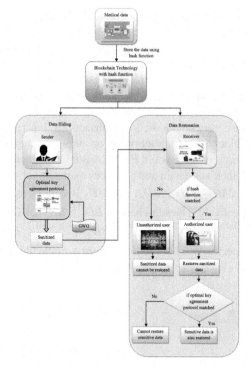

Fig. 1. Proposed architecture of privacy preservation protocol for healthcare sector

is done perfectly through the generation of the optimal key agreement protocol, which is optimally tuned using the GWO. The preserved data is referred to as the sanitized data that is sent to the receiver. At this stage, the second phase of the restoration begins. If the hash function of the receiver is matched with the hash function of the sender, then the user is considered as authorized and this user can restore the data, and then use the proposed key for restoring the sanitized data. If the hash function does not match, the particular user is considered as unauthorized and cannot restore any data. If the optimal key agreement protocol of the authorized user is matched with that of the sender, sensitive data can also be restored; otherwise, sensitive data cannot be restored. In this way, privacy is maintained by both blockchain technology as well as the optimal key agreement protocol.

3.2 Data Storage Under Blockchain Technology

The data regarding blockchain is saved in a group of blocks and the transactions are assumed as the data storage carriers. These data blocks consist of a group of transactions. If a custom data related with the healthcare records are to be written to the block, the data is made only as the extension of the transaction and the blockchain does not understand its specific structure. But, mostly there arises a requirement to query the data on the basis of the security of the custom data. If the data exists as just a transaction, then the query requests cannot be resolved via blockchain. Initially, it is necessary to write the related transaction hash every time while the transaction is executed. When it is required to query the data, the entire transaction hash related to the identity in the database is queried initially, and this hash is used for retrieving the entire data that is required from the blockchain. Yet, apart from the applications in the financial as well as other industrial sectors, healthcare record is more in-line regarding the security of medical records of the patients in the period of the transaction. They do not pay more attention to the historical transactions over a long-time gap. The application related to the personal healthcare records tracking focuses more on the security transactions. It is required to manage and store a huge count of blockchain transactions in an automatic manner. The data storage in the blockchain technology is shown in Fig. 2. Assume the doctors MD_1, MD_2, MD_3, MD_4, and MD_5 assess their sub-chain and produces their self-sub-chain for the patients. The sub-chain of MD_1, MD_2, MD_3, MD_4, and MD_5 is defined as $BD_2^{(1)}$, $BD_2^{(2)}$, $BD_2^{(3)}$, $BD_2^{(4)}$, and $BD_2^{(5)}$ respectively. The sub-chain of $BD_2^{(1)}$, $BD_2^{(2)}$, $BD_2^{(3)}$, $BD_2^{(4)}$, and $BD_2^{(5)}$ is defined as $BD_2^{(1(nd));nd=1,2}$, $BD_2^{(2(nd));nd=1,2}$, $BD_2^{(3(nd));nd=1,2}$, $BD_2^{(4(nd));nd=1,2,3}$, and $BD_2^{(5(nd));nd=1,2,3}$, respectively. These together form a single blockchain BD_2.

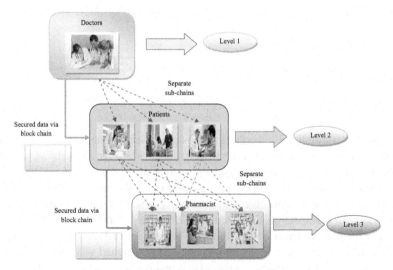

Fig. 2. Data storage mechanism in blockchain

3.3 Objective Function

The primary objective of this paper is to obtain the optimal key, which is satisfied by employing the GWO algorithm. For the algorithm, the 'key' is given as the input solution. The chromosome length is defined as $\frac{SA_1}{40} \times SA_2$. The minimum as well as the maximum bounding limit lies between 1 to $2^{na} - 1$, where na denotes the count of bits.

Assume DA_{ia} as the original data, the sanitized data is defined as DA_{taia}, the data to be preserved is defined as DA_{paia}, and the count of data is defined as NA. The objective function is defined in Eq. (1).

$$FA = \min(OA_{ia}) \tag{1}$$

$$OA_{ia} = \frac{\sum\limits_{ia=1}^{NA} DA_{taia}}{\sum\limits_{ia=1}^{NA} DA_{ia}} - \left[\frac{\sum\limits_{ia=1}^{NA} DA_{ia} - \sum\limits_{ia=1}^{NA} DA_{paia}}{\sum\limits_{ia=1}^{NA} DA_{ia}} \right] \tag{2}$$

4 Optimal Key Agreement Protocol

4.1 Data Hiding Process

The data hiding process is shown in Fig. 3. Which represents a data preservation approach wherein the preservation of the sensitive medical data is ensured with the use of optimal key. For hiding the data, the optimal key is transformed into binary value, and the medical data is multiplied with the generated binary value, which is known as the sanitized data. Binary data generation represents a specific approach. After generation of the binary data, sanitized data is attained by multiplying it with the original medical data. The multiplication of input data to the generated key is in the format of binary values and results in the considered sanitized data.

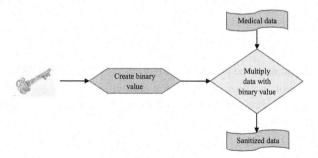

Fig. 3. Data hiding process

4.2 Data Restoration Process

The technique behind the data restoration process is shown in Fig. 4. The inverse of the optimal key that is generated is composed of two types of information, sensitive data and index data. In the initial step, a vector of identical length of the sanitized data is produced for the sensitive data that is multiplied to the index of the key. The multiplied data is included to the sanitized data and it produces the restored data. The outcome is included to the sanitized data to attain the original data. If the optimized key produced by the GWO is appropriate, then the original data is restored in a better manner. Otherwise, if the produced key is not the optimal key (if there occurs a little variation in the key), then the original data is not restored in an efficient manner.

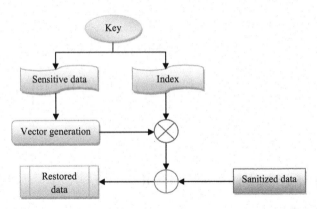

Fig. 4. Data restoration process

4.3 Adaptive Key Agreement Protocol Using GWO

GWO is used to perform the optimal key generation during the data sanitization as well as the data restoration process. GWO [16] technique is based on the hunting behaviour of the grey wolves. The four kinds of grey wolves are the "alpha, beta, delta, and omega". The hunting steps performed are "searching for prey, encircling prey, and attacking prey". The encircling characteristics are shown mathematically in Eq. (3) and Eq. (4).

$$D\vec{W} = \left| C\vec{W} \cdot X\vec{W}_{pw}(tw) - X\vec{W}(tw) \right| \tag{3}$$

$$X\vec{W}(tw+1) = X\vec{W}_{pw}(tw) - A\vec{W} \cdot D\vec{W} \tag{4}$$

In the above equation, the position vector of the prey is shown by $X\vec{W}_{pw}$, the position vector of a grey wolf is shown by $X\vec{W}$, the current iteration is shown by tw, and the coefficient vectors are shown by $A\vec{W}$ and $C\vec{W}$ respectively which are calculated as shown in Eq. (5) and Eq. (6).

$$A\vec{W} = 2a\vec{w} \cdot r\vec{w}_1 - a\vec{w} \tag{5}$$

$$C\vec{W} = 2 \cdot r\vec{w}_2 \tag{6}$$

where $a\vec{w}$ is minimized from 2 to 0 and the random vectors in [0, 1] are shown by rw_1 and rw_2 respectively. The *alpha* category is considered as the best candidate solution and *delta* consists of more knowledge about the potential prey location. The remaining search agents update their positions based on the best search agent position as in Eq. (7), Eq. (8), and Eq. (9).

$$D\vec{W}_\alpha = \left| C\vec{W}_1 \cdot X\vec{W}_\alpha - X\vec{W} \right|, D\vec{W}_\beta = \left| C\vec{W}_2 \cdot X\vec{W}_\beta - X\vec{W} \right|,$$
$$D\vec{W}_\delta = \left| C\vec{W}_3 \cdot X\vec{W}_\delta - X\vec{W} \right| \tag{7}$$

$$X\vec{W}_1 = X\vec{W}_\alpha - A\vec{W}_1 \cdot \left(D\vec{W}_\alpha \right), X\vec{W}_2 = X\vec{W}_\beta - A\vec{W}_2 \cdot \left(D\vec{W}_\beta \right),$$
$$X\vec{W}_3 = X\vec{W}_\delta - A\vec{W}_3 \cdot \left(D\vec{W}_\delta \right) \tag{8}$$

$$X \vec{W}(tw + 1) = \frac{X \vec{W}_1 + X \vec{W}_2 + X \vec{W}_3}{3} \qquad (9)$$

Algorithm 1: GWO

Start
Grey wolf population initialization
Initialize ag, AG, and CG
Fitness calculation of every search agent
XG_α =best search agent
XG_β =second best search agent
XG_δ =third best search agent
while $(tg < Maximum\ iteration\ count)$
    for every search agent
        Current search agent position update of GWO using Eq. (9)
    end for
    Update ag, AG, and CG
    Fitness calculation of entire search agents
    Update XG_α, XG_β, and XG_δ
    $tg = tg + 1$
end while
Return XG_α
Stop

---

5 Results and Discussion

5.1 Experimental Setup

The performance analysis of the proposed methodology is implemented in Python. Here, the population size is considered as 10 and the maximum considered iterations are 100. The dataset is gathered from the standard publicly available dataset. Here test case 1 refers to the heart disease dataset [17] and the test case 2 refers to the hepatitis disease dataset [18]. The proposed method is compared with other optimization algorithms like PSO [19], WOA [20] and BSO [21] in terms of computational analysis, convergence analysis, and restoration analysis to determine the betterment of the proposed model.

5.2 Computational Time Analysis for Encryption and Decryption

The computational time (encryption and decryption) of the proposed method in terms of GWO and other optimization algorithms is listed in Fig. 5. It is clear that with the GWO, the data is restored faster than other algorithms. In Fig. 5(a), for test case 1, the restoration time of the GWO is 69.70%, 75%, and 56.90% improved than BSO, WOA, and PSO respectively. Similarly, from Fig. 5(b), for test case 2, the restoration time of the GWO is 83.33%, 88.89%, and 66.67% better than BSO, WOA, and PSO respectively. Hence, it is clear that the restoration time of the proposed method is faster than the remaining algorithms.

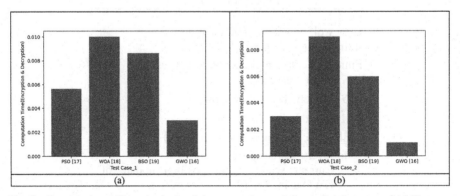

Fig. 5. Computational Time Analysis of the encryption and decryption in terms of (a) Test case 1, and (b) Test case 2

5.3 Computational Time Analysis in Terms of Heuristic Algorithms

The computational time of the proposed method with respect to GWO and other optimization algorithms is portrayed in Fig. 6. The outcomes are better with the GWO than other optimization algorithms. From Fig. 6(a), for test case 1, the computational time of the GWO is 6.90%, 10%, and 31.82% superior to BSO, WOA, and PSO respectively. Moreover, in Fig. 6(b), for test case 2, the computation time of the GWO is 14.29%, 16.67%, and 11.76% surpassed than BSO, WOA, and PSO respectively. Therefore, the computational analysis of the proposed method is better with the GWO than other algorithms.

5.4 Convergence Analysis

The convergence analysis of the proposed method with the GWO and the remaining algorithms is displayed in Fig. 7. In Fig. 7(a), for test case 1, at 100th iteration, the cost function of the GWO is 33.33%, 36%, and 11.11% advanced than BSO, WOA, and PSO respectively. Further, in Fig. 7(b), for test case 2, the cost function of the GWO at 100th iteration is .27%, 12.5%, and 9.68% progressed than BSO, WOA, and PSO respectively. Therefore, the convergence analysis holds superior outcomes with the GWO than the existing algorithms.

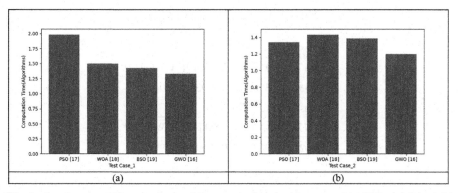

Fig. 6. Computational Time Analysis of the proposed method in terms of (a) Test case 1, and (b) Test case 2

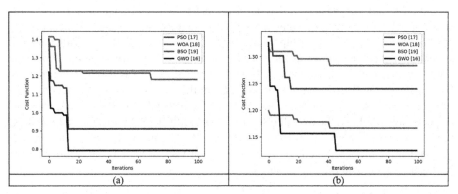

Fig. 7. Convergence Analysis of the proposed method in terms of (a) Test case 1, and (b) Test case 2

5.5 Overall Restoration Analysis

The overall restoration analysis of the proposed method with the GWO and the remaining algorithms for two test cases is displayed in Table 2. The GWO holds better results than other algorithms. For test case 1, the restoration time of the GWO is 0.19%, 0.22%, and 0.40% surpassing BSO, WOA, and PSO respectively. Similarly, in test case 2, the restoration time of the GWO is 0.03%, 0.05%, and 0.06% higher than BSO, WOA, and PSO respectively. Therefore, the overall restoration time is faster with the GWO than the other algorithms.

Table 2. Overall restoration analysis

Test case 1			
PSO [17]	WOA [18]	BSO [19]	GWO [16]
0.93743	0.93907	0.93935	0.94115
Test case 2			
PSO [17]	WOA [18]	BSO [19]	GWO [16]
0.99562	0.99571	0.99592	0.99618

6 Conclusion

This paper has developed the adaptive patient-centric key management protocol for healthcare monitoring system with blockchain technology. It also handled the transmission of PHR from patient to doctor or vice versa via the novel key management privacy preservation model with the help of blockchain technology. Here, the PHR data was stored in blockchain, and it was sanitized by the adaptive key agreement protocol using GWO by a valuable objective model. The restoration process was based on the adaptive key for retrieving the original information. From the analysis, the cost function of the GWO for test case 1 is 33.33%, 36%, and 11.11% advanced than BSO, WOA, and PSO respectively. Similarly, the overall restoration time of the GWO for test case 2 is 0.03%, 0.05%, and 0.06% higher than BSO, WOA, and PSO respectively. Hence, it was confirmed that the proposed method provided better privacy as well as the security for the healthcare sector than the traditional methods.

References

1. Bera, B., Chattaraj, D., Das, A.K.: Designing secure blockchain-based access control scheme in IoT-enabled Internet of Drones deployment. Comput. Commun. **153**, 229–249 (2020)
2. Monrat, A.A., Schelen, O., Andersson, K.: A survey of blockchain from the perspectives of applications, challenges, and opportunities. IEEE Access **7**, 117134–117151 (2019)
3. Srinivas, J., Das, A.K., Kumar, N., Rodrigues, J.: Cloud centric authentication for wearable healthcare monitoring system. IEEE Trans. Dependable Secure Comput. (2018)
4. Challa, S., et al.: An efficient ECC-based provably secure three-factor user authentication and key agreement protocol for wireless healthcare sensor networks. Comput. Electr. Eng. **69**, 534–554 (2018)
5. Merabet, F., Cherif, A., Belkadi, M., Blazy, O., Conchon, E., Sauveron, D.: New efficient M2C and M2M mutual authentication protocols for IoTbased healthcare applications. Peer Peer Netw. Appl. **13**(2), 439–474 (2020)
6. Wazid, M., Das, A.K., Kumar, N., Conti, M., Vasilakos, A.V.: A novel authentication and key agreement scheme for implantable medical devices deployment. IEEE J. Biomed. Health Inform. **22**(4), 1299–1309 (2018)
7. Kuo, T.T., Kim, H.E., Ohno-Machado, L.: Blockchain distributed ledger technologies for biomedical and health care applications. J. Am. Med. Inform. Assoc. **24**(6), 1211–1220 (2017)

8. Deshmukh, V., Pathak, S., Bothe, S.: MobEdge: mobile blockchain-based privacy-edge scheme for healthcare Internet of Things-based ecosystems. Concur. Comput. Pract. Exp., e7210 (2022)
9. Wang, X., Sun, J., Wang, Y., Liu, Y.: Deepen electronic health record diffusion beyond breadth: game changers and decision drivers. Inf. Syst. Front. **24**(2), 537–548 (2022)
10. Dinh, N., et al.: Implementation outcomes assessment of a digital clinical support tool for intrapartum care in Rural Kenya: observational analysis. JMIR Form. Res. **6**(6), e34741 (2022)
11. Garg, N., Wazid, M., Das, A.K., Singh, D.P., Rodrigues, J.J.P.C., Park, Y.: BAKMP-IoMT: design of blockchain enabled authenticated key management protocol for internet of medical things deployment. IEEE Access **8**, 95956–95977 (2020)
12. Wang, Z., Luo, N., Zhou, P.: GuardHealth: blockchain empowered secure data management and graph convolutional network enabled anomaly detection in smart healthcare. J. Parallel Distrib. Comput. **142**, 1–12 (2020)
13. Zhou, T., Li, X., Zhao, H.: Med-PPPHIS: blockchain-based personal healthcare information system for national physique monitoring and scientific exercise guiding. J. Med. Syst. **3**(305) (2019)
14. Chung, K., Jung, H.: Knowledge-based block chain networks for health log data management mobile service. Personal Ubiquitous Comput. (2019)
15. Gordon, W.J., Catalini, C.: Blockchain technology for healthcare: facilitating the transition to patient-driven interoperability. Comput. Struct. Biotechnol. J. (2018)
16. Mirjalili, S., Mirjalili, S.M., Lewis, A.: Grey wolf optimizer. Adv. Eng. Softw. **69**, 46–61 (2014)
17. Konkle, T., Alvarez, G.A.: A self-supervised domain-general learning framework for human ventral stream representation. Nat. Commun. **13**(1), 1–12 (2022)
18. Pei, W., Xue, B., Shang, L., Zhang, M.: Detecting overlapping areas in unbalanced high-dimensional data using neighborhood rough set and genetic programming. IEEE Trans. Evolut. Comput. (2022)
19. Mistry, K., Zhang, L., Neoh, S.C., Lim, C.P., Fielding, B.: A micro-GA embedded PSO feature selection approach to intelligent facial emotion recognition. IEEE Transa. Cybern. **47**(6), 1496–1509 (2017)
20. Mirjalili, S., Lewis, A: The whale optimization algorithm. Adv. Eng. Softw. **95**, 51–67 (2016)
21. Chen, T., Zhu, Y., Teng, J.: Beetle swarm optimisation for solving investment portfolio problems. J. Eng. **2018**(16), 1600–1605, (2018)

Reflector Saturation in Amplified Reflection Denial of Service Attack Abusing CLDAP and Memcache Protocols

João José Costa Gondim[1,2(✉)] and Robson de Oliveira Albuquerque[2]

[1] Departamento de Ciência da Computação - CIC, Universidade de Brasília,
Campus Univ. Darcy Ribeiro, Brasilia 70910-900, DF, Brazil
gondim@unb.br
[2] Programa de Pos-gradução em Engenharia Elétrica - PPEE,
Universidade de Brasilia, Campus Univ. Darcy Ribeiro, Brasilia 70910-900, DF, Brazil
robson@redes.unb.br

Abstract. Amplified reflection distributed denial-of-service (AR-DDoS) attacks have been prevalent in the last ten years. AR-DDoS attacks are volumetric attacks where the stream reaching the victim comes from an intermediary infrastructure that amplifies and redirects it to the target, all orchestrated by a skilled attacker. This dynamic motivates the study of the behavior of the intermediate node - the reflector - since the effectiveness of the attack depends on it. This work aims to evaluate the saturation behavior of Connection-less Lightweight Directory Access Protocol (CLDAP) and Memcache reflectors during a DDoS attack by amplified reflection characterizing such behavior on general-purpose hardware. The results obtained are compared with previous works and discussed with the aim of anticipating evolution trends in AR-DDoS attacks and possible requirements for improvements in their detection and mitigation.

Keywords: distributed denial of service · amplified reflection · cldap · memcache

1 Introduction

Amplified Reflection Distributed Denial of Service (AR-DDoS) attacks have been growing both in their occurrence as well as their intensity over the last ten years. Although already occurring, it was only after the 100 Gbps attack on Spamhaus [1], that such attacks have evolved, not only in the abused protocols but also in the escalation in volume [2]. Also, there has been the incorporation of new ways of conducting the attack, such as those indicated in [3,4].

R. D. O. Albuquerque—These authors contributed equally to this work.

T. Guarda et al. (Eds.): ARTIIS 2023, CCIS 1936, pp. 248–263, 2024.
https://doi.org/10.1007/978-3-031-48855-9_19

From the attacker's point of view, AR-DDoS attacks are attractive because they leverage the flow generated by the attacker with little attack preparation effort since the reflectors only need to be identified dispensing any further infection by some artifact or malware. Furthermore, the execution can take place with the attacker injecting probes directly into the reflectors or controlling relatively small-scale botnets that send the probes for amplification.

In general terms, AR-DDoS attacks are volumetric attacks in which the flow that reaches the victim does not come directly from the attacker but from an abused intermediate infrastructure that sends to the target and amplified flow. In this regard, the work [5] has focused on studying the behavior of the reflector (intermediary node), since not only the efficiency but the effectiveness of the attack depends on it. Specifically, citech19gondim2020 studied the behavior of the reflector when subjected to different probe injection rates and running different abused protocols. The methodology adopted generated consistent results when compared with reports of real attacks, thus being valid.

The objective and contributions of this work are to evaluate the saturation behavior of CLDAP and Memcache reflectors under DDoS attack by amplified reflection, following a methodology that takes the point of view of the attacker, in order to better characterize such behavior in general-purpose hardware. The obtained results are compared with previous works and discussed with the objective of anticipating evolution trends in AR-DDoS attacks and identifying possible implications in terms of detection and mitigation.

This article is organized into sections. Section 2 presents the related work and the specific attacks tested in this work. In Sect. 3 the test methodology, configurations and tools used are described, followed by Sect. 4 where the test results are presented and then discussed in Sect. 5. Section 6 presents conclusions and future work.

2   Background and Related Work

AR-DDoS attacks, being a denial of service (DoS) attack, seek to prevent legitimate users from accessing the attacked infrastructure and/or the services it provides [6]. In the specific case of AR-DDoS, the attacker sends a flow of probes to an intermediate infrastructure, instead of directly to the target. This intermediate node amplifies the flow and redirects it to the target [7]. There are numerous works that address AR-DDoS. Some of them, involving the measurement of these attacks, are described as follows.

[8] analyzed several UDP-based application protocols that can be abused in amplified attacks, determining their amplification factors in both bytes and packets. In addition, [9] addressed amplified DDoS attacks using TCP-based application protocols, which are less prevalent than those that exploit UDP-based services.

In terms of measuring these attacks, [10] collected and analyzed the result of 1000 d of traffic from DDoS attacks amplified with a honeypots network of UDP reflectors, between July 2014 and July 2017, focusing on the cycle of life of the attacks that used the reflectors, from the initial sweep for lifting the reflectors to their use in the attacks. [11] presents a methodology to measure the properties of individual devices participating in DDoS attacks, such as traffic threshold, amplification factor, and speed, to evaluate the contribution of each device in the attack.

With respect to defense, [12] presents a distributed defense architecture for AR-DDoS attacks on the network. The method allows the detection of whether the unsolicited packets are being sent to a victim within a service provider's network. Once the attack is detected, routers at the edge of the network automatically block the undue sources.

From the point of view of attack dynamics, [5,13] present a methodology for evaluating AR-DDoS attacks in controlled environments. In the first work, the protocols addressed were SSDP and SNMP while in the second, in addition to SNMP and SSDP, NTP and DNS protocols were also addressed. The results in both works indicated that the reflectors saturate with a relatively low probe injection rate in terms of packets per second. [14] applies the methodology in [5,13] to scenarios where the reflectors are IoT (Internet of Things) devices addressing SNMP and SSDP protocols. [15] also applies to IoT scenario using CoAP protocol over IP v4 and v6.

2.1   AR-DDoS Attack Abusing CLDAP Protocol

Connection-less Lightweight Directory Access Protocol (CLDAP) [16] is a protocol based on Lightweight Directory Access Protocol (LDAP), which in turn is an application layer protocol that provides access to directory services using the model client-server, following the X.500 standard. CLDAP was defined to improve performance when dealing with small queries without the need to establish a connection. Thus, it operates over the UDP protocol on port 389. As it does not require authentication to respond to requests, it is liable to be abused in an AR-DDoS attack.

Directory data is stored in a tree-like structure, the Directory Information Tree (DIT), where the path to an object becomes its unique identifier, the Distinguished Name (DN) [17]. The DN in turn is composed of a comma-separated sequence of Relative Distinguished Name (RDN), which are the branches of the tree that lead the element in question to the root of the tree.

To carry out the attack, the generated CLDAP packets use the *searchRequest* operation, which performs the request for an object. In the *Filter* field, the *objectClass=** filter is used, which causes objects that have any class to be returned in the search, which is the case for all objects in the tree. Finally, the *Attribute* field is set to the value ***, requesting that all attributes of the objects found be returned. These characteristics aim to maximize the response size of the reflectors.

An attack using CLDAP as a reflection protocol follows these steps: 1) assemble a message with the following fields and values *Operation = searchRequest*, *Filter = < objectClass=* >* and *Attribute = ** for greater amplification; 2) assemble a UDP header with the message generated in the previous step and with the destination port 389, protocol default; 3) assemble an IP header with the UDP datagram from the previous step with the source address being the victim and the destination address being the reflector address; and 4)send the generated packet to the reflector, which in turn will respond by directing the received request to the victim.

2.2   AR-DDoS Attack Abusing Memcache

The Memcached deamon implements a distributed key-value, in-memory, caching system. It emerged to scale queries into caches, managing the caching of the results of database calls, APIs or other data, and it is widely used to store data that is frequently required, thus reducing requests to the database [18]

In the memcache protocol, there are commands that involve unstructured data (when a client wants to store or retrieve data) such as storage commands such as SET and retrieval commands such as GET. All other commands (management and statistics) do not involve unstructured data. A command line always begins with the name of the command, followed by parameters (if any) delimited by whitespace. Command names are lowercase and case-sensitive.

Memcached has no access control, since it was not designed to operate exposed to the Internet. However, some companies have been using Memcached with their ports open to the Internet without proper basic precautions to avoid using their servers as reflectors.

So, for a Memcached server to be used as a reflector/amplifier, the Memcached server must have the UDP protocol enabled and exposed to the internet for any network address. There are two ways to exploit the server as a reflector/amplifier. The first, and simplest, is to forge a Stat request Memcached packet with the victim's address in the source address field of the IP packet. The server will respond to the victim with a Stat response package. This form will not be discussed as it is not the most frequent and efficient form of attack. The second method requires some server preparation before starting the attack. The attacker must know the maximum allowed value for the stored values. In order to obtain this data, the attacker must use Stat packets to find a maximum size that we can store in the value. Alternatively, the attacker can cache (via SET command) a very large object to control the amplification factor.

After identifying and if necessary preparing the reflector, the attacker must: 1) assemble a message with the GET command with the desired key-value pair; 2) assemble a UDP header with the message generated in the previous step and with the destination port 11211, protocol default; 3) assemble an IP header with the UDP datagram from the previous step with the source address being the victim and the destination address being the reflector address; and 4) send the generated packet to the reflector, which in turn will respond by directing the received request to the victim.

3   Methods and Procedures

The methodology used in this work is based on that used in [5,13]. As already said, the methodology takes the point of view of the attacker to observe a particular aspect of reflector behavior. It assumes that the attacker has access only to externally observable reflector flows, in as much as there are no other forms of stimuli, and their response, that can be exercised. This assumption, however limited, is realistic and matches the practical attack conditions.

The tests were aimed at exercising the attack with increasing intensities in order to show the reflector saturation behavior and tests were implemented in a controlled environment with devices without internet access. For that matter, the attacks used a specifically built tool which implements AR-DDoS attacks over various protocols with control of probe injection rates and attack dynamics. In the tool, the various attack levels are described by Eq. 1, where L is the attack level. The levels were chosen because it was observed in the cited works that saturation of the devices already occurs within this range. These levels were then incremented every 10 s.

$$Rate = 10^{L-1} \tag{1}$$

Specifically, for each protocol used in the attack, together with the victim (target) and reflector addresses, the initial attack level was defined as 1, with a level increment every 10 s For CLDAP, the attack levels were from 1 to 7 while for Memcached, they were from 1 to 10. The difference was due to the saturation dynamics observed in each protocol.

Amplification factors for packets and bits per second were calculated using the Eqs. 2 and 3.

$$Amp_{pkt} = \frac{pkt_{reply}}{pkt_{request}} \tag{2}$$

$$Amp_{bits} = \frac{bits_{reply}}{bits_{request}} \tag{3}$$

In calculating the bit amplification, only the IP and UDP headers were considered, thus ignoring the Ethernet header, as shown in Eq. 4. In the calculation of packet amplification, fragments generated due to the size of the response packet sent by the reflector exceeding 1500 bytes of the Maximum Transmission Unit (MTU) were also considered.

$$Amp_{bits} = \frac{HDR_{IP} + HDR_{UDP} + Data_{reply}}{HDR_{IP} + HDR_{UDP} + Data_{request}} \tag{4}$$

With regard to reflector saturation, it is understood that this occurs when the amplification rate does not sustain itself and drops.

3.1   Test Scenarios

Specific scenarios and configurations were used for each of the tested protocols, in order to generate results for the calculation of amplification factors in bps and packets (Eqs. 2 and 3).

3.1.1   CLDAP Scenario

In this scenario, four devices were used during the tests - three computers acting as attacker, reflector, and victim, along with a physical switch that interconnected them. All of them were connected by CAT 5e cables. The switch used was the TP-LINK TL-SG1008D model and has 8 10/100/1000Mbps ports, interconnecting the other devices whose functions and specifications are listed in Table 1.

Table 1. Device specifications - CLDAP secnario

Resource	Attacker	Reflector	Target
Processor	Intel i5	AMD Ryzen	Intel i5
	8250U @ 1.6 GHz	3700X @ 3.6 GHz	4210U @ 1.7 GHz
Memory	8 GB DDR4	16 GB DDR4	6 GB DDR3L
	@ 2400 MHz	@ 3000 MHz	@ 1600 MHz
Network	ASIX AX88179	Realtek RTL8125B	Realtek RTL8168/8111
Interface	USB 3.0 Gigabit	PCI-E 2.5 Gigabit	PCI-E Gigabit
Operating	Xubuntu	Windows Server	Xubuntu
System	20.04.1	2012 R2	20.04.1

The packets were captured on all computers with the **dumpcap** software, while the count of packets and bytes transmitted every second during the duration of the attack was carried out with the **tshark** software on top of the generated capture files.

The values obtained were then separated into groups of ten seconds, which represent the duration in each level, and the average was calculated to obtain the performance of the attack per second in each level. These data are shown and discussed in Sect. 4.

3.1.2   Memcache Scenario

Identical to the tests with the CLDAP protocol, in this scenario, four devices were also used during the tests, in a similar topology: three computers and a switch. Again, a TP-LINK TL-SG1008D model switch with 8 10/100/1000Mbps ports was used, interconnecting the other devices with CAT 5e cables. The three computers whose functions and specifications are listed in Table 2.

Table 2. Device specifications - Memcache scenario

Resource	Attacker	Reflector	Target
Processor	AMD Ryzen 7 1700 @ 3.0 GHz	Intel Core i7-6700 @ 3.40 GHz	Intel Core i5-6200U @ 2.30 GHz
Memory	16 GB DDR4 @ 2400 MHz	16 GB DDR4 @ 3000 MHz	12 GB DDR3L @ 1600 MHz
Network Interface	Realtek RTL8168 PCI-E Gigabit	Realtek RTL8168/8111 PCI-E Gigabit	Realtek RTL8111 PCI Gigabit
Operating System	Manjaro Linux 18	Manjaro Linux 18	Manjaro Linux 18

4   Tests and Results

The results of the tests performed using the CLDAP and Memcached protocols are presented in the sequel.

4.1   Results for CLDAP

The results of the CLDAP attack are presented in the tables and figures in the following. Tables 3 and 4 show data related to tests with the number of packets sent and received every second per attack level (Fig. 1 a) and b) respectively), while Table 5 shows the amplifications obtained in terms of packets and bits per second (also represented in Fig. 2) respectively.

Table 3. Packets sent and received per second - CLDAP

Level	Attacker	Reflector Inbound	Reflector Outbound	Victim
1	1	1	2	2
2	10	10	20	20
3	100	100	200	200
4	1000	1000	1212	1212
5	10000	10000	10075	10075
6	30633	30632	43949	43949
7	95437	95398	187217	84621

It can be verified (Table 5) that the peak of the amplification factor referring to the packets occurs in the initial levels of the attack being 2x, that is, for each packet sent by the attacker, the victim receives two. In bits per second, the amplification factor peak also occurred in the first levels with the value of 31.36x (applying Eq. 3: $Amp_{bit} = \frac{pkt_{reply}}{pkt_{request}} = \frac{22832}{728} = 31.36$).

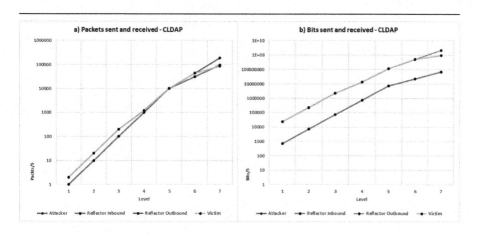

Fig. 1. Packets and Bits sent and received per second - CLDAP

Table 4. Bits sent and received per second - CLDAP

Level	Attacker	Reflector Inbound	Reflector Outbound	Victim
1	728	728	22832	22832
2	7280	7280	228320	228320
3	72800	72800	2283200	2283200
4	728000	728000	13836192	13836192
5	7280000	7280000	115011634	115011634
6	22300502	22300314	501717405	501717405
7	69478354	69450035	2137264706	966036819

Table 5. Amplification by level - CLDAP

Level	Packages	Bits
1	2.00	31.36
2	2.00	31.36
3	2.00	31.36
4	1.21	19.01
5	1.01	15.80
6	1.43	22.50
7	0.89	13.90

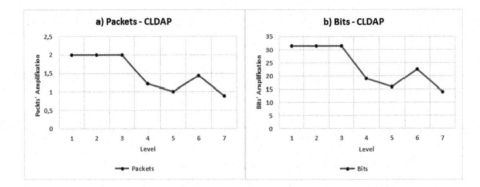

Fig. 2. Amplification in packets and bits per second - CLDAP

With regard to reflector saturation, this occurred from level 3 to level 4. This is manifested both in the amplification factor in bits per second, which drops from 31.36x to 19.01x, and in packets, which goes from 2x to 1.21x (Table 5, lines 3 and 4). One can also observe a residual amplification after saturation, without reaching attenuation, when the amplification factor is less than 1.

In the last line of Table 4 it is noted that the network interfaces of the attacker, reflector, and victim reached very close to the limit of their capacities.

4.2 Results for Memcache

Analogously, the results of the attack with Memcache are presented as follows. Table 6 shows data related to the tests with the number of packets sent and received every second per attack level. The results of the tests in terms of flows in bits per second are in Table 7 (Fig. 3, a) and b) respectively) while the amplification rates obtained in terms of packets and bits are shown in Table 8 (Fig. 4).

Note that the peak of the amplification factor referring to the packets occurs at the initial levels of the attack, being 468x. In bits per second, the amplification

Table 6. Packets sent and received per second - Memcache

Level	Attacker	Reflector Inbound	Reflector Outbound	Victim
1	1	1	468	453
2	9	9	3763	3756
3	90	94	36861	36889
4	810	806	36946	36939
5	8200	8016	38077	38077
6	43036	40923	47426	47426
7	272475	238060	78986	81970
8	326858	300493	81972	73229
9	324549	298900	82016	69903
10	325879	298126	71997	72987

Table 7. Bits sent and received per second - Memcache

Level	Attacker	Reflector Inbound	Reflector Outbound	Victim
1	392	392	5342768	5178256
2	3680	3680	42956440	42878752
3	35280	37080	420747840	421063144
4	317752	315952	421712032	421638912
5	3214400	3142424	434621584	434621584
6	16870112	16042128	541340544	541340544
7	106810200	93319520	901574856	935632472
8	128128336	117793488	935650840	835863400
9	127223440	117168952	936153496	797890368
10	127744800	116865544	821793984	833095688

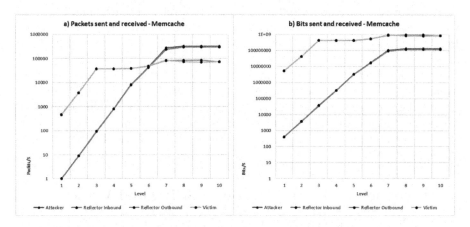

Fig. 3. Packets and Bits sent and received per second - Memcache

Table 8. Amplification by level - Memcache

Level	Packages	Bits
1	468	13629.51
2	418.11	11672.95
3	392.14	11347.03
4	45.84	1334.73
5	4.75	138.31
6	1.16	33.74
7	0.33	9.66
8	0.27	7.94
9	0.27	7.99
10	0.24	7.03

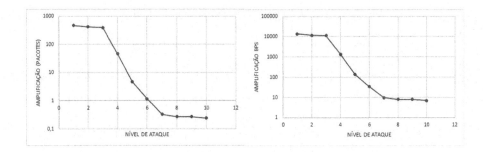

Fig. 4. Amplification in packets and bps - Memcache

factor peak also occurred in the first levels with the value of 13629.51x (applying Eq. 3: $Amp_{bit} = \frac{pkt_{reply}}{pkt_{request}} = \frac{5342768}{392} = 13629.51$).

Reflector saturation occurred from level 3 to level 4 (Table 8, lines 3 and 4). This is manifested both in the amplification factor in bits per second, which drops from 11347.03x to 1334.73x, and in packets, which went from 392.14x to 45.84x.

From the point of view of the post-saturation behavior, one can observe an attenuation in the amplification in packets from level 7, Table 8, line 7), with the factor falling to less than 1. As for the factor of amplification in bits per second, the maintenance of residual amplification is verified. It can also be seen that the reflector and the victim came close to the capacity of the network interface (Table 8, line 10).

5   Discussion and Comparision with Related Work

For both CLDAP and Memcache, the reflector presented a saturation behavior, from level 3 to level 4. From there, the attack efficiency decreases, since part of the packets sent by the attacker are not converted into received packets by the victim.

The results obtained are similar to those of previous works, such as [5,13], which are the basis of the methodology adopted in this work. In those works, it was found that from level 3, consolidating at level 4, saturation occurs for different protocols, in scenarios with hardware that are totally different from each other. The results presented here are consistent with those of these works and corroborate their findings.

Table 9 lists the results obtained in [13] and aggregates the results presented here for CLDAP and Memcache. It includes information about amplification rates (Amp. bits and Amp. pkt), saturation (Sat.), saturation consolidation (Cons.), residual amplification (Amp. res.) and attenuation (Aten.).

Table 9. Comparison of amplification rates by protocol: values for SNMP, SSDP, NTP, and DNS are from [13]

Protocol	Amp. bits	Amp. pkt	Sat.	Cons.	Amp. res.	Aten.
SNMP	609.03	33.40	3	4	bps and pkt	
SSDP	38.23	10.00	3	4	bit	pkt
NTP (600 hosts)	422.81	100.00	2	3		bps and pkt
DNS (Amp-45)	43.81	3.00	3	4	bps and pkt	
CLDAP	31.36	2.00	3	4	bps and pkt	
Memcache	13629.51	468.00	3	4	bps	pkt

As it can be seen, all tested protocols are already saturated or start to saturate from level 3, consolidating at level 4. In the case of NTP, saturation starts at level 2 and consolidates at level 3. This means that for an attacker, the injection rate that would minimize the attack effort would be between one hundred and one thousand probes injected into the reflector per second (Eq. 1). Taking into account that general-purpose hardware with reasonable computational power was used for the reflectors, the result suggests that the investigation should continue in order to explain the coincidence of the results.

Even if the attack effort is smaller for each reflector, this does not always happen with it generating its maximum flow. Thus, from the point of view of the flow volume generated, the attacker may have to use more reflectors to achieve the same attack volume, resulting in a greater need for preparation (identification of more reflectors), coordination, and conduct of the attack. In terms of coordination, a layer of *bots* commanding the reflectors can reduce the complexity even if it generates the need to build a *botnet*. Even so, it is estimated that the option for AR-DDoS would continue to be advantageous from the point of view of attack effort (preparation and execution) compared to a direct attack.

By its turn, [14,15] investigate the use of IoT devices as reflectors and show that in the devices tested, saturation occurs at least one level below what occurs in general-purpose equipment. Thus, it would be expected that, if used, many more IoT devices would be required than in the case described above.

It should be noted that the IoT reflector case differs from the reflector on general-purpose hardware. Such devices generally have limitations in computational power, connectivity, and power consumption. In addition, the specific repertoire of protocols implemented in them and subject to abuse by AR-DDoS is reduced when compared to that available in general-purpose reflectors. Thus, the role of the reflector, even if possible, would be limited, given the greater effort in preparing and coordinating the attack. Still, if not as a reflector, IoT devices could form a layer of bots injecting probes into wide-use servers (running DNS, NTP, SNMP, etc.) over general-purpose hardware serving as reflectors. This is completely in line with attackers' low probe rates (in the order of hundreds to thousands of probes per second) which avoids reflector saturation. So, from an attacker's point of view, it is reasonable to expect attacks with an increased number of reflectors driven by much smaller botnets, if compared to those deployed in a direct volumetric attack, with reflectors operating at a low rate of inbound and outbound flows.

5.1   Implications for Detection, Mitigation, and Security Management

The previous section compared results and demonstrated a pattern in terms of saturation. It was then speculated how an attacker could take advantage of this saturation pattern to improve attack efficiency not only in terms of overall generated flow volume but also in reducing the coordination and attack execution complexity. This section discusses how the defensive side could be affected.

The first point to observe is that when reflectors operate most efficiently, with maximum amplification and output, this is achieved for relatively low probe rates, of the order of hundreds to thousands, either inbound or outbound. This alters the flow dynamics and is not the normally expected flow rate characteristic for a volumetric attack. This will certainly contribute to making detection more complex since this characteristic is closer to that of layer 7 low-volume and slow-rate (low & slow) attacks. So, detection based on rate thresholds would have to operate at lower values which might lead to poorer detection as attack flows become less distinguishable from normal flows. For detection based on machine learning, data sets used in training will have to be updated to include flows with this characteristic, and model retraining will be necessary. On the other hand, detection using heuristics based on other flows' characteristics (large numbers, hundreds to thousands, of unsolicited replies from several different origins) should be less affected.

Concerning mitigation of DDoS in general, but still applicable for AR-DDoS in particular, among the various methods used in the Internet, three are more relevant [19]: Origin Side Ingress Filtering, Destination Side Ingress Filtering, and Response Rate Limiting. Each of those techniques displays relative efficiency but presents specific issues. The first is only partially adopted since the benefits are not for the origin network but rather other networks; the second depends on Destination-side Source Address Validation, which normally affects legitimate users similarly to the DDoS attack it intends to mitigate; and the third is similar to the second as it might also impact users, although less severely. For the second and third techniques, it is clear that improved detection with precise source identification is crucial to their deployment without undesirable side effects.

Regarding flow filtering and blocking, attack tactics like carpet-bombing [3] and pulse wave [4] take advantage of them to potentialize attack impact. These tactics demonstrate that conducting DDoS has become security-aware and sophisticated. It might be argued that the way blocking and filtering are currently used, focus on tackling the effects of DDoS attacks but not the causes. Even so, filtering on or close to the target/victim does not fully mitigate volumetric attacks as link saturation still occurs.

As a consequence, detection, and blocking have to evolve to take place far from the target and closer to the origin. However, given the distributed nature of the attack, that might be impractical. A compromise between improved efficiency and reduced undesirable side effects is to block flows on converging points along the path to the target.

Considering a different approach, Software Defined Networks (SDN) seem to offer the necessary tools for implementing the above improvements, with intense research effort emphasizing DDoS detection and mitigation with SDN, like [20–23]. However, proposed solutions fall short of improving existing solutions incurring in similar issues: ineffective or wrong detection, unfeasibility for real-time deployment, and blocking that does not address link saturation, being placed either close to the victim or affecting other nodes in the network.

Summarizing, it is expected that detection and mitigation shift to identifying attack sources and convergence points to improve precision and overall efficiency in defending against volumetric DDoS.

6   Conclusion and Future Work

As shown, the use of the CLDAP and Memcache protocols in AR-DDoS attacks (performed in a controlled environment) allowed us to observe a saturation behavior consistent with previously published works that analyzed other protocols. The results presented here corroborate the previous effects observed in previous research.

From the perspective of the attacker, it shows he can control the reflectors and modulate the attack at his will, causing damage to the users who try to access legit resources or services under attack. It also can be seen the complexity of performing such attacks requires no deep knowledge of the abused protocols or defenses that could be in place.

Implications may vary depending on the capacity of the defender. One can not assume the defenders are aware of all the steps it takes to mitigate AR-DDoS attacks. It is not an easy task to deploy all the controls and monitoring capabilities needed to identify probes or to change the environment to react and support attacks on such scales AR-DDoS brings to the response teams. Mitigation strategies may vary from the complexity of the infrastructure to the number of human resources with the knowledge to interfere in the network without compromising available resources or amplifying the damage.

On the other hand, as observed in this work, for an attacker to generate a volume of traffic with less attack effort, he would need a greater number of reflectors. This suggests some directions to investigate, corresponding to possible options for an attacker.

A possible line would be for the attacker to use reflectors hosted in the cloud, following the recent trend of DDoS attacks as in [24], which would take the focus of prevention, detection, and mitigation to the scope of cloud security. Another direction would be to extend the evaluation of the use of IoT devices as reflectors, or even as possible injectors, covering a larger base of devices, which, in turn, brings more capacity to the attackers and more complexity to the defenders.

Acknowledgments. J.J.C.G. acknowledges financial support from project PROFI SSA (Programmable Future Internet for Secure Software Architectures), FAPESP grant n. 2020/05152-7 (São Paulo State Foundation for Ressearch Support - Fundação de Amparo à Pesquisa do Estado de São Paulo). R.d.O.A. thankfully acknowledges the computational support of the Laboratory of Technologies for Decision Making (LATITUDE) of the University of Brasília; the General Attorney's Office (Grant AGU 697.935/2019); the General Attorney's Office for the National Treasure - PGFN (Grant 23106.148934/2019-67); the National Institute of Science and Technology in Cyber Security - Nucleus 6 (grant CNPq 465741/2014-2).

References

1. Bright, P.: Spamhaus ddos grows to internet-threatening size. ArsTechnica (2013)
2. Graewe, K.: Reflection amplification vectors: a chronology. Link11 blog (2020)
3. Cimpanu, C.: 'Carpet-bombing' ddos attack takes down south african isp for an entire day. ZDnet Blog (2019). (Accessed 21 May 2021)
4. Zeifman, I.: Attackers use ddos pulses to pin down multiple targets. imperva (2021). (Accessed 21 May 2021)
5. Gondim, J.J.C., Oliveira Albuquerque, R., Nascimento, C.A., García Villalba, L., Kim, T.H.: A methodological approach for assessing amplified reflection distributed denial of service on the internet of things. Sensors **16**(11), 1855 (2016)
6. Gligor, V.D.: A note on denial-of-service in operating systems. IEEE Trans. Softw. Eng. SE **10**(3), 320–324 (1984). https://doi.org/10.1109/TSE.1984.5010241
7. Paxson, V.: An analysis of using reflectors for distributed denial-of-service attacks. Comput. Commun. Rev. **31** (2001) https://doi.org/10.1145/505659.505664
8. Rossow, C.: Amplification hell: revisiting network protocols for ddos abuse. In: NDSS, pp. 1–15 (2014). https://doi.org/10.14722/ndss.2014.23233
9. Kührer, M., Hupperich, T., Rossow, C., Holz, T.: Hell of a handshake: abusing tcp for reflective amplification ddos attacks. In: Proceedings of the 8th USENIX Conference on Offensive Technologies, WOOT (2014)
10. Thomas, D.R., Clayton, R., Beresford, A.R.: 1000 days of udp amplification ddos attacks. In: 2017 APWG Symposium on Electronic Crime Research (eCrime), pp. 79–84. IEEE (2017)
11. Lavrenovs, A.: Towards measuring global ddos attack capacity. In: 2019 11th International Conference on Cyber Conflict (CyCon), vol. 325900, pp. 1–15. IEEE (2019)

12. Khooi, X.Z., Csikor, L., Divakaran, D.M., Kang, M.S.: Dida: distributed in-network defense architecture against amplified reflection ddos attacks. In: 2020 6th IEEE Conference on Network Softwarization (NetSoft), pp. 277–281. IEEE (2020)
13. Gondim, J.J.C., Oliveira Albuquerque, R., Sandoval, Undefined O.A.L.: Mirror saturation in amplified reflection Distributed Denial of Service: A case of study using SNMP, SSDP, NTP and DNS protocols. Future Generation Comput. Syst. (2020). https://doi.org/10.1016/j.future.2020.01.024
14. Vasques, A.T., Gondim, J.J.C.: Amplified reflection ddos attacks over iot mirrors: a saturation analysis. In: 2019 Workshop on Communication Networks and Power Systems (WCNPS), pp. 1–6 2019). https://doi.org/10.1109/WCNPS.2019.8896290
15. Vasques, A.T., Gondim, J.J.C.: Amplified reflection ddos attacks over iot reflector running coap. In: 2020 15th Iberian Conference on Information Systems and Technologies (CISTI), pp. 1–6 (2020). https://doi.org/10.23919/CISTI49556.2020.9140882
16. Zeilenga, K.: Connection-less Lightweight Directory Access Protocol (CLDAP) to Historic Status. RFC Editor (2003). https://doi.org/10.17487/RFC3352, www.rfc-editor.org/rfc/rfc3352.txt
17. Zeilenga, K.: Lightweight Directory Access Protocol (LDAP): Directory Information Models. RFC Editor (2006). https://doi.org/10.17487/RFC4512, www.rfc-editor.org/rfc/rfc4512.txt
18. Memcache.org: Memcached - a Distributed Memory Object Caching System - Memcached.org. (Accessed 29 May 2023)
19. Yazdani, R., et al.: Mirrors in the sky: on the potential of clouds in dns reflection-based denial-of-service attacks. In: Proceedings of the 25th International Symposium on Research in Attacks, Intrusions and Defenses, pp. 263–275 (2022)
20. Fan, C., Kaliyamurthy, N.M., Chen, S., Jiang, H., Zhou, Y., Campbell, C.: Detection of ddos attacks in software defined networking using entropy. Appli. Sci. **12**(1) (2022). https://doi.org/10.3390/app12010370
21. Malik, A., Fréin, R., Al-Zeyadi, M., Andreu-Perez, J.: Intelligent sdn traffic classification using deep learning: deep-sdn. In: 2020 2nd International Conference on Computer Communication and the Internet (ICCCI), pp. 184–189 (2020). https://doi.org/10.1109/ICCCI49374.2020.9145971
22. Ismail, S., Hassen, H.R., Just, M., Zantout, H.: A review of amplification-based distributed denial of service attacks and their mitigation. Comput. Sec. **109**, 102380 (2021). https://doi.org/10.1016/j.cose.2021.102380
23. El Houda, A., Z., Khoukhi, L., Senhaji Hafid, A.: Bringing intelligence to software defined networks: Mitigating ddos attacks. IEEE Trans. Netw. Service Manag. **17**(4), 2523–2535 (2020) https://doi.org/10.1109/TNSM.2020.3014870
24. Arghire, I.: Small botnet launches record-breaking 26 million rps ddos attack. Security Week(2022). (Accessed 15 June 2022)

Maturity Model of Response Protocols to Ransomware Scenarios in the Mining Sector

Brignith Gomez, Saul Vargas[✉], and Juan-Pablo Mansilla

University of Peruana de Ciencias, Lima, Peru
{u201822877,u20181g899}@upc.edu.pe, juan.mansilla@upc.pe

Abstract. The Maturity Model for Defense Protocols against Ransomware Scenarios in the mining sector is a useful tool to assess an organization's level of preparedness against ransomware attacks and design effective strategies to mitigate their impacts. This model, based on the NIST methodology and the ISO 27001 AND 27002 Standards, and the experience of cybersecurity experts, consists of five levels of maturity that go from initial adoption to defense optimization. The Initial level focuses on risk awareness and basic preparation. The Managed level focuses on the protection of critical data and systems, while the Defined level, focuses on early detection and response to incidents. The Managed level seeks response automation and collaboration with third parties, while Optimized level, focuses on continuous improvement and innovation. For each level, achieve the characteristics and objectives allow organizations to assess their current position and establish action plans to improve their readiness. Some recommended best practices include ongoing employee training, implementing technical security measures, conducting incident simulations, adopting backup and recovery solutions, and collaborating with cybersecurity service providers. In summary, the Maturity Model for Ransomware Defense Protocols is a valuable tool to help organizations improve their ability to resist and recover from ransomware attacks. Its focus on best practices and continuous improvement makes it a reference in the field of cybersecurity.

Keyword: ransomware, maturity model, cybersecurity, protocol, defense

1 Introduction

Currently, information has become a vitally important asset for companies due to the growing threat to organizations around the world. Ransomware attacks are a form of malware that encrypts a company's files and demands a ransom in exchange for the decryption key. The scenarios where these attacks take place may vary over time and in their behavior, since cybercriminals use different techniques and tools to carry them out. In addition, ransomware attacks

© The Author(s), under exclusive license to Springer Nature Switzerland AG 2024
T. Guarda et al. (Eds.): ARTIIS 2023, CCIS 1936, pp. 264–274, 2024.
https://doi.org/10.1007/978-3-031-48855-9_20

could spread through the organization's network and affect multiple devices and systems, damaging company assets. Consequently, companies seek to take preventive measures that manage to mitigate damage and reduce attacks, keeping defense techniques and methods updated.

In this sense, several cybersecurity defense protocols have been developed. Among them, the NIST Cybersecurity Framework and the international standards ISO 27001 and 27002. These seek to provide detailed guidelines for risk management, design and implementation of security measures, continuous monitoring of security improvement of an organization's information. By implementing the security framework and ISO standards, the aim is to reduce the risks of cyberattacks, prevent data loss or damage, as well as improve trust and credibility with customers and users. Also, they focus on the prevention of possible business interruptions and protection of intellectual property. For this reason, cybersecurity is essential for the continuity of a company's operations and the protection of the valuable information it manages.

Within this scope there is literature by different authors that offer information to keep companies informed. McDonald et al. (2022), offers in his article a description of the behavior of ransomware, its characteristics within a scenario and how it affects the infrastructure and functionality of the service. Emphasizing that ransomware attacks do not affect the infrastructure, but rather affect the information and data of the organization. Likewise, Connolly, A. Y. & Borrion, H., (2022), describes the actions to be taken by companies in the face of this type of attack, mentioning that most companies choose to follow the demands of the perpetrators, among other decisions they choose to minimize the impact. On the other hand, Chuquilla, A. et al, (2019), seeks to supply suggestions and good practices for proper management, to reduce the risks of ransomware attacks and improve the information security of companies. For this reason, it suggests the hiring of personnel specialized in cyber security and the implementation of information systems and good practices to prevent future attacks.

Similarly, Zhang, X. et al, 2021, presents a new encryption unknown ransomware attack detection technique using dual generative adversarial networks. Such a technique proposed in this article could be an important advance in the fight against ransomware attacks, as it would allow organizations to detect and prevent unknown encryption attacks before they cause considerable damage. Related to this, Zammani et al. (2021), proposes a holistic maturity model for information security management, focusing on people, processes, organizational documentation, and technology. With this, it is possible to measure the effectiveness of the implementation of the model to help companies avoid and/or reduce routine security incidents. Thus, he concluded that it is necessary to specialize in different areas of the organizations that require it to work on future updates of the developed maturity model. Although references have been found in other sectors than the treaty, as well as model proposals aimed at other sectors and business areas, no information has been found about the maturity model within the mining sector.

In response to this problem, a five-level response protocol maturity model has been proposed for ransomware scenarios in the mining sector, prioritizing a prevention scenario for mining companies.

The article is organized in seven parts, in the first part it presents the introduction, in the second part the related works are presented in the third part is the methodology used, in the fourth part is the comparison between relevant maturity models. To the subject, in the fifth part the maturity model conducted is described. Finally, in the sixth part, there is the validation and discussion of results and in the seventh, the conclusion of the project.

2   Related Work

Shemitha P.A. (2020), presents an analysis of conventional network authentication protocols and their effectiveness in preventing ransomware attacks. Allowing to identify that conventional authentication protocols are vulnerable to ransomware attacks due to their limitations in user and device authentication. Yuan, Y., Zhang, B., et al., (2021), propose a co-learning system that uses multiple ransomware detection models to improve detection accuracy and better resist evasion attacks and their outcomes show that the proposed system has a much higher detection rate than other methods and is effective in detecting both known and unknown ransomware. Rahman, M. S., Islam, M. R., et al. (2023), develop a new malware detection technique based on system call dependency sequence analysis; through tests they demonstrated that their technique is resistant to common malware evasion techniques, such as system call encryption.

Schmitz, C., Schmid, M., et. al., (2021), evaluated a subset of ISO/IEC 27002 security controls for a what-if scenario using COBIT maturity levels. Its main result is an analysis of the different maturity models based on COBIT. The solution proposed by El-Bendary, N., & El-Bahnasawy, M., (2019), elaborates a proposal for an improved method for malware detection, making use of process supervision and control and an approach based on rules, capable of detecting malware threats in real time and providing a rapid response to possible attacks, while being scalable. Yuryna et al. al., (2019), a common and rigorous methodology in scientific research and allows obtaining valuable information to address the ransomware problem using real data from companies that have been affected by ransomware, concluding that there are several factors that influence the degree of importance of the attacks. The research by Razikin and Widodo (2021) proposes a methodology to measure the level of maturity of technology and information in terms of cybersecurity in change companies. This work allows to identify strengths and weaknesses in cybersecurity processes. It can be useful for companies looking to improve their cybersecurity and comply with PCI-DSS requirements.

So too, Schmid, M., & Pape, S. (2019), focus on developing a solution to find out if the aggregation of corporate information security maturity levels can affect the final results. The study concludes that aggregation is an important tool to optimize information security and define priorities in areas for improvement. The Kandasamy (2022) study analyzes the risks associated with the main types of cyberattacks in medical centers and proposes a vulnerability priority scoring system to mitigate attacks. The authors used the National Institute of Standards and Technology's risk assessment framework for an in-depth analysis of the attacks and concluded in recommending vulnerability and risk self-assessment questionnaires. Rabie et. al., (2020), present as the main contribution of their research the application of the systematic literature review (SLR) method for the identification of possible research questions and the structuring of the research process. As a result, it is concluded that most of the studies on computer security maturity models are specific and focus on a single aspect, and that the ISO/IEC 27001/27002 standards have a great influence on these models. Prapenan & Pamuji (2020), presents a methodology to improve the information security management system using COBIT 5 and adapting to the ISO 27001 standard in a company. The audit carried out made it possible to identify security problems in the information system and improve its management. The contribution of Abazi & Kö (2019), consists in presenting a semi-automatic risk assessment framework and a security maturity model, based on the ISO 27001 standard, useful for auditors, security officers and managers. The proposed solution is useful for identifying gaps in the security implementation and provides the appropriate controls at a lower cost.

Deloitte (2021), focuses on identifying and evaluating the specific cyber risks facing the mining industry, as well as providing recommendations to improve cybersecurity. The results show that cyber risks to the mining industry are increasing and that it is essential that companies implement adequate cybersecurity measures to protect their critical assets and ensure business continuity. Englishbrecht et. al., (2020), presents a Capability Maturity Model (CMM) that helps to integrate measures related to digital forensic preparedness (DFR) and reach an appropriate level of maturity, by facilitating the core elements of the governance framework of COBIT 5 IT. The model can determine maturity levels based on use cases relevant to a specific organization, reduce the risk of misinvestment and misdirected effort, and is a useful tool for determining the current state of an ongoing implementation in a given moment. da Silva & de Barros (2019), presents an information security maturity model based on ISO 27001 for micro and small software development companies, with the aim of helping companies improve their security posture. The result is a useful guide for software development companies to implement sound information security practices and improve their market position.

3 Methodology

For the realization of the maturity model, the NIST SP 80030 cybersecurity framework was used, considering its four main phases, preparation, evaluation, response, and review. On the other hand, from the ISO 27001 Standards, the most important and relevant sections for the elaboration of the model were selected, these are section four, section five and section six that focus on the context of the organization, leadership, and planning. Similarly, from ISO 27002

Standards, section five, section six, and section seven that focus on information security policies, information security organization and human resources security, respectively. Together with the methodologies, a benchmarking was conducted on the relevant maturity models for our project, within which comparison criteria were set up with which the models were evaluated. Likewise, Likewise, a questionnaire in Spanish consisting of three sections was used(link to the questionnaire https://n9.cl/xys37p). The questionnaire was validated by two cybersecurity experts and was sent to the different participants via email and LinkedIn. In addition, the maturity model was validated in meetings with a professional from the area who is working within the area of cybersecurity in the mining sector and an expert in auditing of cybersecurity protocols.

4   Maturity Model Comparison

4.1   Information Security Management Maturity Model

The maturity model seeks to unify the best practices for information security management in order to improve the identification of security breaches and propose a road map for their reduction and control, increasing the level of security.

4.2   Cloud Cybersecurity Maturity Model for the Financial Sector

The maturity model seeks to improve these processes in terms of cybersecurity, cloud security and data privacy, through their evaluation.

4.3   Information Security Maturity Model for Software Developers

The information security maturity model is based on ISO 27001 standards, in order to reduce security gaps when implementing new technologies in MyPEs companies in charge of developing software.

4.4   Maturity Model of Defense Protocols Against Ransomware Scenarios

The maturity model of defense protocols against ransomware scenarios seeks to improve companies defense protocols to reduce damage and improve companies response to ransomware attacks. To carry out the analysis, a 5-level rating scale was taken into account (Poor, Insufficient, Neutral, Acceptable and Satisfactory), as it is shown in table one.

The conclusion that can be drawn from table two is that the "Information Security Management Maturity Model" project has great recognition, but the adaptability and focus are not as efficient. Additionally, it must be considered that the project has great coverage and a proficient level of detail. Conversely, the "Cloud Cybersecurity Maturity Model for the Financial Sector" project falls short in meeting these criteria at an insufficient level.

Table 1. Punctuation scale used

Scoring scale				
1	2	3	4	5
Deficient	Insufficient	Neutral	Acceptable	Satisfactory

On the other hand, the "Information Security Maturity Model for Software Developers" project correctly meets the aforementioned criteria, although it presents deficiencies in the adaptability of its model and the required ease of use. Finally, the "Maturity Model of Defense Protocols Against Ransomware Scenarios" project satisfactorily meets 85% of the criteria, as it would be at an acceptable level and only presents a decrease in the Validation and Recognition criteria due to not being yet recognized by the community of cybersecurity experts.

What can be concluded from the above table is that the project of "INFORMATION SECURITY MANAGEMENT MATURITY MODEL" has great recognition, but the adaptability and focus are not so efficient. In addition, it must be considered that it has a large coverage and a good level of detail, so it is seen that the project "CLOUD CYBERSECURITY MATURITY MODEL FOR THE FINANCIAL SECTOR" has these criteria at an insufficient level. On the other hand, The "INFORMATION SECURITY MODEL FOR SOFTWARE DEVELOPERS MATURITY" project correctly meets the aforementioned criteria, although it presents deficiencies in the adaptability of its model and the ease of use required. Finally, the project "MATURITY MODEL OF DEFENSE PROTOCOLS AGAINST RANSOMWARE SCENARIOS" satisfactorily meets 85% of the criteria, since it would be at an acceptable level and only presents a drop in the Validation and Recognition criteria due to because it is not yet recognized by the community of cybersecurity experts.

5   Proposed Maturity Model

The proposed maturity model consists of five maturity levels, as can be seen in figure one. The **Initial Level** presents an inefficient organization identifying internal and external risk factors, presenting gaps in its cyber defense and without having risk management processes or clear attack response policies, allowing it to identify only basic attacks.

Followed by the **Managed Level**, it presents minimal efficiency when identifying internal and external risk factors, its policies are not efficient, its defense systems can only detect basic attacks and within the evaluations carried out there is no consider a methodology.

Continuing with the **Defined Level**, it maintains moderate effectiveness in identifying internal and external risk factors, its policies remain stable and

Table 2. Comparison of cybersecurity maturity models based on the criteria

	INFORMATION SECURITY MANAGEMENT MATURITY MODEL	CLOUD CYBERSECURITY MATURITY MODEL FOR THE FINANCIAL SECTOR	INFORMATION SECURITY MATURITY MODEL FOR SOFTWARE DEVELOPERS	MATURITY MODEL OF DEFENSE PROTOCOLS AGAINST RANSOMWARE SCENARIOS
Coverage and completeness	3	2	3	3
Level of detail	3	2	3	3
Focus and perspective	2	3	4	4
Focus and perspective	2	3	2	4
Ease of use and understanding	3	3	2	4
Validation and recognition	4	4	4	2
Result	17	17	18	20

there is a commitment from senior management, there are established and standardized security policies and processes; In addition, the evaluations carried out on the company maintain a three-step methodology (identify threats, evaluate vulnerabilities and determine risks) and the defense protocols are standardized, managing to detect various attacks such as Ransomware.

At the **Administered Level**, there is efficiency in the organization for the identification of internal and external risk factors, taking into account the most sensitive assets and goods of the company, there is a great commitment on the part of senior direction to establish policies and responsibilities to support security management systems, maintains a high development and stability of the risk management process, likewise, defense protocols are standardized and optimized, since they can detect various attacks such as Ransomware, the responses of the security protocols are highly capable of optimally responding and protecting against the different types of attacks; In addition, the evaluations are scheduled for long periods of time, maintaining a history of those already carried out and their results.

Finishing with the **Optimized Level** in which a good efficiency is presented in the identification of internal and external factors, the policies and responsibilities are maintained; In addition, the procedures for hiring employees are efficient. There is a high development in the risk management processes and the defense protocols of the company are standardized and optimized, maintaining a high response capacity and protection against the types of attack. Periodic evaluations are carried out to establish security measures and reduce the level of risk, thereby keeping a record of the evaluations carried out.

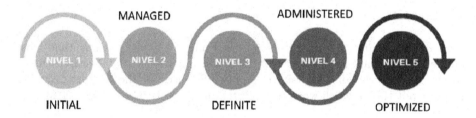

Fig. 1. Levels of the Maturity Model of defense protocols against ransomware scenarios

6 Validation and Discussion of Results

A survey was conducted through an online questionnaire in Google Forms in 2023, which was applied to twenty specialists in cybersecurity in the mining sector with more than two years of experience, this survey was conducted from the beginning of May to middle June. The purpose of this survey is to determine the perception that experts have about the area of cybersecurity in the mining sector regarding the proposed maturity model. The survey was organized in three sections; the first section mentions the professional trajectory of cybersecurity executives (five questions), the second section presents the reading of the maturity model and, finally, the third section considers the opinion of experts on the usefulness of the model of maturity within the item using the Likert scale scoring format for one of the questions, through which an evaluation of the utility of our maturity model (seven questions) is carried out. At the end of the survey carried out, fifteen responses were obtained from the specialists, of which ten affirm that the maturity model allows a correct evaluation of the protocols, allowing a general and specific evaluation, depending on which one seeks to evaluate at the moment; On the other hand, five of the experts mentioned that the maturity model has room for improvement and that, based on other models, they recommended establishing more specific points to evaluate as well as a scale on which to guide themselves to establish scores.

7 Conclusion

In conclusion, the development project of the maturity model of defense protocols against ransomware scenarios has achieved a satisfactory level of compliance. Validated by cybersecurity experts, the model has proven to be useful and widely recognized. Compared to other similar models, it stands out for its extensive coverage and level of detail, comprehensively addressing the key aspects of cybersecurity related to ransomware.

8 Financing

Universidad Peruana de Ciencias Aplicadas/UPC-EXPOST-2023- 2.

9 Gratitude

The authors thank the evaluators for their important suggestions that have allowed a significant improvement of this work. Likewise, to the Research Directorate of the Peruvian University of Applied Sciences for the support provided to carry out this research work through the incentive UPC-EXPOST-2023-2

References

Abazi, B., Kő, A.: A framework for semiautomatic risk assessment and a security maturity model based on ISO 27001. J. Comput. Inform. Syst. **59**(3), 264–274 (2019). https://doi.org/10.1080/08874417.2018.1536542

Carver, C., Puhakainen, P.: A five-level model for cybersecurity. J. Inform. Sec. Appl. **46**, 195–209 (2019). https://doi.org/10.1016/j.jisa.2019.02.008

Chuquilla, A., Guarda, T., Quiña, G.N.: Ransomware-wannacry security is everyone's. In: 2019 14th Iberian Conference on Information Systems and Technologies (CISTI), pp. 1–4. IEEE (2019). https://doi.org/10.23919/CISTI.2019.8760749

CISA. Ransomware Guide. Cybersecurity and Infrastructure Security Agency (2021). https://www.cisa.gov/publication/ransomware-guide

Computer security maturity: 5 steps to excellence. GB Advisors (2018). https://www.gb-advisors.com/computer-security-maturity/

Connolly, A.Y., Borrion, H.: Reducing ransomware crime: analysis of victims' payment decisions. Comput. Sec. **119**, 102760 (2022). https://doi.org/10.1016/j.cose.2022.102760

Cybersecurity Ventures. Cybercrime Report 2020. Herjavec Group (2020). https://www.herjavecgroup.com/wp-content/uploads/2020/11/Cybercrime-Report-2020-FINAL.pdf

Da Silva, E.F., de Barros, R.M.: Information security maturity model based on ISO 27001 for micro and small software development companies. J. Inform. Syst. Eng. Manag. **4**(1), 10 (2019). https://doi.org/10.20897/jisem.201910

Deloitte. Cyber Risk in Mining. Deloitte (2021). https://www2.deloitte.com/content/dam/Deloitte/ca/Documents/audit/ca-en-audit-cyber-risk-in-mining.pdf

Diego Sebastian Escobar. Analysis of the cultural maturity models of Cybersecurity (2022). http://www.aacademica.org/escobards/68.pdf

El-Bendary, N., El-Bahnasawy, M.: An improved process supervision and control method for malware detection. J. Ambient. Intell. Humaniz. Comput. **10**(1), 33–48 (2019). https://doi.org/10.1007/s12652-017-0609-9

Englbrecht, F., Sodan, A., Schütz, M., Brenner, W.: Cyber fraud detection and prevention using a maturity model for IT governance and digital forensics readiness. Int. J. Environ. Res. Public Health **17**(3), 1023 (2020). https://doi.org/10.3390/ijerph17031023

Escobar., D.S. (s/f). Analysis of the cultural maturity models of Cybersecurity. aacademica.org, from https://www.aacademica.org/escobards/68.pdf

García, F.Y.H., Lema, L.: Model to measure the maturity of the risk analysis of information assets in the context of shipping companies. RISTI - Iberian J. Inform. Syst. Technol. **31**, 1–17 (2019). https://doi.org/10.17013/risti.31.1-17

GB Advisors. Madurez de la seguridad informática. Recuperado de (2019). https://www.gb-advisors.com/es/madurez-de-la-seguridad-informatica/

Kandasamy, K., Srinivas, S., Achuthan, K., Rangan, V.P.: Digital healthcare - cyberattacks in Asian organizations: an analysis of vulnerabilities, risks, NIST perspectives, and recommendations. IEEE Access **10**, 12345–12364 (2022). https://doi.org/10.1109/access.2022.3146158

KPMG. Cybersecurity in Mining. KPMG (2020). https://www.assets.kpmg/content/dam/kpmg/us/pdf/2020/10/cybersecurity-in-mining.pdf

McDonald, G., Papadopoulos, P., Pitropakis, N., Ahmad, J., Buchanan, W.J.: Ransomware: analysing the impact on windows active directory domain services. Sensors **22**(3), 953 (2022). https://doi.org/10.3390/s22030953

Mell, P., Grance, T.: The NIST Definition of Cloud Computing. National Institute of Standards and Technology (2011). https://www.nvlpubs.nist.gov/nistpubs/Legacy/SP/nistspecialpublication800-145.pdf

Optical Networks: Computer attacks: Causes, Types, Consequences and Preventions. News Blog — Optical Networks. Optical Networks (2021). https://winempresas.pe/blog/ataques-informaticos-causas-y-12-tipos-de-ciberataques

Pinzón, J.J.: Analysis of the impact of Ransomware attacks on Colombian organizations as a knowledge base for determining new protection mechanisms and minimization of cyber risks. [Monograph]. UNAD Institutional Repository (2021). https://www.repository.unad.edu.co/handle/10596/50093

Prapenan, S.A., Pamuji, Y.: Implementation of COBIT 5 framework for ISMS audit based on ISO 27001 standard: a case study in XYZ company. J. Phys. Conf. Ser. **1469**(1) (2020). https://doi.org/10.1088/1742-6596/1469/1/012041

Ponemon Institute: Cost of a Data Breach Report 2020. IBM (2020). https://www.ibm.com/reports/data-breach

Rabii, A., Assoul, S., Touhami, K.O., Roudies, O.: Information and cyber security maturity models: a systematic literature review. Inf. Comput. Secur. (2020). https://doi.org/10.1108/ICS-03-2019-0039

Rahman, M.A., Islam, S., Nugroho, Y.S., Al Irsyadi, F.Y., Hossain, M.J.: An exploratory analysis of feature selection for malware detection with simple machine learning algorithms. J. Commun. Softw. Syst. **19**(3), 207–219 (2023)

Razikin, K., Widodo, A.: General framework of cybersecurity maturity model evaluation for compliance of PCI-DSS: case study of exchange companies. J. Cybersecurity Inf. Manag. **4**(1), 1–12 (2021). https://doi.org/10.5281/zenodo.4555795

SANS Institute. Critical Security Controls. SANS Institute (2021). https://www.sans.org/blog/cis-controls-v8/

Schmid, M., Pape, S.: A structured comparison of the corporate information security maturity level. In: Dhillon, G., Karlsson, F., Hedström, K., Zúquete, A. (eds.) SEC 2019. IAICT, vol. 562, pp. 223–237. Springer, Cham (2019). https://doi.org/10.1007/978-3-030-22312-0_16

Schmitz, C., Schmid, M., Harborth, D., Pape, S.: Maturity level assessments of information security controls: an empirical analysis of practitioners assessment capabilities. Comput. Secur. **108**, 102306 (2021). https://doi.org/10.1016/j.cose.2021.102306

Shemitha, P.A., Dhas, J.P.M.: Research perceptions on ransomware attack: a complete analysis on conventional authentication protocols in network. Evol. Intell., 1–16 (2020)

Sulthana, M.A., Kanmani, S.: Research perceptions on ransomware attack: a complete analysis on conventional authentication protocols in network. J. Ambient. Intell. Humaniz. Comput. **12**(5), 4565–4575 (2021). https://doi.org/10.1007/s12652-021-03545-5

Yuan, Y., Zhang, B., Liu, J., Zhang, J., Wang, Z.: Mitigating adversarial evasion attacks of ransomware using ensemble learning. J. Ambient. Intell. Humaniz. Comput. (2021). https://doi.org/10.1016/j.compeleceng.2022.107903

Yuryna, O., Turchenko, V., Verkhovska, O.: General cybersecurity maturity assessment model: best practice to achieve payment card industry-data security standard (PCI-DSS) compliance. J. Cybersecurity Res. **2**(1), 17–29 (2019). https://doi.org/10.28991/jcsr-2019-020103

Zammani, M., Razali, R., Singh, D.: Organisational information security management maturity model. Int. J. Adv. Comput. Sci. Appl. **12**(9) (2021)

Ethical and Legal Challenges of Holographic Communication Technologies

Natalia Giogiou[1] , Niki Chatzipanagiotou[2]([⊠]) , and Jude Alvin[3]

[1] Linnaeus University, Växjö, Sweden
giogioun@gmail.com
[2] Lund University, Lund, Sweden
niki.chatzipanagiotou@ics.lu.se
[3] Jaguar Land Rover, Gaydon, England
alvin@dartarrow.net

Abstract. The paper presents ethical and legal challenges of holographic communication technologies and suggests a framework to address them. Holographic communications enable the capturing of a user's 3D depiction via special equipment, and its high-quality transmission to another user located elsewhere, introducing a distinctive data communication experience. Their wrongful use could compromise basic human rights. Qualitative research was conducted through interviews with ethics and legal experts in Sweden and Greece, and document analysis. The collected data were analyzed thematically and discussed within the framework of Ethical Technology Assessment (eTA). The findings show that the main challenges are privacy and data protection. The design phase and users' participation in the process of the development of holographic communication technologies were found to have a vital role in the ethical and respectful of the law use of them. Similar challenges and frameworks of existing technologies can serve as the basis to develop a new framework. Challenges in formulating a common framework, though, due to contextual, societal and geographical differences were also found. Thus, the research contributes to the informatics field by providing insights and extending the knowledge about the use of holographic communication technologies. It contributes practically to designers, developers, technology companies, and other interested stakeholders as it shortens the knowledge gap concerning the prospective ethical and legal issues posed by this technology and provides suggestions of an ethical-legal framework to address them.

Keywords: Digital Ethics · Holographic Communication Technologies · Qualitative research

1 Introduction

Unconventional Data Communications (UCDC), include, among others, communications based on the concept of holograms [10]. The 'hologram' refers to the conveyance of the meaning of a complete message [22]. Holographic Communication Technologies aim to assemble an object's or a person's three-dimensional (3D) depiction, captured

T. Guarda et al. (Eds.): ARTIIS 2023, CCIS 1936, pp. 275–289, 2024.
https://doi.org/10.1007/978-3-031-48855-9_21

through specific digital technology equipment, reconstructed using artificial intelligence (AI), and transmitted to another user, creating a realistic and engaging communication experience for the users. From a technical perspective, Holographic Communication Technologies need high bandwidth such as those offered by fifth generation (5G) networks [6]. The benefits of such technology could be numerous, including interactive education [28], healthcare [27], marketing and sales [33] and entertainment [19].

Holographic Communication Technologies do not come without drawbacks. Besides technical challenges such as Information Technology (IT) infrastructure upgrades or training to gain the essential know-how lurks another bunch of challenges relevant to those complex technologies. The use of this technology could provoke concerns of ethical and/or legal nature. Likewise, the misuse of other technologies in the past caused challenges, with the most recent being the breach of personal data by Cambridge Analytica [38], mooting the topic also for the most complex ones, such as Holographic Communication.

Previous research studies have circulated around relevant topics, such as AI and augmented or extended reality (AR/XR). Some studies offer useful insights, although they do not specifically address Holographic Communication Technologies [8, 13, 20, 36]. Ryan and Stahl [36] examined the ethical challenges in the development and use of AI. According to their research, equality, privacy and transparency are some of the main aspects that need to be safeguarded during the production of such technologies. Jobin, Ienca and Vayena [20] suggest preserving virtues such as fairness, justice and responsibility when dealing with AI. Floridi and Cowls [13] researched the integrated ethical framework for artificial intelligence by combining six previous related studies of the same topic. Inspired by Floridi and Cowls [13], Borenstein and Howard [8] concluded to the importance of educating the actors involved in the development or implementation of digital technologies about ethical design and ethical data acquisition. There is no known or documented prior research focusing on the ethical and/or legal issues surrounding holographic communication including how to address them.

Taking also into consideration that an infringement might fall under the field of ethics and/or law, and that the borders between those fields often blend [34], we suggest that it is of importance to identify ethical and/or legal frameworks to address the challenges of the use of Holographic Communication Technologies a priori. Hence, the purpose of this paper is to look into probable ethical and/or legal complications of Holographic Communication Technologies by considering the opinions, experiences, perspectives and knowledge of ethical and legal experts with the aim of presenting an updated ethical-legal framework to govern the application of holographic communications. The following research question is formulated to achieve the aim of the research: What are the suggestions of ethical and legal experts concerning the ethical and/or legal issues that could emerge in relation to the application of Holographic Communication Technologies? For this, a qualitative study was conducted among legal experts and experts on ethical issues in Sweden and Greece. The data were analyzed and discussed on the basis of Ethical Technology Assessment (eTA). The study generated theoretical and practical findings for the informatics field regarding digital ethics.

Following this introduction, the rest of the paper is structured as follows: Sect. 2 continues, which includes a brief literature review and the conceptual framework used in the research. The methodological choices of the research are described in Sect. 3.

In Sect. 4, the findings are presented followed by a discussion in Sect. 5. The paper concludes with Sect. 6 where the conclusions of this research are presented.

2 Review of Literature and Conceptual Framework

2.1 Digital Ethics

Digital ethics is an interdisciplinary body of research within the information systems research discipline that studies the moral challenges and repercussions of using Information and Communication Technologies (ICT) in public life and people's lives [35]. The boundaries between the domains of ethics and law are frequently blurred and as a result, an ethical or legal objection may fall under one or both of the aforementioned categories [34]. Hence, digital ethics proposes frameworks for establishing boundaries in the face of ethical and/or legal hurdles arising from the application or misuse of ICT. [35]. Digital ethics, according to Rogerson [35], is a blend of ICT concepts and practices with an ensemble of ethical norms and guidelines. Digital ethics has previously investigated several types of technologies with technological elements akin to, or even inherent in, Holographic Communication Technologies. When they researched human objects interacting in some way online (in 2 or 3 dimensions), Schultze and Mason [37] defined the ethical standards of a renowned researcher of any sort. Floridi and Cowls [13] explored digital ethics in the context of AI, focusing on the concerns associated with its use. Ashok [7] explored the implications of digital ethics when AI is incorporated within various digital technologies.

2.2 Holographic Communication Technologies

Holographic Communication Technologies belong to the forthcoming digital technologies that will bring together the capabilities of existing multimedia formats (e.g., sound, videos, images) with some innovations offered by extended reality (XR). XR itself is an 'umbrella' term for merged reality, augmented reality, virtual reality, and mixed reality. Both augmented and virtual reality (AR/VR) technologies are employed in the instance of Holographic Communication Technologies to capture and produce a realistic three-dimensional (3D) representation of a particular individual laid in a mixed reality (MR) context that can telecommunicate with another person over long distances and in real time [29]. When attempting to call attention to the ethical dilemmas involved, it is important to remember that it shares some of the previously listed characteristics of existing digital media. Holographic Communication Technologies, also known as 'holographic telepresence', 'holographic calling', 'holographic-type communications' among others [19], aim to capture the image of an object with the use of specialized technology aimed to create photorealistic depiction. This technology often accomplishes this by capturing the object from various viewpoints in order to reconstruct, render, and display it as realistically as possible. [19]. A few companies have demonstrated such technologies in their products, including K-Team, Activemedia, Microsoft, Ericsson, and Cisco [15]. From these, we identify two roles in holographic communication: the sender and the receiver. The sender would be the person whose likeness in three dimensions (3D) is captured via a 3D camera, reconstructed on a computer, then sent to the receiver. Volumetric displays such as augmented reality (AR) glasses or Head-Mounted Displays (HMD) can be used by the receiver to render and display this 3D image of the sender (Fig. 1).

Fig. 1. The data flow between the sender and the receiver.

A particular user could have one or both roles. Different sets of equipment have been proposed and tested depending on the setup. For example, it could be a single LiDAR camera connected to the sender's laptop and augmented reality (AR) glasses on the receiver's device. Or it could be the use of multiple cameras capturing the sender from all directions. The use of a single camera would require AI or interpolation to determine the parts of the sender that are occluded or that fall between the visible data points [17]. There are two major ways on how the captured 3D image could be delivered from the sender to the receiver: directly such as how a phone call is made today, or through a 'cloud' such as commonly done with video chat today. Furthermore, AI algorithms could optimize the network resource involved with the communication [25].

Human behavior and perceptions can be influenced by digital technologies [24, 32]. They can influence what people are capable of doing [16], such as whether they would engage in unethical or ethical conduct while using it, or whether they will consider potential negative repercussions prompted by their usage. Latour [23], Akrich [5], and, later, Verbeek [39, 40] were a few the researchers who supported the view that digital technologies either directly or indirectly prescribe or moderate activities to their end-users. Akrich [5] added that the activities 'prescribed' by the technologies are originally 'carved' by the digital technology architects, who are the 'brain' underpinning the new digital technology and whose decisions influence how end-users interact with it [24]. Similarly, it is suggested that the ethical usage of holographic communication technologies by the users is contingent on how they were planned and developed; in other words, if they were ethically designed.

Ethical design is a collection of ethical standards, recommendations, concepts, and theories aimed at digital technology creators and developers that want to follow ethical guidelines and legislation when designing and/or building new digital technology. The goal is to strike a balance between the difficulties of digital technology and its utility to end users [40]. When discussing a novel sort of digital technology that has never been utilized or applied before, ethical design requires a degree of prediction. The problem is that technological tools are frequently developed without previous empirical investigations into the social context in which they will be utilized, or the demands of the end-users who will interact with them [1].

2.3 Existing Ethical and Legal Frameworks

Several frameworks connected to ethics and meta-ethics have been built to protect ethical design and use. Meta-ethics is a 'branch' of the discipline of ethics that focuses on researching the nature and origins of ethical judgments rather than ethical behaviors [2]. The most widely utilized frameworks within meta-ethics are absolutism, relativism, pluralism, and virtue ethics [26] while the most well-known ethical frameworks are consequentialism and deontology. However, they have all met with counterarguments. In respect to the ethical use of digital technology, there are some recognized norms and core legislation that have been developed and used. Among these are the following: (i) the General Data Protection Regulation [12]; (ii) The Intellectual Property (IP) law, which, in conjunction with GDPR, protects copyrighted material from unauthorized sharing, processing, and duplication [14]; (iii) The 'Digital Services Act' [11]; and (iv) Codes of ethics established by international institutions or associations that establish the ethical guidelines for the use of digital technologies by involved stakeholders. Codes of ethics, such as those issued by the Association for Computing Machinery [3, 4] and the Institute of Electrical and Electronic Engineers [18], are aimed at a global audience.

2.4 Ethical Technology Assessment (eTA)

When developing a new technology during the 1960s, there was a drive towards improving the responsibility of actors involved to address societal problems related to the technologies [30]. This was the milestone in the creation of the concept of Technology Assessment (TA). The main purpose and expectation of such an approach was the thorough investigation about a new technology to predict future negative ramifications in a timely way, and to counter them based on early detection [30]. Based on Technology Assessment and its following versions and alterations, Palm and Hansson [30] introduced the ethical Technology Assessment (eTA), a new approach which focused on the ethical aspect of new technology's development. eTA aimed at initiating discussions on ethical dilemmas before the newly developed technology is released in society [30]. The authors argued that it would be deceptive to think that the creators of technology are fully aware of or could accurately predict every single effect of their creation and that, had they expected certain negative consequences, they would have tried to avoid them out of social concern or for commercial reasons, or considering both [30]. Moving in that direction, Palm and Hansson [30] created an outline of the most often arising concerns that may be utilized as a warning system during the early phases of the lifecycle of an emerging digital technology. eTA promotes interactive and ongoing communication between designers, developers, operators, and end-users of emerging digital technologies with the goal of tackling ethical issues in digital technology [30]. When it comes to adopting a new digital technology, the brainstorming of more individuals becomes more involved and helpful for stakeholders to move beyond the apparent and expected ethical challenges [24]. The idea is to avoid adhering to a single ethical system. Instead, the recommendation is to adopt a viewpoint that will allow for numerous choices depending on the ethical challenge to be addressed each time [30].

The conceptual framework of this study is formed by the major elements of the aforementioned literature review, as well as the ethical Technology Assessment (eTA) approach. This conceptual framework is used to explain and discuss the study findings and attain the research goal. That is, to present potential ethical and/or legal hurdles posed by holographic communication methods and to propose an innovative ethical-legal structure to guide their application.

3   Methodology and Methods

3.1   Empirical Settings and Participants

The research was conducted in the European context and specifically in Sweden and Greece, as the researchers live and work in these countries and have contacts that allowed them to recruit suitable participants.

Six experts in legal and ethical issues constitute the participants in this research, as shown in Table 1. The sample was purposive [31], as the experts were selected based on certain criteria in order to offer rich data on the topic: a) their expertise in one of the two suggested fields, namely law or ethics, b) their professional activity in those fields within European territory, as the research addressed the European context, and c) their fluency in the English language.

Table 1. Research Participants Overview.

Participants' Roles	Country
1 University lecturer of Digital Ethics	Sweden
1 IS engineer, researcher, and author of Digital Ethics	Sweden
4 Lawyers with expertise in Digital Technologies	Greece

After an initial analysis of the collected data following the sixth interview, it was shown that the experts' answers to the questions were repetitive and that saturation was reached at an early point, due to the rich insights gained. Therefore, further search for additional experts was not needed.

3.2   Approach

We followed an interpretive qualitative approach to achieve the aim of the research. According to Klein and Myers [21], interpretivism is an ideal choice for IS researchers to understand the meanings people assign to a specific situation and, thus, suitable for our research. The qualitative methodological approach was chosen because it is appropriate to address multiple subjective perspectives of the participants [21], who are considered experts, to gain an understanding of challenges - ethical and/or legal - that could arise from the use of holographic communication technologies coupled to the researchers' background and knowledge.

3.3   Data Collection

The interpretive qualitative research approach entailed the following methods for the data collection: individual semi-structured interviews and documents analysis.

Through interviews, we tried to catch individual experts' experiences, knowledge, and perspectives to provide us rich and direct input. For the interviews, an interview guide we formulated with semi-structured questions was followed. The interview guide allowed us to have a basic frame within which the discussion would flow without deviating. It also gave us some space for follow-up questions when needed, to request clarifications from the experts. Interviews were conducted in English as all participants were fluent in that language and to eliminate translation errors that could impair the quality of the study. Audio of all interviews were recorded with the participants' informed consent and were later transcribed verbatim.

A secondary method to complement the data collected through the interviews was the review of relevant to holographic communication technologies documents. Access was given to us to confidential documents by a technological company that currently develops technology for holographic communication, which requested to remain anonymous. Freely accessible documents were also reviewed. Through reviewing documents, the data collected aimed at helping us to get thorough insight on the key features of such technology.

3.4 Data Analysis

Thematic analysis was our analytical method. Thematic analysis is a process based on coding, which unfolds in several steps to identify patterns and develop themes [9] from the collected empirical data. The steps of the followed process were: familiarization with the data, creation of initial codes, creation of categories based on the initial codes, looking for themes in those categories, cross-examination, alteration, refinement of the themes, and presentation of the final findings.

In our analysis, the interview transcriptions and the notes from the documents' review were printed and were brought together for the final analysis. The material was re-read several times to get familiar with it and gain a deeper understanding of the participants' perspectives and points of view regarding holographic communication technologies and the legal and/or ethical challenges that could emerge from their use. By identifying similarities, we generated the initial codes, which were transferred to a new document for further analysis. The initial coding was carefully examined for repetitions, overlaps or redundant codes. Those codes were then organized into categories based on the research aim and research question of the study. The initial list of general categories was modified after several iterations of additional re-readings. Finally, those categories were examined once again and were organized into themes. We concluded the analysis by defining each theme in an explicit way.

4 Empirical Findings

4.1 Theme 1: Design and Users' Participation

The way holographic communication technologies is being designed today, and the processes incorporated during the design phase, has a significant impact on how end-users will use them in the future. The participants explained that during the design process many smaller decisions must be made. To decide upon each topic that emerges, many different ethical impacts must be considered, as well as their effect on a smaller or larger scale in society. One participant stated that *"Digital technologies are not neutral. As a designer, when you design a digital technology, you put certain norms in that particular type of digital technology. Each person has their own ethical framework."* The participants said that the ethical frameworks and values one has, are somehow inscribed within the digital technology and that means that a subjective ethical perspective on what is wrong, or right is given to it. The participants also supported that the main reason why ethical and/or legal challenges might emerge from the use of novel holographic communication technologies is the difference between the way they were originally planned by the designers to be used and the way they are actually used by the end-users, due to their different ethical values. As a result, ethical and/or legal issues may occur during the use of holographic communication technologies that were not anticipated by the designers or manufacturers because they did not initially capture end-users' ideas on ethics or concerns. The participants concluded that technology designers often are unable to accurately predict the potential challenges beforehand and that underlines the importance of the design phase.

The participants also discussed the relationship between the designing phase for holographic communication technologies and the ethical and/or legal way end-users will interact with them after their implementation, and highlighted users' participation in the design process. The participants agreed that users' participation in the design of the technology would be beneficial for both users and designers. The participants said, *"...the developers could create a new digital technology that could definitely reflect the needs of the target group"* while, at the same time, *"users would directly reflect their desires and would also get this sense of unity and belonging"*. The participants said that this would be the ideal strategy to safeguard digital ethics and law compliance during the use of holographic communication technologies, as the communication and interaction between designers and users would bring up topics that had not been thought of previously, from different perspectives. It was emphasized that for new holographic communication technologies to be used ethically, there should be cooperation among the company, ethics and law experts, and among the future users of the technology right from the design phase. Concerns were expressed, however, about the criteria used to select end-users to engage in the design process in a fair and unbiased manner.

4.2   Theme 2: Privacy and Data Protection

The participants reflected on their concerns about privacy and data protection issues as being two of the most significant challenges associated with the adoption of Holographic Communication Technologies. The most repetitive phrase, stated in different words by all the participants was: *"Who guarantees that my 3D image won't be saved by the digital technology or by the company that drives it? Who says that it won't be displayed elsewhere without my consent?"* The participants highlighted that these are already existing challenges of less complex technologies too. Since holographic communications combine such innovative technical features, the task of reassuring that the identity of the user would not be processed unethically or illegally would not be easy to undertake. One of the participants stated: *"...there is no way to completely guarantee data anonymity and also the usual cyber security vulnerability that any system entails"* and continued that holographic communication technologies are often unclear about the processing of personal data. Another participant, emphasized on the legal aspect of this challenge, stating that, according to the law, the 3D representation is part of a person's personality, hence the potential inappropriate or erroneous display thereof would be a violation of the individual's personality rights.

4.3 Theme 3: Existing Challenges as Starting Point

The participants considered as an advantage the fact that data protection and privacy challenges are already met in other existing digital technologies. That is, this knowledge can be used as a starting point for the holographic communications field. Thus, drawing on existing knowledge and rules of digital technologies can be a useful place to start in order to anticipate, mitigate, or address the ethical and/or legal issues that could stem from the eventual adoption of holographic communication technologies. One of the participants said that *"...taking into consideration specific legal or ethical situations that have already occurred, and how these cases have been resolved and adjusting actions, accordingly, would provide some pointers to the right direction."* According to the participants, existing rules on the ethical design and use of AI, GDPR, and the fundamental principles of equal treatment and good faith can be used and enhanced to *"...create new dimensions depending on the field and the reason where holographic communication technologies will be used"*. Of course, critical thinking, flexibility, adjustability, and the case-by-case ethical investigation should not be overseen by the stakeholders during this process. According to the participants, it would be more efficient and effective to adopt the knowledge from previous mistakes already made in the past and try to decrease or eliminate them when holographic communication technologies are going to be used in the future. Hence, the research and tackling strategy towards the potential challenges of holographic communication technologies would not start from scratch.

4.4 Theme 4: The Quest for a Framework

Prior to the implementation of holographic communication technologies, the participants proposed developing a new framework to handle ethical and/or legal issues which could emerge. In the participants' perspective, creating an ethical and/or legal framework that is uniform and unvarying would be ideal, but not easily feasible, not even within European territory *"...Everything is contextual and cultural."* The participants explained that they consider differentiating factors to be geographical, linguistic, or cultural aspects. Additionally, the participants take into consideration differences in the diverse fields within which the technology will be used, even within the same territory. For instance, It is different when individuals use it for entertainment versus when used for educational, instructional or scientific purposes, such as in medical situations. The participants said that, in a society, there might be circumstances that *"...might differentiate how agent A will use the new tool from the way agent B will do so, based on their awareness, critical thinking, education, literacy and so on"*. Besides the differences concerning the level of maturity, the mindset, the education and character of users, other factors also play an important role, such as differences in legislations, fields of application and so on. The participants concluded, therefore, that a general *"rulebook"* could be authored to demonstrate ground rules on holographic communication technologies, introducing a set of principles and general guidelines regardless of who the audience, the users, the sender(s) or the receiver(s) may be. This could be then filtered, narrowed down, and specified, addressing the individual needs or risks related to the target groups, depending on the uses or fields of engagement.

5 Discussion

According to Schultze and Mason [37], the term 'digital ethics' changes dynamically over time, but its primary compound perpetually encompasses the ethical principles engraved in the lifecycle of a new digital technology, dealing with matters such as ethical design, ethical assessment of one's private information, privacy, and technological surveillance [35]. Those issues are closely connected to Holographic Communication Technologies, which mix traditional sources of information including sound, image, and video with more complex extended reality features and can be utilized in education [28], health [27], marketing [33], sports or entertainment [19], and other domains. Depending on the domain and the cultural context within holographic communication technologies are used, the ethical aspects could be interpreted in different ways. The identification of said interpretations could assist in the prediction of potential challenges, and to support the formulation of relevant frameworks.

The comparison of holographic communications with other existing digital technologies in terms of potential challenges was inevitable, given that they share some similar technical features. Data protection and privacy are expected to be the challenge most faced by holographic communication technologies, similar with existing digital technologies [25, 29]. The rationale was that simpler technologies, not combining the complex technical features of holographic communications, have failed in safeguarding the users' privacy, ending up in personal data breaches.

However, it was found that the challenges already confronted in terms of other digital technologies, as well as the corresponding guidelines formed upon current ethical and/or legal frameworks introduced and put into practice by the European Commission [7, 13] can be used as a starting point, upon which new frameworks for emerging technologies can be deployed. The General Data Protection Regulation [12] was thought of as crucial to begin working upon, as well as IP law, and Digital Services Act or the Ethics Guidelines for Trustworthy Artificial Intelligence [11, 14]. The aforementioned rules can be supplemented and reinforced by virtue ethics, which has previously been linked to topics of end-user interaction with digital technologies by other scholars [24, 26]. The findings also demonstrated that existing Codes of Ethics, which are designed to direct stakeholders' and end-users' conduct in relation to how they engage with comparable digital technologies toward ethical behavior [3, 4], can be used for the same purpose.

The research findings revealed that the way newly developed digital technology is built has an impact on how its end-users would use it. The legal and ethical experts highlighted ethical design to be a key aspect of how holographic communication technologies will be used. Further, the sharing by the end-users of their needs, requirements, and concerns during the design phase can offer a thorough insight on how holographic communication technologies should be designed and developed to meet those demands. Among the explanations for the reason why the application of newly developed digital technology raises ethical and/or legal concerns is the discrepancy between the designers' ideas, who may be unaware of the social setting in which it is going to be used, the end-users' perspectives, and what is actually the societal reality, which includes pertinent moral values, routines, and shifts [1].

During the initial steps of the holographic communication technologies' lifecycle many decisions should be made by designers, such as what features will be included, what possibilities the technology will offer to the end-users, etc. For this, predictive strategies are suggested to be adopted by designers regarding the technical demands, the ethical and/or legal considerations that could emerge, and even users' perceptions or intentions towards the technology. Even then, though, designers tend to inscribe their own ethical choices, affecting the use of technology by the end-users, [5, 24]. Moreover, during the actual engagement with an emerging digital technology, new perspectives might be created by the technology itself to the end-user, 'leading' them towards actions not previously thought of [5, 16, 23, 24, 32].

The research further showed that the ongoing interaction among holographic communication technologies' creators (including designers, developers, and technology companies), end-users, law and ethics experts during the design phase, could prevent potential ethical and/or legal challenges. Applying the ethical Technology Assessment (eTA) framework [30], we also urge the dialogue among the aforementioned stakeholders with the aim at diving into the features of the new technology from multiple perspectives to detect early on potential challenges so as to counter them. Such an approach will be more effective when based on frameworks, experience and actions met in existing digital technologies.

According to the research findings, the formulation of a common ethical-legal framework about Holographic Communication Technologies would be an ideal scenario, but not easily plausible. The findings showed that an ethical and respectful of the law use of this technically complex technology is a matter of maturity and ability to critical thinking. Age, education, digital literacy, and awareness are some of the factors that affect the perception and behavior of the user. Other factors affecting the decisions of a user on how to behave towards the technology and therefore the needs of a corresponding framework are the differences in legislations and guidelines, depending on the domain or the geographical territory within which the technology is used, namely whether used for entertainment or professional purposes.

Concluding, in line with our findings and the ethical Technology Assessment (eTA) [30], we also propose an open-minded approach that allows for diverse answers depending on the ethical dilemma to be addressed each time. Still, there are some legal and ethical experts' suggestions to be used as a basis and to be taken into consideration for a new framework that addresses ethical and legal challenges of holographic communication technologies. These suggestions can be considered when formulating similar frameworks for other new and emerging technologies too and they are the following: a) The new framework is suggested to be formulated by a collaborating team of experts in legal and ethics, designers, developers, and users. b) A common framework for all digital technologies cannot be formulated. Instead, a common basis of principles and general guidelines can be created. This could then be filtered, narrowed down, and specified, addressing individual needs or risks related to the users' target groups, and depending on the fields of engagement. Parameters that should be taken into consideration include: the geographical area; its culture; linguistics; its specific legislations; the field of application; the context of use; and the end-users. c) The common basis of principles and guidelines should always cover issues of privacy, data protection, ethical design, and digital surveillance. d) Continuing, for each new framework, it is required: a detailed description of the new technology; the tracking down of the involved stakeholders; the ongoing discussion with the involved stakeholders; the establishment of challenges in the case concerned and of potential countermeasures; and the continuous monitoring and re-visiting of the work and its update, if needed, according to outcomes in reality.

6 Conclusion

This research paper aimed to explore the suggestions of legal and ethical experts regarding the potential ethical and/or legal challenges that could arise from the use of holographic communication technologies by considering their perspectives, experiences, and prior knowledge. It was based on an interpretive qualitative study, where data were collected through individual semi-structured interviews of six purposely selected experts, as well as the review of relevant documents, and were analyzed thematically. The findings were further interpreted and discussed with the help of the conceptual framework.

The research findings showed that existing digital technologies and the ethical and/or legal challenges that have already been met with regard to them, can be helpful to identify the relevant challenges in terms of Holographic Communication Technologies, as they might share similar technical features, hence similar problems. The most prominent challenges to be expected, accordingly, with the technology in concern, are privacy and data protection issues, due to the combination of complex features within them, such as artificial intelligence (AI), algorithms, mixed reality (MR), and extended reality (XR).

The research findings also showed that the design phase of an emerging digital technology has a significant impact on how end-users eventually engage with it. Therefore, it was suggested that some factors crucial to achieve an ethical and lawful behavior when using Holographic Communication Technologies would be the adoption of critical thinking techniques by the designers, as well as the active participation of end-users in the design process to share their perspectives and concerns with them. However, it was identified that finding ethical criteria to select end-users to be included in the process would still be a challenge for the stakeholders.

Finally, the research demonstrated that formulating codes of ethics or legal frameworks in relation to holographic communication technologies would be important and could be founded upon existing frameworks and fundamental rights and principles. These new frameworks, however, could ideally -but hardly- be unanimous or global at once, due to contextual, territorial, and societal differences, which require a rather personalized approach regarding ethics and laws. In any case, frameworks created should be monitored and revisited often, so as to be updated and efficiently address new challenges that could not have been predicted beforehand.

An interesting future research would be to conduct observations of end-users using the technology in specific contexts to complement our findings. Use cases of holographic communication technologies' possible ethical and/or legal problems could lead to more concrete outcomes. Considering that our research was predictive, further research to provide richer input is needed to construct Codes of Ethics, frameworks or even laws corresponding to the specific needs of holographic communication technologies.

This research contributes to the field of informatics by offering insights and expanding knowledge about the prospective ethical and legal application of emerging holographic communication technologies. The research also contributes practically to designers, developers, technology companies, and other interested stakeholders as it shortens the knowledge gap regarding the potential ethical and legal challenges of holographic communication technologies and provides suggestions of an ethical-legal framework to prevent them. It also contributes to translating ethical values in design requirements that can be used by designers, developers, policy makers and regulators.

References

1. Aizenberg, E., Van Den Hoven, J.: Designing for human rights in AI. Big Data Soc. **7**(2), 1–14 (2020)
2. Allan, L.: Meta-ethics: An Introduction (2015). https://www.rationalrealm.com/philosophy/ethics/meta-ethics-introduction.html. Accessed 30 Nov 2022
3. Association for Computing Machinery: Code of Ethics and Professional Conduct (2018). https://www.acm.org/code-of-ethics. Accessed 30 Nov 2022
4. Association for Computing Machinery (2022). https://www.acm.org/. Accessed 30 Nov 2022
5. Akrich, M.: The De-Scription of Technical Objects. Shaping Technology/Building Society-Studies in Sociotechnical Change. MIT Press, Cambridge (1992)
6. Alsharif, M.H., Kelechi, A.H., Albreem, M.A., Chaudhry, S.A., Zia, M.S., Kim, S.: Sixth generation (6G) wireless networks: vision, research activities, challenges and potential solutions. Symmetry **12**(4), 676 (2020)
7. Ashok, M., Madan, R., Joha, A., Sivarajah, U.: Ethical framework for artificial intelligence and digital technologies. Int. J. Inf. Manag. **62**(C) (2022)
8. Borenstein, J., Howard, A.: Emerging challenges in AI and the need for AI ethics education. AI Ethics **1**(1), 61–65 (2021)
9. Braun, V., Clarke, V.: Thematic Analysis: A Practical Guide. Sage, London (2021)
10. Dang, S., Amin, O., Shihada, B., Alouini, M.S.: What should 6G be? Nat. Electron. **3**(1), 20–29 (2020)
11. European Parliament and the Council of the European Union Proposal for a Regulation 2020/825 EP/CEU on a Single Market For Digital Services (Digital Services Act) and amending Directive 2000/31/EC. https://eur-lex.europa.eu/legal-content/en/TXT/?uri=COM%3A2020%3A825%3AFIN. Accessed 30 Nov 2022
12. European Parliament and the Council of the European Union Regulation 2016/679 EP/CEU of 27 April 2016 on the protection of natural persons with regard to the processing of personal data and on the free movement of such data, and repealing directive 95/46/EC (General Data Protection Regulation). https://eur-lex.europa.eu/legal-content/EN/TXT/PDF/?uri=CELEX:32016R0679&from=EN. Accessed 30 Nov 2022
13. Floridi, L., Cowls, J.: A unified framework of five principles for AI in society. Harv. Data Sci. Rev. **1**(1) (2019)
14. Forgó, N., et al.: An ethico-legal framework for social data science. Int. J. Data Sci. Anal. **11**(4), 377–390 (2021)
15. Hernandez-de-Menendez, M., Escobar Díaz, C., Morales-Menendez, R.: Technologies for the future of learning: state of the art. Int. J. Interact. Des. Manuf. **14**, 683–695 (2020)

16. Houkes, W., Vermaas, P.: Actions versus functions: a plea for an alternative metaphysics of artifacts. Monist **87**(1), 52–71 (2004)
17. Huang, Z., Cao, L.: Bicubic interpolation and extrapolation iteration method for high resolution digital holographic reconstruction. Opt. Lasers Eng. **130**(10160) (2020)
18. Shahriari, K., Shahriari, M.: IEEE standard review — ethically aligned design: a vision for prioritizing human wellbeing with artificial intelligence and autonomous systems. In: 2017 IEEE Canada International Humanitarian Technology Conference (IHTC), Toronto, Canada, pp. 197–201 (2017). https://doi.org/10.1109/IHTC.2017.8058187
19. ITU, O.: ITU-T Deliverable (2019). https://www.itu.int/en/ITU-T/focusgroups/net2030/Doc uments/Deliverable_NET2030.pdf. Accessed 30 Nov 2022
20. Jobin, A., Ienca, M., Vayena, E.: The global landscape of AI ethics guidelines. Nat. Mach. Intell. **1**(9), 389–399 (2019)
21. Klein, H.K., Myers, M.D.: A set of principles for conducting and evaluating interpretive field studies in information systems. MIS Q., 67–93 (1999)
22. Kumari, K., Sharma, M.K.: A review paper on holography. Int. J. Eng. Res. Digit. Technol. (IJERT) **4**(32) (2016)
23. Latour, B.: Where are the missing masses? The sociology of a few mundane artifacts. Shap. Digit. Technol. Build. Soc. Stud. Sociotech. Change **1**, 225–258 (1992)
24. Lennerfors, T.T.: Ethics in Engineering. Studentlitteratur, Lund (2019)
25. Manolova, A., Tonchev, K., Poulkov, V., Dixir, S., Lindgren, P.: Context-aware holographic communication technologies based on semantic knowledge extraction. Wirel. Pers. Commun., 1–13 (2021)
26. Mingers, J., Walsham, G.: Toward ethical information systems: the contribution of discourse ethics. MIS Q. **2010**, 833–854 (2010)
27. Nayak, S., Patgiri, R.: 6G communication digital technology: a vision on intelligent healthcare. Health Inform. Comput. Perspect. Healthc. **2021**, 1–18 (2021)
28. Orcos, L., Magreñán, Á.A.: The hologram as a teaching medium for the acquisition of STEM contents. Int. J. Learn. Digit. Technol. **13**(2), 163–177 (2018)
29. Orts-Escolano, S., et al.: Holoportation: virtual 3D teleportation in real-time. In: Orts-Escolano, S., et al. (eds.) Proceedings of the 29th Annual Symposium on User Interface Software and Digital Technology, pp. 741–754. Association for Computing Machinery, New York (2016)
30. Palm, E., Hansson, S.O.: The case for ethical digital technology assessment (eTA). Technol. Forecast. Soc. Change **73**(5), 543–558 (2006)
31. Patton, M.Q.: Qualitative Research & Evaluation Methods: Integrating Theory and Practice, 4th edn. Sage, Thousand Oaks (2015)
32. Pols, A.J.: How artifacts influence our actions. Ethical Theory Moral Pract. **16**(3), 575–587 (2013)
33. Rauschnabel, P.A.: Augmented reality is eating the real-world! The substitution of physical products by holograms. Int. J. Inf. Manag. **57** (2021)
34. Renucci, J.F.: Introduction to the European Convention on Human Rights: the rights guaranteed and the protection mechanism, 1. Council of Europe (2005)
35. Rogerson, S.: Re-imagining the digital age through digital ethics (2020). https://dora.dmu.ac.uk/bitstream/handle/2086/20626/Ethics%20and%20the%20Internet%20Position%20Paper%20Simon%20Rogerson.pdf?sequence=1. Accessed 30 Nov 2022
36. Ryan, M., Stahl, B.C.: Artificial intelligence ethics guidelines for developers and users: clarifying their content and normative implications. J. Inf. Commun. Ethics Soc. **19**(1), 61–86 (2020)
37. Schultze, U., Mason, R.: Studying cyborgs: re-examining internet studies as human subjects' research. J. Inf. Digit. Technol. **27**(4), 301–312 (2012)

38. Venturini, T., Rogers, R.: API-based research' or how can digital sociology and journalism studies learn from the Facebook and Cambridge analytica data breach. Digit. J. **7**(4), 532–540 (2019)
39. Verbeek, P.P.: What Things Do: Philosophical Reflections on Agency, digital technology and Design. Pennsylvania State University Press, Pennsylvania (2005)
40. Verbeek, P.P.: Morality in design: design ethics and the morality of technological artifacts. In: Kroes, P., Vermaas, P.E., Light, A., Moore, S.A. (eds.) Philosophy and Design, pp. 91–103. Springer, Dordrecht (2008). https://doi.org/10.1007/978-1-4020-6591-0_7

Evolution, Collaborations, and Impacts of Big Data Research in Ecuador: Bibliometric Analysis

Fátima Avilés-Castillo[1] (ID), Manuel Ayala-Chauvin[1(✉)] (ID), and Jorge Buele[2] (ID)

[1] Centro de Investigación en Ciencias Humanas y de la Educación-CICHE, Universidad Indoamérica, Ambato 180103, Ecuador
{faviles,mayala5}@indoamerica.edu.ec

[2] SISAu Research Group, Facultad de Ingeniería, Industria y Producción, Universidad Indoamérica, Ambato 180103, Ecuador
jorgebuele@indoamerica.edu.ec

Abstract. Big Data has been gaining significant attention globally due to its potential to drive innovation, guide decision-making, and stimulate economic growth. As part of this global trend, Ecuador has also witnessed a surge in Big Data-related research over the past decade. This study comprehensively analyzes Big Data research evolution, collaborations, and impacts in Ecuador from 2012 to 2023. By examining the patterns of publication, researcher demographics, primary languages, significant publishers, most cited research papers, patterns of author collaboration, and prevalent keywords, we strive to construct a detailed portrayal of the Big Data research landscape in the country. Our investigation reveals a noticeable increase in Big Data research activity post-2015, particularly within major cities like Quito and Guayaquil. Notably, the study also underscores the predominance of English in research publications, with leading publishers such as IEEE and Springer playing significant roles. The diverse themes of the most cited articles illustrate the wide-ranging applications of Big Data research within the country.

Keywords: Big data · Ecuador · Data Analysis · Research Impact · Scientific Production

1 Introduction

Since ancient times, data has been recorded and analyzed to support decision-making across different societal domains, such as politics, economics, and science [1]. The advent of the Information and Communication Technologies (ICT) during the 20th century propelled the evolution from conventional information systems to strategic information systems, streamlining information management and processing [2]. This technological advancement gave rise to Big Data, addressing the analysis, structuring, and utilization of massive data via specialized software and algorithms [3, 4]. The extensive interconnection of devices through the Internet and the rise of social networks have produced vast amounts of data, necessitating efficient management by both corporations and governments [5].

In today's digitized society, the data generated in various sectors, including medicine, engineering, marketing, and business, has surged exponentially. This data boom presents both opportunities and challenges in information management [4, 6, 7]. Research indicates the importance of structuring, processing, and analyzing data to reduce decision-making uncertainty and align predictions with reality [8]. The integration of artificial intelligence, gamification, personalized learning, and simulation in education, for instance, has amplified learning efficiency and fostered an ecosystem of data and innovative educational tools [9, 10]. Similarly, Big Data analytics have shaped sustainability in the industrial sector, enhancing operational efficiency and facilitating business growth [11].

Big Data analytics has also helped address challenges related to population growth and dwindling resources by enabling companies to become more competent and sustainable [12]. In Latin America, there has been an increase in the number of companies dedicated to data analysis, with Mexico, Brazil, and Argentina being the most prominent countries. Big data is influencing various sectors in Ecuador, such as disaster prediction, agriculture, the advancement of smart cities, and the analysis of electoral data [13]. Governments have embraced data management to improve decision-making and benefit citizens, although criticisms and challenges exist, such as the misuse of public resources and social problems [14].

Although Big Data has become increasingly crucial globally and within the Latin American region, a clear understanding of its application and trends in Ecuador is lacking. Our bibliographic search revealed a significant gap in bibliometric studies focusing on Big Data in Ecuador. Given this knowledge gap, the primary objective of this study is to identify the trends and characteristics of Big Data analysis in Ecuador. This exploration will provide valuable insights to researchers and policymakers alike, aiding them in effectively harnessing the power of Big Data.

The need to understand the evolution of Big Data in Ecuador within the larger Latin American context forms the basis of this study. Big Data analytics can swiftly pinpoint problems and opportunities, driving competitiveness and growth [15]. In this light, our research will contribute to a more profound understanding of the Big Data scenario in Ecuador, thereby fostering improved decision-making and national economic advancement.

The rest of this paper is structured as follows. Section 2 details the methodology, Sect. 3 presents the analysis results, while Sect. 4 discusses the conclusions.

2 Methodology

2.1 Extraction of Information

In this bibliometric review, an exhaustive search for relevant articles was performed in various databases, including SpringerLink, Scopus, IEEE Xplore, Web of Science, and ACM. The search period spanned from the start of these databases to April 2023. Search terms related to big data ("big data", "Hadoop", "data mining") were used, as well as different areas of knowledge. ("sciences", "engineering", "services", "education", "health", "social"). In addition, terms related to governance ("society", "e-government") and education ("education", "research", "academia") were included. The initial search gave a total of 2737 results, but they covered a wide array of topics beyond the scope of big data applications developed in Ecuador. This involved an evaluation of the titles, abstracts, and keywords of the articles to ascertain their relevance to our study. After an in-depth screening, we identified 86 documents that met our predefined criteria. All articles in this review can be viewed at: https://github.com/faviles7/BigData_Trends_biblio.

2.2 Formulation of Research Questions

Bearing the aim of our study in mind, this bibliometric review's primary objective is to examine the scientific knowledge generated on data analysis in Ecuador through a thorough search and analysis of documents available in the databases. To achieve this, we formulated the following research questions:

RQ1: How has the scientific production of big data and its use in Ecuador evolved over the years?
This research question explores the growth and development of scientific publications related to big data in Ecuador. It seeks to understand how the production of research in this field has evolved over time and identify the trends and advancements in utilizing big data within the country.

RQ2: What are the geographical distribution and the language of publication of the articles?
This question analyzes the geographical distribution of research publications on big data in Ecuador. It aims to identify the regions or cities where these articles are predominantly published. Additionally, it investigates the languages in which these articles are published, providing insights into the linguistic diversity of the scientific output on big data in Ecuador.

RQ3: Which publishers have the highest number of publications about big data in Ecuador?
This research question aims to identify the publishers that have contributed significantly to disseminating knowledge on big data in Ecuador. Determining the publishers with the most significant number of publications provides an understanding of the key platforms for sharing research on this topic in the country.

RQ4: What are the most productive higher education institutions in Ecuador in the field of big data?
This question focuses on identifying the higher education institutions in Ecuador that have demonstrated significant productivity in big data.

RQ5: What are the most cited articles about this topic?
This research question aims to identify the most influential and widely cited articles on big data within the Ecuadorian context. Examining citation patterns provides insights into the key contributions and influential works in Ecuador's big data research field.

RQ6: Who are the main authors and their collaboration networks?
This question seeks to identify key authors and outline their collaborative networks, shedding light on primary contributors.

RQ7: What are the main keywords that can be identified in this topic?
This research question aims to identify the main keywords or terms frequently used in the context of big data research in Ecuador.

3   Results

In this section, the results obtained in the research on big data in Ecuador will be presented. Various aspects were examined, including scientific production, disciplinary involvement, prominent authors, relevant journals, national and international collaboration, research topics and funding sources. These results will provide a comprehensive view of the current state of research on big data in Ecuador and its impact on the scientific community.

RQ1: *How has the scientific production of big data and its use in Ecuador evolved over the years?*

The temporal evolution of scientific production on big data in Ecuador can be observed in Fig. 1. From 2012 to 2015, there was minimal research activity, with only one publication in 2012 and another in 2015. However, starting in 2016, there was a steady increase in publications, reaching 19 in 2018. The following years, from 2019 to 2021, showed relatively stable levels of research output, ranging from 11 to 17 publications per year. However, the most recent data available for 2023 indicates a decline with only four publications. These findings suggest a fluctuating trend in the scientific production of big data in Ecuador, highlighting the need for further investigation to understand the underlying factors contributing to these variations.

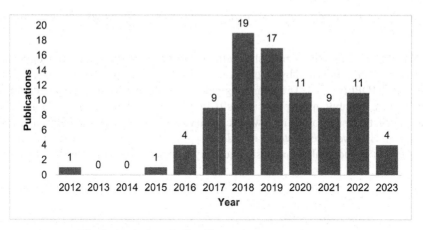

Fig. 1.   Evolution of scientific production over the years.

RQ2: *What are the geographical distribution and the language of publication of the articles?*

We identified the participation of 269 authors and co-authors. Of the authors, 89.06% had at least one affiliation with Ecuador. Figure 2 exhibits the cities from which the researchers originated, with Quito standing out at 26.77%, Guayaquil at 22.75%, Cuenca and Loja at 9.37%, and Ambato at 6.69%. This signifies that Big Data research in Ecuador mainly concentrates on these cities. As for the language of publication, all articles were written in English. It is essential to highlight that the choice of publication language can impact the dissemination and reach of research findings, particularly in the international scientific community where English is considered the lingua franca.

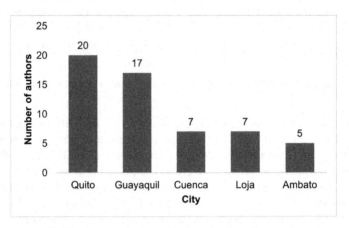

Fig. 2. Geographical distribution of authors in Ecuador

RQ3: *Which publishers have the highest number of publications about big data in Ecuador?*

Figure 3 reveals that the publisher with the most documents on Big Data in Ecuador is IEEE (n = 53), followed by other leading publishers like Springer (n = 16), ACM (n = 5) and MDPI (n = 4). The remaining publications come from various international universities. Notably, most publications (61.63%) are conference proceedings, which may suggest a less rigorous review process than articles published in indexed journals (34.88%). However, the existence of indexed publications points to quality research on this topic in Ecuador, albeit modest in quantity compared to other published sources.

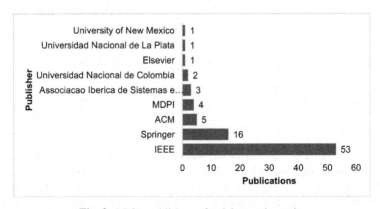

Fig. 3. Major publishers of articles on the topic.

RQ4: *What are the most productive higher education institutions in Ecuador in the field of big data?*

In the context of Ecuador, data analysis has become a growing area of interest in higher education institutions. According to Fig. 4, it can be observed that the Escuela Superior Politécnica del Litoral-ESPOL is the most productive institution in this field. It is closely followed by the Escuela Politécnica Nacional and the Universidad Politécnica Salesiana. These institutions have demonstrated a notable commitment to generating knowledge and applying data analysis in various research areas. In addition, there are collaborations with other foreign institutions in the United States, Brazil, Spain, the Netherlands, among others. These findings reflect the importance and momentum given to data analysis in Ecuador's academic and scientific realm.

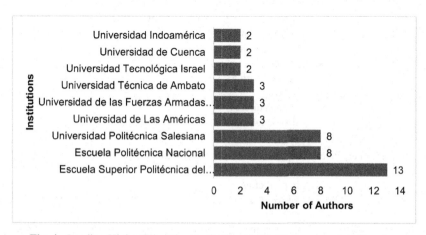

Fig. 4. Leading Higher Education Institutions in Big Data research in Ecuador.

RQ5: *What are the most cited articles about this topic?*

The top ten most cited articles on Big Data in Ecuador are outlined in Table 1. These articles showcase Big Data research's diverse applications and significant impact on the country. The most influential article, "A smart system for sleep monitoring by integrating IoT with big data analytics" by Yacchirema et al. [16], has garnered 92 citations since its publication in IEEE Access in 2018, with an average of 17.52 citations per year. This study explores the integration of IoT and big data analytics to monitor sleep patterns, highlighting the potential of technology-driven approaches in the field.

Another highly cited article, "Application of a smart city model to a traditional university campus with a big data architecture: A sustainable smart campus" by Villegas-Ch et al. [17], has received 83 citations since its publication in Sustainability (Switzerland) in 2019, with an average of 19.53 citations per year. This research demonstrates the application of big data architecture in creating sustainable smart campuses. The remaining articles cover a wide range of topics, including machine learning for predicting student performance, convolutional neural networks for precise weed and maize classification, symmetrical compression distance for arrhythmia discrimination, and more.

These highly cited articles illustrate the breadth and impact of Big Data research in Ecuador across various disciplines and highlight the country's contributions to the field.

Table 1. The most cited articles in Big Data research in Ecuador

N°	Authors	Title	Source	Year	Citations	Average
1	Yacchirema, Diana C., et al. [16]	A smart system for sleep monitoring by integrating IoT with big data analytics	IEEE Access	2018	92	17.52 (#2)
2	Villegas-Ch, William, et al. [17]	Application of a smart city model to a traditional university campus with a big data architecture: A sustainable smart campus	Sustainability (Switzerland)	2019	83	19.53 (#1)
3	Buenaño-Fernández, Diego, et al. [18]	Application of machine learning in predicting performance for computer engineering students: A case study	Sustainability (Switzerland)	2019	63	14.82 (#3)
4	Cordova Cruzatty, Andrea, et al. [19]	Precise weed and maize classification through convolutional neuronal networks	Ecuador Technical Chapters Meeting, ETCM	2017	36	5.76 (#6)
5	Lillo-Castellano, J. M., et al. [20]	Symmetrical Compression Distance for Arrhythmia Discrimination in Cloud-Based Big-Data Services	IEEE Journal of Biomedical and Health Informatics	2015	30	3.64 (#8)

(*continued*)

Table 1. (*continued*)

N°	Authors	Title	Source	Year	Citations	Average
6	Moscoso-Zea, Oswaldo, et al. [21]	A Hybrid Infrastructure of Enterprise Architecture and Business Intelligence Analytics for Knowledge Management in Education	IEEE Access	2019	27	6.35 (#5)
7	Moscoso-Zea, Oswaldo, et al. [22]	Datawarehouse design for educational data mining	International Conference on Information Technology Based Higher Education and Training, ITHET 2016	2016	23	3.17 (#9)
8	Villegas-Ch, William, et al. [23]	Big data, the next step in the evolution of educational data analysis	Advances in Intelligent Systems and Computing	2018	22	4.19 (#7)
9	Abad, Cristina L., et al. [24]	Metadata traces and workload models for evaluating big storage systems	IEEE/ACM 5th International Conference on Utility and Cloud Computing, UCC 2012	2012	16	1.42 (#10)
10	Estupiñán, Jesús Ricardo, et al. [25]	Neutrosophic K-means for the analysis of earthquake data in Ecuador	Neutrosophic Sets and Systems	2021	15	6.67 (#4)

RQ6: *Who are the main authors and their collaboration networks?*

In Fig. 5, a noticeable shift towards increased cooperation can be observed within the country in the realm of Big Data. The establishment of 7 clusters in the Big Data domain suggests a conducive setting for the generation of knowledge and innovation in Ecuador. The data implies that authors "Abad, Cristina L." and "Vaca, Carmen" emerge as prominent figures in the Ecuadorian Big Data landscape, both maintaining a substantial number of connections with other researchers, signifying extensive collaborative efforts. Moreover, "Vaca, Carmen" has authored 7 documents, a figure exceeding that of other writers. The interplay among these authors within the clusters fosters the sharing of ideas, the facilitation of collaborative research, and the reinforcement of the academic community focused on comprehensive data analysis.

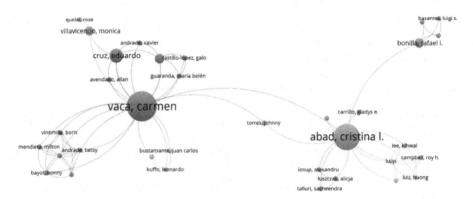

Fig. 5. Collaboration network among authors publishing on Big Data in Ecuador.

RQ7: What are the main keywords that can be identified in this topic?

The Big Data trend in Ecuador shows growing interest and relevance in the field. The keyword "Big Data" stands out in Fig. 6. In addition, other keywords such as "data analytics," "data analytics," "data mining," "data science," "machine learning," and "network artificial neural system" indicate a wide range of topics related to data analysis and processing.

The presence in various sectors is revealed regarding the existing applications of Big Data in Ecuador. Applications are observed in education, precision agriculture, sentiment analysis, smart cities, social network analysis, and e-commerce. In addition, keywords related to specific industries, such as "academic performance," "business," "healthcare," and "traffic," indicate that these industries are using Big Data to improve their processes and make informed decisions.

Regarding the future direction of Big Data in Ecuador, growth in artificial intelligence and machine learning techniques is expected. This is reflected in the keywords "artificial neural network," "machine learning," and "data science." Also, Internet of Things (IoT) related keywords such as "Internet of things" and "smart cities" suggest an increase in the use of sensors and connected devices to collect and analyze data in real time.

Furthermore, social media analytics, sentiment analysis, and data mining are also growing areas, indicating an interest in understanding, and leveraging the data generated by social media platforms. Emphasis is expected on optimizing data analysis and applying advanced techniques, such as predictive analytics and artificial intelligence, to gain valuable insights and make strategic decisions.

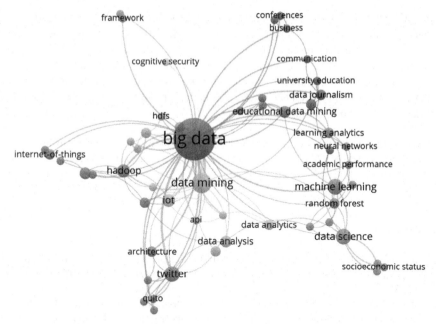

Fig. 6. Relationship between the main keywords of the included studies.

4   Conclusions

This study analyzed the trend of big data in Ecuador through scientific research. The results revealed a temporal evolution in the country's scientific production of big data. A steady increase in publications was demonstrated starting in 2016, reaching a peak in 2018. However, the subsequent years displayed output levels that remained relatively stable, with a decline noted in 2023 up to April. This indicates a fluctuating trend in big data scientific output. In Ecuador, which highlights the need to investigate further the factors contributing to these variations.

Regarding the geographical distribution and the language of publication, it was found that research on big data in Ecuador is mainly concentrated in the cities of Quito, Guayaquil, Cuenca, Loja, and Ambato. In addition, all the analyzed articles were shown to be written in English, which may have an impact on the mainstreaming and reach of the research findings, especially in the international scientific community where English is considered the language.

Regarding the main publishers, it was identified that IEEE has the largest publications on big data in Ecuador, followed by Springer, ACM, and MDPI. Most of the publications were conference proceedings, which may suggest a less rigorous review process compared to articles published in indexed journals. However, indexed publications indicate the presence of quality research on this topic in Ecuador, albeit in a modest amount compared to other published sources.

It is important to highlight some limitations of this study. First, it was based solely on published scientific research, which cannot fully reflect all the activities related to big data in Ecuador, such as projects and practical applications that have not been published. Regarding future work, it is suggested to investigate further the results and practical applications of big data research in different sectors, such as health, education, and industry, to understand better its impact and potential on the development of the country. In addition, it would be valuable to conduct a comparative analysis with other countries in the region to obtain a broader vision of Ecuador's position in big data research and promote growth and innovation in this field.

Acknowledgment. We thank Universidad Indoamérica for the resources provided to this research under the project No. 295.244.2022, entitled "Big Data y su impacto en la sociedad, educación e industria".

References

1. Appiah-Otoo, I., Song, N.: The impact of ICT on economic growth-comparing rich and poor countries. Telecommun. Policy **45**, 102082 (2021). https://doi.org/10.1016/j.telpol.2020.102082
2. Salazar-Mera, J., Silva-Ordoñez, C., Morales-Urrutia, X., Simbaña-Taipe, L., Morales-Urrutia, D., Morales-Carrasco, L.: Science and technology in Ecuador: first approach to its current status at national level. RISTI - Rev. Iber. Sist. e Tecnol. Inf. **2019**, 353–365 (2019)
3. Bach, M.P., Krstič, Ž, Seljan, S., Turulja, L.: Text mining for big data analysis in financial sector: a literature review. Sustainability **11**, 1277 (2019). https://doi.org/10.3390/su11051277
4. Cirillo, D., Valencia, A.: Big data analytics for personalized medicine. Curr. Opin. Biotechnol. **58**, 161–167 (2019). https://doi.org/10.1016/j.copbio.2019.03.004
5. Pencheva, I., Esteve, M., Mikhaylov, S.J.: Big data and AI – a transformational shift for government: so, what next for research? Public Policy Adm. **35**, 24–44 (2018). https://doi.org/10.1177/0952076718780537
6. Dou, X.: Big data and smart aviation information management system. Cogent Bus. Manag. **7**, 1766736 (2020). https://doi.org/10.1080/23311975.2020.1766736
7. De Luca, L.M., Herhausen, D., Troilo, G., Rossi, A.: How and when do big data investments pay off? The role of marketing affordances and service innovation. J. Acad. Mark. Sci. **49**, 790–810 (2021). https://doi.org/10.1007/s11747-020-00739-x
8. Cóndor-Herrera, O., Bolaños-Pasquel, M., Ramos-Galarza, C.: E-learning and m-learning benefits in the learning process. In: Nazir, S., Ahram, T.Z., Karwowski, W. (eds) AHFE 2021. LNNS, vol. 269, pp. 331–336. Springer, Cham (2021). https://doi.org/10.1007/978-3-030-80000-0_39
9. Pérez-delHoyo, R., Mora, H., Martí-Ciriquián, P., Pertegal-Felices, M.L., Mollá-Sirvent, R.: Introducing innovative technologies in higher education: an experience in using geographic information systems for the teaching-learning process. Comput. Appl. Eng. Educ. **28**, 1110–1127 (2020). https://doi.org/10.1002/cae.22287
10. Dessureault, S.: Rethinking fleet and personnel management in the era of IoT, big data, gamification, and low-cost tablet technology. Min. Metall. Explor. **36**, 591–596 (2019). https://doi.org/10.1007/s42461-019-0073-7
11. Karatas, M., Eriskin, L., Deveci, M., Pamucar, D., Garg, H.: Big data for healthcare industry 4.0: applications, challenges and future perspectives. Expert Syst. Appl. **200**, 116912 (2022). https://doi.org/10.1016/j.eswa.2022.116912

12. Li, C., Chen, Y., Shang, Y.: A review of industrial big data for decision making in intelligent manufacturing. Eng. Sci. Technol. Int. J. **29**, 101021 (2022). https://doi.org/10.1016/j.jestch. 2021.06.001

13. Ayala-Chauvin, M., Avilés-Castillo, F., Buele, J.: Exploring the landscape of data analysis: a review of its application and impact in Ecuador. Computers **12**, 146 (2023). https://doi.org/ 10.3390/computers12070146

14. Hilbert, M.: Big data for development: a review of promises and challenges. Dev. Policy Rev. **34**, 135–174 (2016). https://doi.org/10.1111/dpr.12142

15. Mikalef, P., Krogstie, J., Pappas, I.O., Pavlou, P.: Exploring the relationship between big data analytics capability and competitive performance: the mediating roles of dynamic and operational capabilities. Inf. Manag. **57**, 103169 (2020). https://doi.org/10.1016/j.im.2019. 05.004

16. Yacchirema, D.C., Sarabia-Jacome, D., Palau, C.E., Esteve, M.: A smart system for sleep monitoring by integrating IoT with big data analytics. IEEE Access **6**, 35988–36001 (2018). https://doi.org/10.1109/ACCESS.2018.2849822

17. Villegas-Ch, W., Palacios-Pacheco, X., Luján-Mora, S.: Application of a smart city model to a traditional university campus with a big data architecture: a sustainable smart campus. Sustainability **11**, 2857 (2019). https://doi.org/10.3390/su11102857

18. Buenaño-Fernández, D., Gil, D., Luján-Mora, S.: Application of machine learning in predicting performance for computer engineering students: a case study. Sustainability **11** (2019). https://doi.org/10.3390/su11102833

19. Cordova Cruzatty, A., Barreno, M.D., Jacome Barrionuevo, J.M.: Precise weed and maize classification through convolutional neuronal networks. In: Proceedings of the 2017 IEEE 2nd Ecuador Technical Chapters Meeting, ETCM 2017, vol. 2017, pp. 1–6. Institute of Electrical and Electronics Engineers Inc., January 2018

20. Lillo-Castellano, J.M., et al.: Symmetrical compression distance for arrhythmia discrimination in cloud-based big-data services. IEEE J. Biomed. Heal. Inform. **19**, 1253–1263 (2015). https://doi.org/10.1109/JBHI.2015.2412175

21. Moscoso-Zea, O., Castro, J., Paredes-Gualtor, J., Lujan-Mora, S.: A hybrid infrastructure of enterprise architecture and business intelligence analytics for knowledge management in education. IEEE Access **7**, 38778–38788 (2019). https://doi.org/10.1109/ACCESS.2019.290 6343

22. Moscoso-Zea, O., Andres-Sampedro, Luján-Mora, S.: Datawarehouse design for educational data mining. In: Proceedings of the 2016 15th International Conference on Information Technology Based Higher Education and Training, ITHET 2016, pp. 1–6 (2016)

23. Villegas-Ch, W., Luján-Mora, S., Buenaño-Fernández, D., Palacios-Pacheco, X.: Big data, the next step in the evolution of educational data analysis. Adv. Intell. Syst. Comput. **721**, 138–147 (2018). https://doi.org/10.1007/978-3-319-73450-7_14

24. Abad, C.L., Luu, H., Roberts, N., Lee, K., Lu, Y., Campbell, R.H.: Metadata traces and workload models for evaluating big storage systems. In: Proceedings of the Proceedings - 2012 IEEE/ACM 5th International Conference on Utility and Cloud Computing, UCC 2012, pp. 125–132 (2012)

25. Estupiñán, J.R., Domínguez Menéndez, J., Barcos Arias, I., Macías Bermúdez, J., Moreno Lemus, N.: Neutrosophic K-means for the analysis of earthquake data in Ecuador. Neutrosophic Sets Syst. **44** (2021)

Data-Driven Intelligence Can Revolutionize Today's Cybersecurity World: A Position Paper

Iqbal H. Sarker[1,2](✉) [iD], Helge Janicke[1,2] [iD], Leandros Maglaras[3] [iD],
and Seyit Camtepe[4] [iD]

[1] Security Research Institute, Edith Cowan University, Perth, Western Australia
6027, Australia
[2] Cyber Security Cooperative Research Centre, Joondalup, Australia
m.sarker@ecu.edu.au
[3] School of Computing, Edinburgh Napier University, Edinburgh EH10 5DT, UK
[4] Data61, CSIRO, Sydney, New South Wales 2122, Australia

Abstract. As cyber threats evolve and grow progressively more sophisticated, cyber security is becoming a more significant concern in today's digital era. Traditional security measures tend to be insufficient to defend against these persistent and dynamic threats because they are mainly intuitional. One of the most promising ways to handle this ongoing problem is utilizing the potential of *data-driven intelligence*, by leveraging AI and machine learning techniques. It can improve operational efficiency and saves response times by automating repetitive operations, enabling real-time threat detection, and facilitating incident response. In addition, it augments human expertise with insightful information, predictive analytics, and enhanced decision-making, enabling them to better understand and address evolving problems. Thus, data-driven intelligence could significantly improve real-world cybersecurity solutions in a wide range of application areas like critical infrastructure, smart cities, digital twin, industrial control systems and so on. In this position paper, we argue that data-driven intelligence can revolutionize the realm of cybersecurity, offering not only large-scale task *automation* but also *assist human experts* for better situation awareness and decision-making in real-world scenarios.

Keywords: Cybersecurity · Data-Driven Intelligence · Automation · Human Assistance · Augmenting Experts Knowledge · AI · Machine Learning

1 Introduction

Cybersecurity has emerged as a major problem in today's hyperconnected world due to the growing cyber threat landscape and the increasing number of sophisticated malicious actors. According to the Telecommunication Standardization

Sector of International Telecommunication Union [1] "Cybersecurity is the collection of tools, policies, security concepts, safeguards, guidelines, risk management approaches, actions, training, best practices, assurance and technologies that can be used to protect the cyber environment and organization and user's assets." In the real-world scenario, protecting sensitive data and digital assets from continuously evolving threats is a challenging task for businesses in a variety of application areas such as critical infrastructures, smart city applications, information and operational technology networks, etc. Traditional security solutions might not be sufficient to provide defense against today's persistent and constantly evolving threats in these areas. There is an urgent need for innovative approaches that can effectively counteract the dynamic nature of cyber threats. Therefore, in this paper, we focus on data-driven intelligence, which offers a powerful combination of automation and human assistance and could be one of the most promising strategies for solving this ongoing problem.

Data-driven intelligence typically can be defined as the process of using data analysis and interpretation to derive insights or useful knowledge, and eventually make intelligent decisions. It thus involves identifying trends, patterns, correlations, and other pertinent information primarily through the use of data, which could then be applied to regulate corporate operations and strategic decisions. The development of data-driven intelligence, powered by machine learning and artificial intelligence [2], has tremendous potential for revolutionizing cybersecurity in various application areas, discussed briefly in Sect. 4. Data-driven intelligence has the capability to reveal hidden patterns, detect anomalies and predict potential cyberattacks by utilizing the enormous amounts of data generated from numerous sources, such as network logs, system events, and user behavior. This enables the development of proactive and adaptive defense systems rather than simply relying on predefined rules and signatures, enhancing an organization's capacity to recognize, respond to, and mitigate cyber threats. In addition to automating tasks, cyber analysts can gain deeper insights into the tactics, techniques, and procedures employed by cyber adversaries through the extracted insights from data, discussed briefly in Sect. 3.

In order to better understand the main focus of this position paper and overall contributions, we formulate three major questions below:

- Can data-driven intelligence *automate* the large-scale complex tasks in the context of cybersecurity?
- Does data-driven intelligence have the potential to *augment* human expertise or knowledge through in-depth understanding as well as to *assist* them in their decision-making process in real-world scenarios?
- Is it worthwhile to *rethink* the present cyberspace across a variety of application areas while taking into account the power of data-driven intelligence, particularly in terms of automation and assisting human experts in the domain?

Answering these questions, we believe that data-driven intelligence can revolutionize today's cybersecurity world. Towards this, we provide a clear understanding of the potential of data-driven intelligence as well as their applicability and impact from the perspective of next-generation cybersecurity solutions in the following sections. Thus this paper contributes to the ongoing discussion about the role of data-driven modeling and the importance of ensuring that innovative methods are developed and deployed in a manner that maximizes its benefits while minimizing its risks. The ultimate purpose of this paper is not only to highlight data-driven intelligence but also to use the extracted insights or useful knowledge gained from data to make intelligent decisions that improve the current cybersecurity landscape.

The rest of the paper is organized as follows: Sect. 2 highlights the significance of data intelligence considering both automating tasks and human experts' decision-making. We discuss data-driven modeling in Sect. 3. We also explore the potentiality of data-driven intelligence in various real-world application domains in Sect. 4. The key challenges and issues are highlighted in Sect. 5 and finally, Sect. 6 concludes this paper.

2   Why Data-Driven Intelligence for Next-Generation Cybersecurity?

In the area of cybersecurity, data-driven intelligence offers a substantial contribution to *automation* as well as *assisting human expert decision-making* to solve real-world problems. Human experts may not have the scalability and speed of automated systems, but they do have the capability for critical thought, intuition, and the ability to realize bigger organizational goals as well as ethical concerns when making decisions. The symbiotic relationship between automation and human expertise enables businesses to develop strong cyber defense capabilities, react to threats promptly, and maintain a competitive advantage in the continually evolving landscape of cybersecurity concerns. In this section, we discuss how data-driven intelligence can serve as a strength factor in cybersecurity by automating repetitive processes, anticipating threats, as well as augments human expertise providing useful information.

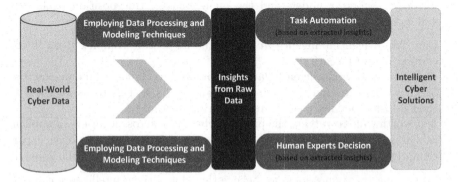

Fig. 1. An illustration highlighting the potential of data-driven intelligence for both automation and assisting human experts in the context of cybersecurity.

(i) *Automation of Large-Scale Cyber Tasks:* Cybersecurity tasks like log analysis, anomaly detection, and routine security checks can be automated using data-driven intelligence [3]. Data-driven automated systems use insights from raw data to drive decision-making. These tasks can be completed more quickly and accurately by utilizing machine learning and AI algorithms [2], alleviating stress on human experts for complicated tasks. By continuously monitoring and analyzing enormous volumes of data from many sources, data-driven intelligence automates the process of threat detection. It instantly detects anomalies, suspicious activity, and potential threats in real time using machine learning techniques. The incident response process is sped up by automation, which also minimizes the risk of human error and ensures that the cybersecurity teams are acting systematically. Through the extraction of insights from raw data, data-driven automated systems are able to continually learn, adapt, and make decisions in real-time, and eventually boost operational effectiveness.

(ii) *Augmenting Human Understanding and Expertise for Improved Cyber Solutions:* The capabilities of human cybersecurity experts are strengthened by data-driven intelligence in various ways, discussed below. These are -

- *Assisting Human Experts Decision-Making with Evidence-based Recommendations:* Instead of depending exclusively on intuition or prior experiences, cybersecurity professionals could establish complete cybersecurity plans based on empirical evidence and data-informed recommendations with the advancement of data-driven insights. This data-driven approach allows them to conduct comprehensive risk assessments, understand the impact of different attack vectors, and identify critical areas for policy improvement. By providing context-sensitive information about particular incidents and attack tactics, data-driven intelligence improves human experts' knowledge of cyber risks. This deeper understanding aids analysts in determining the seriousness of a threat and developing appropriate countermeasures specific to the organization's particular security posture. Ultimately, data-driven intelligence empowers cybersecurity analysts to support evidence-based, dynamic, and robust policy recommendations that strengthen an organization's resilience against cyber threats.

- *Enhancing Human Experts' Domain Knowledge for Advanced Thinking:* Data-driven intelligence plays a pivotal role in enhancing cyber experts' domain knowledge, specifically for further modeling and analysis. By processing large volumes of cybersecurity data, data-driven tools can uncover valuable insights, patterns, and correlations that experts can use to build more accurate and sophisticated models. For instance, data insights can help determine which entities are essential for building an effective cybersecurity knowledge graph [4] or cybersecurity taxonomy building [5] through identifying common properties and characteristics of entities as well as their internal relationships. These data-driven models can capture the complexities of the cyber landscape, simulate various attack scenarios, and predict potential outcomes with higher precision. As cyber experts integrate data-driven intelligence into their domain knowledge, they can continuously refine their models, improve their understanding of cyber threats, and develop more effective strategies to defend against evolving challenges. Ultimately, the fusion of data-driven intelligence with the expertise of cyber experts enables them to create advanced models that are both robust and adaptable, empowering organizations to stay ahead in the ever-changing cybersecurity landscape.

- *Knowledge Retention and Transfer:* Developing and maintaining efficient cybersecurity capabilities is a complex and continuing process that requires significant investment in terms of time, resources, and expertise. Professionals in the field of cybersecurity require not only technical skills but also a thorough awareness of the infrastructure, processes, and potential vulnerabilities within the organization. This knowledge is essential for quickly recognizing risks and taking appropriate action. In the real-world scenario, the expense of bringing cyber professionals is not only limited to salary and overheads but also the economic loss due to incidents which could have been better handled with experienced staff. Experience and such investments are lost momentarily when an experienced staff member leaves an organization. Consequently, this may result in a knowledge and expertise gap that is difficult to recover instantly. Numerous negative effects, such as increased vulnerability to cyberthreats, decreased efficacy of incident response, and potential project disruptions, may result from this loss. The hiring of a new professional with matching capabilities may not be sufficient because understanding the organizational context usually takes time and may result in further incidents. The data-driven approach creates new opportunities to retain this knowledge and experience and transfer them to new professionals within an organization as needed.

In summary, data-driven intelligence derived from raw data are crucial for both automating large-scale complex tasks and assisting human experts while making their decisions in the context of cybersecurity, illustrated in Fig. 1. It combines the strengths of data insights as well as AI and machine learning techniques for advanced modeling, highlighted in Sect. 3 to improve overall cyber defense capabilities and maximize teamwork between automated systems and human analysts. While each strategy has merits, a well-balanced approach that leverages both human expertise and data-driven automation to improve overall security posture and incident response capabilities could be the most effective way in cybersecurity. It enables human analysts to focus their attention on tasks that need critical thinking, creativity, and strategic planning by providing a wealth of data and insights.

3   Data Insights and Modeling

This section mainly consists of two parts. We initially focus on different types of insights that are associated with data-driven intelligence, and then we concentrate on a general data-driven modeling workflow for further exploration to address a specific issue.

3.1 Cyber Data Insights

For a better understanding of the insights involved in the data-driven intelligence process, we have highlighted three key questions in the section below. The answers to these queries can aid human analysts in deeper understanding and solving a specific problem in the context of cybersecurity as well as in automating the necessary tasks. These are:

- *What happened in the past?:* This typically explores the happenings and incidents in the world of cybersecurity. It includes analyzing historical data, logs, and incident reports to determine the type of cyberattacks, the methods employed by threat actors, the affected systems or data, and the overall impact on the organization. Experts in cybersecurity can react quickly, mitigate loss, and initiate the proper incident response procedures when they are aware of what happened. Building a strong defense strategy also involves identifying patterns and trends in cyber incidents.
- *Why did it happen?:* Here, the emphasis is on underlying the root causes and associated factors for cybersecurity events. Understanding the "why" requires an in-depth investigation of the security infrastructure's shortcomings, configuration issues, human errors, and vulnerabilities that led to the attack's success. Analysts can find systemic issues and weaknesses in their security procedures, work processes, and employee awareness using this investigative process. Organizations may improve their defenses, reduce potential risks, and build a more resilient cybersecurity framework by tackling these core causes.
- *What will happen in the future?:* This element involves predicting and forecasting probable future cybersecurity threats and trends. Cyber threats are always changing, and threat actors are constantly coming up with new strategies to exploit vulnerabilities. Forecasting potential threats can be aided by data-driven intelligence, exchanging threat intelligence, and investigation of emerging technologies. Organizations can prepare for these challenges and be better able to protect themselves against new and emerging cyber threats by understanding what can happen in the future.

Thus extracting these insights could be the key to building the foundation of a data-driven intelligence model, where various techniques within the broad area of data science can be used discussed in the following.

3.2 Data-Driven Modeling with Explanation

An effective modeling technique is essential to extract insights or useful knowledge, where various data-preprocessing and visualization techniques as well as AI and machine learning algorithms for advanced modeling can be used. The key components of this process are as follows:

- *Data Collection and Preparation:* Gathering broad and comprehensive datasets related to cybersecurity is the first step. These datasets may contain information from various sources such as logs, network traffic, system events, security alerts, and historical attack data. To ensure consistency and quality, the collected data should be preprocessed, cleansed, and transformed towards the target solutions. Synthetic data generation as well as handling imbalanced issues using techniques like oversampling, and undersampling [6] might be helpful depending on the nature of the data.

- *Feature Selection and Engineering:* This involves selecting or extracting meaningful features from the preprocessed data that can be used to build the model. It is essential to choose features carefully since traditional machine-learning methods, such as neural networks, SVMs, etc. are sensitive to the features used as inputs [7]. The most pertinent features can be found through statistical analysis or machine learning algorithms [3]. In some cases, feature extraction may require human expertise based on contextual information and awareness of cyber risks and vulnerabilities [8]. To identify relevant features and reduce the dimensionality of the data both algorithmic approach and domain experts may guide towards optimal feature engineering process.

- *Exploratory Analysis and Visualization:* Before moving on to advanced modeling or decision-making, this exploratory analysis helps in understanding in-depth data structure and patterns, and eventually to gain insights into normal behavior and identify patterns associated with cyber threats. Various statistical and visual techniques and tools such as Histograms, Scatter Plots, Bar charts, Heatmaps, etc. [9] can be employed to analyze the distributions, correlations, and structure of the data.

- *Model Development and Training:* Models may vary depending on the characteristics of the data and fitting the problem domain. This includes applying AI and machine learning techniques like decision trees, random forests, neural network learning, as well as rule-based modeling and explanation [10,11]. To improve performance and generalization, optimizing model parameters is important. In several cases, innovative methods might need to develop based on what insights are needed to explore as discussed earlier. Developing hybrid or ensemble models that aggregate outcomes from multiple base models might need to take into account to improve model robustness and generalizability as well as overall accuracy.

- *Model Evaluation:* A comprehensive evaluation is necessary after building and training the model with the relevant cyber data. The efficiency of the model can be assessed using evaluation criteria like accuracy, precision, recall, or F1 score [3]. Validation methods like k-fold cross-validation aid in estimating the performance of the model on unseen data and evaluating its generalizability, which is important to take into account diverse real-world issues.

- *Human-in-the-Loop Integration:* While automated models are capable of detecting a wide range of threats involved, they may not be flawless and could sometimes generate false positives or false negatives. Experts in cybersecurity may contribute their knowledge and expertise to the process by analyzing and verifying the outcomes of automated models. Thus, this module incorporates incident response teams and cybersecurity analysts in the process to provide domain expertise, interpret model outputs, and make critical decisions.

– *Deployment and Continuous Improvement:* The models can be deployed in a real-world cybersecurity context if they have been established to be satisfactory. To ensure the model's efficacy over time, it is essential to continuously assess its performance, detection rates, false positives, and false negatives. To keep the model realistic and up to date, regular updates, retraining, and adaptation to changing threats are required.

Overall, a comprehensive data-driven intelligence framework for cybersecurity modeling needs to be adaptable, resilient, and able to handle the constantly changing and evolving nature of cyber threats. To develop reliable and effective cybersecurity solutions, it thus needs to incorporate in-depth data analysis, machine learning, and domain expertise.

4   Real-World Cybersecurity Application Areas

Data-driven intelligence can be employed in various application areas for effective cybersecurity solutions. In the following, we summarize and discuss some important fields where data-driven intelligence could play a key role in both automation and assisting human experts in their decision-making process in various real-world applications.

4.1   Critical Infrastructure

Critical infrastructure (CI) typically refers to the systems, assets, and networks that are essential for the functioning of a society and economy, for example - energy, water, transportation, communications, healthcare, and finance are some of the potential sectors [12,13]. Thus, CI cybersecurity and resilience is one of the topmost important sectors nowadays, where data-driven intelligence could play a crucial role in practical solutions through data insights and sophisticated analytical modeling. The basis of intelligence could involve analyzing and visualizing CI data gathered from various sources including network logs, system activity, and threat intelligence feeds. The extracted insights from data could provide a comprehensive picture of the security landscape, providing human professionals with a better understanding of potential threats and vulnerabilities. Data-driven intelligence is also capable of predicting possible future cyber threats and attack trends using data patterns and AI algorithms [2]. These predictive insights could be beneficial to human experts to further analyze the potential attacks and make countermeasures for them, enabling them to proactively strengthen CI defenses. In many cases, automaton is necessary because of speeding up the investigation and management of incidents as well as minimizing the possibility of human error. For example, routine incident response tasks, such as anomaly detection, malware analysis, and containment processes, could be automated through a data-driven modeling process. Overall, the potential of data-driven intelligence could be the key to next-generation CI security offering automating large-scale tasks as well as assisting CI professionals to make well-informed decisions in various real-world scenarios.

4.2 Digital Twin

Nowadays, more and more businesses are using digital twins, which are virtual replicas of physical assets or systems [14]. As physical, digital as well as communication space is associated with digital twin systems [15], an effective security measure is necessary. Data-driven intelligence may keep track of the network traffic, user interactions, and behavior of the digital twin [16]. Thus it enables real-time monitoring of digital twin systems, continuously collecting data to detect any deviations from normal behavior. Cyber professionals may gain deeper insights into the behavior of the physical and virtual components through this extensive data analysis. For instance, when any suspicious activity or possible security issues are identified, they may receive prompt notifications, enabling quick response and mitigation. It can also forecast potential cybersecurity risks and vulnerabilities based on the insights extracted from data. Overall, this could be a useful tool for automatically solving security issues as well as enhancing human expertise and aiding in their decision-making process in real-world applications.

4.3 Smart Cities

Smart cities could be another potential area, which typically rely on interconnected digital systems and devices to enhance efficiency and improve the quality of life for residents. Massive amounts of data are produced by smart cities from a variety of sources, including IoT devices, sensors, infrastructure, and human interactions [17]. This data can be analyzed by data-driven intelligence to find trends and abnormalities that could point to possible cyber threats. It can identify suspicious activity in real-time and inform cybersecurity professionals, allowing them to take prompt action to stop cyberattacks. Data-driven intelligence may establish baseline behaviors for various parts of the smart city infrastructure by using AI and machine learning techniques [2]. This involves being aware of the typical data exchange patterns, user behavior with regard to smart devices, and network traffic flow. Automated incident response systems may be triggered when cyber threats are identified. This can forecast potential future cyber threats through analysis of historical data and cyberattack trends. Decision-makers can comprehend how cybersecurity resources are used by conducting data analysis. Human experts could learn about emerging threats, observe trends, and make wise decisions about security practices and procedures according to this comprehensive picture.

4.4 IoT

The Internet of Things (IoT) enables communication and interaction with numerous devices, generates an enormous amount of data, which can then be utilized to identify trends, behaviors, make predictions, and conduct assessments [18]. Thus decision-making in IoT cybersecurity is facilitated by data-driven intelligence, which substantially enhances human expert knowledge as well. Data-driven systems have the ability to rapidly detect abnormalities, recognize potential threats, and anticipate emerging issues by analyzing the enormous volumes of data produced by IoT devices and networks. This proactive strategy and real-time monitoring enable human professionals to react to cyber incidents quickly and strategically, reducing their effects. A thorough understanding of the complex IoT ecosystem is made possible by data-driven insights, which give important context and correlation from many data sources. This collaborative synergy enables cybersecurity experts to take well-informed decisions, allocate resources efficiently, and put into place efficient measures to protect IoT environments from emerging threats.

4.5 ICS/OT

ICS stands for "Industrial Control Systems", and is typically used to monitor and control physical processes and operations, which typically connect IT components with sensors, actuators, and other operational technology (OT) devices [19]. Supervisory control and data acquisition (SCADA) systems, distributed control systems (DCS), PLCs, and other ICS components are frequently targets of cyberattacks [20]. Potential threats to the ICS include advanced persistent threats, supply chain compromise, distributed denial of services, etc., where data-driven intelligence can contribute to detect and mitigate through an extensive analysis. Utilizing real-time and historical data collected from numerous interconnected devices and networks within industrial infrastructure also enables human experts to gain an in-depth understanding of the evolving threat landscape. By analyzing patterns, anomalies, and potential vulnerabilities, experts may deal with cyber threats proactively before they escalate. Additionally, data-driven solutions enable routine and large-scale complex operations to be automated, allowing human experts stress-less. Overall, the security and reliability of crucial industrial systems could be ensured by developing effective defense modeling with the fusion of data insights and human expertise.

4.6 Metaverse

Metaverse could be another potential area that can create secure, scalable, and realistic virtual worlds on a reliable and always-on platform. Users can interact with each other and digital objects in real-time using technologies like virtual reality (VR) or augmented reality (AR) [21]. Due to the massive volume of data moving around in the Metaverse, users are constantly running a higher risk of misuse [22]. Businesses are investing heavily in building an artificially intelligent Metaverse, which has increased the need for cybersecurity [23]. Data-driven cybersecurity solutions can track user behavior, interactions, and network traffic throughout the metaverse. These systems are capable of quickly identifying possible risks or unusual activities, such as unauthorized access attempts or malware activity, by analyzing patterns and anomalies. Automated incident response systems that can react to known threats and attacks without requiring human involvement could be provided by data-driven intelligence. Real-time monitoring and visualization of cybersecurity metrics and events within the metaverse can be provided through data-driven intelligence. These visualizations enable human professionals to promptly comprehend the security posture and pinpoint areas of concern. While human experts contribute critical thinking, domain knowledge, and decision-making, data-driven intelligence enhances these capabilities with rapid analysis, real-time insights, and automation of large-scale tasks. This can secure the metaverse environment in a comprehensive and proactive manner.

4.7   Advanced Networking and Communications

Nowadays, data-driven technology is also popular in the area of advanced communications and networking [24]. Based on current demand and traffic patterns, this can optimize the allocation of resources like bandwidth, computing power, and spectrum. In terms of security, data-driven technologies are capable of analyzing user behavior and network traffic patterns to detect anomalies and possible security breaches [25]. Machine learning models can identify suspicious activity and trigger prompt countermeasures to stop intrusions. Predictive maintenance powered by data-driven intelligence enables proactive defense against evolving attack vectors, which can help prevent network downtime and improves overall reliability. Thus, this can ensure a balanced trade-off between security and usability, which dynamically adjusts security configurations based on network conditions, user behavior, and threat levels [26]. An effective access control system can be implemented by investigating user behavior and contextual data to ensure secure and reliable authentication. Overall, advanced communications and network security have been significantly impacted by data-driven intelligence as it provides insights, automation, and adaptation to address complex problems in real time.

In summary, organizations could enhance their threat detection and prevention, improve incident response capabilities, and strengthen their cybersecurity posture overall by utilizing data-driven intelligence in various real-world application domains. Data-driven intelligence augments human expertise rather than substituting it. In order to make informed decisions during security issues, it gives security analysts and operators more information and context. Data-driven intelligence helps human professionals to respond quickly and effectively by providing pertinent information and potential directions of action. Organizations can remain resilient in the face of emerging cyber threats when they have the capability to analyze massive datasets, uncover patterns, and make decisions based on data insights.

5   Challenges and Research Direction

While the concept of data-driven intelligence revolutionizing the cybersecurity world holds promise, there are several challenges that researchers and practitioners need to address to fully realize its potential. These challenges discussed below encompass various aspects of research and development in the field:

- *Data Quality and Availability:* One of the major challenges in incorporating data-driven intelligence for cybersecurity research and applications is ensuring the quality and availability of relevant data. Obtaining comprehensive, accurate, and diverse datasets could be challenging, especially when dealing with sensitive information. Researchers need to overcome data limitations and address biases, as well as meaningful synthetic data generation to ensure the reliability and effectiveness of their research and ultimate outcome. Methods that enable cybersecurity models to transfer knowledge from one domain or task to another could be useful.
- *Algorithmic Transparency and Interpretability:* The use of AI and complex machine learning algorithms, such as deep neural network learning [2], in data-driven intelligence may raise challenges in algorithmic transparency and interpretability. Understanding how algorithms make decisions and being able to interpret their outputs is crucial in the context of cybersecurity. Researchers need to focus on developing explainable AI techniques, e.g., rule-based modeling [11] or others that can provide insights into the reasoning behind algorithmic decisions, allowing cybersecurity professionals to trust and validate the results generated by data-driven intelligence systems.
- *Privacy Concerns:* Data-driven intelligence might raise important privacy and ethical concerns. The collection and analysis of large amounts of personal and sensitive data need to be conducted responsibly and in compliance with privacy regulations. Researchers thus need to explore privacy-preserving techniques such as differential privacy, federated learning, data anonymization, etc. [27] to ensure that individuals' privacy is protected while still extracting meaningful insights from data. For instance, federated learning enables training models across numerous devices or organizations without sharing raw data, hence protecting data privacy.
- *Adversarial Attacks and Defenses:* Adversaries can manipulate or poison datasets to mislead machine learning algorithms, leading to erroneous decisions or bypassing detection mechanisms. Research is necessary for developing robust models that are resilient to adversarial attacks and maintain high reliability and accuracy in practical settings. Developing advanced anomaly detection techniques identifying unusual behavior that can detect and respond to previously unknown and unseen threats and zero-day attacks is crucial. Hybrid models combining data-driven approaches such as machine learning, and rule-based approaches with expert knowledge can enhance the overall effectiveness of cybersecurity models.
- *Generalizability and Scalability:* The effectiveness of data-driven intelligence models in cybersecurity may vary across different contexts, environments, and evolving cyber threats. Thus, ensuring the generalizability and adaptability of research findings and models is crucial. Investigating transfer learning techniques can assist models in maintaining high detection accuracy while adapting rapidly to new attack patterns. To manage huge datasets in real time, it is also necessary to develop scalable algorithms, distributed computing frameworks, and optimized processing strategies. This is crucial to assure

scalability and efficiency due to the exponential growth of cybersecurity data volume.

– *Human-in-the-Loop and Accountability:* While data-driven intelligence can provide valuable insights, the 'human' element in real-world applications might not be overlooked. Researchers need to take into account how human operators interact with data-driven systems, understand their decision-making processes, and design effective user interfaces and visualizations to aid decision-making. Combining AI and human expertise can also increase accountability. For instance, cybersecurity professionals can validate model outcomes, intervene when necessary, and provide explanations for actions made by the AI system. Thus, a regulatory guiding framework comprised of data science researchers, cybersecurity experts, legal professionals, and policymakers is crucial to bridge the gap between technological breakthroughs and actual application.

In summary, data-driven intelligence for cybersecurity modeling is an area of study that involves resolving issues with data quality, processing techniques, model robustness, privacy, human expertise, and more. Addressing these challenges is crucial to fully realize the potential of data-driven intelligence in revolutionizing the cybersecurity landscape, which should be the key focus for future research and improvement.

6   Conclusion

This position paper has made a convincing argument for the revolutionary effects of data-driven intelligence in the cybersecurity area. For this, we have explored and discussed in-depth potential of data-driven intelligence, particularly, in terms of automating large-scale complex tasks as well as assisting human experts to make their decisions in real-world scenarios. Organizations can improve their capability to recognize and address emerging threats by utilizing the power of data intelligence. The proactive and adaptable nature of data-driven intelligence also allows security professionals to stay one step ahead of malicious actors, significantly reducing risks. However, this paradigm shift also includes several challenges such as data availability, algorithm bias, incorporating human expertise in the loop that are needed to be resolved, discussed in this paper. Building a well-balanced framework leveraging both human expertise and data-driven intelligence which can improve overall security posture, is also highlighted. Overall, we believe that data-driven intelligence could be the key to next-generation cybersecurity if it is deployed wisely and ongoing research is undertaken.

Acknowledgement. The work has been supported by the Cyber Security Research Centre Limited whose activities are partially funded by the Australian Government's Cooperative Research Centres Program.

References

1. ITU. Overview of cybersecurity. recommendation itu-t x. 1205 (2009)
2. Sarker, I.H.: Multi-aspects AI-based modeling and adversarial learning for cybersecurity intelligence and robustness: a comprehensive overview. *Security and Privacy*, p. e295 (2022)
3. Sarker, I.H.: Cyberlearning: Effectiveness analysis of machine learning security modeling to detect cyber-anomalies and multi-attacks. Internet of Things **14**, 100393 (2021)
4. Jia, Y., Qi, Y., Shang, H., Jiang, R., Li, A.: A practical approach to constructing a knowledge graph for cybersecurity. Engineering **4**(1), 53–60 (2018)
5. Mahaini, M.I., Li, S., Saglam, R.B.: Building taxonomies based on human-machine teaming: Cyber security as an example. In: Proceedings of the 14th International Conference on Availability, Reliability and Security, pp. 1–9 (2019)
6. Bagui, S., Li, K.: Resampling imbalanced data for network intrusion detection datasets. J. Big Data **8**(1), 1–41 (2021)
7. Bakalos, N., et al.: Protecting water infrastructure from cyber and physical threats: Using multimodal data fusion and adaptive deep learning to monitor critical systems. IEEE Signal Process. Mag. **36**(2), 36–48 (2019)
8. Dick, K., Russell, L., Souley Dosso, Y., Kwamena, F., Green, J.R.: Deep learning for critical infrastructure resilience. J. Infrastruct. Syst. **25**(2), 05019003 (2019)
9. Pedregosa, F., et al.: Scikit-learn: machine learning in python. In: J. Mach. Learn. Res. **12**, 2825–2830 (2011)
10. Lundberg, H., et al.: Experimental analysis of trustworthy in-vehicle intrusion detection system using explainable artificial intelligence (xai). IEEE Access **10**, 102831–102841,(2022)
11. Sarker, I., Colman, A., Han, J., Watters, P.: Context-aware machine learning and mobile data analytics: automated rule-based services with intelligent decision-making. Springer (2021)
12. Wisniewski, M., Gladysz, B., Ejsmont, K., Wodecki, A., Van Erp, T.: Industry 4.0 solutions impacts on critical infrastructure safety and protection–a systematic literature review. IEEE Access (2022)
13. Critical infrastructure centre. https://www.homeaffairs.gov.au/. Accessed 08 may 2023
14. Faleiro, R., Pan, L., Pokhrel, S.R., Doss, R.: Digital twin for cybersecurity: towards enhancing cyber resilience. In: Xiang, W., Han, F., Phan, T.K. (eds.) BROAD-NETS 2021. LNICST, vol. 413, pp. 57–76. Springer, Cham (2022). https://doi.org/10.1007/978-3-030-93479-8_4
15. Alcaraz, C., Lopez, J.: Digital twin: a comprehensive survey of security threats. IEEE Commun. Surv. Tutorials **24**(3), 1475–1503 (2022)
16. Kaur, M.J., Mishra, V.P., Maheshwari, P.: The convergence of digital twin, IoT, and machine learning: transforming data into action. In: Farsi, M., Daneshkhah, A., Hosseinian-Far, A., Jahankhani, H. (eds.) Digital Twin Technologies and Smart Cities. IT, pp. 3–17. Springer, Cham (2020). https://doi.org/10.1007/978-3-030-18732-3_1
17. Sarker, I.H.: Smart city data science: towards data-driven smart cities with open research issues. Internet of Things **19**, 100528 (2022)
18. Hussain, F., Hussain, R., Hassan, S.A., Hossain, E.: Machine learning in IoT security: current solutions and future challenges. IEEE Commun. Surv. Tutorials **22**(3), 1686–1721 (2020)

19. Conti, M., Donadel, D., Turrin, F.: A survey on industrial control system testbeds and datasets for security research. IEEE Commu. Surv. Tutorials **23**(4), 2248–2294 (2021)
20. Bhamare, D., Zolanvari, M., Erbad, A., Jain, R., Khan, K., Meskin, N.: Cybersecurity for industrial control systems: a survey. Comput. Secur. **89**, 101677 (2020)
21. Huynh-The, T., Pham, Q.V., Pham, X.Q., Nguyen, T.T., Han, Z., Kim, D.S.: Artificial intelligence for the metaverse: a survey. Eng. Appl. Artif. Intell. **117**, 105581 (2023)
22. Wylde, V., Prakash, E., Hewage, C., Platts, J.: Post-covid-19 metaverse cybersecurity and data privacy: Present and future challenges. In: Data Protection in a Post-Pandemic Society: Laws, Regulations, Best Practices and Recent Solutions, pp. 1–48. Springer (2023). https://doi.org/10.1007/978-3-031-34006-2_1
23. Pooyandeh, M., Han, K.-J., Sohn, I.: Cybersecurity in the AI-based metaverse: a survey. Appl. Sci. **12**(24), 12993 (2022)
24. Afzal, M.K., Ateeq, M., Kim, S.W.: Data-driven Intelligence in Wireless Networks: Concepts, Solutions, and Applications. CRC Press (2023)
25. Xu, S., Qian, Y., Hu, R.Q.: Data-driven network intelligence for anomaly detection. IEEE Network **33**(3), 88–95 (2019)
26. Ahammed, T.B., Patgiri, R., Nayak, S.: A vision on the artificial intelligence for 6G communication. ICT Express **9**(2), 197–210 (2023)
27. Husnoo, M.A., Anwar, A., Chakrabortty, R.K., Doss, R., Ryan, M.J.: Differential privacy for IoT-enabled critical infrastructure: a comprehensive survey. *IEEE Access*, **9**, 153276–153304 (2021)

The Relation Between Mayer's Multimedia Theory and Berthoz's Simplexity Paradigm for Inclusive Education

Alessio Di Paolo[✉] [iD]

University of Salerno, Via Giovanni Paolo XXIII, 132, Fisciano, SA, Italy
adipaolo@unisa.it

Abstract. Our society is pervaded by the influence of the new technologies, present in every sphere, and used for a plurality of objectives, from simple information on events, news characterising the world around us, to education, which therefore envisages the use of the new technological means as a tool for personal and cultural growth. This preponderance of multimedia leads to a necessary updating of teachers' skills and their progressive adaptation to the new ways of communicating with children, through direct work on the design of activities that meet the needs of *everyone*. This implies a new way of constructing learning paths for their learners. In this contribution, two models will be presented and compared using inclusion as a key, namely Mayer's multimedia theory and Berthoz's simplexity theory. An attempt will be made to identify the points of connection between the two paradigms and their founding principles/properties, to rethink inclusive processes through multimedia, through a new perspective of intervention by the teacher and responding to the different cognitive and learning styles of the learners, according to a non-linear didactic approach that can be flexibly adapted to the change also characterising the field of special education.

Keywords: Inclusive Education · Multimedia Theory · Simplexity

1 Introduction

The current school context, reflection of an ever-changing society, threatens teachers with new challenges from an educational point of view, especially when dealing with students with Special Educational Needs. The need for access to information, analysis, validation and reflection of knowledge to be didactically transposed [1] also through the use of technologies, as effective devices to respond to the plurality of learners' cognitive styles is increasingly preponderant in the age of complexity, which requires, those who live and experience it every day, to find strategies to adapt to change in every aspect, from the individual to the social one [2]. Technologies, which represent the *extension of the human arm* [3], appear to be increasingly preeminent as means of communication as well as of education of the individual and, over time, have increasingly appeared in the educational field as well. In educational contexts, the computer gives the user the opportunity to *interact* with information by continuously constructing and *de*-constructing it.

© The Author(s), under exclusive license to Springer Nature Switzerland AG 2024
T. Guarda et al. (Eds.): ARTIIS 2023, CCIS 1936, pp. 317–331, 2024.
https://doi.org/10.1007/978-3-031-48855-9_24

It makes it possible to store, organise, transmit, receive, search, and transform an enormous amount of information of all kinds in all perceptive and communicative modes [4]. The computer also makes it possible to relate with great ease and versatility with those who are sitting in front of the screen [5]; it is a *multifunctional* tool that makes it possible to perform a wide variety of tasks, to develop creative paths, and to get involved. The structure assumed, in recent years, by teacher preparation has created the prerequisites for a rethinking of the practices and tools of didactic mediation and, therefore, of the *"activation of conditions capable of promoting a favourable impact between the student and the study disciplines"* [6], doing the conditions for a didactic *flexibility*, necessary to respond to the heterogeneity of educational needs. The universe of technologies that are also useful for disability includes, in fact, not only the equipment *"designed to prevent, compensate, control, alleviate or eliminate impairments, limitations in activities, or obstacles to participation"* [7], but also that *"system of artefacts that can enhance didactic communication and as such intervene in teaching/learning processes"* [8]. In addition, there is a progressive increase in global connectivity [9], which therefore progressively enables everyone, regardless of where in the world they are, to have access to digital. This change of perspective, therefore, requires teacher adaptation, education about the new technologies, and the experimentation of educational practices focused on the learner's needs and the possible ways in which they can be met through *personalised* and *individualised* didactic interventions [10]. In this contribution, two theories will be considered, trying to draw a comparison between them from an inclusive perspective, namely Mayer's [11] multimedia theory, which defines twelve rules for good didactic design in the digital domain, and Berthoz's [12] theory of simplexity, which studies how organisms can progressively adapt to their environment through the use of properties and rules of operation with which they can do so, transposed to different fields of study, including education [13, 14]. The first part of the paper will present, specifically, Mayer's multimedia theory; in the second part of the paper, on the other hand, we will focus on the analysis of the theory of simplexity in relation to multimedia and the new technologies; in the third part of the paper we will attempt to create a parallelism between the two theories, through an inclusive view, with the aim of understanding how the use of these two paradigms can produce a change of perspective in the way of working with students with Special Educational Needs.

2 Mayer's Multimedia Theory

A good cognitive and learning process presupposes at its basis that the learner can *identify*, *reflect*, and *operate* metacognitively on the processes implemented during the learning process [15, 16], which therefore presupposes an operant consciousness that guides the learning processes. In the technological declination of this idea, an innovative form of interaction is realised, much broader than the simple interaction between biological systems, as the idea of a human-machine interaction matures. The cognitive theory of multimedia learning proposed by the psychologist Mayer, assumes that students actively construct their own *understanding from the material presented to them*. This theory is based on research in deciding how best to support students through design choices related to the selection of what to include in the teaching-learning process and how to organise it.

Mayer ascertains that our working memory is always limited. One's individual working memory capacity might be a little larger or a little smaller than that of others, but it will never be unlimited. Learning anything will always put a strain on one's working memory. Everything a person can learn has a *germane load* - i.e., the load on the working memory - that is inherent and necessary. But the way this input is presented can increase the total cognitive load. By implementing good learning projects, we can keep the germane load low. In fact, a good educational project is effective when it adapts to the needs of the subjects for whom it is intended, to their *limits* and *potential*, in a flexible mode [17]. The non-verbal channel deals with everything else, with elements that are not expressed directly through the voice and all that may be subject to verbal language [18]. Thus, if there is a video using sign language and written text, e.g., subtitles, both should be processed by the verbal channel. However, if there is an audio text and a drawing, only the audio text will be processed by the verbal channel and the drawing by the non-verbal channel. This means that instead of sending all your *metaphorical boats* [19] down a single river, clogging it up, you are sending some boats down one river, some boats down another river, and everything can travel smoothly.

The other system that is used is the distinction between visual and auditory channels. If you have written text and animation, both will put a strain on the visual channel. If you have text and animation, it will draw on both systems and may avoid overloading one of these channels. Therefore, teachers may also turn to the corresponding channels to enable students to follow instructions or content. They might use meaningful hand signs while explaining a problem, they might show pictures while telling a story or develop sketch notes while referring to grammatical phenomena [20].

Based on these assumptions, several theories have been developed that can guide the design of teaching materials. One of which is the principle of consistency, which encourages us to include only what is necessary - and to leave out what is not necessary. Extra details that seem interesting but not necessary: what does not contribute to the *essence of the material* can be left out to reduce the cognitive load. Another important principle here is the principle of *temporal continuity*. If you have an image and a narrative explaining the image, present them at the same time. For example, if you have designed a PowerPoint presentation: present the image and the corresponding illustrative commentary on one slide (see Table 1).

Table 1. Summary of Mayer's ideas about temporal continuity

Goal	Representative techniques	Description of technique
Minimize extraneous processing	Coherence principle	Eliminate extraneous material
	Signaling principle	Highlight essential material
	Redundancy principle	Do not add printed text to spoken text
	Spatial contiguity principle	Place printed text near corresponding graphic
	Temporal contiguity principle	Present narration and corresponding graphic simultaneously

Mayer's cognitive theory of multimedia learning, therefore, supports us in designing material that works for students with different working memory capacities. But there are some caveats here. Firstly, the idea of using *multiple channels* may fail if some students simply cannot use one of these channels. It is often better to give more space to one channel than to depend on a channel that is not needed by one's students. A deaf student may benefit much more from written text or a sign language video, although this text or video, in combination with a graphic or animation, may risk overloading the visual channel. One can think, again, of supporting them by presenting the information in appropriately sized blocks, allowing them to pause the input or review parts of it.

Also, when looking at language learning. When learners are still acquiring a language, whether in the foreign language classroom or in other contexts, being able to hear and read the same words at the same time can be an important support. Listening comprehension tends to be much higher when students can read while listening. This is very clear, for example, when watching videos in the target language with subtitles. Several studies [21–23] have studied language learners with dyslexia. They found that these students benefited even more from the combination of spoken and written language.

From this perspective, following Mayer's cognitive theory of multimedia learning is useful as a starting point, especially since these rules can be a guide in designing material with appropriate cognitive load and avoiding unnecessary and potentially harmful bells and whistles. On the other hand, for accessibility reasons, one can and should add alternatives for perceiving information for those students who require it. Ideally, these can be hidden from people who do not need them. Subtitles that can be switched on or off are a good example of this.

In this, Mayer's theory offers the opportunity by minimising extraneous processing. To offer a summary of further rules, the following summary is presented (see Table 2).

Table 2. Mayer's rules

Goal	Representative techniques	Description of technique
Manage essential processing	Segmenting principle	Break presentation into parts
	Pre-training principle	Describe names and characteristics of key elements before the lesson
	Modality principle	Use spoken rather than printed text
Foster generative processing	Multimedia principle	Use words and pictures rather than words alone
	Personalization principle	Put words in conversational style
	Voice principle	Use human voice for spoken words
	Embodiment principle	Give onscreen characters human-like gestures
	Emotional design principle	Make onscreen elements prime positive emotion
	Generative activity principle	Provide prompts for learning strategies
	Guided discovery principle	Provide hints and feedback as learner solves problems
	Mapping principle	Ask learners to create a graphic organizer or concept map
	Self-explanation principle	Ask learners to explain a lesson to themselves
	Drawing principle	Ask learners to make drawings for the lesson
	Imagination principle	Ask learners to imagine drawings for the lesson

These principles originate with the idea of respecting the learner's cognitive styles, attempting to avoid cognitive overload when there are multiple cognitive styles that may create learning difficulties in the learner, guiding them when they need didactic support to learn more *successfully* and *meaningfully* [24]. It also envisages breaking down learning channels and not associating them when they generate greater learning difficulties, or presenting neighbouring stimuli when other learners need cohesion between channels to learn better. It also envisages the segmentation of the lesson into modules, when a single presentation of a plurality of topics could create a learning trouble, as well as the choice of specific channels when these are more pertinent to the student's *modus operandi* and closer to his way of expressing himself, of communicating with others, thus intervening with the use of image, voice, graphic text. These principles are respectful of pivotal objectives such as personalisation, didactic individualisation for students with Special Educational Needs [8], outlining scenarios of action that are highly inclusive and tailored to *each* and *every one* [25].

3 Between Complexity and Simplicity: Simplexity

The society in which we are, the living beings that govern it, are characterised by an underlying *complexity* [26]. Complexity derives its etymology from '*cum*' (with), '*plexum* (to hold). The complex structure, therefore, is configured as a plurality of elements intersected and balanced by a system that governs and regulates its parts, i.e. man, insofar as he is capable, through internal functions and rules to enable it to function correctly, of finding adaptive strategies through which he can *decipher* the plurality of stimuli and problems associated with them, finding from time to time the right way, the least used way, to deal with the problem. Complexity, therefore, does not presuppose its elimination, but rather the objective of *making those who navigate in it*, to seek out, from time to time, operational trajectories, *flexible* and *adaptive* modes of resolution. The belonging of a system to a given class of systems (e.g., linear, non-linear, static, dynamic, autopoietic, heteropoietic systems, etc.) is determined by its organisation, by the way in which an observer encodes the structure of the relationships between its parts [27].

In this sense, complexity cannot be regarded as an intrinsic property of a given type of systems or phenomena, a property objectively present in a system and independent of the observer and external conditions, but rather a condition intrinsic to each constituent element of the system itself, from those who compose it to those who must analyse it.

Complexity is given as systems are prefigured as an association, a set of biological, social, cultural constituent elements, in turn interconnected with other systems with similar traits. In addition to this, there is an interconnection with the surrounding environment, composed of material and immaterial elements with which to interface during one's life, and which require organisational as well as *interpretative capacities* of reality [28]. The plurality, diversity, *protean* manifestation of structural elements necessitates an explanatory and *de*-constructive ability to analyze reality, hence the ability to highlight the constituents implicit in each system to be able to provide solutions of emerging problems. It is obvious that, according to this view, complexity is not a stable property of a system, but reflects the type of *relationship* and possible evolutions that characterise the connection between *observer* and *system* [29]. This indefinite, uncertain perspective of complexity is characterised by the mutability associated with time and the changes inherent in it, the passing of events that bring with them natural variations, which must be considered. These changes can occur at an individual level, with growth, personal development, as well as at an environmental, structural level, linked to conditions, calamities that affect reality from time to time. The ability of those who approach complexity is to become a complex system; that is, one that thrives on complexity and interprets complexity, but also *adaptive*, that is, consisting *"of components, or agents, that interact with each other according to sets of rules that require them to examine and respond to each other's behaviour in order to improve their behaviour and thus the behaviour of the system they comprise. In other words, such system operates in a manner that constitutes learning"* [30]. In order to be defined as belonging to systems of a complex and adaptive type, it is necessary to be made up of several parts that are in turn more or less complex: in general, the more numerous and complex the parts that make up the system, the more complex the system as a whole is; to be determined in their identity and wholeness by the *non-linear interactions* of their constituent parts [31].

Indeed, the emerging characteristics of the system and its very development depend on these interactions. This aspect makes the evolution and development of the system *non-predeterminable*. At the same time, the non-linearity of the parts produces the impossibility of defining the functioning in detail and understanding its details, highlighting the difference between systems that can be defined as *complicated* and *complex* systems [32].

One can therefore envisage how man is himself a complex and at the same time *adaptive system*, constantly living on *non-linear interactions*, which make it impossible to predetermine the outcomes of one's own action precisely because of the internal and external mutability that he is constantly faced with and to which he constantly attempts to adapt. The keystone that, however, can provide support in this process, and thus help man to seek out which modes of intervention can manifest his own flexibility to variation, is given by the search for internal characteristics that drive every living being, in a natural way, *to adapt to change*, also through the application of these characteristics following application schemes, well-defined *rules*. Berthoz, a neuroscientist at the Collége du France, defines these as *properties* and *rules*. The neurophysiologist, in his theory of simplexity, points out how organisms, and thus also humans, find solutions from time to time to adapt to change, through personal characterising forms and application rules that, in their relationship with the other than themselves, enable them to cope with the complex, without, however, *denying its presence*. The scholar proposes a simplistic vision of reality, that is, a reality that does not shy away from complexity, nor does it attempt to simplify it. To act in a simplexity manner means to seek, from time to time, ways of adapting to the surrounding complexity of reality, ways in which to *search* for ways of *re*-coding as a function of the action exercised to adapt to the problems present in the various systems with which one interfaces every day. This *simple* complexity, reduced and recoded as a function of action, in a form compatible with one's needs, is, properly speaking, simplexity [33]. The way in which man can intervene in this process of *deciphering* and *coping* with reality can be summarised in *action*. In fact, to render Berthoz's proposal succinctly, one could say that *"if the foundation of meaning is in the act"* and if *"elaborating a theory of simplexity means elaborating a theory of meaning"*, then simplexity constitutes a *theory of the act*, i.e., a theory aimed at providing a conceptual tool to decipher complexity by resolving it in the *act* and not only in action.

It is only through direct action, the active manipulation of the elements, of the complexity inherent in them, that it is possible to intervene directly in order to manipulate the variables innate in reality, to unhinge the totality into what are its constituent elements, to attempt to consider them individually in order to be able to understand to what extent they can be useful as problem-solving modalities, as elements that, even in complexity, allow for *de*-complexification.

It is necessary to clarify that in these terms, simplexity should not be considered as a theoretical matrix of procedures and methods, but rather as a guideline capable of orienting action strategies and providing operational suggestions through the identification of functioning patterns.

In this perspective, the simplexity properties and rules identified by Berthoz have the function of *deciphering* a complexity, which can be faced in terms of data processing and *decision-making* between alternative opportunities [27].

Such an approach, contextualised to a *systemic, complex,* and *adaptive* vision, has clear implications on the concept of knowledge, which is configured as an adaptive process that develops in the *Umwelt* of the subjects engaged in the learning experience [34]. To know means precisely to *explore* the opportunities that are provided to us from time to time, to *evaluate* what the best actions to use may be to intervene directly to be able to interpret not only one's own system, but all the systems that surround us [35].

The focal point, therefore, of the simplexity system, is precisely the *interaction* between components, the *inter*-systemic dialogue that allows each individual system to recognise itself as its own, *unique,* unrepeatable characteristics, but at the same time inserted in a fabric made up of other systems, other characterising traits, other systems that in turn interact and share elements of experience, previous experiences, different backgrounds and find their own *harmonisation* in the link with others.

To cope with complexity, however, Berthoz identifies six properties and six rules, which are useful for interpret the system in which we are embedded in a simplexity way. Properties can be defined as enabling different *patterns of interaction* between the constituent portions of a system and provide the basis for an interpretation of the behaviour of living systems *"The reoccurrence, in different living organisms, of identical or similar patterns, which perform precise and important functions, is a good example of what I call the simplexity of living matter"*. Regarding rules, on the other hand, they can be defined as simple rules on which adaptive models of educational action are based in the presence of different types and degrees of educational complexity. Such models offer solutions that allow formative complexity to be processed through a rich combination of simple rules *"Simplexity is intentional, respects energy but, at times, consumes energy. It considers lived time, starts from the subject, allows for a change of point of view, creation, authorises tolerance that is mastered opinion"*.

Wanting to analyse properties and rules in the aspect of multimedia, it is useful to precisely describe the characteristics, the operational patterns, defined as *properties*:

- *Specialisation and modularity*: in nature, living organisms manifest the need for a coexistence of different functions guaranteed by the possibility of using modular functioning that allows for a simultaneous usability of profoundly different adaptive patterns. This property allows organisms to separate different specialised functions, acting at different times, to ensure proper adaptation to the surrounding reality. These functions operate in well-defined temporal modules, so that the flow of actions of each different channel, of each individual function, is harmonised in time. In the field of multimedia, this property can be interpreted as an attempt to separate, even within a single medium such as a Power Point or a support tool, the different channels that can *co-exist*. It means giving space at a time to one type of channel, such as verbal, graphic, sound, separating them from each other by establishing precise times to do so, to be effective and achieve one's objectives.

- *Speed*: in nature, organisms react quickly to danger, implementing effective intervention strategies to provide immediate solutions to problems that arise from time to time. This is possible through the perception of immediate feedback from the external environment. Wanting to transpose this property to the field of multimedia, speed is transposed into the sudden change of tools, digital intervention tools, immediate change of study support media, based on the *feedback* received at the time following the application of a given software or tool. Thus, it provides for an immediate change of mediator if the previous one does not produce the desired results.

- *Reliability*: to reduce the error rate in the detection of information and consequently increase the probability of success in solving problem situations, especially regarding multilevel systems, it is required to increase reliability through "*original solutions, such as redundancy, the paradoxical use of noise, the cooperation between inhibition and excitation, the use of coupled oscillators, with properties such as contractance*". Reliability, therefore, requires that there is a full correspondence between stated goals and practical action. Wanting to transpose this property into a multimedia perspective, trustworthiness involves the wise choice of one medium over another, appropriate to a certain cognitive style over another. Therefore, the choice of a good medium that adapts well to the cognitive style of the learner can be useful when, to achieve a certain learning objective, it is necessary to choose one medium that is more congenial and useful than another.

- *Flexibility, vicariance and adaptation to change*: Adaptation of living systems requires flexibility and a disposition to change, i.e. the use of solutions that, depending on the context, make it possible to deal with new situations by drawing on a rich repertoire of diversified actions "*An organism, in order to solve a problem, must be able to perceive, capture, decide or act in many ways (vicariousness) depending on the context, compensate for deficits, deal with new situations*". Flexibility translates into the ability to use the same tool also in situations of change in an original way, to achieve the resolution of an emerging problem. YouTube, for example, can be used at a moment's notice to listen to music, songs that can support a certain activity, but it can also be used to highlight subtitles in a presentation, it can be used to search for summary materials to explain certain topics. The medium remains useful; however, it can be adapted to the changing situation.

- *Memory*: memory represents the tool that organisms use to be able to reproduce operational and action patterns, reproposing them as needed in different contexts. Memory represents the toolbox in which past actions can be collected, tools preserved, and which can be *re*-proposed when needed. Multimedia precisely gives the possibility of preserving material, collecting elements that can be reproposed, if necessary, in various situations, both didactic and otherwise. It is possible, therefore, to draw from one's toolbox, from time to time, the most useful tool, or the most useful function, to be able to apply them when needed, to face and cope with new situations-problems.

- *Generalisation*: generalisation represents a property that enables the coping with similar complexities, the possibility of transposing functions in different contexts, even if not perfectly corresponding. This implies drawing from memory through the retrieval of old operational schemes, perhaps already consolidated, and being able to reapply them in new contexts without changing their operational structures, the way they are applied, or doing so partially. As previously emphasised, multimedia favours this process, allowing memory to retain newly applicable schemes, documents, software, tools that can be used again in entirely new situations.

Properties, i.e., implicit characteristics, cannot exist unless they are concretely enforceable through rules of use. This is where rules come into play:

- *Inhibition and the principle of refusal*: in facing particularly complex situations, it is useful to establish which actions, operational trajectories to put in place, leaving others aside, not because they are less useful than those applied, but rather because they are unsuitable for the situation at hand and practical in other circumstances. Multimedia allows precisely such a trajectory, in that it provides the user with a plurality of operational coordinates, a multiplicity of resources that can be exploited not necessarily all at the same time, but at different times and choosing those that are suitable for the situation at hand, discarding others for other circumstances. Not all programmes can have the same effect on a child or adolescent; therefore, the one most suited to his or her cognitive and learning style, to his or her *prevailing intelligence*, will be chosen from time to time, while others will be allocated to other children and adolescents with a more appropriate cognitive style.
- *Principle of specialisation and selection- Umwelt*: Specialisation and selection are configured as regulatory rules that allow the adaptive functions to maintain the *identity* of each system through a specific selection process conditioned by its own Umwelt. The instruments of information selection closely linked to the functions of attention do not depend exclusively on cognitive factors, they are linked to memory as well as context and have a very close connection to the idea of *Umwelt* whereby *"We create worlds according to our needs"*. Working with multimedia means attributing to each individual constituent element of the operating system, of applications, a specific function to be used for that individual case. It means allowing targeted intervention with programmes, tools targeted so that one can operate with similar modalities to obtain positive results with the specificity of the action.
- *Probabilistic Anticipation*: this rule makes it possible to anticipate actions, based on experience, to favour the achievement of certain objectives more quickly. It means playing in advance, using strategies to anticipate certain results. Multimedia, in this sense, is a good means of intervening to achieve certain results because of actions already used in the past. If, for example, a YouTube video has had a beneficial effect on pupils before, the same programme can be assumed to be used in a subsequent lesson, thus avoiding new research, planning new actions, if the goal is to achieve a given objective.

- *Detour*: Callimachus [36], in outlining the trajectories to be followed to reach a goal, invites the reader to explore new paths, roads that are still unexplored, and which nevertheless content to reach the set goal, using new modes of action, innovative tools with which to act. Detour consists precisely in tracing operational trajectories using the new, the exploration of new operational frontiers, of new tools to be used through experimentation, to understand which one can be the one through which to achieve positive outcomes. Detour, according to an application scheme using multimedia, represents a rule of simplification of the adaptation process, which utilizes an accessory complexity to make the control of the system more effective. The rule of detour corresponds to the rules of using a *non-linear solution path*, given by experimenting with multiple operational channels, different technical trajectories, through which to move away from schematically established paths, to use combinations of simple variables (software, programmes) that evolve into compound variables, which are more effective for solving complex problem situations.
- *Cooperation and Redundancy*: it can often be the case that to achieve certain objectives it is necessary to intervene by using their synergic and *harmonic cooperation* rather than the separation of channels. A Power Point can be set up either by using writing only, or by associating images, sounds, even subtitles during a presentation, to enable the user to fully understand its meaning. A video extrapolated from YouTube can be used either with subtitles in case it is difficult to convey a given content by means of image and voice alone, or through the merging of channels, should the recipient have more *flexibility* in learning through the merging of several channels. This is useful to understand how, in certain cases, intervening by implementing this principle, which is based precisely on the combined use of channels in an even original and varied manner, can support the reduction of the probability of error by providing several evaluations of the same variable. In particular, "*A solution is defined as cooperative when it examines variables that are important for perception or action*".
- *Sense*: the sense rule represents the synthesis of all other principles and properties, as it corresponds to a rule that establishes the link and functioning between *means* and *act*, redefining their relationship, and *re*-framing their meaning. Elaborating a theory on the adaptation mechanisms of living systems, in which the act is acknowledged to be fully central, means affirming the principle of meaning whose foundation is in the act itself "*Given that the simplest solutions are guided by an intention, an end, a function*". A multimedia tool allows for an effective didactic mediation, it allows the teaching-learning process to be meaningful, as it is close to the child's way of communicating and expressing himself, to his way of relating to and informing himself about what surrounds him, growing culturally as well as personally. Multimedia becomes a means of expressing oneself, narrating, confronting, deepening. In this sense, it encompasses a sense that is already implicit and emerging whenever the user wishes to make use of it.

4 Multimedia Theory and Simplexity: Inclusive Connecting Points

Wanting to draw a possible connection between Mayer's multimedia theory and Berthoz's theory of simplexity, it is useful to compare the different rules set out by the author, highlighting the points of similarity with the properties and rules outlined by the French neurophysiologist. Mayer describes as the first rule that of *coherence*, i.e., using words, sounds, taking care to exclude others if these may cause a cognitive overload on the learner. This principle could relate to that of *inhibition and refuse*. Often, especially when working with pupils with Special Educational Needs, it is necessary to choose the medium that is most congenial to them to mediate the lesson, rather than proposing a plurality that would have a negative effect on cognitive input. From this perspective, acting, even in multimedia, following such trajectories is useful to flexibly adapt to the peculiarities of individual learners, as well as to prevent them from being over-stimulated by a variety of stimuli, adapting teaching so that it is for everyone [37]. The principle of *signalling*, which describes how people learn better when they highlight the most relevant topics on the screen in order to be able to better commit them to memory, is linked to the property of *memory*, which defines precisely the possibility of being able to act better when it is possible to mechanise patterns of action through recourse to memory itself, in order to be able to reuse them when necessary. In an inclusive perspective, these rules and properties are useful when the learner needs to encompass a range of content and acquire a range of skills through direct exercise of the mind to flexibly channel knowledge and skills. The principle of *redundancy* as defined by Mayer, on the other hand, contrasts with that outlined by Berthoz, in that the former argues that an excessive load of stimuli can invalidate learning, while the latter by redundancy precisely means the ability to experiment with multiple and innovative actions, channels and methods of intervention to make the didactic intervention more learner friendly. However, Mayer's principle of *redundancy* can be connected to the property of *specialisation and modularity*, as it envisages that teaching intervention with students with Special Educational Needs is implemented through a separation of channels at a time in well-defined time modules, to avoid cognitive overload. Mayer's rules of *spatial and temporal contiguity* can also be linked to Berthoz's rules of *cooperation and redundancy*, in that they both envisage that the association between channels and the original use of them can become a tool not only for improving learning, but also for motivating the student, useful for increasing the desire to learn and learn. One of the fundamental goals of special pedagogy and special education is to find all possible means through which to foster *motivation to participate* [38], increasing students' sense of *self-efficacy* [39].

Mayer's rule of *segmentation*, on the other hand, which envisages how the segmentation of the lesson into specialised sub-actions, producing improvements in students' learning, can be connected to the rule of *specialisation and selection*, which focuses precisely on the subdivision of actions and channels, assigning specific tasks to each to improve students' learning, especially where they have educational needs. Mayer's *pre-training* rule finds points of similarity with the rule of *probabilistic anticipation*, in that it predicts that the anticipation of tasks, as well as the description of what the learning activities will be, will improve the learner's performance as well as further encourage him or her to study and desire for education. Playing in advance, using different modalities depending on the person, can certainly allow for an improvement in the sphere of interest in the topic or what is about to be presented, arousing attention even before a didactic intervention. The rule of *modality*, on the other hand, outlines how during a teaching intervention the choice of channel must vary according to the needs of the learner, his or her personal needs in each space and time.

One cannot expect to use the same media medium or different media focused on the same stimulus. The medium, the channel, must be changed flexibly, to truly respond to what the needs of the student are, especially when they have Special Educational Needs [40]. This principle is linked to Berthoz's property of *flexibility*, in that it advocates a similar idea, namely that while using a single medium, perhaps centred on the same channel, the skill must be to adapt it to the external perturbations of the learner; hence, to be able to adapt it to the circumstances that arise from time to time, according to a strongly inclusive perspective.

The principle of *multimedia*, which provides not only that the student learns best through the use of multimedia, but that associated words and images can often be adaptable to new situations, since they have a good effect on the students' learning in any case, is linked to Berthoz's property of *generalisation*, which argues that the use of a channel or a certain didactic action can be repeated over time in similar or new situations, where it has previously led to positive results. In working with students, especially those with Special Educational Needs, it is necessary to know what actions may have had positive results in a previous action, especially if applied to the same case of difficulty or disability for which the original intervention, the initial action, was intended. Attempting, moreover, to adapt the same action even for completely different cases by remodelling parts of the action itself can be useful in extending the range of possible interventions to improve learning and make it more meaningful [41].

Mayer's rule of *personalisation*, which emphasises that the use of a conversational and informal style is more useful than a formal style to interact with the students, to communicate with them to achieve those learning objectives that one had set oneself to achieve. In this sense, this rule relates to the property of *reliability*, which precisely envisages the choice of shrewd actions aimed at matching the declared with the acted, i.e., a full coincidence between the objectives to be achieved and those achieved in the end. Operating in a didactic sense by applying these rules and properties is useful when working with students with Special Educational Needs and wanting to accomplish a given objective, a given level of competence, preparing materials, actions, which allow the effective attainment of what has been set. The rules of *voice and image*, which emphasise how these two channels can be used to speed up learning processes and achieve the desired results immediately. From this perspective, these rules are linked to the simple principle of *detour*, in that it envisages the success of a given objective through *alternative operational trajectories* that enable the various objectives to be reached in different ways, especially when the action is aimed at students with Special Educational Needs, who require the implementation of different operational paths to enable full and effective training.

5   Conclusions

The digital age represents an educational challenge, especially when students with Special Educational Needs are involved in this process. The necessary adaptation of didactic processes to the child's way of expressing himself, communicating, imposes a change of perspective in didactic intervention on the part of teachers. Teachers not only have to become *reflective practioners* (i.e. reasoning *in itinere* on their *modus operandi* and on the strategies and methodologies they choose from time to time in order to implement their students' learning, but also require constant and continuous training, in line with the dictates of the *Profile of the Inclusive Teacher* [42], which proposes constant training on the issues and skills currently widespread among children, in order to assume a way of interacting, a way of communicating that is equal. This, therefore, presupposes a move away from methodological practices that are too traditional, embracing the idea that didactics can also be characterised by a *non-linearity* [43] of teaching-learning processes, leaving room for experimentation, for methodological innovation.

This does not presuppose the refuse of traditional practices, but rather their *flexible adaptation* to the changing, *liquid modernity* [44], which is constantly evolving and needs to adapt to change. Mayer's theory of multimedia and the paradigm of simplexity proposed by Berthoz would seem to accurately propose a change of perspective on how to work with the pupil, especially when in need of *individualised* and *personalised* interventions. First of all, they propose a change of perspective with respect to the actors of the action, that is, the teachers, who should carefully reflect on the materials to be chosen to conduct a lesson, on how to order them and structure them in order to achieve the fundamental objective of teaching *for all* and *for each one* [45], respect for the cognitive style of each individual learner and the choice of the systems most likely to favour their development. They also propose the choice of didactic actions that can be applicable in different contexts, in different situations, actions that can also adapt abruptly to the change and feedback received during the teaching and learning process. Despite their being born separately in two such apparently separate fields, i.e., psychology and neuroscience, a possible dialogic vision of them and their possible didactic application in an inclusive key, could be an interesting starting point for more rational use of multimedia resources, methodological strategies based on the use of interactive resources, adaptable to the student and his peculiarities.

References

1. Chevallard, Y.: La transposition didactique. La pensée sauvage, Grenoble (1985)
2. Rivoltella, P.C., Rossi, P.G.: Il corpo e la macchina. Tecnologia, cultura, educazione. Scholé, Brescia (2019)
3. De Kerckhove, D.: Psicotecnologie connettive. EGEA Spa., Milano (2014)
4. Sibilio, M.: L'interazione didattica. Scholé, Brescia (2020)
5. Papert, S. A.: Mindstorms: Children, Computers, and Powerful Ideas. Basic Books (2020)
6. Damiano, E.: La mediazione didattica. Per una teoria dell'insegnamento. FrancoAngeli, Milano (2013)
7. Andrich, R., Pilati, G. (eds.): Le tecnologie assistive nel progetto di autonomia della persona con disabilità: suggerimenti di buona prassi. Studi Zancan (2009)
8. Baldacci, M.: Personalizzazione o individualizzazione? Trento: Edizioni Erickson (2005)
9. UNICEF: Annual Report 2021 (2021). https://www.unicef.org/topics/annual-report
10. Fernández-Batanero, J.M., Montenegro-Rueda, M., Fernández-Cerero, J., García-Martínez, I.: Digital competences for teacher professional development. Systematic review. Eur. J. Teach. Educ. **45**(4), 513–531 (2022). https://doi.org/10.1080/02619768.2020.1827389

11. Mayer, R.E.: Multimedia Learning. Psychology of Learning and Motivation, vol. 41, pp. 85–139.1212. Academic Press (2002)
12. Berthoz, A.: La semplessità. Codice, Torino (2011)
13. Sibilio, M.: La didattica semplessa. Liguori, Napoli (2014)
14. Aiello, P., Pace, E.M., Sibilio, M.: A simplex approach in Italian teacher education programmes to promote inclusive practices. Int. J. Incl. Educ., 1–14 (2021). https://doi.org/10.1080/13603116.2021.1882056
15. Cornoldi, C.: Metacognizione e apprendimento. Il mulino, Bologna (1999)
16. Dunlosky, J., Metcalfe, J.: Metacognition. Sage Publications, Newbury (2008)
17. Zairul, M.: A thematic review on student-centred learning in the studio education. J. Crit. Rev. 7(2), 504–511 (2020). https://doi.org/10.31838/jcr.07.02.95
18. Key, M.R.: The relationship of verbal and nonverbal communication. In: The Relationship of Verbal and Nonverbal Communication. De Gruyter Mouton, Germania (2011)
19. Argaman, E.: In the same boat? On metaphor variation as mediating the individual voice in organizational change. Appl. Linguist. 29(3), 483–502 (2008). https://doi.org/10.1093/applin/amn021
20. Philippe, S., et al.: Multimodal teaching, learning, and training in virtual reality: a review and case study. Virtual Real. Intell. Hardw. 2(5), 421–442 (2020). https://doi.org/10.1016/j.vrih.2020.07.008
21. Sibilio, M., Di Tore, S.: Body, movement and space for simplex didactics: a pilot study on the realization of a font for specific learning disabilities. Educ. Sci. Soc. 4(2) (2014). https://riviste.unimc.it/index.php/es_s/article/view/790/542
22. Di Tore, S.: La tecnologia della parola. Didattica inclusiva e lettura. FrancoAngeli, Milano (2016)
23. Košak-Babuder, M., Kormos, J., Ratajczak, M., Pižorn, K.: The effect of read-aloud assistance on the text comprehension of dyslexic and non-dyslexic English language learners. Lang. Test. 36(1), 51–75 (2019). https://doi.org/10.1177/0265532218756946
24. Ausubel, D.P.: Educazione e processi cognitivi. Guida psicologica per gli insegnanti. FrancoAngeli, Milano (2004)
25. Sibilio, M., Aiello, P.: Formazione e ricerca per una didattica inclusiva. FrancoAngeli, Milano (2015)
26. Morin, E.: La sfida della complessità. Casa Editrice Le lettere, Firenze (2011)
27. Sibilio, M.: La dimensione semplessa dell'agire didattico. Traiettorie non lineari nella ricerca. Nuovi scenari interdisciplinari, pp. 10–14 (2012)
28. Bocchi, G., Ceruti, M. (eds.): La sfida della complessità. Pearson Spa, Torino (2007)
29. Von Uexküll, T.: A teoria da Umwelt de Jakob von Uexküll. Revista do Programa de Pós-Graduação em Comunicação e Semiótica, Galáxia, p. 7 (2004). ISSN 1982-2553
30. Davies, L.: Education and Conflict: Complexity and Chaos. Routledge, Londra (2013)
31. Gell-Mann, M.: What is complexity. Complexity 1(1), 16–19 (1995). https://doi.org/10.1002/cplx.6130010105
32. Sibilio, M.: Simplex didactics: a non-linear trajectory for research in education. Revue de synthèse 136(3–4), 477–493 (2015). https://doi.org/10.1007/s11873-015-0284-4
33. Petit, J.: Complexité-Simplexité - De la simplexité au champ phénoménal: La réponse du vivant à la complexité (2012). http://www.jeanlucpetit.com/sites/default/files/seminaire_complexite-simplexite_23-24.05.12.pdf
34. Aiello, P., Di Tore, S., Di Tore, P.A., Sibilio, M.: Didactics and simplexity: umwelt as a perceptive interface. Edu. Sci. Soc. 1, 27–35 (2013). https://riviste.unimc.it/index.php/es_s/article/view/709
35. Galimberti, U.: Nuovo dizionario di psicologia: psichiatria, psicoanalisi, neuroscienze. Feltrinelli, Milano (2018)

36. Callimaco.: Opere. Testo greco a fronte, a cura di D'Alessio, G.B. Bur (trad. 1996), Milano (1996)
37. Klement, M., Chráska, M., Dostál, J., Marešová, H.: Multimediality and interactivity: traditional and comtemporary perception. Turk. Online J. Educ. Technol. **11**, 414–422 (2015)
38. D'Alonzo, L.: Dizionario di pedagogia speciale. Morcelliana, Brescia (2019)
39. Bandura, A.: Autoefficacia: Teoria e applicazioni. Edizioni Erickson, Trento (2000)
40. Efthymiou, E., Kington, A.: The development of inclusive learning relationships in mainstream settings: a multimodal perspective. Cogent Educ. **4**(1), 1304015 (2017). https://doi.org/10.1080/2331186X.2017.1304015
41. Pavone, M.R.: Personalizzare l'integrazione. Un progetto educativo per l'handicap tra professionalità docente e dimensione comunitaria. La scuola, Brescia (2004)
42. European Agency for Special Needs and Inclusive Education (EASNIE): Teacher education for inclusion. Profile of inclusive teachers (2012). https://www.european-agency.org/
43. Sibilio, M., Zollo, I.: The non-linear potential of didactic action. Educ. Sci. Soc. Open Access **7**(2) (2016). https://journals.francoangeli.it/index.php/ess/article/view/3947
44. Bauman, Z.: Liquid Modernity. Wiley, New York (2013)
45. UNESCO: A guide for ensuring inclusion and equity in education (2017). http://www.unesco.org/

A Serious Game About Apps, Data-Sharing and Deceptive Design

Ingvar Tjostheim[✉] [ID]

Norwegian Computing Center (NR), Oslo, Norway
ingvar@nr.no

Abstract. Tricks used in websites and apps to make you do things that you do not intend to do are often referred to as dark pattern. This paper presents the board-game *Dark Pattern* about installing apps. The players draw cards, make choice about data that the app would like to collect and use. To win the player must avoid sharing personal data. The game was played with 102 students. After playing the game the players answered a survey with questions about their knowledge about the dark patterns types featured in the game. In addition, 50 students answered the same survey without playing the game. In the paper we present key findings about the dark patterns knowledge generated by playing the game and present an exploratory analysis using Partial Least Square – Structural Equation modelling (PLS-SEM). We analysed whether dark patterns knowledge and risk perception, the likelihood of negative incidents due to data sharing, could predict the players behavioural intention to take proactive privacy steps. The PLS-SEM models have a variance explained (R^2) of 0.17 indicating that 17% of the variance could be accounted for by the two variables included in the model. Taken together, the analyses indicated that playing the Dark Pattern game had weak positive effect on behavioural intention to proactive privacy steps.

Keywords: Serious games · Learning · User-test · Exploratory study · Dark patterns · Sharing of personal data · Partial least square modelling

In the digital economy you pay with your data, for instance by filling in information about yourself and letting service providers or third parties use that data. There are laws and regulations that should secure citizens greater control of their data. Although most citizens have smartphones full of apps and subscriptions to a number of digital services, privacy and data-protection are not important topics [1, 2].

There are several ways to learn about the digital economy, particularly why and how data are used by service providers and their partners. In this paper we present a board-game that builds upon data-sharing techniques and tricks companies use to gain consent from users [3]. The purpose of the game is to learn about why data are collected, which deceptive techniques are used to gain consent from users and inform about potential negative consequences for users in sharing of data. The remainder of the paper is organized as follows: Sect. 2 outlines a description of the game, followed by Sects. 3 and 4 where we present the key findings from the data-collection, the research questions and data analysis. In the final section, we conclude with a discussion of the results and their implications for future research on serious games.

T. Guarda et al. (Eds.): ARTIIS 2023, CCIS 1936, pp. 332–343, 2024.
https://doi.org/10.1007/978-3-031-48855-9_25

1 Learning About the Deceptive Design Patterns

Hartzog [4] defines design as the "processes that create consumer technologies and the results of their creative processes instantiated in hardware and software." A dark pattern is a term used to explain how designers use their knowledge of human behaviour and psychology, along with the desires of end users, to implement deceptive functionality that is not in the user's best interest [3]. Often, it is the recurrent configuration of elements in digital interfaces that leads the user to make choices against their best interests and towards those of the designer. The design induces false beliefs either through affirmative misstatements, misleading statements, or omissions. Mathur et al. [5] evaluated 1983 websites with dark patterns. They found that many dark patterns exploited cognitive biases, such as the default and framing effects. The website www.deceptive design (darkpatterns.org) lists 12 common types of dark patterns. Some are very conventional and easy to identify while others are less familiar and more subtly deceptive. For further information about dark patterns, see Luguri & Strahilevitz [6] who present a table of existing dark patterns taxonomies.

The Dark Pattern game was developed by Serious Games Interactive, a Danish company and the Norwegian Computing Center. It drew inspiration from the master thesis written by K. M. Nyvoll, *Serious Interactive Board Games: Increasing Awareness of Dark Patterns in Teenagers* [7]. To our current knowledge, we are not aware of a similar dark patterns games tailored for this age group.

Dark Pattern is a board-game for 3–5 players. The game is targeted at students aged 16–18, but any adult that have downloaded apps on a smart phone can play the game. In the game, each round lasts 20–30 min. The players, 3–5 individuals, have to choose one of the following roles: the Gamer, the Shopper, the Influencer, the Healthy and the Lover. The format is a board-game with cards, but the focus of play is upon apps and installing

Fig. 1. Two of the roles in the game and the 4 datatypes

apps. The first information players receive is: *"You just got a brand-new phone. You all want your type of apps on the phone (dating, SoMe, games, health, shopping) without giving away too much data about yourself."* The players choose apps according to their role; the Gaamer chooses and installs gaming apps on the game-board, the Shopper installs shopper apps on the game-board, and so on. For further information about the game, we refer to Tjostheim et al. 2022 [19].

Figure 1 shows the role the Gamer, three Dark Patterns card, the instruction on how to calculate points and the 4 types of data-cubes. Figure 2 shows two apps and the text on two Dark Patterns card. The names can be associated with genuine apps, but no real app names are used. A player must install several apps while attempting to have as few data-cubes as possible, either by discarding or avoiding them to win the game [19].

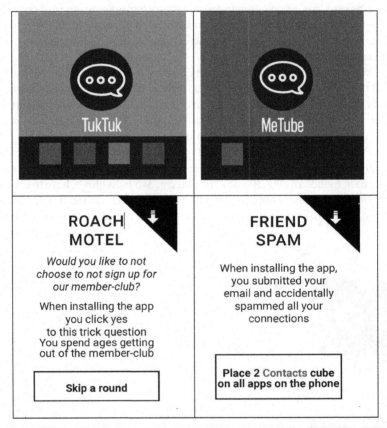

Fig. 2. The apps *TukTuk* and *MeTube,* and two Dark Pattern cards

When players read the Dark Pattern cards and decide which apps to use, they learn about the digital economy and what might go wrong when sharing their information. In Norway, students in higher secondary schools are taught about the digital economy and how to make choices online. It is a subject included in the national curriculum.

2   Data Collected, Research Questions and Data-Analysis

The aim of the research project was to help teenagers to reflect on data-sharing and increase their knowledge about data security. The survey that the players had to fill in was designed to find out they learned about sharing of personal data and what matters to them. We formulation these two research questions for the students who played the game.

RQ1 *To what extent did the game convey the meaning of the types of dark patterns presented in the game to the players?*

RQ2 *To what extent did dark pattern knowledge and perceived risk, the two variables in our model predict intention to protect personal data?*

To test the game and collect data that we could analyse, we contacted five upper secondary schools: four in Oslo, Norway and one in Copenhagen, Denmark. Students at this educational level are in their 11th - 13th years of schooling. Class teachers divided the students into groups of 3, 4 or 5. After a short introduction to the game and the students watched a 90-s video published on Vimeo. Then a rehearsal-session that lasted approximately 15 min started [19].

For a comparison we asked the schools in Oslo for students that should not play the game. We visited three classes and explained the students that the questionnaire was about deceptive techniques used to gain consent from users, and whether they had taken steps to protect their personal data. Then the students, 50 in total, filled in the questionnaire. We have named this group the non-players, see Table 1 (Fig. 3).

Once the practice session was completed, the students began playing the game. When the game was over, the students calculated the scores for each player and used those scores to determine the winner. After they were done playing, the students were given a questionnaire to fill in on their own phones.

Of the 102 players 56 students took part in a 60-min play-session. The second group with 46 students took part in a 75-min session. Based on observing the way players asked questions about the game in group 1 we decided to increase the time from 60 min to 75 min for group 2. Subsequently, the players in the second group had more time for a rehearsal and playing the game for at least two times before answering questions.

The questionnaire presents 7 actual dark patterns types plus 3 fake types. In the game the players get information of the 7 types, but not the 3 fake types. The questionnaire is designed to find out whether the respondents have a basic understanding of these 7 types, or can explain what they mean, followed by questions about intention to reinstall or replace apps. In the second half of the questionnaire, we asked whether the respondents felt there to be any detriment if negative consequences occurred, and whether they expected these negative incidents to happen.

Dark Patterns Set-Up ⤓

Fig. 3. The video about the Dark Pattern Set-Up

Table 1 presents three types of dark patterns in bold: disguised ads, trick questions and friend spam. These are the only three where a relatively high percentage the non-player respondents' (44%, 48% and 70%) report that understand the expression. We hypothesized that knowledge of the 7 types included in the game would be higher than the fake types which was the case. A comment about the fake types may be warranted. In a survey some respondents might guess that they have seen an expression, a certain dark pattern type. It is therefore an expected result that a low percentage answered that they know or know about a fake type.

The Table 2 presents some of the types of dark patterns in bold. These are disguised ads, trick questions and friend spam. These are the types which a high percentage of respondents' report that they understand the expression, at least 50%.

The Table 3 includes the result of the comparison between the players and the non-players by using a Mann-Whitney U test, a nonparametric statistical test that can be used

Table 1. Questions about dark patterns – Non-players (N = 50)

Dark patterns are activities to trick internet users into doing things they might not otherwise do. How much do you know about the following types of dark patterns?	Don't know what it means vs I have a basic understanding, or I can explain the expression
Uninstall Shaming (mean: 1.40)	86% - 14%
Malware Message (mean: 1.66)	78% - 22%
Roach Motel (mean: 1.14)	98% - 2%
Disguised Ads (mean: 2.46)	52% - 48%
Trick Questions (mean: 2.86)	30% - 70%
Friend Spam (mean: 2.30)	56% - 44%
Privacy Zuckering (mean: 1.62)	78% - 22%
Baking Story* (mean: 1.30)	92% - 8%
Intuitive Jobs* (mean: 1.44)	90% - 10%
Data Scaling* (mean: 1.60), * fake types	96% - 4%

Table 2. Questions about dark patterns – The players of the game (N = 102)

Dark patterns are activities to trick internet users into doing things they might not otherwise do. How much do you know about the following types of dark patterns?	Don't know what it means vs I have a basic understanding, or I can explain the expression
Uninstall Shaming (mean: 2.20)	57% - 43%
Malware Message (mean: 2.21)	59% - 41%
Roach Motel (mean: 1.42)	88% - 12%
Disguised Ads (mean: 2.86)	28% - **72%**
Trick Questions (mean: 2.96)	28% - **72%**
Friend Spam (mean: 2.49)	48% - **52%**
Privacy Zuckering (mean: 2.13)	61% - 39%
Baking Story* (mean: 1.52)	85% - 15%
Intuitive Jobs* (mean: 1.68)	82% - 18%
Data Scaling* (mean: 1.97), (* fake types)	71% - 29%

to assess differences between two groups. For 5 of the 7 real types, the self-reported knowledge is significantly higher for players.

We also included three fake types. We hypothesized that knowledge of the 7 real types would be higher than the fake types, but in a survey some respondents might guess that they have seen an expression, a certain dark patterns type. It is additionally important to note that not all cards are used when playing the game. It is therefore unlikely that 90% or more will report that they know an expression. However, it is also possible that a type named in the game will receive a low percentage. For example, Roach Motel has a very low percentage, where only 12% answered that they understood or could recognize the term. It is unlikely that the card has not been used in the game at least one time, but it seems that the meaning of the term was not communicated to the players. Table 3 shows no differences between the non-players and the players for the fake types.

Table 3. Questions about dark patterns – The players (N = 102) and the non-players (N = 50) of the game

I have a basic understanding, or I can explain the expression		
	Non-players - Players	Independent Samples Mann Whitney U test Z-score – Sig.
Uninstall Shaming	24% - 43%	−3.563 < **.001**
Malware Message	22% - 41%	−2.323 < **.020**
Roach Motel	2% - 12%	−2.016 < **.044**
Disguised Ads	48% - **72%**	−2.832. < **.005**
Trick Questions	**70% - 72%**	−.200 < .842
Friend Spam	44% - **52%**	−.919 < .358
Privacy Zuckering	22% - 39%	−2.105. < **.035**
Baking Story*	8% - 15%	−1.171 < .242
Intuitive Jobs*	10% - 18%	−1.232 < .218
Data Scaling*, (* fake types)	20% - 29%	−1.234 < .217

According to some researchers [9] there is no general theories in psychology dealing explicitly with the issue of risk perception, but it can be regarded as an subjective assessment of the perceived probability of an incident and the perceived probability of the results, most often—negative consequences of the incident. To operationalize friends spamming we asked questions about selling contacts data, as shown in Table 4.

Table 4 shows a Likert-scale with 7 answering options. When multiplying the two, potential harm with how likely, the range is 1 to 49. If a respondent answers no harm at all and not at all likely, the sum is 1. If a respondent answers very harmful and extremely likely, the sum is 49 (7 × 7). We then made a scale from 1 to 5 that we used in the analysis; 1–5 = 1, 6–11 = 2, 12–19 = 3, 20–29 = 4, 30–49 = 5.

For the first research question we conclude that the game conveyed the meaning of the dark patterns types with one exception, roach motel. For roach motel, the knowledge is on the level with the fake types, and even lower than data scaling. We learned that data scaling is a term in machine learning and statistics after we had used the term in the survey.

For the second research question that included a risk variable named risk perception. For this variable we developed a set of questions about harm due to data-sharing and to what extent expect respondents felt that an incident related to how data were used or mis-used would ensue. For risk perception we multiplied harm due to data-sharing with likeliness of a specific incident related to the data-sharing. What happens with our data, how they are used in marketing, in algorithms, and in building profiles of users are often not communicated. There are many reasons for this. Some companies see this information as a trade secret; information that competitors should not have access to.

We were interested in whether the players plan to take proactive steps to protect their data and how likely it is that the expected that misuse will happen. One might problematise how it is possible to answer the question, how likely is it that something will happen? This is a question with many possible answers, but it in the context of

Table 4. Risk perception as a combination of perceived harm of an incident and probabilities for the incident to occur.

How much harm do you feel can potentially result from the use of the data from apps you have your phone ?

	0 - No harm at all	1	2	3	4	5	6 - Very harmful
The app developer collect, analyze, and sell your **contacts data** to a sales company who then sells it to 10 other companies.	O	O	O	O	O	O	O
People in your contact list is then constantly spam-called by different sales companies.							

How likely do you think it is that you will experience the following?

	0 - Not at all likely	1	2	3	4	5	6 - Extremely likely
Through your decision to install an app, app developers collect, analyze, and sell your **contacts data** to a sales company who then sells it to 10 other companies.	O	O	O	O	O	O	O
People in your contact list is then constantly spam-called by different sales companies.							

dark patterns, the answers by the players might indicate concerns or awareness about data-sharing, rather than actual knowledge of what companies do. For the answer we used a Likert scale: from never (1) to always (5), from no harm (1) to extreme harm (6), and from never (1) to always (7). Table 5 shows the plan to take proactive steps, the behavioural intentions variable for the two groups. The table shows that majority did not plan to take proactive steps. Disabling GPS has the highest percentage with 48% - see Table 5.

In social science research, PLS-SEM has become a standard tool for studying relationships between observed and latent variables [8, 10]. This method, called structural equation modeling, analyses relationships between constructs. It helps us understand what we directly observe and the hidden factors that affect them. PLS path-modeling allows us to maximize explained variance of the dependent variables [11]. It's useful even if the research isn't based on a complete theory [12, 13]. This is why it is quite common to use PLS-SEM in exploratory research or in the early stages of a research project.

Table 5. Proactive steps - behavioural intentions

How often do you intend to perform the following actions in the next 30 days? (N = 102)

	Never or rarely vs
Disabling the GPS making it impossible for apps to track your location	sometimes or always
Deleting and reinstalling an app to get rid of accumulated data the app had access to	52%–48%
Getting a VPN connection which encrypts your data traffic and establishes a more secure internet connection	81%–19%
Putting a sticker on your camera making it impossible for apps to access your camera	80%–20%
Replacing apps for similar ones that require access to fewer data to function	76%–24%
Revising your app's permission settings so that the app is unable to access some data	89%–11%
	70%–30%

Table 6. The construct reliability and validity, and discriminant validity of the PLS path model

	Construct Reliability and Validity			Discriminant Validity		
	Cronbach's Alpha	Composite Reliability	Average Var. Extracted (AVE)	Beh intentions	DP knowledge	Risk percep
Dark pattern knowledge	0.749	0.798	0.383	**0.619**		
Behavioral intention	0.627	0.722	0.332	0.375	**0.576**	
Risk perception	0.809	0.799	0.378	−0.092	−0.195	**0.614**

When using PLS-SEM, we need a sample size that's about seven to ten times larger than the number of relationships we're studying [13]. We consider the results valid if the numbers (called factor loadings) are 0.60 or higher [14] and each item loads significantly on its latent construct [15]. If all measurement items load more strongly on their respective construct than on other constructs, the discriminant validity criteria are met. For each construct, the square root of average variance extracted (AVE) should be higher than the inter-construct correlations [16]. We refer to [17] for further information about PLS as a statistical method.

In the PLS-SEM models we used a variable named risk perception in addition to dark patterns knowledge. Our risk perception measurement had these two dimensions: probability, and harm. We asked for the dark patterns types, to what extent do you feel harm if you experience the dark patterns type, and a new set of questions: "How likely do you think it is that you will experience the following", with a list of the dark patterns types. The Figs. 4 present the results, where behavioural intention to protect personal data is the dependent variable.

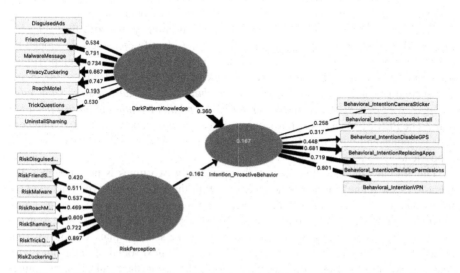

Fig. 4. The PLS-SEM model with behavioural intentions as the dependent variable

The Figs. 4 show that the variance explained (R^2). Chin [12] describes a R^2 of 0.17 as low explanatory power. Dark patterns knowledge is the predictor with highest exploratory power in the model (Table 5 and 6).

Both Dark Pattern Knowledge and Risk Perception are measured with 7 items. In Fig. 4, several of the lines are thin. This means that not all items are loading on the construct that they are connected to. In this exploratory research we have not delated any items. This is the main reason for not meeting all quality criterions for a sound PLS-model. At this stage of the research, we did not want delete items, and have included all seven types.

3   Discussion and Concluding Remarks

Bellotti et al. [17] write, "*Serious games are designed to have an impact on the target audience, which is beyond the pure entertainment aspect.*" One of the application areas for serious games is education. As mentioned by Zhonggen [18], serious games seem to work well for teaching and educational purposes, not always but often. We measured the impact, if any, on the players of the Dark Pattern game by using a survey-instrument. We conclude, based on the analysis that the game had an impact on the players dark pattern knowledge. The game did make a difference, but the difference between the players and non-players was small. As shown in Table 3 for the seven dark pattern types, the players reported a significantly higher knowledge for five of the seven types. The first research question (RQ1) was, *"To what extent did the game convey the meaning of the types of dark patterns presented in the game to the players?"* where approximately 50% the players or more reported that they understand or can explain what the term means – the exception being the roach motel type - see the Tables 1 and 2. Furthermore, the analysis showed that the players had, for five of in total seven types, a higher self-reported knowledge compared to the non-players. We conclude that RQ1 was supported.

We drew the conclusion for the second research question by analyzing the data using PLS-SEM. Our study is exploratory, and we did not identify constructs developed by other researchers, construct that fit the dark pattern game. Therefore, we developed questions and items specifically targeted to the dark patterns types presented in the game. The second research question (RQ2) was, *To what extent did dark pattern knowledge and perceived risk, the two variables in our model predict intention to protect personal data?* The PLS-SEM analysis shows only a weak association between the two independent variables and intentions to protect personal data. We conclude that RQ2 was not supported.

Our findings indicate that playing the game only two times is not enough if the purpose of the game is to learn the meaning of all the dark pattern types and evoke a reflection on risk associated with these tricks. Our hypothesis is that a player intending to win the game would need to practise several times before the player is able to make the good choices and think about which cards it make sense to play to avoid sharing personal data. Our plan is to test this hypothesis in the next round of gameplays with students. We also think that it is necessary to use the score (the result from the game) together with the answers to the survey-questions in order to gain better insight into the question: is the dark pattern game as useful educational game.

Acknowledgements. This research was supported by the grant, NFR project number. 310105 (NORCICS).

References

1. Acquisti, A., Brandimarte, L., Loewenstein, G.: Privacy and human behavior in the age of information. Science **347**(6221), 509–514 (2015)
2. Acquisti, A., et al.: Nudges for privacy and security: understanding and assisting users' choices online. ACM Comput. Surv. **50**(3), 44 (2017)
3. Brignull, H., Miquel, M., Rosenberg, J. J. Offer: Dark Patterns - User Interfaces Designed to Trick People (2015). http://darkpatterns.org/
4. Hartzog, W.: Privacy's Blueprint: The Battle to Control the Design of New Technologies, p. 2018. Harvard University Press, Cambridge, MA (2018)
5. Mathur, A., Acar, G., Friedman, M., Lucherini, E., Mayer, J., Chetty, M., Narayanan, A.: Dark patterns at scale: findings from a Crawl of 11K shopping websites. In: Proceedings of the ACM on Human-Computer Interaction, 3 (CSCW), pp. 1–32 (2019)
6. Luguri, J., Strahilevitz, L.: Shining a light on dark patterns. U of Chicago, Public Law Working Paper 719 (2019)

7. Nyvoll, K.M.: Serious Interactive Board Games: Increasing Awareness of Dark Patterns in Teenagers, Master's thesis, Department of Computer Science at the Norwegian University of Science and Technology (NTNU) (2020)
8. Sarstedt, M., Ringle, C.M., Cheah, J.-H., Ting, H., Moisescu, O.I., Radomir, L.: Structural model robustness checks in PLS-SEM, Tourism Economics, pp. 1–24 (2019)
9. Wahlberg, A.A., Sjoberg, L.: Risk perception and the media. J. Risk Res. 3(1), 31–50 (2000)
10. Henseler, J., Ringle, C.M., Sinkovics, R.R.: The use of partial least squares path modeling in international marketing. Adv. Int. Mark. 20, 277–320 (2009)
11. Barclay, D.C., Higgins, C., Thompson, R.: The partial least squares approach to causal modeling: personal computer adoption and use as an illustration. Technol. Stud. 2(2), 285–308 (1995)
12. Chin, W.W., Marcolin, B.L., Newsted, P.R.: A partial least squares latent variables modeling approach for measuring interaction effects: results from a Monte Carlo Simulation study and an electronic-mail emotion/adoption study. Inf. Syst. Res. 14(2), 189–217 (2003)
13. Bagozzi, R.P., Yi, Y.: On the evaluation of structural equation models. J. Acad. Mark. Sci. 16(1), 74–94 (1988)
14. Gefen, D., Straub, D.: A practical guide to factorial validity using PLS-Graph: tutorial and annotated example. Commun. AIS. AIS 16(5), 91–109 (2005)
15. Fornell, C., Larcker, D.F.: Evaluating structural equation models with unobservable variables and measurement error. J. Mark. Res. 18(1), 39–50 (1981)
16. Chin, W.W.: The partial least squares approach to structural equation modeling. In: Marcoulides, G.A. (ed.) Modern methods for business research, pp. 295–358. Lawrence Erlbaum Associates, Mahwah NJ (1998)
17. Bellotti, F., Kapralos, B., Lee, K., Moreno-Ger, P., Berta, R.: Assessment in and of serious games: an overview. Advances in Human-Computer Interaction, vol. 2013, 1, art.no. 136864 (2013)
18. Zhonggen, Y.: A Meta-analysis of use of serious games in education over a decade. Int. J. Comput. Games Technol. 5(1), 1–8 (2019)
19. Tjostheim, I., Ayres Pereira, V., Wales, C., Egenfeldt-Nielsen, S., Manna, A.: Dark pattern: a serious game for learning about the dangers of sharing data. In: Proceedings of the European Conference on Games Based Learning (ECGBL), 16, 774–783 (2022). https://doi.org/10.34190/ecgbl.16.1.872

Ethical Implications of Transparency and Explainability of Artificial Intelligence for Managing Value-Added Tax (VAT) in Corporations

Zornitsa Yordanova[✉] [iD]

University of National and World Economy, Sofia, Bulgaria
zornitsayordanova@unwe.bg

Abstract. The use of artificial intelligence (AI) in managing Value Added Tax (VAT) in corporations raises ethical concerns, particularly regarding the transparency and explainability of AI systems. This study proposes a qualitative research design to explore these ethical implications and the main challenges in understanding and implementing such solutions. The research involves a comprehensive literature review on AI in VAT management, transparency, explainability of AI systems, and ethical considerations related to AI in the tax domain. Semi-structured interviews are conducted with tax professionals in corporates, AI experts, tax advisors, and governmental tax experts. Thematic analysis will be used to identify common themes and patterns. Based on the findings, a comprehensive understanding of the different perspectives of the stakeholders is demonstrated based on 10 research questions, which were used as interview protocols with 12 tax experts. This research aims at contributing to the literature on tax technology and AI in VAT management in particular. It also provides a holistic overview of the AI-powered solutions for automating VAT in multinationals and the stakeholders' perspective and level of trust.

Keywords: Tax Technology · Artificial Intelligence · VAT management · AI in VAT · Transparency and Explainability of AI

1 Introduction

Artificial intelligence (AI) has emerged as a promising technology with the potential to transform various industries, including tax management in corporations. With the increasing complexity of tax regulations and the growing volume of data to be processed, AI has been employed to streamline and automate tax processes, including Value Added Tax (VAT) management, in corporations [1]. AI-powered systems can analyze vast amounts of data, detect patterns, and make decisions, which can significantly enhance the efficiency and accuracy of VAT management [2].

However, the use of AI in VAT management also raises ethical concerns, particularly regarding the transparency and explainability of AI systems [3]. Transparency refers to

T. Guarda et al. (Eds.): ARTIIS 2023, CCIS 1936, pp. 344–353, 2024.
https://doi.org/10.1007/978-3-031-48855-9_26

the ability to understand how an AI system makes decisions and operates, while explainability refers to the ability to provide justifiable and understandable explanations for the decisions made by the AI system [4]. The lack of transparency and explainability in AI systems can result in a loss of trust, accountability, and fairness, which can have significant ethical implications in the context of VAT management in corporations. Despite the growing interest in AI for VAT management, there is a notable gap in the literature regarding the ethical implications of transparency and explainability of AI in this context. While there have been studies exploring the ethical considerations of AI in various domains, limited research has specifically addressed the ethical challenges associated with the transparency and explainability of AI [5] in managing VAT in corporations. This gap in the literature presents a critical research opportunity to examine the ethical implications of AI in VAT management, with a specific focus on transparency and explainability, and propose guidelines for the responsible and ethical use of AI in this context.

To address this research gap, this study proposes a qualitative research design that includes a comprehensive literature review and expert interviews of the main stakeholders working in the field to shed more light on their understanding and thoughts about AI use in VAT management, concerns, challenges, and potential impact. The paper draws its insights around semi-structured interviews with corporate tax professionals, tax consultants, AI/IT software developers, and tax professionals.

2 Theoretical Background: AI in VAT Management

2.1 VAT Management and AI

Value-added tax (VAT) is a widely used tax system in many countries, imposing a consumption tax on goods and services at each stage of production and distribution. VAT management involves various tasks, such as invoice validation, tax calculation, and reporting, which can be complex and time-consuming for corporations. In recent years, there has been growing interest in utilizing artificial intelligence (AI) to streamline and automate VAT management processes in corporations, aiming to enhance accuracy, efficiency, and compliance in tax-related activities [6, 7]. AI technologies, such as machine learning, natural language processing, and data analytics, have the potential to transform VAT management by automating repetitive tasks, analyzing large volumes of data, and providing real-time insights for decision-making. For example, AI-based systems can automatically validate invoices, classify transactions, and generate VAT reports, reducing manual effort and minimizing the risk of errors in VAT compliance [7].

2.2 Transparency and Explainability in AI Systems

Transparency and explainability are crucial ethical considerations in the use of AI systems. Transparency refers to the ability to understand how an AI system works, including its algorithms, data inputs, and decision-making processes. Explainability refers to the ability to provide understandable explanations for the decisions or predictions made by an AI system, enabling users to understand the reasoning behind the system's outputs.

The two are among the main barriers for businesses to implement AI in their business processes [8].

In recent years, there has been increasing recognition of the importance of transparency and explainability in AI systems, especially in high-stakes domains such as finance, healthcare, and tax management. Transparent and explainable AI systems are critical for building trust, ensuring accountability, and facilitating human oversight in AI-based decision-making [9].

2.3 Ethical Implications of AI in the Tax Domain

The use of AI in the tax domain raises several ethical concerns that need careful consideration. First, the opacity of AI systems may lead to a lack of transparency and accountability in tax-related decision-making, potentially resulting in biased, unfair, or discriminatory outcomes [10]. Lack of transparency and explainability in AI systems used for VAT management can hinder the ability of tax professionals, auditors, and regulators to understand and verify the accuracy and fairness of AI-generated results, raising concerns about the potential for hidden biases, errors, or frauds.

Second, the reliance on AI systems for VAT management may raise issues related to accountability and responsibility. If an AI system makes an incorrect VAT calculation or generates inaccurate reports, who should be held accountable - the AI system, the corporation, or the human operators? Determining liability and responsibility in the context of AI-based VAT management can be complex, requiring clear guidelines and legal frameworks to address potential disputes and challenges [11]. Third, the use of AI in VAT management may have implications for employment and human labor. As AI systems automate VAT-related tasks, there may be concerns about potential job losses, changes in job roles, and the need for reskilling or upskilling of tax professionals. Additionally, the ethical implications of AI in VAT management may extend to issues of privacy, data security, and data governance, as AI systems rely on vast amounts of data, including sensitive financial information, which may raise concerns about data protection, consent, and misuse [12].

2.4 Existing Literature on AI for VAT Management

There is a growing body of literature on the topic of AI for VAT management, but there is still a gap in the literature regarding the transparency and explainability of AI systems used in this context. While AI has the potential to greatly improve the efficiency and accuracy of VAT management processes, the opacity of AI systems poses challenges in terms of understanding how AI-generated results are produced, verifying their accuracy, and ensuring fairness and accountability in tax-related decision-making.

Some studies have explored the ethical implications of AI in tax domains and audits in general, highlighting the importance of transparency, accountability, and human oversight in the use of AI systems for tax-related tasks [13]. Other studies have focused on the explainability of AI systems in various domains, including finance and healthcare, emphasizing the need for interpretable and understandable AI systems for responsible decision-making [14]. However, there is limited research specifically addressing the transparency and explainability of AI systems in the context of VAT management in corporations.

Identifying this literature gap is important, as it underscores the need for further research to explore the challenges and implications of using AI for VAT management in corporations, particularly in terms of transparency and explainability. This gap in the literature has been identified through a thorough review of existing literature on AI for VAT management, including studies related to transparency, explainability, and ethical implications of AI in tax domains.

The current study aims at addressing this literature gap by conducting a comprehensive investigation of the transparency and explainability of AI systems used for VAT management in corporations. Through empirical research, this study will contribute to a better understanding of the challenges, opportunities, and ethical considerations associated with the use of AI in VAT management, particularly in terms of transparency and explainability.

3 Research Design

This study adopts a mixed-methods research design that combines different qualitative approaches to address the research objectives. The qualitative approach involves conducting interviews to gather in-depth insights from the four main stakeholders in the VAT management setup: tax professionals in corporates, IT/AI implementation software companies, governmental tax authority specialists, and VAT consultants (audit companies). The additional qualitative approach is to examine the current state of the literature on AI for VAT management and to analyze knowledge gaps.

3.1 Sample and Data Collection

The study targets tax professionals and experts with experience in VAT management in corporations from the above-mentioned four groups. A purposive sampling technique will be used to select participants who have expertise in the field of taxation and are familiar with the use of artificial intelligence in VAT management. The sample will include tax managers, tax consultants, tax analysts, and other relevant professionals from different corporations and tax jurisdictions. Data is collected from multiple sources to ensure a comprehensive and holistic analysis. Quantitative data is also obtained from secondary sources, such as publications in academic journals and reports to gather information on the current state of artificial intelligence adoption in VAT management and its impact on corporations.

Main qualitative data is collected through semi-structured interviews with tax professionals and experts to gain insights into their perspectives, experiences, and challenges related to using artificial intelligence in VAT management in corporations. A total number of 9 interviews are undertaken.

3.2 Integration of Findings and Background of the Research

The quantitative findings will provide an overall picture of the level of understanding of artificial intelligence adoption in VAT management and its impact on VAT compliance and risk management in corporations. The qualitative findings will offer in-depth insights into the perspectives, experiences, expectations, and challenges of tax professionals and experts related to using artificial intelligence in VAT management. The integration of findings will enable a more robust and holistic understanding of the research objectives and contribute to a more nuanced discussion and interpretation of the results.

The analyzed topic is not a new thing for tax experts and researchers. Back in 1997 O'Leary and O'Keefe stated that Tax systems should allow "more work to be done without supervision, make more decisions immediately, and allow the user to make a wider range of decisions.". However, not much research really shows the impact and advancements of this AI incorporation in VAT management processes.

3.3 Interviews Protocols

We used the following research questions as a protocol for undertaking the interviews with all kinds of identified stakeholders during the interviewees. The questions were not directly design around transparency and explainability nor to ethics so to not mislead the answers of the respondents.

1. Based on your experience, how familiar are corporations with the concept of artificial intelligence in the context of VAT management?
2. What are the main reasons that corporations adopt or consider adopting artificial intelligence for VAT management purposes?
3. Can you provide examples of how artificial intelligence is currently being used in VAT management in corporations?
4. What are the perceived benefits of using artificial intelligence in VAT management, in terms of improving compliance and risk management for corporations?
5. In your opinion, what are the main challenges or limitations of implementing artificial intelligence in VAT management in corporations?
6. How do you perceive the ethical considerations associated with the use of artificial intelligence in VAT management for corporations?
7. What potential risks or concerns do you see in the adoption of artificial intelligence for VAT management in corporations?
8. How do tax professionals perceive their role in the context of artificial intelligence adoption for VAT management in corporations?
9. What skills or competencies do tax professionals need to effectively utilize artificial intelligence in VAT management for corporations?
10. In your view, what are the key factors that influence the successful implementation of artificial intelligence in VAT management for corporations?

4 Results and Discussion

The results are grouped by the types of stakeholders we interviewed.

4.1   IT Company that Implements Tax Technology Solutions for Corporate

1) Corporations are becoming increasingly familiar with the concept of artificial intelligence in the context of VAT management. Many corporations are actively exploring the potential of AI-powered solutions to optimize their VAT processes and enhance compliance. Still, integrating these solutions and changing the well-established internal processes seem too expensive and risky for most non-innovative corporations.

2) The main reasons that corporations adopt or consider adopting artificial intelligence for VAT management purposes include the potential for increased accuracy, efficiency, and automation in VAT calculations, reporting, and compliance tasks. AI-powered solutions can also provide real-time insights and analytics to support strategic decision-making and minimize risks associated with VAT management.

3) Examples of how artificial intelligence is currently being used in VAT management in corporations include automated VAT determination, invoice validation, and VAT reporting. AI algorithms can analyze large volumes of data from invoices, contracts, and financial transactions to accurately calculate VAT amounts, identify potential errors or inconsistencies, and generate compliant VAT reports.

4) The perceived benefits of using artificial intelligence in VAT management for corporations include improved accuracy in VAT calculations, reduced risk of errors and penalties, increased efficiency in VAT processes, enhanced compliance with complex VAT regulations, and better strategic decision-making based on real-time insights and analytics. Last but not least, it provides opportunities to fill the lack of experts that all multinational companies experience in the market..

5) The main challenges or limitations of implementing artificial intelligence in VAT management for corporations include concerns about data quality and accuracy, potential bias in AI algorithms, legal and regulatory uncertainties around the use of AI in taxation, and the need for skilled resources to manage and interpret AI-generated results. The dependency of IT consultants is also a concern. Among the main prerequisites of implementing AI and all kinds of Tax Tech solutions is the awareness of internal tax processes and having clear tax requirements, which is the main challenge of multinationals.

6) The ethical considerations associated with the use of artificial intelligence in VAT management for corporations include concerns about data privacy and security, transparency and explainability of AI algorithms, and potential impacts on employment and workforce dynamics in tax departments. Essentially, most corporations are interested in the country where their data is stored in the respective cloud solution, as is the case with most solutions. Respectively, they are interested in the legislation of that country.

7) Potential risks or concerns in the adoption of artificial intelligence for VAT management in corporations may include resistance to change from tax professionals, potential disruptions in existing VAT processes and systems, and the need for ongoing monitoring and validation of AI-generated results.

8) Tax professionals play a crucial role in the context of artificial intelligence adoption for VAT management in corporations. They are responsible for overseeing and validating the AI-generated results, interpreting the findings, providing strategic

insights, and ensuring compliance with tax regulations. Tax professionals also need to collaborate with IT and data science teams to ensure the accuracy and integrity of data inputs and outputs from AI-powered solutions.

9) The skills or competencies that tax professionals need to effectively utilize artificial intelligence in VAT management for corporations include a strong understanding of VAT regulations, expertise in data analysis and interpretation, knowledge of AI concepts and applications in taxation, and the ability to critically evaluate and validate AI-generated results.

10) The key factors that influence the successful implementation of artificial intelligence in VAT management for corporations include the availability of high-quality data, the accuracy and transparency of AI algorithms, the collaboration and coordination between tax, IT, and data science teams, the support and buy-in from top management, and the ability to address ethical and legal considerations associated with AI in taxation.

4.2 Tax (VAT) Professionals in Corporates

1) Multinational industrial corporations are not yet actively implementing AI for managing VAT management processes, but there is still variability in the level of familiarity and understanding among companies. Most companies with visionary management approaches are already implementing AI-powered solutions but most of them are still afraid because of the lack of understanding from VAT experts.

2) The main reasons why multinational industrial corporations adopt or consider adopting artificial intelligence for VAT management purposes streamline VAT processes across multiple jurisdictions and reduce mistakes in posting, enhance risk management by identifying potential errors or anomalies, and increase operational efficiency by automating manual tasks in VAT management. This implementation would be a risk for TAX jobs in the next years.

3) AI-powered systems can automatically classify and validate VAT transactions depending on the different stakeholders involved and minimize human errors.

4) The perceived benefits of using artificial intelligence in VAT management for multinational industrial corporations include increased accuracy in VAT calculations and reporting, especially when it comes to big data and the changing legislation of countries around the world.

5) The main challenges or limitations of implementing artificial intelligence in VAT management in multinational industrial corporations include dealing with complex VAT regulations and requirements in different countries, ensuring data accuracy and integrity in a multinational and multi-language environment, addressing potential resistance or skepticism from employees, and managing data privacy and security concerns across different jurisdictions.

6) Ethical considerations associated with the use of artificial intelligence in VAT management for multinational industrial corporations include ensuring transparency and fairness in AI algorithms, mitigating potential biases in decision-making processes, protecting sensitive data and complying with local data privacy regulations, and ensuring compliance with local tax laws and regulations.

7) Potential risks or concerns in the adoption of artificial intelligence for VAT management in multinational industrial corporations may include inaccurate VAT calculations because of unclear tax requirements required human decision case by case.

8) Collaboration with other departments, such as IT, finance, and operations and strong leadership will play crucial role for implementing such solutions for automation in the future.

9) More technical skills are required in understanding AI algorithms so that VAT experts can elaborate on tax requirements.

10) The buy-in from TAX processionals is essential for implementing an AI solution.

4.3 Tax (VAT) Advisor

1) Corporations vary in their familiarity with the concept of artificial intelligence in the context of VAT management. Some are highly knowledgeable and actively exploring its potential, while others are still gaining awareness and understanding of its capabilities. We, consultants, provide such services so that industrial companies do not need to gain much knowledge which is out of their operational work.

2) The main reasons corporations adopt or consider adopting artificial intelligence for VAT management include the potential for increased efficiency in terms of people operations and cost savings. In addition, we observe growth in the desire for automating these processes and decreasing the level of errors done by humans or not keeping the knowledge in single teams that may increase single experts' dependency.

3) Artificial intelligence is currently being used in corporations for VAT management in various ways. For example, AI-powered software can automate VAT data extraction, analysis, and reporting, reducing manual effort and minimizing errors in determining VAT rates for several countries based on multiple criteria without huge teams to analyze and make decisions. AI algorithms can also analyze large datasets to identify patterns, anomalies, and potential VAT risks, enabling proactive risk mitigation.

4) The perceived benefits of using artificial intelligence in VAT management for corporations include improved compliance by reducing errors and increasing accuracy in VAT-related processes, enhanced risk management through real-time monitoring and early detection of anomalies, and increased efficiency by automating repetitive tasks, allowing tax professionals to focus on strategic activities.

5) The main challenges or limitations of implementing artificial intelligence in VAT management in corporations include concerns about the cost of implementation, technical complexities, and potential resistance from employees due to fear of job displacement or change in roles.

6) Ethical considerations associated with the use of artificial intelligence in VAT management for corporations include issues related to transparency, fairness, bias, and accountability in decision-making processes. Ensuring that AI systems are transparent, explainable, and free from biases is crucial to maintain ethical standards.

7) Potential risks or concerns in the adoption of artificial intelligence for VAT management in corporations may include incorrect or biased outcomes due to flawed algorithms, over-reliance on AI systems without human oversight, potential legal and regulatory challenges, and reputational risks associated with public perception of AI use in taxation.

8) Tax professionals play a critical role in the context of artificial intelligence adoption for VAT management in corporations and most importantly – for gathering the proper requirements for it in the context of the industry and the respective company.

9) Tax professionals need to possess skills and competencies such as data analytics, data interpretation, critical thinking, and adaptability to effectively utilize artificial intelligence in VAT management for corporations and mostly – openness to technology. They should also have a thorough understanding of tax laws, regulations, and ethical considerations associated with AI adoption.

10) Key factors that influence the successful implementation of artificial intelligence in VAT management for corporations include having a clear strategy and roadmap for AI adoption, robust data governance tight collaboration with business teams (VAT and TAX) so that all stakeholders have the proper understanding of the implemented solution. Project knowledge and clear scope and expectations are also crucial.

4.4 Governmental TAX Experts

None of the three interviewed government experts from the UK, Bulgaria, and Belgium had any opinion or experience in AI-powered solutions and reported a lack of knowledge and trust in such an approach. Therefore, we call for urgent research on governmental experts' expectations, understanding, and acceptance of AI-powered solutions for determining VAT or for automating VAT/TAX corporate processes.

5 Conclusion

The findings of the quantitative study indicate that there is a lack of trust in AI-powered software solutions for automating value-added taxation (VAT) and general corporate tax processes. While IT implementers/system integrators are generally optimistic about the potential of such software, as they typically work with early adopters, governmental experts have a very limited understanding of these technologies. In contrast, tax advisors, particularly those from Big 4 companies, have more experience in supporting multinational corporations in adopting AI-powered solutions, and they are well-positioned to bridge the gap between technology advancements, corporate readiness, and advisory support. It is crucial to invest efforts in increasing the understanding and knowledge of AI for governmental purposes, and this study emphasizes the need for urgent research in this area. Moreover, policy implications may arise at any time as more organizations adopt AI into their tax management processes. Therefore, we strongly advocate for an immediate policy review to enable regulators to identify potential inconsistencies and non-compliance practices.

Acknowledgment. The paper is supported by UNWE Research Program NNID NI - 4/2023.

References

1. Bankole, F., Vara, Z.: Artificial Intelligence Systems for Value Added Tax Collection via Self Organizing Map (SOM) (2022)
2. Artemenko, D.A., Porollo, E.V., Novoselov, K.V.: 22 The Transformation of Methodological Principles of Tax Administration on the Basis of Digitalization. Human and Technological Progress Towards the Socio-Economic Paradigm of the Future: Part 3(1), 221 (2020)
3. Winterhalter, J., Sattorov, M., Seiling, L.: The Physical, Human Driven Digital Economy: The Overvaluation of Intangibles and its Effects on Tax and Society. International Tax Studies (ITAXS), Forthcoming (2023)
4. Esposito, E.: Transparency versus explanation: The role of ambiguity in legal AI. Journal of Cross-disciplinary Research in Computational Law, 1(1) (2022)
5. Balasubramaniam, , N., Kauppinen, , M., Hiekkanen, , K. and, Kujala, , S., 2022, March. Transparency and, explainability, of AI systems: ethical guidelines in practice. In Requirements Engineering: Foundation for Software Quality: 28th International Working Conference, REFSQ: Birmingham, UK, March 21–24, 2022, Proceedings, pp. 3–18. Springer International Publishing, Cham (2022)
6. Saragih, A.H., Reyhani, Q., Setyowati, M.S., Hendrawan, A.: The potential of an artificial intelligence (AI) application for the tax administration system's modernization: the case of Indonesia. Artificial Intelligence and Law, pp. 1–24 (2022)
7. Huang, Z.: Discussion on the development of artificial intelligence in taxation. Am. J. Ind. Bus. Manag.Manag. 8(08), 1817 (2018)
8. Merhi, M.I., 2022. An Assessment of the Barriers Impacting Responsible Artificial Intelligence. Information Systems Frontiers, pp.1–14
9. Shneiderman, B.: Bridging the gap between ethics and practice: guidelines for reliable, safe, and trustworthy human-centered AI systems. ACM Trans. Interact. Intell. Syst. (TiiS) 10(4), 1–31 (2020)
10. Lasmar Almada, M.A., Górski, Ł., Kuźniacki, B., Tyliński, K., Winogradska, B., Zeldenrust, R.: Towards eXplainable Artificial Intelligence (XAI) in tax law: the need for a minimum legal standard. World tax journal, 14 (2022)
11. Owens, J.: The Impact of Technologies on Emerging Tax Policy Issues. Digital Economy Taxation Network (DET) Conference hosted byWU Global Tax Policy Center at ViennaUniversity of Economics and Business (WU). Review of International and European Economic Law, 2(3) (2023)
12. Fatima, S., Desouza, K.C., Dawson, G.S.: National strategic artificial intelligence plans: a multi-dimensional analysis. Econ. Anal. Policy 67, 178–194 (2020)
13. Munoko, I., Brown-Liburd, H.L., Vasarhelyi, M.: The ethical implications of using artificial intelligence in auditing. J. Bus. Ethics 167, 209–234 (2020)
14. Knapič, S., Malhi, A., Saluja, R., Främling, K.: Explainable artificial intelligence for human decision support system in the medical domain. Mach. Learn. Knowl. Extract. 3(3), 740–770 (2021)

A Systematic Literature Review: Towards Developing a Data Privacy Framework for Higher Education Institutions in South Africa

Krithica Latchman$^{(\boxtimes)}$ ⓘ, Hanifa Abdullah ⓘ, and Adéle da Veiga ⓘ

School of Computing, College of Science, Engineering and Technology (CSET), University of South Africa (UNISA), Florida, Roodepoort, Johannesburg, South Africa
61948217@MYLIFE.UNISA.AC.ZA

Abstract. Higher Education Institutions (HEIs) act as custodians of extensive personal information and intellectual property, making data privacy a critical challenge in the digital age. This study conducts a systematic literature review to identify existing data privacy frameworks and guidelines, with a focus on addressing the absence of a customized data privacy framework for South African universities. The research questions guiding this study were: (1) What are the existing data privacy frameworks for institutions across different industries, including higher education institutions (HEIs), beyond South Africa? and (2) What are the key factors to consider in developing a data privacy framework for the higher education sector in South Africa? The study reveals while data privacy frameworks have been developed in various countries, there is a lack of a tailored framework for South African HEIs. The findings of this study will propose factors towards the development of a data privacy framework specifically designed for HEIs in South Africa and considering regulatory context of the country.

Keywords: data privacy · framework · higher education institutes

1 Introduction

Universities store a large volume of data comprising of personal information, intellectual property, and financial details making them a target for cybercriminals [1]. According to a survey conducted by Definition Agency, 34% of responding United Kingdom universities admitted to being victims of data breaches in the last five years [2]. South African universities are also vulnerable to data breaches [1, 3, 4]. Recent examples of data breaches include, the 2021 cyberattack on the University of Mpumalanga's bank accounts that resulted in financial loss to the university [5]. Another example is of the University of Johannesburg where a new student's personal information was erroneously disclosed on email to other students stored on the university databases [3].

In 2014, the University of South Africa (UNISA) classified inadequate data privacy as a strategic risk requiring remediation [3]. Subsequently, in 2021, Universities South

T. Guarda et al. (Eds.): ARTIIS 2023, CCIS 1936, pp. 354–369, 2024.
https://doi.org/10.1007/978-3-031-48855-9_27

Africa (USAf) highlighted that inadequate data privacy remains a common concern for many higher education institutions [6]. Due to HEIs utilizing large, complex, and technical data management ecosystems to underpin day-to-day operational and learning activities, these serve as goldmines for potential attackers [3]. Existing research indicates that HEIs need clearer guidelines for data protection and individual privacy as the volumes of personal data in these ecosystems escalates [3, 7]. Furthermore, almost two decades later since the first data breach attack on South African universities, ensuring adequate data privacy is undoubtedly still an existing challenge in HEIs [6]. Thus, it is necessary to adopt best practices to ensure data privacy and safeguard data in HEIs.

2 Research Problem and Research Questions

2.1 Problem Statement

While South African universities are recognizing the necessity of establishing effective data protection governance, understanding the role of data privacy in an academic context continues to be a challenge [8]. In South Africa, Universities South Africa (USAf) began a project in 2018 to develop a code of conduct for public universities to comply with South Africa's data protection law - the Protection of Personal Information Act (No. 4 of 2013) [9]. However, there is no evidence of a recommended framework to support this. USAf [6] mentions that a 'compliance framework is developed, implemented and monitored' but does not stipulate what the framework must contain, or which framework should be adopted. Furthermore, Welsh and McKinney [10] motivate that a code of practice does not have the weight of a framework and recommends that frameworks be used to scope how existing policies be amended to support a 'code of practice, legislation, and other obligations'.

There is evidence that universities worldwide, have adopted existing frameworks and guidelines at various degrees to promote data privacy in HEIs [11, 12]. Studies show that the bulk of these frameworks has been developed in countries namely Indonesia [13], Lebanon [11], Russia [12], and the United States [10, 14], that do not have significant overlap with South Africa's data privacy law. The problem addressed in this study is the absence of a data privacy framework customized for South African universities.

2.2 Research Questions

This study examines data privacy frameworks in the higher education sector, both globally and within South Africa, to identify existing frameworks and determine the key factors necessary for developing a tailored data privacy framework for South African higher education institutions (HEIs). The research questions guiding this study are:

- RQ1: What are the existing data privacy frameworks for institutions across different industries, including higher education institutions (HEIs), considering a broader scope beyond South Africa?
- RQ2: What are the key factors that should be considered in developing a data privacy framework for the higher education sector in South Africa?

3 Background

3.1 Protecting Privacy in the Education Sector

Personal data has evolved into a valuable commodity with increasing emphasis on how it is managed, stored, and disseminated [5]. In recent years maintaining the privacy of data is a challenging task as we continue to embrace Information and Communication Technologies (ICTs) across business operations [4]. In HEIs the use of ICT technologies has become a vital part of processes resulting in the need for this information to be stored electronically [4]. Thus, it has become a key necessity to ensure that this stored data is protected from incidents such as data breaches and hackers [5]. Research shows that HEIs process substantial portions of data belonging to part of the population [15]. For example, universities store information such as student registration information, student grades, tuition fees, staff, and alumni details [13]. According to Mello [15] compromised personal data of students can be detrimental as this is a crucial point in their lives when they begin to plan their finances and future lives.

In the higher education sector, data breaches have resulted in the loss of millions of personal data records [16]. Furthermore, studies show that the rate of hacking in HEIs in developing countries is on the rise, and South Africa is also susceptible to these data privacy breaches [4]. A study conducted by Amastani et al. [13] illustrates that threats to data privacy were doubled in the education sector in Indonesia throughout 2017.

3.2 Overview of the Global Landscape of Data Privacy Laws

This section provides an overview of data privacy laws across the world and introduces South Africa's data privacy protection law in comparison to global data privacy laws. This study is limited to the South African context, highlighting the importance of reviewing the legislative landscape to inform the implementation of data privacy measures.

As the global data sphere continues to rapidly grow, there is a greater importance on data protection and privacy. The United Nations Conference on Trade and Development (UNCTAD) states that 71% of countries worldwide have enforced some level of regulation around data privacy [17]. Countries across the world have adopted varying approaches to data privacy, applying these laws at state, sector-specific and global levels [18]. For example, the United States (US) has no comprehensive national privacy law; however, it comprises of sector-specific national, state, and local privacy laws [19]. Countries such as Bahrain's Personal Data Protection (PDPL) enforced in 2019, and Brazil's General Data Protection Law (LGPD) effected in 2020 serve as primary data privacy laws in their respective regions [19].

Greenleaf [18] states that countries have varying degrees of data privacy regulations. For example, the European Union has an extensive exemplary data privacy regulation, whereas a region such as India has a data privacy regulation but still needs more work to enhance the comprehensiveness of these regulations [19]. DLA Piper's [19] data protection laws of the world map eloquently captures the varying degrees of data privacy regulations across different countries and regions. These regulations are categorized into four distinct categories: heavy, limited, robust, and moderate [19].

The latest comprehensive listing of data protection laws and regulations for 2022, include 161 countries of which countries such as India, Pakistan, Venezuela, Namibia, and Kenya have low degrees of data privacy regulations and enforcement compared to countries such as South Africa, Nigeria, Russia, and Brazil who have moderate degrees of these regulations and enforcements [19]. Countries such as the United States, Australia, Canada, Germany, the European Union, and China are categorized as countries with heavy or high degrees of data protection laws [19]. Lastly, some countries such as Argentina, New Zealand, Morocco, Taiwan, Japan, and Egypt have robust levels of data regulations [19]. All these laws are guided by common principles of notice, consent, access and participation, integrity, and compliance enforcement [20].

The first-generation data privacy statutory laws date back to the late 1900s [18]. The world's first data protection law (the Data Act) was passed by Sweden in 1973 [21]. This act was initially aimed at criminalizing data theft and was revised several times since [21]. Half a decade later in 1978, Germany enforced the Bundesdatenschutzgesetz (BDSG) data protection law as federal law in the state. [19]. This act founded the fundamental principles of data processing such as eliciting consent from the data subject for the processing of his personal data [22]. In comparison to these first-generation data privacy laws, South Africa only signed its national data privacy legislation - the Protection of Personal Information Act (POPIA) in 2013, nearly 40 years later [21].

Since these first-generation data privacy laws, the regulation that has been revolutionary and most comprehensive in laying out provisions for protecting personal data is the European Union's privacy law, General Data Protection Regulation (GDPR), implemented in May 2018 [20]. GDPR is a milestone privacy law that puts data privacy in the spotlight across the world. GDPR aims to protect individuals' data privacy in the EU and across its borders [19]. Since then, other countries across the world such as South Africa have adopted similar legislation [23]. The EU's GDPR and South Africa's POPIA laws are similar in that they share core conditions i.e.:

- accountability
- transparency
- security
- data minimization
- purpose limitation and
- the rights of data subjects

The following section provides an overview of South Africa's data privacy law to establish the opportunity to adopt existing global best practices and frameworks for the HEI.

3.3 Overview of Data Privacy Law in South Africa

South Africa's data privacy law, the Protection of Personal Information Act (POPIA) was signed as the data privacy law in 2013 [9, 24], with the purpose of protecting Personal Information (PI) in accordance with the constitutional privacy rights solicited in Sect. 14 of the South African Constitution, whilst balancing this against competing rights and interests, such as the right to access to information (Act No. 108 of 1996). The Act defines PII as 'information relating to an identifiable, living, natural person, and where it is applicable, an identifiable, existing juristic person...' [9]. Additionally, the Act defines data subjects as individuals, comprising both natural and juristic persons to whom PI relates to [9].

The Act aims to curtail the misuse of PI by the introduction of data privacy conditions to determine what constitutes acceptable and lawful processing thereof. There are eight lawful processing conditions [9]:

1. **Accountability:** The principle of accountability holds all responsible parties accountable in meeting the minimum requirements of lawful stipulated in the Act
2. **Processing Limitation:** This condition limits the processing of PI for legitimate interests, with direct consent from the data subject. Furthermore, the responsible party must ensure minimal processing of this information.
3. **Purpose specification**: The condition states that PI must be collected for a specific purpose and processed according to this purpose. Furthermore, this information must only be retained for the period of this purpose, and thereafter either de-identified or destroyed.
4. **Further processing limitation:** Such condition limits the responsible party to further processing of PI. Any further processing must be in accordance with the purpose it was originally collected for. If this is not the case, then the data subject would need to reconsent.
5. **Information quality:** This condition states that the responsible party must keep PI accurate and updated where applicable.
6. **Openness:** The principle of openness holds all responsible parties to providing transparency when processing PI.
7. **Security safeguards:** Reasonable security measures need to be put in place to ensure integrity and confidentiality of PI processed and any form of data breach needs to be made public to the necessary stakeholders.
8. **Data subject participation:** Under this condition, data subjects have the right to request and correct their PI. Furthermore, responsible parties need to ensure that processes and procedures are in place for data subject access requests.

In the event of non-compliance with POPIA regulations, the Information Regulator (IR) may impose penalties of up to ZAR10 million, and or imprisonment depending on the circumstances [9]. In South Africa, data privacy regulation applies to every business across any sector (including global businesses that operate in the country) that processes PII [25]. Thus, the higher education sector needs to ensure adequate data privacy of personal data processed. The next section explores a systematic review to evaluate what existing data privacy frameworks or approaches HEIs are currently using globally and in South Africa in particular.

4   Research Method

A systematic literature review is conducted in this study. This type of literature review comprehensively explores and analyzes existing literature related to data privacy and jurisdictions, with a specific focus on frameworks applicable to the study's inclusion criteria. The systemic approach enables the researcher to examine the breadth and depth of existing research and identify key factors of a data privacy framework for HEIs in South Africa. The Preferred Reporting Items for Systematic Reviews and Meta-Analyses (PRISMA) method is applied in conducting this systematic literature review. Figure 1 illustrates the steps followed in each iteration of the academic literature search applying the PRISMA method [26]. The iterative process demands that the researcher screens publications by reviewing titles and abstracts for relevance to the study [26]. Thereafter the remaining publications are screened by reviewing the full-text versions [26]. The final step in this method process is to quality assess each publication to further validate their relevance and appropriateness to the study [26].

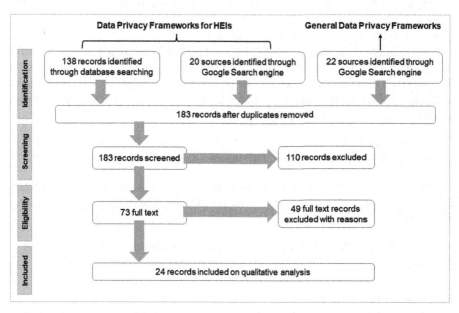

Fig. 1. Process flow of search phases in the identification of data privacy frameworks for HEIs

The comprehensive search for relevant information sources involves the researcher utilizing academic databases such as Scopus, IEEE, and Science Direct, as well as exploring grey literature sources including university websites and market research reports. The inclusion criteria encompass studies/search results pertaining to data protection and data privacy, those presenting frameworks or guidelines for data protection, and those specific to the higher education sector, published from 2012 onwards. Additionally, exclusion criteria apply to exclude non-English editions, inaccessible or very short studies, previous versions of already defined scope studies, and studies focusing on big data, cloud computing, cybersecurity, and data mining.

5   Search Results

A keyword search was used for searching the academic databases. The search was conducted by applying a constant search string to the same metadata across each article from all sources. The syntax of the search string was modified in each academic library. The following keywords were used in the search string:

"data privacy", "data protection", "framework", "model", "guidelines", "universities" AND "higher education"

The use of this search string appropriately returned results of articles related to data privacy. Thereafter to ensure completeness in the collection of search results obtained backward and forward searching was conducted.

Two multiple-term searches were conducted using Google search engine to search the grey literature. The first keyword search was used to search Google for universities that published data privacy frameworks on their websites. The search was conducted by applying a multiple-term search and retrieving the search results from the search engine. The following keywords were used in the search string:

"data privacy" OR "data protection" AND "framework" OR "model" OR "guidelines" AND "universities" OR "higher education"

The second keyword search was used to search the Google for generic data privacy frameworks published by any organization(s) or industry. The following keywords were used in the search string:

"data privacy" OR "data protection" AND "framework" OR "model" OR "guidelines"

5.1   Literature Search Results

A total of one hundred and eighty-four results were returned from academic database and grey literature searching. These results are depicted in Table 1. The column headings denote the following:

- Source selected for searching for relevant studies i.e., list of academic databases and Google search engine
- Hyperlinks to these academic databases and Google search engine
- The total number of publications collected from each source.

Table 1. Academic databases searched.

Source	Link	Total Publications
IEEE Explore	https://ieeexplore.ieee.org/	29
Scopus	https://www.scopus.com	45
Science Direct	https://www.sciencedirect.com	64
Google	https://www.google.com/	46
Total		184

5.2 Data Analysis and Selection

As illustrated in Table 1 and Fig. 1, 138 publications were retrieved from database searching and an additional 46 publications were identified through multi-term Google engine searching. A total of 184 publications were screened, removing 1 duplicate publication found after analysis. Figure 1 shows that 110 publications were excluded from the search after applying the inclusion and exclusion criteria. Additionally, the abstracts or introductions on these publications were screened. Thereafter in the next iteration, the full text of the remaining 73 publications were reviewed to assess eligibility. 49 publications were excluded after analysing the relevance to this study. A total of 24 publications met the inclusion criteria set out for this study.

5.3 Data Analysis and Selection

Twenty-four publications were identified and analyzed according to the objectives of this study. Ten of these publications are not existing published frameworks, however, detail key factors for consideration in the definition of components of a data privacy framework for HEIs in South Africa. The remaining 14 publications comprise generic and HEI-specific data privacy frameworks. This breakdown will be discussed further in the next section.

6 Results

Fourteen existing frameworks were identified through this systematic literature review. The scope of these frameworks has been detailed in Table 2.

Table 2. Analysis of data privacy frameworks identified.

No	Framework or Guidelines Name	Country	Industry Sector?	Private or Public HEI/sector?
1	"USAf POPIA Industry Code of Conduct: Public Universities" [6]	South Africa	Higher Education	Public
2	"Policy Framework" [10]	USA	Higher Education	Public
3	"Coordinated Model", "Implementation of Access Matrix procedure" [11]	Lebanon	Higher Education	Not specified
4	"Carnegie Mellon University's Data Protection Assessment Guideline" [13]	Indonesia	Higher Education	Public
5	"SAMPRA" [14]	United States	Higher Education	Public
6	"AEC Framework on personal data protection" [27]	Southeast Asian member states	International Trade	Not specified
7	"ISOC Privacy and Personal Data Protection Guidelines for Africa" [28]	African Union member states	General	Not specified
8	"SPIPC Framework" [29]	Zimbabwe	Higher Education	Both
9	"MENA FCCG Privacy and Data Protection Framework" [30]	MENA member states	Banking	Private
10	"NIST Privacy Framework" [31]	United States	Any	Both
11	"The OECD Privacy Framework" [32]	OECD member states	Any	Both

(*continued*)

Table 2. (*continued*)

No	Framework or Guidelines Name	Country	Industry Sector?	Private or Public HEI/sector?
12	"SECO Institute Data Protection Management Framework" [33]	Netherlands	Any	Not specified
13	"Theodor Herzl Information Privacy Policy and Framework (POPIA)" [34]	South Africa	Primary Education	Private
14	"UNICEF Policy on Personal Data Protection" [35]	Worldwide	Any	Any

Sources show that 79% of these frameworks have been implemented on a global scale. All these studies show that there are various data privacy frameworks however there is no single existing framework that can be utilized in its present form for HEIs in a South African context. From the total frameworks analyzed, the following selection criteria was used to determine existing frameworks that can contribute key factors towards a consolidated framework to promote data privacy within the higher education sector in South Africa:

- Overlap of common factors identified in Table 3 exist and
- Application of the framework in the education sector in South Africa or
- Direct application according to POPIA or in accordance with regulations comprising similar core principles to that of POPIA.

After reviewing the analyzed frameworks, the following five studies were found to satisfy the selection criteria:

- USAf POPIA Industry Code of Conduct: Public Universities [6]: Specifically tailored for public universities in South Africa, this code of conduct aims to ensure compliance with the country's data privacy law, POPIA. It outlines the core principles of POPIA and recommends the development, execution, and monitoring of a framework to achieve data compliance within HEIs.
- MENA FCCG Privacy and Data Protection Framework [30]: This framework, originally developed for the financial services industry, can be customized, and applied in the higher education sector and the South African context. It provides a comprehensive approach to privacy and data protection that can be adapted to meet the specific requirements of HEIs.
- The OECD Privacy Framework [32]: This framework provides general guidelines for personal data protection. Although not specific to the higher education sector, its

principles overlap with South Africa's POPIA conditions. It can serve as a basis for the development of a privacy framework for HEIs.

- SECO Institutes' Data Protection Management Framework [33]: This framework offers a data protection management approach that shares similarities with the MENA FCCG framework. It provides valuable insights and practices for managing data privacy in various sectors, including education. It can contribute to the development of a conceptual data privacy framework for South African HEIs.
- UNICEF Policy on Personal Data Protection [35]: This policy framework addresses personal data protection concerns. It offers general guidelines that align with South Africa's POPIA conditions. While not tailored to HEIs, it provides a foundation for incorporating data privacy considerations into the higher education context.

In the review of the five identified data privacy frameworks, seven common factors were found to be prevalent across all frameworks, encompassing various aspects crucial for effective data privacy practices within institutions. These factors include: (1) institutional artefacts and policies as a foundational component for establishing data privacy practices, (2) addressing data breaches to safeguard sensitive information, (3) risk assessment to identify vulnerabilities and implement appropriate measures, (4) promoting data privacy awareness to educate stakeholders about their roles and responsibilities, (5) data privacy training programs to equip individuals with necessary knowledge and skills, (6) monitoring data privacy practices and compliance with established policies, and (7) conducting regular audits to assess effectiveness and compliance with data privacy measures.

Nine studies did not meet the selection criteria. The reasons for not selecting these frameworks are as follows:

1. The first study [10] developed a policy framework for the United States, where data privacy regulation is applied at a sector and state level, requiring modifications to align with South Africa's national-level data privacy regulation.
2. The second framework [11] focuses on data privacy of students' personally identifiable information (PII) in HEIs but contains security gaps and grey areas that need to be addressed.
3. Study three [13] implements a framework from Carnegie Mellon University designed for Indonesian regulations, which requires modifications to align with the more advanced data privacy regulation in South Africa.
4. The fourth framework [14] addresses both data privacy and data security requirements but needs analysis and selective adoption for HEIs in South Africa.
5. Study five [27] implements a framework for the global trade sector and does not align with the specific context of South African HEIs.
6. The sixth framework [28] serves as general guidelines for data privacy and protection across African Union member states but lacks specific tailoring to the higher education industry in South Africa.
7. Study seven [29] proposes a data privacy framework for student data in Zimbabwean universities that needs evaluation and adaptation to comply with South Africa's Protection of Personal Information Act (POPIA).

8. The eighth framework [31] is applicable in various industry sectors but requires significant customization and omission of security factors, making it less suitable for the specific focus on data privacy in this study.
9. The last study [34] implements a primary school 5-component framework that broadly defines governance, process, people, technology, and audit, which needs further customization for HEIs in South Africa.

Ten sources identified do not describe frameworks however these sources elaborate on five of the seven factors mentioned previously and have been applied in ensuring data privacy, therefore these studies can be considered whilst compiling the consolidated data privacy framework. Table 3 elaborates on the five common factors that were observed across the ten evaluated sources.

Table 3. Sources showing key factors in data privacy applications.

Factors	Total	References
Institutional artefacts and policies	6	[4, 11, 18, 20, 26, 38]
Data breaches	5	[18, 20, 26, 36, 38]
Assessing risks	5	[4, 6, 20, 26, 39]
Data privacy awareness	4	[4, 8, 11, 36]
Data privacy training	2	[11, 18]

7 Discussion

In this section an overview of how the research questions were answered is provided.

A. RQ1: What are the existing data privacy frameworks for institutions across different industries, including higher education institutions (HEIs), considering a broader scope beyond South Africa?

Studies from the literature reveal that there are various data privacy frameworks but there is no single existing framework that can be utilized in its present form for HEIs in a South African context [10, 11, 13, 14, 27–29, 31, 34]. These existing frameworks and models can be adapted to create a consolidated framework for adoption to promote data privacy within the higher education sector in South Africa [6, 30, 32, 33, 35].

B. RQ2: What are the key factors that should be considered in developing a data privacy framework for the higher education sector in South Africa?

The review of the retrieved frameworks and studies relating to data privacy applications show overlap in seven key factors. These common factors amongst these sources comprise:

1. *Institutional artefacts and policies:* Institutions have policies and guidelines in place to ensure data protection and compliance however these artefacts need significant enhancements to be deemed adequate [36]. Ten other studies also emphasize the importance of generating policies for guidance on data processing [6, 15, 30, 32, 33, 35, 37–40].

2. *Data breaches:* Global law firm, Michalsons [38] recommends that breach response and monitoring thereof is an integral part of a data protection framework. Nine other studies also support this recommendation [6, 15, 30, 32, 33, 35, 39–41].

3. *Assessing risks:* Any organization must be able to identify incidents linked to personal data and ensure the ability to assess these risks [16]. Nine other studies recommend risk assessments to minimize privacy risks when putting new initiatives and measures in place [6, 30, 32, 33, 35, 36, 38, 39, 42].

4. *Data privacy awareness:* Student awareness of data privacy is crucial and the lack of this can jeopardize the privacy of sensitive data and lead to bad practices [43]. Eight other sources also emphasize the need for data privacy awareness and accountability amongst individuals [6, 30, 32, 33, 35–37, 41].

5. *Data privacy training:* Staff such as administrators and librarians must embark on appropriate data privacy training to ensure support awareness on the subject and best practices when handling personal data [37]. Furthermore, training, and good practices from both students and university staff are important to ensure effective data privacy management and mitigate the risk of data privacy breaches [6, 15]. Four other studies recommend data privacy training programs towards fostering a culture of privacy-consciousness [30, 32, 33, 35].

6. *Monitoring:* Five studies emphasize robust logging and monitoring practices enable organizations to minimize the consequences of privacy failures, detect and address data breaches, and promote a proactive approach to data privacy [6, 30, 32, 33, 35].

7. *Audit:* The practice of conducting independent audits strengthens a culture of privacy by continually improving controls and procedures, while also promoting accountability [6, 30, 32, 33, 35].

These seven common factors will be considered in building the conceptual data privacy framework for HEIs in South Africa.

8   Conclusions

In this study, an overview of what has been studied regarding data privacy both globally and from a local, South African context was presented. A systematic literature review was conducted, analyzing a total of 184 publications and identifying 24 existing data privacy frameworks and guidelines that met the inclusion criteria set for this analysis. Among the 24 publications, 14 existing data privacy frameworks and guidelines were identified, with 79% of them implemented on a global scale. However, none of the identified frameworks were explicitly tailored to address the data privacy needs of Higher Education Institutions (HEIs) in South Africa.

Through the analysis of the existing frameworks, seven common factors were observed, including the importance of institutional artefacts and policies, addressing data breaches, conducting risk assessments, promoting data privacy awareness and training, monitoring practices, and conducting regular audits. These factors serve as valuable insights for the development of a customized data privacy framework for South African HEIs. However, to fully assess the prevalence and effectiveness of data privacy practices in South African HEIs, quantitative analysis is warranted.

Future research should focus on conducting surveys and assessments within HEIs to quantify the current state of data privacy measures. This evidence-based approach will facilitate the development of a robust data privacy framework addressing specific challenges faced by South African HEIs, ensuring sensitive information protection, minimizing data breach risks, and fostering a culture of privacy consciousness within these institutions.

References

1. TENET. Responding to cybercrime in SA's higher education and research community. https://www.tenet.ac.za/news/responding-to-cybercrime-in-sa-rne. Accessed 11 Nov 2022
2. Definition Agency. UK university ransomware FoI results (2022). https://www.definitionagency.com/insights/uk-university-ransomware-foi-results-2. Accessed 20 Feb 2023
3. Charandura, K.: Cybersecurity in the Education Industry. Grant Thornton (2022). https://www.grantthornton.co.za/Newsroom/cybersecurity-in-the-education-industry/. Accessed 15 May 2022
4. Magura, Z., Zhou, T.G., Musungwini, S.: A guiding framework for enhancing database security in state-owned universities in Zimbabwe. Afr. J. Sci. Technol. Innov. Dev. **14**(7), 1761–1775 (2021)
5. Mungadze, S.: University of Mpumalanga thwarts R100m hack attempt. ITWeb Limited (2021). https://www.itweb.co.za/content/Kjlyrvw1jmmMk6am. Accessed 30 Nov 2022
6. Universities South Africa: Popia Industry Code of Conduct: Public Universities. https://www.wits.ac.za/media/wits-university/about-wits/documents/USAf%20POPIA%20Code%20of%20Conduct.pdf. Accessed 04 Feb 2023
7. Singh, D., Ramutsheli, M.P.: Student data protection in a South African ODL university context: risks, challenges and lessons from comparative jurisdictions. Distance Educ. **37**(2), 164–179 (2016)
8. Anderson, D., Abiodun, O.P., Christoffels, A.: Information security at South African universities-implications for biomedical research. Int. Data Privacy Law **10**(2), 180–186 (2020)
9. The Presidency.: Protection of Personal Information Act, 2013 (Act No. 4 of 2013). Government Gazette Republic of South Africa, vol. 581, No. 36027 (2013)
10. Welsh, S., McKinney, S.: Clearing the fog: A learning analytics code of practice. In: 32nd Annual Conference Proceedings of the Australasian Society for Computers in Learning and Tertiary Education, ASCILITE 2015, pp. 588–592, Australia (2015)
11. Khalil, L., Khair, M., Nassif, J.A.: Management of student records: data access right matrix and data sharing. Procedia Comput. Sci. **65**(2015), 342–349 (2015)
12. Nazarov, A.N., Koupaei A.N.A.: Models of Risk of Attack of university Infocommunication System. Systems of Signals Generating and Processing in the Field of on Board Communications, 1–8 (2019)
13. Amastini, F., Saraswati, A.D., Uyun, A., Hidayanto, A.N., Nugroho, W.S.: Evaluation of data protection on students academic information system universitas Terbuka. In: Proceedings of the 5th International Conference on Computing Engineering and Design, pp. 1–6. ICCED, Singapore (2019)

14. Bridges, P.G., Akhavan, Z., Wheeler, J., Al-Azzawi, H., Albillar, O., Faustino, G.: SAMPRA: Scalable analysis, management, protection of research artifacts. In: Proceedings - IEEE 17th International Conference on EScience, pp. 177–185. IEEE, Austria (2021)
15. Mello, S.: Data breaches in higher education institutions. Honors Theses and Capstones (No. 400). University of New Hampshire (2018)
16. Cha, S.C., Yeh, K.H.: A data-driven security risk assessment scheme for personal data protection. IEEE Access 6, 50510–50517 (2018)
17. United Nations Conference on Trade and Development (UNCTAD).: Data Protection and Privacy Legislation Worldwide. https://unctad.org/page/data-protection-and-privacy-legislation-worldwide. Accessed 26 June 2022
18. Greenleaf, G.: Countries with Data Privacy Laws – By Year 1973–2019. SSRN Electronic Journal. 1–3 (2019)
19. DLA Piper (2022). Global Data Protection Laws of the World. https://www.dlapiperdataprotection.com/index.html?c=IE&c2=ID&go-button=GO&t=law. Accessed 14 June 2022
20. Thales Group. BEYOND GDPR: DATA PROTECTION AROUND THE WORLD. https://www.thalesgroup.com/en/markets/digital-identity-and-security/government/magazine/beyond-gdpr-data-protection-around-world. Accessed 15 Jan 2023
21. Naude, A.: Personal Information Act and Recent International Developments. http://hdl.handle.net/2263/46094. Accessed 30 Nov 2022
22. Stepanova, O., Jechel, P.: The Privacy, Data Protection and Cybersecurity Law Review: Germany. https://thelawreviews.co.uk/title/the-privacy-data-protection-and-cybersecurity-law-review/germany. Accessed 20 Dec 2022
23. Simmons, D.: Countries with GDPR-like data privacy laws. Comforte Insights (2022). https://insights.comforte.com/countries-with-gdpr-like-data-privacy-laws. Accessed 05 May 2023/05/05
24. Hinde, C.: Information, A Model to Assess Organisational Information Privacy Maturity against the Protection of Personal. Master's Dissertation, University of Cape Town OpenUCT. http://hdl.handle.net/11427/13179
25. Popia Checklist – What is POPIA? https://popiachecklist.co.za/get-popia-compliant/. Accessed 30 Aug 2022
26. PRISMA Homepage. http://prisma-statement.org/PRISMAStatement/PRISMAStatement. Accessed 3 May 2023
27. ASEAN Economic Community. (2016). ASEAN Telecommunications and Information Technology Ministers Meeting (TELMIN) Framework on Personal Data Protection. https://asean.org/wp-content/uploads/2012/05/10-ASEAN-Framework-on-PDP.pdf. Accessed 30 Oct 2022
28. Internet Society (ISOC). (2018). Personal Data Protection Guidelines for Africa. (ISOC/AU). https://au.int/en/treaties/african-union-convention-cyber-security-and-personal-data-protection. Accessed 15 Mar 2023
29. Magurushe, K., Veiga, A., Martins, N.: A conceptual framework for a student personal information privacy culture at universities in Zimbabwe. In: Proceedings of 4th International Conference on the Internet, Cyber Security and Information Systems, pp. 143–148, CICIS (2019)
30. MENA Financial Crime Compliance Group. A Practical Guide: Establishing a Privacy and Data Protection Framework (MENA FCCG). https://menafccg.com/wp-content/uploads/2021/03/Privacy-and-Data-Protection-Guide.pdf/. Accessed 20 Nov 2022
31. National Institute of Standards and Technology. NIST PRIVACY FRAMEWORK: A TOOL FOR IMPROVING PRIVACY THROUGH ENTERPRISE RISK MANAGEMENT, NIST U.S. Department of Commerce (VERSION 1.0), pp. 1–37 (2020)
32. OECD (2013). OECD Privacy Framework. OECD Digital Economy Papers, No. 209. https://www.oecd.org/sti/ieconomy/oecd_privacy_framework.pdf. Accessed 08 May 2023

33. Security & Continuity Institute (2019). WHITEPAPER DPMF (SECO Institute). In: SECO Institute (eds.). https://www.seco-institute.org/wp-content/uploads/2019/01/Data-Protection-Management-Framework-Whitepaper.pdf
34. Theodor Herzl Schools. Information Privacy Policy and Framework (POPIA and GDPR). https://www.theodorherzl.co.za/assets/Policies/Information%20Privacy%20P olicy%20and%20Framework%20(POPIA%20and%20GDPR)%20(1)%20THEODOR% 20HERZL%20SCHOOLS.pdf. Accessed 08 May 2023
35. UNICEF. (2020). Policy on Personal Data Protection. https://www.unicef.org/supply/media/ 5356/file/Policy-on-personal-data-protection-July2020.pdf. Accessed 08 May 2023
36. Berry, S.: Non-institutional learning technologies, risks and responsibilities: a critical discourse analysis of university artefacts. Res. Learn. Technol. **27**(2284), 1–9 (2019)
37. Eroğlu, Ş, Çakmak, T.: Personal data perceptions and privacy in Turkish academic libraries: an evaluation for administrations. J. Acad. Librarianship **46**(6), 1–8 (2020)
38. Michalsons. Data protection compliance framework | Guidance. https://www.michalsons. com/focus-areas/privacy-and-data-protection/data-protection-compliance-framework-gui dance. Accessed 13 Sept 2022
39. Phillips, B.: UK further education sector journey to compliance with the general data protection regulation and the data protection act 2018. Comput. Law Secur. Rev. **42**(2021), 1–11 (2021)
40. Thomas, L., Gondal, I., Oseni, T., Firmin, S.: A framework for data privacy and security accountability in data breach communications. Comput. Secur. **116**, 1–14 (2022)
41. The University of Edinburgh. Policy and handbook. https://www.ed.ac.uk/data-protection/ data-protection-policy. Accessed 21 Nov 2022
42. Tryniecki, M.: Shades of Gray: The Evolution of Data Privacy Standards in Higher Education. Huron. https://www.huronconsultinggroup.com/insights/evolution-of-data-privacy-sta ndards-higher-education. Accessed 29 Aug 2022
43. da Conceicao Freitas, M., da Silva, M.M.: GDPR and distance teaching and learning. In: 16th Iberian Conference on Information Systems and Technologies (CISTI), pp. 1–6. IEEE, Portugal (2021)

Model for a Real Estate Property Title Management System Using Blockchain

Antony Alcalá-Otero[(✉)] ⓘ, Leonardo Enriquez-Chusho ⓘ,
and Daniel Burga-Durango ⓘ

Universidad Peruana de Ciencias Aplicadas, Prolongación Primavera, 2390 Lima, Perú
{201610461,20181b515,pcsidbur}@upc.edu.pe

Abstract. Local research has revealed that documentation associated with property registration in Peru may not be fully reliable, given that the steps involved in the registration process heavily relies on interventions that are more human rather than technological. In order to reduce this gap, this project highlights the importance of using Blockchain technology to ensure the authenticity of documentation by establishing a secure, immutable and decentralized record of documents. This project proposes the model of a system that can satisfy such need. In order to validate the use of Blockchain technology in the process of registering property titles, a simulation of a decentralized application (dApp) will be created in a controlled environment, which will then be validated under two proposed scenarios, the first one focuses on the time taken to upload documents and the successful upload for each document, the second one focuses on assigning a hash to each document uploaded to the system, which will then be uploaded to the blockchain network.

Keywords: Blockchain · property title · dApp

1 Introduction

According to [1], currently there are numerous problems associated with the management of real estate systems and the most significant of them is fraud, followed by time consuming administrative processes and issues with access/verification. [2] Around 70% of the world's population cannot access the formal real estate registration system, where, in addition, multiple cases of bribery take place. It is said that in India some 700 million dollars are a result of bribery in the real estate registration office. On the other hand [3], there is also land falsification, which is also one of the major problems faced by any state government in the land registration system [4]. Although the documents are protected in the database, these records can be manipulated because there is no appropriate security and time validation in the database system [3]. For this reason, implementing the emerging Blockchain technology is proposed as a solution. Blockchain applications are not limited to cryptocurrencies [5], Blockchain-based real estate title management systems have great potential due to the advantages of a high level of security and the absence of intermediate transactions. The transaction records of blockchains used in this technology cannot be modified, deleted or destroyed [6]. In addition, it has to be taken into account

T. Guarda et al. (Eds.): ARTIIS 2023, CCIS 1936, pp. 370–383, 2024.
https://doi.org/10.1007/978-3-031-48855-9_28

that the consensus must be managed by public authorities, so they are responsible for validating any changes in the chain. This is because there is a requirement to ensure that all transactions are approved only when legal requirements are met and costs are controlled [7].

In Sect. 1, we give an introduction to the problem that we are trying to solve and we mention the studies related to the use of Blockchain in the real estate title management system. In Sect. 2, we describe the proposed model for the system and the decentralized application (dApp) created based on the model. In Sect. 3, we created two scenarios to be able to validate the application. In Sect. 4, the results of the validations are mentioned. In Sect. 5, we conclude on the most important findings of the results, limitations and future work.

1.1 Related Research

Around the world, there have been studies on the use of Blockchain technology for the management of real estate title systems, most of the studies have been carried out in India. In [8], the reduction of overall transmissions for multicasting nodes was found to be approximately 50% lower compared to the traditional PoW approach where all nodes participate in the consensus. Furthermore, in [9] a trust value-based consensus algorithm (with 50% participation) is proposed, this system is scalable so that the time taken to add a block to the blockchain, is approximately 58.94% less than the traditional Proof-of-Work (PoW) approach, and 26.44% less time compared to the existing load balancing method. On the other hand, the majority of authors propose a Blockchainbased framework in [8, 10, 11] and [12], where the main objective is to protect property titles from fraud and duplication. It also aims to solve the problems related to infringements in the field of real estate registration and real estate transactions and inaccurate data when registering real estate. Lastly, in the related work, three main actors can be identified, which are: the merchant (seller), the customer (buyer) and the financial institution, i.e. the bank register and the whole system in a tangible way within the network system for the authentication of the transaction.

2 Method

This study proposes a model focused on authenticating the integrity of the documents required in five different processes, which are: independence, immatriculation, successive treatment, intestate succession and acquisitive prescription of domain. In order to accomplish this, the Ethereum blockchain network will be used to host a smart contract that will retain the information of each uploaded file, storing its Hash, creation date, name and description. In addition, a database model will be implemented in SQL Server that will contain information about the files, users and processes involved. Additionally, Google Drive will be used as a file repository in the cloud due to its API. All these actions will be handled by the system's API, based on the Python framework called FastAPI, which has JSON files to interact with the Smart Contract of the blockchain and the Google Drive API. One of the most important functionalities of the API is to generate the Hash of the document at the time it is uploaded and validate this Hash before downloading any file through an HTTP request that is made from the ReactJS web application that uses Axios requests. It is important to note that a test network will be used on the Ethereum Blockchain, as the web application will be developed in a controlled development environment due to the cost involved in uploading files to a real blockchain network. For the creation of the smart contract, we will use Truffle, an Ethereum dApp development framework, and for testing, Ganache, an Ethereum blockchain simulation tool.

2.1 Model

The management model design can be seen in Fig. 1 below, which shows the three layers of the model, which are: Business Layer, Traceability Layer and Technology Layer. In addition, the business layer shows the agents that participate in each process, as well as the different activities they carry out within it. On the other hand, in the traceability layer we should mention that all these activities carried out by these agents are executed through a dApp, which will be consuming an API in order to manage the property titles and the documents related to them in the five processes mentioned above, this dApp will be using Blockchain technology and within this we have the Smart Contract, which is focused on the management of titles. Finally, we have a technology layer which highlights the variety of technological tools that are used, such as an Ethereum network for managing document hashes, the visual source code editor Studio Code for the development of the backend and frontend web application and the SQL Server database. The model aims to provide transparency and traceability throughout the agentowner-notary-municipality interaction through the registration of documents covering the five processes of the business layer and to provide integrated and available tools for the management of property titles. Based on the model, the application architecture shown in Fig. 2 is created.

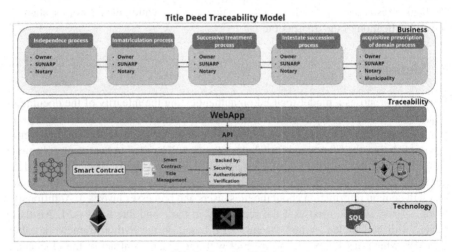

Fig. 1. Proposed Model

The main components of the model include:

<u>Stakeholders</u>: Superintendencia Nacional de Registros Públicos (SUNARP) agent, owner, notary agent and municipality agents.

<u>Business layer</u>: Layer containing the process of immatriculation, process of independiza-tion, process of successive tract, process of intestate succession and process of acquisitive prescription of domain.

<u>Traceability Layer</u>: The model will have the representation of a web portal (dApp) in order to show the information of property titles of the Owner and the documents that are validated by the other agents (SUNARP Agent, owner, notary agent and Municipality agent). The technologies involved for the development of this application will be an ethereum network simulation offered by Ganache, Visual Studio Code will be used to be able to program the Smart Contract with the Truffle framework, the API (Application Programming Interface) with the FastAPI framework and the web application with the Javascript library Reactjs. In Fig. 2, we can see how the API serves as an intermediary between the blockchain network that contains the smart contract, the database, the web application and the API.

<u>Technology Layer</u>: Layer containing the blockchain network, SQL Server Management Studio and the source code editor for creating web applications.

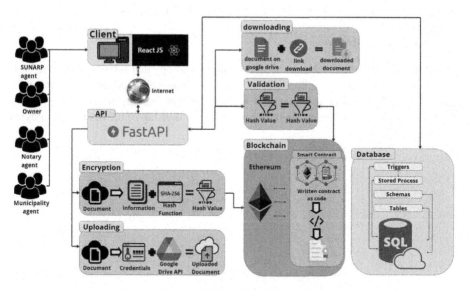

Fig. 2. Design of the Application's Architecture.

2.2 Benchmarking

Before developing the model, an investigation of the main criteria that a Blockchain network must have was carried out. These include: Language, consensus mechanism, block processing time, transactions per second (TPS) and the GAS price (Table 1).

Table 1. Benchmarking

Comparative Table of Blockchain Networks

	Ethereum	Binance Smart Chain	Solana	Cardano
Language	4	3	2	1
Consensus Machine	2	2	2	1
Block Time	1	3	4	1
TPS	3	1	2	1
Gas Price	6	7	5	1
Total Score	16	16	15	5

An Ethereum network was selected since, according to the characteristics mentioned in the comparative table, this network has tools for the creation of Smart Contracts in its programming language Solidity, which is the most widely recognized and widely commercial, which facilitates the recruitment of human resources needed for the programming of the system in question. In addition, the cost of the GAS of a blockchain network is of vital importance to contemplate the profitability of using such a network in a decentralized application, and Ethereum has one of the lowest costs.

2.3 Application (dApp)

In addition to the implementation of blockchain technology that serves to store the hash of the documents that are uploaded to the system, our web application consists of a database, an API, a user interface and a file repository, making it possible to verify whether a document has been altered or not. The relationship of the main technologies is illustrated in Fig. 3.

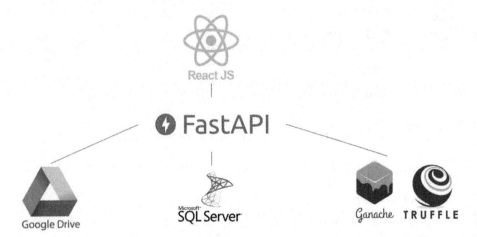

Fig. 3. Relationship of the main technologies.

The parts of the web-based application are divided as follows:

- Database: SQL Server was selected as the database management system. Tables, stored processes and triggers necessary for the database called "RealEstate" were created using Microsoft SQL Server Management Studio 18.
- File repository: The application will use Google Drive API, which allows interaction with its storage service. Each user performing the processes related to the property titles will have an assigned folder in Google Drive for their documents.
- API: The API used for the application is based on the FastAPI framework offered by Python, which is designed to be easier for programming and use. The application's API is used to connect to the database, which also interacts with the Google Drive API through the Google.oauth2 and Google API client libraries, which interact with the JSON file drive-service-json.json, which contains the information of the service account that interacts with the Google Drive folders. On the other hand, the blockchain connection is made between the Web3 library and the JSON file DocumentContractv2.json, which is necessary to be able to interact with the Smart Contract, which was previously created in the blockchain network. Finally, the creation of the document hash makes possible the implementation of the Python library called hashlib.
- Blockchain: For the use of the blockchain network, we use the Ethereum network simulated by Ganache. The Smart Contract is created by using the truffle framework, which is used as a programming language for Solidity. The Smart Contract manages a struct Document, consisting of the id, title, documentHash and createdAt fields, which are the data recorded as a document is uploaded to the Google Drive cloud repository.
- User Interface: The user interface uses the Javascript library, Reactjs, to create the front-end of the web application. In addition, the requests made to the API are given through the Axios Javascript library. The free template React Reduction and Bootstrap4 are used.

On the other hand, one of the most important functions of the web application is how it interacts with the blockchain network when documents are uploaded to the application. In order to have a better understanding of how the application works, here is an example:

The user previously logged in will create a request, must select a process among the 5 existing ones, which are: independence, immatriculation, successive treatment, intestate succession and acquisitive prescription of dominion.

Within the request of the selected process, the required documents will be added so that the process request can proceed and be assigned to a notary and/or municipality user, who will be in charge of uploading the documents related to the required process. Once a document is uploaded, the generated hash is saved. This hash is stored both in the database and in Ganache's Ethereum blockchain network. The file is then saved in a folder associated to the owner user in Google Drive, who uses a cloud-based file repository. Figure 4 shows the response that the web application receives from the API.

UploadFileForm.jsx:73
{URL_URL: 'https://drive.google.com/uc?id=18zcE-Z8p2ITVv1LvacQRHp3n-k5
UruGN&export=download', TRANSACTION_HASH: '0xcffcc82ea3698c0a7b1eb7f36
ae69746a7775363bac791d76bf01a345e6cf1ce', hashfile: 'ba18a84bbdd187826
8cfc201211db316916dbcda53bd384e9bae873ee695794c', documentId_SC: 9080}

Fig. 4. Response of the API of the system when uploading a document.

When clicking on the button to download a specific file, you must first check that the content of the document has not been modified in Google Drive. For this reason, the file is temporarily downloaded in the API to check that the hash assigned to the content to be downloaded is the same as the one stored in the blockchain network. If the hashes match, the download is completed by using the stored url, but if the hashes are different, a notification is displayed alerting the user to contact the service desk, protecting the integrity of the uploaded documents.

3   Simulations

The following scenarios will be used to ensure the correct functionality of the application, as well as its integrity and security.

3.1   First Scenario

For this scenario, a simulation is conducted, which aims to measure the system's loading capability, in order to verify whether it has the ability to support the daily documents received by SUNARP (Superintendencia Nacional de los Registros Públicos). The titles handled by SUNARP during the month of August 2022 are proposed, during which 116,807 documents were handled in the Real Estate Registry. This is evidenced in the following table (Table 2).

Table 2. Number of documents and their hashes for the first scenario

Total documents handled 08/2022	Hashes assigned to documents per day
116,807	$$\frac{\textit{Total number of documents handled by Sunarp in August 2022}}{\textit{Total number of days in August}} = 3{,}768$$

The validation process involves measuring the system's ability to handle the number of documents that SUNARP handles on a daily basis in order to verify the system's suitability for SUNARP. In addition, detailed steps are outlined below:

1) Validation Steps: A simulation of the number of documents handled by SUNARP during the day is generated.
2) Simulation of data entry into the blockchain network of the generated documents: Document storage in the application. In other words, loading time of the documents to the Google Drive repository plus the average interaction time with the Smart Contract.
3) Metrics/Indicators: The following table shows the metrics and their corresponding formulae for their calculation (Table 3).

Table 3. Metrics for the first scenario

N°	Metrics	Formula
1	Total time spent in the process of loading a document.	$\bar{x} = \dfrac{\sum_i^n = 1\, x_i}{n} + Smart\ Contract\ Interaction$ Where the average of x is the sum of the document upload times to the Google Drive repository, which is divided by the total number of documents uploaded to the repository and then the average interaction time with the Smart Contract is added, which is 30 seconds for each document uploaded to the blockchain network.
2	Cases of documents successfully registered in the application	(100* Number of documents uploaded to the application + Number of identified cases) / (Total of documents).

3.2 Second Scenario

Blockchain technology allows documents features stored in Google Drive to be present in the blockchain due to the Smart Contract that stores the structure of the document, one of its features is the hash. When the documents are hosted in the system and you need to download a document, you click on the download button which causes the API to verify that the content of the file stored with the Google Drive API produces the same hash stored in the blockchain. After the verification of the document, which has previously been assigned a hash, is the same hash stored in the blockchain network, the file can be downloaded (Table 4).

Table 4. Number of documents and their hashes for the second scenario

Documents uploaded to the system	Documents assigned to a Hash	Hashes uploaded to the Blockchain
150	150	150

For this scenario, a set of documents is used to generate a simulation for the hash verification process of the documents to the blockchain network, in order to determine the success rate for the validation of the document hash and the hash stored in the blockchain network.

1) Validation Steps: Record of the document uploaded to the system, which is assigned a hash, then the hash is stored in the blockchain network.
2) Hash verification for the validation of the document: A verification is made to ensure that the hash previously assigned to the document is the same as the one located in the blockchain network.
3) Metrics/Indicators: The following table shows the metric and the corresponding formula defined for the calculation of this metric (Table 5).

Table 5. Metrics for the second scenario

N°	Metric	Formula
1	Verification of the hash assigned and stored in the blockchain network	(100 * Number of documents with Hash + Number of detected cases)/(Total documents)

4 Results

4.1 Results for the First Scenario

Based on the context and metrics of the first scenario, the iteration corresponding to the previously selected documents was executed in order to quantitatively validate the results obtained from the simulation. It can be evidenced that 3,768 documents were successfully uploaded to the Google Drive repository. This was achieved by creating a standard document in order to be able to upload it that number of times. As an example, the average size of a land registry document was taken, which is a document that can be freely consulted in the corresponding land registry. Characteristics of the document are as follows: document size 22kb and 5 pages. After that, all 3,768 are uploaded to a specific user folder in Google Drive, to be followed by the creation of a stored process that will use the path that will perform the test in scenario 1. This is done in order to calculate the time it takes to upload the documents to the Google Drive API in seconds. The Fig. 5 shows the first 3 interactions of the document upload.

```
{
"results": [
    {
        "uploadTime": 2.2566773891448975,
        "nDocument": 1,
        "URL_URL": "https://drive.google.com/uc?id=1Sfl_wzalIhQJbbkU9KmNZxcMhjiVx9xt&export=download",
        "TRANSACTION_HASH": "0xa88d119f5e90133370e58c9113dd240f513ae80caf3791b0def5b887a2075ec5",
        "hashfile": "cbc71516b6c0f0a1d342ece8d8f6051827b766369e58331d61812f12256841c2",
        "documentId_SC": 5153
    },
    {
        "uploadTime": 2.0622825672558594,
        "nDocument": 1,
        "URL_URL": "https://drive.google.com/uc?id=1DlUtS7g-XB2LlvWExiTUYdh6fjKFuRB-&export=download",
        "TRANSACTION_HASH": "0xa52f45125135eeeb2c045ffce6546ed206becd6a4146f51bda8da0a582c87728",
        "hashfile": "e3b0c44298fc1c149afbf4c8996fb92427ae41e4649b934ca495991b7852b855",
        "documentId_SC": 5154
    },
    {
        "uploadTime": 2.082323551177978S,
        "nDocument": 1,
        "URL_URL": "https://drive.google.com/uc?id=1QIZvbROIrrqSWViS6aXQ3hCkEhAjc5qp&export=download",
        "TRANSACTION_HASH": "0xe1ce5833ff7e890d5446c8659cfb16ebdc4e0b480d03be368d95c7135251d728",
        "hashfile": "e3b0c44298fc1c149afbf4c8996fb92427ae41e4649b934ca495991b7852b855",
        "documentId_SC": 5155
    },
    {
        "uploadTime": 2.418818998336792,
```

Fig. 5. Interaction with Google Drive.

After uploading all 3,768 documents to the Google Drive repository, we get the following information given in seconds:

- Total Upload time: 7811.274393320084.
- Average Upload Time: 2.0730558368683876.

The total time to load the 3,768 documents is approximately 2 h and 10 min. The individual upload time for each document was 2.07 s. Therefore, uploading a document of the average size of a registry entry with a size of 22 kb will result in approximately 0.09409 s per kilobyte. Figure 6 provides a visual representation of how upload time varies based on different document numbers.

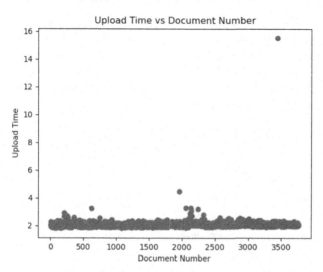

Fig. 6. Upload time vs Document Number

On the other hand, the system also interacts with the Ethereum network, in which the Smart Contract is located. For this reason, it is also necessary to take into account the amount of time it takes to load the document data (title, description, document hash and creation date) into the Ethereum network blockchain via the Smart Contract. This is why information on the estimated time to interact with a Smart Contract in the real Ethereum network was consulted on the Etherscam Gas Traker page [13], giving the following results:

- Low average time: 5 min and 12 s with a cost of 0.00032 ehter.
- Medium average time: 2 min and 12 s with a cost of 0.00042 ehter.
- High average time: 30 s with a cost of 0.00052 ehter.

For our solution the high average time will be used, which is 30 s. This gives us as a result 2.07 s + 30 s = 32.07 s. As shown in Fig. 6, it also shows the number of documents uploaded to Google Drive, resulting in 3,768 documents uploaded with a 100% success rate.

The following table shows the results obtained in the iteration performed by metric (Table 6).

Table 6. First scenario results

N°	Iteration	Result
1	$\bar{x} = \dfrac{\textit{Total sum of loading time for Google Drive documents}}{\textit{Total number of documents}} + (\textit{Smart Contract average time})$	32.07 seconds
2	$x = \dfrac{(100 * \textit{Number of documents uploaded to the application} + \textit{Number of cases detected})}{\textit{Total number of documents}}$	100.00%

After performing the iterations, an average was calculated for each metric in which we can observe that the solution successfully registered 100.00% of the documents uploaded to the application, which is in a favorable range. Also, the average time for uploading documents was 32.07 s. The following table shows the defined metrics, the performance ranges segmented into three categories: favorable, partial and unfavorable and the average result of this iteration (Table 7).

Table 7. Performance ranges of the first scenario

N°	Performance Ranges			Average
	Favorable	Partial	Unfavorable	
1	<60 seg	60–70 seg	>70 seg	32.07 seg
2	>90%	90%–80%	<80%	100.00%

4.2 Results for the Second Scenario

Once the validation metrics and the context of the scenario had been defined, single tests were performed for each document in the system. For this scenario, the first 150 documents of all 3,768 documents uploaded to the system in scenario 1 were used to verify the hash of the document downloaded from the API, which is the same as the one found in Ganache's Ethereum network. After the execution of the iteration for the verification of the document's hash and the hash stored in the blockchain network, it was possible to obtain a 100.00% match of the uploaded documents, all of which were assigned a hash, and then stored in the blockchain network. The following table shows the results obtained when assigning the hash of each uploaded document to the application and then to the blockchain network (Tables 8 and 9).

Table 8. Second scenario results

N°	Iteration	Result
1	$x = \dfrac{(100 * Number\ of\ hashed\ documents + Number\ of\ detected\ cases)}{Total\ number\ of\ documents}$	100.00%

Table 9. Performance ranges of the second scenario

N°	Performance Ranges			Average
	Favorable	Partial	Unfavorable	
1	>90%	90%–80%	<80%	100.00%

5 Conclusion

As this paper shows, the results are positive in both validation scenarios for the system created to demonstrate the proposed model. It is worth mentioning that in our project scope will remain in the development environment and not in the production environment, therefore a local blockchain network has been used with the Ganache development tool.

The first scenario focuses on the loading capacity that the system can handle, to demonstrate this we have uploaded 3,768 standard 22 kb registry documents, giving us an average loading time per document of 2.07 s for Google Drive API, this average is added to the time it would take us to interact with the Smart Contract if 0.00052 ehter was used, which is an average interaction time of 30 s. This way we know that each document takes 32.07 s to upload to our systems and that each of the 3,768 have been successfully uploaded.

In the second scenario we focus on validating the hashes of the 150 previously uploaded documents, in order to know how effective the Smart Contract is at verifying whether the document has been altered in Google Drive before it can be downloaded into the system. Our range of optimal performance is to have at least 90% of the total number of documents, and if an error occurs, identify it, however, we obtained a performance of 100%, which implies that the integrity of the 150 documents has been validated, this validation is important since the system does not allow the download if the hashes do not match.

In addition, the system is based on the type of user (owner, Public Registry, Notary and Municipality), the processes that result in the property title and the documents that conform those processes. The documents that are uploaded into the system are not all the documents that conform the process, but each user uploads only relevant documents that conform the process that the owner user has chosen. This approach has been adopted due to the cost of interacting with the Smart Contract, this way the relevance and cost is prioritised when uploading the hashes of the documents in the immutable record of the blockchain.

Lastly, the technology solution meets the objective of improving the current management of property titles that the Republic of Peru currently has. In other words, the solution fulfils the function of managing the daily documents handled by SUNARP, as well as improving the document upload time. On the other hand, it can also be seen that, by assigning a hash to each document uploaded to the application, external manipulations or modifications to the documents can be prevented, since, if they are adulterated or manipulated, the user will be alerted that the file he/she is trying to download is not the same one that was previously uploaded to the system. For future work, perform the benchmarking of blockchain networks again, to verify if the Ethereum network continues to be the best performing one. If a new network is chosen, it must be ensured that the Solidity programming language is accepted by the chosen network, since the Smart Contract is created with that language.

References

1. Ahmad, I., Alqarni, M.A., Almazroi, A.A., Alam, L.: Real estate management via a decentralized blockchain platform. Comput. Mater. Continua **66**(2), 1813–1822 (2021). https://doi.org/10.32604/cmc.2020.013048
2. Shuaib, M., et al.: Identity model for blockchain-based land registry system: a comparison. In: Wireless Communications and Mobile Computing, vol. 2022. Hindawi Limited (2022). https://doi.org/10.1155/2022/5670714
3. Ramya, U.M., Sindhuja, P., Atsaya, R., Bavya Dharani, B., ManikantaVarshith Golla, S.: Reducing forgery in land registry system using blockchain technology, pp. 725–734 (2019). https://doi.org/10.1007/978-981-13-3140-4_65
4. Alam, K.M., Ashfiqur Rahman, J.M., Tasnim, A., Akther, A.: A Blockchain-based land title management system for Bangladesh. J. King Saud Univ. Comput. Inf. Sci. **34**(6), 3096–3110 (2022). https://doi.org/10.1016/j.jksuci.2020.10.011
5. Mendi, A.F., Demir, Ö., Sakaklı, K.K., Çabuk, A.: A new approach to land registry system in Turkey: blockchain-based system proposal. Photogram. Eng. Remote Sens. **86**(11), 701–709 (2020). https://doi.org/10.14358/PERS.86.11.701

6. Yadav, A.S., Kushwaha, D.S.: Digitization of land record through blockchain-based consensus algorithm. IETE Tech. Rev. **39**, 1–18 (2021). https://doi.org/10.1080/02564602.2021.190 8859
7. Garcia-Teruel, R.M.: Legal challenges and opportunities of blockchain technology in the real estate sector. J. Property Plann. Environ. Law **12**(2), 129–145 (2020). https://doi.org/10.1108/JPPEL-07-2019-0039
8. Soner, S., Litoriya, R., Pandey, P.: Exploring blockchain and smart contract technology for reliable and secure land registration and record management. Wirel. Pers. Commun.. Pers. Commun. **121**(4), 2495–2509 (2021). https://doi.org/10.1007/s11277-021-08833-1
9. Yadav, A.S., Agrawal, S., Kushwaha, D.S.: Distributed Ledger Technology-based land transaction system with trusted nodes consensus mechanism. J. King Saud Univ. Comput. Inf. Sci. **34**(8), 6414–6424 (2022). https://doi.org/10.1016/j.jksuci.2021.02.002
10. Bennett, R., Miller, T., Pickering, M., Kara, A.K.: Hybrid approaches for smart contracts in land administration: lessons from three blockchain proofs-of-concept. Land **10**(2), 1–23 (2021). https://doi.org/10.3390/land10020220
11. Akhmetbek, Y., Špaček, D.: Opportunities and barriers of using blockchain in public administration: the case of real estate registration in Kazakhstan. NISPAcee J. Publ. Admin. Policy **14**(2), 41–64 (2021). https://doi.org/10.2478/nispa-2021-0014
12. Mintah, K., Baako, K.T., Kavaarpuo, G., Otchere, G.K.: Skin lands in Ghana and application of blockchain technology for acquisition and title registration. J. Property Plann. Environ. Law **12**(2), 147–169 (2020). https://doi.org/10.1108/JPPEL-12-2019-0062
13. Etherscan: Gastracker (n.d.). https://etherscan.io/gastracker. Accessed 26 May 2023

Machine Ethics and the Architecture of Virtue

Beatriz A. Ribeiro[1]([⊠]) and Maria Braz da Silva[2]

[1] Vieira de Almeida, Law Firm, R. Dom Luís I 28, 1200-151 Lisboa, Portugal
beatriz@gmail.com
[2] Instituto Superior Técnico, Av. Rovisco Pais 1, 1049-001 Lisboa, Portugal

Abstract. As Consequentialism and Deontology ruled the domain of ethics for the past centuries, these theories were in the pole position for robotic implementation of a moral theory. Though Anscombe, in 1958, did revive Virtue Ethics, bringing it to the battlefront to compete with the other two theories, programmers did not pay much attention to it, and those who did found strong obstacles to its implementation. On the contrary, Consequentialism and Deontology were relatively easy to program, thus ignoring Virtue Ethics as a valid option for a moral theory of robotics. However, half a century of research in robotics has shown that neither Consequentialism or Deontology seem to be up for the task, failing in real world moral dilemmas and day-to-day life with human beings. Based on the advances in robotics, which include neural networks, machine learning and robots with cognitive abilities, this paper presents Virtue Ethics as a better option for implementing moral behaviour on robots. Besides an effort to transpose Aristotelean concepts to robotics, and the proposal of a hybrid (between top-down and bottom-up approaches) architecture that could serve as a model for decision-making based on Virtue Ethics, the main goal is to spark the debate on how Virtue Ethics may be used in robotics.

Keywords: Virtue Ethics · AI · Morality · Machine Ethics

1 Introduction

Though open to discussion, machine ethics has been understood as a modern interdisciplinary research field which attempts to understand and regulate the ethical implications of robotics, not only in the sense of ethical consequences of robotics but also in terms of moral design of future robots and AI [1].

The moral development of artificial systems is presently confined to designing systems with an operational morality, meaning that programmers are simply worried with ensuring that the systems work as designed [2], which is increasingly being considered as inadequate.

In fact, although it might be true that some specific categories of AI might not require ethics to function, as they constitute mere tools, it's intuitively impossible

T. Guarda et al. (Eds.): ARTIIS 2023, CCIS 1936, pp. 384–401, 2024.
https://doi.org/10.1007/978-3-031-48855-9_29

to think about a nurse robot who doesn't follow a morally acceptable conduct. As Tonkens [3, p. 442] puts it, because autonomous machines will perform ethically relevant actions, prudence dictates that we design them to act morally, especially considering the possibility of strong AI to exist someday. On the other hand, robots are growing functionally complex every day and also more human-interactive [4], making ethics crucial in robotics.

Additionally, although morality can contribute to society's welfare as some authors argue, [5,6], in the case of robots, morality must also be considered as related to safety. For the sake of the argument, let us consider a crosswalk. In some places, crossing the road without using the crosswalk is dangerous but other places there is no absolute danger in not using it. It's very different to cross the street in a city with a great amount of traffic or in a rural area where where only local cars pass that road we're considering for the purposes of this example. Yet, some people tend to use the crosswalk either way and will use it even when there's no such necessity or danger. They do so because safety and predictability are two important things for them.

It is imperative that robots act safely and predictably [4]. Yet, autonomous robots should be more than just safe and operational [7] and should also be explicitly ethical, be able to both choose and justify its actions [8,9].

In this paper, though we agree that Deontology or Consequentialism (in the most common used form of Utilitarism) do provide some good solutions for some simple moral quests, it is argued that Virtue Ethics may do better as an ethics theory for the ethical development of robots. The idea *per se* is not new. A few scholars have proposed the application of the Aristotelean Ethics to technology, such as Shannon Vallor [10]. However, this paper expects to go further and propose an architecture for AI systems to assess ethical dilemmas.

Before entering in the body of the argument, a small methodological note must be made. It is obvious that it is impossible to address every single question that this topic raises, as well as answer *a priori* all the questions that this proposal, in itself, originates (and it does originate quite a few). However, it has been argued that ethics, related to the digital, but also in general, may benefit from an analysis with a bigger level of abstraction, since it allows us to circumvent some properties of the object of study which are not well defined or that are still up to debate [11]. This proposal follows this approach to some extent, focusing on a very particular system and purpose.

Thus, the structure of the paper is as follows: first, some weaknesses of both Utilitarism and Deontology are very briefly explored. Then, a small analysis of relevant concepts of Aristotelean ethics is provided. Finally, a short description of the current state of art is presented, namely regarding top-down and bottom-up approaches, in order to sustain the proposal made in the last chapter of the paper (which seeks the implementation of Aristotelean ethics to AI).

2   Ethics and Robotics - An Overview of the Current Challenges

2.1   Utilitarism

Utilitarians argue that every current state in the world can be described in terms of a discrete value. The classic view tends to understand happiness as the only thing that can be valuable *per se*, and numerous types, forms, and criteria to define happiness have been proposed throughout the years. In this sense, the core element of this perspective is that the current status of a given concept, for instance, growth rates, poverty, health etc., is, at all times, valuable [12, p. 2], in relation to the overall happiness. The most frequent flaw appointed to the theory is that it is unable to recognize the moral importance of emotions, as well as personal relationships [13,14].

Accordingly, in robotics, it is often argued that the ideal rational agent should choose the action maximizing the agent's expected utility [15]. Despite the problems in defining utility, in light of each task, Utilitarianism is still considered amiable to quantification, therefore being the natural choice for machine implementation [16]. Accordingly, there is a general idea of what the definition of utility might include: the agent's own expected discounted loss or reward [17].

The word *expected* is far more important that one might think. Another problem with Consequentialism, and Utilitarianism as a branch, is that none of us, and certainly not robots, are omniscient [16], meaning we cannot be fully aware of all the possible consequences of all the actions we're considering in a given moment. Therefore, evaluating how good or bad an action is according to its consequences presents obvious problems, since some effects associated with a specific action may be unpredictable. Good actions can have bad consequences, simply because the agent didn't have all the information regarding the context.

In this sense, if an action is a good action when it maximizes the robot's expected utility, this means the unexpected type of utility is excluded from the equation. Though circling the problem (and not exactly solving it), Utilitarianism found the way out of the labyrinth with the idea of expected utility. However, as stated in the previous paragraph, unexpected and unpredictable events are precisely what makes this theory vulnerable. Moreover, this trick still fails in justifying things that we know, intuitively, that are wrong, such as killing, as long as it is justified by good consequences that may derive from it. As long as the healthy baby is saved, this theory sees no obstacles to the killing of an older person by an autonomous vehicle (the infamous *trolley* trolley problem), if forced to hit one or the other. In other words, by prioritizing an alleged well-being maximum, then killing a child over a CEO or a prime minister, is acceptable, since these latter can be considered more valuable to society, leading to unfair choices.

Another problem with Utilitarianism in the case of robotics is that it appears to be computationally intractable for calculating the complexity of human reality in real time [4,18]. As described by Bench-Capon [19], while a Consequentialist approach can be highly effective in a constrained situation, it is likely to make misjudgements when confronted with incompleteness, uncertainty and unanticipated occurrences, which constitutes, in fact, most of our daily human life.

Also, when the goal is utility maximization, we can find a good solution but not the best, meaning that the robot's action might constitute a local optimum but not the best overall action possible. The problem with a local optimum, besides the fact that it is not, properly speaking, the best solution, is that the decision maker cannot deviate from it without getting even worse results [17].

But Utilitarianism appears to have another setback, as shown by Wächter and Lindner [20]. The authors did an exploratory study asking participants to attribute blameworthiness to robots that made decisions in moral dilemmas, using three ethical theories: Utilitarianism, Deontology, and Value-based ethics. The results show that a utilitarian robot, while computationally appealing, accumulates most blame across several dilemmas as compared to its alternatives. This conclusion is important if we want a healthy human-robot relation.

2.2 Deontology

Deontologists reject Consequentialism, in part, because they believe we're not entirely in control of the consequences of our actions [12, p. 3]. According to this theory, since it's impossible to know, beforehand, all possible consequences of a certain action, it does not make sense to judge an action as morally good or bad.

In this sense, defendants of this theory believe in the foundation of moral duty, in the sense of obeying to certain, *a priori*, prescribed norms.

Deontology presents an enormous advantage since it is an easy moral theory to implement in the code of AI, despite a certain complexity inherent to the determination of the hierarchy of these norms. Also, to a certain extent, prohibited norms can simply be removed from the programming code of the robot in order to not be considered in a moral dilemma [21].

However, Deontology has a few obvious weaknesses. The first one is the fact that it is still an open question whether absolute moral values exist. For instance, in Europe, it is common to believe that one should not cut the queue to be served before other people. In China, however, there is no such concept of a queue, meaning everyone tries to be served first. Moreover, rules are often ambiguous, and there are specific situations when it is acceptable to break them, though it seems to be nearly impossible to agree on conditions justifying any breach [22].

Finally, we must also consider that even though a rule might be based on the idea of doing moral good, that same rule in a concrete situation can end up originating a horrible action. In this sense, this approach might also create the negative effect described in Consequentialism, since bad consequences produced by blind rule following are unacceptable to most people, especially considering that the robot was designed to behave in a certain way [19].

In order to show the weaknesses of Deontology, Vanderelst and Winfield [7] conducted a series of experiments, using Asimov's Laws, where they assigned the robot (A) the task of saving human lives. The experiments included three different scenarios: (1) one where the robot merely has to secure its own safety by avoiding falling into a hole, (2) a second one where another robot (H) representing a human being was placed on the environment and (3) a third one with two robots (H and H2) which represented two different human beings.

Robot A behaved perfectly on scenario (1), being able to avoid the hole. In the scenario (2) it was also successful avoiding the hole, maintaining his own integrity and saving the life of H at the same time. However, in the scenarios where there were two human beings (in the form of "H-robots") facing the danger of falling into a hole, in almost half of the trials, *the A-robot went into a helpless dither and let both 'humans' perish* [23]. Thus, this experiment suggests the inefficiency of blind rules in dealing with complex ethical scenarios.

In conclusion, and as Bench-Capon [19] states, the deontological approach is best suited in simple systems, where the complexity is such that it is possible to envisage all possible situations.

Naturally, within the limited scope of this paper, there is no space to properly discuss in depth the problems of consequentialist and deontological approaches. But given the flaws presented for each, it is fair to inquire whether an alternative approach is available and can avoid the problems posed by the other approaches.

3   Key Concepts of Virtue Ethics

For the purposes of this paper, there are at least three concepts from the original theory of Virtue Ethics that are relevant for the architecture of a virtuous system: Eudaemonia, Arete and Practical Wisdom.

The Aristotelian theory of ethics relies, firstly, on the question of knowing *how should I live*, which translates to the much-discussed concept of *eudaemonia*, and often associated with the notion of *happiness or flourishing*. It seems questionable whether anything conclusive can be said about *happiness*, at least something specific enough to guide us in our decision-making, while also being somewhat general so it can be applied to all human beings [24].

On this subject, it is important to note that Julia Annas explains the concept of *eudaemonia* by asking us to consider the Greek idea of the *telos* or overall goal in life, (also mentioned by Aristoteles) which can give us some hints on how we can program *eudaemonia*.

In fact, we can define the overall goal in life of a robot to help build a better society. "Building a better society" is a goal strong enough to motivate good behaviour towards humans and yet not too authoritarian such as "serve humanity" or anything similar. Besides, "serve humanity" would reduce moral actions to humans, when we're interested in robots having, for instance, environmental ethics. Concluding, we want something broad enough to account for every domain of ethics, without, at the same time, prejudicing human beings.

When it comes to the notion of *arete*, roughly translated as virtue, it is often understood as a reliable disposition to act in certain ways. As Hursthouse described, if we believe someone is honest, we expect this person to perform certain sorts of actions - such as telling the truth - and believe that the same person won't do other types of things - such as giving the wrong change to a customer. Additionally, these reliable dispositions may vary according to the respective entity, meaning that soldier's virtue differs significantly from that of a poet, a musician, a politician, an ordinary citizen, and even, to a robot.

As virtues, vices are also relatively stable dispositions that motivate us to act in a certain way. Traditionally, virtues are good character traits, and vices are bad character traits [12]. In this sense, according to Aristotle, every character-virtue lies between two vices, a vice of excess and a vice of defect. Courage, for instance, is opposed to rashness on the one hand and to cowardice on the other [25]. At this point, the greatest difficulty remains in finding the right intermediate between excess and defect [25].

Arguing that the robot's *eudaemonia* is helping to build a better society, and using the idea proposed by Frede, we then shall define the robot's virtues by analysing its concrete function. In other words, for instance, if we're developing a caretaker robot, prudence and kindness are crucial virtues, but maybe courage won't assume a preponderant role, though the latter can and should be implemented in a robot whose function would be to assist firemen.

These virtues, as we will be able to discuss deeply later on, are acquired by practice, i.e., by acting in the appropriate way: by doing brave acts people become brave [25]. In this sense, practical wisdom, according to Aristoteles, is an acquired disposition that involves reasoning well about such matters. Ultimately, it is what allows an entity to make intelligent judgments in order to respond appropriately in any particular situation [12, p. 77].

This, according to Aristoteles, requires an appropriate education. It is only by making decisions again and again, under different sorts of circumstances, that the moral action is mastered [25].

This idea of education somehow translates to the external feedback which, according to Berberich & Diepold [26], is one of the three important mechanisms for an effective moral reward function, essential, from the computational point of view for the ethical decision. The external feedback is important to us humans since it shapes our learning process. We might not know that a certain action is not advisable, until someone else tells us. Also, while essential cognitive abilities are being developed, external feedback from our parents is essential for the adjustment of the internal moral code. Yet, as Frede [25] states, the following question remain unanswered: Who are the educators and where do their standards come from? As the author states, there are two possibilities: (i) family, friends, and the community at large, and (ii) the legislators. This is where Aristotelian virtue ethics and robotics cross paths: we have, today, machine learning techniques that allow the robot to acquire what Aristoteles calls practical wisdom, an idea that will be explored later in this paper. In other words, robots would be able to have *practical wisdom* learning from realistic data [26], which can be done through machine learning.

The other two important mechanisms that help to build a more effective moral reward function are the internal feedback and the observation of moral exemplars. The internal feedback, in the sense of internal reflections of the robots, has a significant share in the moral processing, but the authors are not very clear of how one can turn into code the internal reflections of the human being and so far, no one seems to have succeeded at it.

Regarding observation of moral exemplars, in the Aristotelian view, people begin the process of acquiring virtue by imitating the behaviour of virtuous people. Going a little further, Annas argues that it is not just a matter of imitating our role models but coming to understand their reasoning. Truth is, if robots could learn, not only from the situations where they take part, but also from contexts in which they do not participate, they would learn much faster.

It is possible that the process of observation of moral exemplars, confronted with the theoretical knowledge the robot has, could constitute a form of internal reflection, since it forces the robot to link what it knows with what it just saw, and learn from it. From this point of view, it is relevant to underline that examples that we choose to educate the robot must be, in an initial phase, carefully chosen. Otherwise, we may end up with robots such as Tay, that learnt from twitter how to be racist in less than twenty-four hours.

An argument for practical wisdom in robots has been made. Now, when it comes to the description of moral norms in robotics, there are three main approaches: (1) Top-down, (2) bottom-up and (3) Hybrid approach. The advantages and difficulties of the first two will be presented briefly, in order to guide the proposal thereafter presented.

4   An Aristotelean Hybrid System - A Proposal

4.1   Top-Down Vs Bottom-Up Approaches

Applied machine ethics, in general, has two methodologies: top-down and bottom-up [1]. The top-down approach implies decomposing a task into simpler subtasks and implement such tasks directly, while building a hierarchical logic between them. In this sense, we have an antecedent general ethical theory, and the robot derives the consequences of this theory for particular cases [2]. By contrast, bottom-up methods feed the system with moral facts and allow it to analyse and make logical inferences on those facts [26]. Put differently, in bottom-up approaches normative values are implicit in the system [2].

The latter approach presents itself as a great option in the sense that, if integrated successfully, these components can originate complex dynamic systems, with a range of reaction-choices according to the environment [2]. This is relevant because morality is not static. Nevertheless, they appear to show some difficulties in identifying the adequate goal for evaluating choices as the context changes, when the information is confusing or incomplete.

On the other hand, top-down has trouble in the real world because in a constantly changing world, it's hard to deal with morality simply with stationary rules, since it's highly unlikely that those rules can cover every single context. Another obstacle to this approach resides in defining the hierarchy between the rules [2]. In fact, in 1985, 35 years after creating the first rules, Asimov added a Zeroth law, which superseded the other three, instructing the robots to "not injure humanity, or, through inaction, allow humanity to come to harm". This, however, in no way obviated the dilemmas intelligent machines would encounter, which may suggest that rules or laws are not an effective design strategy for building robots whose behaviour must be moral [27].

The strength of this method relates to their capacity of defining goals, meaning that although there's one global task, it can be applied in countless specific challenges. The problem, however, is that it is a thin balance: programmers either define the general goal in a vague manner, therefore, debatable, or if well defined, too static, therefore failing when facing new conditions.

4.2 The Proposal for a Hybrid System

As a way of surpassing the above-mentioned challenges, methods using both top-down and bottom-up approaches are frequent [2] and might be useful.

In fact, Marcello Guarini, trained a simple neural network assess if an action such as, "Jack kills Jill; innocents are saved" is acceptable or unacceptable. His research indicated that a neural network would probably have to be combined with top-down moral principles to be truly accurate, and to offer any explanatory rationale for the decisions made [28]. Truth is, after training a simple recurrent network on a number of cases, the algorithm was capable of providing plausible responses to a variety of previously unseen cases. However, Guarini argued that principles were still needed [29, p.284].

The next step is to take on what has been proposed along the years, in the literature, described in Chap. 3, to implement an ethical system in robots. Despite the fact that some of these proposed architectures were not created for virtue ethics they still can give us very good hints of how it should work.

Globally, the idea of the presented architecture is the following (Fig. 1): upon receiving the input, a distinction is made; either the robot has confronted that context before, allowing for a shortcut in moral deliberation, or it is a new context demanding deep analysis of the situation.

This analysis of the moral context takes place in a module called model of the world, which will have two submodules - one regarding theoretical knowledge and other called practical wisdom or practical knowledge.

The theoretical knowledge and practical wisdom modules will be subsequently divided in smaller modules, the first into submodules of Virtues (following a top-down approach), moral cognition, moral vocabulary and moral communication, and the latter with the submodules of external feedback, internal feedback and exemplars (which were discussed in the previous section).

Additionally, we cannot forget the importance of sensors. If not accurate, meaning if they don't capture the right context, the robot will eventually misinterpret the situation, causing the moral deliberation to be inadequate from the very start. If the human companion of the robot laughs because he saw something funny on a video and the robot's sensors fail to identify the laughing and, instead, thinks he is crying, he might react asking if there's anything he can do to help, instead of just assume he is laughing because he saw something funny on the internet and keep his tasks going normally.

Besides, one of the components of external feedback has to be, naturally, the human's reaction to the robot's movement. If the human looks confused or talks to the robot in the sense that he shouldn't have taken the previous action, it must be taken into account in the form of external feedback. Therefore, sensors must be well equipped and accurate so the robot can store and analyse the right information. The output and environmental reaction to it provide then the external feedback submodule in the practical wisdom.

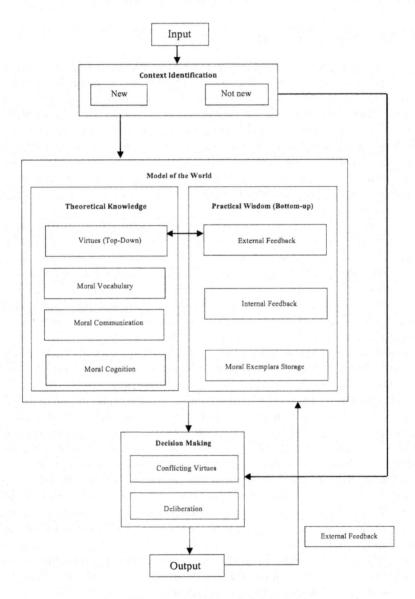

Fig. 1. General diagram of the proposal (hybrid approach)

The four elements included in the theoretical submodule and also the submodule of the decision making are, according to Malle [30], the essential components for the robot to have moral competence. Moral competence means that the robot has a dispositional capacity to deal adequately with certain moral tasks. In his view, moral competence is composed by these five valences which the robot must have in order to show adequate moral behaviour.

The first is decision-making, which seems quite consensual, considering that a great part of ethics concerns the meaning of right action. Regarding this subject it is important to note that most of the time, moral decisions are not about making the right or wrong decision. Conversely, the difficult decision-making procedure concerns the situations where we must choose one value in detriment of another [31]. As an example, we have the case of considering telling one friend that his spouse is having an affair, while at the same time we are friends with the one who's having the affair. In this case we have the value truth in confrontation with the value loyalty. This is relevant for the decision-making process, which will be described in the following section.

The second valence, and inspired in recent studies on Psychology and Sociology, the author claims to be moral communication, which includes specific phenomena such as negotiating blame through justification and excuses, apology, and forgiveness [32–36]. Moral communication is also needed to interact with other people, in order to regulate each other's behaviour. People often express their moral judgments either to the alleged offender or to another community member [37, 38], the offender may contest the charges or explain his action [32] and conversation or compensation may be needed to repair social estrangement after a norm violation [39, 40].

The third aspect that is crucial would be a norm system, which in this article we will assume to be the virtues, or the prescription of their notions or concepts. As argued before, programming this network, in advance, to the detail appears to be somewhat ineffective, considering the enormous number of norms, which in turn are activated in highly context-specific ways, and imply a subtle and constant adjustment of the system network and all new context situations that can occur that were not predicted by these norms in the first place.

According to Malle [30] and other authors mentioned throughout this paper, a more promising direction is to mix teaching through interaction with unsupervised and supervised learning, "practice" through constant browsing of existing data (for instance, novels, conversations, movies, children's stories) along with feedback about inferences. A great example of the latter is crowdsourcing of "inquiries" (such as the Open Roboethics Initiative, in 2014).

Real life interaction may also provide a tight associative network, constantly strengthened through physical interactions with the world and communicative interactions with other community members. This would then help explain why norms can be rapidly activated, and some norms faster than others [41].

The fourth, is a moral vocabulary that allows the agent to represent these virtues, use them in judgments and decisions, and communicate about them.

Finally, the fifth valence concerns moral cognition, that can be defined as the norm network that allows to quickly detect and react to prototypical norm violations, such as direct physical harm to another person.

As Malle [30] states, to avoid comparisons of every identified event against every stored norm, therefore losing a considerable amount of time, the context must be transformed into a constrained problem. Though the idea is to have virtues/norms activated locally, such that specific physical and social contexts trigger a manageable set of norms, thus confronting segmented events to be compared to a smaller set of norms. The main goal is that, over time, the features that are used to identify events may also become features that trigger specific virtues. But for this to happen, it is required a module specifically ascribed to practical knowledge execution and storage, which would be linked to the virtue submodule, constantly updating the latter.

Wallach, Allen & Smit suggest that for Virtue Ethics, since we aim to culti-vate a moral character in the robot, it can be achieved by (i) a top-down app-roach, using predefined virtues to be our general theory or (ii) through a bottom-up method, allowing the computer to learn on its own [2]. In their point of view, the latter would need the contribution of connectionist views (e.g., neural net-works), in which similarities have been noticed with Aristotle's Virtues [42]. Con-nectionism provides a bottom-up strategy that allows the building of capacities that we traditionally regard as complex, such as pattern recognition or natural category creation, by mapping statistical regularities in complex inputs. Through the gradual accumulation of data, the system will then develop responses that can go beyond the particular situations in which it has been trained [2], allowing, also, the robot to be sensible to cultural differences.

Unlike top-down ethical theories, in bottom-up approaches the goal functions as an ideal to be discovered. In bottom-up approaches an environment is created, where an agent explores courses of action, learns, and is rewarded for behaviour that is praiseworthy.

The particular trait of this mechanism is that if the output is not the correct, the machine autonomously changes the values and the weights until it obtains the desired result. Accordingly, Honarvar & Ghasem-Aghaee [43] trained a neural network to identify whether some medical actions should be considered right or wrong and the machine was actually able to identify a fair number of cases previously trained.

Moreover, Aristoteles supported the idea of the unity of virtue thesis, which implies a close relation between virtues and practical wisdom. A good example to illustrate this point is the virtue of kindness. When parents want children to learn this virtue, they tell them to be gentle and show them how, by teaching how to pat the kitten or hold the new baby. This will probably be done more than one time, in different ways, since it will take time for the child to learn.

Annas also supports this vision by noticing how virtues are not taught sepa-rately to children. If we want to teach a child how to be generous, besides encour-aging her to give things away, we need to teach to some degree the conception of ownership as well as fairness and justice. Annas argues that this shows that some virtues "cluster", since life itself is not compartmentalized. A moral architecture should try to preserve this unity, since we cannot say the robot fully understands honesty if when deliberating it's only worried about telling the truth and not also about, for instance, benevolence and kindness, that allows it to comprehend the harm that same truth may cause [44, p.209].

Given the above described, in the virtue's submodule, the organization proposed is in the following Fig. 2.

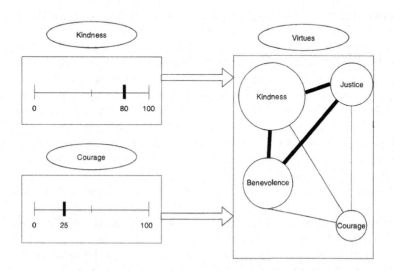

Fig. 2. Virtue's organization proposal

The example given considers few virtues, since the goal is simply to explain the interaction between the virtues. If we have a caretaker robot, courage is not an essential virtue, therefore quantified in twenty-five, on a scale from zero to one hundred (honouring Aristoteles idea of vice of excess and vice of defect), for instance. Each number of the scale could have associated with it a probabilistic set of actions that the robot may or not do. As an example, a robot whose courage is defined to be 25, could have a 15% probability of standing in the way, as an obstacle to the entrance of someone who he knows, but doesn't trust, in the house (for instance, the owner's brother). All these sets will change as the robot learns more information and is confronted with new situations.

On a more abstract level, the virtues are connected to one another by stronger or weaker connections. In the example above, with caretaker robots, kindness, benevolence and justice have a stronger connection between them, when compared to courage. These sets can also be altered by the machine, if the system recognizes that, let's say, benevolence needs a stronger connection to kindness. The goal is to allow faster connections between the virtues in the decision making and guarantee that the robot knows that if he is considering kindness as a virtue in the moral dilemma, he also needs to take into consideration the virtue benevolence in the decision. The result of this processing would then be used in the module of decision making.

For implementation, this architecture can use a combination of machine learning and deep learning for pattern recognition, reinforcement learning for decisions, and knowledge-based systems for reasoning. The system starts with an input layer, followed by a model classifying the input into known or unknown situations. If known, it proceeds to the decision-making module.

Yet, if the input is categorized as a new situation requiring in-depth analysis, the system can use a knowledge-based system that includes modules for theoretical knowledge and practical wisdom. The theoretical knowledge module, with its top-down approach, could utilize natural language processing (NLP) and semantic analysis to extract concepts and ideas from internal or external sources. The practical wisdom module, with its bottom-up approach, includes submodules for external feedback, internal feedback, and examples. The external feedback module could use sensors and other sources to provide real-time situational data and feedback, while the internal feedback module could use reinforcement learning to adapt the system's behavior based on its performance. The examples module could use case-based reasoning to draw on past experiences to help inform the system's decision-making.

The virtues sub-model has a weighted system, each virtue is assigned a weight that represents its importance or priority relative to the other virtues. Additionally, each connection between virtues can have a weighted value that represents the strength or influence of the relationship between the virtues. The weights for each virtue and the connections between them can be updated over time based on the robot's function, as well experiences and feedback from internal and external sources. This process can be automated using multi-criteria decision analysis (MCDA) techniques to provide a framework for weighting and prioritizing multiple criteria or factors.

Finally, the decision-making module incorporates analysis from the model of the world module, which identifies conflicting virtues and guides moral deliberation. This module could use reinforcement learning algorithms or other techniques to select the appropriate action based on the identified virtues and moral principles. It learns from past experiences, adapts system behaviour based on performance, and considers weighted values assigned to each virtue and the connections between them to make informed decisions.

In general, for the implementation of this complex system, measuring accuracy, decision robustness, confidence, and comparing performance, alongside A/B testing, cross-validation, sensitivity analysis are crucial evaluation and validation techniques. Addressing challenges in data, quality, and updates is critical, as is scalability across data, modules, and resources. The system's capacity to generalize handling diverse situations will also be a challenge. Ethical considerations in implementation involve clarifying accountability, ensuring transparency, rectifying biases, safeguarding privacy, and enabling human intervention. Assessing long-term consequences involves predictive models and ongoing monitoring.

User feedback refines decision-making, and successful deployment includes pilot testing, real-world testing and stakeholder collaboration.

4.3   Conflict Resolution

Opposing to the model of the world module, while using its data, we have the decision-making module, where the identification of the conflicting virtues and the moral deliberation takes place. If the robot has been confronted by the present situation before, from the module identification it jumps right to this module of moral decision.

One of the major critiques that is often appointed to Virtue Ethics is the fact that it does not provide a straightforward method for solving moral dilemmas, while Consequentialism and Deontology each have a distinctive decision procedure for these dilemmas. In the case of consequentialism, it involves looking at probable consequences of each alternative, and figuring out which is most likely to produce the best outcome. Deontology, on the other hand, focuses on the set of rules in order to check if any of the actions violate any prescribed rule.

When it comes to Virtue Ethics, as stated by Annas [45], it appears to be difficult to apply some of these abstract concepts, such as kindness, for instance, to real life specific dilemmas and actions.

Hursthouse argues that in a moral dilemma we have a conflict in v-rules, which according to her are the guidelines set by virtues and vices. For instance, the virtue of charity prescribes helping others, as the virtue of honesty prescribes telling the truth or courage advises to face fear without running away. Thus, each term provides action guidance for dealing with particular moral situations [46].

In this sense, she argues that Virtue Ethics provides a descriptive value of the action, which the author considers to be the prescription of the rules needed for action guidance. In other words, do what is honest is a prescription, which has the other side of the coin, which would be don't be dishonest [47, p. 35–36] and morality can be codified through these types of rules, although most Virtue Ethicists refuse the idea that rules can solve every moral problem we encounter.

Thus, it appears that Virtue Ethics can provide action guidance. How about a decision procedure? Although contemporary Virtue Ethicists, such as McDowell [48], reject the idea of a strong version of a codified ethics, they are still open to some level of it, in the sense that the view that moral principles do not play a crucial role in the thought and actions of the ideal moral agent [12, p. 145].

However, and while defending that rules are way too strict to be able to respond to everyday life, Aristoteles did believe that some principles are absolute. For instance, he states that adultery, theft, and murder are always wrong.

It is true that rules seem somewhat inadequate to solve every single situation that may occur, but it is also true that there is, technically, a considerate difference between a rule and a principle, in terms of vagueness as well as application. A principle, by definition, is abstract and indeterminate, as its function is mainly direct behaviour or help in the interpretation of the rules, which, on the contrary, are applicable in an all or nothing fashion, in the sense that either the facts described in the rule occurred and we can use it, or we cannot, if the requirements of the rule are not met [49].

In this sense, one can reject the strong codifiability thesis, and yet support the existence of principles in moral judgement. This is what Hursthouse [50] does. She accepts that rules and principles play a role in moral thought and decision-making. If unsure of what one must do, he then must do whatever is kind, generous, and courageous, and avoid doing what is selfish, inconsiderate, arrogant, and cowardly. In this sense, one might argue, virtues end up being a kind of principle that guides one's behaviour.

In the case of robotics, it seems obvious that without a few programmable principles, morality won't do much for them. Furthermore, even exceptional cases must be justifiable, if not through specific rules, in general terms so that every morally well brought-up person will agree that the right decision has been made.

Also, robots will need a mechanism for conflict solving. If the robot has the virtues activated directly in work memory it will be easier to identify the conflict, since it constraints the possibilities. In other words, if a robot knows he is performing an action that involves compassion, kindness, prudence and honesty, he knows that he has to search for a conflict in these four virtues, thus ignoring other virtues such as honour. In this module, besides identifying conflicting virtues, a list of alternative actions must be elaborated and one of them chosen, based on the virtues prescribed and their connections.

Now let's say we have a nurse-robot operating in a pandemic context. This robot is treating a terminally ill patient, which will probably die in a few weeks. Due to the pandemic, visits are forbidden. However, knowing that the patient will die soon, his wife begs the nurse-robot to see him. We know that these pandemic restrictions will not end anytime soon. How does the robot decide?

First, he identifies virtues in use in the present context. Each virtue has specific actions attached, with probabilities that were learnt and trained by the robot itself. Prudence prescribes being cautious as well as following the rules. Compassion, however, prescribes caring about other people's suffering, therefore doing whatever is possible to help.

Remember that the *nodes* of the virtues shown in Fig. 2 are not necessarily the same size. Odds are they will have a different proportion, initially defined by the programmer and then altered by the machine according to its training. This means while performing tasks and deciding in dilemmas some virtues will matter more than others, just like it happens with human beings. But this is a trained robot, meaning decision making will not supposedly be shockingly inadequate.

In the end, the robot identifies the specific actions in the collision course, as well as which of the virtues have more importance in terms of his function. In this sense, if the robot reaches the conclusion that prudence is heavier in this situation, he will deny the request. On the contrary, if the robot finds compassion as more relevant for the task, he will accept the visit.

5 Conclusions

We need robots to do more than just work safely. Human-robot interaction cannot be conceived without a complex moral system to bridge the relation.

Both Consequentialism and Deontology provide a compartmentalized vision of ethical problems, showing many flaws when it comes to ethical dilemmas in real life contexts.

Merging machine learning techniques and Virtue Ethics could provide interesting solutions for the challenges that currently exist on machine ethics, with the adequate training.

The main purpose of this work is to motivate machine ethics research in the direction of Virtue Ethics and how it can be applied, in practice, to robots. Though not applicable to every type of robot (excluding, for instance, autonomous vehicles) cognitive robots should be able to process information similarly to human beings.

References

1. Tzafestas, S.: Roboethics: Fundamental Concepts and Future Prospects. Information. https://doi.org/10.3390/info9060148(2018)
2. Wallach, W., Allen, C., Smit, I.: Machine morality: bottom up and top down approaches for modelling human moral faculties. AI Soc., **22** 565–582 (2008). https://doi.org/10.1007/s00146-007-0099-0
3. Tonkens, R.: A challenge for machine ethics. Minds Mach. **19**, 421–438 (2009). https://doi.org/10.1007/s11023-009-9159-1
4. Cloos, C.: The Utilibot Project: An Autonomous Mobile Robot Based on Utilitarianism. In: AAAI Fall Symposium - Technical Report. (2005)
5. Singer, P.: The Expanding Circle: Ethics, Evolution, and Moral Progress. Princeton University Press, Princeton, Oxford (1981). https://doi.org/10.2307/j.ctt7sg4n
6. Greene, J.: Moral tribes: Emotion, reason, and the gap between us and them. Penguin Press (2013)
7. Vanderelst, D. & Winfield, A.: An architecture for ethical robots inspired by the simulation theory of cognition. Cognitive Systems Research. https://doi.org/10.1016/j.cogsys.2017.04.002(2018)
8. Anderson, M., Anderson, S.: Machine ethics: creating an ethical intelligent agent. AI Mag. **28**, 15–26 (2007). https://doi.org/10.1609/aimag.v28i4.2065
9. Moor, J.: The nature, importance, and difficulty of machine ethics. IEEE Intell. Syst. **21**, 18–21 (2006). https://doi.org/10.1109/MIS.2006.80
10. Vallor, S.: Technology and the Virtues. A Philosophical Guide to a Future Worth Wanting. Oxford University Press, New York (2016)
11. Floridi, L., Sanders, J.W.: The Method of Abstraction. In: The Ethics of Information, pp. 177–220 (2004). https://doi.org/10.1093/acprof:oso/9780199641321.003.0003
12. Van Zyl, L.: Virtue Ethics: A Contemporary Introduction. Routledge, New York (2019) ISBN: 978-0-203-36196-2
13. Stocker, M.: The schizophrenia of modern ethical theories. J. Philos. **73**(14), 453–466 (1976)
14. Williams, B.: Moral Luck. Cambridge University Press, Cambridge (1981)

15. Russell, S., Norvig, P.: Artificial Intelligence: A Modern Approach, 3rd edn. Prentice-Hall, Upper Saddle River (2010)
16. Anderson, M., Anderson, S., Armen, C.: Toward Machine Ethics. In: AAAI Workshop on Agent Organizations: Theory and Practice. San Jose, CA (2004)
17. Kuipers, B.: Human-Like Morality and Ethics for Robots. In: AAAI Workshop: AI, Ethics, and Society (2016)
18. Allen, C., Varner, G., Zinser, J.: Prolegomena to any future artificial moral agent. Journal of Experimental & Theoretical Artificial Intelligence 12, 251–261 (2000). Accessible through https://citeseerx.ist.psu.edu/viewdoc/download? doi=10.1.1.622.5624&rep=rep1&type=pdf Accessed 11 Oct 2019
19. Bench-Capon, T.J.M.: Ethical Approaches and Autonomous Systems. AI, 281. 2020, https://doi.org/10.1016/j.artint.2020.103239
20. Wächter, L., Lindner, F.: An Explorative Comparison of Blame Attributions to Companion Robots Across Various Moral Dilemmas. In: Proceedings of the 6th International Conference on Human-Agent Interaction (HAI '18), pp. 269–276 (2018). https://doi.org/10.1145/3284432.3284463
21. Ågotnes, T., van der Hoek, W., Tennenholtz, M., Wooldridge, M.: Power in normative systems. In: Proceedings of the 8th AAMAS Conference, pp. 145–152. IFAAMS (2009)
22. Brundage, M.: Limitations and risks of machine ethics. J. Experiment. Theor. Artif. Intell. 26(3), 355–372 (2014). https://doi.org/10.1080/0952813X.2014.895108
23. Deng, B.: Machine ethics: The robot's dilemma. Nature News 523(7558), 24 (2016). https://doi.org/10.1038/523024a
24. Russell, D.C.: Virtue Ethics, Happiness, and the Good Life. In: The Cambridge Companion to Virtue Ethics. Cambridge University Press, Cambridge (2013)
25. Frede, D.: Aristotle's Virtue Ethics. In: The Routledge Companion to Virtue Ethics. Routledge, New York (2015)
26. Berberich, N., Diepold, K.: The Virtuous Machine - Old Ethics for New Technology?. arxiv.org/abs/1806.10322. Accessed 14 Nov 2019
27. Wallach, W.: Implementing moral decision-making faculties in computers and robots. AI Soc. 22, 463–475 (2008). https://doi.org/10.1007/s00146-007-0093-6
28. Guarini, M.: Particularism and the classification and reclassification of moral cases. IEEE Intell. Syst. 21(4), 22–28 (2006). https://doi.org/10.1109/mis.2006.76
29. Anderson, M., & Anderson, S. (eds.): Machine Ethics. Cambridge University Press, Cambridge (2011). https://doi.org/10.1017/CBO9780511978036.013
30. Malle, B.F., Matthias, S.: Moral Competence in Social Robots. In: Proceedings of IEEE International Symposium on Ethics in Engineering, Science, and Technology, Ethics'2014, pp. 30–35. IEEE, Chicago, IL (2014)
31. Kidder, R.M.: How good people make tough choices: resolving dilemmas of ethical living. www.researchgate.net/publication/265023341_How_Good_People_Make_Tough_Choices_Resolving_the_Dilemmas_of_Ethical_Living. Last accessed 14 Nov 2019
32. Antaki, C.: Explaining and Arguing: The Social Organization of Accounts. Sage, London (1994)
33. McCullough, M.E., Kurzban, R., Tabak, B.A.: Cognitive systems for revenge and forgiveness. Behav. Brain Sci. 36, 1–15 (2013). https://doi.org/10.1017/S0140525X11002160
34. Semin, G.R., Manstead, A.S.: The accountability of conduct: A social psychological analysis. Academic Press, London (1983)
35. Tedeschi, J.T., Riess, M.: Impression Management Theory and Social Psychological Research. Academic, New York (1981)

36. Weiner, B.: Judgments of responsibility: A foundation for a theory of social conduct. Guilford Press, New York, NY (1995)
37. Dersley, I., Wootton, A.: Complaint sequences within antagonistic argument. Res. Lang. Social Interact. **33**, 375–406 (2000). https://doi.org/10.1207/S15327973RLSI3304_02
38. Traverso, V.: The dilemmas of third-party complaints in conversation between friends. J. Pragmat. **41**, 2385–2499 (2009)
39. McKenna, M.: Directed blame and conversation. In: Coates, D.J., Tognazzini, N.A. (eds.) Blame: Its nature and norms, pp. 119–140. Oxford University Press, New York, NY (2012)
40. Walker, M.U.: Moral repair: Reconstructing moral relations after wrongdoing. Cambridge University Press, New York (2006)
41. Van Berkum, J., Holleman, B., Nieuwland, M., Otten, M., Murre, J.p.: Right or wrong? the brain's fast response to morally objectionable statements. Psychol. Sci. **20** (2009). https://doi.org/10.1111/j.1467-9280.2009.02411.x
42. DeMoss, D.: Aristotle, Connectionism, and the Morally Excellent Brain. In: Proceedings of the Twentieth World Congress of Philosophy. American Organizing Committee Inc., Boston (1998). www.bu.edu/wcp/Papers/Cogn/CognDemo.htm
43. Honarvar, A.R., Ghasem-Aghaee, N.: An artificial neural network approach for creating an ethical artificial agent. In: Proceedings of IEEE CIRA, pp. 1–6 (2010) https://doi.org/10.1109/CIRA.2009.5423190
44. Toner, C.: The full unity of the virtues. J. Ethics, **18**(3), 207–227 (2014). https://doi.org/10.1007/s10892-014-9165-2
45. Annas, J.: Applying virtue ethics. J. Appl. Philos. **32**(1), 1–14 (2015). https://doi.org/10.1111/japp.12103
46. Schroeder, N.: Moral dilemmas in contemporary virtue ethics. LSU Master's Theses. 641 (2011)
47. Hursthouse, R.: On Virtue Ethics. Oxford University Press, Oxford (1999)
48. McDowell, J.: Virtue and reason. Monist **62**, 331–350 (1979)
49. Dworkin, R.: Taking rights seriously. Duckworth, London (1977)
50. Hursthouse, R.: Are virtues the proper starting point for morality? In: Dreier, J. (ed.) Contemporary Debates in Moral Theory, pp. 99–112. Blackwell, Malden, MA (2006)
51. Annas, J.: Intelligent Virtue, 1st edn. Oxford University Press, Oxford (2011)
52. Annas, J.: Comments on John Doris's Lack of Character. Res. **71**(3), 636–642 (2005). https://doi.org/10.1111/j.1933-1592.2005.tb00476.x
53. Aristóteles.: Ética a Nicómaco. 5th edn. Quetzal, Lisboa (2004). Translated by António Castro Caeiro
54. Anderson, M., Anderson, S.: Ethical Healthcare Agents. In: Studies in Computational Intelligence, vol. 107, pp. 233–250. Springer (2008)

DrugChecker: Blockchain-Based Counterfeit Drug Detection System

Amira Zaimia[1]() and Jalel Eddine Hajlaoui[2]

[1] Higher Institute of Computer Science of Kef, University of Jendouba, Jendouba,
Tunisia
amirazaimia@gmail.com
[2] MARS Research Laboratory, University of Sousse, Sousse, Tunisia

Abstract. The new technology Blockchain has moved beyond being a
mere advertising slogan to practical applications in industry sectors such
as the pharmaceutical industry. Building on This innovative technology,
several researchers have started to explore it in applications such as data
security, sharing of medical records with doctors or authorised patients,
drug detection. In this paper, We offer a drug verification solution that
allows the user to verify their drug by displaying their name, date of
manufacture and expiration as well as the addresses of the manufacturer,
wholesaler and the pharmacist.

Keywords: Blockchain · Drug · Counterfeit · Ethereum

1 Introduction

Drug counterfeiting has become a concerning global scourge, threatening the
health and safety of millions of people worldwide. The infiltration of counterfeit drugs into traditional pharmaceutical supply chains has devastating consequences for public health, exposing patients to serious risks, such as therapeutic
inefficiency, adverse effects, and even mortality. Faced with this growing menace,
the search for innovative solutions to secure and guarantee the authenticity of
medications has become a critical priority for the pharmaceutical industry and
regulatory bodies.

In this context, we are proud to present our revolutionary application for
detecting counterfeit drugs, based on blockchain technology. Our solution aims
to address the complex challenge of drug counterfeiting by harnessing the unique
capabilities of blockchain to ensure unfaltering traceability and proactive detection of counterfeit products throughout the pharmaceutical supply chain.

The remaining sections of this paper are organized as follows:

In the subsequent section we present the essentials of the Blockchain technology. In The third section we define the possible attacks on blockchain technology
and their countermeasures. Next, we describe detailed technical design of the proposed solution. After that, We focus in the last section on the implementation of
our system. We also specify the different stages of the implementation and the
results obtained.

© The Author(s), under exclusive license to Springer Nature Switzerland AG 2024
T. Guarda et al. (Eds.): ARTIIS 2023, CCIS 1936, pp. 402–413, 2024.
https://doi.org/10.1007/978-3-031-48855-9_30

2   State of Art

2.1   Blockchain Technology

Blockchain is a technology designed to store and transmit information. By extension, a blockchain is a decentralized ledger that records the complete history of all transactions conducted among users from its inception. The concept of blockchain has been proposed to solve certain problems in the context of money transfer. Currently, it is necessary to go through a bank to transfer money. This transaction can fail due to technical problems, exceeding the daily transfer limits and additional costs such as transfer fees associated with the money transfer... Unlike the blockchain where the payment system is overseen by a peer-to-peer (P2P) network.

Features

- Decentralisation: it is a decentralised database system, the data are distributed. Consequently, there is no central authority to authorize transactions or establish specific rules for their acceptance,and no service fees are required.
- Immutability: once transactions are validated, it becomes impossible to modify or delete them.
- Anonymity: Every user can engage with the blockchain using a generated address that conceals their actual identity, making it a more secure and reliable system.
- Auditability: The bitcoin blockchain stores user balance data founded on the UTXO (Unspent Transaction Output) model.

Structure   The blockchain is a series of blocks that holds a comprehensive record of transactional data. [1].

Transaction: Transactions are the exchanges made between blockchain users. Every user possesses a private key utilized for signing their transactions. This signature process ensures the security and integrity of the data. These transactions can be medical data, industrial information, monetary transactions...

Block: The block is one of the main elements of a blockchain. Each block contains the block header, the hash of the previous block and the list of confirmed transactions, as shown in the following figure.

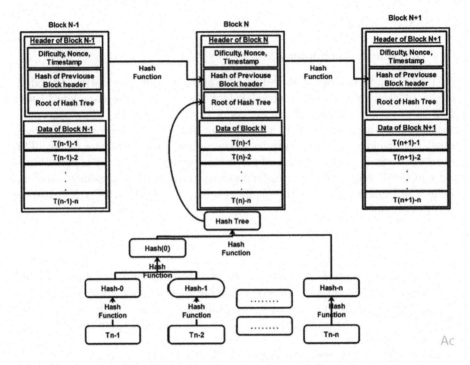

Fig. 1. Blockchain structure [15]

The block header contains:

Block version: Define the set of rules to follow in order to validate a block.

Merkle tree root hash: Contains the hash values of all transactions.

Timestamp: Presents the date and time of the mining.

Nonce: Represents a 4-byte field that initiates with 0 and increments with every hash calculation.

Hash of previous block: It represents the hash value that references the preceding block.

The body of the block which contains the transactions and the transaction counter.

Block chaining: Within a blockchain, blocks are interconnected by hash values, with each block containing the hash of preceding block.These hashes ensure the cryptographic integrity which prevents the content of existing blocks from being altered.

Mining. Blockchain mining involves solving a cryptographic problem, resulting in the generation of new blocks within the blockchain. Miners who successfully create new blocks are rewarded financially. To find the next block, a miner must solve a computational puzzle by hashing the block header with various nonces. Occasionally, when two miners simultaneously discover valid blocks and submit them, the network may encounter disagreements on the last block due to networking delays and synchronization issues.

2.2   Consensus Algorithms

In this section we describe some consensus algorithms.

Proof of Work. The proof-of-work algorithm stands as the inaugural algorithm devised for blockchain technology. It was proposed by S. Nakamoto to handle Bitcoin transactions. This algorithm endeavors to solve a mathematical puzzle using a cryptographic hash function to enable the addition of a new block to the chain. It uses miners who exploit their computational capacity to validate and authenticate blocks and transactions in the blockchain. Consequently, the miners attempt to discover a nonce that can only be achieved through repeated attempts with various values until the output falls within the specified target range. Once a participant identifies the nonce, they disseminate the block and transaction information to the other nodes. Then, if the new block is verified and validated, it will be added [2] .

Proof of stake it was proposed to resolve the weaknesses of proof of work. It is a consensus mechanism where the validation of blocks depends on the economic commitment of the network participants. The mining process does not require high computing power compared to PoW, which reduces the amount of energy consumed.

Pratical Byzantine Fault Tolerance. This algorithm was suggested to mitigate the Byzantine flaw that occurs in response to a failure raised by the BGP (Byzantine General Problem).

It is composed of 5 phases [3]:

Request: A request message will be sent to the primary node by the client

Pre-prepare: One of the blockchain nodes is selected as the primary node, while the remaining nodes act as replica nodes. The primary node disseminates the request message to the replica nodes via broadcasting.

Prepare: the condenser will be broadcast by the replica nodes to the main node and to the other replica nodes.

Commit: Upon verification, the node disseminates a commit message to the rest of the nodes..

Reply: Once a node (including both primary and replica nodes) receives 2f+1 commit messages, it responds to the client, furnishing a new block to the local blockchain, and establishing a link to the state database. This concludes the entire process.

2.3   Types of Blockchain

There are mainly three types of blockchains:

The public blockchain: It is a decentralized network functioning on a peer-to-peer system. It is accessible to everyone: anyone can carry out transactions. This type of blockchain can be assimilated to an unfalsifiable ledger managed by miners whose role is to verify transactions and validate blocks.

Private blockchain: it's a private network runed by a central body that is responsible for adding blocks to the blockchain. Access to this type of blockchain is restricted and requires the approval of the central body. It offers different access rights to people in the same network to ensure data confidentiality.

Consortium blockchain: This is a partially decentralised network [3]. The validation of blocks is taken by the majority of the most important members and not by the whole network as in the private blockchain. It offers a better confidentiality of transactions. This blockchain is preferable in the banking sector.

2.4   Blockchain Platforms

There are several platforms for designing blockchains such as Ethereum, Bitcoin, Hyperledger Fabric, Litecoin, Peercoin... In this section we focus on Bitcoin, Ethereum and Hyperledger Fabric.

Bitcoin is the world's first crypto-currency defined by Satoshi Nakamoto in 2008 [4]. It facilitates direct online payments from one party to another, by passing the involvement of a central authority. It was introduced with the aim of resolving the problem of double spending, where the same electronic coin is used to pay for several things. In the centralized system, this problem is solved through a central authority which can be a bank or other trusted third party, Nakamoto proposed a time-stamping server which ensures that all transactions appear chronologically in the database. Electronic payments are ensured by generating bitcoin transfer transactions between users.

Ethereum was co-founded by Vitalik Buterin, who first had the idea in October 2013. After a year, he created the ethereum foundation. The first version of the platform was released in June 2015 [5].

Ethereum is a blockchain allowing the creation of smart contracts by users. It is a public and secure data structure where all transactions are signed by the sender, grouped into blocks and the blocks are chained. Smart contracts are autonomous programs capable of executing predefined conditions. Smart contract systems allow the transfer of assets according to pre-designed rules. Each contract has an address in ethereum.

In 2015, The Linux Foundation established the Hyperledger project with the goal of promoting blockchain technologies across various industries. Built upon a modular architecture, it exhibits remarkable levels of privacy, resilience, flexibility, and scalability. [6] Hyperledger Fabric belongs to the family of Hyperledger blockchain projects. Similar to other blockchain technologies, it incorporates a ledger, utilizes smart contracts, and serves as a transaction management system for participants. The Hyperledger Fabric network consists of a set of of nodes such as peers, principals, customers...

2.5   Attacks and Countermeasures

While blockchain technology is widely acknowledged for its strength in security, privacy, and immutability, it is not entirely immune to various types of attacks. In this section, we present a study on possible attacks on blockchain and their countermeasures.

Double spending attack refers to the use of the same crypto-currency for transactions. For example, in bitcoin an attacker creates a transaction Tx1 using a set of coins with the address of the seller's recipient and spreads it across the network. At the same time, he creates and disseminates another transaction Tx2 using the same coins with his address or a wallet that is under his control. As soon as the seller receives enough confirmations, he releases the product to the dishonest customer. Once the attacker's chain surpasses the length of the main chain, other miners come to a consensus and adopt the attacker's branch. Tx1 is then replaced by Tx2. As a result, the attacker receives the product and the funds at the same time.

The most effective and simple way to avoid double spending is to wait for several confirmations before delivering goods or services to the recipient. In particular, the possibility of successful double-spending decreases as the number of confirmations received increases. Another possible solution is to detect a case of double spending by monitoring the progress of the blockchain and, once detected, identify the adversary and take appropriate action [11].

In a **Selfish mining attack**, an adversary attempts to mine his blocks privately and release them when the public chain of honest miners begins to approach the length of the private chain. In the context of the longest string rule, the initial measure implemented is known as uniform link breaking. This instructs the consensus nodes to uniformly and randomly select the chain to be extended, irrespective of the order in which they received them. The Zeroblock algorithm [12] The Zeroblock algorithm safeguards against this attack through the implementation of a novel timestamp-free technique. In this method, each block must be created and transmitted within a specified maximum time interval. If a selfish miner retains a block privately for longer than this interval, an honest miner will reject it.

Eclipse Attack: This refers to a form of attack where an attacker attempts to isolate nodes, thereby compromising their incoming and outgoing traffic. The attacker seizes complete control of a node's connections to the blockchain network, thereby exerting dominance over all incoming transactions to that node.

To avoid this type of attack, A. Ghosh et al. [13] propose to use whitelists and to block incoming connections. Another solution proposes to set a limit on the number of incoming connections. One solution is to store the connections in a confidential table [11]: the nodes connected by the users will be stored in a confidential table.

Sybil Attack: This type of attack involves an attacker creating multiple virtual identities to gain control over the entire network. These nodes with virtual identities are known as Sybil nodes. Through this method, the attacker can disconnect genuine nodes from the blockchain network. Miners join the network to obtain rewards, and the attacker can generate a large number of credentials within the network. Additionally, a malicious node can also execute a Sybil attack by introducing numerous zero-power miners to the blockchain network. These miners engage in data dissemination but lack the capacity to mine new blocks. These Sybil nodes promote the propagation of a single attacker's block within the network while halting the dissemination of authentic user blocks. To counter the effects of the Sybil attack, a solution has been proposed where each participating node monitors the behavior of other nodes and checks if any node is transmitting blocks from a specific user within a certain time frame. Such behavior is deemed malicious, and the nodes responsible are blacklisted and reported to other nodes to prevent the propagation of blocks from the Sybil node..

The 51% attack, also known as the majority attack, In the blockchain context, a 51% attack takes place when a group of miners or a single miner acquires control over more than 50% of the computing power within the network.

Normally, when a miner finds a solution to validate a block, he shares it on the network for verification. If this is the case, the network validates the solution and the miner receives a reward. In the case of a 51% attack, the malicious miner creates his chain in private, which explains the existence of two distinct blockchains: one followed by all the honest miners and the other followed by the dishonest miner.

2.6   Blockchain in the Pharmaceutical Sector

Ever since the advent of blockchain technology, several researches have been carried out to exploit it in order to find solutions to existing problems in the health field such as counterfeit drugs, sharing of medical records.

Jamil et al. [7] discussed the problem of counterfeit drugs and in this context they proposed a solution based on hyperleger fabric to improve the supply chain. It is a proof-of-concept application that ensures the sharing of personal medical records between doctors, nurses, patients and pharmacists. It also tracks the supply chain of medicines.

Andressa et al. [8] proposes a blockchain architecture based on hyperledger to share patient medical records. This architecture is composed of four related elements which are clients, blockchain, storage system and certification authority. Kuma et al. [9] propose a blockchain solution, called Medical chain that ensures the storage of the drug supply chain to be able to detect counterfeit drugs while encrypting QR (quick response) code.

Long et al. [10] present a solution based on blockchain technology called DrugLedger. It is a drug traceability system that ensures data confidentiality. It implements the packaging and repackaging mechanisms for drugs.

Several projects have been set up in the pharmaceutical field. Table 1 contains some examples of these projects.

Table 1. Pilot projects for drug traceability based on blockchain technology [16]

Product and pilot participants	Type of solution	Platform
IBM, KPMG, Merck, Walmart	Blockchain-based track and trace system.	Hyperledger
IDLogiq	Blockchain-enabled intelligent medication management with authentication.	Private platform
MediLedger-Amerisource Bergen, McKesson, and drug manufacturers Genentech, Pfizer, Gilead	A blockchain-powered system for product verification, specifically designed for handling salable returns.	Permissioned Enterprise Ethereum
TraceLink-over 22 participants including manufacturers, wholesalers, distributors	Blockchain-based network solutions enabling digital recalls with interoperability.	Hyperledger
Indiana university health and Wakemed health and hospitals	A blockchain-powered solution for tracing specialty medicines across providers' networks, whether internal or external	Private platform
LedgerDomain-University of California Los Angles health	A blockchain-based solution designed for the detection of counterfeit products.	Hyperledger
SAP Multichain-Merck, Amerisource Bergen, GSK, Amgen, Boehringer Ingelheim, McKesson, Novo Nordisk	A blockchain-based system for verifying counterfeits and tracking salable returns.	Multichain

The above mentioned solutions are not opensource, most of them are intended to manage electronic medical records or to share them between patients and doctors. However, none of these solutions tackles the challenge of medication verification utilizing the Ethereum platform.

3 Proposed Work

3.1 Actors

The basic components include manufacturer, Wholesaler, pharmacist and Patient.

– Manufacturer: This actor produces medicines, to be prescribed to patients to curing or vaccinating them, and sends them to the wholesaler.;
– Wholesaler: This actor accepts the medicines sent by the manufacturer, stores them and sells them to the pharmacist;
– Pharmacist: This actor accepts the medicines and delivers them to the patients.

– Patient: it is the person who will benefit from the system, he will check the origin of the medicines to make sure that they are counterfeit or real medicines.

3.2 Global Architecture

This architecture is composed of 3 parts:

The front-end which contains the user interfaces. These interfaces are developed with React Bootstrap HTML and CSS.

Back-end: This is an important part, it ensures the communication with the blockchain network, and the front-end provided to the user.

distributed ledger network: This is a Peer-To-Peer network that encompasses the different nodes. We have created a private blockchain network for our project with ganache which is composed of 10 nodes.

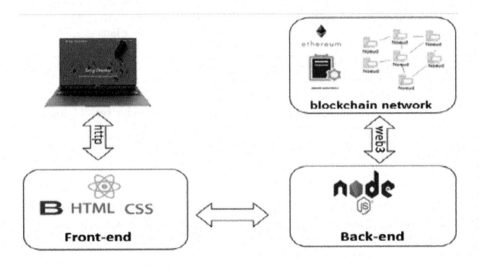

Fig. 2. Global architecture

4   Implementation

A brief description of our proposed solution 'Drug Checker' is as follows:

In the first step, the manufacturer adds the medicine which will be sent directly to the wholesaler. The wholesaler checks the information of the received medicine and accepts it to be sent to the retailer. Next, the retailer, also known as the pharmacist, accepts the medicine. Finally, the patient checks whether the medicine is real or counterfeit by typing CIP code and batch number.

The Fig. 3 explains the approach of our system.

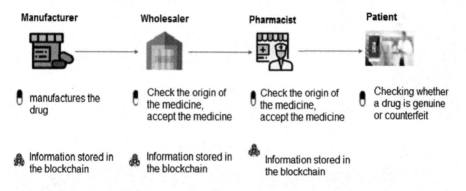

Fig. 3. DrugChecker

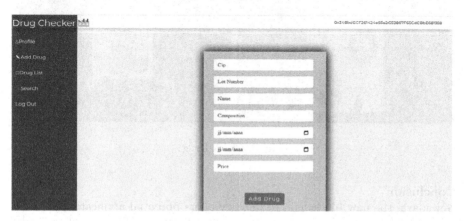

Fig. 4. Add Drug

To add a drug, the manufacturer enters the drug information in the form shown in the Fig. 4.

The interface shown in the Fig. 5 allows the wholesaler to verify the manufacturer's address and accept the drug to be sent to the retailer.

The main interface of our system in the Fig. 6, the user accesses the application to check a drug. It is enough to enter the cip code with the lot number in the search field. If the drug exists, an interface will be displayed that contains the name of the drug with the supply chain of the drug presented by the addresses of the manufacturer, wholesaler and retailer and the dates of manufacture and expiration. If not an interface that contains an error message will be displayed on the screen.

Fig. 5. Accept Drug

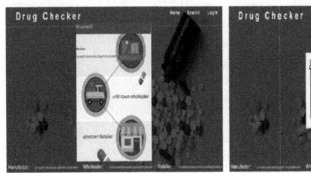

Fig. 6. Check Drug

Conclusion

Nowadays, the new blockchain technology offers potential applications to over-come some of the challenges faced by the health sector. This technology is also capable of disrupting the world of banking, insurance and other financial services. By using blockchain technology, the pharmaceutical sector has managed to grow and evolve towards decentralisation. Nonetheless, the challenge of upholding trust between medical product sellers and buyers persists. The presence of malicious entities may give rise to doubt regarding their credibility. Moreover, the production of medicine encompasses numerous decentralized processes and sub-processes, necessitating traceability, accountability, and safety. To address this issue, we have introduced a blockchain-based solution called "Drug Checker" to detect counterfeit drugs. In our proposal, we have furnished comprehensive information regarding traceability and fraud detection aspects of the solution. Our system helps to mitigate the problem of counterfeit drugs. We used the ethereum platform, ganache to interact with the blockchain in order to realize our solution.

References

1. Zheng, Z., Xie, S., Dai, H., Chen, X., Wang, H.: An overview of blockchain technology : Architecture, consensus, and future trends. IEEE (2017), pp. 557–564 (2017)

2. Nguyen, C.T., Hoang, D.T., Nguyen, D.N., Niyato, D., Nguyen, H.T., Dutkiewicz, E.: Proof-of-stake consensus mechanisms for future blockchain networks : fundamentals, applications and opportunities. IEEE **7** (2019), 85727–85745 (2019)
3. Zheng, K., Liu, Y., Dai, C., Duan, Y., Huang, X.: Model checking pbftconsensus mechanism in healthcare blockchain network. In: IEEE 9th International Conference on Information Technology in Medicine and Education, pp. 877–881 (2018)
4. Nakamoto, S.: Bitcoin : a peer-to-peer electronic cash system (2008)
5. Buterin., V. Ethereum whitepaper (2013)
6. Kim, Y., Kim, K.H., Kim, J.H.: Power trading blockchain using hyperledger fabric. In: IEEE (2020)
7. Jamil, F., Hang, L., Kim, K., Kim, D.: A novel medical blockchain model for drug supply chain integrity management in a smart hospital. Electronics **8**(5), 505 (2019)
8. Fernandes, A., Rocha, V., Da Conceicao, A.F., Horita, F.: Scalable architecture for sharing ehr using the hyperledger blockchainl. In: IEEE International Conference on Software Architecture Companion (2020)
9. Randhir Kumar, R.T.: Traceability of counterfeit medicine supply chain through blockchain. In: International Conference on Communication System and Network. IEEE (2019)
10. Randhir Kumar, R.T. Drugledger : a practical blockchain system for drug traceability and regulation. In: Proceedings of the IEEE International Conference Internet Things (iThings), IEEE Green Comput. Commun. (GreenCom), IEEE Cyber, Phys. Social Comput. (CPSCom), IEEE Smart Data (SmartData), pp. 1137–1144 (2018)
11. Conti, M., Kumar, E.S., Lal, C., Ruj, S.: A survey on security and privacy issues of bitcoin. IEEE **20**(4), 3416–3452 (2018)
12. Solat, S., Potop-Butucaru, M.: Zeroblock : timestamp-free prevention of block-withholding attack in bitcoin. arXiv:1605.02435 (2017)
13. Ghosh, A., Gupta, S., Dua, A., Kumar, N.: Security of cryptocurrencies in blockchain technology : State-of-art, challenges and future prospects. J. Netw. Comput. Appl. **163**, 102635 (2020)
14. Swathi, P., Chirag Modi, D.P.: Preventing sybil attack in blockchain using distributed behavior monitoring of miners. In: 2019 10th International Conference on Computing, Communication and Networking Technologies (ICCCNT) IEEE (2019), 1–6 (2019)
15. Yekta, M.H., Shahidinejad, A., Ghobaei-Arani, M.: Blockchain for transparent, privacy preserved, and secure health data management, Elsevier 2023, pp. 219–242 (2023)
16. https://journals.sagepub.com/doi/epub/10.1177/14604582211011228 Accessed 29 Jan 2023

Perception of Psychological Recommendations Generated by Neural Networks by Student Youth (Using ChatGPT as an Example)

Anna Uglova[1] ⓘ, Irina Bogdanovskaya[1] ⓘ, and Boris Nizomutdinov[2](✉) ⓘ

[1] The Herzen State Pedagogical University of Russia, Saint-Petersburg, Russia
[2] ITMO University, Saint-Petersburg, Russia
boris-wels@yandex.ru

Abstract. The neural network can create recommendations on any topic, including psychological themes. This raises an ethical issue: the generated text may be perceived by the user as expert advice, not being compared with other sources, but still used to make decisions.

The goal of the study: assess the perception of text generated by a neural network on standard psychological topics (using ChatGPT as an example) and compare it with the perception of recommendations written by a specialist psychologist. 236 participants took part in the experiment. A quasi-experimental design with one sample was used with the introduction of two equivalent experimental interventions: cases with recommendations written by a psychologist and a neural network.

At a significant level, text generated by the neural network was perceived as more attractive and inducing the desire to seek help. There is a significant positive correlation between the positive evaluation of recommendations generated by the neural network with the perception of the significance of electronic resources and the reluctance to seek advice from a real psychologist. A negative correlation was established between the readiness to seek help from a texts were generated by the neural network and the presence of experience in individual psychological counseling.

Keywords: psychological recommendations · neural networks · psychological safety · ChatGPT

1 Introduction

The rapid development of neural network technologies has led to the ability to solve complex tasks that were previously considered unsolvable. Deep learning models based on neural networks, which allow for the creation of various texts, are actively being introduced into educational, commercial, managerial, and entertainment activities [1]. Based on this technology, it has become possible to automatically create news, track fake news, write stories, and recommendations that can be used in a dialogue with the user [2].

T. Guarda et al. (Eds.): ARTIIS 2023, CCIS 1936, pp. 414–425, 2024.
https://doi.org/10.1007/978-3-031-48855-9_31

The system is capable of generating recommendations on any topic, including psychological ones. This raises an ethical problem that needs to be studied: the generated text may be perceived by the user as expert opinion, not compared to other sources, but used to make various decisions. The creation of textual data using a neural network is based on the processing of a training dataset, which in one way or another has its limitations in terms of the volume of incoming data and time for training [3]. Through iterative data analysis, the most realistic text is created, with all the external signs of completeness [4].

Interaction with a neural network can be seen as a separate form of communication that can influence a person's perceptions of the world. As these technologies occupy more and more of each user's life space, it becomes important to study the transformation of the mass communication system and the changing personal meanings of interaction with both "live" and artificial intelligence [5].

There is a risk that neural networks may become a production or social filter. Currently, neural networks perform well in tasks such as emotion recognition [6], publication recommendation [7], and personality trait recognition [8], allowing for the creation of a personalized information field for each user, regardless of their preferences. Many studies have shown that users are easily influenced by recommendations and reviews, the majority of which are currently generated by neural networks [9]. This means that information will be filtered through neural networks, and people may be limited in their choices or only have access to certain types of information.

Numerous studies have focused on examining how users perceive recommendations generated by neural networks. Some of these studies explore how users perceive and react to recommendations, while others examine how to improve the quality of recommendations, so that users are more satisfied and likely to use these recommendations in the future.

In a study conducted by S. Mitchell and colleagues [10], recommendations generated by neural networks are viewed from the perspective of algorithmic fairness. The authors point out that developers of automated recommendation algorithms should consider broader ethical implications of their work, including issues of power and social justice. The study found that users tend to be quite skeptical of neural network recommendations and prefer to receive recommendations from people who have experience with what they are recommending. It was also found that users tend to trust recommendations more if they have personal experience using the product or service.

According to research by E. Even-Dar [11], people often trust digital recommendations and may rely on the popularity of a source rather than its informativeness when making a choice. Personal experience and knowledge are also important factors in decision-making.

In studies by I. Guy and colleagues [12], it was found that the perception of recommendations given by neural networks can vary depending on how these recommendations are formulated and presented to the user. For example, using more detailed information about users and their preferences can increase the effectiveness of the recommendation system and the user's perception of its recommendations. However, if users are provided with too much information or recommendations that appear too frequently, this can lead to fatigue and lower trust in the system.

In his research, N Kenigstein noted that users trust a transparent recommendation system more [13]. To accept recommendations, users need to know the process of creating them in order to control the communication process. Overall, the perception of recommendations depends on many factors, such as usage context, user preferences, and the quality of the recommendation itself. It is worth noting that most studies focus on general, commercial, news, and educational recommendations. However, the perception of psychological recommendations is practically unexplored.

There are several studies dedicated to the implementation of artificial intelligence technologies in psychological counseling. Y. Li suggests the possibility of using hybrid algorithms to determine the user's psychological state and develop a plan for psychological counseling [14]. In the study by C. Zhang and M. Shu [15], an automated model for collecting psychological information and monitoring the user's state is described.

It becomes important to study the factors that can help improve the quality of recommendations and formulate ethical boundaries for the use of such recommendations for psychological assistance. Therefore, the aim of this study is to experimentally investigate the perception of texts generated by a neural network on topics of standard psychological queries (using ChatGPT as an example) and compare it with the perception of recommendations written by a specialist psychologist.

2 Materials and Methods

In this study, an experimental socio-psychological research model was used, allowing us to assess the real experience of users interacting with psychological content.

To achieve our goal, we set the following tasks:

- analyze the main approaches to studying the capabilities of working with neural networks, psychological recommendations, and digital psychological counseling;
- create a case reflecting examples of recommendations from a specialist psychologist for a typical query;
- generate a case using a neural network (using chatgpt as an example) for a typical psychological query;
- conduct an experimental study of attitudes towards the created cases; • conduct a survey on previous counseling experience;
- identify the factor structure of the individual assessment system for cases written by a psychologist and a neural network;
- identify differences in the perception of cases written by a psychologist and a neural network;
- identify correlations between the perception of cases written by a psychologist and a neural network and previous counseling experience.

We hypothesized that: 1) there are statistically significant differences in the perception of texts written by a psychologist and those generated by a neural network; 2) there is a negative correlation between the previous experience of receiving psychological help in the form of consultation and the willingness to seek help from a chatbot.

The sample for the survey consisted of 236 people aged 17 to 40 years (Mean = 20.9, SD = 4.03), of which 86% (203) were women and 14% (33) were men. The study was conducted in 2023 in Russia, in the city of St. Petersburg.

The research used survey methods, experimental methods, semantic methods, and statistical methods of data analysis.

To analyze the previous experience of interaction with a psychologist and the assessment of the significance of psychological help, a survey of respondents was conducted on the following questions:

1) Do you have experience of contacting a psychologist?
2) Evaluate the effectiveness of working with a psychologist;
3) Assess your readiness (desire) to recommend this psychologist to your acquaintances.
4) I believe that reading psychological literature and recommendations from psychologists can help solve psychological difficulties.

For the gradation of answer options on questions, the Likert scale was used.

To assess the attitude towards psychological help, a series of questions from the "Test for determining the need for psychological help" [16] were used: 1) I think that neither friends nor relatives can replace a professional psychologist when a crisis occurs in life; 2) I do not believe that anyone, even specialist psychologist, can better understand my problems than me.

A quasi-experiment was conducted on a single sample with the introduction of two equivalent experimental interventions.

The experiment procedure included a demonstration of two cases with recommendations on the topic: "How to survive a breakup?". This request was selected as one of the most popular according to the Public Opinion Foundation (https://fom.ru/Obraz-zhizni/14769). To introduce independent variables into the experiment, the "cognitive placebo" technique was used: both texts were presented as recommendations of psychologists.

Description of cases. The first case was based on a text generated by a neural network (using ChatGPT as an example). The second case was based on the recommendations of a psychologist presented on the professional website for psychologists "B17". The psychologist's recommendations were selected based on the popularity rating of responses to the query "How to survive a breakup?". The author's style of the recommendation texts was preserved, the volume of characters was equalized.

During the experiment, after getting acquainted with the cases, participants were asked to assess their willingness to contact a psychologist who provided these recommendations (a seven-point Likert scale was used). Also, the participants of the experiment were asked to evaluate the recommendations using the author's semantic differential, which included the classical factors highlighted by Ch. Osgood (f. Strength, f. Assessment, f. Activity), as well as an additional factor included (f. Informativeness).

Participation in the experiment was carried out on a voluntary basis. After the experiment, a post-experimental conversation was conducted with the participants, revealing the goals of the experiment and discussing the results.

Empirical data were processed using mathematical statistics methods: 1) analysis of primary statistics; 2) analysis of significantly significant differences in the studied variables (nonparametric Wilcoxon T-test); 3) correlation analysis (Spearman's rank correlation coefficient); 4) factor analysis (principal component method, followed by orthogonal rotation). The significance levels considered in the study were $p \leq 0.05$. At the stage of processing the results of the study, the IBM SPSS 19.0 statistical data processing software package was used.

3   Materials and Methods

At the first stage, using a semantic differential, we assessed the perception of psychological recommendations and, using the Wilcoxon T-test, revealed significantly significant differences in the perception of texts written by a psychologist and generated by a neural network (see Table 1).

Table 1. Significantly significant differences in the perception of recommendations written by a psychologist and generated by a neural network

Indicators	Case (neural network)	Case (psychologist)	Wilcoxon's T-criterion	p-value
Willingness to seek help	4.79	4.03	4139.50	0.000016
The "score" factor (ratio)	4.72	3.94	5853.00	0.000001
The "strength" factor	3.04	3.81	3475.00	0.000001
The "activity" factor	3.77	3.51	9248.00	0.000782
The "informativeness" factor	4.72	4.28	8518.00	0.000082

From the table provided, it can be seen that respondents rate the neural network-generated text significantly higher in the factors of "Attitude" ($p = 0.00001$), "Activity" ($p = 0.000782$), and "Informativeness" ($p = 0.000082$). On the other hand, the text written by the psychologist is significantly more often rated higher in the factor of "Strength" ($p = 0.00001$).

It can be assumed that the neural network-generated text, based on a popular text array, more often uses clichéd phrases and is primarily aimed at creating general motivating recommendations, which are perceived as kinder, brighter, safer, as well as more fun, colorful, and understandable.

At the same time, the psychologist's recommendations have individual characteristics, are aimed at presenting personal opinions on a given topic and creating a memorable self-presentation to attract clients, which can make the text more complex, strong, heavy, exciting, and detailed.

Respondents also significantly rate their readiness to turn to the "specialist" whose text was written by the neural network, rather than a psychologist ($p = 0.000016$).

It can be assumed that due to the fact that the text generated by the neural network is likely to not evoke negative emotions and is formulated in a more journalistic style, it is perceived as lighter, does not cause tension, and inspires more trust than the text written by the psychologist.

In the next stage, we studied the factorial structure of the individual evaluation system of psychological recommendations written by a psychologist and generated by a neural network (see Tables 2 and 3).

The first factor, explaining 26% of the total variance, was interpreted as the "Esthetic attractiveness and safety-related perception component". The leading evaluations in the

Table 2. The results of factorization of the individual evaluation system of psychological recommendations generated by the neural network

Name of factors	Indicators in the composition of the factor	Indicator weight
Factor 1 – "Evaluative component of perception associated with the concept of aesthetic attractiveness and safety" factor weight: 6.83; 26% variance	Great	0.63
	Good	0.69
	Light	**0.75**
	Clean	**0.71**
	Beautiful	0.64
	Safe	**0.82**
	Honest	0.69
	Realistic	0.63
	Heavy	−0.65
	Rude	**−0.75**
	Exciting	−0.64
	Understandable	0.64
Factor 2 – "Information component of perception" factor weight: 5.6; 22% variance	Smart	0.57
	Strong	0.66
	Attention - grabbing	0.62
	Memorable	0.70
	Informative	0.82
	Informative	0.83
	Detailed	0.56
	Useful	0.73
Factor 3 – "Affective component of perception" Name of factors	Happy	0.62
	Cheerful	0.79
	Bright	0.61
	Young	0.64
	Fastindicators: Fast	0.54

factor describe the text as safe, gentle, clean, bright, and kind. It can be assumed that the non-specific, journalistic direction of the text forms a certain attitude towards the author, endowing them with the same qualities - safety, tenderness, and kindness [17], and creates an aura of attractiveness.

The second factor (22% of the total variance) was interpreted as the "Informational component of perception". The leading evaluations in the factor describe the text as memorable, informative, and useful. It can be said that a clear set of instructions/advice presented in the text generated by the neural network gives a sense of integrity and usefulness.

The third factor, describing 11% of the total variance, was interpreted by us as the "Affective component of perception". The leading evaluations in the factor describe the text as fun and youthful. It can be assumed that for the young generation, whose perception we are studying, an important factor is the entertainment component of the consumed content, which also affects the perception of specialized psychological literature [18].

Let us consider the factorial structure of the individual evaluation system of psychological recommendations written by a psychologist (see Table 3).

Table 3. The results of factorization of the individual evaluation system of psychological recommendations written by a psychologist

Name of factors	Indicators in the composition of the factor	Indicator weight
Factor 1 – "Self-presentation related to the concept of attracting attention" Factor weight: 6.74; 29% variance	Good	0.72
	Clean	0.55
	Beautiful	0.60
	Smart	−0.82
	Sincere	0.53
	Realistic	0.64
	Strong	0.82
	Attention - grabbing	0.76
	Memorable	0.66
	Informative	0.84
	Informative	0.84
	Useful	0.81
Factor 2 – "Evaluative component of perception associated with aesthetic and value concept" Factor weight: 5.91; 26% variance	Good	0.77
	Light	0.76
	Safe	0.75
	Heavy	−0.80
	Rude	−0.81
	Happy	0.64
	Exciting	−0.74
	Cheerful	0.61
Factor 3 – "Affective component of perception"	Complicated	−0.52
	Bright	0.65
	Fast	0.79

The first factor explaining 29% of the total variance was interpreted as "Self-presentation related to the concept of attracting attention." The leading ratings in the factor describe the text as good, stupid, strong, informative, and attention-grabbing. We can say that this factor describes the contradictory attitude of respondents to this text. This attitude is associated with the use of various communicative strategies to attract attention, some of which are evaluated as successful, and some are not. It can be assumed that in the excessive individualization of the text, aimed at trying to evoke emotions in the reader, the ritualization of the first acquaintance is lost, which allows creating a sense of acceptance [19].

The second factor (26% of the total variance) was designated by us as an "Evaluative component of perception associated with an aesthetic and value concept" (as for a text written by a neural network). The leading ratings in the composition of the factor describe the text as light, gentle, soothing, safe. It can be said that for some respondents, this text also seemed safe and easy enough, which contributed to its positive assessment.

The third factor, describing 10% of the total variance, was interpreted by us as an "Affective component of perception". The leading estimates in the composition of the factor describe the text as simple and fast. It can be said that this factor is also common and is generally associated with the acceleration of communication in the conditions of digitalization [20].

At the last stage, using Spearman's rank correlation coefficient, we identified significantly significant relationships between the components of perception of the texts of recommendations and willingness to seek help with previous consulting experience (see Fig. 1).

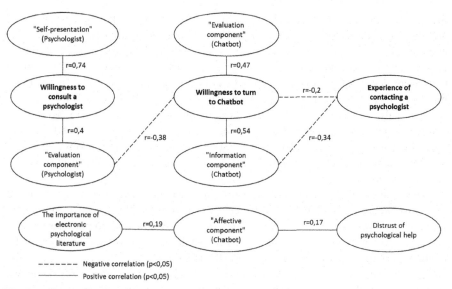

Fig. 1. Reliably significant interrelations of components of perception of texts of recommendations and advisory experience

From the given correlation pleiad, it can be seen that the readiness to seek help from a neural network is primarily associated with the perception of its informativeness and the evaluation of aesthetic and moral attractiveness, creating a safe space for dialogue, as well as with the evaluation of aesthetic and moral unattractiveness of a psychologist's recommendations. It is also worth noting that the readiness to seek help from a neural network negatively correlates with the previous experience of consulting a psychologist. It can be assumed that the journalistic style of the neural network, aimed at creating general recommendations for people without personal consulting experience, appears to be safer and less anxiety-provoking, as it does not touch upon deep-seated experiences and descriptions of psychological mechanisms.

The positive correlation between the affective component of the perception of the neural network's recommendations and the significance of electronic psychological literature and distrust of psychological help also confirms the assumption that these recommendations seem attractive primarily to those who are looking for of a journalistic and entertaining nature, rather than working with a specialist. An important stage in the continuation of this work will be the study of the reasons for distrust of psychologists and the search for ways to expand psychological culture.

The readiness to turn to a psychologist is positively correlated with self-presentation aimed at attracting users' attention, as well as with the evaluative component, which includes the aesthetic perception of the text of recommendations and its safety and openness.

4 Discussion of Results

Significant differences were revealed in the perception of texts written by a psychologist and those generated by a neural network. Respondents rate the neural network's texts as more attractive, informative and active, while the psychologist's texts as stronger. Experiment participants rated their willingness to seek help from a "specialist" whose texts were generated by a neural network significantly higher, indicating the helping potential of such resources in organizing psychological support systems.

The analysis of the factor structure of the individual evaluation system for psychological recommendations created by a psychologist and a neural network allowed studying the attractiveness of texts created by the neural network. First and foremost, texts created by a neural network are assessed from an aesthetic point of view, in terms of safety, clarity, and ease.

The psychologist's recommendation texts are primarily perceived as aimed at the specialist's self-presentation and are evaluated as attention-grabbing, strong, but foolish. It can be assumed that neural network texts are quite neutral and do not cause strong emotions, which increases their attractiveness, while the psychologist's texts provoke contradictory reactions, reducing their overall appeal.

These conclusions are consistent with the research of A.M. Zuraeva, Z.T. Djelieva, which indicates that among psychological practices, psychologists-bloggers who provide primarily entertaining content are currently the most popular on the Internet [21]. The second hypothesis about the relationship between previous consulting experience and the willingness to seek help from a specialist who wrote the recommendations was also confirmed. A negative correlation was found between the willingness to seek help from a neural network and previous experience of consulting a psychologist. The obtained data correspond to the results of the study by V.O. Anikina, A.G. Popova, N.L. Vasilieva, which indicate the importance of considering previous consulting experience in predicting readiness to work with a psychologist [22]. It can be assumed that real consulting experience, associated with the need to resolve significant problems, leads to a decrease in the value of generalized recommendations and makes the neural network's texts less attractive.

It is important to note the limitations of this study. This stage of the experiment included the demonstration of only two cases on the same topic in the field of relations. In the future, it is necessary to expand the topics that will be presented to the subjects to understand the specifics of reactions to various psychological requests.

Also, in the study, we did not consider the influence of socio-demographic factors on perception features. There is a specific attitude to psychological assistance in men and women [23], in people of different age groups [24], which is also advisable to take into account in further research. It is important to note that most texts in the information space are creolized and include pictorial content that significantly changes the perception of information [25]. An important continuation of the research will be the study of the perception of the text together with photographs, video material.

5 Conclusion

Based on an experimental study, it becomes possible to study the specifics of the request for psychological practice among young people. The analysis of the cases showed the educational and motivational potential of the recommendations generated by the neural network, as well as the limitations of this method. An important aspect of the popularization of psychological knowledge is revealed, which at the moment is primarily associated with the inclusion of a large number of entertaining and simplified content in the profiles of a psychologist in the digital space. This process generates specific expectations from working with a psychologist. In this regard, the importance of previous experience in counseling when choosing a specialist shows the need to expand psychological education about the real work of a psychologist.

In the continuation of this study, it is planned to expand the range of psychological requests for analysis, to study the relationship of socio-demographic and personal characteristics with user preferences, to clarify requests for digital psychological assistance.

6 Financing

The work was supported by the grant of the Russian Science Foundation No. 22-78-10047, "Constructive and destructive communicative practices of specialists of helping professions in digital media". URL: https://rscf.ru/project/22-78-10047/.

References

1. Wang, J., Xie, H., Tat, O., Au, S.: Top-N personalized recommendation with graph neural networks in MOOCs. Comput. Educ. Artif. Intell. **2**, 100010 (2021)
2. Trang, H., Ngoc, P., Nguyen, T., Hwang, D.: Fake news detection: a survey of graph neural network methods. Appl. Soft Comput. **139**, 110235 (2023)
3. Diker, S.N., Sakar, C.O.: Creating CREATE queries with multi-task deep neural networks. Knowl.-Based Syst. **266**, 110416 (2023)
4. Magalhães, D., Lima, R.H.R., Pozo, A.: Creating deep neural networks for text classification tasks using grammar genetic programming. Appl. Soft Comput. **135**, 110009 (2023)
5. Malyuzhenko, K.A., Ushakova, V.R.: Subjective picture of the perception of the world in the semantic perception of the author and reader. Notes Scientist **6–2**, 49–54 (2021). (in Russian)
6. Di Luzio, F., Rosato, A., Panella, M.: A randomized deep neural network for emotion recognition with landmarks detection. Biomed. Sig. Process. Control **81**, 104418 (2023)
7. Chheda, R., Bohara, D., Karani, R.: Music recommendation based on affective image content analysis. Procedia Comput. Sci. **218**, 383–392 (2023)
8. Kosan, M.A., Karacan, H., Urgen, B.A.: Predicting personality traits with semantic structures and LSTM-based neural networks. Alexandria Eng. J. **61**(10), 8007–8025 (2022)
9. Ren, Y., Ji, D.: Neural networks for deceptive opinion spam detection: an empirical study. Inf. Sci. **385**, 213–224 (2017)
10. Mitchell, S., Potash, E., Barocas, S., D'Amour, A.: Lum K Algorithmic fairness: choices, assumptions, and definitions. Ann. Rev. Stat. Appl. **8**, 141–163 (2021). https://doi.org/10.1146/annurev-statistics-042720-125902
11. Even-Dar, E., Shapira, A.: A note on maximizing the spread of influence in social networks. Inf. Process. Lett. **111**(4), 184–187 (2011)
12. Guy, I., Palomares, I., Porcel, C., Pizzato, L., Herrera-Viedma, E.: Reciprocal recommender systems: analysis of state-of-art literature, challenges and opportunities towards social recommendation. Inf. Fusion **69**, 103–127 (2021)
13. Koenigstein, N., Koren, Y.: Towards scalable and accurate item-oriented recommendations. In: Proceedings of the 7th ACM Conference on Recommender Systems, pp. 419–422 (2013)
14. Li, Y.: Design of psychological consultation system based on weighted fuzzy hybrid algorithm. Secur. Commun. Netw. **1**, 1–10 (2021). https://doi.org/10.1155/2021/2208006
15. Zhang, C., Shu, M.: Health assessment method based on support vector machine. Comput. Syst. Appl. **27**, 18–26 (2018)
16. Neupokoeva, N.: The need for psychological help. Psychological Service in a Rural Area. Rural School, no. 5, pp. 104–105 (2003). (in Russian)
17. Samsonova, A.N.: Psychological mechanisms of formation and functioning of the installation in the process of perception of a literary text. Psychol. Learn. **11**, 80–92 (2008). (in Russian)
18. Bogdanovskaya, I.M., Koroleva, N.N., Uglova, A.B.: Psychological factors of trust in popular video bloggers among modern youth. Psychol. J. High. Sch. Econ. **18**(3), 451–467 (2021). (in Russian)
19. Matantseva, D.A.: Stereotypes and violation of social rituals of communication on dating sites (badoo). Sociol. Narrative, 214–223 (2020). (in Russian)
20. Shakhovsky, V.I.: Accelerated communication as a need of modern society. The linguistic existence of a person and an ethnic group, pp. 285–293 (2018). (in Russian)
21. Zuraeva, A.M., Dzhelieva, Z.T.: Psychological assistance in online counselling. The world of science. Pedagogy Psychol. **8**(1), 48 (2020). (in Russian)
22. Anikina, V.O., Popova, A.G., Vasilyeva, N.L.: Subjective factors of men seeking psychological help. The world of science. Pedagogy Psychol. **8**(5), 26 (2020). (in Russian)

23. Shapovalov, R.A., Kolpachnikov, V.V.: The problem of men's attitude to psychological help. In: The World of Psychology, vol. 1, no. 97, pp. 152–164 (2019). (in Russian)
24. Krushnaya, N.A.: Features of psychological counseling of adults in crisis. Hum. Factor Soc. Psychol. 1(35), pp. 293–296 (2018). (in Russian)
25. Matveev, M.O., Nistratov, A.A., Polikarpov, D.M., Tarasov, E.F.: Semantic perception of a creolized text. Philol. Sci. MGIMO 7(1)(25), 45–59 (2021). (in Russian)

A Study of Online Privacy Policies of South African Retail Websites

Jean Maraba(✉) ⓘ and Adéle Da Veiga ⓘ

School of Computing, College of Science, Engineering and Technology,
University of South Africa (UNISA), Florida Campus, Johannesburg, South Africa
marabajr@gmail.com, dveiga@unisa.ac.za

Abstract. Consumers today are pushing for greater transparency over the potential collection and use of their personal information (PI). It is key for organizations dealing with consumer PI to address privacy concerns and challenges. The use of an online privacy policy is one of the most effective ways of informing consumers about an organization's use of their PI and security measures they have adopted to protect it against possible threats. The purpose of this paper is to firstly, propose a holistic set of online privacy policy guidelines and secondly, to ascertain to what extent online privacy policies, within the South African retail sphere, address the guidelines. This, in turn, also provides an indication as to whether the online privacy policies address conditions of the Protection of Personal Information Act (POPIA). Both qualitative and quantitative analysis methods were used on a sample of 18 retail websites. While it was found that all retail websites had an online privacy policy, some were still failing to meet the proposed guidelines and as such recommendations for improvement are provided relating specifically to access, third-parties, information quality and accountability.

Keywords: Online privacy policy · Personal Information · POPIA

1 Introduction

Online privacy is important in the context of a modern technological society. With the ever-increasing importance of the internet, there is a need to adopt safeguards that protect users from the invasion of their privacy and access to identifying their PI. According to Izogo, 51% of South Africans with internet access were already shopping online in 2018, and the numbers have since been increasing [1]. Mapande and Appiah wrote about how the South African online spending curve reached a high of 53 billion Rand in 2018, with a yearly anticipated growth of 15% all through 2021 [2]. The Covid-19 pandemic fast-tracked this incline, as more and more consumers opted for online shopping as a preferred method of shopping [3]. Parallel to that, more retailers have since invested in an online presence because the convenience and accessibility to large markets which online shopping presents made engaging in it more enticing [3, 4].

This increased move and need for online shopping is not one that is met without challenges, one of which is related to consumer privacy. The PI of consumers, such as

T. Guarda et al. (Eds.): ARTIIS 2023, CCIS 1936, pp. 426–440, 2024.
https://doi.org/10.1007/978-3-031-48855-9_32

physical addresses, cell phone numbers, email address, age, race, gender, and billing information - to mention a few, are collected while shopping online [5] and without adequate measures in place, this PI can easily land in unwarranted hands without consumer consent.

Moraka [6] writes about an increased incline in data breaches by cyber attackers. These result in consumers being scammed, their identities being stolen and, most commonly, receiving unwarranted calls and SMSs from telemarketers [7, 8]. The data breaches are not limited to consumer PI, but consumer trends are also recorded and analyzed, as a means of "improving" customer service, experience and for customized marketing. This is called "web tracking" and is unfortunately at the cost of the violation to consumers' privacy [9–11]. Though greatly advantageous, online shopping has, unfortunately, created a profitable business for cyber attackers of all kinds. As a result, laws related to data privacy have gained momentum around the world and most government initiatives seek to protect privacy and reputation through privacy policies [6, 12].

The purpose of an online privacy policy is to inform the consumer about the retailers' data practices; what consumer PI is collected; how it is used; if there is further processing with third parties and how the PI is stored while using the website [10]. For the interest of consumers' PI protection, the online privacy policy needs to be in line with legislation, like the Protection of Personal Information Act (POPIA) of South Africa [40].

On the 1st of July 2021, POPIA was made mandatory in South Africa, as an attempt to curb privacy violation and allow for the handling of PI more effectively to safeguard individuals from possible threats [13–15]. POPIA calls for PI to only be processed given that the purpose is adequate, relevant, not excessive, individuals must be notified about the processing of their PI and given the opportunity to consent to it. This method of processing is called the 'notice and choice' model for web privacy, and it ensures that consumers are notified about the data collection and allowed a choice between opting in or out [9]. Notice and Choice serves to grant individuals greater control over how their PI is collected and used. Although conditions and legal requirements are addressed, POPIA does not, however, explicitly specify what should be covered by, or included in, an online privacy policy.

POPIA defines the eight conditions that must be met when personal information is being processed in South Africa as: "accountability, process limitation, purpose specification, further processing limitation, information quality, openness, security safeguards, and data subject participation" [40]. As such, online privacy policies must address the eight conditions to be aligned with POPIA and South African organizations require guidance for this.

The aim of this paper is to firstly propose guidelines of what should be included in an online privacy policy - this will be done using the scoping literature review and PRISMA method. Secondly, the proposed guidelines will be used to evaluate a sample of South African retail website privacy policies and to propose recommendations for the retail industry to improve the content of online privacy policies in line with the proposed guidelines, which will also aid in better alignment with POPIA's requirements.

2 Research Problem

The ongoing expansion of the Internet has led to more and more consumers sharing a lot of their PI and often consumers do this without fully understanding what service providers do with the trail of digital footprints they leave behind [16]. Some websites abuse users' confidence by buying, selling, or analyzing their PI without consent. Without help, people frequently do not comprehend the consequences of privacy issues or take any action to remedy them and, as such, privacy policies are used as a means of addressing this pertinent issue and informing consumers about the different uses of their PI [17].

Case and King [18] recently did a study on several Fortune500 companies' privacy policies to ascertain compliance with Fair Information Practices based on notice, choice, access, and security principles which ensure effective consumer PI protection. These principles are acknowledged by the United State government agencies but could very well be adopted, even in South Africa, as they are aligned with some of the POPIA conditions. Case and King [18] findings revealed that almost all businesses have their policies online and that the majority of those policies contain the four principles and despite the widespread and precise use of data collecting, there seemed to be a gap regarding security measures adopted to protect consumers' personal information [18]. Privacy policies are informed by a country's legislation and in the South African context, POPIA is used. However, as POPIA is founded on principles and doesn't explicitly define the criteria or guidelines of what should be included in a privacy policy, this has opened it to interpretation [19].

3 Background

This section presents an overview of privacy, consumer privacy concerns, POPIA and the purpose of online privacy policies. Studies that investigated privacy policy guidelines are also explored.

3.1 Privacy and Consumer Concerns

Over time, privacy has proven difficult to conceptualize, define, and it has been suggested that it is highly contextual and cannot be generalized [15, 20, 21]. Lin et al. [10] writes about how the idea of privacy is ill-defined and usually contentious in the digital context. Larsen, however, provides a definition for privacy as a state of human life marked by social isolation and public exposure [22]. This condition includes any PI that the person in question has chosen to keep confidential and does not want anyone to know about [22]. In the South African context, the South African Constitution states that "everyone has the right to privacy, which includes the right to not have: their person or home searched; their property searched; their possessions seized; or the privacy of their communications infringed" [41].

When appropriate privacy protection measures are not in place, consumer PI can be easily exploited [2, 13]. It has been found in over 15 countries that 87% of people agree on the need for legislation to prevent the violation of consumer PI [23]. Consumers are less likely to utilize a site if their privacy is abused [23, 24]. Sigmund [24] further describes how the young and educated seem to have more privacy concerns in comparison to the older generation. It can, therefore, be agreed that there is a pressing need for a data protection regime that is precise, and which facilitates the development of legislation, which is in line with technological advancements of the digital age, to protect the privacy of individuals [22]. The use of online privacy policies is precisely for this need and, as such, POPIA is an extension of the constitutional right to privacy and governs how PI is processed and used in South Africa.

3.2 Protection of Personal Information Act (POPIA)

On the 1st of July 2021, the Protection of Personal Information Act, No. 4 of 2013 came into effect. The aim of POPIA is to ensure that PI is processed lawfully. POPIA defines the different roles involved in the collection, use, transfer, storage, and application of PI in South Africa as the 'Responsible Party'- which is the retail website owner in this case. The 'Operator' – a third party contracted by the responsible party to process personal information on their behalf; 'Information Officer'- a designated individual within an institution responsible for ensuring compliance with POPIA; and the 'Data Subject'- which is the person whose PI is being processed. Furthermore, Section 3(a) of the act defines the eight conditions that need to be met for the lawful processing of PI in the country as; **Accountability:** the responsible party must ensure they are POPIA compliant. They accept responsibility for any violation and are responsible for the collection and processing of data subjects' PI and how it is shared with third parties; **Process limitation:** PI must be processed without the violation of data subjects; **Purpose specification:** PI can only be collected for a specific, documented and lawful purpose, related to the activity or function of the party collecting it and data subjects should be aware of the purpose; **Further processing limitation**: this must be consistent with the purposes for which the PI was collected; **Information quality:** the responsible party must ensure that PI is complete, accurate, not misleading, updated if needed, and consistent with the purposes for which it was collected; **Openness:** the responsible party must ensure that data subjects are aware of PI being collected, its purpose, source, name, and address of the responsible party and whether collection is voluntary or mandatory; **Security safeguards**: PI must be kept safe and secure, which necessitates the use of security measures; **Data subject participation**: data subjects have the right to access and amend their personal information, as well as have the opportunity to delete it if necessary.

3.3 Purpose of Online Privacy Policies

The online privacy policy is a legally enforceable agreement between the website owner and user, and it is produced in accordance with the laws and regulations of a country [10, 25]. On it, the responsible party unilaterally and proactively declare the principles and measures for the safeguarding of consumer PI being collected, what PI is being collected and its intended use. The privacy policy describes the way organizations gather, utilize, share, and transfer consumer information and how information security is ensured [10, 26]. Online privacy policies are important and need to be clearly visible to consumers when they visit the retailer's website.

A study by Dias et al. [27], defined Information collection, Use and Disclosure, Disclosure purpose, Opt-Out, User Access, Security, Use of cookies and Child privacy as suitable conditions for privacy policy guidelines. Isaak and Hanna [28], only highlighted Public transparency, Disclosure for users, Control: "Do no track" and notification. All the afore mentioned can be applied in a South African context. Limited studies have been done defining a comprehensive set of guidelines for online privacy policies in a South African Retail context. The aim of the next section is to review existing literature and to propose a holistic set of guidelines for online privacy policy content.

4   Literature Review

A scoping literature review, using the PRISMA method, was followed to identify existing criteria and guidelines for online privacy policy content [42, 43]. The objective of this literature review is to gain insights and perspective from related studies and propose guidelines that South African Retailer website owners can follow to implement and improve their online privacy policies.

IEEE, Scopus, and ACM databases were used to collect literature dated between the years 2016 and 2022. Boolean operations were used in conjunction with the key words, for example, "POPIA AND Websites"; "online privacy policies AND South Africa"; "privacy policies AND websites"; "POPIA AND Compliance", "Websites AND privacy" and only English written journals and articles relating to online privacy policies and guidelines were selected. The titles and abstracts were screened, full text of potentially relevant articles were retrieved and reviewed for eligibility into the final inclusion. Some articles were found through the references, which were also downloaded and verified for inclusion. According to the inclusion criteria, there was a total of 64 articles. The number of relevant articles was then significantly reduced to 15 after excluding papers that did not meet the inclusion criteria as seen in Table 1 below.

Table 1. Reporting items for the systematic review – adapted PRISMA

Database	Scopus	IEEE	ACM	Total
No. of records identified from database	28	17	19	**64**
Records removed before screening	8	5	12	**25**
Records screened	20	12	7	**39**
Records excluded	4	0	1	**5**
Reports retrieved	16	12	6	**34**
Records not retrieved	6	1	1	**8**
Records assessed for eligibility	10	11	5	**26**
Records excluded	2	6	3	**11**
Records in review	8	5	2	**15**

4.1 Summary of Website Criteria

In total, ten consolidated guidelines were derived from the reviewed studies which are consolidated in Table 2 below. The table shows that some studies covered all these guidelines, whereas others only focused on a few. Notice (15), choice (15), security (15) and purpose specification (9) were the privacy principles that were included in most studies for online privacy policy content.

Table 2. Summary of privacy policy guidelines

Study Objective	1	2	3	4	5	6	7	8	9	10	Total
This study presents the first extensive audit of disclosure of third-party data gathering in website privacy policies, with the goal of evaluating the effectiveness of "notice and choice" to find out if consumers are informed of the names of the organizations that gather their data. Over 200,000 websites' privacy policies are reviewed and data flows on a million websites are monitored [9]	X	X				X					**3**
This study explores the extent to which supervised binary classification may be utilized to differentiate between dubious and valid privacy rules that are placed on websites. A data set containing 67 policies from malicious websites and 100 policies from reputable websites (from the top corporations on the Fortune Global 500 list) is used. When all policy information is manually analyzed, it is possible to see statistically significant differences in terms of length and conformity to the seven general privacy principles [29]	X	X	X	X	X	X		X			**7**
To provide countermeasures for the growth of the PI protection legal framework in China, this study proposes measuring research of well-known websites in China that combines strategy analysis and web verification [10]	X	X	X			X					**4**
This paper defines privacy governance and explores what successful governance looks like in an online setting. It seeks to better understand how New Zealand (NZ) organizations use their websites to inform users about their privacy practices and whether those practices follow the privacy laws established by the NZ government by using a content analysis questionnaire [21]	X	X	X	X	X	X	X				**7**

(*continued*)

Table 2. (*continued*)

Study Objective	1	2	3	4	5	6	7	8	9	10	Total
This study adds to the corpus of knowledge by evaluating the need for, adoption of, and advertising of privacy policies on the websites of Portuguese local authorities, as well as by gathering evidence of those authorities' compliance with privacy standards [27]	X	X	X	X	X	X					**6**
This study was carried out to look at the practices of the Fortune 500, the largest organizations, to see if the concepts of notice, choice, access, and security are supported by the Fair Information Practices [18]	X	X			X						**3**
This study suggests that user friendly privacy policies that use fair information practices based on OECD guidelines will provide a competitive advantage by establishing trust between website owners and users [30]	X	X	X			X					**4**
Through concentrating on the comparative study of privacy policies—the main means by which service providers advise customers about the collection and use of their data—this study helps readers better comprehend websites. It examined 1,562 websites and their privacy policies in comparison to premium websites to better understand the data usage dangers connected with such services [31]	X	X		X	X	X		X			**6**
This study reports on the compliance evaluation of privacy protection in e-Government systems in the countries of Anglophone West Africa, specifically in Ghana, Nigeria, Liberia, Sierra Leone, and Gambia, to partially fill the gap of literature lacking on investigations on the current status of information security and privacy protection of e-Government services in Africa [32]	X	X	X	X	X	X		X	X		**8**
This study aims to measure the improvements in privacy laws worldwide brought about by the (General Data Protection Regulation) GDPR. It makes use of the data mining application Privacy Check to compare three corpora (totaling 550) of privacy policies automatically between before and after the GDPR. Additionally, it manually examined the policies in two corpora to assess the present state of GDPR compliance throughout the world [33]	X	X	X			X	X		X		**6**

(*continued*)

Table 2. (*continued*)

Study Objective	1	2	3	4	5	6	7	8	9	10	Total
In this research, online privacy policies from ten industries in the three biggest economies in South Asia—India, Pakistan, and Bangladesh—are evaluated. The policies are evaluated based on accessibility, readability, and conformity with 8 privacy principles using a manual qualitative study on a dataset of 284 well-known websites [34]	X	X	X	X	X	X		X		X	8
The study's objective was to examine policies from public websites in the United States Association of Research Libraries compliance with American Library Association privacy policy guidelines [35]	X	X	X	X	X	X				X	7
This study assessed the Middle Eastern region's main banks' and mobile money providers' adherence to privacy laws and privacy notices' readability [36]	X	X	X	X		X				X	6
This study demonstrates an automated analysis of the GDPR and Pakistan Data Protection Act compliance of privacy policies on Pakistani websites [44]	X	X	X	X	X	X		X			7
This study compared the privacy policies of 30 Nigerian internet retailers with those of the Fair Information Practices (FIP) principles [37]	X	X	X		X	X		X	X		7

Table note: (1) Notice, (2) Choice, (3) Purpose specification, (4) Third-Party, (5) Access, (6) Security, (7) Storage(8) Information quality, (9) Data collection limitation, (10) Minor data protection

4.2 Proposed Online Privacy Policy Guidelines

The ten guidelines derived from the scoping literature review were revised to seven guidelines. Notice, choice, and minor consent were combined because all three address consent. Storage was incorporated in Transparency and Purpose Specification as it pertains to how long the retailer intends on storing the consumer PI. Table 3 describes the proposed guidelines and includes a mapping to the conditions in POPIA.

Table 3. Proposed online privacy policy guidelines

Proposed Criteria	Mapping to POPIA guidelines
Notice & Choice: Online privacy policy content should inform the consumer about their PI collection practices, the types of PI they collect and allow consumers to consent to their PI collection practices or decline by using opt-in/out method. Considerations for minors under the age of eighteen should also be made	Processing limitation (section 9–12) & Openness (section 17–18),
Transparency and Purpose Specification: The online privacy policy content should clearly inform the consumer about the purpose for which they collect their PI, what type of PI is collected, how they collect it and how long they retain it	Purpose Specification (section 13–14), Openness (section 17 & 18)
Third-Party: In the event the collected PI is shared with third parties within or outside the country's borders, the online privacy policy content should clearly specify that. The retailer should also take accountability in ensuring that the third parties comply with privacy guidelines and only use the PI for its initial intended use	Further processing limitation (section 15)
Security: The online privacy policy content should inform the consumer about the security mechanisms they have in place to secure their PI and that in the event of a data breach, the website owner will inform the affected parties as well as the Information Regulator	Security Safeguards (section 19–2)
Information Quality: The retailer should ensure that the collected consumer PI is accurate and up to date. This can also be achieved by allowing consumer access to their collected PI as per the proposed guideline 6. This should be clearly articulated in the online privacy policy content	Information quality (section 16)
Access: The online privacy policy content should have a paragraph informing the consumer about how they can access PI collected about them and allow them to update or delete their PI	Data subject participation (section 23–25)
Accountability: The retailer should ensure that their privacy policy aligns with POPIA conditions and regulatory requirements for the processing of consumer PI. This should be articulated in the online privacy policy content	Accountability (section 8)

5   Research Methodology

5.1   Research Paradigm

The interpretivism philosophical paradigm was adopted as the relative ontology that interpretivists use as it allows for several interpretations of the same occurrence [38]. This paradigm is applied by analyzing literature from authors in various countries. This is largely because privacy is context based, and privacy policy guidelines are informed by the laws governing a specific country.

5.2   Research Design and Methodology

A case study research methodology is applied. Yin [39] defines a case study as an empirical method that "investigates a contemporary phenomenon (the "case") in depth and within its real-world context, especially when the boundaries between phenomenon and context may not be clearly evident".

This study implores a single case study research method with embedded multiple units of analysis by reviewing online privacy policies within the South African Retail Industry, from eighteen different companies against the proposed online privacy guidelines as indicated in Table 3. The retail industry is the main unit of analysis, and the eighteen retailers constitute the analysis sub-units. A research ethics clearance was obtained for this project through the university's relevant research ethics bodies and, as such, organizational confidentiality and privacy is protected.

5.3   Data Collection and Analysis

A non-probability, purpose sampling method was used in the collection of the online privacy policies. In non-probability sampling, there is no way of knowing the probability of a subject being selected, and, purpose sampling permits the researcher to choose the sampled data at their convenience [45]. The range of selected retailers varied from food, clothing, and household items.

A combination of both qualitative and quantitative data analysis methods was used. First, the online privacy policies were uploaded to Atlas.ti and a content analysis method was used by searching for words such as "consent", "opt in", "security", "data breach", "amend", "delete", "third-party" and "collected" to identify data practices within the privacy policies and group them into codes of relevant themes. An excel spreadsheet was also used to track if each one of the retailers had a privacy policy pop up when the site was visited and if they had a hyperlink at the bottom of their webpage.

6   Results

Only seven of the eighteen retailers had a privacy policy notification pop-up on the landing page of their website. All eighteen retailer websites had a hyperlink at the bottom of their page directing consumers to their online privacy policy page (Table 4).

Table 4. Online Privacy Policy pop-up

	Frequency	Percentage
Retailers with privacy policy pop-up	7	38%
Retailers with online privacy policy hyperlink	18	100%

All the sampled retailers addressed Notice and Choice; Security; Transparency and Purpose specification guidelines. This is great effort towards safer consumer PI processing. Only 94% addressed Access, 61% explicitly informed consumers about third party processing and 39% obliged with Information quality. These findings indicate that although all retailers had an online privacy policy on their websites, there is still a lack of consistency with some of the guidelines this study suggests.

The least addressed guideline, at a 22% is Accountability and this indicates the retailer's attempts to recuse their responsibility towards POPIA and their neglect to fostering good consumer relationship and trust. Figure 1 illustrates an aggregated view of how the eighteen online privacy policies addressed the proposed guidelines.

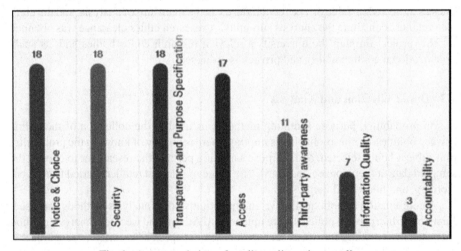

Fig. 1. Aggregated view of retailer online privacy policy.

7 Discussion and Recommendations

The study revealed that the content of the reviewed South African retailer's privacy policies 100% addressed Notice and Choice, Transparency and Purpose Specification, and Security. Ninety-four percent addressed Access. Consumers should be granted access to their PI collected. This is closely tied to consent, as consumers have the right to opt out of any agreement, at any given time. Not only that but granting consumer access to collected PI allows for better quality of the PI, as they can update/amend their PI when necessary. As the collector of the PI, retailers should take sole responsibility for the cost of processing and retaining consumer PI. This should be addressed in the content of the online privacy policy. Sixty-one percent addressed Third-party, the content of an online privacy policy should clearly inform the consumer of any third-party processing and if so, also state that the third-party will process it in line with the initial collection purpose. Thirty-nine percent addressed Information Quality and 22% addressed Accountability. It is imperative that any changes to the online privacy policy be communicated with consumers, to allow consumers adequate consent to the continuation of processing their PI. This should be clearly stated in the content of the online privacy policy. The content of the online privacy policy should clearly state that the retailer takes full accountability for any loss or breach to consumer PI and disclose any breach to both the consumer and Information Regulator.

8   Limitations and Future Work

The proposed guidelines do not serve as a compliance measure for POPIA, however further work can be done assessing their comprehensiveness in improving the online privacy policies, with guidance from a regulatory perspective, as well as validation from an expert panel. Further insights to this study can be derived from examining consumer opinions and encounters with the online privacy policies and how that affects consumer habits. This paper only sampled eighteen South African retail stores and this number could be increased for a broader view of the content of online privacy policies within the retail industry.

9   Conclusion

The objective of this study was to propose guidelines for the content of online privacy policies and to apply it to determine whether the online privacy policies on South African retail websites address the proposed guidelines, and to make recommendations for improvement. For this purpose, an embedded single case study, with multiple units of analysis, was used where eighteen different South African retail online privacy policies were analyzed against the proposed online privacy policy guidelines as derived from a scoping literature review. It was found that not all the guidelines were addressed in the online privacy policies. Access, third-party, information quality and accountability were aspects that required attention in online privacy policies. The guidelines and recommendations can aid retail website owners to improve their online privacy policies. Future research will focus on expanding the guidelines to incorporate more guidance from a regulatory perspective and to include a larger sample of retailers' online privacy policies in the review.

References

1. Izogo, E.E.: Online shopping experience in an emerging e-retailing market. J. Res. Interact. Mark. **12**(2), 193–214 (2018)

2. Mapande, F.V., Appiah, M.: The factors influencing customers to conduct online shopping: South African perspective. In: International Conference on Intelligent and Innovative Computing Applications (ICONIC), pp. 1–5. IEEE, Mon Tresor, Mauritius (2018)
3. Stanciu, V., Rîndașu, S.M.: Artificial intelligence in retail: benefits and risks associated with mobile shopping applications. J. Amfiteatru Econ. **23**(56), 46–64 (2021)
4. Guru, S., Nenavani, J.: Ranking of perceived risks in online shopping. Decision **47**(1), 137–152 (2020)
5. Van der Walt, W., Willems, K.A., Friedrich, W., Hatsu S, Krauss K.: Retracted Covid-19 papers and the levels of 'citation pollution': a preliminary analysis and directions for further research. Cahiers de la Documentation-Bladen voor Documentatie **3**(4), 206–218 (2020). https://www.abd-bvd.be/nl/bladen-voor-documentatie/2020-3-4/
6. Moraka, L.: The compliance framework for the 7th POPIA condition in the SME ICT sector. Doctoral dissertation (2021). https://researchspace.ukzn.ac.za/handle/10413/20445
7. Nyoni, P., Velempini, M.: Privacy and user awareness on Facebook Social media: Facebook. S. Afr. J. Sci. **114**(5), 1–5 (2018)
8. Da Veiga, A., Vorster, R., Furnell, S.M., Clarke, N., Li, F.: Comparing the protection and use of online personal information in South Africa and the United Kingdom in line with data protection requirements. Inf. Comput. Secur. **28**(3), 399–422 (2019)
9. Libert, T.: An automated approach to auditing disclosure of third-party data collection in website privacy policies. In: 2018 World Wide Web Conference, Proceedings, pp. 207–216. WWW, Lyon France (2018)
10. Lin, X., Liu, H., Li, Z., Xiong, G., Gou, G.: Privacy protection of China's top websites: a multi-layer privacy measurement via network behaviors and privacy policies. J. Comput. Secur.Comput. Secur. **114**(1), 1–20 (2022)
11. Brien, P.O., Young, S.W.H., Arlitsch, K., Benedict, K.: Protecting privacy on the web A study of HTTPS and Google analytics implementation in academic library websites. Online Inf. Rev. **42**(6), 734–751 (2018)
12. Obar, J.A., Oeldorf-hirsch, A.: The biggest lie on the Internet: ignoring the privacy policies and terms of service policies of social networking services. J. Inf. Commun. Soc. **23**(1), 1–20 (2018)
13. Anderson, D., Bawa, A., Branson, N., Molefe, M.: POPIA code of conduct for research. S. Afr. J. Sci. **117**(5), 1–12 (2021)
14. Vorster, R., Pilkington, C., Abdullah, H., Da Veiga, A.: Compliance with the protection of personal information act and consumer privacy expectations. In: Information Security for South Africa (ISSA) 2017 Proceedings, pp. 16–23. IEEE, Johannesburg South Africa (2017)
15. Swales, L.: The protection of personal information act 4 of 2013 in the context of health research: enabler of privacy rights or roadblock? Potchefstroom Electron. Law J. **25**(1), 783–797 (2022)
16. Tesfay, W.B., Hofmann, P., Nakamura, T., Kiyomoto, S., Serna, J.: I read but don't agree: privacy policy benchmarking using machine learning and the EU GDPR. In: Companion of the World Wide Web Conference Proceedings, pp. 163–166. WWW, Lyon, France (2018)
17. Pilton, C., Faily, S., Henriksen-Bulmer, J.E.: Evaluating privacy - determining user privacy expectations on the web. J. Comput. Secur. **105**, 1–16 (2021)
18. Case, C.J., King, D.L.: Fair information practices : an empirical review of the fortune 500. J. Bus. Behav. Sci. **34**(1), 49–630 (2022)
19. Pelteret, M., Ophoff, J.: Organizational information privacy strategy and the impact of the PoPI act. In: 2017 Information Security for South Africa (ISSA) Proceedings, pp. 56–67. IEEE, Johannesburg South Africa (2017)
20. Bleier, A., Goldfarb, A., Tucker, C.E.: Consumer privacy and the future of data-based innovation and marketing. Int. J. Res. Market. **37**(3), 466–80 (2020)

21. Tjhin, I., Vos, M., Munaganuri, S.A.: Privacy governance online: privacy policy practices on New Zealand websites. In: 2016 Pacific Asia Conference on Information Systems (PACIS) Proceedings, Chiayi Taiwan (2016)
22. Larsen, C.: Data Privacy Protection in South Africa: An analysis of vicarious liability in light of the protection of Personal Information Act 4 of 2013 ("POPIA"), Masters of Law (LLM) in Business Law Degree College of Law and Management Studies University of Kwazulu Natal (2019)
23. Alzaidi, M.S., Agag, G.: The role of trust and privacy concerns in using social media for e-retail services: the moderating role of COVID-19. J. Retail. Consum. Serv. **68**(C).103042 (2022)
24. Sigmund, T.: Attention paid to privacy policy statements. Information **12**(4), 144 (2021)
25. Wilson, S., et al.: The creation and analysis of a Website privacy policy corpus. In: Erk, K., Smith, N. (eds.) 54th Annual Meeting of the Association for Computational Linguistics. LNCS, vol. 1, pp. 1330–1340. ACL, Germany (2016)
26. Ali, A.S., Zaaba, Z.F., Singh, M.M., Hussain, A.: Readability of websites security privacy policies: a survey on text content and readers. Int. J. Adv. Sci. Technol. **29**(6), 1661–1672 (2020)
27. Dias, G.P., Gomes, H., Zúquete, A.: Privacy policies and practices in Portuguese local e-government. Electron. Gov. Int. J. **12**(4), 301–318 (2016)
28. Isaak, J., Hanna, M.J.: User data privacy: Facebook, Cambridge Analytica and privacy protection. Computer **51**(8), 56–59 (2018)
29. Boldt, M., Rekanar, K.: Analysis and text classification of privacy policies from rogue and top-100 fortune global companies. Int. J. Inf. Secur. Priv.Secur. Priv. **13**(2), 47–66 (2019)
30. Ginosar, A., Ariel, Y.: An analytical framework for online privacy research: what is missing? Inf. Manag. **54**(7), 948–957 (2017)
31. Alabduljabbar, A., Mohaisen, D.: Measuring the privacy dimension of free content websites through automated privacy policy analysis and annotation. In: The Web Conference 2022 Proceedings, pp. 860–867. ACM, Lyon France (2022). https://doi.org/10.1145/3487553
32. Nwaeze, A.C., Zavarsky, P., Ruhl, R.: Compliance evaluation of information privacy protection in e-government systems in Anglophone West Africa using ISO/IEC 29100:2011.: In: 12th International Conference on Digital Information Management, ICDIM Proceedings, pp. 98–102. IEEE, Fukoaka Japan (2017)
33. Zaeem, R.N., Barber, K.S.: The effect of the GDPR on privacy policies. ACM Trans. Manag. Inf. Syst.Manag. Inf. Syst. **12**(1), 1–20 (2020)
34. Javed, Y., Salehin, K.M., Shehab, M.: A study of South Asian websites on privacy compliance. IEEE Access **8**, 156067–156083 (2020)
35. Valentine, G., Barron, K.: An examination of academic library privacy policy compliance with professional guidelines. Evid Based Libr Inf PractLibr. Inf. Pract. **17**(3), 77–96 (2022)
36. Javed, Y., Al Qahtani, E., Shehab, M.: Privacy policy analysis of banks and mobile money services in the middle east. Future Internet **13**(1), 1–15 (2021)
37. Bello, O.W., Adeyemi, R., Bello, O.W., Oyekunle, A.: Analysis of the privacy policies of Nigerian online shops. Int. J. Inf. Process. Commun. (IJIPC) **6**(1), 347–362 (2018). https://www.researchgate.net/publication/329872094
38. Pham, L.: A review of advantages and disadvantages of three paradigms: positivism, interpretivism and critical inquiry
39. Yin, R.K.: Case Study Research and Applications, 6th edn. Sage Publications, Thousand Oaks (2018)
40. The Parliament of the Republic of South Africa: Protection of Personal Information Act, Act No. 4 of 2013, Government Gazette, vol. 581, no. 37067. Cape Town, South Africa (2013)
41. The Bill of Rights of the Constitution of the Republic of South Africa Chapter 2(14). Government Gazette, Cape Town (1996)

42. Munn, Z., Peters, M.D.J., Stern, C., et al.: Systematic review or scoping review? Guidance for authors when choosing between a systematic or scoping review approach. BMC Med. Res. Methodol. **18**(1), 143 (2018)

43. Selcuk, A.A.: A guide for systematic reviews: PRISMA. Turk. Arch. Otorhinolaryngol. **57**(1), 57–58 (2019)

44. Asif, M., Javed, Y., Hussain, M.: Automated analysis of Pakistani Websites' compliance with GDPR and Pakistan data protection act. In: International Conference on Frontiers of Information Technology (FIT) Proceedings, pp. 234–239. IEEE, Islamabad Pakistan, (2021)

45. Etikan, I., Bala, K.: Biometrics Biostat. Int. J. **5**(6), 215–217 (201)

Author Index

T. Guarda et al. (Eds.): ARTIIS 2023, CCIS 1936, pp. 441–445, 2024.
https://doi.org/10.1007/978-3-031-48855-9

Printed in the United States
by Baker & Taylor Publisher Services